The African American People

The African American People is the first history of the African American people to take a global look at the role African Americans have played in the world. Author Molefi Kete Asante synthesizes the familiar tale of history's effect on the African people who found themselves forcibly part of the United States with a new look at how African Americans in later generations impacted the rest of the world. Designed for a range of students studying African American History or African American Studies, *The African American People* takes the story from Africa to the Americas, and follows the diaspora through the Underground Railroad to Canada, and on to Europe, Asia, and around the globe.

Including over fifty images documenting African American lives, *The African American People* presents the most detailed discussion of the African and African American diaspora to date, giving students the foundation they need to broaden their conception of African American History.

Molefi Kete Asante is a Professor of African American Studies at Temple University. He is the author of sixty-eight books, including *An Afrocentric Manifesto* and *The History of Africa: The Quest for Eternal Harmony* (Routledge).

The African American People

A Global History

MOLEFI KETE ASANTE

Routledge
Taylor & Francis Group

NEW YORK AND LONDON

First published 2012
by Routledge
711 Third Avenue, New York, NY 10017

Simultaneously published in the UK
by Routledge
2 Park Square, Milton Park, Abingdon, Oxon OX14 4RN

Routledge is an imprint of the Taylor & Francis Group, an informa business

Library of Congress Cataloging-in-Publication Data
Asante, Molefi K., 1942–
 The African American people : a global history / by Molefi Kete
Asante.
  p. cm.
Includes bibliographical references and index.
1. African Americans–History. 2. African Americans–Social
conditions. 3. African Americans–Intellectual life. 4. United
States–Civilization–African American influences. 5. United
States–Race relations–History. 6. African diaspora. I. Title.
 E185.A796 2012
 305.896'073–dc23
                    2011025880

ISBN: 978-0-415-87254-6 (hbk)
ISBN: 978-0-415-87255-3 (pbk)
ISBN: 978-0-203-14580-7 (ebk)

Typeset in Avenir and Dante
by Keystroke, Station Road, Codsall, Wolverhampton
Printed and bound in the United States of America on acid-free paper
by Edwards Brothers Inc.

Contents

List of Illustrations

Tables

Preface

The movement of human history is like a massive star with numerous flares intermittently jutting out into space. At any time one flare might extend out beyond others and assume the role of the dominant edge of the star. In African American history, observers have often seen various flares leaping out as leading themes. For example, there was a phase in historiography where African redemption was the principal approach to African American history. But eventually the Redemptionists who wanted to demonstrate that black people (Africans) were just as capable of achievements and contributions as other people soon discovered that their approach to history was self-effacing and defeatist. They thought that if they could demonstrate the precise event or phenomenon considered by whites to be the one marking blacks as inferior, they could describe the reasons for such thinking, thereby obliterating the racist idea of black incapability. Of course, whenever the Redemptionist historians showed that blacks had achieved in this or that capacity, it was often taken by the racist ideologues to be a form of blacks just imitating whites, and this thinking consequently robbed the Redemptionists of their victory. Another form of African American history was based on the "Great Man" idea. During the early part of the twentieth century we were inundated with histories that highlighted Frederick Douglass, Booker T. Washington, William E. B. Du Bois and other great men as examples of the black race. This book, on the other hand, has pushed toward a more complex, eclectic portrayal of the African American in a global context. Africans born in the United States have traveled to many countries and influenced the cultures, arts, music, and education in faraway regions of the world. Often when African American history is written, those individuals who left the United States to become expatriates are forgotten and marginalized. While this project strives to include the global reach of the African American, I am the first to admit that this book, as a first attempt at this high goal, has still not included many of the outstanding achievements of African Americans abroad.

In the early 1990s I had occasion to invite Lilly Golden, a second-generation African Russian, to my home in Philadelphia. Dr Golden had been an expert on Africa for the Soviet Union, and after the thaw in political relations between the two nations she had come to the United States. Lilly's daughter, Yelena Khanga, accompanied President Mikhail Gorbachev to the United States in 1987. Americans had Condoleezza Rice, but Russians had Yelena Khanga.

Lilly Golden herself was the daughter of an African American, Oliver John Golden, and a Jewish American, Bertha Golden, who moved to the Soviet Union in 1931 with sixteen black experts in cotton production. However, Lilly was born in the Soviet Union, educated in Moscow, and married to a Tanzanian, the father of her Yelena. What I learned from listening to Lilly Golden speak about blacks in Russia as she sat in my living room was enough to make me want to write expatriates into the narrative of African Americans. While we know a little about blacks in the old Soviet Union and in Russia from the works of Hugh Barnes, Lilly Golden, and others, this knowledge has not been widely disseminated. For example, we know that Alexander Pushkin, the iconic and legendary Russian writer, was of African descent, but few readers would be aware that there had been blacks in Russia long before the Russian Revolution in 1917. Langston Hughes took twenty-two African American filmmakers and the famous singer Paul Robeson to Russia under the auspices of the Comintern. Some of the descendants of African American expatriates, such as the actor James Lloydovich Patterson, make their own history in the country of their birth, in his case, Russia. There are thousands of African Americans living in Africa, Europe, South America, Asia, and Australia who carry with them intense cultural styles and behaviors that have been shaped by the peculiarly rich history of Africans born in the United States of America.

An increasing number of African Americans have recent roots in the Caribbean and South America, though their earlier origins are on the continent of Africa. Earl Graves, the founder of Black Enterprise magazine and Eric Holder, the first black Attorney General of the United States, both have ancestors from Barbados; Pearl Primus, the dancer, and Kwame Ture, the fiery leader of the Student Nonviolent Coordinating Committee, had Trinidadian backgrounds; and both Marcus Garvey and Colin Powell had Jamaican ancestors. The list of African Americans whose parents or grandparents immigrated to this country from Costa Rica, Cuba, Puerto Rico, Colombia, the Bahamas, Honduras, Brazil, Jamaica, and Haiti is long. In addition, newer immigrants from Nigeria, Ghana, South Africa, Congo, Egypt, Sudan, Senegal, Gambia, Guinea, Somali, and Zimbabwe have enriched the African American experience, making it one of the quintessential ethnic experiences in the United States.

I have written this book fully aware of the recent trend in historiography to move away from the narrations of individual lives except in extended biography. I am conscious of the time in which we live and the tremendous pressures on academic historians to discover the bizarre, the odd, and the unusual in order to announce something novel. But that is not the book I have written; I have written a volume to tell a coherent narrative about the memory of African American people as experienced by numerous makers of this history. These makers of history are both well-known individuals and not so well-known ones; they are gradualists in political terms as well as radicals; they are nationalists as well as integrationists; and they all have rebelled against the conditions of prejudice, discrimination, and racism. If anything creates solidarity between the various groups of black people in America, it is the struggle against white privilege and the racial domination brought with it. Since the beginning of enslavement, African Americans have been on the road to freedom. It was never far from us and we also had with us always the stirring narratives of how others overcame the strangleholds of slavery and discrimination.

Therefore, this book has characteristics that are linear *and* thematic, especially in the latter chapters, where our information is so dense that it is impossible to arrange a completely linear account without taking into consideration artistic, social, or religious spurs that may go off in other directions than the main story. Yet I have tried to maintain as much distance as is possible in a closely wrought history of one's own people. To write about African Americans in American history is a different project than writing African American history, and few have succeeded in this task. This work is not modeled on other histories and it centers itself as much as possible in the voice of the African American. This is the type of history I have sought to write.

In his towering study of the black struggle for freedom *There is a River*, Vincent Harding explained how he had told the story and "provided a rigorous analysis of the long black movement toward justice, equity, and truth" (Harding, *There is a River*, New York: Harcourt, Brace, 1981, p. xi). There was for him this strong tension between being an objective historian and being a subjective responder. Fortunately, I have experienced no such strivings because I did not set out to tell an objective narrative but a useful one, based on the best facts that I could amass, and in so doing I believe that I have advanced the resilience and nobility often hidden from other histories of the African American population.

Another tendency in my narrative is to include global activities of African Americans. It is not enough to write history of blacks inside the fifty states; we must see where African Americans have gone, carrying the same torch of freedom. This is why I have deliberately highlighted the international involvement of African Americans. I cannot claim the discovery of any new documentation to the general facts of African American history, but I can claim that this work is meant to demonstrate the extent to which African Americans have made their way in the world; and this is a new perspective on the facts, some of them often shoved to the margins. The irresistible will of the people to survive and to "make good" danced in the lights on the stage with Josephine Baker, sang alongside Marian Anderson in Washington, and fought with Joe Louis in the ring with every challenger. This is what I wanted to capture in this book.

Among contemporary historians, I have been blessed to know and read the works of Daryl Zizwe Poe of Lincoln University, Darlene Clark Hine of Northwestern University, Michael Gomez of New York University, Robin Kelley of the University of Southern California, and Michael Tillotson of the University of Pittsburgh. As a student at the University of California, Los Angeles, I sat at the feet of Boniface Obichere, Gary Nash, Ronald Takaki, Mazisi Kunene, and Terrence Ranger, and from both groups of historians, a few of whom I argued against, I have learned that the pursuit of history, especially African American or African history, requires a lengthy period of sorting out the facts, which must be presented in an intelligent manner as rational discourse. Yet my methods have remained Diopian. That is, I have attempted to see history not simply as a linear narrative, though progression does imply some form of linearity, but I have discovered facts and ideas from every discipline I could to include in discussing the narrative of African Americans. In this regard I have followed the work of Cheikh Anta Diop a historian, anthropologist, physicist, and politician who demonstrated the ability to amass information from many disciplines in order to provide clarity on an important topic. I have tried to do this from a historical perspective. To the extent that I have missed something, and I am sure I have missed a lot, it is due to my inadequate ability to grasp all that I have experienced. Nevertheless, I seek to tell these events from the angle of the African person as agent—not simply what happened *to* us, but what we did. The reason one tries to do as much as one can to track down the little-known fact, to explain the seemingly contradictory actions of historical agents, and to make sense of the unusual characteristics that aggregate in certain circumstances is to provide the reader with a coherent and comprehensible narrative.

The quest for identity has been an active part of the African American political and social experience. One of the reasons the great dramatist August Wilson could write plays for each decade of the twentieth century was because he knew that the struggle for identity in a people so long lost from their sense of place must be one that we return to decade after decade.

The quest for belongingness occurs in the African American population because we are often confounded by the reality of where we are, given our resources, our strengths, and our wills. Why is this a question that is frequently asked in the African American community? If we are truly citizens of America since the end of the Civil War and the Fifteenth Amendment, then what is this strange nagging feeling we have about the way our fellow citizens speak of us, insinuate about us, threaten us, and try to entrap or block us? Yet, throughout American history we have fought in the wars, built the roads, harvested the crops, written the books, researched and explored the sciences, all in efforts to demonstrate that African Americans, too, belong to this nation. Simultaneously, African Americans have never forgotten Africa, the distant yet always rising star on our experiential horizon, and have pursued a collective, though often tortured, path toward achieving a rapprochement with our origin on that continent.

I have introduced two conventions in the text. The first is the use of the African term for ancient Egypt, "Kemet," used interchangeably with the Greek-derived "Egypt." The second is that I have spoken of Africans in America prior to the end of the enslavement as Africans and only after 1865 do I refer to Africans born in the United States as African Americans. Prior to the end of bondage, Africans were generally without citizenship and in some places barely invested by white slaveholders with humanity.

I think that history can be structured around our lived experiences which give us progression but must also succumb to the burdens of discontinuities, fits-and-starts, and cycles that return one to the place from which one left like a merry-go-round or some *déjà vu* encounter.

Increasingly since the 1890s, when African Americans became more European Christian than African in religion, there has been a strong Christian explanatory element in the historiography concerning Africans in America. Some highlight this Christian explanation as the reason for African American survival; others see it as just a part of the process of ultimate acceptance by white American society. Of course, many reject this type of historical analysis, and object to the narrowing focus of the black journey. Nothing will negate the contribution of Hoodoo, Vodun, agnostic, atheist, Yoruba, Muslim, Akan, and even Jewish votarists among African Americans, though the Christian element gained ascendancy in the twentieth century. While I recognize the role of the church in the way African Americans have described historical experiences, I am not beholden to that viewpoint because I see it as limited and limiting in the construction of a usable history. When I write about a usable history I am referring to explanatory narratives that provide the reader with justifications for striving to excel. What could be a higher purpose, for example, than a human being who is on the road toward the greatest achievement possible within his or her frame of time? I consider some histories of the African American to be slave histories, bounded examples of people captured and held by ideas that strangle all authentic purpose, thus making the recipient of such ideas silly, inarticulate, and ineffective in their own lives. The church has not saved us from ourselves and cannot fill the great gulfs that remain unfilled in our lives.

Who saved African Americans from enslavement, for example? What songs did our ancestors sing when they were captured and taken into slavery? Whose god authorized and sanctified the keeping of human beings in chains? And why should an African American find the elements of that history usable in a genuine manner? No, this is not a history articulated by the Christianity of African people, although I would be the first to admit that the role of the church has been important in defining the maladies that are suffered by the African community. One could reasonably discuss the place of the Christian religion in the overthrow of the gods of Africa and arrive at a more interesting quest for authentic history, but alas, that is reserved for another volume.

This history is not a history of politicians, as so many histories tend to be, nor do I intend to carry on a dialogue only between the regular heroes of the African community. Rather, my aim is to join together a congress of attitudes and responses, individual and collective actions, personal and public behaviors that are an amalgamation of centered narratives of those who are considered heroes with those that suggest agency in their lives on behalf of African people. The turbulent ruptures of our history in America have often been caused by caustic interventions of racism, prejudice, discrimination, and violence. My aim, therefore, as a historian, is to perform the magic of piecing together the torn parts of the past by arranging them around the principal ideas of centrality and agency.

There is a way to formulate narratives of African Americans that does not rely simply on the notion that African Americans have been victims and that whites in America have been victimizers. This is why I have always contended that there were victories, authentic victories, of black people during the enslavement—indeed, even on the slave ships. We were not unfeeling stones, nor pieces of wood, though we were treated like chattel. Our ability to make argument with our kidnappers, sometimes silently, but always rationally in our heads; our articulation of our grievances in our music and field hollers; our sense of what was wrong and what was right filled our waking moments and tossed us in our grass bottom cots at night; and our sensitivity to those who had been raped, whipped, abused, and punished allowed us to curse the day we first laid eyes on the ships from Europe. My narratives of this history could never be merely the narratives of victims when so many people were victors.

I can only claim a composite historical experience for African Americans if I tried to enlarge the field of critical inquiry to include the narrative experiences outside of the United States. This has rarely been done, and in this book I have given voice and presence to those blacks that left the United States to find new ways of living, working, and seeing in other parts of the world. They have not all been successful but enough African Americans have left the United States to work and live in places like Zimbabwe, Tanzania, Ghana, China, Japan, France, Britain, Germany, Russia, Sweden, and Brazil for historians to try to integrate these narratives into the larger tapestry of African American history. Of course, no history is complete, and indeed I have discovered as this manuscript goes to press new narratives in other places that have to be integrated into the movement of African Americans. I, as an African historian with a perspective, must seek to impose some order and sequence on these actions without abandoning the fundamental principles of telling the truth about social forces and cultural crises as far as I can discern from the written and documentary record. For the privilege of writing this manuscript, I give *dobale* to John Hope Franklin, Vincent Harding, St. Clair Drake, Lerone Bennett, and John Henrik Clarke.

Acknowledgments

A book project of this magnitude depends upon many people; this one has been no different. I would like to thank Maggie Lindsey-Jones, Emma Wood and the other editors at Routledge for their incredibly brilliant guidance during this process. My acquistion editor Kimberly Guinta has always been constant in her vision and devoted to the project in the deepest way. I appreciate her confidence in me. Furthermore, my relationship with Routledge, Taylor and Francis, continues to be phenomenal and I cannot show enough gratitude to the people who have had confidence in my work. Perhaps this project will justify their devotion to excellence.

Chapter Time Markers

7 Million BCE	Appearance of *Sahelanthropus tchadensis* in Chad
250,000 BCE	Appearance of *Homo sapiens* in Africa
15,000 BCE	Nubian material culture develops
7000 BCE	Nabta Playa lays foundation for Nile Valley cultures
3400 BCE	Writing appears in Kemet
2800 BCE	Imhotep builds Sakkara Step Pyramid
2300 BCE	Harkhuf explores Northeast and Central Africa
1503 BCE	Hatshepsut sends emissaries to Somalia (Punt)
790 BCE	King Pianky of Nubia invades Kemet
300 BCE	Rise of Ghana Kingdom in West Africa
290 CE	Axum conquers Nubia
1062 CE	King Tenkhamenin expands Ghana Empire
1240 CE	Sundiata, king of Mali, defeats Emperor Sumanguru of Ghana
1311–12 CE	Mali emperor Abubakari II sends ships across the Atlantic Ocean
1324 CE	Mali emperor Mansa Musa travels to Mecca with a huge entourage
1492 CE	Emperor Sunni Ali Ber dies and leaves a weakened empire
1594 CE	Timbuktu falls to the Moroccans

Time before the Time   1

The African Cradle (7 Million BCE–700 CE)

Important Terms and Names

Sahelanthropus tchadensis	Nubia
Monogenesis	Kush
Polygenesis	Kemet

African Origins

The first Africans entered the English North American colony of Jamestown, Virginia, in 1619, yet African history in America begins neither at the Virginia settlement, nor in 1619. The history of Africans in America is far more complex and comprehensive than is suggested by merely referring to that place and date. The varied narrative of Africans in America can only be told as a long journey of resistance and liberation, oriented toward the nobility and grace that mark the best character of a resilient people. Just as other populations have moved or been moved from one place to another, the African American today is a product of human movement from the most ancient of times until the most recent.

Mobility

Mobility marks the human species, and the earliest example of human beings moving from one place to another is found on the continent of Africa. After the origin of *Homo sapiens* somewhere in the fertile river valleys of a pristine East Africa, human beings traveled throughout our native continent, crossed into Asia and Europe, and populated the earth. In a profound sense the narrative of Africans in the Americas, South and North, might be said to transcend geography, deserts, oceans, forests, cultures, and even time. Indeed, African American history opens us up to what Winston Van Horne has termed transgenerationality, transculturality, and transcontinentality.

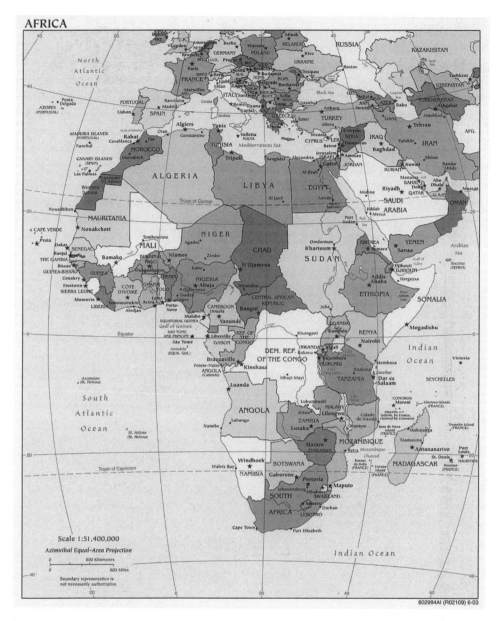

Figure 1.1 Map of Africa

The global reach of African American history starts in a unique way with the emergence on the African continent of resilient, curious, and durable ancestors. Thus, the historical narrative is not simply one that starts and ends in Africa—although that history is itself rich and vital. Rather, it moves across the globe. Humans share a common ancestry.

We feel and experience human kinship in many forms in a lifetime; that is our existential condition. However, the peculiarities of human interaction have from time to time produced unbearable grief, anxiety, pain, and suffering. This occurs when our journey through life is challenged by divisiveness, slavery, genocidal wars, ethnic cleansings, and other cruelties. Yet out of these conditions emerges the incredible rise to human fulfillment and completeness that some refer to as glory.

While it is true that all humans can trace their ancestry to the African continent, perhaps the so-called Middle Passage Africans—those in the Caribbean and the Americas—hold a more recent and emotional attachment to Africa as their ancestral home than any other group of people living outside of the African continent. It is the "Mother Land," as the name of a contemporary documentary film by Owen Shahidah reminds us. The Middle Passage Africans who entered the English colony as enslaved Africans in seventeenth-century Virginia have written a dramatic narrative across the face of the American continent and have demonstrated in every field the international reach of their influence.

Lessons of Biology and Anthropology in African Origin

The genetic mother of the mitochondrial DNA of the human race appears to have emerged in Africa about 250,000 years ago. In effect, scientists believe that this First Mother gave her genetic information to the nearly 7 billion people on the earth today.

Scientists Vincent Macaulay et al. report that both modern human mitochondrial DNA (mtDNA) and the male-specific part of the modern human Y chromosome have a recent origin in Africa and were dispersed throughout the rest of the world less than 100,000 years ago.[1] This conclusion substantiates the antiquity and the origins of modern humans in Africa, although recent evidence suggests that Denisovans whose remains were found in the caves of Siberia, Neanderthals found in the Neander Valley of Germany, and "hobbits"—dwarf hominids—found on Flores Island in Indonesia, existed for a while alongside modern *Homo sapiens*. However, all species of hominids are traced to the continent of Africa regardless of where their bones are found today. Mitochondrial studies have shown that everyone, inside and outside of Africa, is descended from one African mother.

To understand how scientists arrived at their conclusion about the origin of humans in Africa one must consider the time before recorded history. Historians refer to this time as *prehistory*. During prehistory there existed small-brained, human-like creatures called *hominids*. The oldest fossilized hominid is called *Sahelanthropus tchadensis* and it lived nearly 7 million years ago in what is today the African country of Chad. *Sahelanthropus* is the most recent common ancestor to humans and chimpanzees. Found in the region occupied by the Tebou people of Chad, the fossil remains of *Sahelanthropus* suggest that the archaeological evidence for the African origin of human beings is as dramatic as the biological evidence from mitochondrial DNA. Prior to the discovery of *Sahelanthropus tchadensis* scientists had found other old fossils that pointed to African origin. They referred to these remains as *Australopithecines*. The earliest example of these is *Australopithecus afarensis*, referred to by the Ethiopians as *Dinqnesh* and by Americans as *Lucy*. Indeed, the Ethiopian scholar Ayele Bekerie says, "Dinqnesh, we insist, and not Lucy, is a 3.1-million-year-old human-like species found in the Afar region of the Rift Valley of Ethiopia."[2] Dinqnesh was bipedal and much shorter than modern humans. In 1974 a team of American and Ethiopian archaeologists led by Donald Johanson found Dinqnesh or Lucy's fossilized skeleton remains—everything but her skull—curled up like a fetus in the semi-arid region of Ethiopia. According to scientists, she lived 4.2 million years ago. Her environment was rich with water, food, and natural places for shelter and protection such as rock ledges or huge trees. In fact, archaeologists have discovered so many fossils in East Africa that they refer to it as the "cradle of the species," the original home of humankind.

Scientists believe that human beings are the result of *monogenesis*—one common African origin. This belief replaced an earlier theory which contended that humans developed in many places at the same time. Most scientists believe that this polygenesis theory is inaccurate, as well as the more recent conclusions of Christy G. Turner II that Africans and Europeans are derived from a more recent common Southeast Asian source, based on his identification of two basic dental clusters.[3] In fact, Turner compares dental samples from North Africa with archaeologically derived Near Eastern dental samples to suggest that the temporal changes in the North African teeth were due to population replacement or admixture from the north. It is further argued that Afro-Asiatic was introduced into Africa along with the migrating immigrant farmers and herdsmen from the Near East 10,000 to 7,000 years ago. This theory has not been universally accepted by other scientists but is potentially significant in anthropological research. There is nothing in Turner's argument that displaces the emergence of *Homo sapiens* on the African continent, however. A conclusion of Turner's thesis is that humans left Africa and returned to Africa, and that this is the change reflected in the North African dental samples. Of course, Shomarka Keita, following another track, has established the fact that in the available Y chromosome data of the Afro-Asiatic language family—for which reliable genetic data exist—most Afro-Asiatic speakers share the lineage defined by Yap descendant PN2/215/M35. It was further found that that a key lineage—the M35/78—was shared between the populations in the locale of original Egyptian speakers and modern Cushitic speakers from the Horn of Africa.[4] Even with reports by scholars such as Keita and others who explore the package of culture, biology, and language, the overwhelming biological and archaeological evidence still points to an African origin of humanity and an early human migration from Africa of people settling in other parts of the world.

Civilizations and Cultures

It is a stunning achievement of the human spirit that within the past 250,000 years early humans in Africa have created the fundamentals of the civilizations that are now shared by the world. Regardless of the simplicity or complexity of the concepts, attributes, models, rituals, inventions, sciences, or arts of humanity, scholars have clearly determined that it was on the African continent that *Homo sapiens* first conceived the thoughts and crafted the tools that have made the modern world. Although the earth is thought to be 13 billion years old, dinosaurs who ruled the earth for 175 million years disappeared about 75 million years ago, *Sahelanthropus tchadensis* walked the earth 7.2 million years ago, the prehistoric Stone Age began a mere 4 million years ago, *Australopithecus sadiba* fell into an open cave in South Africa 2 million years ago, and *Homo sapiens* appeared on earth about 250,000 years ago. We are a late species. Nevertheless, we have been as active as—or more active than—any other species in arranging the earth, as best we could, for our own happiness and expansion. On the African continent humans emerged and immediately began the process of securing their own reproduction by devising codes of conduct, social units, and kinship structures. They also experimented with food gathering and preparation; it was not always clear what was fit to eat and what would kill you. Shelter from storms, natural fires, dangerous animals, and other humans was essential for any group that would survive. The naming of things, the memory of events and personalities, the memorializing of the dead, and the care of the young all had to become a part of the archival and active knowledge of the early communities in Africa. Out of these knowledge communities larger clusters of people would develop into mutually beneficial settlements. We often refer to these large societies as civilizations, meaning that there are common elements in their approach to achieving the ends of human happiness. These commonalities are sometimes expressed as language, spiritual beliefs, kinship styles, narratives of origin, responses to the environment, agricultural practices, gender relationships, and political structures.

Nubia, the Land of the Bow (15,000 BCE–300 CE)

The recent book *Black Genesis: The Prehistoric Origins of Ancient Egypt* by Robert Bauval and Thomas Brophy—like the earlier book *Black Athena* by Martin Bernal—has continued along the avenue taken by the African intellectual Cheikh Anta Diop in his monumental *The African Origin of Civilization*: that the earliest civilizations were black civilizations. Bauval and Brophy argue that the discoveries at Nabta Playa and the work of earlier explorers such as Ahmed Hassanein Bey (called the greatest desert explorer of all time), Rosita Forbes, and Gerhard Rohlfs demonstrate that the black people of southern Egypt, Libya, and Sudan were the creators of the earliest cultures in the Sahara and along the Nile. Indeed, in 1921 Hassenein, accompanied by Rosita Forbes, made a journey deep into the southwest desert, where they met with the Tebu's king, Herri, and were told of the ancient sites in the area. When Bauval and Brophy journeyed to the site of Nabta Playa in 2008 they would declare it to be the source of ancient Egyptian civilization. Their argument and that of other scholars continues the uncovering of information that challenges much racist thinking as well as much *place of origin* apprehension found in many Africans in the Diaspora.

One of the earliest known African civilizations was that of Nubia, a society dating back to the middle of the New Stone Age (15,000–3400 BCE) which was the first community to make use of the special material and agricultural gifts of the Nile Valley. We now know that the age of human development in Nubia stretches back farther than we had previously thought.

In 1981 the shuttle *Columbia* carried a radar-imaging camera that could record images through the sands of the Sahara. Once NASA scientists analyzed the photographs, they discovered dried-up riverbeds, ancient settlement areas, and other evidences of human activity. Yet when Robert Bauval and Thomas Brophy traveled to the same area to study the megaliths of Nabta Playa, the place seemed to have no life whatsoever. What it does have, however, is some of the oldest megaliths in the world. They are situated about 200 miles west of Abu Simbel—at one time located in Nubia but now found in the south of the modern country of Egypt (whose recent national boundaries are the products of numerous political alignments and realignments).

Scientists believe that with the rising of the sea levels about 14,000 years ago, profound changes occurred in the earth, including rain and monsoon rain in parts of Africa that are now dry as a bone. By 9000 BCE, human artifacts appear in the sediment around the megaliths. It is likely that humans occupied a fertile Sahara region for thousands of years and it is no wonder that the remnants of those settled areas hovered along the banks of the Nile in Nubia.

Several major African kingdoms developed in the vicinity of Nubia. Kush, Meroë, and Napata were the names of three key kingdoms in that region; however, Kemet—ancient Egypt—and Kush were the most significant in history. Using the Nile and the sun, a combination that would produce flourishing civilizations for thousands of years, these two civilizations would rival any in the world.

All people of Nubia lived along the fertile, narrow banks of the river as it flowed northward to the sea. Their land was blessed with a temperate climate, fertile soil, and a good supply of water. Nubia became a great kingdom in its own right and was approximately 1,100 miles long, running from a few hundred miles south of the present Khartoum (the capital of the modern country of Sudan) to Aswan (in present-day Egypt). Unfortunately, most of the area that was marked by this great civilization, and that of Kush, was flooded by the building of the Aswan High Dam. It is believed that more than 200 historical sites, many of them tombs of nobles, temples to the ancient deities of Nubia and Kush, and places of historic battles and deeds of Nubians, have been destroyed. The governments of Egypt and Sudan also forced nearly 100,000 Nubians from their homes during the building of the High Dam in the 1960s. In fact, some Nubians who had been living in Egypt were moved 28 miles away while the Sudanese Nubians were relocated 370 miles from their ancestral homes.

The Egyptian government in the 1960s was also forced by international pressure to move one of the largest Nubian temple sites in the Nile Valley, the Abu Simbel temples of Ramses and Nefertari, to a new location above the lake created by the dam. The Egyptians made an attempt to dig for artifacts in the area but the harm done to the historical record of Egypt and Nubia can never be repaired and the forced migration of the people produced a sustained anger and bitterness among them. Notwithstanding the popular images of Kemet created by the Egyptologist Zahi Hawass, the indigenous Nubian people of the Nile Valley—the original inhabitants—still insist that the Arab culture in its expansive dimension has attempted to minimize the blackness of the ancient Egyptians. They point out that Kemet was black thousands of years before the arrival of Arabs from Arabia in the seventh century of this era.

Nubian society developed from a series of scattered villages built around kinship groupings along the fertile banks of the Nile. The Nubians established farms, made mud-brick houses, planted fruit trees, and fished. The crops grown on their farms were often cassava, rice, and bananas. They mastered the technique of building houses that were cool during the hot sun of the day and warm during the cool of the night. Their building techniques did not end with houses. They constructed tool-making sites and shrines and temples where they performed religious ceremonies. They designed and made pottery, baskets, and weapons of war. All of this happened before writing appeared in Egypt, around 3400 BCE. Thus, Nubia was the one of the birthplaces of knowledge and its application to daily life.

As we know, powerful kingdoms grew up in the territory that was Nubia. One of the most important was the civilization of Kush, but other magnificent cities such as Meroë and Napata existed in the same general region. It was Kush, however, that competed with its neighbor Kemet for military and political impact for thousands of years.[5]

Kush: The Land of the Lion Warriors

Kush was a kingdom located in the territory that had been called Nubia. Many kingdoms had originated in this narrow, fertile valley, south of Kemet, along the Nile River in today's Sudan. Kush was located in an area that reached north from present-day Khartoum in Sudan to Aswan in Egypt. By the eighth century BCE Kush had created a mature civilization based upon the indigenous culture of its people. The Kushites had their own religion, an aggressive fishing enterprise, agricultural projects, and were producing beautiful art. The people, in addition to demonstrating considerable skill in the production of grain and the distribution of meats from hunt, had mastered the art of war. A combination of the ancient people of Nubia and Dinka, the multiethnic population of Kush constituted a pluralistic government noted for its use of the bow and arrow. In fact, some have argued that its name means "land of the bow"—a name given by the literate Kemetic people who had both seen the results of a Kushite attack and allied themselves to Kush during the reigns of several Kemetic kings, notably Senursert, Mentuhotep I, and Ramses II.

During the eighth and seventh centuries BCE, Kush expanded its military reach, increased the construction of ancestral tombs, paid homage to the deities with huge displays of dramatic ritual, and built, out of respect and devotion, massive temples to honor the gods and goddesses of the land.

In nearly one thousand years of existence, Kush had sixty-seven kings or queens, from King Kashta in 760 BCE to King Malequerebar in 320 CE. The early civilization of Kush placed a remarkable emphasis on revitalizing the entire Nile Valley from the south to the north. The kings and queens built numerous shrines and restored monuments from Napata to Mennefer, an area covering more than a thousand miles.

When Kemet had grown weak because of internal political squabbles among its ruling families, the kingdom of Kush under the leadership of its king, Kashta, led an invasion into Kemet in 750 BCE. The ease with which Kashta defeated the Kemetians suggests the weakness of Kemet's southern borders. Neither the cataracts nor the desert could prevent the military might of the Kushites from advancing northward. Kashta took the title of pharaoh of Upper and Lower Egypt and made Napata, his capital city, the first city of the realm. Residents of Waset, the city that had been the capital for several centuries, paid homage to Napata in Kush.

By 728 BCE, Piankhi, Kashta's son and successor, mounted a second attack on Egypt. He so utterly defeated the Egyptians, the cousins of the Kushites, that in his conquest he ended the bitter rivalries of the northern families, conquered the Libyan invaders of Egypt, built fortresses and modernized the temples, repaired the public buildings, and increased the national support for the priesthood in Waset.

Piankhi ruled from Waset itself as the first king of the twenty-fifth dynasty. His conquest of Egypt was more direct and aggressive than his father's. After twenty years as ruler of Napata, Piankhi led an army toward Waset. He marched to the city because he heard of the movement of a young prince named Tefnakhte who was threatening Upper Egypt from his base in Lower Egypt. Once in Waset, Piankhi showed his devotion to Amen, the great deity of the city, and reasserted Kushitic rule over Upper Egypt. He conquered the rebellious princes and rulers and consolidated Kushitic power over the entire valley. Piankhi's brother,

Table 1.1 Four great Kushite kings of united Kemet

Piankhi	728–716 BCE
Shabaka	716–700 BCE
Shabataka	700–690 BCE
Taharka	690–664 BCE

Shabaka, succeeded him in 716 BCE. Piankhi's sons Shabataka (700–690 BCE) and Taharka (690–664 BCE) succeeded Shabaka.

One of the most impressive of all Kushite kings was Taharka, Piankhi's son. He became ruler in 690 BCE and spent much of his time in Egypt. He was crowned in Memphis. He took his mother more than a thousand miles from Napata to Memphis to witness his installation as the king of Upper and Lower Egypt. But although Taharka restored monuments, reclaimed wastelands and made them profitable, organized the priesthood to be more effective in aiding the sick, and built obelisks and new temples, his rule was plagued by the Assyrians, an Asian people from an area that is in today's Iraq.

Miriam Maat Ka Re Monges claimed in *Kush: The Jewel of Nubia* that most people fail to give Kush the credit it deserves for bringing Egypt its last golden age. According to Monges, the revitalization of the Nile Valley civilizations provided by the Kushite kings was responsible for giving Egypt a golden age several hundred years prior to its being overcome by the Greeks in 332 BCE.[6] This period in history, often referred to (as in the February 2008 issue of *National Geographic Magazine*) as the "Era of the Black Pharaohs" as if the majority of the African leaders of Kemet were not black, was directed by the Kushite kings, who did not see Kemet as foreign to their own country.[7] It was in fact the gift of Nubia, the land the Kushites had inherited, and therefore their conquest of Kemet was seen by them as a way to return it to the righteousness and harmony of the ancestral wisdom.

The Idea of Monarchy

The Nubians were the earliest humans to develop the concept of *monarchy*, a form of government headed by a supreme ruler such as a king or queen. An incense burner and other relics were discovered during an expedition in 1967 conducted by archaeologists from the University of Chicago.[8] These relics contain images of a crown, the façade of a palace, and other symbols of kingship. They existed long before similar images appear in Egypt. The idea of the divine kingship is now believed to have originated with the Nubian Africans in the fourth millennium BCE. rather than with the Egyptian Africans, thus pushing the idea of the royal crown back several hundred years. Many of the ideas that were found later in Egypt had already occurred in Nubia. There had been a constant interplay between these two ancient African communities, such was their nature; sometimes they would compete and at other times they would unite in alliance.

Kemet: The Black Land along the Nile

Kemet rose along the Nile under the brightest of suns. It stretched along the Nile River from what is present-day Aswan north to the Mediterranean Sea and lasted from 3400 BCE to the conquest by Alexander the Great in 333 BCE. The land of Kemet, as it was called until the Greeks renamed it Egypt, was the home of the most majestic civilization of antiquity. It would transcend Nubia and thrust African achievements into the rest of the world. Here we would find the beginning of philosophy, astronomy, mathematics, geometry, architecture, and medicine. No other ancient people are credited with as many basic inventions and creations for civilization as the people of Kemet. They were the children of the Nile River.

The Nile gave life to everything that grew on its banks. Without the Nile, the country of Egypt would be nothing but a desert. The annual flooding of the Nile, which was different from the Nile in Nubia, brought silt down from the interior of Africa to the Nile Valley. It also wreaked havoc on private property boundaries and livestock. The people of Egypt came together to manage the overflowing of the Nile and in the process created responses and solutions to annual problems that advanced human sciences. For example, geometry was created when they used ropes to measure the land when the flooding of the Nile destroyed property boundaries, and the Egyptian calendar was based on the coordination of the rising of Sirius, the brightest star in the heavens, with the annual flooding of the Nile.

The Nile provided a means of transportation for the shipbuilding industry and the quarrying of stone for large building projects located downstream. Large stones could be transported down the river during the flood period. Massive carved stones used as obelisks or stelae for historical purposes were usually cut from stone at Aswan in southern (Upper) Kemet and floated along the river to various construction sites.

On the other hand, as the Nile was regular in its inundation, so the sun was a constant in its heat. It rarely rains in Egypt and so the people used their time productively in agriculture, mastery of the sciences and arts, rites and celebrations, and the constructing of temples and tombs. Even during the flooding they just moved to higher ground and continued to work. The sun was a steady reminder of stability and regularity. Some historians have suggested that this stability was a sort of stagnation, perhaps slowing their progress. Certainly stability could also be the hallmark of a civilization that has mastered the necessary requirements for maintaining order and harmony. The idea that conflict is itself the motive for civilization is vastly overstated, and the importance of stability grossly underrated.

Egypt developed a unique civilization with a centralized government that united forty-two different areas along the Nile. Menes, who is sometimes called Narmer, the king of the first *dynasty*, united the various groups of Upper Egypt to the south and Lower Egypt to the north into one nation. Before Menes united them there were only a collection of clans of various ethnicities settled along the river. These districts were referred to as *sepats*; the Greeks later called them *nomes*. A leader who was called a *nomarch* headed each one of these groups. These *nomarchs* were like small kings over their own people. Menes' union in 3200 BCE marked the first time in history that such a feat had been achieved. Therefore, Menes is called the Father of the Nation for founding a multiethnic, pluralistic society that went beyond kinship bonds. Kemet would continue to produce value for humanity in epic proportions for hundreds of years.

Egypt gives us Imhotep, the first multidimensional personality in recorded history, who built the first pyramid, prescribed the first medicines, and served as an administrator for the king. There are written records about many aspects of his life, including his career, his parents, and even what he believed and thought on certain issues. Imhotep lived around 2800 BCE. He was an architect, a prime minister, a physician, a philosopher, a scribe, and a historian. Imhotep was so great that later generations worshipped him as a god. His name comes from the root word "hotep," which means "peace" in ancient Egyptian (or ciKam, the language of Kemet). Thus, his name means "he who comes in peace."

The people of Kemet had two other names of endearment for their land. They called it Ta-Mery, meaning "beloved land." The word "Ta" in ancient Egyptian meant "land" and the word "Mery" stood for "beloved". They also called the country Ta-Wy, the Two Lands, referring to Upper and Lower Egypt. This indicated the two different geographical parts of the country originally united by Menes. It is sometimes argued that the two lands referred to the fertile areas near the river and the desert sands away from the river. However, the Kemetians lived mainly along the green river valley and would most likely have been referring to the kingdoms in the north and the kingdoms in the south. The king wore two crowns—the red crown of Lower Kemet, and the white crown of Upper Kemet—neither of which represented the desert.

In a global African sense, and especially for Africans in the Diaspora, often disconnected from constant and continuous contact with continental values, customs, and traditions, Kemet represents the majestic fountain from which spring many classical African concepts. Kemet is in relationship to the African continent as Greece is to Europe and China is to Asia. Indeed, one can say that each area of the globe can claim classical civilizations that produce values worthy of emulation. Africa has its Kemet and Nubia; Asia has India and China; and Europe has Greece and Rome. These are civilizations that can be studied as the source for many surrounding cultures.

The Earliest Golden Age (3150 BCE–2700 BCE)

The period of major achievement in construction and exploration, named for the important town of This, is referred to as the Thinite Period. During this time many significant achievements were made in the Nile Valley; for example, Imhotep built the first pyramid for King Djoser during this period. The pyramid was called the Sakkara Step Pyramid because it was constructed like giant steps, and its complex contains the oldest masonry building in the world. Following Imhotep's example, much later, in the Thinite period, others whose names are not recorded constructed the Great Pyramids of Giza in honor of kings Khufu, Khafre, and Menkaure. They remain among the greatest wonders in the world because of their size, majesty, endurance, and longevity.

The Old Kingdom (2700 BCE–2190 BCE)

Harkhuf, an adventurer and high official of Egypt, tells of his travels during the Old Kingdom from Kemet to places deep in the interior of the continent. He and his caravan of camels and donkeys traveled more than a thousand miles across the Sahara Desert to the Ituri rainforest in Central Africa, where he visited societies of small people, possibly the Mbuti or the Ituri people. It is expeditions such as Harkhuf's which clearly show that Africans explored their continent before any external explorers set foot on the desert or in the forest, and knew about areas far beyond their own region. Harkhuf went on three explorations into the interior of Africa around 2300 BCE. His explorations and journeys show the contact between ancient Egypt and other parts of the continent, but this was hardly a one-way process since many of the individuals who entered Kemet from Nubia, Congo, Punt, Axum, or other areas also made their journeys back and forth across the continent. Harkhuf's journey simply demonstrates the cultural exchange and trade that flourished among African kingdoms. In one of his diaries Harkhuf declares:

> I have come here from my city,
> I have descended from my nome,
> I have built a house, set up its doors,
> I have dug a pool, planted sycamores,
> The king praised me,
> My father made a will for me.
> I was one worthy.[9]

Harkhuf made several long explorations from Kemet. During his third exploration he visited the kingdom of Yam, which was located in the southern part of contemporary Sudan. On his arrival he both gave and received gifts. On his return down to Kemet he said, "I came down with three hundred donkeys, laden with incense, ebony, oil, panther skins, elephants' tusks, throw sticks, and all sorts of good products." The products of Yam became a visa for Harkhuf when he passed through other kingdoms. For example, when the ruler of Irtjet, another kingdom in contemporary Sudan, saw the gifts from the king of Yam that he had brought with him, Harkhuf reports that he was allowed to pass through the country. In fact, he writes, "the ruler escorted me, gave me cattle and goats, and led me on the mountain paths of Irtjet—because of the excellence of the vigilance I had employed beyond that of any companion and chief of scouts who had been sent to Yam before." Apparently others had gone before Harkhuf to Yam, but returned with little or no success. Furthermore, an empty-handed traveler might not be so easily disposed to write about his adventures. Harkhuf's narrative is a statement of triumph, vision, and personal mastery.

The Middle Kingdom (2000 BCE–1786 BCE)

War between Egyptians doomed the Old Kingdom. The Middle Kingdom came into existence following the first intermediate period of warfare between Egyptians. The country was led out of confusion and internal strife by kings from Upper Egypt around 2000 BCE. A dynasty led by Mentuhotep I came to power and restored the temples, built palaces, improved administration of the agricultural lands, and established military supremacy over Egypt's neighbors to the north and to the south. The Middle Kingdom was a period of great building under the leadership of kings such as Mentuhotep I and Mentuhotep II. During this period Senursert I and Senursert II established themselves as great conquerors, defeating nations around the Mediterranean, including Syria, and regions around the Black Sea in Southwestern Asia. In fact, Herodotus, writing in his book *Histories* nearly 1,500 years later, would refer to the physical evidence of Kemetians in what became the Abkhazian region of the Black Sea. He writes that the "Colchians must be Egyptians because like them they have black skin and wooly hair."[10]

As the Middle Kingdom grew weaker because of internal divisions and the growing presence of Asians, that is, people who had come from Southwest Asia to the Delta region, Kemet lost political control over the country. Numerous warlords took charge of districts they claimed as their own, weakening further the power of the central government. However, the greatest threat came from the Delta region where the Asians had flowed into Kemet from the northeast. The Hyksos, or Hekaw Khasut, a people from Southwest Asia, created a separate government around the Delta region, which is in Lower Egypt, and ruled from 1786 BCE to 1650 BCE. Like later invaders of Egypt, the Hyksos gained power by becoming part of the existing political system. They were finally defeated at the gates of the city of Avaris by King Kamose, the last king of the seventeenth dynasty and predecessor to the Ahmosian Dynasty.

The New Kingdom (1552 BCE–1069 BCE)

The third period was called the New Kingdom. During this time Egyptian rulers from Upper Egypt reasserted the power of the central government and reunited the main centers of Egyptian authority such as the authoritative temples at On, Mennefer, Abydos, and Waset. This reunited area stretches from Cairo to Luxor in modern Egypt. The first king of the eighteenth dynasty was Ahmose. He succeeded in driving the Hyksos from Egypt and established the first dynasty of the New Kingdom (1567 BCE–1085 BCE). No more fabled dynasty exists in Egypt's history. This was the age of Hatshepsut (1503 BCE–1482 BCE), the world's first imperial queen, ruling in her own right as leader of a great empire. She sent an expedition to visit the queen of Nubia and king of Punt and received gifts of incense, animals, trees, and precious stones, all recorded on the walls of her funerary temple. Also during this period Tuthmoses III, the greatest conqueror of antiquity in terms of personally led war missions, annexed Syria, Palestine, Lebanon, and Nubia to Egypt. Tuthmoses III is credited with personally leading more military campaigns against the opponents of Kemet than any other per-aa (pharaoh in Hebrew). In fact, no ancient leader is credited with more successes than Thutmoses III.

During the New Kingdom the boy king Tutankhamen, whose tomb discovery popu-larized Egyptian history because it was found intact, ruled Egypt. He died when he was eighteen years of age without having made any memorable achievement in the life of Egypt. He was buried in the Valley of the Kings in Upper Egypt near the city of Waset, previously called Thebes by the Greeks, called Luxor today by the Arabs. All the tombs of the New Kingdom kings were meant to last forever. They were supposed to be secret but in actuality many of them were broken into and the gold objects stolen long before the modern era. Only the tomb of Tutankhamen, placed among sixty or more temples, remained intact until the twentieth century when the Englishman Howard Carter, an amateur archaeologist, discovered it in 1922. Carter found that the tomb of Ramses VI was carved just above that of King Tutankhamen and the rubble from Ramses VI's tomb had for centuries covered the burial place of Tutankhamen. When it was discovered, the tomb contained golden pendants, jewelry, ivory beads, golden stools, a golden mummy case, and numerous stones. King Tutankhamen owes his place in history not to any political or social transformations, but to the remarkable artifacts and works of art found in his tomb and recovered for future generations.

Egypt would last for eleven dynasties after Tutankhamen before its glory would fade. However, other states in Africa were ready to take their walk in the bright sunlight of history. One such state had been preparing since the days when its sons defeated Egypt and annexed it to Kush, making it a united country along the Nile for more than a thousand miles. This was the Nubian Empire that ruled from Napata and Waset. It would later become the victim of the powerful Axumite kingdom to its south and east.

Axum: The Rival to Rome

Axum has often been called Ethiopia, a word that was used as a general term for Africa by some early writers. Ethiopia is a Greek word that means "burnt faces." The nation of Axum was a specific kingdom within the boundaries of today's Ethiopia but is not to be identified as the exact same country as the borders have changed through the years. Often called Abyssinia, modern Ethiopia dates its history from ancient Axum.

Historical Axum rose to become one of the most inventive kingdoms of the world by the third century CE. Indeed, its fame had spread so wide that historians and scholars in other parts of the world saw Axum as among the most organized and efficient kingdoms of its day. The prophet Mani (216–276), a Persian philosopher, teacher, and writer of importance, who became the founder of Manicheism, a belief that the flesh was evil and one had to work to conquer it at all costs, wrote in a book called *Chapters* that there were four great empires in the world: Axum, Rome, Persia, and China. Rome formed the core of modern Italy, Persia became Iran, and China has remained China for centuries. Axum morphed into the present Ethiopia.

As Axum grew into an empire it established a commercial capital called Adulis, known for its physical beauty, official residences, public buildings, and the wealth of its citizens. It was the trading center of the Axumite Empire. This city of shining buildings and intelligent citizens was the brightest jewel of the realm. While the city of Axum, the namesake of the empire, would become the most identified city within the kingdom, Adulis would rival its political capital for world attention and become the face of the empire.

There were many languages spoken in Axum by the seventh century. Among the languages were Ge'ez, Latin, Greek, Arabic, Egyptian, Farsi, Meroitic, and other African languages. The Axumites wrote about their lives and their empire in striking dramas, history, and comedy. Indeed, the ancient writings of the Axumite Empire tell their story in fascinating details. Stelae, that is, stones with writing on them, specifically erected to provide historical information, have been found throughout the area occupied by the empire. But since not everything was history, the people of Axum wrote about their feelings, their religion, and their interactions with other people.

Borrowing a great deal, it seems, from the Nubians and Kemites, the people of Axum recorded their achievements for posterity. In addition to their writings we have many artifacts that reveal a very active civilization in commerce and artistic developments. The ancient Axumites created and erected monoliths, like the *tekken* of Kemet, that were massive in scale. These obelisks, as they are sometimes called, were meant to demonstrate the power and authority of the Axumite people. They built stelae, huge altars, throne bases, and other large stone structures. They also built houses for the nobles and elites that would be called mansions or palaces. They were built mainly in Axum but also in Adulis and Matara, where there are ruins of palaces and elaborate villas of the highest artistic quality. They reflect attention to detail and design representative of Axum's glory during the years of pre-eminence as an African empire. In design the house complex often seen in Axum was directly related to the concept of the African compound, where many structures serving different functions are connected by a common courtyard or walled-in walkway. Thus, a family might use one small building for storage, another for sleeping, another for visitors, another for entertainment, and so forth. It is common in the West for people to have all functions under one roof. When Christianity ruled in Axum their architects soon employed the huge stone culture on a monumental scale in the creation of Christian churches and tombs of kings.

It is difficult to discover an empire in antiquity with as much copper, gold, pottery, glass, and as many precious stones and ceramics as Axum. Anything we can imagine would only be a pale copy of the robust original. Using these huge pieces of art for religious and ceremonial purposes meant that the empire had to constantly remind the subjects of the central authority of the government. A strong military force, under the authority of the king, insured the success of the people's memory.

Axum was an industrial hub for East Africa. One of the principal metals used for warfare and agriculture was iron, although it was not only a metal used for work and war; it was also used to make utensils for worship. One could say that iron was the metal of work, worship, and warfare while gold was more frequently used in Axum for mystery, ritual, and personal ornamentation.

Gold vessels were regularly employed in the ceremonies and church rituals. Although gold never reached the popular use in Axum that it had in Kemet and Nubia in terms of gold jewelry, it was actually the most sought-after metal among the wealthy landholders and urban merchants. Yet it was the pottery that revealed for future generations the depth of the Axumites' love for their civilization and belief in the glory of their kings. In the pottery we see how the Axumites decorated jars, vases, bowls, and urns with their history. The ancient people of Africa, especially along the Rift Valley, could be identified by their pottery to the extent that one could truly say that by their pottery you can know the people.

Three periods are recognized in Axumite history: dawning, glowing, and brilliant. These represent the eras during which the empire of Axum started, matured, and reached its zenith in power and majesty. The dawning stage ran from about 500 BCE to 200 BCE; the glowing stage from 200 BCE to 99 AD; and the brilliant stage from 99 CE to 900 CE.

During the dawning stage Axum's architectural and cultural styles were being developed and the culture expressed itself in art and sculpture that has been found throughout the ancient land. It was during this stage that the people of Axum first became acquainted with the Arabian people of Yemen. They first met, as one would think, trading with each other across the Red Sea. Soon the interactions were such that commerce brought them into conflict and they occasionally occupied each other's land. The Axumites influenced the culture of Yemen to the degree that one can still find remnants of the Axumite culture in some of the small towns of Yemen. The architecture of Yeha and Haoutlti-Melazo in Axum can be found in Yemen. Undoubtedly the interactions went both ways as there are linguistic items that the two languages came to share because of the trade and political relationship. But in this early era there was already evidence of the growing military prowess of the Axumite people.

The glowing stage brings the Axumites into the Christian era. Axum's involvement in southern Arabia becomes weaker due to Axum's concentration on its own internal problems, rebellions against the central power, internal squabbles over the kingship, and the growing threats from other African nations. At the same time the country is producing majestic art with beautiful pottery and vases. Its key centers of influence have increased from the powerful Axum and the dynamic Adulis to other cities such as Yeha, Gobo-Fench, Fekya, and Li'Lay-Addi. These towns were the most vigorous in the empire and may have been among the most important centers of commerce, trade, and gossip in the whole of Africa during the glowing period of Axumite history.

In Adulis, scholars have found more than sixty different inscriptions on the most ancient buildings. These inscriptions suggest that Axum was actively engaged in communication with other nations and kingdoms and that the historical events recorded are evidences of the lively discourse in thought, ceremony, and ritual in the city.

The brilliant stage was the time of the greatest influence and power of the Axumite kingdom. Indeed, the society reached its full glory about the same time as Rome, but two important neighbors—Nubia in Africa and Saba in Arabia—were in decline. Nubia had controlled the Nile and Saba had controlled much of the Red Sea trade. With Axum's rise at the expense of both of those countries, it gained enormous wealth and status, changing the political equation both in Africa and in Arabia. This impacted the extensive outreach of Rome, which had from time to time depended upon Saba and Nubia for its extended trade routes. It was now evident that it would be to Axum that Rome would turn to protect its ships in the Red Sea against the constant problem of pirates. To further cement its friendship with Rome, Axum agreed to prevent the Beja from attacking Rome's southern flank in the south of Egypt. Rome had ruled Egypt since 30 BCE and the death of Cleopatra. Axum was the mightiest nation in Africa in the fourth century CE, exercising power and authority over politics and commercial activities in the region.

In one inscription the King of the Adulis area wrote, "Having commanded the peoples closest to my kingdom to preserve the peace, I bravely waged war and subjugated in battles the following peoples . . ."[11] There follows a long list of defeated enemies, including Sennar, a country that was located near the Abay River and had become a major source of irritation to the Axumite Empire. There was also a country that was described as a land of "high mountains, cold winds, and mist," which could have been some other area of the present country of Ethiopia, or part of Kenya or Uganda. These areas are known for their mist and cold weather. The king of Axum had a monument erected for himself just in case the Adulis region thought that it did not have to pay allegiance. The conquering king, whose name does not appear on the stelae, having been rubbed out, says that he defeated all of his neighbors in the surrounding territories. In fact, he did more than defeat all the people who lived on the border with Egypt. He "again made the road from Egypt to Axum a thoroughfare."[12]

Heliodorus, a Greek, wrote a historical novel called *Aethiopica* around 280–300 CE set in the time Persia ruled over Egypt, which was considerably earlier than the writing of the novel. In the novel, Nubia is described as being at the height of its power. Also in the novel there are lots of triumphal celebrations with different nations that have been conquered walking past the Nubian king so that he could review his conquered subjects. The kings came by, some of them bowing, others kneeling, and still others falling completely to the ground before the conqueror. However, when the king of Axum passed by the Nubian king, the novelist writes, the Axum king is standing erect, paying no tribute, and appearing as the last king to come before the Nubian. The Nubian expressed friendship with the Axum king and treated him as an equal. It would not be long before the Axumites conquered the Nubians. Even Axum's neighbors were thought by fictional writers to respect its power. Around 290 CE the king of Axum invaded Nubia and added it to his empire. In fact, the last king of Meroë whose name we know, Teceridamani, does not even appear in historical records after 254 CE. There were six Meroitic kings after him, yet these kings remain anonymous because their names have worn off of the stone stelae.

The evidence of the Axumite Empire's glory is everywhere, in all fields, during this time. Axum was the most advanced civilization Africa had produced so far. It had superseded both Kemet and the Nubian kingdoms of Kush and Meroë, and was a center of philosophical thinking and writing. Some of the wisest people lived in the towns of Axum and Adulis and some of the most respected artists, writers, and religious figures impacted the world from the Axumite kingdom. They were outstanding in architecture, writing, language, religion, statesmanship, government, and bureaucracy. With the assistance of a well-developed bureaucracy, made so because of the emergence of the Ge'ez language and the church, the Axumites practiced an international politics that was advanced for its time.

At this point in Axum's history the culture was distinctively different from Nubia's or Kemet's; it was no mere replay of the earlier civilizations, but had emerged essentially on its own in Africa, away from the mainstream of the Nile Valley civilizations. Eventually, Axum had more contact with the Red Sea kingdoms and nations, including Yemen and Punt (Somalia). But its locus of power and center of culture would always remain the African continent. This was its source of religious, philosophical and aesthetic ideals.

Axum, the lodestone and magnet of the empire, sat high on the plateau beyond the mountains one had to cross on the eight-day journey from Adulis. The city was the seat of government and power. From this town the king ruled over the entire empire, sending out edicts, imposing taxes, minting coins, and raising an army in time of war. Its public buildings were grand, much like the rectangular buildings of Nubia and Kemet, but with the addition of tiers or floors that alternated in projecting outward and recessing inward.

By the brilliant age Axum was a deeply Christian country, the new religion having completely replaced the traditional religion based on the ancient deities in the capital city by the third century BCE. Of course, there were outlying areas where Christianity had not reached and did not reach during the entire period of the Axumite Empire. The grandeur of the structures in Axum might yet be related to the religious beliefs because the huge, monolithic dimensions and spaces of the buildings reflected a transcendent idea. The Axumites mostly used granite for building and created the obelisks entirely out of granite, much as the earlier cultures of the Nile Valley had used the stone for their massive monuments.

Kaleb's tomb at Axum and the Giant Stelae, both meant to be funerary monuments to the kings, represent significant achievements in memorial architecture. The huge structures are elaborately carved and show repetition of characteristically African aesthetic designs.

Public writings seem to have flourished during this time as well. The public decrees by officials, either the king or his representatives, show a civilization that took communication seriously. Almost every public building had a written inscription, in keeping with the tradition established by the African kingdoms and empires of the Nile Valley. In its public form, writing appeared everywhere. Thus, once again it is inaccurate to speak of African civilization as being without writing. There was as much or more writing in African antiquity as in any other ancient civilization. Just as there were large areas of Europe, North America, South America, Asia, and Australia without writing, so it was on the continent of Africa. But we have seen in previous discussions how the continent that gave the world writing also produced items based on the skill of writing. It was not just a dead skill but a very positive and vital activity of the people.

By the third century CE the Axumites began to use natural resources for everyday purposes. Gold, silver, and bronze were used to make coins throughout the empire. The Kemetic and Nubian civilizations, which did not make much use of coins, and the Axumites were the first Africans to mint their own coins and to use them in external trade.

For their internal trade they used bronze coins, but they relied mainly on a system of bartering. Axumite potters began to make pottery in new shapes and colors that were both beautifully decorated and functional. Clearly, international trade helped to influence the local artisans, but it is equally clear that Axum was not just a receiver of ideas but also a place that impacted on others.

In the middle of the fourth century CE, according to a sixth-century historian named Rufinus who wrote the book *Ecclesiastical History*, a Syrian Christian was on his way to India through the Red Sea when he became shipwrecked. His two sons, Aedesius and Frumentius, were adopted by King Ella Amida of Axum and raised in the palace. When King Amida died and his son, Ezana, became king, the two young Syrians Aedesius and Frumentius were brought into the court as advisors regarding the Christian nations and peoples. Ezana I ruled over a large kingdom that included the Beja, Arabia, Saba, Abyssinia, and Meroë. Most of these people had their own religions and they believed in their own gods. However, with the influence of Aedesius and Frumentius, who may have been in their teen years during the time of the shipwreck, many people in the Axumite state turned away from the ancient Axumite deities of Mahrem, Beher, Meder, and Astar. The two young Syrian men became enamored with the Axumite culture, passionate about Christianity, and began to study all forms of Christian theology, including Arianism, which was named for Arius, a priest who lived in Alexandria during the latter part of the third century BCE.

The Beja represented the most difficult nation to subdue for the Axumites. Ezana I succeeded in defeating them by sending his two brothers, She'azana and Hadefa, to head the Axumite army during the decisive battle with the Beja. These two generals had become the country's leading military strategists and Ezana I wanted them to plan the conquest of the Beja once and for all. This ancient people had harassed the Kemites and the Nubians, and now Axum was prepared to end the irritation of their hostile raiding parties. When the battle was over, the Beja recognized the supremacy of Axum. As an act of complete authority over their enemies, She'azana and Hadefa made the Beja soldiers, led by six of their surviving kings, walk to the court of Ezana I. The walls took four long months because it involved the royal houses of Beja, wives, children, and animals.

When they arrived in Axum the Beja bowed to the Axumite king. Ezana I could have killed the kings before the people, as some conquering kings would have done, but his mercy and generosity knew no bounds. He let the Beja keep their families together, their animals, and the use of their language. Such was his respect for the Beja that he did all he could to assist them. He ordered that 25,000 long-horned cattle, clothing, and food be given to the Beja kings. There was great rejoicing among the Axumites and the Beja. The Axumite king understood clearly the ancient African wisdom that said, "The sun will shine on those who stand before it shines on those who kneel." There was no need to further humiliate the ancient Beja people. In one way the moving of the Beja anticipated the twentieth-century removal of many Beja, Nuba, and Nubians during the construction of the Aswan High Dam. The Beja people remain a strong ethnic group in northeast Africa even into the twenty-first century.

The country was a magnet for ideas. People came to the land from afar to trade, to study, and to see the wonderful objects that had been created by the Axumites. Its growing intellectual class was made up increasingly of religious thinkers, philosophers, and debaters. In the sixth century, Cosmas Indicopleutes, a Greek writer and visitor, wrote that he found "everywhere in Axum and Adulis churches of Christians, bishops, martyrs, monks, and recluses by whom the Gospel of Christ is proclaimed."[13] It is more likely that Indicopluetes found people "willing to be martyrs" than actual martyrs in Axum and Adulis, but nevertheless he was quite impressed with what he saw. About 300 years later al-Yaqubi wrote that there were "mighty cities of the Abyssinians visited by Arab merchants of Dahlak." Perhaps unbeknown to al-Yaqubi the Arabs had knowledge of the Axumite kingdom even earlier, because we know that in the seventh century the king of Ethiopia gave protection to Muslims who had fled Arabia.

A century earlier, in 528 CE, the Axumite Empire had invaded Arabia, and ruled the Yemenite area until 575 CE when problems at home forced the large contingent of troops kept in Yemen to return to support the king in his contest with pretenders to his power. In fact, the power of the home base had to be preserved in order to continue the kingdom. So great was the military power of Axum in defending itself from attack that its neighbors, Sennar and Meroë, still paid taxes and gave gifts to the Axumite king well into the seventh century. Thus, Axum is said in the book *Periplus of the Erythraean Sea* to be a "place to which all the ivory is brought from the countries beyond the Nile."[14]

Axum's importance had to do with the sophisticated nature of its political and economic relationships with the rest of the world. It traded with India, China, Sri Lanka, Rome, Punt, Greece, Zanzibar, Persia, Kemet, Arabia, and Nubia. Its history is rich with the stories of the Queen of Sheba's visit to King Solomon and with the Gabaza Axum being the place where the Jewish Ark of the Covenant is kept, having been moved by King Menelik I from Jerusalem through Elephantine to the mountain kingdom of Axum.

The Mighty Niger Basin Civilizations

The Niger River rises in the Djallon Mountains in a small village called Tembakounda in the country of Guinea, a tropical land on the West African coast. The mighty Niger River flows eastward for 2,590 miles alternately through desert and grasslands. Near Timbuktu it takes an almost 90-degree turn toward the south through the countries of Niger and Nigeria. It enters the rainforest in Nigeria and flows to the Atlantic Ocean.

Fabled cities in African history are located near or on the shores of this mighty river: Niani, Timbuktu, Gao, Jenne, Loripeni, Bonny, Nembe, Onitsha, and Niamey are just a few. Many of these cities were in the ancient kingdoms of Ghana, Mali, and Songhay. Millions of people along the Niger use the river as their source of transportation and commerce. Great cities have been built on its banks because it has brought nations together and cemented friendships and trade for several thousand years.

The agricultural crops that were harvested along the river Niger consisted of rice, millet, maize, cocoa, peanuts, bananas, palm oil, and cassava. In fact, the contemporary agricultural industry is complemented by a river industry in construction of boats, cargo ships, paddle-wheel boats, and canoes which has its origin in antiquity. But the use of the Niger as a route for transporting goods is often limited since only a thousand miles of it is navigable all the time. The caravans carrying valuable gold and salt for trading relied upon the camel routes through the desert. These trade routes cross the areas where the great empires of Ghana, Mali, and Songhay once held sway.

Ghana: The Emergence of Imperial Power

Ghana was a strong, military kingdom in West Africa, established long before any other. It arose around 300 BCE among the Soninke and Susu people. It was located in today's Mali and western Senegal, and reached northward into Mauretania. Few early kingdoms in any continent have been more acclaimed than Ghana, which started the process in West Africa of uniting conquered people into one political body with a paramount king.

Ghana emerged as the Sahara Desert expanded and Sahelian people spread to the edge of the western savanna grasslands. Already by 100 BCE there were settled farming villages along the Senegal and Niger rivers as well as along the shores of Lake Chad farther to the east. Numerous other rivers in the western part of Africa supported village development. Small industry flourished around the creation of farm implements and home-building materials. Extraordinary efforts were made to maintain ancestral shrines, often erected near the farms. Families would live in villages and travel daily to their farms before the sun rose, pause for noon meals and relaxation, and then work until the sun set. This was the traditional pattern of West African farming.

This environment made it possible for farmers to grow a great variety of foods such as yams, melons, cassava, and beans. Men went out hunting and cleared the land for farms, and women and children did most of the planting, weeding, and harvesting. Women also threshed and ground grain. We know from historians who wrote of the empire that women in Ghana were treated with dignity. They often held high posts and were of high status in the realm. They played an active role in producing the wealth of the empire and also in producing the ruler since ancient Ghana was *matrilineal*, meaning that lineage is traced through the mother's line of descent.

One of Ghana's most illustrious rulers was King Tenkhamenin, who was responsible for expanding the territory in 1062 CE. From the money he collected taxing the caravans crossing his territory carrying gold from the south and salt from the north, he was able to employ a standing army of paid soldiers. These soldiers subdued the warring factions and settled the differences between rival ethnic groups, hence unifying various factions behind the king.

Al-Yaqubi, a historian-traveler, describes some of the duties and prestige related to the king: "The king of Ghana is a great king. In his territory are gold mines, and under him a number of kingdoms, among them the kingdom of Sugham and the kingdom of Sama. In all this country there is gold." Yaqubi's observations are critical to our understanding of the significance of Ghana. To be a great king means to Yaqubi that there was widespread appreciation for his wealth, that he had political power, which meant knowledge and skill in bringing together diverse peoples and kingdoms under his authority, and that he occupied a territory that had many gold mines.

In 1067 CE we learn from another writer—al-Bakri, an Arab geographer—that Ghana was the title of the king. All kings were called *ghanas*, the name of the clan from the original village, Wagadu, around which the kingdom and empire grew. Thus, all references to the ancient empire of Ghana must be understood as references to the name of the kings of the empire that had its capital at Kumbi Saleh.

The Royal Court

The ghana or emperor, who resided in Kumbi Saleh and headed the great empire, could put two hundred thousand soldiers in the field at one time, forty thousand of them armed with bow and arrows. He could sit in state and be surrounded by ten pages holding shields and gold mounted swords. To the right of the king, as he sat in state, were the sons of the princes of the land, colorfully dressed with golden plaits in their hair. The governor of the city was said to sit in front of the king and around him were his prime ministers in the same position. The gate of the assembly hall was usually guarded by dogs who wore around their necks collars of gold and silver. The people would announce the beginning of the meeting by playing a drum called the *deba*. Everyone would gather when they heard the deba.

Ceremonies and assemblies were important events in Ghana, but administration of the towns, cities, and villages was the king's main responsibility. When the villages grew into towns and, in some cases, cities, the kings had to use governors to manage the affairs of the larger communities. In modern times in West Africa kings are known to have celebrations that are called "debas," usually misnamed "durbars," which relate to the ancient call of the deba drum that brought people together for important occasions.

Some of the major cities of the Ghana Empire included Kumbi Saleh, Awdaghast, Walata, and Wagadu. The wealth accumulated by the people of the small farming village of Wagadu played a vital role in filling Ghana's treasury. It was strategically located on the road used by caravans transporting gold from southern regions of West Africa located in the general area of today's Ghana to Morocco, a country in the north. If they were carrying salt from the Sahara Desert to Wangara in the south, in the area of present-day Senegal, they would pass right through the center of Wagadu just south of the bend of the Niger.

Gold and salt were the key products in the Sahara trade, and were largely transported and sold by Muslim merchants who came from the north. The routes through the Sahara

Desert from the savanna northward to the Mediterranean coast passed through many small villages. Since gold was plentiful in the forest regions of present-day Ghana, Nigeria, Sierra Leone, and Senegal, these areas were important to the Ghana Empire and were often referred to as "Wangara" or the "Wangara States." Villagers sought to control the supply of gold to the north by determining who would be allowed to pass through their territory to engage in trade. The vessel of choice for transporting the gold was a hollow feather, a sort of quill repository.

A barter system of exchange existed. Salt from the Sahara region was exchanged for gold. Salt is an important commodity. In hot climates salt is needed to prevent dehydration, the loss of important body fluids. The trade between the gold-bearing and the salt-bearing regions was a natural interaction between two equally needy areas. In the central area of the Sahara, around Taghaza, people often built houses out of salt.

Of course, there is no record that the people of the forest built houses out of gold. They mined quite a lot of it and it amply supplied their trading needs. In mining the gold, there was a division of labor: the men would dig for the gold and the women would wash it in the many steams that cut through the forest region.

Ghana became a major trading kingdom during the ninth century CE. Its trading relationship with a network of kingdoms to the south of the savanna region and to the north of the desert made it the central player in the West African market for gold, salt, silk, beads, horses, kola nuts, cotton, leather, and glass beads. People from places far and near gathered within its borders to trade and talk of adventures along the caravan routes. A young girl of Ghana could meet young girls from Arabia, southern Europe—especially al-Andalus—as well as from the Cayor kingdom of Senegal. She could also see men trading the beautiful glass beads that came from Venice and Amsterdam, and if she followed the customs of the times and did not speak, she could overhear traders from the Wangara states in the south speaking of the great amounts of gold they carried. The music in the air came not only from the instruments but also from the nonstop chatter about commerce.

Interactions between West African kingdoms and the north had occurred for centuries and it was not unusual for diplomatic relations to occur. The king of Diuafunu visited Morocco to meet the Almoravid leader, Ali ibn Yusef, in the twelfth century. We know also that a ninth-century delegation from the Rustamid imam of Taherti was sent to the emperor of Africa with gifts. Some claim that this delegation may have been sent to Gao.[15] Nevertheless, we now know many delegations passed between the north and the south, and delegations were exchanged regularly between the West and North African capitals. Correspondences between the leaders of the West African kingdoms and other governments have survived in Arabic sources. Although these are not full letters they do give us enough information to imagine what the situation was during the African medieval period. The governor of Sijilmasa in the north sent a letter to the king of Ghana, the most powerful king in West Africa during the early part of the thirteenth century. The letter says:

> We are neighbors in benevolence even if we differ in religion; we agree on right conduct and are one in leniency towards our subjects. It goes without saying that justice is an essential quality of kings in conducting sound policy; tyranny is the preoccupation of ignorant and evil minds. We have heard about the imprisonment of poor traders and their being prevented from going freely about their business. The

coming to and fro of merchants to a country is of benefit to its inhabitants and a help to keeping it populous. If we wished we would imprison the people of that region who happen to be in our territory but we do not think it right to do that. We ought not to forbid immorality while practicing it ourselves. Peace be upon you.[16]

Ghana lasted for nearly fifteen hundred years. In 1240 CE Sundiata, the young king of Mali, the Mande-speaking kingdom, defeated the great empire.

Mali: The Flowering of the Empire (1240 CE–1400 CE)

Sundiata's name is one of the most recognized of African names. As a young boy he was very sickly, but the epic narrative of his life, told brilliantly by Djibril Tidiane Niane in *Sundiata: An Epic of Old Mali*, is found not in his weakness but in the discipline and commitment he manifested in overcoming all obstacles to his success.[17] Sumanguru, the emperor of Ghana, defeated his father's army and caused great suffering in the small kingdom of Mali. The Ghana emperor killed most of the royal children but spared Sundiata Keita because of his poor health. The sickly youth vowed to become a great leader. The eminent historian Djibril Tidiane Niane says that by the time he grew into manhood, Sundiata had become a warrior, an athlete, and an intelligent diplomat.

At the battle of Kirina, Sundiata's smaller army met the main forces of Ghana on a blustery day in 1240 CE when Sumanguru had summoned all of his wise men, his counselors, and his prophets to his side. But neither the dust from the wind nor the words from the soothsayers could help the army of Ghana. Sumanguru's forces were crushed and within a few years Sundiata had swallowed up the entire Ghana Empire. He replaced it with the Mali Empire built around the royal family of the Mandinka people. Mali was located in an area that would include today's Senegal, Guinea, and Mali. Its capital, Niani, was on the Niger River, and major cities included Niani, Gao, Jenne, Timbuktu, Koukya, and Kirina. Under Sundiata's leadership, Mali grew much larger than Ghana. The large kingdom occupied all of what had been Ghana's territory and took advantage of the trade in salt and gold.

The word Mali is an Arab version of the Mande word meaning "the dwelling-place of the king." The kings of Mali were called *mansas*, and the greatest mansa of all was Mansa Musa.

Mansa Musa, who succeeded Sundiata, came to the throne in 1307 CE because his brother Abubakari II abdicated to search for the limits of the ocean. In 1312 CE Abubakari II set sail on the Atlantic Ocean. He was perhaps the most famous of the African mariners to sail the Atlantic, but he was by no means the first. As early as the eighth century BCE Africans sailed to the Americas as captains of their own ships—centuries before the Europeans. Evidence of the African presence in the Americas can be found in many artifacts and utensils, most impressively in the gigantic head sculptures of the Olmec civilization in central Mexico. The similarities between Olmec and African culture—the pyramids, smoking pipes, pottery, folk narratives and dramas, and carved figures—are striking. While there is no proof that Abubakari ever arrived in the Americas before the Europeans, it is clear now that some Africans did and that they left a lasting impression on the native people.

Mansa Musa Becomes King of Mali

This is Mansa Musa's account as told to writer Al Omari:

> We belong to a house which holds the kingship by inheritance. The king who was my predecessor did not believe that it was impossible to discover the furthest limit of the Atlantic Ocean and wished vehemently to do so. So he equipped 1,000 ships filled with men and the same number filled with gold, water, and provisions enough to last them for years. And said to the man deputed to lead them "do not return until you reach the end of it, or your provisions and water give out." They departed and a long time passed before anyone came back. Then one ship returned and we asked the captain what news they brought. He said, "Yes, O Sultan, we traveled for a long time until there appeared in the open sea a river with a powerful current. Mine was the last of those ships. The other ships were on ahead but when they reached that place they did not return and no more was seen of them and we do not know what became of them. As for me, I went about at once and did not enter that river." But the Sultan disbelieved him. Then the sultan got ready 2,000 ships—1,000 for himself and the men whom he took with him and 1,000 for water and provisions. He left me to deputize for him and embarked on the Atlantic Ocean with his men. That was the last we saw of him and all those who were with him, and so I became king in my own right.[18]

Mansa Musa came to power as king because his brother had the heart of an explorer. But Mansa Musa clearly had the heart of a king. He conquered the people who lived on the Atlantic coast, expanding the empire to the west and northwest. He also conquered the Amazighs in the north. He ruled the expanded Mali Kingdom for twenty-five peaceful years. Mansa Musa became a devout convert to Islam and traveled to Mecca in 1324 CE.

Mansa Musa was quite knowledgeable concerning Islam. He would have known that the first muezzin was Bilal, the Ethiopian who was a friend of Muhammad, the prophet. In Islam, *muezzins* call the faithful to prayer. He would have been familiar with the Five Pillars of Islam. One of those pillars was the pilgrimage to Mecca, called the hajj. He would have heard his own muezzins cry, *"Allah hu akbar,"* that is, "God is great!"

Mansa Musa left his kingdom in 1324 CE with 500 servants, each bearing a golden staff. His caravan boasted more than one hundred camels carrying gold. Mansa Musa's legendary trip to Mecca remains one of the most storied trips in history. In fact, al-Omari, writing about the pilgrimage as it came to Cairo, says:

> The people of Cairo earned incalculable sums from Mansa Musa, whether by buying and selling or by gifts. So much gold was current in Cairo that it ruined the value of money. That is how it has been for twelve years from that time, because of the great amounts of gold Mansa Musa's people brought to Egypt and spent there.[19]

Songhay: One Last Great Stand of African Unity

Once again, like Tenkhamenin of Ghana and Mansa Musa of Mali, a king of great courage and military prowess arose in the large, semi-arid Sahel region of West Africa and defeated the reigning empire. As in the previous empires in the region, Songhay's economy depended mainly on the trade in salt and gold. Under the leadership of the Songhay conquerer, considerable improvements had been made since the reign of the Mali kings. Now a system of weights and measures set a uniform value on the gold and salt. This development eased tensions between merchants, making trade agreements smoother. The imaginative Sunni Ali Ber was the great king of courage who conquered Mali and brought about these significant improvements.

In 1468 CE Sunni Ali Ber saw Arab Muslims as intruders into West Africa and he sought to return the people to their traditions. He defeated the Mandinka, allies of the Arab Muslims, at Timbuktu and went from town to town subduing the Malian army. But Songhay was entering the midnight of West African imperial power; the daylight had steadily declined in the warfare between states, and even with Sunni Ali Ber's remarkable splash of brilliance, the stage had been set for the end of the empire.

By 1475 CE, when Sunni Ali Ber consolidated his power, there was evidence of the coming decline. The city of Timbuktu, once the great capital, had been succeeded by the trading center of Gao, also situated on the Niger River. Sunni Ali Ber grew up in the area where the Niger River makes a bend in present-day Burkina Faso and Niger. From this base he was able to create the largest empire ever established in West Africa. Just as the kings of Mali were called mansas, the kings of Songhay were called askias. Songhay was centered on a small ethnic group also called Songhay. From their local power base the Songhays conquered all neighboring peoples, gathering them under their conquering emperor. When Sunni Ali Ber had completed his work, the Songhay Empire superseded the Mali Empire. Sunni Ali Ber practiced both his traditional religion and the religion of Islam, setting a pattern that would last in West Africa for hundreds of years.

Sunni Ali Ber died in 1492 CE, one of the most significant dates in African history. His death meant that even the great Askia Muhammad, the devout Muslim who succeeded him, would not be able to hold back the disintegration of the West African empire. By force of personality and force of arms, Sunni Ali Ber had held the great empire together. Askia Muhammad was more devoted to the Koran (Qur'an)—the Muslim holy book—than Sunni Ali Ber, and, like Mansa Musa during the Mali Empire, Askia made a journey to Mecca. While his pilgrimage to Mecca was not as grand as Mansa Musa's, the positive results of his journey were significant to the kingdom. As he traveled through Egypt and into Saudi Arabia he assembled an impressive group: scholars, mathematicians, poets, musicians, engineers, and architects. This group greatly enhanced and expanded the educational system of Songhay. The University of Sankore was central to Songhay's educational system because here all the learned men of the kingdom gathered to debate the newest learning and the most appropriate response to challenges in art, science, and agriculture.

At the height of the empire, scholars from Arabia, Europe, and other parts of Africa journeyed to the fabled cities along the Niger to study religion, art, oratory, ethics, and astronomy. Ahmed Baba, the most distinguished of a long line of scholars, served as the last vice chancellor of the University of Sankore in Timbuktu. He was the author of at least forty-two books covering topics including astronomy, law, science, theology, rhetoric, and logic. Such a rich legacy gave way to the struggles over leadership, but then again, the legacy of struggle itself is also a part of all human history. The necessity of struggle would reappear in African American history.

When Askia Muhammad died, Songhay declined quite rapidly. The cities of Timbuktu, Gao, Jeno-Jenne, and Jenne fell into squalor and stagnation and the Moroccans destroyed the major centers of trade and commerce in 1594 CE.

Timbuktu Falls

The day the Moroccan army stormed into the ancient city of Timbuktu, it was hot and dry. Despite the heat, scores of students listened to the eloquent professor, Ahmed Baba, as he lectured outside the mosque by the wall of his 1,600-book library. He was teaching his students at the University of Sankore about the origins of the Songhay Empire. The year was 1594 and the University of Sankore was among the greatest centers of learning in the world. The students who had gathered to hear Baba speak were thrilled at the opportunity to learn from the most eminent professor in Sankore's history.

As the Moroccans drew closer to the university, the scene for the Songhay people was frighteningly similar to an earlier attack. In 1590, some 5,000 Moroccans had invaded the empire hoping to seize control of the wealth of Songhay, particularly its rich gold and salt mines. Although the Moroccans never succeeded in discovering where the gold mines were, they took complete control of the salt mines at the town of Taghaza, which is now a part of southern Morocco.

But on that hot day in 1594 the Moroccans were after more than gold and salt. Forcing their way quickly through the streets, the Moroccan soldiers could smell the sweet success of victory. They could hear Ahmed Baba's calm voice as he lectured, completely unaware that danger was just around the corner. Within minutes, Ahmed Baba, the last great professor of the University of Sankore, was grabbed from behind, shackled in chains, and carried away by the invading Moroccan army. Ahmed Baba's arrest brought to an end one of the many glorious periods in African history. Songhay's defeat signaled the beginning of one of the stormiest and most traumatic periods in the history of the African people. While the empire faded into the background, the culture that produced the mighty political institutions continued well into the twenty-first century when the eminent historian and culturalist Hassimi Maiga became the paramount leader of the Songhay—the amiiru of Songhay—in 2010.

Conclusion

The history of human origins in Africa is the history of the human race. Only in Africa do we have such a preponderance of information about our beginnings. From the first evidences of hominids in Chad 7 million years ago to the presence of *Homo sapiens* in Ethiopia, Kenya, and Tanzania nearly 300,000 years ago, we are telling an African and a human narrative. Migrations from East Africa to other parts of the continent and the earth mean that we all bear some connection to the African continent.

Great kingdoms and empires that rose in Africa along the riverbanks produced riverine societies that remain until this day. Complexes of societies in the Nile Valley, the Niger River area, the Limpopo River region, and the Congo River valley represent our earliest responses to the environment in a variety of ways. It is out of these responses that humans developed the capacity for kingdoms and empires. Wielding the powers that came with knowledge and force, early leaders of clans built larger communities and molded slightly diverse peoples into states that could protect themselves against other states.

Kemet, Nubia, Axum, Ghana, Mali, Songhay, Kongo, and Monomatapa are the eight great civilizations of the continent. From these kingdoms and empires have come numerous civilizations as offsprings of these motherlodes and they in turn have given birth to still others. Thus, Ghana produces Cayor, and Cayor produces Wolof kingdoms. In the south, Monomatapa gives birth to Rozvi, and then we have Shona kingships. In many instances these are the same people, that is, they inherit from the same ancestor and their forms of culture are similar. This chapter sets the stage for African Americans because Africa remains the most recent home of the majority of African Americans. Forced migration may have been the reason huge numbers of Africans are found in the Americas but clearly the possibility of Africans crossing the 1,500 miles to South America is not out of question.

Additional Reading

Adams, William Y. *Nubia: Corridor to Africa*. Princeton, NJ: Princeton University Press, 1984.

Ade Ajayi, J. K. and Michael Crowder, eds. *History of West Africa*, 3rd ed., 2 vols. Harlow, England: Longman, 1984.

Bernal, Martin. *Black Athena: The Afroasiatic Roots of Classical Civilization*. New Brunswick, NJ: Rutgers University Press, 1987.

Diop, Cheikh Anta. *The African Origin of Civilization*. New York: Lawrence Hill, 1974.

Grimal, Nicholas. *A History of Ancient Egypt*. Oxford, England: Blackwell, 1983.

Johnson, Samuel. *History of the Yorubas*. Lagos: CMS, 1921.

July, Robert. *A History of the African People*, 5th ed. Prospect Heights, IL: Waveland, 1998.

Levtzion, Nehemiah. *Ancient Ghana and Mali*. London: Methuen, 1973.

Maiga, Hassimi O. *Balancing Written History with Oral Tradition: The Legacy of the Songhoy People*. New York: Routledge, 2008.

Oliver, Roland. *The African Experience: Major Themes in African History from Earliest Times to the Present*. New York: HarperCollins, 1991.

Reader, John. *Africa: A Biography of the Continent*. New York: Knopf, 1998.

Stringer, Christopher and Robin McKie. *African Exodus: The Origin of Modern Humans*. New York: Holt, 1997.

Thornton, John. *Africa and Africans in the Making of the Atlantic World, 1400–1689*. New York: Cambridge University Press, 1992.

Chapter Time Markers

3400 BCE	Menes unites Kemet (ancient Egypt)
631 CE	General El As occupies Egypt from Arabia
711 CE	African Muslims (Moors) invade Hispania
732 CE	Charles Martel defeats Moors at Poitiers
1240 CE	Sundiata, king of Mali, defeats Sumanguru, emperor of Ghana
1591 CE	Songhay defeated by the Moroccan army
1619 CE	Africans arrive at Jamestown, Virginia
1761 CE	Phillis Wheatley kidnapped in Senegal

The Broken Links

2

Terms and Names

Karnak

Ausar

Amen

Garamantes

Jenne

Sunni Ali Ber

Urbanization

Loango

Goree

Elmina

Badagry

The State of African Society

Complex societies with artisans living and working in cities existed in Africa prior to the arrival of Europeans and Arabs.[1] In every section of the continent, by the tenth century of the Common Era Africans had established organized communities that were engaged in trade and commerce with their neighbors and had created councils, societies, and civil authorities to deal with factional problems. In addition, professionals serving as healers, mental therapists, and surgeons worked to treat personal and societal conditions. This was the state of Africa before the arrival of the Arab and Europe people.

No African state waited for outsiders to teach the laws of governance, politics, art, society, organization, or religion; these attributes were found in the most isolated of states and in some places where the people have been considered stateless. What one found in the Twa or San societies, for example, could be seen as simpler than what one could see among the Hausa, Yoruba, Zulu, or Kikongo, but the evidence suggests that the Twa and San societies had enough organization and structure to be seen as functioning units organized for procreation, kinship rituals, ancestral commemorations, symbolic and actual hunts, and yearly festivals.

Families existed before states, and states existed before empires. In Africa we find the emergence of vast families with several lineages often emanating from one Great Mother.

Some of these families became clans and the clans constituted the first great step toward a unified ethnic group. As numerous families and clans united, the hereditary or chosen leader of the clans—often the elder of the group—assumed more power. With a visionary leader, such as Menes was for ancient Kemet, African clans could combine their strengths and become mighty states. Thus, the uniting of Kemet by Menes around 3400 BCE was the first example in history of the formation of a national state, on the basis of the conquest of forty-two clans.[2]

Each African nation came into being with an obligatory treasure of traditions, concepts, and practices. These were translated into the way of life of the people played out on the environmental and relational canvas of their own history. Africans confronted huge challenges to human society and won those battles with resilience and grace. Who would have thought that mighty nations could be founded on the dry soil of the Sahel? What visionary would have insisted that a people of the rainforest carve out civilizations from the aggressive encroachments of plants, trees, and grasses that have no resting moments for growth? The physical challenge was itself one of the most powerful obstacles to society and yet in every case the African conquered the natural condition and made societies. The ruined cities of Dananombi, Khami, Dhlo Dhlo, Mapungubwe, and Zimbabwe are just a few of the hundreds of cities and towns built from the granite of the southern African plateau. Indeed, the builders of the southern African cities used the materials they found in their environment as their compatriots did in the forest and desert regions of other parts of the continent. Africans created institutions, values, ideas, and structures of society by attending to the fundamental philosophies discovered in their communities by sage wisdom, that is, the wisdom of elders who had experienced various transformations in the environment and society and could therefore speak from an accumulation of knowledge and facts.

Asante and Mazama documented numerous African creation narratives, ethical philosophies, and foundational values in their massive *Encyclopedia of African Religion*.[3] Among the earliest philosophies of life in the world is the idea of Maat, one of the oldest concepts in African history.[4] Maat is at the beginning of the ancient Kemet idea of value and virtue. What governed the early Africans along the Nile River was the belief in the permanence of Maat. It existed as a concept to be accepted as real, genuine, and basic to the operation of society. The per-aa was the chief protector of Maat in the society, but this meant that the per-aa has to be Maat in order for it to permeate the rest of the society.

Maat, according to Maulana Karenga, is a category of right. In fact, Karenga says, "the central category by which Maat is understood is the right with its expansive range of meaning, indicated in its various forms: rights, rightness, rightful, rightfulness, righteous, righteousness, upright, and uprightness."[5] Maat is at the core of all activities to eliminate evil and to restore right in the world. Understandably, the ancient Africans felt that during the creation of the universe only Maat, as a concept, existed with the divine creator. In some senses Maat was the first human attempt to define an ethical position for human relationships, extraordinary happenings, and personal morals. As the Kemites saw it, the aim of the human was to achieve Maat; the objective of the divine was to ensure that Maat would exist in society. Thus, the Karengean seven-fold construction of Maat as truth, justice, righteousness, order, harmony, balance, and reciprocity defined the extent of the range of this early African idea.

Among the beliefs of Africans during the period of dynastic Egypt was the idea that human life was the prelude to eternal life. No religious tradition in the world is as ancient as this on the question of eternal life. Written on the walls of the temples and on the great tombs, the words "Eternal Life" are at the center of the ancient belief in human transcendence over time. Throughout the Pharaonic period the priests believed that the objective of life on the earth was nothing more than an introduction to everlasting life, *ankh neheh*.

There was a genuine philosophical basis for the belief in eternal life. Since the primeval Ausar had been killed by his brother, Set, and yet resurrected by the agency of his sister and companion, Auset, it was possible for humans to consider the possibility of their resurrection. Ausar was the example for humans of the conquest over death. He becomes the god of the resurrection, bringing into existence the eternal optimism of life forever.

Over the ancient years the narrative was clear—Ausar was murdered by his brother, Set, and was subsequently resurrected by the love of his sister and wife, Auset. This regenerative love becomes symbolic of the promise of eternal life. The cycle of destruction, death, and rebirth was known in Kemet by the constancy of the annual inundation of the Nile River. It would flood, seeds would be planted, the harvest achieved, and the floods returned each year. Heru, called Horus by the Greeks, was the son of Ausar and Auset. This would be the world's first holy family; the father, mother, and child. In fact, Auset and Heru would form the first Madonna and Child in religious history. Images of Auset and Heru adorned the walls of many temples and were found in numerous tombs. Venerated throughout the land, the holy family triad was repeated in various ways in many temples. For example, at Karnak the temple featured the triad of Amen, Mut, and Khonsu.

The ancients described Ausar as a human king who taught husbandry, created the first legal code, and established the rituals for honoring ancestors; these actions constituted the basis for human civilization. During rites of passage, initiates would often take on the name of Ausar, alongside their own names, as an indication of their commitment to the principles of the ancient king. Later it became the practice of kings to take on the name of Heru when they were installed as a representation of the son who fought to restore good to the land by defeating Set. Of course, the role of Auset in the elevation of Ausar and Heru was primary.

Kemites, the people of Kemet, depicted Auset on coffins and tomb walls along with her sister, Nebhet, with outstretched wings to show the protective embrace of the people. More significantly, she would also embrace Ausar in a protective manner, thus demonstrating that the woman, the wife, the partner, was not someone would sat on the sidelines, but was actively engaged in the process of maintaining Maat in the society.

The role of Auset as protector is seen when she nurtures Heru, when she engages the society as the redeemer, and by her actions of restoring the society to its order and balance. But Auset is also the protector of the rule of Ausar and the one who gives birth to heaven and earth. She is the one who shelters the weak and is the mother of all the gods. The names and attributes of Auset are more numerous than those of any other deity in ancient times. She is called the "Mistress of the House of Life," "One Who Knows How to Make Right Use of the Heart," "Light Giver of Heaven," "Lady of Powerful Words," "The Moon Shining Over the Sea," and "She Who Restores the Balance."

Auset gave power to her son, Heru, which made him more powerful than any rival. She had gotten Ra to reveal his hidden name and had made Ausar the god of the resurrection while, all the time, maintaining her role as the Great Mother. She was the "Mistress to the Gods who Knew Ra by His True Name". No female in history had achieved this type of power and influence prior to Auset. In fact, it may be that no other person had demonstrated such an incredible insight into the nature of humanity. Here at the beginning of all African religious history, all sacred writings, and all value creations is the one story that sets this ancient African narrative as the fundamental basis for society. All values, concepts of ancestors, rituals of remembrances, solemn processions, names of gods, and ideas of order find their origin here along the Nile River.

Reincarnation as a concept is related to Maat. In fact, among African people the idea is centered on the continuation of the life of the ancestors. A child born today can be viewed as a reincarnation of someone in the ancestral line. It is different from the late Hindu idea of humans being reincarnated as animals. In African traditions a person may be reincarnated only within his or her family and therefore this philosophy establishes the idea of continuous life. All reincarnation is communal and therefore a reason for discovering in a community the proper rituals of remembrance. If you want to be reincarnated then you follow the patterns of community that constitute the warrant for reincarnation.

Social ideas are at the core of any understanding of the nature of African society. To have children, for example, is one of the highest values of African life. Without children a person cannot have those who would keep alive memory. To live and not to have children who will ritualize you after death is to be truly dead. Fertility establishes community and reaffirms continuity. Nothing serves the community more than ritual ceremonies to the ancestors as forces to weave together the living and the dead.

Ancestral reverence in Africa is almost universal. The idea is to encourage children to remember the traditions. One begins the process as a young person respecting those who are older than oneself. Subsequently one learns to respect elders who are next to the ancestors. In following the concept of ancestral reverence the person maintains the familial and communal bases of all ethics. The reason this is important in the African sense is that character is the source of everything social. Trust depends upon character, and without character the relationship between the living and the dead, the various generations, and the immediate family breaks down. This belief is the reason Africans have come to establish the family as the key to all human sciences.[6]

It is no wonder that African Americans reacted against the desecration of the ancient burial place in New York in May 1991 during preparations for a large construction project. It was not long after demonstrations and protests that the burial place was commissioned by the National Park Service as a special monument to what was the largest pre-Revolutionary African cemetery in America. Adam Clayton Powell III and Maya Angelou declared that they were in support of preventing any building on the site if there could not be recognition of the cemetery's importance in a reverent way for blacks. Who would want to defame the graveyard or demean the dead buried there during colonial times?

Character is the highest virtue in African philosophy. The traditionalists believe that character is the value that opens up all other virtues. The Yoruba people use the word "iwa" to mean character but they normally add the word "pele" to mean "good character." The ethical system demands character before love, character before mercy, character before wealth, and character before belief; the catchment of character contains all other virtues. A sacred text of the Yoruba, the *Odu Ifa*, has a very precise statement about iwa. Maulana Karenga translated the Yoruba text into English as *Odu Ifa* and argues in an important essay that "The position of good character as the major moral value in Ifa tradition can be seen in several passages in the *Odu Ifa*, the sacred text of the Ifa tradition."[7]

What Karenga understands is the fact that character is central to human growth and development. Without character a person is like a bird without wings: one is unable to fly and to develop any sense of personal transformation. The person who seeks destiny can only find it in the search for character. This is why the Yoruba's sacred *Odu Ifa* says, "Character is all that is required. There is no destiny that needs to be called unfortunate in Ifa. For character is all that is required."[8]

Whether one is speaking of the ancient Kemites or the more modern Akan people of Africa, the Yoruba teaching on character resonates with all of them. It is the central characteristic of a value system based on trust and human dignity. Karenga writes, "As in Maatian teaching, good character is a memorial for those who have it and provides a path to life after death in this world and the next." Moreover, it links character and sacrifice, a key practice and focus in Ifa tradition, saying, "Your sacrifice is in vain if your character is deficient."[9]

These are a few African values that were in play when the continent experienced the invasion that brought European Slave Trade operations to the coastal cities. Africa was no blank sheet waiting for processing by Europeans who came with higher values, but had developed systems of human organization, and greater virtue. It would take centuries before Africa was completely dominated by the foreign ideas that essentially turned African cultures on their heads. It would take missionaries, mercenaries, and merchants dedicated to the idea of white or European supremacy, as strongly as the Third Reich was dedicated to the inferiority of the Jews, for Africa to be laid waste by the rape of the continent. Only by realizing what was lost, not just in terms of material or monumental culture, but in terms of values, attitudes, concepts, and human relationship, can we understand the depth of the poverty that Africa experienced at the hands of invaders.

How Was Slavery Introduced?

Africa has experienced two foreign invasions in search of humans for slavery—the Arab Slave Trade from the East and the European Slave Trade from the north. Both began as interactions for trade, with Africa being the principal reservoir of goods. The two penetrations were equally damaging to the African community and each had its own peculiar method of attacking the trajectory of African history. Although the Arab Slave Trade started earlier than the European Slave Trade, the first beginning in the ninth century and the latter beginning in the fifteenth century CE, they were both catastrophic for African people and their cultures. Indeed, the terror of the Sahara Passage, with its excruciating heat and cold, was as traumatic as that of the Middle Passage inasmuch as Africans were kidnapped from ancestral homes and taken across many miles of sand to locations that were alien to them. Pekka Masonen of the University of Tampere wrote an important essay ("Trans-Saharan Trade and the West African Discovery of the Mediterranean World") that contended the Sahara was never a barrier to civilizations in the same sense as the Atlantic Ocean separated worlds.[10] As the caravans traveled across the Sahara they took salt, gold, ivory, and, in many instances, people. What Masonen's essay suggests is that Africa always had an interactive relationship internally as well as with people from outside of Africa. The Sahara, rather than being a barrier, was a gateway to the goods and commodities in various parts of the continent. Those who argued that there was no contact between one part of Africa and others were convinced that Africans were inferior, this having been the predominate European and Arab view during the time of the enslavement. Writers looked to Greek, Jewish, Phoenician, Roman, Arab, and even Chinese influences whenever an African creative contribution was made. Of course, this was an attempt to remove Africans from Africa, if not physically, certainly intellectually. It is now rare to discover this sentiment among scholars but it is sometimes concealed in a neutral rendition of the argument that Africans, especially those in the Sahel and the Forest regions, could not have produced anything of value. Ideas of state formation, metallurgy, sculpture, art, urbanism, philosophy, and medicine were seen as being borrowed from other cultures. Racist interpretations claimed that nothing original occurred in Africa.

It is false to claim that Africa was simply a passive receiver of culture from elsewhere. In fact, it is an archaic attitude that seeks to advance the idea that Africans were incapable of exploration or travel from their own villages. Initially the trade between African kingdoms in the south and north appeared to be based on the traditional commodities of salt, gold, and ivory. Yet one could not escape the reality of the interaction of ideas, concepts, myths, and philosophies. The people of the south did not engage their brothers and sisters in the north with empty hands or minds, as is often suggested. Commercial interaction between the people brought benefits to all. Traders were often explorers, great storytellers, and bringers of gossip about lands adjacent to their own. In Bilad al-Sudan, "The Land of the Blacks," gold was said to be as plentiful as stones. Masonen is correct to question why the West African discovery of the northern part of Africa has not been as eagerly pursued by historians as the Arab and European discovery of other parts of the continent.[11] Scholars have not discovered an enormous corpus of documents written by West Africans about their experiences with the north and this has left the impression that West Africans did not impact the northerners. However, the lack of documentation does not mean that there was no impact. We know, of course, that written accounts by Arabs and later by Europeans allow us to speculate on the worldview of Africans. Furthermore, African scholars have begun to aggressively use other markers to indicate African agency.[12]

Encounters for the Historical Record

According to the fifth-century-BCE Greek historian Herodotus, the Garamantes, an ethnic group of Libyans, are said to have traversed the Sahara in chariots looking for the Ethiopian troglodytes or cave-dwellers.[13] No one knows when West or North Africans began moving into the desert to live, hunt, or search for escaping enemies. The story of the Garamantes, while useful, tells us nothing about the earliest contact in the desert region. It is to be expected that humans have been traveling in and across the desert for thousands of years inasmuch as human civilization, human migration, and human exploration occurred first on the African continent.

The desert was actually crossed at the isohyets between Morocco and Mauritania, and in other places, for thousands of years. Even as the desert expanded, it left the area of equal rainfall between the north and south in the Western Sahara. Another thesis that has been advanced is that Africans had chariots that could have crossed the desert between the north and south in ancient times. Paintings on cave walls depicting chariots give proof that the people either had them or imagined them. Whatever the truth of this thesis, we know that the two-wheeled light chariots could only have been used for transporting a few people, not for carrying lots of raw materials.

Herodotus writes of Nasomonians, young people of Libya, traveling to the south where they met small black men who took them to their capital town. The area was swampy and appears to have been the Niger inland delta. According to Marinus of Ture, another Greek writer, a Roman merchant named Julianus Maternus went with the king of the Garamantes to a land called Agisymba where there lived many rhinoceros. This must have been in the area of Chad since this would have been the closest site of rhinoceros during African classical antiquity.

Western archaeologists have found evidence of the early contacts between Romans and West Africans in some objects that appear to be Roman. These items, dated to the third century CE, were found in Abalessa in Ahaggar, in the tomb of Queen Tin Hinan. This was not a common or consistent encounter because we know of only two Roman coins found further south, and these were found in southern Mauretania near Senegal. While it is possible that these coins may have been transplanted to the area during the Islamic period, we know that other objects were found at the exciting site of Jenne-Jenó, that is, the old Jenno. In 1976, European-style beads and a Hellenistic statuette depicting a feminine Janus that suggests a relationship to Cyrenaica in the second century were found in the country of Niger. Most scholars believe that the encounter across the Sahara was more extensive than we currently know, given the fact that the excavations of the tumuli in the Niger bend have not been thoroughly explored or examined.

The fearless Garamantes with their galloping horses could have established the long routes between themselves and others in the Sahel region. This is a history that cannot be fully written at this time, given the extensive archaeological records that still remain buried or hidden in the Sahara. With time and more intense research—as we are seeing in African universities—the role of the Amazighs, the so-called Berbers, the Tamasheks, often called Tuaregs, and the Garamantes will be clarified. But for now we believe that the nomadic people who lived near the Senegal River area in the west may have pushed their way to the north at the start of the rainy season and returned to the south during the dry season. This pattern appears reasonable given the need for pastures in southern Morocco and the Atlas mountain region. Interactions with people from Europe or Asia are almost certain to have happened. Gold, salt, ivory, and copper may have been the first commodities traded between these people. Since gold appeared in abundance in the south, it was taken to the north and traded for dates, beads, fabrics, and perhaps even animals such as cattle. Prior to the conquest of the Americas it is estimated that two-thirds of all gold circulating in North Africa, Southwest Asia, and Europe came from West Africa. Whatever the nomadic people could not produce in the south, they may have brought with them from the north when they returned during the dry season.

It is likely that the camel was the animal that carried on its back the burden and the promise of trade between African people. Horses and mules are notorious for dying in the difficult conditions of the desert. Long distances could only be overcome by the careful cultivation of the dromedary as a beast of transport, for even water could now be taken long distances by the travelers. The earliest camel bones found in West Africa were discovered in Senegal and dated to the third century of this era, around 250 CE. Thus, the dromedary, often thought by those who dismiss African creativity to have been brought by the Romans to North Africa, had been domesticated before the Roman penetration into West Africa. In fact, since there are no wild camels in Africa, they had to be domesticated by the African people themselves.

Urbanization and various forms of state organization occurred in West Africa independently of any outside influences. Internal trade and creative exchanges made possible the development of wealth that spurred state formation and empire building. There are no evidences of external invasions in West Africa during the time of the rise and development of the great Ghana kingdom around 300 BCE to 300 CE. It would last until the thirteenth century after sustaining Islamic influences from the ninth century CE, through to its defeat by Sundiata in 1240.

Arab influences and Islamic culture entered Egypt in the seventh century CE and began a long period of domination of the indigenous peoples and societies. The massive Umayyid caliphate stretched from the Pyrenees to the Indus River, influencing all of North Africa, and in the process swallowed up the local industries, nascent networks of traders, and native medical and spiritual leaders into a vast cauldron of religion and trade based on the Koran and gold as a monetary system.

The endless search for gold led the Muslim armies deeper and deeper into West Africa, where they found abundant gold mines. There was no gold in North Africa except the recirculated gold in Egypt that had come from Nubia and further south. The Islamic armies did find gold in southern Spain and perhaps some in Sicily, but the greatest amount of gold was to be found in West Africa. Regular trade was established between the conquered territories in North Africa and the still independent regions of West Africa, creating several principal trans-Sahara routes. By the ninth century the famous terminals in the north were Sijilmasa and Taherti, while the southern terminals were Jenne, Adwaghast, Kumbi Saleh, and Tadamakka. The "Big Three" routes across the desert were from Awdaghast to Sijilmasa, making use of the isohyet between Mauritania and Morocco; the route from Timbuktu to Ifriqiya; and the route from Kufra to Siwa—the western, central, and eastern routes respectively. Longer routes could send traders as far away as Cairo, and once Islam took hold of kings and nobles in the west, some would travel in giant caravans all the way to Mecca. However, in all cases the old tried-and-true route would be used for some of the distance.

Islamic expansion had a serious impact on the nature of African communities in the north and west. The emergence of the Fatimid caliphate as a rival to the Umayyads of Spain brought a third Islamic force into the contest for strength, support, and wealth. Already the Abbasids of Baghdad were making their power felt in the eastern world and the Fatimids made the western trade route the most used, the most important, and the best developed. Ibadites at Wargla controlled the central route. However, once the Fatimids transferred their capital site from Ifriqiya to Cairo in 971 CE they sought gold from the ancient Nubian mines and did not have to rely on West Africa.

In place of the Fatimids along the Western route rose the Almoravids, who would become the most successful forces in Western Africa, uniting their forces in Spain, Morocco, Western Sahara, Mali, and Mauritania. The word "Almoravids" is a Spanish transliteration of the Arabic "al-Murabitun," meaning literally "ready for battle."

The Muslims had conquered the Iberian Peninsula in the eighth century CE and had increasingly tightened the screws on their subjects. When Tariq ibn Ziyad landed his African armies on Gibraltar in 711 CE it was one of the first times in recorded history that an African army had invaded European territory. The collapse of Visigoth military power allowed the North African Muslim army to occupy most of Hispania and to rename it al-Andalus. The Islamic forces would not be stopped until a united army under the leadership of the Frank commander, Charles Martel, defeated them at the Battle of Poitiers in 732 CE, preventing the takeover of Tours in France. Yet by the eleventh century the Almoravids were fighting wars against the Christians and the new Muslim princes of al-Andalus, as well as the Almohads in the Maghreb in North Africa. Yusef ibn Tashfin went to al-Andalus at the invitation of Muslim princes in 1086 to help them defend against Alfonso VI, king of Leon and Castile. However, Tashfin defeated the Christians but went on to remove all of the Muslim princes, annexing their states to the Almoravids. When he died at the age of 100, Yusef ibn Tashfin was called the *Amir al Muslimin*, the leader of the Muslims. At this time the Almoravid golden dinar was the most important currency in the Mediterranean region.

The African Muslims had to confront many problems after the death of Yusef ibn Tashfin. His son, Ali ibn Yusef, fought several wars to bring regions of Iberia (al-Andalus) back under control, but the times were different and the French moved southward to assist Alfonso VII of Leon—the Almoravids had a succession of losses. Thus, by 1139 Afonso I of Portugal could claim a victory at the Battle of Ourique, and less than ten years later, in 1147, Lisbon was rescued and reclaimed by Portugal. By 1492 the African Muslims would lose all of the Iberian Peninsula and turn their attention southward toward Africa.

Consequently, nearly a hundred years after the defeat of the Moors in Spain, Morocco invaded Songhay in 1594, sacked the main cities, and exiled the leading Songhay intellectuals, including Ahmed Baba, to Morocco. Under the leadership of Judar Pasha, a Spanish-born eunuch who had been elevated by Ahmed I, the Moroccan king, an invasion force of 6,000 soldiers armed with eight English cannons and eighty Christian personal guards for Judar Pasha made the difficult trek across the Sahara to Songhay. Judar's army destroyed the salt mines in Taghaza and destroyed the industrious city of Gao, the capital of Songhay, and assaulted Timbuktu and Djenne, leaving them in smoke. Because Songhay's leaders had felt that the desert would ruin Judar's army, they were surprised to discover the Moroccan army at their doorstep. Askia Ishaq II, emperor of Songhay, placed 40,000 troops, including cavalry, on the battlefield, and the two determined armies met in one of Africa's most decisive contests in the Battle of Tondibi in March 1594. The superior weapons of the Moroccans and the introduction of gunpowder into the battle equation gave the Moroccans one of their best days in the war. Less than thirty years later, in 1619, twenty Africans arrived in Jamestown, Virginia, to began the difficult African journey in the English colony of America.

Prior to the defeat of Songhay in 1594 the contact arena for Africans and Arabs had been limited to the isolated "foreign" quarters set up by African kings. While there was no racial discrimination in the modern sense, the Africans were clear that the religion and the living styles of the Arabs were different. Those who spent numerous years in the West African towns as traders usually intermarried with the locals and in some cases married the local women and moved away to the north. As agents of North African trading associations, these early Arabs helped to develop a pattern that still has some residual elements in African towns—separate Muslim quarters. In these quarters on the edge of the desert, in most instances the Arabs could practice their own religion and cook their own foods.

Those who left West Africa for the north and those who came to West Africa from the north had to deal with sickness and warfare. If cavalry were to be used, the horses had to be closely watched because of the prevalence of trypanosomiasis, which could be deadly for horses. One illustration of the importance of the environment is the 1544 expedition undertaken by Sultan Muhammad al-Mahdi to control the mines in Songhay. When Askia Ishaq I refused to give him the rights to the mines, a war broke out and a combined force of the Songhay Empire forced the Moroccans out of the Sahara.

African conversion to Islam was neither monolithic nor sudden. It was often peaceful but could just as easily occur because of royal decree. Why did the Africans accept Islam? There are numerous theories: the religion of Islam shares many values with traditional Africa; the religious leaders of Islam brought news of the wider world; the social prestige of associating with those who had access to written texts; and the possibility of rewards and gifts for converting to the new ideology. Some people were forced by arms to accept the religion and to change their names. One must be careful not to state categorically that Islam came only by force or that it came into West Africa only through peaceful conversion.

Sunni Ali Ber and the Decline of Imperial Africa

It is probably true, as Masonen claims, that "Islam remained for a long time as a cult of the courts and commercial centres."[14] Most of the kings of the medieval African empires adopted Islam politically but their kingdoms and empires were not Muslim states. They held no mass allegiance to Mecca and the majority of the people in the empires were not Muslim. In reality the kings preferred Islam as a court cult but not as a religion that would challenge their positions as divine kings—something that was anathema to Islam.

Sunni Ali Ber's death in 1492 sped the arrival of the European slave trade to West Africa. Although a centralized government would control most of the powerful states for another hundred years, the death of Sunni Ali Ber sounded the death knell for African empires. Ber had been a military genius who had achieved unity among many nations, bringing them into the fold of Songhay. When he ascended the throne of Gao in 1464 as a member of the royal Sunni dynasty, the future looked bright for the remnants of the Mali Empire. It took Ber only twenty-eight years to change the fortunes of Gao and make it the center of the Songhay Empire. Under his reign the Songhay Empire took in all of the great cities of learning of West Africa such as Jenne, Niane, and Timbuktu. From his powerful post as emperor of Songhay, Sunni Ali Ber was able to keep back the Arab invasion from the Sahara as well as to unify the country under his rule. Arab slavery had gone on for several centuries and Sunni Ali Ber's opposition to it brought him into direct conflict with some of the intellectual and merchant classes. Consequently, he engaged in political conversion to Islam for trading purposes but became an enemy to the Muslims, which is why he is still regarded by Islamists as an enemy of Islam. It was not so much that he was an enemy of Islam as that he was a supporter of the indigenous people of Songhay and an enemy of the enslavement of Africans.

His place as a military emperor in Africa is alongside that of Thutmoses III, Ramses II, and Sundiata. He would build the greatest army ever seen in West Africa with a huge infantry, a fleet of ships operated by the brilliant Sorko people of fishing fame, and a cavalry that could put 200,000 horsemen in the field in a military engagement. He was able to sustain his power because of the discipline of his army.

By the time of his death by drowning in 1492 he had captured Timbuktu from the Tuaregs in 1468, who had taken the city from Mali in 1434. Akil, the Tuareg king, left the city for Walata when he saw his army being badly defeated by the Songhay. It is recorded that Sunni Ali Ber killed the imams, ran the Muslim scholars out of the city, and closed down the foreign markets. Later, in 1473, after he had laid siege to Jenne for seven years, seven months, and seven days, Sunni Ali Ber captured the city.

Although Sunni Ali Ber had running battles with the Mossi he never completely conquered them. However, the Mossi had destroyed Walata and Sunni Ali Ber considered them weakened by their campaign and went after them throughout the Western Sudan. He drove them back to Ouagadougou, pacifying them in 1486, so that they were no longer a threat.

Sunni Ali Ber then turned his armies on the Fulani of Massina and Gurma, refusing to allow them peace in his empire, until he finally defeated them militarily so that they were no longer a threat. Returning from his victory over the Gurma, his horse stumbled and he fell into a river, weighed down by his military armor, and died. Sunni Ali Ber had been a great African champion but he was unable to prevent the continual penetration of Islam and slavery from across the Sahara. Furthermore, the year of his death, 1492, was the year Christopher Columbus took his voyage to the Americas. Africa's future was bleak from that period forward.

The Arab Slave Trade

Arab merchants and imams participated in the enslavement of thousands of Africans. No records of the type that accompanied the European Slave Trade exist for the Arab Slave Trade. The estimate of the numbers of Africans who were enslaved across the desert range from 9.3 million to 20 million people taken from West Africa, Chad, Sudan, Ethiopia, and other areas of the continent to enslavement in North Africa and Southwest Asia. As in the Middle Passage across the Atlantic Ocean, the proportion of Africans who died during the Hot Passage across the Sahara Desert may have been as high as one-third.

The trans-Saharan assault on Africa opened the doors for the arrival of the Portuguese on the West African coast. This contact would create new trade patterns, factories for commodities and later for enslaved Africans, and a decline in the trade with North Africa. Centuries of trans-Saharan trade gave way to a more nimble trade between the Iberian Peninsula and West Africa. Just as Portugal was feeling its way south in search for a new route to Asia, the West African kingdoms were experiencing numerous upheavals caused by political intrigues, death in the royal houses, and sporadic wars. Prince Henry the Navigator (Dom Henrique), Lord of the Order of Christ, son of King João, had begun to send ships to probe the west coast of Africa, and when the first Africans were taken to Lisbon in the fifteenth century it created an excitement among the upper classes. Portugal had thrown off the Moorish conquest long before the Spaniards and had found its way to Africa out of curiosity, wealth, and the search for a new route to the east. While rounding the African continent, however, the Portuguese found themselves often enough on the African coasts.

Africa, Slavery, and History

Despite the Arab inroads into North and West Africa, it would take the Portuguese, Spanish, and Dutch to open up the massive removal of Africans from the continent across the West African Ocean. The Atlantic, as it is now called, was the largest body of water Africans in the empires of Ghana, Mali, and Songhay knew about, and they did not refer to it after the name of the mythical Atlantis. In whatever language of West Africa they used, whether Mandinka, Wolof, or Akan, by the fifteenth century they knew the sea as the deep Waters of Abubakari, so indelibly had his name been associated with the sea's history because of his fourteenth-century voyages.

How a people could fall from such tremendous heights in arts, religion, science, military prowess, and human relations to being enslaved by Arabs and Europeans in the worst manner could be the subject of many books. However, in a book on the global African American experience one must attempt to provide a rational account of these events in order to make sense of the subsequent history of African people in the United States and throughout the world.

What the Arabs maintained, and the Europeans later supported, was the separation between people and the categorizing of groups into superior and inferior humans. This was not an African behavior and had never become a part of the worldview of any African society. Such a foreign notion that humans could be divided into superior and inferior was to wreak havoc on the unsuspecting African people for nearly a thousand years. It would begin with the Arabs and end with the Europeans. Both groups came to the African world with the same general principles, although the details were certainly different and distinct—so different that they would be the source of Arab and European conflicts.

The singular core idea of both groups, Arabs and Europeans, seemed to reside in their religious beliefs. They had arrived as in-groups and out-groups, saved and unsaved, heathens and infidels, free and slave, by way of their fundamental adherence to religions that gathered them in groups which were superior to others who were outside of those groups. Herein was the initial mistake of the African world. Africans had a different view of humanity, one based on an extensive history of interaction over thousands of years on the African continent with diversity. They did not see diversity and difference as anything other than the variety of humans peopling the earth. No sense of categorizing by rank, status, or rights had yet come to play in the arena of African ideals.

When Africans invited General El As to come from Arabia to help them throw off the Romans in 631 CE they had no conception of what this would mean for them or the continent. El As did not come just with military expertise, though he was strong in that suit; he came with a conviction about his religion. Allah, like Jehovah of the Jews, was a jealous God who did not tolerate other gods. Thus, when the religious zealots of Islam made their way into the continent and across the north of it, they came with both the military and the religion. The idea that if you did not believe in Islam meant you were a heathen or an infidel carried with it all of the warrants necessary for a true believer to see a practicing African as a victim, a second-class citizen, an inferior—indeed, a slave. By the same token the Europeans would use the same logic to attack Africans as well as claiming that Africans could be enslaved because they did not have a soul, or that Africans were heathens and therefore outside of the grace of God. It would not be long before the longships of the whites waited, like predators, in the bays, harbors, and rivers of West Africa for human cargo. Thus would begin the legacy of slavery that would affect every African either directly or indirectly.

Capture and Kidnapping

The Portuguese capture of seventy Africans from a village near the Senegal River in 1441 brought the universe of Europe, with its preconceived notions of adventure, novelty, law, and brutality, into direct clashes with the African universe with its traditions, innovations, rituals of respect, hospitality, humanity, and wisdom. This encounter would change forever the nature of the world. In a mere sixty years Africans would be enslaved in San Domingo, other Caribbean lands, and in South America. After all, one of the pilots—Pedro Alonso Niño, known as El Negro—on Columbus' third voyage was a black man. Thirty Africans accompanied Vasco Núñez de Balboa during his exploration of the Pacific Ocean area. Numerous other Africans traveled to the American West in search of golden cities.

History is not prediction and none of the Africans could have predicted in 1619 that the Dutch ship that brought them to the Jamestown, Virginia, settlement would be followed by thousands of others. In some ways the entry of this small band of brothers and sisters into the English colony represented the last frontier of the despicable practice of buying and selling Africans across the sea. A chapter was opened that would not close for another 246 years.

Stunned, it seemed, by the complexion of Africans, whites in North America were no different from the whites who had earlier contact with Africans on the continent or in Cape Verde. "These people are all blacke, and are called Negros, without any apparel, saving before their privities," wrote one sailor.[15] Furthermore, although the people were black, "they were civill."[16] Blackness and nakedness, the condition in which many Africans were held, made an impact on many of the European travelers. It would take the Black Codes, coming decades later, to define the proper clothing of enslaved Africans.

When John Rolfe wrote in his diary that "twenty negars" arrived in Virginia in 1619 it was evidence of the earliest presence of Africans in the English colony. This was one year before the pilgrims landed at Plymouth Rock in the Mayflower, but nearly one hundred years after blacks had been in Spanish and Portuguese colonies. Oscar and Mary Handlin argued in 1950 in a famous article, "Origins of the Southern Labor System," that Africans were not immediately enslaved in Virginia.[17] The system of indentured servitude that existed for poor whites was the type of labor pattern that greeted the first Africans in Jamestown. But within fifty years blacks had been so degraded in condition that perpetual enslavement was finally imposed by the will of the colony. Although the article by the Handlins was used to argue that race prejudice did not occur until after slavery, others argued that racism preceded enslavement and that many whites believed that blacks were inferior even before slavery. Since Africans had already been enslaved in Santo Domingo and Brazil it was not difficult to imagine that Virginians would have been influenced by what was happening in the rest of the Americas.

Two cultures, heretofore practically unknown to each other, met on unequal terms. The representatives of the older of these cultures, the African, entered Jamestown therefore as indentured servants; the English culture had defeated the indigenous people of the area and established their own colony in which they were the masters, thus setting up what would become the fundamental pattern of relationships between Africans and Europeans in North America for more than two centuries.

Slavery in the American Colonies

In fact, although slavery had existed in some form since the 1640s, in Virginia it was only formalized in law around 1671, when there were about 2,000 Africans in the colonies.[18] In 1705, after the end of the British Royal Africa Company's monopoly on the slave trade, the laws governing the treatment of Africans was codified into one comprehensive slave code. Thus the era of African enslavement began in North America on a note of European legal agreement that Africans should be enslaved.

Slavery has an ancient history, yet it captures our modern imagination because of its relentless and peculiar form of human bondage. Examples of oppressive modern labor practices are often called slavery, as when a Saudi Arabian businessman holds a Filipino against her will, or an American employs a Mexican and works him for endless hours without relief, knowing that the Mexican without legal immigration papers will not report abuses for fear of deportation. In these cases, of course, we often have individuals who have been lured into horrible situations because they were willing to "sell" their labor for food and shelter. People are taken advantage of and their liberties are curtailed, but these examples are not comparable either in scale or abuse to chattel slavery that uprooted millions of Africans.

So vast an operation was the European Slave Trade that it ravaged towns and villages along the West African coast, and the interior, for three centuries of dogged destruction of the African homeland to build a white homeland in the ancestral territory of another people. Languages were lost, histories were obliterated, customs and traditions distorted, and beautiful and peaceful places turned into bloody patches of the most dastardly deeds known to humans. Names like Loango, Whydah, Elmina, Badagry, Calabar, Gorée, and a thousand others were written in the book of infamy during the slave trade. Africans, young and old, but mostly pre-teens and teens, were captured and sent into bondage in the Caribbean, South America, and the English colonies.

These were not nameless humans. These were not people without history and potential; they were, each of them, treasure chests of possibilities. When Phillis Wheatley was kidnapped in Senegal in 1761 she was barely seven years old. She had been born in 1754 in a literate society of Muslim teachers where she was familiar with daily study, reading the Koran, and listening to instructions. In addition, her Peul and Wolof ancestors had expanded the Cayor Empire far into the interior of the continent, and Phillis Wheatley—who may have been named Binta or Koumba—had participated in the same rituals, songs, games, and festivals dedicated to the fishermen that went out for days on the ocean.

Phillis Wheatley was brought to Boston in 1761 and sold to John Wheatley as a servant for his wife. Wheatley learned English quickly and soon read the Christian Bible, to the amazement of her captors. Speaking and reading with fluency few whites had mastered, the young Wheatley was soon writing her ideas on paper. Always in poor health because of the lack of warmth in the Boston winters, and perhaps because of intense loneliness due to the loss of her own family, Phillis Wheatley suffered illnesses at an early age. John and Susannah Wheatley found her to be a poor domestic and eventually resolved to let her study Latin and Greek classics. At fifteen years of age Wheatley published her first poem, and six years later, in 1773, her book, *Poems on Various Subjects*, was published with the assistance of the Wheatleys.[19] Thus, Wheatley was the first enslaved African to publish a book and only the third woman to publish a book of poems in the English colonies. After the publication of her book, John Wheatley emancipated Phillis Wheatley. She achieved some international fame for her ability to write poems, largely because so many whites believed, falsely and ignorantly, that it was impossible for an African to write English. Wheatley was for many whites an oddity, an exotic being, someone who could do something that was nearly impossible to imagine. A black woman who writes books—imagine that!

Meanwhile, in America Phillis Wheatley was an object of equal curiosity and was received by the political and social leaders of the day, including George Washington, to whom she wrote a poem. Voltaire, known for his racist views, was quite surprised at Wheatley's command of English and referred to her work as "very good English verse."[20] Nevertheless, fame and attention did not bring Wheatley wealth or a decent life and she lived in poverty after marriage in 1778 to John Peters, a free Bostonian African. She tried to find a publisher for her second book of poetry, which has never been found, but apparently never succeeded. Her death in 1784 came in the midst of colonial political turmoil that would lead to the establishment of a new nation but not freedom for Africans.

One could have thought that Massachusetts, with its great beacon of intellectual light, Boston, might lead the United States toward freedom for the enslaved, but instead Massachusetts had followed Virginia into the abyss of enslavement. Neither Massachusetts not Virginia began with slavery—they had begun with indentured servants—but in the middle of the seventeenth century both colonies had moved swiftly to perpetual servitude for Africans.

Slavery did not officially arrive in Virginia until several decades after Africans arrived in Jamestown. This legislation was soon followed by Massachusetts, which also legislated that Africans could be held in perpetuity as slaves. Indentured servants quickly vanished and the preponderance of enslaved Africans overtook all human relations in the North American colony. From the middle of the seventeenth to the middle of the nineteenth centuries the dissonance between personal greed and personal morality overwhelmed the labor situation. Greed reigned until the stallions of moral indignation were finally awakened in the early nineteenth century and, with the added energy of liberated and free Africans, overwhelmed the forces of perpetual slavery. But even before the nineteenth century, Phillis Wheatley in her indomitable manner—quiet, studious, and with bombast—placed a slow nail in the coffin of black inferiority and raised the possibility of an eventual freedom for all enslaved Africans.

Obviously there was a fundamental hypocrisy among those individuals who attempted to degrade Africans as less than whites while seeking to declare their own liberty. What could be any more revealing of this attitude than the whites in America who declared for their own independent rights while they held in bondage more than 100,000 Africans?

Thomas Jefferson went so far as to pledge his fortune, which included nearly two hundred enslaved Africans, in support of the belief that all men, except Africans, were created equal and endowed with inalienable rights to life, liberty, and the pursuit of happiness. This remarkable ability to erase Africans, who were considered inferior, was nothing short of an amazing moral contradiction. Slaveholding founders of the American ideal of liberty based their own drive for independence on high-sounding words and doctrines that they denied to the humans they held in bondage. This was a contradiction that would plague the entire history of the American nation. There would attempts to argue away this contradiction by speaking about the ideals in the Declaration of Independence and the Constitution, but the fact remained that the formers of the American nation had little respect for Africans and thought of themselves as fundamentally better than them.

Africans Protest against Slavery

In a remarkable stroke of collective clarity about their own liberty, Americans met in Philadelphia on July 4, 1776, and made a declaration:

> We hold these truths to be self-evident, that all men are created equal, that they are endowed by their Creator with certain unalienable Rights, that among these are Life, Liberty and the pursuit of Happiness. That to secure these rights, Governments are instituted among Men, deriving their just powers from the consent of the governed. That whenever any Form of Government becomes destructive of these ends, it is the Right of the People to alter or to abolish it, and to institute new Government, laying its foundation on such principles and organizing its powers in such form, as to them shall seem most likely to effect their Safety and Happiness.

Yet they could not see how their enslavement of Africans was a contradiction of their own desires for themselves. How could those who prosecuted the most heinous crimes against Africans utter the most beautiful words of liberty? Of course, this conundrum did not escape the former Massachusetts governor Thomas Hutchinson, who observed in his "Strictures upon the Declaration of the Congress at Philadelphia" that there seemed to be some discrepancy between the "declaration that all men are created equal and the practice of depriving more than a hundred thousand Africans of their rights to liberty."[21] The Englishman Thomas Day said it was truly "something ridiculous in nature to see an American Patriot signing resolutions of independence with one hand while holding a whip over enslaved Africans with the other."[22]

The thread that held these contradictions together was the acceptance of the idea that Africans were chattel, property. By the time of the Declaration of Independence in 1776, the British colonies of North America had experienced more than one hundred years of steady indoctrination in the legal idea that Africans were chattel and in the moral idea that Africans had no rights to life, liberty, or the pursuit of happiness that whites had to respect.

Nevertheless, Africans in America had by 1776 established their own tradition of fighting for freedom. There was no separation in their minds about the value of one human as opposed to another. The Africans were the true freedom fighters, the authentic seekers of the ideal of treating all humans equally. The situation had boiled for more than one hundred years. By the late eighteenth century the African population had become familiar with the narrative of American history that had isolated them as a foreign class, on the margins of white society. However, examples of African nobility in war and peace, in negotiations and in protests, were constant among the free blacks of the North, while in the South those who could, sought all means to escape.

Conclusion

In this chapter we have generally explored the origin and activities of Arab and European enslavers of Africans during a period of 1,000 years. Although we have not been able to delve into the specific details of these extensive encounters, we have demonstrated that the contacts between Africans and Arabs, and Africans and Europeans, may have begun as commercial encounters but soon became trade in humans. Resistance to these activities would define a major theme in African history and lay the groundwork for a collective sense of identity that would emerge in the Americas as group consciousness based on sharing similar experiences. Europe dominated the slave trade from the sixteenth century to the nineteenth century and occupied the major port cities of West Africa during this time.

Chattel slavery emerged in the American nation as something that distinguished itself from other forms of bondage. White Americans defined Africans as chattel and set in motion a new orientation toward human beings. Africans were not human, but property, things, to be bought and sold, used and abused, at the will of the slaveholder. This concept of enslavement created a human population that would be held in perpetuity in bondage just as a person would hold land or animals. Some enslaved Africans, like Phillis Wheatley, demonstrated intelligence, capability, and ingenuity that would contradict the rhetoric of inferiority promoted by whites. Nevertheless the system of enslavement endured, and the rise of protests by blacks in the North, gave new urgency for the nation to find an end to enslavement.

Additional Reading

Asante, Molefi Kete. *African American History: A Journey of Liberation*. Saddle Creek, NJ: PPG, 2001.

Berlin, Ira. *Many Thousands Gone: The First Two Centuries of Slavery in North America*. Cambridge, MA: Belknap Press, 1998.

David, David Brion. *The Problem of Slavery in Western Culture*. Ithaca, NY: Cornell University, 1990.

Gutman, Herbert. *The Black Family in Slavery and Freedom*. New York: Pantheon, 1976.

Jordan, Winthrop D. *White over Black: American Attitudes toward the Negro, 1550–1812*. Chapel Hill, NC: University of North Carolina Press, 1968.

Kolchin, Peter. *American Slavery, 1619–1877*. New York: Wang, 1993.

Wright, Donald R., *African Americans in the Colonial Era: From African Origins through the American Revolution*. Arlington Heights, IL: Harlan Davidson, 1990.

Chapter Time Markers

Africans Confront the American Situation

3

War and Exploration (1770–1829)

Important Terms and Names

Crispus Attucks
Zumba
Nanny
Yanga
Peter Salem

Racism
Chattel Slavery
Cheikh Anta Diop
Eric Williams
York

Stirrings of Contradictions

There were no smooth flights to freedom for most Africans who sought self-expression. In every situation there was danger and the possibility of disrespect and even death, yet nothing could be as dear to them as their freedom from perpetual bondage, and so, as others would likely do, they risked their lives to attain it. They would confront war, lynching, and hostile racial attitudes but would never end their relentless advance toward freedom.

On March 5, 1770 a confrontation between a group of men and British troops in Boston resulted in Crispus Attucks, James Caldwell, and Samuel Gray being shot dead. Attucks, an African dockworker who had run away from slavery, was considered the first casualty in the American Revolution. Those killed became symbols for the ensuing struggle between the British authorities and the Americans. Attucks, who was apparently mixed Native American and African, was celebrated for demonstrating that Africans, although still oppressed, would fight for their liberty.

By 1775 there may have been 500,000 Africans in the colonies including both enslaved and free people. However, the condition of blacks in the land was different from that of whites, who saw themselves as the rightful owners of the land that was occupied by the Native Americans. The dispossession of Native Americans occurred as the enslavement of Africans progressed, both processes happening during the time that whites were feeling exploited by taxation from Britain. When the war with the British broke out, the African population was just as engaged as the whites, since the condition of enslaved Africans depended to a large degree on the political position and attitude of their white owners. Free blacks had to choose their political position as well, and the choice was not clear. On both sides of the War of Independence there were both slaveholders and anti-slavery votarists.

Given these circumstances some black people made their choices largely on the basis of their own vision of the future. If you thought that the government, that is, the British authorities, was going to offer a better deal for Africans, you were more likely to fight for the redcoats. On the other hand, if you felt that your chances and that of the black population would be better under a new government of the settlers, then you chose to fight on the side of the revolutionaries.

African Profiles of Valor in the Revolutionary War

There were numerous examples of Africans who exceled as supporters of the American colonists.[1] On April 19, 1775 Peter Salem, an African who had been freed from slavery, distinguished himself in the first battle of the war for independence. Like Crispus Attucks, the first man to be killed challenging the British with a group of colonists in Boston in March 1775, Peter Salem believed that he should fight for freedom from Britain. He joined the Minutemen of Framingham and marched to the center of the town. When the Minutemen, those who could be ready at a minute's notice, heard that the British were marching toward Concord to destroy stores of arms, they took up their muskets and rushed toward Concord. Other young Africans—Cato Bordman, Cuff Whittemore, and Job Potama—met the Minutemen and marched with them to the rendezvous with history. Seven hundred British troops met 350 Minutemen at Concord. When the battle started, Peter Salem and the other Minutemen held their ground until the British retreated toward Boston. The battle was furious, with men running from fence to wall, from pillars to posts, from wells to houses, firing and reloading, running and dodging behind trees. Brave men fought that day and quite a number of them were Africans. In addition to the African fighters already named were Prince Estabrook, Cato Wood, Pomp Blackman, and Isaiah Bayoman—courageous defenders of a liberty that most of them did not have and would never see. Others would join the struggle at Concord and elsewhere, including Pomp Fisk, Caesar Weatherbee, Cuff Whittemore, Barzillai Lew (a veteran of the French and Indian War), and Prince Hall (a prominent black leader after the war), as well as Salem Poor, who wintered with Washington at Valley Forge in 1777–1778. Their names are stamped forever on the pages of history as ardent supporters of freedom.

When the battle at Concord was over, the Minutemen had lost ninety men but the British had lost more than 300, with many bleeding from severe injuries as they dragged their tired and wounded bodies back to Boston. Africans had served their cause with courage and dignity but they would be tried again at the Battle of Bunker Hill.

Preparation for the Battle of Bunker Hill occurred on June 16, 1775, two months after Concord. State militias from Rhode Island, Connecticut, and New Hampshire had essentially surrounded the British at Boston. Since there was no organized colonial army the men who took to the streets to fight against the British were volunteers eager to defend their strike for liberty. Africans were just as passionate about this as whites. So the veteran fighter Peter

Salem, a leading black patriot, was joined by nearly 1,200 others, many black, lying in wait for the British at Breed's Hill outside the city. The battle began at sunrise on June 17, 1775 when the British formed a battle line with their 2,200 soldiers marching slowly and steadily toward the Americans.

Guns blazed as one of the bloodiest battles of the revolution raged. Africans were in the thick of the battle, fighting without fear, and with a vigor that would later earn them recognition for their bravery. The citation written in Peter Salem's honor called him a "brave and gallant soldier." While Peter Salem won great honor, he was not alone as a black soldier. When the British major John Pitcairn shouted for them to surrender, Salem took aim and felled him. While the colonists had to retreat, they had sent a message to the British Empire that they would fight for independence.

Bunker Hill had been a bitter battle for the Africans and the whites; many had died, and even more were wounded.[2] The Americans soon formed the Continental Army under the leadership of George Washington, a Virginian. Peter Salem and other Africans joined the army, but some colonies forbade Africans to join the army. Africans often preferred to fight rather than to be enslaved but slave-owners felt that, since the enslaved were property, if the Africans were killed they would have to suffer economic loss. The bottom line was their largest concern.

Figure 3.1
George Washington. Image courtesy of Charles L. Blockson Afro-American Collection, Temple University Libraries.

Contest for African Allegiance

Great Britain contested the Continental Army for the Africans' allegiance. In November 1775 Lord Dunmore, a loyalist of Great Britain and governor of Virginia, promised freedom to any African who fought for the British. Perhaps he knew that since Washington was a major slave-owner it would be difficult—almost impossible—for him to allow enslaved Africans to fight. Thousands of Africans ran away from enslavement to join the British. Lord Dunmore had seen that Africans had proved to be good soldiers and wanted them to enlist. The Continental Army finally agreed to accept all soldiers, black or white, so long as they were fit. Only Georgia and South Carolina, believing that blacks should not be encouraged to kill whites, even the enemies of the colonies, refused to allow Africans to serve in their militias.[3]

The British drove George Washington's Continental Army from New Jersey into Pennsylvania and were soon trying to take the entire Hudson River area of New York. This led to a strategic error where British general John Burgoyne surrendered his entire army to the Americans at Saratoga, New York. The French and other European countries came to the aid of the Americans. By October 1781 Lord Cornwallis had surrendered another British army to Washington at Yorktown, Virginia. There would be no British victory in the American colony.

However, the British had forced the Americans to consider one strategy that would become a lingering question in future wars. During the organization of the Continental Army in July 1775 George Washington had forbade the enlistment of African troops and had further refused the re-enlistment of blacks who had fought at Lexington, Concord, and Bunker Hill. Like their common leader, Washington, the colonial militia in other states refused to enlist black troops. The Americans figured that if they enlisted black soldiers it would lead to Africans leaving their enslavers without permission, and so there was no effective way of enrolling blacks into the army. Secondly, they argued that blacks with guns could endanger the white social order. Indeed, blacks who used guns to shoot white people would create an unsustainable instability in the relationship between whites and blacks. Yet a third argument, although contradictory, was that blacks were too cowardly to fight.

On the other hand, the British took advantage of the racist positions of the Americans—attitudes they may have had themselves—and recruited black soldiers to fight for the Crown. The British recruited Africans from Maryland to Georgia, starting a rumor among the whites that the British would incite the Africans to revolt against slavery. One of the most daring and direct appeals was made on November 7, 1775 when Lord Dunmore of Virginia, forced out of Williamsburg and seeking to raise soldiers against the marauding Americans who had captured the fields and small towns, desperately issued a proclamation which offered to free any black person who joined "His Majesty's Troops."[4] Ralph Henry, a twenty-six-year-old slave of Patrick Henry, joined Lord Dunmore's troops. Some have argued that Dunmore offered the appeal to blacks when he realized that he had only 300 men and his army had been driven from Williamsburg. Although a large number of blacks wanted to join Dunmore's forces, only about 800 joined since the governor had to run to warships for protection and black volunteers could not reach the forces. Furthermore, Dunmore's battered forces, half of the 600 black, lost the Battle of the Great Bridge in December 1775 and he essentially had to end his recruitment efforts. He had struck at the heart of the rebellious colonists by offering blacks freedom. It was a psychological blow of the greatest degree. Washington had proclaimed of Dunmore, "If that man Dunmore is not crushed before the Spring he will become the most dangerous man in America. His strength will increase like a snowball running down a hill. Success will depend on which side can arm the Negro faster."[5] By December 30, 1775, Dunmore was defeated and Washington had black troops fighting on the side of the Americans.

Nevertheless, numerous blacks still escaped from slavery during this period and joined the cause of the loyalists. The British employed blacks as laborers, road builders, and food gatherers from outlying farms. In fact, black loyalists were most prominent in Georgia and South Carolina. There are reports that blacks who remained loyalists carried out attacks against colonists as late as 1786. More blacks joined the forces of the loyalists than joined the side of the Americans. Indeed, many blacks died of typhus and smallpox, as they were often without medical care during their service for the British. Hundreds of Africans abandoned the war effort when the British did and sailed to New York City, the new British headquarters. One black leader left in the war was Colonel Tye, who conducted guerrilla raids in the area of Monmouth County, New Jersey, for four years until he was killed in battle in 1780. Tye and his band of twenty-five loyalists created a whirlwind of havoc in New Jersey by spiking cannons, ambushing American troops, plundering villages for food, and killing as many officers as possible. Tye's interracial band was one of the earliest guerrilla groups fighting for the Crown. While Tye's death ended his career, many of his men joined the British in retreating to Acadia, now Nova Scotia, and then to Jamaica or Sierra Leone.

York and the Exploration of the North American Continent

Between the end of the Revolutionary War and the beginning of the War of 1812, American leaders made as much advance as possible in understanding the vast expanse of the North American continent. It was not until William Clark, York, and Meriwether Lewis, however, crossed the continent from the east to the west and back again that Americans truly grasped the extent of the land.[6]

York, a black man who grew up with William Clark and was enslaved by Clark, made his mark on American history by becoming the first African in historical time to cross the continent north of Mexico. There was the story of Estevanico—who lived between 1500 and 1539, and is often referred to as Esteban the Moor from Morocco—who was one of the first Africans to arrive in the continental United States. He was an enslaved African who was one of four survivors of the 1533 Spanish Narváez expedition and journeyed with Andrés Dorantes de Carranza, Álvar Núñez Cabeza de Vaca, and Alonso del Castillo Maldonado across the southwestern part of the United States. So while there were Africans traveling with Spanish explorers, as they had traveled with Columbus before, the first African to actually walk across the continental United States was York of the Lewis and Clark expedition.

York accompanied Lewis and Clark on the expedition to the Pacific Ocean and back to the east between1803 and 1806. York and Clark were roughly the same age and York had been given to Clark by his father in a will dated July 24, 1799. On October 29, 1803, York and Clark, who would become co-commander of the expedition with Meriwether Lewis, joined nine others, stepped aboard the Corps keelboat, and set off on their journey from Louisville, Kentucky.

York's contribution to the expedition was definite and significant. Although York was enslaved he performed his duties and responsibilities with dignity, expertise, and discipline. He explored the American West with his eyes wide open and, though he could not read or write, left his achievements in the journals of William Clark. He was considered strong, a great swimmer, an excellent chef, a mighty hunter, and a remarkable presence among the Native Americans, who found him an easy communicator and an expert dancer. On December 26, 1803 Clark wrote, "Corps. White house & York Commce sawing with the Whip Saws," showing that York carried out his duties even though he remained enslaved.[7] York is mentioned again on April 7, 1804 when he accompanied the captains to St Louis. Clark entered, "Set out at 7oclock in a Canoo with Cap Lewis my servant & one man at 1/2 past 10 arrived at St. Louis."[8] Then Clark writes on May 14 that "2 of us & york."[9]

On June 5 it is reported that York swam to a "Sand bar together Greens for our Dinner," indicating that he was involved in meals for the captains and that he could swim fairly well.[10] On September 9, 1804 Clark says "Derected My Servent York with me to kill a Buffalow."[11] Clark had grown up with York in Kentucky and felt comfortable hunting with him. Enslaved Africans were usually prohibited by law from having firearms except on the frontier and were issued a license by a magistrate, which had to be applied for by their masters.

York finally reached the tidal waters of the Columbia River. He then walked nineteen miles to the Pacific Ocean to become the first African man to have crossed the continent to the Pacific Ocean. By now the party had been joined by Sacagawea and hence it became the first truly multicultural expedition in American history, with a Native American woman, an African man, and white men reaching the south Oregon shore.

Clark drafted a notice that the expedition was sent out by the government to explore the interior of the continent. Every person was mentioned, including "York, a black man of Captain Clark's."[12] These notices were given to local Indians and a passing ship's captain.

Later, while exploring Yellowstone River, Clark named a small stream "York's Dry River," the second geographic feature named for his enslaved African.[13]

The expedition made it to St Louis about noon on September 23, 1806. York had gone across the continent and back and had seen many sights but would remain enslaved to Clark for another ten years. But when York returned to daily life, he asked Clark for freedom or to be hired out to be close to his wife. Clark refused at first and then, ten years after the expedition, gave him freedom. It is believed that York, the explorer, died in 1832.

The War of 1812

It has often been thought that one war leads to another. And so it did with the end of the Revolutionary War in 1781. Neither Britain nor America felt that the war was complete—although the Americans had declared independence and had established a Continental Congress, Britain was not pleased with the new government. In 1803 Britain had begun to seize American ships, especially slave ships, and impress their crews into service for Britain. Later in 1807 they would increase the intensity and coverage of their seizures and force the Americans to react. Already the American Constitution had declared that slavery was not to be permitted on the seas after 1807, but there was limited will among American politicians to hold to this standard. Jefferson had declared that America did not have the resources to patrol the seas. Britain, on the other hand, exercised its right to seize American ships. The USS *Chesapeake* resisted the demands from the crew of the British HMS *Leopard*, which resulted in three American deaths and eighteen Americans wounded. According to the British, since they were at war with France they could not allow any American ship to engage in commerce with France. On the other hand, France sought to interdict American ships headed to England. American industry and commerce suffered because of the contest between the two superpowers, France and Britain. Jefferson's Embargo Act of 1807 tried to force France and Great Britain to change international shipping policies. Neither the British nor the French agreed to change their policies immediately. However, when Napoleon in 1810 exempted the United States from French restrictions, even though Britain had compensated the United States for the USS *Chesapeake* incident, France had pulled off a political victory. In 1811 President James Madison discontinued all trade with Britain, which caused Britain to attempt to change its laws against American shipping. It was too little too late and on June 1 Madison asked Congress to declare war. By June 18 the Congress had granted Madison's wish and the United States and Britain went to war for the second time in twenty-five years.

The state of New York raised two regiments of 2,000 black soldiers to fight the British. The soldiers who had been enslaved were promised freedom. Hundreds of black sailors joined the U.S. Navy, the one service where blacks had always been welcomed. The United States had fewer ships than the British but it had three superior vessels—the USS *Constitution*, dubbed "Old Ironsides"; the USS *President*; and the USS *United States*. They were the fastest ships and the most armored ships in the world. Whites refused to allow black sailors to serve on those ships; however, black sailors did serve on Captain Oliver Perry's ship, the USS *Lawrence*, and Lieutenant Thomas McDonough's ship, the USS *Saratoga*. Perry's six-ship flotilla patrolled Lake Erie and on September 10, 1813 his squadron faced a British squadron led by Captain Robert Barclay. Most of the British fire struck the USS *Lawrence*, killing eighty percent of its crew. Perry had to transfer to the *Niagara*. He continued the battle and soon forced a British surrender. The 100 black sailors who fought with him represented more than a quarter of his sailors, although Perry complained that when he asked for seamen he had only received blacks, soldiers, and boys. Commodore Isaac Chauney took issue with Perry, declaring that of the best men of his own ship, many were Africans.[14]

As had been the case during the Revolutionary War, Africans also fought for the British. In 1814, 5,000 enslaved blacks joined the Royal Navy from the Chesapeake Bay region. In some battle arenas black sailors made up as much as twenty percent of the navy force of both sides in the war. The sailors could emigrate to Canada or the West Indies if they fought for the British. When the British invaded Maryland they used more than 1,500 black marines, who inflicted a heavy defeat on the Americans.

So as we can see, both the Americans and the British employed black marines during the War of 1812. However, the only all-black militia existed in Louisiana, and while it was a slave state, there were 4,600 free blacks by 1809. Some of these Africans had emigrated from Haiti and were veterans of the revolution in San Domingo. Free blacks who owned property and paid taxes for two years were recruited to serve in the navy. Louisiana law, since it was still a slave state, did not permit blacks to serve as officers, although three blacks served as second lieutenants. To defend his territory against a threatened British attack, Governor William

C. C. Claiborne needed black soldiers. He assured General Andrew Jackson that it was necessary to have these black troops, who had fought quite nobly under the Spanish. Thus, Andrew Jackson had 500 blacks out of his 6,000 troops defending New Orleans. When the War of 1812 was over, blacks had once again proved themselves to be the equal of any soldiers.

The Origins of American Racism

Thus, the origin of racism in the seventeenth century became a basis for categories of slavery, subordination, and hegemony. Although today we are aware that the race myth is problematic, the European colonists and slave traders of the seventeenth and eighteenth centuries were sure that race was genetic, and that biological differences constituted the basis for white superiority over blacks. Therefore, what Africans experienced was the construction of the hegemonic idea itself where whites went beyond ritualistic racial bigotry; they created an oppressive systematic form of sinister dehumanization of Africans. The leading opinion-makers, philosophers, and theologians of the European enslavers organized the category of blackness as property value. Africans were, in effect, without soul, spirit, emotions, desires, and rights. Chattel could have neither mind nor spirit.

There was an almost unanimous chorus of European thinkers who believed in the inferiority of Africans. Thomas Henry Huxley, considered a progressive in his time, wrote in 1871 that "No rational man, cognizant of the facts, believes that the average negro is the equal, still less the superior, of the white man . . . The highest places in the hierarchy of civilization will assuredly not be within the reach of our dusky cousins."[15]

Georg Hegel argued in 1828 that spirit was the leading national characteristic because it contained the past and the future in a pregnant moment of the present. All people had spirit, emotion, and desires. Yet even Hegel would consider Africans to be outside of history, as Africa was no part of history. No Western thinker since Plato was more influential than Hegel, and yet his thinking on Africa painted an image that continues in some circles until today. Hegel wrote:

> The peculiarly African character is difficult to comprehend, for the very reason that in reference to it, we must quite give up the principle which naturally accompanies all our ideas—the category of Universality. In Negro life the characteristic point is the fact that consciousness has not yet attained to the realization of any substantial objective existence—as for example, God, or Law—in which the interest of man's volition is involved and in which he realizes his own being. This distinction between himself as an individual and the universality of his essential being, the African in the uniform, undeveloped oneness of his existence has not yet attained; so that the Knowledge of an absolute Being, an Other, and a Higher than his individual self, is entirely wanting.[16]

Thus, Hegel is as much a purveyor of a racist attitude about Africans as he is a believer in the inferiority of black people. In Hegel's thinking, Africans could have no notion of the abstract in art or religion, as in God or as in Law, where the human will was involved in society. And yet, before him was the evidence of thousands of years of African history; indeed, a history which predated the civilizations of Europe stared back at him when he looked south. Actually, the earliest names of a supreme being had been uttered on the African continent before they were spoken anywhere else in the world. What Hegel was doing was establishing the basis for an argument of European superiority. Furthermore, he commented:

> The Negro, as already observed, exhibits the natural man in his completely wild and untamed state. We must lay aside all thought of reverence and morality—all that we call feeling—if we would rightly comprehend him; there is nothing harmonious with humanity to be found in this type of character. The copious and circumstantial accounts of Missionaries completely confirm this, and Mahommedanism appears to be the only thing which in any way brings the Negroes within the range of culture.[17]

One has to remember that this was the nineteenth century, and enough material existed in the narratives of a few adventurers from Europe to Africa to disprove Hegel's opinions. Nevertheless, he pursued the most ignorant lines of argument. What is the meaning of Hegel's statement of the African that "there is nothing harmonious with humanity to be found in this type of character"?[18] Setting Europeans up as the standards by which others are to be judged, Hegel observed or believed that Africans were so far away from the European way of thinking and behaving that they could not have any relationship to their environment, to concepts, to religion, to philosophy, or to consciousness. This was completely inaccurate but it was the type of thinking that placed Africans on the defensive for 300 years. Just to twist the dagger once again, Hegel writes:

> At this point we leave Africa, not to mention it again. For it is no historical part of the World; it has no movement or development to exhibit. Historical movements in it— that is in its northern part—belong to the Asiatic or European World. Carthage displayed there an important transitory phase of civilization; but, as a Phoenician colony, it belongs to Asia. Egypt will be considered in reference to the passage of the human mind from its Eastern to its Western phase, but it does not belong to the African Spirit. What we properly understand by Africa is the Unhistorical, Undeveloped Spirit, still involved in the conditions of mere nature, and which had to be presented here only as on the threshold of the World's History.[19]

Therefore, Europe's most impressive thinker of the nineteenth century dismisses Africa and establishes the basis for future arguments about African culture and character. No wonder the writing of African history has been clouded by Eurocentric racism. Hegel takes the two civilizations of Africa that are well known in the West, Egypt and Carthage, and accredits them to forces outside of Africa. In fact, neither Egypt nor the Carthage that invaded Rome was anything other than African in content and character. Egypt, or Kemet, as the Africans called it, was a black civilization, or, as Cheikh Anta Diop declared in *The African Origin of Civilization*, a "Negro civilization."[20] It was neither European nor Asian; it was African and black. On the other hand, Carthage or Khart-Hadesh, New City, was settled in Africa by Queen Elisa and about 150 Phoenicians and Cyprians. There are many legends and rumors about this settlement, and archaeology has not established any clear evidence that this site was actually settled as claimed. For example, Timaeus gives the date for the founding of Carthage as 814 BCE, the same date he gives for the founding of Rome. This has caused some people to argue that the story is legendary and that the characters are not real. Yet I think it is important to make another salient point about this history.

Justinian records that a king of Tyre made Elisa and Pygmalion joint heirs of his kingdom.[21] However, when he died, the people preferred Pygmalion alone as the ruler even though he was a young boy. Elisa married Acerbas, her uncle, who was a high priest, and second in power to the king. It was believed that Acerbas had lots of gold buried and so the young king had him murdered. Elisa, believing that her life was in danger, wanted to escape Tyre, so she devised a plan to move into the palace with her brother as a way to convince him that she was appeased. He was pleased that his sister would be coming to the palace and sent attendants to help her move. She ordered them to throw bags of gold into the sea, apparently Acerbas's gold, but in reality only sand. Elisa told the attendants that these bags were offerings to her late husband's spirit. She then persuaded the attendants to join her in leaving Tyre since Pygmalion would be angry when he learned that they had thrown the gold into the sea. Thus, a small party of attendants and servants went with Elisa to Cyprus. When they got there a priest of Jupiter agreed to join the expedition so long as he could bring eighty young women who were prostituting themselves at the seashore, to become wives of men in the party. When the party set sail they eventually made it to the northern coast of Africa, where they asked the local people for a bit of land for a temporary refuge.

The greatest personality of Carthage was Hannibal, the son of Hamilcar Barca, who lived from 248 BCE to 183 BCE. If we accept Timaeus' date of 813 for the founding of Carthage in Africa, it is 565 years before the appearance of Hannibal, the African general who led elephants across the Alps. There is no way that a small colony of 150 people could have landed on the northern African coast from Phoenicia and remained among the local African population without becoming over time submerged into the African culture. Furthermore, they would have intermarried enough with the local population that they would have lost all characteristics of their Phoenician identities within four or five generations, not to speak of what would have happened in twelve to fifteen generations! Hannibal was an African, a black man, who was born in Africa of African parentage and rose to become one of the great military strategists of all time.

Combating the many opinions of Western thinkers who have raided the treasury of African historical information and left the coffers full of myths and artifice has been a major aspect of African American history for decades. Indeed, the works of W. E. B. Du Bois, Carter G. Woodson, Benjamin Quarles, Anna Julia Cooper, Maria Stewart, Alice Dunbar, John Henrik Clarke, John Hope Franklin, John Jackson, Yosef Ben Jochannon, Asa Hilliard, William Leo Hansberry, and others have attempted to set the record straight as to African history. George G. M. James, a Guyanese teaching at Pine Bluff, wrote *Stolen Legacy* and published it in 1956.[22] It was a shocker of a book because James, a student of Greek, Latin, and Hebrew, argued that Greek civilization was really nothing more than stolen African civilization. There would then be an outpouring of powerful works by John Jackson, *Introduction to African Civilization*; Chancellor Williams, *The Destruction of Black Civilization*; and Yosef ben-Jochannan, *Black Man of the Nile and His Family*, that would reset the narrative of African history.[23] However, these harbingers of truth had to crawl over the rubble of racism and prejudice in order to gain attention. Whether personality, movement, character, or behavior moves history along, one cannot say with any certainty. But what we do know is that the argument for national economic conditions having a lot to do with the course of history is an abiding one.

Marx would argue that it was not ideas or national personalities that ruled history, but the economic conditions of human lives, and that all alienation was economic and social, not spiritual or metaphysical. New interpreters of slavery would fall upon this idea as the most salient explanation of the relations between whites and blacks. Indeed, Eric Williams would write in *Capitalism and Slavery* that it is the heart of the slavery phenomenon. Since slaveholders owned enslaved people, these people, who were not human in the sense of rights and aspirations, according to whites, were simply means of production and capital accumulation.[24] We could have been robots as far as the slaveholders were concerned.

Actually, the enslavement was something far more brutally inhuman in its end result because although Africans were defined legally as chattel, Africans could be hurt physically and mentally. One has to understand that the enslaved Africans were not laborers but slaves, and slaves in the mind of the capitalists-colonialists were less, much less, than laborers. The alienation was deeper than any social or economic conditions could render humans; blacks were, in the minds of some whites, sub-human. There is the moral and ethical problem of the human situation during the enslavement. Chattel produced chattel. Humans defined as chattel made products and created wealth that is directly linked to the present condition of status in the West.

Let me add here the sentiment of Eric Williams in *Capitalism and Slavery* that the triangular trade stimulated British industry. Matt Wrack in reviewing the brilliant book *The Making of New World Slavery: From Baroque to the Modern, 1492–1800*, by Robin Blackburn, demonstrated that Williams' thesis remains valid.[25] It was Williams' idea that capitalism ushered in the era of racism because the massive movement of millions of Africans across the ocean caused new justifications to be developed around human interactions. One could argue, however, that there was a convergence of conditions and situations that produced the European response to human difference, not simply capitalism. New approaches to hierarchy based on biological arguments, the expansion of Christianity into other nations, and the rise of Enlightenment reasoning gave way to attempts to make racial categorizing a part of the European construction of societies.

What can anyone say about the awful horrors of the European Slave Trade and the American and Caribbean practice of the slave system? Words cannot express the massive scale of the operation, where the population of enslaved persons swelled to over 6 million in the Americas by 1850. Prior to the greatest holocausts of the centuries, the European enslavement of Africans and the subsequent centuries of resistance were the historical moment that defined the modern world.

No one could have dreamed or planned a more deadly tragedy to last for centuries than the organizers of slavery. Olaudah Equiano's account of his capture and enslavement was enough for many British and American whites to declare themselves opposed to the practice of slavery.[26] There is inherent in the prosecution of the slave system a contradiction to the Enlightenment notion of progress because here, in the activities of slavery, were millions of small tragedies that produced one great terror. As Eric Williams understood, it was during this period of enslavement of Africans that whites equated blackness with slavery and with inferiority. While slavery may have existed, as the apologists claim, in other parts of the world, it was never the hellhole of horror created by European chattel slavery. In both scale and form, nothing that had gone before equaled what Africans experienced. In 1829 David Walker declared that no people had been as cruel and barbarous as the white Christian Americans.[27]

Unquestionably the transformation of agriculture and the exploration of the Americas assisted in the emergence of a European desire for free labor. New lands for exploitations and new plantations for agricultural goods meant a need for workers. After the failure of British and Irish emigrants as indentured servants who would work for three, five, or seven years for the plantation, the colonial plantation owners looked to enslaved Africans to carry out their work. In 1638 there were 2,000 indentured whites and only 200 Africans in Barbados, but by 1653 the island had 20,000 enslaved Africans and 8,000 indentured Europeans.[28] Indeed, Eric Williams explained that the search for a secure labor source produced the rise in the slave trade of Africans. An intermediate step between indentured Europeans to enslaved Africans was the enslavement of local native people. His argument was that it was not the color of the worker but the cheapness of the worker that produced the origin of slavery. Of course, this position is debated by some historians who claim that Europe was far closer to the plantations, had large supplies of unemployed workers, and was capable of delivering for the plantations English-speaking workers. Nevertheless, Williams' thesis that slavery did not originate with racism but that racism was the consequence of the enslavement has remained a major component of our modern interpretation of slavery.

Bacon's Rebellion in 1676, one hundred years before the Declaration of Independence, shook the foundations of the nascent system of servitude and slavery in the American colonies because it involved enslaved Africans, white servants, and freemen. No plantation owner wanted a system where whites and blacks would combine in a solid phalanx against the system. They were terrified of group solidarity. Soon there were laws against whites and blacks socializing, and the enforcement of laws limiting perpetual slavery to Africans and heathens only, thus setting the white servants on a different paths which ultimately led to the end of the indenture system. According to Williams' analysis, white opposition to slavery was weaker in those colonies where the enslavement of Africans was demanded by law.[29]

Impact of the Slave Trade

Africans who were not kidnapped were often purchased with goods manufactured in Britain, France, Portugal, and Holland. Because of British dominance on the seas, during the seventeenth and eighteenth centuries Africans were largely transported on British ships. The sugar, cotton, molasses, and indigo produced in the Americas by Africans created new British industries. Furthermore, the maintenance of the plantation system, including owners and the enslaved, produced new markets for British companies. By the middle of the eighteenth century there was hardly any British town of any size that was not in some way connected to the slave trade or colonial rule. Thus, the accumulation of capital in England that helped to fuel the Industrial Revolution was made on the back of the trade. Just as enslaved Africans made the sugar colonies the sweetest prizes of imperialism in the Caribbean, so the Africans in the American South made cotton king of the realm in Manchester.

The Nature of Human Bondage

Various forms of human bondage still exist in the world today. As horrendous as they seem to us with our modern sensibilities, they are nothing compared to the massive holocaust that struck the African continent during the great disaster called the European Slave Trade. This search for wealth was equivalent to the madness of a gold rush; it was the iconic capitalist venture of its era, just as information technology might be today. If a European person was not in the game, he or she felt that they were missing out on an opportunity for great wealth. Given the strength of the idea that Africans were property, chattel, that could bring great wealth, some Europeans dubbed Africans "Black Gold."

Let us see now if we can shed more light on the meaning and processing of the term chattel slavery. This term is at the very core of the debasement of Africans that accompanied this massive transfer of people against their wills from one continent to another. Chattel slavery has been rudely misunderstood, treated almost gingerly as though it is a decent term to describe a quaint practice that was acceptable to high society. Yet it is clear that the people who were being enslaved had achieved more in antiquity than the enslavers; the mere invention of the gun separated the whites from blacks. Europe had invented almost nothing prior to 1500 and had been seen as less developed than Africa in the fifteenth and sixteenth centuries.

James Blaut wrote in *The Colonizer's Model of the World: Geographical Diffusionism and Eurocentric History* that Europe used its geographical position to amass large amounts of the world's wealth and this aggrandizing behavior has contributed to Western dominance.[30]

There are reasons for the way chattel slavery has been understood or misunderstood by contemporary society. In the first place, there is this belief that the forced migration of Africans to the Americas and Caribbean was simply the outgrowth of a demand for labor on the part of an expanding Western economy. The theory is that the population decimation of the Native Peoples in the Americas and Caribbean led to a more intense demand for labor for the production of goods and metals. Labor, of course, is one thing; chattel slavery is an entirely different thing.

Thus, from the fifteenth to the nineteenth centuries the colonizing empires, led by Portugal and Spain but eventually dominated by the Dutch and English, found an over-whelming demand for labor that could not be satisfied by the ordinary settlement of European colonists. They were unable to meet the demands of the commercial, agricultural, and mineral production.

Although by 1650 there were 800,000 white settlers in the Americas and Caribbean, the demand for labor persisted and was coexistent with the requirements for larger profits.[31] The whites exploited the Native Peoples, eliminating them at a horrendous rate through work, disease, and sport. Ultimately, what this situation led to was a demand for even more labor as Africans were kidnapped, captured, and bargained for on the coast of Africa and transported to areas that became Peru, Ecuador, Colombia, Brazil, Venezuela, Guatemala, Nicaragua, all of the major islands, and many of the minor islands in the Caribbean, Mexico, and the United States. Such massive removal of Africans from Africa set the foundation for the extensive African Diaspora. Despite the risks to themselves and their human cargo, the captains of the ships believed that their activities would increase their wealth. So, they engaged in the slave trade without thought for themselves and certainly with little thought for the lives of Africans who suffered during the Middle Passage. According to the demand-for-labor theory, because Europeans, with the exception of some northern Europeans, did not migrate in high enough numbers due to the cost of transportation and resettlement, the only way that the colonies could survive was to turn to the enslavement of Africans.[32]

While slavery was not unknown in Europe, it is safe to say that it was more common in Eastern and Southern Europe than it was in Northern Europe prior to the sixteenth century. The Iberian Peninsula actively practiced slavery during this time but by the fifteenth century even in Spain there was a waning of the enslavement of Arabs, Moors, Jews, Berbers, and Slavs. Africa was relatively unexploited; there had been religious enslavement—the Arab Slave Trade—prior to the sixteenth century, but there was no culture of slavery in Africa, and no chattel slavery.

The English word slave comes from the Middle English *sclave*, which originates in the Old French *esclave*, which can be found in the Medieval Latin *sclavus*. This term is related to the Greek *sklabos*, from *sklabenoi*, Slavs, of Slavic origin. The word *sklabenoi* is closely linked to the Old Russian *Slovene*. It is thought that the contemporary word slave is directly related to the Slavic people, many of whom were sold into slavery.

Europe also practiced indenture and serfdom. Neither of these forms of service, one with a time period attached to it, and the other with land attached to it, could be compared to the chattel slavery of Africans. Serfdom is not the same as slavery. Sometimes this is confused in the mind of the contemporary person. The current usage of the term chattel slavery is not synonymous with serfdom. European serfs were considered to have rights because they were human beings. Enslaved Africans were people who had neither rights nor freedom of movement, and were not paid for their labor because they were seen as "things." Aside from providing food and shelter, the enslaver had no responsibility to the enslaved, but would allow the enslaved no space to have responsibility for him- or herself.

Now let us turn the screws a little bit tighter on chattel. One reason the enslavement of Africans was chattel slavery rather than slavery is because in the English language it is possible to confuse a certain idea of servitude with slavery. An African who was enslaved had no personal or private rights and was expressly the property of another person, to be held, used, or abused as the owner saw fit. Imagine the hell of this predicament and you are on the edge of the nightmare of chattel slavery.

In R. C. Smedley's *History of the Underground Railroad in Chester and the Neighboring Counties of Pennsylvania* there is an indicting account of what it meant to be chattel.[33] Smedley tells it this way:

> Two women from Alabama narrated the wretched and degrading treatment imposed on them and others in the rice swamps and cotton plantations of the far South. During the very busy season in time of cotton picking they were compelled to work all day, and during moonlight nights until nearly morning, not being allowed time to rest, nor to eat, but had to carry a small bag of corn around their neck from which they might pick the grains and eat while at work, while the driver with his whip kept them going continually to the utmost limit of their strength. The field hands were kept in a state of nudity, and when allowed to sleep at night they were huddled together in a pen; and with ball and chain attached to each to prevent their running off, were thus left to lie

down and sleep together like so many brute beasts. These two women were assisted by a sea captain to make their escape.[34]

Two events in the British-occupied areas of the Caribbean and the Americas must be seen as contributing to the ideological foundation of chattel slavery. The first event was in Barbados and the second was in South Carolina. Slavery was established in Barbados in 1636 but it would take nearly thirty more years for the colonists to refine their legal basis. Indeed, the Barbadian Slave Code of 1661 was the first code establishing the English legal base for slavery in the Caribbean. It was adopted by the American colony of South Carolina in 1696, introducing the basic guidelines for slavery in British North America. Ten years earlier, in 1686, South Carolina had established a slave's position as freehold property, which meant that such an individual, as property, could not be moved or sold from the estate. This was similar to serfdom in medieval Europe. However, by the time South Carolina adopted the ideas of the Barbadian Slave Code, the African had been degraded to chattel, giving the enslaver absolute control and absolute ownership. Actually, the South Carolina law meant that enslaved Africans, Native Americans, and mulattoes could be bought and sold like any property, and the condition of their children would also remain that of the enslaved. In a more refined ideological sense, chattel kept producing chattel, even when it was one human giving birth to another. Virginia had made its own law in 1662 creating the status of chattel for Africans, providing that they were slaves for life and that their condition as slaves was transmitted to their posterity. Supposedly the slave status passed to descendants through the mother, as in the Virginia 1662 statute that read as follows: "All children born in this country shall be held bond or free only according to the condition of the mother."[35] However, the colony of Maryland provided in 1664 that "whatsoever free-born English woman shall intermarry with any slave shall serve the master of such slave during the life of her husband; and that all the issue of such free-born women, so married shall be slaves as their fathers were."[36] So, in some cases the condition of the mother, if she were white and free-born, was changed to one of enslavement so that the children would continue to be enslaved. They would, of course, take the condition of the father and be chattel as well. I think what you can see is that a game was being played here.

The enslavers knew that Africans were human and knew that a white could be married to an African or have children by an African woman, but to maintain the ideological subterfuge these situations had to be redefined inside of the slave code itself. A white woman could become, by virtue of her marriage to a black man, black herself. However, a white man who had children by a black woman remained triumphantly white, although his children were chattel.

But Where Does This Idea of Ownership of a Person Begin?

The word "chattel" is akin to the word "cattle" and in fact both words share a common origin in Medieval Latin and Old French. The word "capital" comes from the same root. Thus, chattel slavery means that one person has total ownership of another. There are two basic forms of chattel: domestic chattel, with menial household duties; and productive chattel, working in the fields or mines. Those closest to the enslaver by virtue of space were the domestics and they were usually accorded a higher status in slave society. But to say higher status is not to say much when the idea of chattel slavery was that the human was not a human but a thing. It is not so much that Africans were dehumanized, as is often mentioned, but that African humanity was considered an inferior form of humanity. This is the meaning of chattel. Just as you would not consult your dog, you would not consult a chattel slave. Just as you would not concern yourself with the comfort of a tool, a plow, or a hammer, you would not concern yourself with an enslaved African's comfort. What is chattel is not human in the mind of the enslaver, but nevertheless human in reality. A chattel could not have protection under law, although there were many codes to regulate the use of the enslaved.

New laws were enacted to strip the enslaved of all protection of previous laws. There was hardly any restraint on the enslaver's will, lust, and physical force. If a white person murdered an enslaved person, it was only a misdemeanor punishable by a small fine, a sort of nuisance tax. An enslaved person could only attack a white person in defense of his own enslaver's life. Africans were executed for plotting their own freedom, for burning corn in the fields or stacks of rice, or teaching reading and writing to another African.

The Negro Act of 1740 in South Carolina also established death for teaching another African "the knowledge of any poisonous root, plant, or herb."[37] Since Africans were chattel, laws had to be passed to insist that Africans be dressed. Some enslavers refused to clothe the enslaved. This is one of the dubious achievements of the Barbadian Slave Code. Enslavers complained but they had to dress their slaves, as it was considered quite erotic to see well-developed young African men and women walking around in the nude. But if chattel had to be dressed, what kind of fabric had to be used? The law said that slaves could not dress "above the condition of slaves" and that their clothes could only be made from a list of coarse fabrics.[38] Furthermore, since Africans were chattel there was no reason for them to assemble. Indeed, those Africans who violated these provisions were subject to flogging.

Thus, Africans who had been brought to the slave colonies during the sixteenth century had uncertain legal status. Some were even considered indentured servants; others could own slaves themselves. However, by the middle of the seventeenth century Africans who entered the Caribbean and the Americas were firmly established as chattel property.

The European Slave Trade and the Law of the Admiralty

European capitalism and the European Slave Trade were the twin engines of world dominance from the late 1400s through the second half of the twentieth century. The fact of the matter was that while labor was necessary for the sugar, tobacco, and cotton plantations, slave labor was unnecessary unless one wanted to have excessive profits—greed without limits. In the process, human beings from Africa were trampled underfoot and called chattel, one more piece of property to go with the real estate, firearms, and textiles that became keys to the triangular trade. No wonder it was an accepted practice for European sea captains on the way from Africa to the Americas to throw their human cargo overboard if they were low on food or potable water.

The British Admiralty made the British Isles not only the master of the sea but also the master of the slave trade. One might reasonably argue that the Law of the Admiralty, often called Maritime Law, figured in the legal definitions used in the Barbadian Slave Code. There was some legitimacy—or, at least, slave-owners assumed legitimacy—when it came to their plantations in Barbados.

Since the Law of the Admiralty relates to events happening on the sea or in regard to the spoils of war, such as capture, rebellion, or mutiny and property, those who landed their vessels in the Caribbean or in the Americas took the law into their own hands.[39] In fact, I believe that the notion of command enforcement to maintain discipline on a ship was transferred to land.

There were two aspects to this law: (1) how to control the crew in the middle of the sea, and (2) how to control goods, prizes, and property, real and personal. Of course, since we are talking about a landed situation in Barbados, the idea of punishment was also included when it came to the enslaved Africans. We have rarely looked at chattel within the context of Maritime Law that involves navigation and commerce, and yet surely the Law of the Admiralty that obtained on the sea often spilled over to the land.

Defined as "things," Africans had no rights either on the sea or on land; we were without any protection although the captains of the ships became essentially the masters of all they surveyed. When one thinks of the fact that, to a large degree, Admiralty Law emerged out of the difficult conditions of seafaring, where the crew had no right to privacy, to trial by jury, or anything else considered rights, it is easy to see how this legacy from *Corpus Juris Civilis* of Justinian influenced the creation of rules and laws governing the treatment of Africans.[40] Privileges existed by the will of the captain; there could be no rights under this type of jurisdiction. The only response to this type of situation by an aggrieved or group of aggrieved was to mutiny, that is, to rebel against the privileged position of the captain. This was usually considered reason enough for execution if the mutiny failed. The history of rebellions of Africans in the Americas is long, bloody, and often heroic, as in the cases of Yanga of Mexico, Nat Turner of the United States, Nanny of Jamaica, and Zumba of Brazil.

There are two implications of the creation of chattel Africans: (1) the invention of the white race, and (2) the commodification of the African. In the first instance, out of a heterogeneous group of Europeans who did not claim to be of the same race and, as Smedley understood, did not perceive themselves in a common way, there was invented, Allen argued, a new reality, "the white race."[41] What the enslavers knew that they had in common was that they were not black. So long as they could not find any African in their ancestry, they could become a part of this new creation, a formation of white people who were a reaction to the blackness of the enslaved Africans. This was an all-class formation— a white person could emerge from any class and be considered more privileged than a black from any class, even if one observed that the black, for example, was a descendant of African royalty.

But for white planters Africans were troublesome chattel, a fact that made a lie of the idea that the enslaved were not human and could not think. Enslaved Africans assaulted the system of enslavement and sought to bring the system down by burning cornfields, making machinery inoperative, and slowing down their own physical labor.

Of course, in recent years what we have now seen is that whiteness has become a property in the same racist societies that gave us blacks as chattel property.[42] There is a great difference between the two forms of property, however. In the case of the property rights of whiteness one is speaking of privilege based on the acquisition of whiteness. In the United States there was a time when only English people, Germans, and Scandinavians were whites. Over the centuries, Italians, Irish, Hungarians, Jews, and Turks have become white, meaning essentially that they have participated in the privilege structure of a racist society.

On the other hand, the commodification of Africans established a pattern that would become the fundamental method of transferring wealth in a capitalist society. Who could accumulate wealth by dispossessing Africans? The whites could do it because they had acquired the privilege of whiteness regardless of their origins by virtue of the Africans being defined as chattel. Thus, accumulation by dispossession became one of the principal ways Africans in the United States were systematically constrained and restrained, economically, socially, and psychologically.

Vast wealth from the European Slave Trade fueled the British economy at the same time that Africans were being reduced to things. A commodity could have no rights, no feeling, no sentiments, no religion, and no thoughts. While it is good and decent that recently Britain celebrated the bicentennial of the British abolition of the slave trade by marking the end of slavery with stamps, exhibitions, speeches, and memorial services, one still asks: If slavery was wrong, irreligious, and immoral in 1807, why not in 1707 or 1657?

One cannot truly see the value of abolition without discovering what it was that was abolished. Prior to 1807 the British Parliament passed numerous laws and regulations to encourage and support the trade in human beings. Yes, of course one could argue that this was before the giants of abolition really transformed public opinion. Nevertheless, one cannot forget, even if one wanted to, that in Liverpool the economy thrived on the building of slave ships and the transport of Africans from the continent to the Americas. Nothing is more authentic at this moment in history than the recognition that a great wrong was done to African people and that cities such as Bristol, Nantes, Bordeaux, Lisbon, and Liverpool stood in the center of the chaos on one side of the ocean as Charleston, Savannah, Norfolk, Philadelphia, Baltimore, and New Orleans stood in the center in North America. No wonder the poet James Weldon Johnson wrote:

> Stony the road we trod, bitter the chastening rod
> Felt in the days when hope unborn had died.
> Yet with a steady beat, have not our weary feet
> Come to the place for which our parents sighed?[43]

But it was David Walker in 1829 who put the situation most precisely. He wrote:

> the result of my observations has warranted the full and unshaken conviction, that we, (coloured people of these United States,) are the most degraded, wretched, and abject set of beings that ever lived since the world began; and I pray God that none like us ever may live again until time shall be no more. They tell us of the Israelites in Egypt, the Helots in Sparta, and of the Roman Slaves, which last were made up from almost every nation under heaven, whose sufferings under those ancient and heathen nations, were, in comparison with ours, under this enlightened and Christian nation, no more than a cypher—or, in other words, those heathen nations of antiquity, had but little more among them than the name and form of slavery; while wretchedness and endless miseries were reserved, apparently in a phial, to be poured out upon our fathers, ourselves and our children, by *Christian* Americans![44]

Walker's passionate reaction to enslavement was a testament written in the names of the millions of Africans who felt the same emotions but were unable to voice their sentiments. He firmly states:

> I count my life not dear unto me, but I am ready to be offered at any moment, For what is the use of living, when in fact I am dead. But remember, Americans, that as miserable, wretched, degraded and abject as you have made us in preceding, and in this generation, to support you and your families, that some of you (whites) on the continent of America, will yet curse the day that you ever were born. You want slaves, and want us for your slaves ! ! ! My colour will yet, root some of you out of the very face of the earth ! ! ! ! ! ! You may doubt it if you please. I know that thousands will doubt—they think they have us so well secured in wretchedness, to them and their children, that it is impossible for such things to occur.[45]

Walker died in 1830 soon after he had published the third edition of the *Appeal to the Coloured Citizens of the World*. After his death some blacks claimed that he was murdered for his opinions, yet the *Appeal* continued to agitate the white population.

The American Colonization Society

The presence of Africans in the American colony created uneasiness in the minds of some whites. They knew that the colony could not long sustain a population of two peoples, one enslaved and the other free, and that inevitably there would come a time when the enslaved would seek their own freedom. At the turn of the nineteenth century nothing could have convinced some of the whites of the possibility of danger inhering from the enslaved in their midst more than the Haitian Revolution in 1804. A liberated nation of former enslaved Africans created such havoc in European circles that white Americans were willing to consider any scheme to remove Africans. Out of this intense fear and the concomitant debate was born the American Colonization Society with the purpose of sending some Africans back to Africa.

The white leaders who met in Washington in 1816 to form the American Society for Colonizing Free People of Color of the United States, usually called the American Colonization Society, were among the major slaveholders and politicians in America. Bushrod Washington, a nephew of George Washington, was a prominent member and so was Henry Clay, the compromiser. Both were among the outstanding whites in attendance. No Africans, enslaved or free, were invited to the meeting. Those present claimed that they wanted to abolish slavery gradually and compensate the enslavers for their property. They also wanted to send emancipated Africans to Liberia. They did not think that whites would ever support outright emancipation.

Yet slaveholders like Andrew Jackson, John Tyler, John Randolph, and Francis Scott Key helped to create chapters of the ACS in several northern states. Abolitionists like Lewis Tappan, William Lloyd Garrison, Gerritt Smith, and Arthur Tappan held to the belief that there was something good in the proposition to send Africans back to their native land.

Sierra Leone had been opened up as early as 1787 for resettlement of Africans. Britain, already frightened by the prospect of a large black population in its midst, carved out of the territory of the Mandinka, Kru Temne, Peul, and Bullom people a colony for 500 destitute black men and women from England. They arrived in 1787 and were joined in 1792 by 1,200 more Africans from Nova Scotia, who had fought on the loyalist side in the Revolutionary War. These immigrants had originally begun their journeys in the American South but after the British defeat they retreated to Nova Scotia. The conditions in that cold and unfriendly climate, in addition to the lack of economic possibilities, left them bitter, disappointed, and happy to go to Sierra Leone. Jamaican Maroons, runaways, after a long struggle against the slaveholders of Jamaica, had signed a treaty with Britain, but were deceitfully taken to Canada in 1800. British humanitarians ran the colony and increased its population dramatically after 1807, when recaptured Africans from slave ships were settled in the colony. More than 58,000 Africans from all over the continent were disembarked at Freetown.

An African American Migration

Businessman and seaman Paul Cuffee strode through the early nineteenth century as a larger-than-life mover and shaker in the black community in Massachusetts.[46] He was skilled, wise, and adventurous in an era when a person born of African and Native American heritage was not thought by whites to be capable of much. Cuffe had become a prosperous shipowner and an ardent campaigner for the rights of African people. He was invited by England's Royal African Society to visit Sierra Leone and in 1811, with nine other African seamen, Cuffe set sail for the colony. When they arrived in Freetown, Cuffe immediately saw opportunities for trade and commerce between the black populations in Africa, the Caribbean, and North America. He might be called one of the first true practitioners of a Pan-African vision. When he returned to Massachusetts he organized the Friendly Society of Sierra Leone in order to advance his ideas. He was able to convince thirty-eight emigrants to move from the United States to Sierra Leone in 1815. There was an international group of blacks on the voyage, including people from Congo, Haiti, and Senegal. In some respects this was the very first official migration of Africans from America returning to Africa.

Liberia Assumes a Role

Liberia, liberty, a country whose origins as a modern nation are wrapped tightly in the fabric of hope and despair, optimism and pessimism, what could be and what was to come, soon succeeded Sierra Leone as a destination for formerly enslaved Africans. After all, Britain never had as many domestic Africans as the United States, which had an endless supply ready to leave. Liberia was the natural home of the Vai, Kru, Kissi, Grebo, Bassa, Kpelle, and Mandinka as well as many other linguistic groups. Thus, the settling of Americo-Liberians, as they were called, created political and social confusion and instability that would last for decades.

In 1816 the American Colonization Society had established the colony of Liberia as a home for free blacks despite much criticism. The first ship to set sail for Liberia was the *Elizabeth*. It carried eighty passengers intent on making their new home in Africa. When they found it difficult to acquire land in Liberia they moved on to Sierra Leone, where they found refuge. The next year thirty-three Africans from the United States landed at Cape Mesuardo, later called Monrovia after the United States president James Monroe. Sixteen thousand Africans went to Liberia from 1821 to 1854. Forty-one ships were chartered between 1848 and 1854 by the American Colonization Society to carry thousands of migrants who had been born in the South or who lived as free people in the North. Some had been freed from slavery on the condition that they leave the United States. Of course, this was often extremely difficult because some blacks believed that white masters wanted them out of the country in order to have free access to their wives and daughters. Still others knew that their belligerence and intolerance for enslavement would create serious problems and cause their deaths had they remained in bondage, and therefore chose to leave.

Elite Opposition to Back-to-Africa

The idea of migrating to Africa, however, would meet head-on with another idea born in the urban life of free Africans. They would argue that they were not Africans but "colored" Americans who should be shown the same respect as white Americans. In this argument the "free" Africans of the North attempted to thrust themselves into the heart of the discourse on citizenship and humanity. They recognized their connection to Africans enslaved in the South and to those still enslaved in the North but they felt that they were in every way Americans, even if colored. Such an attitude gave birth to various institutions and organization with the purpose of "proving" that the "Negro" was in every way as capable as the white person.

James Forten

One of the leading interpreters of the "colored" theme, James Forten, had been born in Philadelphia on September 2, 1766. He was born free and despised any talk of sending Africans back to Africa. Although Forten's parents, Thomas and Sarah Forten, were free, he was the grandson of enslaved Africans. He would make a major contribution to the economic condition of other blacks in Philadelphia because of his industrious spirit. Forten attended the Quaker School set up by Anthony Benezet for "African" children. By the time he was eight years old he was apprenticed to Robert Bridges' sailing business. His father worked at the same company but was killed in a boating accident when Forten was still only nine years old. Nevertheless, Forten took on other obligations in the sailing industry, so determined was he to support his family. He mastered the sailing business, learned how to make sails, how to repair them, and how to outfit ships. As a teenager during the Revolutionary War he worked on the *Royal Lewis* until the British captured him. When he returned to Philadelphia he was given the foreman's position at work and soon his

Figure 3.2
James Forten, abolitionist and wealthy businessman. Image courtesy of Charles L. Blockson Afro-American Collection, Temple University Libraries.

boss, Bridges, chose to retire. Thus, in 1798 Forten became the leader and owner of the sailing loft. By 1800, after establishing himself as a formidable businessman, James Forten was a force in local politics. He supported temperance, women's suffrage, and full citizenship for all Americans. In fact, he led the organizing of a petition that asked the United States Congress to free all Africans. Thomas Jefferson was running for president and was peeved by the audacity of Forten in asking Congress to free all enslaved Africans. Nevertheless, Forten persisted in his advocacy for his enslaved brothers and sisters, denouncing the Pennsylvania legislature for prohibiting enslaved Africans from emigrating from other states.

Forten joined forces in 1817 with Richard Allen, a renowned preacher and founder of the African Methodist Episcopal Church, to form the Convention of Colored Peoples. They were successful in gaining the support of the major intellectual and political giants in the African American community, among them Samuel Eli Cornish, Henry Highland Garnet, and William Wells Brown.

Figure 3.3
Richard Allen, founder of the longest continuous black organization in the United States, the African Methodist Episcopal Church. Image courtesy of Charles L. Blockson Afro-American Collection, Temple University Libraries.

Of course, Brown became by the middle of the nineteenth century one of the most formidable African intellectuals. Yet because of his race he felt restrained, constrained, and actually oppressed in American society. This is why he wrote in *The American Fugitive in Europe* after a particularly impressive conference in Paris:

> The day after the close of the Congress, the delegates and their friends were invited to a soirée by M. de Tocqueville, Minister for Foreign Affairs, to take place on the next evening (Saturday); and, as my colored face and curly hair did not prevent my getting an invitation, I was present with the rest of my peace brethren.
>   Had I been in America, where color is considered a crime, I would not have been seen at such a gathering, unless as a servant.
>
> (William Wells Brown, The American Fugitive in Europe:
Sketches of Places and People Abroad, Boston: John P. Jewett, 1855, p. 73).

Figure 3.4
William Wells Brown, first major
African American historian. Image
courtesy of Charles L. Blockson
Afro-American Collection, Temple
University Libraries.

Samuel Cornish

Samuel Cornish was a preacher, an abolitionist, and an editor of great significance to the advancement of black organizations. He had been born in Sussex County, Delaware, in 1795 of free parents. When Cornish was twenty years old he made his way to Philadelphia, where he came under the influence of the Reverend John Gloucester, who founded the first black Presbyterian church. Gloucester found Cornish very eager to be educated and taught him the elements of speaking in public, biblical interpretation, and the liturgy. In 1819 Cornish was licensed to preach and then he moved to the New Demeter Street Presbyterian Church in 1821. Gloucester died of tuberculosis in 1822. Cornish, who had gained exceptional knowledge, praised his mentor for his training. He married Jane Livingston and they had four children. Cornish became an itinerant preacher seeking to build Presbyterianism among black people.

Cornish's reputation rests mainly on his work as an abolitionist and not as a minister. In 1827 and 1828 he was a popular agent for the New York African Free Schools, encouraging parents to send their children to school. In 1831 the First Annual Convention of the People of Color asked him to serve as an agent to collect funds for a college for Africans to be built in New Haven, Connecticut. Because of the local white opposition and the strident arguments of some blacks against the idea, the college was never completed.

John Brown Russwurm

Perhaps Cornish's most important public action was when he joined with John Brown Russwurm to create the *Freedom's Journal* newspaper, which appeared on March 16, 1827. Russwurm had been born in Port Antonio, Jamaica, of an English father and an enslaved African woman. He was taken by his father at eight years of age and sent to Quebec, where his father thought he would receive better treatment and an education. When the boy was a teenager he moved to Maine to live with his father and stepmother, Susan Blanchard. When Russwurm's father died he remained in the care of his stepmother and her new husband. They assisted him in going to Bowdoin College. By the time he joined Cornish and became the junior editor of *Freedom's Journal*, Russwurm was firmly convinced that whites would not treat Africans fairly in the United States and so he became a strong believer in colonization. Although Samuel Cornish initially remained with the paper only six months, Russwurm taking complete editorial control by September, he was a pivotal figure in assisting with circulation because of the many black families he knew. Little did Cornish know, however, that he would later have to assume the duties of the editor in 1829 because the supporters of the paper disagreed with Russwurm's defense of the American Colonization Society. Ultimately, Russwurm took leave from the United States in 1829 and went to Liberia, where he became the governor of the Maryland colony.

Freedom's Journal was out of publication for two months and Cornish started it again under the name *The Rights of All*. In 1832 he served for a few months as pastor of the First African Presbyterian Church in Philadelphia, where he had first received his training under John Gloucester.

An able organizer with a penchant for structure, Cornish became a leading member of William Lloyd Garrison's American Anti-Slavery Society in 1833. He served on the executive board of the American and Foreign Anti-Slavery Society for nine years, participated in the American Missionary Society, which eventually incorporated Cornish's Union Missionary Society, which he had assisted in founding, and served as vice president and president of the AMS for several years.

With more experience and less liberalism as a person, Cornish assumed the role of editor of another newspaper, *The Colored American*, in 1837. This paper received financial support from the white abolitionist Arthur Tappan. Philip A. Bell, an associate of Cornish, became a newspaper editor in California. One could see from Cornish's associations that he was becoming less inclined toward radical solutions. Like Russwurm earlier, who had come under verbal fire from the black community and some whites for his views on the American Colonization Society, now Cornish, much older than some of his fiery contemporaries, found himself explaining his conservative views. He wrote an editorial in 1837 opposing demonstration by blacks against the enforcement of fugitive slave laws. If words can break social, political, and fraternal bonds, no words ever severed such a powerful union as that between Samuel Cornish and David Ruggles of the New York Vigilance Committee, which was dedicated to helping fugitives as against Cornish's seeming weakness in the face of a mortal threat to runaways. Cornish soon moved to Belleville, New Jersey, and found himself facing hard times. He had not been paid his salary as an editor and the *Colored American* was not making money. Yet he believed that outside of New York he would find a less hostile environment for his four children. Not long after he had moved to New Jersey his younger son drowned and the older son had to endure taunts and prejudice in the public school. Once again Cornish moved, always looking for the ideal situation for his family in a racist country. He took his family to Newark, New Jersey, in 1840 and pastured a church there for a few years. But when his wife died in 1844 he found himself back in New York, where he started the Emmanuel Church and preached for the congregation until 1847. Tragedy embraced his family with a tight grip when his older daughter died in 1846 and his younger daughter became ill and died, insane, in 1855. His own health declining rapidly, Cornish moved to Brooklyn, dying there in 1858.

Life did not give Samuel Cornish an easy pass; he grasped whatever it threw his way and he never took his eyes off the goalpost: the full rights of African people. Like so many extraordinary personalities who by the force of their wills shape their times and the institutions they either start or inherit, Cornish brought with him all the mistakes and weaknesses of his humanity. Nevertheless, we are able to speak of him today because his ambition was to become a servant for the people despite his personal flaws, and in this goal he succeeded admirably.

Free Blacks in the North Go to College

One of history's longstanding debates surrounds the first black to finish college in the United States. It seems that Edward Jones was the first African to complete college. He graduated from Amherst College in Massachusetts on August 23, 1826. Jones eventually migrated to Sierra Leone, where he planned to become a teacher and leader of the new Sierra Leone settlement. In fact, he became the principal of Fourah Bay Christian Institute, which was later to become Fourah Bay College. His father, Jehu Jones Jr., opened the first African Lutheran church in Philadelphia. A second black graduate is often credited with being the first, probably because Edward Jones had moved to Sierra Leone: John Brown Russwurm graduated from Bowdoin College on September 6, 1826. Both men received their Master's, Russworm in 1829 and Jones in 1830.

Conclusion

Africans in the period before the Civil War made incredible advances despite the huge obstacles they faced. With resilience and ingenuity they petitioned the government, established free African societies, joined self-help organizations, became preachers, and studied in any college that would permit them to become scholars. A people with an eye on the final mark of freedom continued to march toward the goal, with Richard Allen, Samuel Cornish, John Brown Russwurm, James Forten, and others breaking through barriers to assert their freedom. Yet in the South, where the vast majority of blacks labored in difficult circumstances, there was little hope and no advancement.

Fighting in two wars, the American Revolutionary War and the War of 1812, Africans played key roles in the American victories. They showed no fear and sought to demonstrate what really needed no proof: that they were humans with all the capabilities and weaknesses of other humans. Assuming the stance that they would prove that they were the equal to all men, Africans leaped at the chance to fight in the wars. They were content to finish what they had started.

Thus, a generation that had seen active resistance to the American Colonization Society and David Walker's militant pamphlet *An Appeal to the Coloured Citizens of the World* stood at the precipice of a great internal war knowing that it had done all it could to save the millions of blacks enslaved in the South. While there were different routes to the goal of African dignity and disagreements over the strategies to employ, there was enough unity among the African leaders in the North that a common phalanx appeared to exist in the community. Of course, as is always the case, there were blacks who neither participated nor voiced opinions about the condition of other Africans, but nevertheless enough activists were present, intelligent, and fearless enough to fight the battles for freedom that would open doors for their posterity.

Additional Reading

Genovese, Eugene D. *From Rebellion to Revolution: Afro-American Slave Revolts in the Making of the Modern World*. Baton Rouge: Louisiana State University, 1979.

Hinks, Peter P. *To Awaken My Afflicted Brethren: David Walker and the Problem of Antebellum Slave Resistance*. University Park: Pennsylvania State University Press, 1997.

Quarles, Benjamin. *Black Abolitionists*. New York: Oxford University Press, 1969.

Staudenraus, P. J. *The American Colonization Movement, 1816–1865*. New York: Columbia University Press, 1961.

Chapter Time Markers

Freedom and Revolution without End

4

Important Terms and Names

Harriet Tubman
Fugitive Slave Law
Nat Turner
Charles Deslondes
Gabriel Prosser
Denmark Vesey

Ira Aldridge
Benjamin Banneker
Black Seminoles
Amistad
Mary Ann Shadd
Martin Delany

Taking the Shape of Freedom

By the opening of the eighteenth century the shape of the coming struggle for freedom was clear in the variety of African resistance to enslavement and prejudice. Perhaps there had never been a more turbulent era on the North American continent than that from 1739 to 1889. This period includes petitions, resistance in the courts, participation in the American Revolution battles, the Civil War, and its aftermath. Blacks vowed to express themselves in the fullest human ways possible. They would not be restricted by the limits that had been set by whites. In the South, enslaved Africans would find the courage to rebel against the oppressive system, while in the North free blacks would demonstrate their skills and talents in science and the arts in efforts to overcome all constraints on their intellectual and artistic development. Thus, from rebellions to individual narratives of expressive power, the eighteenth- and nineteenth-century Africans found the will to express freedom.

Stono Rebellion

One of the earliest slave revolts to take place in the English colonies happened on Sunday September 9, 1739, when an explosive uprising that killed sixty whites shocked the South

Carolina colony. An African from Angola, named Jemi, led a band of twenty enslaved Africans on a general rebellion at the banks of the Stono River. Seeing themselves as warriors intending to free all blacks from enslavement, they broke into Hutchinson's store, gathered some guns and ammunition, called for their freedom, secured the consent of others along the way, and began to kill overseers. When the rebels reached the Edisto River they were ambushed by nearly one hundred armed whites who had been alarmed and warned about the roving fighters. Most of the rebels were killed and those not killed were captured and sold into slavery in San Domingo and Jamaica.

American historians have debated what caused the revolt.[1] It is clear what caused the debate: the need to understand why people were tired of enslavement and wanted their freedom. There is nothing subtle about the will of any mass of people to throw off their shackles if they believe they have a good chance of winning. Obviously, the charismatic Jemi knew that the conditions were ripe for revolt. He was aware that a malaria epidemic had struck Charleston and there was general panic in the white population. Jemi also probably knew that the whites had passed a new law in August 1739 called the Security Act that required all white men to carry firearms to church on Sundays. Jemi figured that the best time to strike at the plantation was when the slave-owners were at church with their guns.

After the Stono Rebellion, the South Carolina authorities moved quickly to reduce all provocations for rebellion. The colony set some laws for slave-owners and tightened the screws on what Africans were allowed to do.[2] Masters, for example, were penalized for imposing excessive work or brutal punishments of slaves that could sow discord and cause Africans to want to rebel. Furthermore, the whites created opportunities for some blacks to learn the Christian doctrine—especially the verses that would assist in keeping the enslaved from rebelling. In a colony that already had more blacks than whites in the 1740s the Assembly also imposed a prohibitive duty on the importation of new slaves from Africa and the West Indies. The general attitude was that South Carolina was already black enough. The authorities also tightened control over the enslaved. The Assembly enacted a new law requiring a ratio of one white for every ten blacks on any plantation and passed the Negro Act of 1740, which prohibited enslaved people from growing their own food, assembling in groups, earning money they could keep without giving it to their owners, and learning to read. The colonial authorities sought to control who should eat, and what Africans could eat, as well as to insure that no one amassed any great amount of money that the slave-owners did not know about. Their assessment was that knowledge was dangerous for the enslaved. Indeed, even Africans who were free in the North felt the stigma of racism and sought to overcome it by hard work, diligence to task, and application of their skills to practical issues. Such was the case with Benjamin Banneker.

Benjamin Banneker

In the late eighteenth century Benjamin Banneker made a series of discoveries and calculations that made him a precursor of the coming creativity of the enslaved African. Benjamin Banneker came into the American world of slavery as a direct contradiction to the idea that Africans could not think. He became a mathematician and astronomer, and from 1792 to 1797 was perhaps the best mathematician in the United States. Banneker was an astronomer who calculated ephemerides (locations of the stars and planets) for widely circulated almanacs. In effect, he was one of the early scientists who popularized, for a public whose ability to read was limited, the use of tables of star and planet locations for farming and other uses.[3]

Banneker was born on November 9, 1731 in Baltimore, Maryland, to a free African, Robert, who had purchased his freedom and married Mary Banneky, the free daughter of an Englishwoman and an African man. His father had a farm that was the source of the family's economic foundation, and with his three sisters Benjamin passed a fairly comfortable life in rural Baltimore. After completing his chores on the farm young Benjamin would study reading and writing from his mother and grandmother, and by the time he was ten years old he was reading the Bible to his family at evening meals. He was sent to a Quaker country school, one of the few schools that accepted black children, and he excelled in mathematics. He attended the school for no more than four seasons but soon began to teach himself history, geometry, and literature. So eager was he to master all the learning he could that he would read by the lantern at night when all the rest of the family was fast asleep in their beds.

By the time he was twenty-five he had inherited his father's farm. Intelligent, and clever about business and agricultural trends, Banneker soon expanded the farm to undertake tobacco cultivation. This made his life quite easy and in his leisure he could still pursue his mathematical and scientific interests. He was thirty years old when he constructed the first successful clock ever made by an African and one of the first made in America. Banneker's achievement was heralded by his neighbors and brought to the attention of leading figures in the national government. He had never seen a clock prior to the construction of his own remarkable wooden version; however, he had seen a pocket watch. With precision and care, Banneker artistically carved the toothed wooden wheels and gears of the clock out of seasoned elm wood.

Banneker's interest in astronomy, strong since his teens, peaked when he was about fifty-eight years old. At that time he became involved in the serious study of astronomy on the encouragement of his farming neighbor, George Ellicott, who shared several English books on astronomy as well as a telescope. Just with the these books and an old telescope Banneker taught himself the science of astronomy, becoming the leading scientist in his region. He projected the lunar and solar eclipses and began in earnest an attempt to commercialize his knowledge. This proved a daunting task because few people were interested in buying his observations, but this did not matter to Banneker, who kept making his calculations. Finally, in 1791, Major Andrew Ellicott, a surveyor of new lands for development, was asked by the government to survey the ten square miles for the new Federal Territory that was to become the new American capital. During this period Pierre Charles L'Enfant, an architect, engineer, and artist with offices in New York, had managed to have the ear of George Washington and to have the president's approval to design the city itself with places for all the public buildings. Ellicott was in charge of the survey of the district and L'Enfant in charge of the design of the city. However, Andrew Ellicott, the brother of Benjamin Banneker's neighbor, told the commissioners who had been placed in charge of the overall project that L'Enfant was unable to have the plan engraved and had refused to give a copy of the plan to Ellicott. In this dispute, Andrew Ellicott won the argument and with the assistance of Benjamin Banneker was able to complete the design of the city. Soon thereafter George Washington removed

L'Enfant from the project and he died a very poor man, after spending many years fighting to have the government pay him for his work. On the other hand, Ellicott and Banneker must be credited with the final plan for the national capital. Ellicott asked Banneker to work with him as an assistant, and when the baselines and boundaries of the district and the outline of the city had been drawn and approved, Banneker went back to his farm. The following year he published in Baltimore the work *Benjamin Banneker's Pennsylvania, Delaware, Maryland, and Virginia Almanack and Ephemeris, for the Year of Our Lord, 1792; Being Bissextile, or Leap-Year, and the Sixteenth Year of American Independence.*[4] After the publication of this first almanac he was able to publish four more times until 1797.

Having worked with Andrew Ellicott as an assistant on planning of the District of Columbia, Banneker decided to forward a copy of his calculations to Thomas Jefferson, who was secretary of state. In the letter accompanying his calculations, Banneker demonstrated his courage and integrity by criticizing Jefferson's pro-slavery view, and urged an end to the enslavement of Africans. For Banneker, it was clearly a case of hypocrisy to anyone who could see that there was little difference between the right of whites to struggle against the British and the right of blacks to fight for their freedom. Who could not see this? Although Jefferson would become an intellectual icon of the American Revolution, his position on slavery sullied his historical record.

Regardless of his personal feelings, however, Jefferson acknowledged the letter and forwarded it to the Marquis de Condorcet, who was the secretary of the Academy of Sciences in Paris. Banneker was a prodigious worker and attempted to promote his work in the most productive channels. In fact, the correspondence between Banneker and Jefferson was published as a pamphlet in 1793. Few creative minds equaled that of Banneker in this period of American history. Using every opportunity to publish his papers, he included Dr Benjamin Rush's proposal "A Plan for an Office of Peace" alongside his almanac in 1793. Fortunately for Banneker, the abolition societies in Maryland and Pennsylvania embraced him and assisted in the broadcast of his work; after all, it was another demonstration that Africans were the intellectual equal of, and in some cases the superior to, the general population of whites. Everything scientific was of interest to Banneker—he continued to make his ephemeridic calculations until 1804 and he also computed the seventeen-year cyle of the locust.

Banneker neither married nor had any children. He died on October 9, 1806, having carved out of his life memorabilia that amounted to his almanacs, manuscript journals, and a commonplace book where he entered his calculations and observations. He was buried on the family farm. Like Phillis Wheatley, Benjamin Banneker was a strong representative of the capability and capacity of the African person during a time when whites were questioning black intelligence.

Ira Frederick Aldridge

Not quite a year after the death of Benjamin Banneker, the great actor Ira Frederick Aldridge was born on July 24, 1807 in New York City.[5] He would become a stage actor at the worst of times for blacks who sought roles other than the stereotypical roles of the subservient African. Yet with an industry and energy unique for his time, Ira Aldridge succeeded in making his career on the London stage, becoming the first African actor to have a bronze plaque at the Shakespeare Memorial Theatre at Stratford-upon-Avon.

When Aldridge died, on August 7, 1867 in Łódź, Poland, he had risen far above his beginnings. His parents were Daniel and Luranah Aldridge. They sent him to the African Free School when he was thirteen years old. Started by blacks in an effort to further the education of their children, the African Free School was one of the first initiatives of self-determination. Aldridge became interested in plays after seeing them acted out by white actors in the Park Theatre from his balcony. As fortune would have it, the young Aldridge appeared to have been born in the right place and to have lived in New York's theatre district at the right time. Soon he was acting himself and by 1820 he had played the role of Rolla in *Pizzaro* and the roles of Romeo and Hamlet from Shakespeare. His performances were all associated with the company at the African Grove.

Increasingly Ira Aldridge found it difficult to secure the kind of professional acting he desired in the United States, due to discrimination and ridicule. To him, acting was serious and he saw himself, even then, as a professional, seeking to make the art of acting his life career. After exploring all avenues for continuing his work in the United States, he was convinced that he had to leave for England. He emigrated to England and then became a dresser to the British actor Henry Wallack. Soon Aldridge is acting on stage at the Royalty Theatre, where he is called a gentleman of color. Later, when he appears at the Royal Coburg, he is called "the American Tragedian" from the African Theatre. However, Ira Aldridge's ambition was to become an important Shakespearean actor. To this end he devoted himself to the study of Shakespeare, and when he eventually performed on the London stage in the character of Othello he created a sensation in theatrical circles. Not only did Ira Aldridge master the delivery of the passages but he also understood the depth of emotion expressed in Shakespeare's writing. London's reaction to Aldridge had something to do with the expectations of an African actor as well as the unfamiliarity of many people with intelligent and talented blacks.

In 1825 Ira Aldridge established himself as one of the most sought-after young actors in London. He was in many plays, creating everywhere discussion and speculation, and causing audiences to marvel at his brilliant acting though he was not yet twenty.

Ira Aldridge became a major actor in the British Isles, playing in Scotland, Wales, and Ireland. Racism was never far from him as some critics ventured to criticize his race and others took cheap shots at his diction. Nevertheless, the audiences continued to appreciate his work, and when he toured Europe in 1852 and in 1858 he found great success in Germany, Prussia, Bulgaria, and Russia. He met Leo Tolstoy, Mikhail Shchepkin, and Taras Shevchenko in Russia while studying the language and seeking to connect with the country of the great black writer Alexander Pushkin, whom he admired.

When Aldridge returned to England he purchased property and applied for British citizenship. He toured Russia again in 1862. Married twice, once to a British woman and then, when she died, to a Swedish woman, Aldridge never returned to the United States. While the Civil War raged in the United States he maintained a steady schedule of performances and appearances, where he often spoke in support of the Union cause. He spent his final years mostly in Russia, whose language he had learned well enough to be able to read Pushkin. Aldridge is buried in the Łódź Evangelical Cemetery and the Society of Polish Artists of Film and Theatre maintains the grave.

Gabriel Prosser's Revolt

Because history is never in a straight line and humans live and die in various parts of the world making different achievements, one can always discover areas where the scholar sincerely asks, "How can these personalities or events be linked?" Seven years before the first performance of Ira Aldridge, Gabriel Prosser had organized a massive rebellion in the South. Yet Aldridge, living in New York, grew up in a growing urban environment connected to Prosser and other blacks because of discrimination and harassment. In the South, danger lurked and occasionally pounced in the form of an African upon the suspecting yet inadequately protected white plantation owners. No weapons or suspicions have been strong enough to deter a people bent on freedom from striking to break their bonds. Even if they died in the tens, scores, or hundreds, they knew that their descendants would one day rise up against the oppression that sucked the life out of their bodies and caused them to be psychologically and economically stunted or, worse, killed. The turbulent situation of the enslaved African in the American South, with the unrelenting toil, physical exhaustion, and beatings, rapes and sexual indignities that accompanied the status of human chattel, was a constant generator of danger, fear, trepidation, and suspicion.

One of the most detailed conspiracies in complexity ever conceived by an enslaved African occurred during 1800.[6] Gabriel, a name given to him by his slave-owner, Thomas H. Prosser of Henrico County, Virginia, was a harbinger of a century of rebellions and revolts. It came to pass that in the same year as Gabriel's revolt, 1800, Nat Turner and John Brown, two American revolutionaries of historic proportion, were born and Gabriel, the archangel of African salvation, began preaching liberation to enslaved Africans around Richmond.

By all accounts Gabriel was an impressive man. He was a "fellow of courage and intellect" as well as a formidable orator.[7] However, it was in his organizational ability that his genius showed. He was able to surround himself with other brave men and women. They intended to purchase "a piece of silk to make a flag on which they would write 'death or liberty.'"[8] Gabriel is said to have been over six feet tall, but not so tall as Jack Bowler, who was four inches taller. Bowler believed that "we had as much right to fight for our liberty as any men."[9] He joined ranks with Gabriel to strike for freedom. Nanny, Gabriel's wife, made her voice and her actions known in the conspiracy as well. Solomon and Martin, Gabriel's two brothers, used their network to spread the word that there would be a general rebellion. Solomon also led in the making of swords to be used in the attacks. Martin vehemently opposed what he saw as delay in the plan believing that too many people knew of it and it was only a matter of time before the white slaveholders knew as well. He told his brothers, "Before I would any longer bear what I had borne, I would turn out and fight with a stick!"[10]

There is a hint that word of the conspiracy reached Governor Monroe during the spring of 1800 because in a letter to President Thomas Jefferson, dated April 22, the governor spoke of "fears of a negro insurrection."[11] The urgency of the situation demanded that the enslaved Africans combine their skills to produce swords, spears, and bayonets in addition to the 500 bullets that they had made by spring. Each Sunday Gabriel staked out the city of Richmond, going into the town and learning important markers and paying attention to the location of weapon stores and possible houses with arms. The enormous plot, with attention to the smallest details, such as who would signal the leaders when they saw armed whites coming out of church and who would resupply the weapons that were lost in battle, had been kept secret for several months. Although the length of time of the plot gave the planners opportunity to take care of all details, it also meant that the planners were more likely to be discovered. On August 9, 1800, J. Grammer of Petersburg wrote a letter to Augustine Davis of Richmond in which he said that he was apprehensive about the enslaved population's restlessness. This letter was passed to Dr James McClurg, who informed the military authorities and the governor.[12] But the most damaging revelation and the rumor that essentially killed the plot was made when Mosby Sheppard, whose enslaved the Africans Tom and Pharaoh, told him that blacks were planning a rebellion. Tom and Pharaoh are footnotes in African American history and are unrecorded in most books but their tattling unraveled one of the most elaborate plots in the history of slavery. Tom, Uncle Tom, and *tomming* became an idea illustrating the willingness of some blacks to compromise their own freedom. Later Harriet Beecher Stowe would write a book called *Uncle Tom's Cabin* and the name would be planted forever in the canons of subservience. Similarly, the African who had the name Pharaoh discredited his own immediate family but also the title that had been bestowed upon the earliest African dynasty of kings.

The governor, rattled by the extent of the plot, quickly appointed three additional armed assistants for his family and asked for the use of the federal armory at Manchester. In addition, he put cannons at the capitol building, called 650 white men into action as a temporary militia, and told every militia commander in the state to be on alert.

On the evening of the revolt, about sunset, there was a major thunderstorm with lightning, hail, and thunder of the most terrible kind that brought down torrential rains. There was so much water that the Africans could not pass over Brook Swamp and therefore were stopped from entering Richmond itself. With the passage impossible and the leaked word about the plan adrift among the whites, the rebellion was doomed.

Nevertheless, 1,000 Africans on horseback and on foot, armed with swords, scythes, bayonets, and some homemade guns, met about six miles outside the city. But there was no way that Gabriel wanted to lead the men and a few women to their death in the storm. It pained him to the core of his soul that he could not bring to bear on the slavery system the punishment he believed it deserved. Neither could he now defend his people, those who had shown their willingness to fight and to die for freedom, who stood without the defensive measures that would be necessary to fight off the better-armed and better-equipped white militias of the state.

The next day the rains stopped and an aroused and angered state mustered all of its forces to arrest as many blacks as possible. It is believed that even some of those who reported the plot were caught up in the dragnet that was used to snare scores of African people. Gabriel was urged to flee by his compatriots and he took a schooner down the river but in Norfolk was recognized as a fugitive by two other blacks, who reported him to the authorities. So close to freedom and the liberation necessary to fight another day, Gabriel was brutalized, shackled in chains, and returned to Richmond, where he was quickly convicted and sentenced to hang. Hoping that the captured Gabriel, under torture, would talk and reveal more information, the authorities delayed his execution until October 7. Governor James Monroe interviewed Gabriel and is said to have reported, "From what he [Gabriel] said to me, he seemed to have made up his mind to die, and to have resolved to say but little on the subject of the conspiracy."[13] One of the reasons that Gabriel remains an icon of bravery and intelligence is that he refused to reveal his plans or his people even in the presence of certain death. If he were to die, which the state surely intended for him, then his death should not come with any revelations.

Monroe, most likely with Jefferson's blessing, unleashed an orgy of killings in an effort to ease the fear in the white community. The American heroes of white people's freedom hanged the most iconic representative of freedom for the oppressed in Virginia. On October 7, the day Gabriel was hanged, fifteen other rebels were sent to their deaths. Twenty-one other people had been executed prior to October 7 and four had been scheduled to die afterward. In fact, no one really knows for certain how many Africans died as a result of the plot because it is suspected that some plantation owners carried out their own capital sentences on their enslaved plotters. There were reports that some committed suicide in prison, but whether their death was self-inflicted or not is surely unknown, given the various means that whites used to eliminate blacks in prison.

The Haitian Revolution

As Africans throughout the United States agitated, planned, and carried out revolts against slaveholders, they were buoyed by the powerful uprising of the enslaved Africans in San Domingo, the richest slave colony in the Caribbean. The names of revolt leaders such as Mackandal, Boukman, and Cécile Fatiman preceded those of the revolutionary generals Toussaint L'Ouverture, Dessalines, and Christophe but together they made one grand phalanx of courageous Africans who fought for their freedom and won it in 1804. Although the battles had been waged for many years when Dessalines defeated the French Army at the Battle of Vertières, it was the first time that an army of Africans had defeated a major European army. Blacks everywhere rejoiced that the shackles of slavery had been permanently broken in the newly renamed country of Haiti.

Denmark Vesey's conspiracy

The Haitian Revolution of 1804 inspired Denmark Vesey's 1822 conspiracy. Vesey had been enslaved in the Caribbean, possibly the Virgin Islands, and by the time he was sixty years old was fed up with the brutality that he saw around him. However, seeking to be as organized and as determined as the Haitians, Vesey spent considerable time in preparation for his revolt in Charleston, South Carolina. He worked as a carpenter and found a number of Africans who agreed with his arguments for a massive and sustained rebellion. He believed that he would receive support from Haiti, at that time called San Domingo. White planters had blacks whose job or desire was to tell the plantation owners all they heard among other blacks. For some reason, these blacks believed that by telling they would insure their own safety, security, and privilege. Oftentimes the whites would take the information but then punish the bringer of the information as someone who had been corrupted by the preaching of the revolutionaries. In the case of the Vesey Conspiracy there were tattlers who ran to the whites with plans for the plot. The informers told of a major organized revolt led by Denmark Vesey that would have upset the balance of power in Charleston. More than 130 Africans, including Vesey, were arrested. Forty-seven were found guilty of the plot, thirty-seven were executed and twelve were pardoned.

Whites were greatly agitated by the plan. It struck them as bold and sinister for two reasons. In the first place, they did not consider Africans capable of organizing against them. This was unthinkable, given the fact that whites thought of Africans as inferior. So ingrained in their consciousness was the idea of Africans as without thought, without the ability to lead and plan, that their racist constructions of reality wanted to deny the possibility of a revolt. Secondly, they were told in the trials that between 3,000 and 9,000 Africans were involved in the planned rebellion. This fact alone caused many slave-owners to fear that their enslaved Africans had participated. Punishment of the strongest Africans on plantations began almost immediately. Whites felt that they had to control the rise of any leader cadres.

Many rumors grew and swirled around this case.[14] Whites would say, "Did you know that they had a list of names of all their conspirators?" Others would try desperately to hunt down this list. Still others would say, "You know they had 300 daggers and 250 pike heads that they had stashed away for the revolt?" Meanwhile, there was no documentary evidence that pointed to the actual number of potential rebels. In the end, forty-nine people were accused of a conspiracy and all were executed.

The Louisiana German Coast Rebellion

Charles Deslondes was a free African born in San Domingo who could no longer stand to see women and children and fellow Africans beaten near to death for the slightest transgression. Therefore, during the Christmas celebrations of December 1810 Deslondes had organized a close group of Africans to prepare for war with the slave-owners.[15] Deslondes believed that the slaveholders had become increasingly vile and vicious as they had become wealthier and more profligate.

On January 8, 1811 he led a group of thirty to forty men along the "German Coast" of Louisiana in a killing spree against white plantation owners. Initially Deslondes, who because he was from San Domingo was familiar with the Haitian revolt, struck the whites with cane knives and clubs until he and his men were able to secure a few guns. They fought for their freedom and that of the other enslaved Africans for three days but could not find sufficient ammunition to withstand the organized and heavily armed Louisiana militia.

Inspired by Toussaint L'Ouverture and Dessalines, Deslondes believed that he could create the same conditions in Louisiana and cause a general uprising there as well. However, his revolt was bogged down by lack of weapons and tactical plans. The whites captured some of the fighters and executed nearly one hundred blacks as they suppressed the rebellion. Many Africans escaped and others quietly re-entered their plantation lifestyles. Yet in a gruesome display of their ability to be brutal, the white executioners placed the heads of sixteen black freedom fighters on posts along the road leading to the plantation where Deslondes had started the revolt. The estimate of the number of rebels varies, with Herbert Aptheker claiming as many as 500 and Eugene Genovese saying that it was closer to 400.[16] Genovese became increasingly conservative in his social, political, and scholarly work after the publication of his book *Roll, Jordan, Roll*.

Nat Turner's Rebellion

Turner's rebellion found its energy in the most charismatic leader of the Southampton region of Virginia and North Carolina. In August, 1831, the dynamic Nat Turner turned the entire plantation slavocracy into a frightened killing field. It was an August of nerves, a time of testing, an ultimatum to the manhood of Africans who had seen the oppressive condition. Scores of black men would decide after listening to Nat Turner that it would be safer to kill the whites than to live with them. Turner grew up with a belief that he would be a deliverer.[17] He had always felt, since he was a teenager, that he had been divinely chosen to make a difference in the lives of his people. If Turner was not the one to lead the rebellion, then who else would do it? Thus, he prepared himself for his mission with diligence, given completely over to the vision he had of the future. Everything around him spoke to him of his leadership, whether it was how he was treated by his peers, the deference they showed him, or in the leaves on the plants in the field, the mysterious *veves* that seemed to have been written in blood. The report of his last speech and the account of his activities, although recorded by a white man, showed the clear and profound insight Nat Turner had of his place in the history of his people and his determination to fight until death for liberation. This is why he could say that when the time came he organized his core group of men, secured their commitment to fight to the death, asked them not to tell a word to anyone, and then they began the task.[18]

Black Seminole Rebellion

The Black Seminole rebellion of 1835–1836 must be considered one of the major African revolts in the United States. It was a rebellion of enslaved Africans against the misery of slavery. Various scholars, including John Hope Franklin, Eugene Genovese, Stanley Elkins, and Herbert Aptheker, have written of the rebellion as a contingent of Maroon Africans joining with the Seminoles to fight the United States Army. However, we now know that there were nearly 400 enslaved Africans who joined the Maroons in the battle against their plantation owners. Although several top historians have omitted to mention or neglected the Black Seminole rebellion, it was one of the largest actions against the United States government by enslaved Africans. All one has to do is to compare the size and extent of the Black Seminole rebellion with those of other revolts.

Table 4.1 African rebellions compared

Date	Name	Africans Involved	White Deaths	Black Deaths
1712	New York	40	9	27
1739	Stono Rebellio	80	25	50
1800	Prosser Rebellion	2,000	0	35
1811	Louisiana revolt	500	2	200
1822	Denmark Vesey	49	0	49
1831	Nat Turner	80	65	300
1838	Black Seminoles	1,200	400	400

Sengbe and the *Amistad* Mutiny

Those who love freedom must strike when they can. The story of fifty-three Africans who mutinied aboard the Spanish schooner *La Amistad* is one of the world's most inspiring narratives.[19] In July 1839 *La Amistad* left Havana to go to another Cuban port but in the process it was taken over and diverted. Led by Sengbe Pieh, an African from the west coast of Africa, possibly Sierra Leone, the enslaved mutinied, and killed the captain and the ship's cook. Although they were unaware of Western navigation techniques, the enslaved forced two of the white sailors to sail the ship to Africa while the others were put over the side in boats. Instead of sailing to Africa, the two white navigators steered the boat north and after fifty days landed in Long Island in New York State. The boat was seized by a United States naval vessel and escorted to New London, Connecticut, where Sengbe Pieh and other Africans were accused of piracy and murder.

The case became a *cause célèbre* for the abolitionist community. Defended by the abolitionists, the mutineers had their case sent to the United States Supreme Court. The former president John Quincy Adams (1767–1848) argued their case with brilliance and eloquence. The administration of President Martin Van Buren sought to return the Africans to their slaveholders. However, on March 9, 1841 the Court ruled that the Africans had to be set free because the slave trade was illegal and they were eventually returned to their Mende homeland.

The *Amistad* victors may not have known, but their actions fitted a general pattern of resistance found in the African world at the time. In fact, the enslaved Moses Gottlieb played a pivotal role in the 1848 St Croix Rebellion that was essential in bringing to an end slavery on that island. Inflamed by a decree from Denmark that babies born to enslaved parents would be free at birth on July 28, 1847 but freedom would not come for other Africans until twelve years later, Gottlieb planned several secret meetings of leading men and women and planned a revolt. Gottlieb was a field slave yet he knew how to read and write and bitterly resented slavery. Widely loved and respected by other Africans, he emerged as the sole leader of the rebellion that erupted on July 3, 1848 as thousands of blacks declared their freedom from slavery. Gottlieb then had to end the revolt, which was difficult, because he had unleashed the full fury of his people. The Danish were frightened by his personal power and charisma. The people called him "General Buddhoe" as a sign of endearment. The Danish immediately emancipated all enslaved persons; however, because he was so powerful, the new governor had General Buddhoe arrested and sent to Trinidad. Once he landed in Trinidad he was robbed of all his possessions and warned never to re-enter the Virgin Islands, yet General Buddhoe remains firmly entrenched as one of the islands' greatest heroes.

The trial of the *Amistad* Africans and the subsequent discussion and debate pushed the elegant and dignified Sojourner Truth to begin her own crusade against the evil practice of human slavery. Enslaved in the North, able to converse in Dutch and English, and determined to be free and free others, she got up one day and claimed a new name and a new purpose to "sojourn" and to tell the "truth." In 1843 she began her campaign against slavery and for its complete abolition. Few men or women ever equaled the simple cadence, and the powerful periods of Sojourner Truth.[20] Of all the people who worked to create a spirit of freedom, few excelled Sojourner Truth. Born in Hurley, New York, in 1787 as Isabella Baumfree, she died in Battle Creek, Michigan, at the age of eighty-six in 1883. She struggled as a young woman to make her way through servitude and in the bitterness of her time in bondage she claimed her own victory over enslavement. At the age of forty-six she changed her name because she had a vision that God wanted her to travel and to tell the truth about the treatment Africans received at the hands of evil people. When she was born, slavery was still allowed in the state of New York and it did not end there until 1827. But because her master would not free her she ran away with her youngest son.

One day when the great Frederick Douglass had concluded a very dismal assessment of the condition of enslaved blacks, Sojourner Truth, his equal in eloquence, rose from her seat and stood her six-foot frame straight as an arrow and asked him, "Frederick, is God dead?" No God of hers would allow Africans to suffer in perpetuity. She was a militant campaigner for women's rights as well as for the rights of her people.

During the war Sojourner Truth encouraged President Abraham Lincoln to urge Northern Africans to support the war effort. By her own will she organized a group of women to serve as nurses for wounded Union soldiers. When the war was over she continued to serve as a nurse for the recently emancipated Africans in the South. By 1875, when she published her narrative, her reputation had been firmly established as a freedom fighter.

A contemporary of Sojourner Truth's was Ellen Craft, but their circumstances and situations were entirely different. Yet in her own way Craft demonstrated her dislike for the conditions of her life. Born in Clinton, Georgia, she was the child of her mother's master. The master's wife was so jealous of Ellen that by the time she was eleven she was given as a slave to the master's legitimate daughter. Ellen could not take this treatment, and when she was older she married another African named William, who was an expert carpenter. After working all day, she and William would talk almost all night about escaping. Since Ellen looked white, they thought up a scheme that would get them to Philadelphia. Ellen would shave her head, dress like a man, wear green tinted glasses, and feign a limp; William would play her servant traveling with her to Philadelphia, where she would seek expert medical attention. They were able to get a train to the North under those conditions. When they arrived in Philadelphia the abolitionists were able to secure passage to England for them. The book *Running a Thousand Miles for Freedom* was published in 1860, detailing their exploits. In England they had five children, worked and saved their money, and in 1868, a few years after slavery had been abolished in the United States, they returned and bought a farm, where they opened a trade school. Such were the type of men and women, made of steel, who wore down enslavement. All were not equally brave or courageous and some became casualties of the violent and oppressive circumstances, but other Africans fought to be free at any cost.

Henry "Box" Brown was born at the Hermitage Plantation, about ten miles from Yanceyville, Virginia, in Louisa County around 1815. When his slaveholder, John Barrett, died, in 1830, Brown, who had spent his early years with his parents and siblings, a rare situation, was separated from his family and sent to work in the tobacco factory of William Barrett, John's son. His four sisters and three brothers were sold to other plantations, except Martha, who was kept by William Barrett as his mistress or "keep miss."

While working in the Richmond tobacco factory, Henry married Nancy in 1836. She was enslaved to a different slaveholder. They eventually had three children but when she was pregnant with their fourth child in 1848, Nancy and her children were sold to another enslaver in North Carolina, away from Virginia and Henry Brown. He was crushed, distraught, and bitter. In the First African Baptist Church in Richmond he sang in the choir but could get no solace from religion. However, he found a free black man, James Caesar Anthony Smith, who agreed to help him escape. His pain was great at the thought that he would never see his wife or children again, and after many months of mourning he decided that he would leave enslavement. Smith knew a white shoemaker who was a gambler and a drunk and agreed to help them if they paid him a small price. Brown came up with the plan to have himself put in a box and shipped to Philadelphia from Richmond. Samuel Alexander Smith, the white Smith, is said to have held Africans in bondage himself, but he was willing to help Brown. The white Smith contacted James Miller McKim, a leader of the anti-slavery movement in Philadelphia, and told him to look out for a box that was being delivered to him. Brown had one particularly severe close call when he was turned head down for hours as the box was being transferred on the steamboat at the Potomac River port at Aquia Creek for the up-river trip to Washington.

Brown nearly died and later wrote that "I felt my eyes swelling as if they would burst from their sockets; and the veins on my temples were dreadfully distended with pressure of blood upon my head,"[21] but he explained that he was resolved to "conquer or die." The parcel arrived in Philadelphia on March 24, 1849 and McKim took the delivery. With trepidation the anti-slavery office opened the box and out popped Henry Brown. After twenty-six hours of confinement in the box, Brown came out alive and in freedom. He later wrote, "I had risen as it were from the dead." He was henceforth called Henry "Box" Brown.

The Fugitive Slave Law

No more vile law to hold people in bondage had been written since the preceding half century than the Fugitive Slave Act of 1850.[22] Thousands of Africans were so disturbed by the law that they fled the United States. Others, who were free, moved farther to the north, as close as possible to the Canadian border. In fact, the law stated that anyone who escaped from slavery would be returned to their slave-owners if captured, even if they were caught in a free territory. This meant that a black person who escaped and made her way to California could be grabbed by a white person and literally dragged back into slavery in Louisiana. Some blacks in the United States moved to Ontario, where they established communities in Toronto, Buxton, Hamilton, Elgin, and Owen Sound. A group of 600 blacks left California and made their way hundreds of miles north to Vancouver Island in 1858 when they could manage to acquire the resources to leave. Most of the settlers ended up in Victoria. Men such as Joshua Howard, Mifflin Gibbs, and Peter Lester led the expatriating blacks. An energetic society, these new settlers became farmers, gardeners, politicians, lawyers, and business people. Many of them opened small businesses as seamstresses, carpenters, and barbers. A few blacks from the California wagon group went to Salt Spring Island as well as the mainland of British Columbia.

The Fugitive Slave Law of 1850 was a game-changer. It meant that everything that had happened during the first half of the century had to change. People could no longer assume that their freedom—if they had been manumitted, if they had purchased their freedom, or had escaped—was genuine freedom. At any time they could be, in the language of the novel by Charles Fuller, snatched.[23] The law was a continuation of the philosophy that had been adopted during the first so-called fugitive slave law in 1793, but the 1850 version was more expansive, and even more sinister than the earlier law. Now it was clear that if magistrates and marshals refused to carry out the law they would be charged the price of the labor that was lost by the African escaping and remaining free. Indeed, the dirty secret was that the authors of the law intended to obscure the question of free labor by insisting throughout the document that Africans who ran away were fugitives from labor. No more hellish euphemism had ever come out of the United States Congress. This law was an integral part of the "Compromise of 1850." The anti-slavery leaders gained the admission of California as a free state, and the prohibition of slave-trading in the District of Columbia. At the same time, the slavery party got concessions that included slaveholding in Texas and the passage of the Fugitive Slave Law. A deal had been struck that would cause tremendous hardships on families living in the North after escaping from bondage. Pressures would be placed on the Quakers and other abolitionist sympathizers to turn in escaped Africans. It would be a decade or so before the battle to end slavery would start but it would have been caused by incidents like the passage of this law. What it meant for Africans was that they could no longer feel safe in the North—they had to travel to Canada, where the laws were less hostile to men and women seeking freedom.

The Anthony Burns Incident

Some black people risked everything to escape the South during this period. One of the more telling cases of escape and capture was the story of Anthony Burns, who boarded a ship in Alexandria, Virginia, in March 1854 and made his way to Boston, where he worked in a clothing store owned by Lewis Hayden, an abolitionist. However, on May 24, 1854, Burns' slave-owner snatched him under the Fugitive Slave Law as he was returning home from his job. Two days later a black and white group of abolitionists, led by Lewis Hayden and Thomas Wentworth Higginson, stormed the courthouse to release Burns. When the dust had settled on that May 26, thirteen people had been arrested and one guard had been killed. The next day the city of Boston was overrun with federal troops and abolitionists as Burns was taken to court. Robert Morris, an African American attorney, and Richard Henry Dana Jr represented Burns before U.S. Commissioner Edward Loring. At the end of the arguments Loring ruled in favor of the slave-master. Fifty thousand people lined the streets on June 2, 1854 to watch 2,000 marines escort a shackled Anthony Burns to a waiting ship to be taken back to Virginia. A huge wooden coffin draped in black with the sign "Liberty" written on it was suspended from a pole on State Street. Flags were turned upside down and black cloth draped the windows of buildings as the drama of Burns' return unfolded in what was one of the most poignant statements of the clash between freedom and slavery.

Martin Delany States His Case

Martin Robinson Delany was born in Charlestown, Virginia, on May 6, 1812 during a period when America and Britain were still settling their differences.[24] From the time of his birth to parents who traced their ancestry to African royalty, Delany would be free neither of controversy nor of leadership. A brilliant man, he would become a journalist, physician, army officer, and judge. However, it was his nationalist sentiment, so intensely dedicated to finding peace for black people, that would make him a national hero among the black intelligentsia. When his parents moved from what became West Virginia to Chambersburg, Pennsylvania, when he was ten years old to find a better racial climate, it was a lesson that was well learned by the younger Delany. At nineteen he was sent to an African American school in Pittsburgh and met Kate Richards, whom he married in 1843. They had eleven children and Delany was a devoted family man, believing that his children should be raised in a society of freedom. The same year he married Kate Richards he also founded a newspaper, *The Mystery*, which he dedicated to the abolitionist cause. For him, as for the more enlightened of his Northern colleagues, there could be nothing less than unrestricted equality for black people. Frederick Douglass convinced him to serve as co-editor of the *North Star,* his own paper, which Delany did for two years and then left to study medicine at Harvard.

After training at Harvard, Delany put his medical schooling into practice, trying to raise the level of health in the black community. He was forty years old when he started the

Figure 4.1 Martin Delany, one of the original leaders of self-determination and self-definition among blacks. Image courtesy of Charles L. Blockson Afro-American Collection, Temple University Libraries.

profession of physician and although he would go away from it from time to time, it was the one job that he continued throughout his life. Researching and writing on the black condition was something else that kept him busy. He published the book *The Condition, Elevation, Emigration, and Destiny of the Colored People of the United States, Politically Considered* in 1852. Despite all that he had experienced and seen as an abolitionist and physician, and given his familiarity with the political direction of the country heading toward war, he advocated for a separate country for black people. He could not see the possibility of unrestricted freedom for Africans in America and he did not trust whites to protect the safety of black people, even if freedom came to the enslaved in the South. The only answer, as Delany saw it, had to be emigration out of the United States to Africa, Canada, or South America. He would live in Ontario for a few years just to see how it could be where blacks were free, and although he opposed the Liberia experiment because of the ill intentions of the organizers, he kept an open mind toward emigration to other sites in Africa. To this end, he traveled to the land of the Yoruba, in what is now Nigeria, and negotiated with local kings for settling African Americans in their country. He reported this in a document called "The Official Report of the Niger Valley Exploring Party" in 1861. While others talked about projects and programs, Delany was willing to put his money and his life on the line for the deliverance of African people from misery and constant harassment.

Fearless, Martin Delany had come of political age during the debate over the Fugitive Slave Law and, like many of his compatriots, some who had moved to Canada before he had, he felt that the time had come for blacks to fight alone, if necessary, to defend their freedom in the North. At a historic meeting in Pittsburgh on September 30, 1850, he had been asked, along with Mayor Hugh Fleming, to say a few words to an immense crowd at Market House, the largest mass assembly in Pittsburgh's history, twelve days after the Fugitive Slave Law was enacted. Here is what Martin Delany said to the crowd, addressing his words to the mayor:

> Honorable Mayor, whatever ideas of liberty I may have, have been received from reading the lives of your revolutionary fathers. I have therein learned that a man has a right to defend his castle with his life, even unto the taking of life. Sir, my house is my castle; in that castle are none but my wife and my children, as free as the angels of heavens, and whose liberty is as sacred as the pillars of God. If any man approaches that house in search of a slave, I care not who he may be, whether constable, or sheriff, magistrate or even judge of the Supreme Court, nay, let it be he who sanctioned this act to become a law [President Millard Fillmore], surrounded by his cabinet as his bodyguard, with the Declaration of Independence waving above his head as his banner, and the constitution of his country upon his breast as his shield, if he crosses the threshold of my door, and I do not lay him a lifeless corpse at my feet, I hope the grave may refuse my body a resting place, and righteous Heaven my spirit a home. O, no! He cannot enter that house and we both live.[25]

It is this Delany—this militant, strong, and confirmed human, whose search for freedom led him to Africa and to advocacy of separation of blacks from whites—who found such turbulence in his own political life that even blacks questioned his understanding of the racism they faced in the South. When Delany returned to the States from abroad, he discovered that the Civil War was in force and he immediately joined up to take part in the conflict. He convinced President Abraham Lincoln to appoint him as a major in the infantry in charge of recruiting all African units for the Union Army. He, like Douglass, was quite successful in this work and when the war ended he was offered a position in South Carolina with the Freedmen's Bureau and as a Republican politician. He remained in the South for several years and in 1874 narrowly lost an election to be lieutenant governor of South Carolina. But as the Union Army moved out of the South, and the white Democrats gained the upper hand over the Republicans, blacks and whites, he could see that the Democrats would soon control the state. In what was considered by many blacks a slap in the face to their efforts, Delany switched parties and cast his lot with the Democrats, who did not have a liberal bone in their political body. He had been feared as a politician and he had been respected as a black leader, but he lost respect for the white Republicans who did not deliver on their promises for rehabilitating black people in the South, and so he supported the former Confederate general Wade Hampton for governor in 1876. When Hampton was elected he gave Delany a judgeship in Charleston. This surprised lots of people, and Delany's operation of his office won the respect of both races in South Carolina. However, the black masses held him at a distance when it came to trying to understand a black Democrat. Actually, Delany barely escaped serious injury or death on October 16, 1876 when a group of African Americans confronted him on the issue of supporting the Democrats. This misunderstanding caused Delany to redouble his efforts to establish a homeland for blacks. According to the *News and Courier*:

> When it was understood that Col. M. R. Delany who is probably the most intelligent man of his race in the State was to be one of the speakers on the Democratic side, your correspondent asked Mr Bowen if they would hear him speak. "Yes, " replied Mr Bowen, "I reckon I can keep them still but it will be just about as hard as to hold a wild elephant or a lion without tying him."[26]

But when Delany began to speak, the crowd of 500 African citizens "started to beat their drums and left in a body. They would not listen to 'De damned Nigger Democrat.' In vain the chairman called them to come back and shouted to them to stop their drum beating. They paid no attention to his orders. They marched off and the women crowded around the wagon with their bludgeons, with threats, curses and imprecations."[27]

Delany was urged to speak, and when he started, the audience surrounded the wagon where he was standing and began to interrupt him. He said that

> he had come to South Carolina with his sword drawn, to fight for the freedom of the black man; that being a black man himself, he had been a leading abolitionist; that he had warned them against trusting their money to the Freedman's Bank; and that they had, to their sorrow, paid no heed to his warnings. His only object was to give them warning now that the northern white people were altogether in sympathy with the southern whites.[28]

Ullman explains that the audience had been told not to bring any weapons but the African citizens brought their guns and hid them in the swamps, and when someone opened fire indiscriminately on the whites, Delany, and a few other blacks, took refugee in a brick farmhouse until the trouble had passed.[29]

Delany was undeterred in his commitment to using whatever means necessary to secure black rights even if some of his own people did not understand him. His dedication to the separation of blacks from whites and the creation of a black homeland intensified, and so in 1878 he co-sponsored the Liberian Exodus Joint Stock Steamship Company, which sent an ill-fated emigration group to Africa. During the following year he wrote *The Principia of Ethnology*, where he contended that there was value in projecting pride, dignity, nobility, and purity of the races and that the African race had as much right to do the same as other races. With the hardening of racial lines and the visible emergence of race hatred in the South, Delany lost the support of the whites and had lost the trust of many blacks. He returned to medicine and then went into business in Boston. He died on January 24, 1885.

Mary Ann Shadd and Henry Bibb

Mary Ann Shadd established her persona as one of the most courageous, brilliant, and active leaders during the middle of the nineteenth century. She was born in October, 1823 to freeborn abolitionists, Harriet and Abraham Shadd, in Wilmington, Delaware. When she was ten years old Mary Shadd moved with her family to West Chester, Pennsylvania, where she attended a Quaker school for six years. By 1840 she had started her own school for black children. But ten years later, with the passing of the racist Fugitive Slave Law of 1850 in the United States, and talk about fugitives being arrested and sold into slavery, she made her way north to Canada. Knowing the possibility of being taken into bondage, Shadd and her brother Isaac, a lover of freedom, traveled to Windsor, Ontario, and settled there. Soon after she had arrived in her new home, Shadd went about setting up a school for black and white children with the support of the American Missionary Association. Of course, Shadd was not an island; she was a member of the local community and her activities created conflicts with Henry Bibb, one of the leading black Canadians of the day. Bibb felt that Shadd's work endangered the lives of the fugitives, and his paper "The Voice of the Fugitive" wrote negatively of Shadd's character. Martin Robinson Delany, a free man who, as we have seen, had published the newspaper *The Mystery* in 1843, often wrote for Bibb's paper. Bibb had his own considerable narrative to tell and to protect and he felt that Shadd, newly arrived in Canada, had not spent sufficient time learning the lie of the social territory. He had been born in Kentucky on May 10, 1815, the son of a white man, Senator James Bibb, and an enslaved African woman, Mildred Jackson, who worked on the plantation of William Gatewood. Bibb had six siblings, all sold to different plantation owners. He had little contact with his mother and by the age of ten he had made his first attempt to escape slavery. Brought back, he married as a teenager and became enraged when his wife's slave-owner forced her into prostitution with white men. Finally, in 1837, Henry Bibb was able to successfully escape and make his way across the Ohio River to Cincinnati, Ohio. Unhappy in freedom without his wife and children, Bibb returned to the South for his family, but they were captured and sold to various slave-owners. Once again, Bibb was able to organize an escape but the family could not make it across the river and were recaptured. He never saw his wife and children again. Bibb was sold to a Cherokee farmer. He promptly escaped, crossed the river, and made his way to Detroit, Michigan, where he lectured against slavery. The Liberty Party, which had been formed in 1840, was like an intellectual home to him. While traveling in the North lecturing against slavery he met Mary Miles of Boston. They were married in 1848. Bibb's book *Narratives of the Life and Adventures of Henry Bibb* was published in 1849. When Bibb met Josiah Henson, an older, wizened elder in the community and a fellow abolitionist activist, he believed that he had found a heroic partner with whom he could fight against slavery and racism. They formed the Refugee's Home Colony for escaped Africans in Sandwich Township, Ontario, right after the passage of the Fugitive Slave Act.

Refusing to be silenced by Bibb, Mary Shadd brought her own skills and intellect to bear on the founding of her own newspaper, *The Provincial Freeman*, in 1853. A year later, in 1854, Henry Bibb, at the young age of thirty-nine, died. Neither Shadd nor the black community rejoiced in the death of Bibb because everyone knew that, even with his disputes with Shadd, he was a promoter of black interests. Joining with Samuel Ringgold Ward, an outstanding orator and leader, Mary Shadd used the paper to promote moral reform. It ceased publication after a few issues but she and Ward resurrected it in Toronto a year later. It was published until 1859.

Bibb had his intellectual heavyweights, Josiah Henson and Martin Delany, but Mary Shadd had Samuel Ringgold Ward, the equal of any activist or orator of the day. He had been born in Maryland in 1817 and while still a teenager had escaped with his mother to New Jersey. In 1834, when he was seventeen years old, Ward was beaten by a pro-slavery mob in New York. He fought back but was outnumbered. When the dust cleared, Ward was arrested, although he had been the person attacked. This experience hardened him and caused him to dedicate his life to assisting other Africans in escaping bondage. He was a fierce anti-slavery activist, speaking on behalf of freedom throughout the North. He was a partisan of the Liberty Party and also gave support to the Free Soil Party. By the time he joined with Mary Shadd he had been a teacher, a minister, and an editor. Ward preached for two predominantly white churches, a Presbyterian church in South Butler, New York, and a Congregationalist church in Cortland, New York. The Fugitive Slave Act underscored for Ward the danger that all blacks, free and unfree, were facing in the United States. He left for Canada and never returned to the United States. He wrote his memoir *The Autobiography of a Fugitive Negro* in 1855. He died in Jamaica in 1864.

Mary Shadd's life was a dance of actions, movements, and styles that inspired a Canadian spirit of integration. She felt that Bibb, Henson, and Delany were too much inclined to support separate schools and churches for blacks. Mary Shadd believed that this nationalist philosophy would undercut the search for freedom and therefore she worked for the equality and integration of blacks in all institutions.

Soon Shadd was joined in Canada by her mother, father, and siblings. In 1856 Mary Shadd married a Toronto barber, Thomas F. Cary. She made her home in Chatham, Ontario, making her living as a teacher and editor. In 1858, John Brown, on a tour of the black community in Ontario, held one of his meetings in the home of Mary Shadd and her husband, Thomas Cary.[30] Three years later she would publish *Voice from Harper's Ferry* as a tribute to John Brown. Cary died in 1860 and Mary Shadd Cary took her two children back to the United States, where she served as a recruiting officer in Indiana to enlist blacks as volunteers for the Union Army. At the close of the war she taught school in Wilmington, Delaware, and then moved to Washington, where she taught school and attended Howard

University School of Law. She received her law degree in 1883, the second black woman to do so in the United States. Her career as an intellectual did not cool off when she earned the law degree; in fact, she wrote numerous articles for *The National Era* and *The People's Advocate*. Susan B. Anthony, Elizabeth Cady Stanton, and others joined Shadd Cary in the fight for women's suffrage. She became the first black woman to cast a vote in a national election and one of the first to testify before a committee of the House of Representatives. Shadd Cary died on June 5, 1893 in Washington.

Henry McNeal Turner

When the Fugitive Slave Law of 1850 was passed, Henry McNeal Turner, who would become the greatest African Methodist Episcopal leader since Richard Allen, was a precocious sixteen-year-old. He was born in Newberry Courthouse, South Carolina, to Sarah Greer and Hardy Turner. His father's father was a white plantation owner and his maternal grandfather was from the Mandinka royal clan. When David Greer, the name he was given, arrived from Africa he had the markings of the Mandinka coat of arms tattoed on his arms. Instead of selling him into the slavery the owners decided to send him to live with a Quaker family. The young Turner learned to read and write and received a rudimentary education of the kind free Africans could get in South Carolina. He was employed as a janitor for a law firm when he was fifteen. He became increasingly involved in advocacy for the Africans he saw in slavery. The lawyers at the firms spoke highly of his intelligence, diligence, and high moral behavior.

Preaching and Opening the Eyes of the Blind

In 1853 Turner was licensed to preach for the African Methodist Episcopal and three years later married Eliza Peacher, the daughter of a wealthy African American builder in Columbia, South Carolina. Two years after that, Henry McNeal Turner was given a pastorate in St Louis, Missouri. He later preached in Baltimore and Washington. Turner's magnificent generosity of spirit and dynamic personality allowed him to befriend two powerful legislators, Charles Sumner and Thaddeus Stevens, two of the most important political supporters of the African American community. When they encouraged him to assist in the recruitment of African Americans for the war effort, he immediately organized meetings in his own churchyard for recruits and made himself available to the army as a chaplain.

After the war Turner spent several years traveling around Georgia as an evangelist for the AME. In this position he saw the dire conditions of the black population, which touched him deeply, so much so that he began to condemn the government for not really changing the economic and social circumstances of African people. He became a political force in 1867 after the passage of the Reconstructions Acts. Turner had seen the venom of the white population in other southern states after the war and he believed that the trouble in the land was still unsettled. After the riots in New Orleans in 1866 there would be others during the Reconstruction Period, some turning into massacres of black people.

The Hamburg Masssacre

One of the most disturbing outbreaks of violence was the Hamburg, South Carolina, Massacre. On July 4, 1876 two white men in a buggy happened upon a black militia drilling in the center of town during the centennial celebrations. Seeing the black men in military uniforms angered the whites and angry words were spoken. Days later the Democrats in the state demanded that the black militia be disbanded as they did not want black men walking the streets with guns. White gun clubs and would-be neo-Confederates descended upon the small, predominantly black town and fought with forty blacks holed up in the armory. Whites called upon white Georgians to rush in a cannon to assault the blacks in the armory. After days of fighting, one white man was killed and the blacks ran low on ammunition. Twenty-nine blacks were eventually taken as prisoners. However, five blacks considered leaders were shot down in cold blood. Others escaped and ran away. The massacre of Hamburg was etched deeply in the psyche of the newly freed African Americans.

Leading Reconstruction Riots

1868	Opelousas, Louisiana
1868	Camilla Massacre, Georgia
1869–71	Jackson County War, Florida
1870	Eutaw, Alabama
1870	Laurens, South Carolina
1871	Meridan, Mississippi
1873	Colfax Massacre
1874	Vicksburg, Mississippi
1874	New Orleans, Louisiana (Liberty Place Riot)
1874	Coushatta, Louisiana
1875	Yazoo City, Mississippi
1875	Clinton, Mississippi
1876	Ellenton, South Carolina
1876	Hamburg, South Carolina

Threats and Reactions

Bishop Henry McNeal Turner was a member of the Georgia state constitutional convention and was elected to the Georgia House of Representatives, representing the city of Macon. A year later, in 1868, the white legislators voted overwhelmingly to expel all black members of the House of Representatives on the grounds that office should not be held by those who came from servile backgrounds. This was the year of the Camilla Massacre in Georgia. In response to the strident voices of the whites, the eloquent and fearless Turner gave one of the most powerful speeches ever given in the Georgia legislature, but in the end it did not persuade the whites. Their minds were made up: they were white supremacists of the hardcore variety and felt that no black should ever occupy the Georgia legislature. In reaction to Turner's speech, whites threatened Turner physically. U.S. president Ulysses S. Grant appointed Turner to be postmaster of the city of Macon.

Leaving Macon under a cloud of charges about his adminstration of his office, Turner went to the Georgia coast, where he served as pastor of the St Philip's AME church in Savannah. By 1880 he was so well known in the church that he could run for bishop. After winning the battle to be the bishop of the church, Turner became the first AME bishop to ordain a woman, Sarah Ann Hughes, to the position of deacon, in 1885. He sent missionaries to Cuba and Mexico as well as to Sierra Leone, Liberia, and South Africa. When his wife, Eliza, died in 1889, Turner married three more times: Martha Elizabeth DeWitt in 1893; Harriet Wayman in 1900; and Laura Pearl Lemon in 1907. Turner traveled to Africa four times between 1891 and 1900.[31] The idea of migration was in the discourse air and Pap Singleton's internal migration had gained attention when Henry McNeal Turner decided to organize the International Migration Society. He organized two ships with more than 500 emigrants to travel to Liberia in 1895 and 1896. Although there were some problems, with some emigrants complaining about disease in Africa, the majority remained and Turner kept his pledge to support all back-to-Africa programs. He died on May 8, 1915 in Windsor, Canada. He is buried in Atlanta, Georgia.[32]

Harriet Tubman and Revolutionary Seizure of Property

Harriet Tubman's is the most legendary name in the African pantheon in North America. No single individual stood for justice, righteousness, fairness, and resistance to enslavement and discrimination any more boldly and directly than Tubman. Her courage and intelligence were extraordinary and without compromise. Although she is often compared to other heroes of the African world such as Nehanda, Yenenga, Nanny of Jamaica, and Yaa Asantewa, Tubman was uniquely gifted with a personal hatred of slavery and a bravery bordering on foolhardiness, the combination of which prepared her for a historic role in black liberation. She is credited with personally escorting 300 Africans to freedom on more than twenty separate missions. Such missions entailed hundreds of miles of walking, navigating through rough terrain, crossing swamps, streams, and rivers, outwitting professional slave-catchers, and evading hunting dogs.

Tubman was born in 1820 outside of Bucktown, Maryland, on the Eastern Shore, an area that is well known for famous African Americans such as Frederick Douglass and Maulana Karenga. Harriet married John Tubman, a free black man who unfortunately did not approve of her desire to be free. Constant argument between them finally caused Harriet to escape from the Dorchester County, Maryland, plantation, where she had been enslaved, and from the reactionary views of John Tubman. Once she had escaped, Harriet Tubman made twenty trips to the South to deliver Africans to freedom. Her first trip was to retrieve her sister, nieces and nephews, and other members of her family from Baltimore. She worked in Philadelphia and Cape May, Jersey, to gain money for her missions. Tubman became a model for courage and freedom. On at least eight of her missions she collaborated with the courageous Thomas Garrett and William Still, two extraordinary leaders against slavery. In fact, it was Still who wrote the book *Underground Railroad* that popularized her name. Tubman was one of his favorite personalities. She never lost a "passenger" on her freedom train. In fact, she was adamant that reluctant Africans explain to her why they would not want to leave slavery. When they showed trepidation and fear, she would take her gun and point it at them and say, "Before I'd see you a slave, I'd see you dead and buried in your grave."[33] No one refused to travel with her to freedom and none of her people were ever recaptured. White southerners offered a $40,000 reward for her capture. John Brown visited her in Canada and told her of his plans. During the Civil War Harriet Tubman worked as a spy for the Union Army. She lived in Philadelphia, St Catherines, Ontario, and finally settled in Auburn, New York. She died in 1913.

Josiah Henson

b. June 15, 1789
d. May 5, 1883

"My earliest employments were, to carry buckets of water to the men at work, and to hold a horse-plough, used for weeding between the rows of corn. As I grew older and taller, I was entrusted with the care of master's saddle-horse. Then a hoe was put into my hands, and I was soon required to do the day's work of a man; and it was not long before I could do it, at least as well as my associates in misery.

"A description of the everyday life of a slave on a southern plantation illustrates the character and habits of the slave and the slaveholder, created and perpetuated by their relative position. The principal food of those upon my master's plantation consisted of corn-meal, and salt herrings; to which was added in summer a little buttermilk, and the few vegetables which each might raise for himself and his family, on the little piece of ground which was assigned to him for the purpose, called a truck-patch.

"In ordinary times we had two regular meals in a day: breakfast at twelve o'clock, after labouring from daylight, and supper when the work of the remainder of the day was over. In harvest season we had three. Our dress was of tow-cloth; for the children, nothing but a shirt; for the older ones a pair of pantaloons or a gown in addition, according to the sex. Besides these, in the winter a round jacket or overcoat, a wool-hat once in two or three years, for the males, and a pair of coarse shoes once a year.

"We lodged in log huts, and on the bare ground. Wooden floors were an unknown luxury. In a single room were huddled, like cattle, ten or a dozen persons, men, women, and children. All ideas of refinement and decency were, of course, out of the question. We had neither bedsteads, nor furniture of any description. Our beds were collections of straw and old rags, thrown down in the corners and boxed in with boards; a single blanket the only covering. Our favourite way of sleeping, however, was on a plank, our heads raised on an old jacket and our feet toasting before the smouldering fire. The wind whistled and the rain and snow blew in through the cracks, and the damp earth soaked in the moisture till the floor was miry as a pig-sty. Such were our houses. In these wretched hovels were we penned at night, and fed by day; here were the children born and the sick—neglected."[34]

The *Dred Scott* Decision

The idea that all blacks anywhere and at any time could be declared slaves was one of white supremacy's most desperate attempts to reduce the African to nothing.[35] The United States Supreme Court under Chief Justice Roger B. Taney declared in March, 1857 that all Africans, enslaved as well as free, were not and could never become citizens of the United States. Furthermore, the Court said that the 1820 Missouri Compromise was unconstitutional and therefore slavery was permitted in all states and territories.

The case before the Court was *Dred Scott v. Sanford*.[36] It had come to the Supreme Court because Dred Scott was a slave who had lived in the free state of Illinois and the free state of Wisconsin before moving back to the slave state of Missouri with his slaveholder. Scott had appealed to the highest court in the land, believing that he would be granted his freedom. However, Taney, a white supremacist and supporter of slavery, wrote in the majority opinion that because Scott was black he was not a citizen and therefore had no rights before the Court. He certainly could not sue a white man! Taney made it clear that it was his opinion that the makers of the Constitution wanted to affirm that blacks

> had no rights which the white man was bound to respect; and that the Negro might justly and lawfully be reduced to slavery for his benefit. He was bought and sold and treated as an ordinary article of merchandise and traffic, whenever profit could be made by it.[37]

For Taney and the Court's majority Dred Scott was pure and simply nothing more than chattel who could be moved into and out of free and slave states just as a white man could take a plow into and out of free and slave states. Intent on linking his argument to the Declaration of Independence, Taney said of the Declaration's phrase that "all men are created equal" it was clearly not intended to include blacks because "It is too clear for dispute, that the enslaved African race were not intended to be included, and formed no part of the people who framed and adopted this declaration."[38]

The Court's opinion started a fierce campaign against the racist ideology that was the foundation of the Court's philosophy. Most abolitionists saw this decision as one of the saddest moments in their struggle for a progressive society. On the other hand, for one reason or another, Frederick Douglass said after the decision that "my hopes were never brighter than now."[39] It is likely that Douglass believed that the severity of the ruling, the awful stench of it in human terms, and the impossibility of its being policed meant that the nation would rise up against slavery and reject it outright. Unfortunately, Douglass would have to wait for the Civil War to see his vision realized.

One could imagine that the Court's decision weighed heavy on Frederick Douglass, whose entire adult life had been one of struggle against the institution of slavery. He had escaped from bondage as a young man, worked his way up to become one of the most highly sought-after anti-slavery speakers, and yet any white Southerner could conceivably track him down and drag him back into the abyss of endless hell. This meant that he had to sharpen his own strategic tools for the survival of those he loved as well as himself. There was no question in his mind that the intent of the Fugitive Slave Act was to dampen the spirit of the blacks in the North and to make it almost impossible for them to venture onto the platform against slavery. Consequently, even the great Douglass, yet to become more luminous, had to travel to Canada and then settle in Rochester, New York, from where he could, if necessary, reach Canada quickly.

John Brown and the Raid on Harpers Ferry

On October 16, 1859, when the white abolitionist John Brown marched into Harpers Ferry to take over the United States Armory, there were five Africans in his group of twenty-two men. Lewis S. Leary, Dangerfield Newby, John A. Copeland, Shields Green, and Osborne P. Anderson were free and courageous men who were willing to risk their lives alongside equally brave white men who despised the savage system of slavery. The first two, Leary and Newby, perished in the initial raid; Copeland and Green were captured, imprisoned and executed; and the fifth, Anderson, was never captured, having escaped into the backwoods of Virginia and probably northward into Ontario.[40]

Brown has been rewarded with immortality by his deeds. Some whites considered him to be irrational for his actions; others, believing in the idea of freedom, saw John Brown as the quintessential symbol of justice against an evil system. He became, for all time, the abolitionists' guardian. He knew, even on the eve of his execution by hanging on December 2, 1859, that civil war was inevitable: "I, John Brown, am now quite certain that the crimes of this guilty land will never be purged away but with blood."[41]

Harpers Ferry became an iconic place in history. Storer College was founded in the town after the Civil War in honor of John Brown. In 1881 the famous orator and abolitionist Frederick Douglass delivered one of his most powerful panegyrics in praise of John Brown. The second meeting of the Niagara Movement was held at Storer College in 1904 in recognition of the importance of the location for African American freedom. Walking at the break of day to the site of John Brown's last defense, the conferees experienced the deep emotion of the place, some of them shedding tears as they walked, and others overcome with dread, as they finally entered the fort ready for their great work in establishing the National Association for the Advancement of Colored People. For many years after the raid on Harpers Ferry, children in the black communities recited orations singing the praises of Leary, Newby, Copeland, Green, and Anderson alongside the name of John Brown.

The Epic of the People: Out of the Fire of Brutality

Du Bois called the highly elegant and textured songs that developed during the antebellum age "sorrow" songs because of their mournful quality. These songs, however, acquired the name "Spirituals" because the early analysts of African culture thought that the songs reflected the deep religious emotion of the African. In some ways these were the first uniquely American songs to be derived from this nation's experiences. Unlike the English ballads and Irish jigs that had dominated the music of the colonies, the Spirituals seemed to come directly from the life of the Africans in the Americas. Although these songs had emerged over a long period of time they did not become known in a larger public sense until after the Civil War. Whites certainly did not intend to promote anything creative from the enslaved African population prior to the end of the war and Africans had no way to project the music other than in the collective ensembles in the cotton, tobacco, and sugar cane farms.

Piecing together strands of black life, myths, overheard Christian religion, a spirit of awe, and fundamental African rhythms, the enslaved Africans were able to create a testament to the resilience, resistance, and optimism of the people. The songs were impressive, meant to announce the majesty of a people in the midst of suffering, sweat, and blood. I have often referred to these Spirituals as "the epic of the people" because they contain the seeds of the classical traditions of African Americans. Expressing the most profound responses to the condition of involuntary servitude with a "soul" that produces an ethos of optimism is like a heroic journey through the worst kind of opposition one can imagine. This is what the collective makers of the Spirituals imagined; this is their conquest as Africans in a bizarre circumstance. Without reading and writing for the most part, Africans enslaved in North America used their songs and their speech to reflect the trauma of the slave experience. Most of these songs appeared after Nat Turner's Revolt of 1831 because Turner had shown how one could use the religion, the snippets of the white man's religion that were overheard, to build a theology of revolt; this theology could also produce resistance songs and victory songs in the very presence of slavery's guile.

The makers of these songs did not know that they were carrying the weight of an entire people on their shoulders; they were essentially writing their own existential narratives that became, by virtue of unanimity, the will of those whose physical toil and psychological burdens were lightened by grandeur of song. Nothing could express the desire for new world, a different and better condition, a more equitable circumstance, than a palliative such as:

> There is a balm in Gilead to make the wounded whole.
> There is a balm in Gilead to heal the sin-sick soul.
> One of these mornings bright and fair, I'm gonna lay down my heavy load.
> Gonna take my wings and cleave the air, I'm gonna lay down my heavy load.

The songs seemed to have arisen spontaneously but they were the products of a profound reflection. The great songs, the African emotional tapestry, were affirmations of humanity and spirit, but also the wish for an eternal life that would be free from slavery's deprivation of family, pleasure, opportunity, and perpetual punishment.

No one knows the number of songs that were created by enslaved Africans, but the production was constant and more than 500 have been recorded and mentioned in literature. Some of them have become standard enough to be called classical poetry of the enslavement period. They are not all religious; some are the highest forms of folk culture.

> Mary wore three links of chain,
> Every link was Jesus' name;
> Keep your hand on that plow, hold on.
> Hold on. Hold on.
> Keep your hand on that plow, hold on!

However, because of the nature of slavery, the Africans had to be surreptitious when it came to speaking about freedom from bondage, and some of the songs were cast in the cryptic biblical language of the church in order to serve as an instrument for communicating with each other and to confound the slaveholders. Thus, one could sing:

> Run to Jesus, shun the danger,
> I don't expect to stay here much longer.

Perhaps a more popular song in this genre is the following:

> Steal away, steal away, steal away to Jesus,
> Steal away, steal away home.
> I ain't got long to stay here.

Very few enslaved Africans were Christian in any sense of the word prior to the end of the Civil War, although the presence of the religion among free blacks in the North—particularly in its African Methodist Episcopal, the African Methodist Episcopal Zion, and African Baptist forms—meant that elements of the religion penetrated the great cotton curtain behind which Africans lived during the enslavement. Those small fragments were often magnified by the belief that goodness must overcome evil, that the universe had to have a moral order, and that redemption and justice were parts of human life. These were purely thoughts brought into the enslaved African world through un-African religion. Most Africans believed in African religious ideas or maintained, as much as possible, their connections to the spirit world through ancestral attachments; less than fifteen percent of Africans were Christian when slavery ended. It would take a massive missionary effort on the part of Northern white churches and the AME to "convert" the newly freed Africans to Christianity as a method of bringing "civilization" to the 4.5 million liberated Africans. Yet during the enslavement songs of deliverance were often couched in faint religious terms unrecognizable by many whites.

> There ain't but one train on this rail track,
> All night long.
> Straight up to heaven and straight right back.
> Do Lord, deliver poor me.

Among the more popular songs are "Sometimes I Feel Like a Motherless Child," "Deep River," "There is a Balm in Gilead," "Wade in the Water," "Joshua Fought the Battle of Jericho," "Swing Low, Sweet Chariot," and "Go Down Moses." Some of the songs reflected the secular sentiment of running away with no reference to religion at all:

> When the sun comes back and the first quail calls,
> Follow the drinking gourd.
> For the old man is a-waiting to carry you to freedom
> If you follow the drinking gourd.

What could have been more powerful or perceptive than this song that could be used as escaping Africans walked by plantations? This song told other Africans how to look at the night sky and follow the Big Dipper as a way to the north. All one had to do was to look to the sky for the sign.

Some of the more direct and confrontational songs were actually created during the war for emancipation when African volunteers would sing the great majestic song "Oh Freedom!"

> Oh freedom, oh freedom,
> Oh freedom over me. And before I'll be a slave,
> I'll be buried in my grave,
> And go home to my Lord and be free!

The first published collection of Spirituals came out in 1867, two years after the Civil War. It was called *Slave Songs of the United States.* There had not been a wide recognition of the power of these songs until this period, although whites had remarked here and there about the depth of these moving songs. However, the publication of this collection and the rise of the Fisk College Jubilee Singers as a group to travel and raise money for the college made the songs popular. The Jubilee Singers started in 1871 to take the songs to Europe and throughout the United States, but it was probably Antonin Dvořák, the Czech composer, who brought the music to the wider world in a critical way. Almost all white Americans composers and musicians ignored the Spirituals until Dvořák proclaimed them masterful through his New World Symphony.

Conclusion

This chapter has focused on the numerous instances of African resistance to slavery and brutality. Heroic men and women dedicated their lives and resources to freeing their brothers and sisters during the most intense period of the enslavement. Between 1825 and 1855 the condition of Africans in the slaveholding states had reached a nadir after a couple hundred years of oppression. Every avenue was explored to end bondage from petitions and agitation to revolt and insurrection. Among the major attempts to free blacks from slavery were the revolts of Denmark Vesey, Gabriel Prosser, and Nat Turner. These are iconic and well known, but the Stono Rebellion, the Deslandes Uprising, and the Seminole Wars must be understood as being just as important as the more famous rebellions.

There were few blacks that could write, and if they could, they did not necessarily write against slavery. This is why David Walker must be considered one of the most important figures of the early nineteenth century. What is so remarkable about his pamphlet *An Appeal to the Coloured Citizens of the World* is the way it consolidates current historical, political, and social knowledge to make his argument that "the white Christian Americans are the most barbarous people on the face of the earth and the Negroes are the most abject and perse-cuted." In this chapter we have seen that Walker was a product of an environment which the American Colonization Society had begun to poison with the idea of sending Africans, especially Africans who were considered impossible to break, back to Africa. This movement had split the sentiment in the black community in the North ten years or so before the appearance of Walker's pamphlet.

Strong streams of logic and emotion flowed from the words and actions of Harriet Tubman, Frederick Douglass, Martin Delany, Bishop Henry McNeal Turner, and the blacks who collaborated with the brave John Brown. They were called insane for their love of liberty, militant for their determination, and radical for their objective to overturn the system of slavery. Nevertheless, these devotees of freedom defied all the odds and brought a degree of optimism to other blacks and their allies that leaned the nation toward a split with its past of enslavement.

Additional Reading

Abzug, Robert H. *Cosmos Crumbling: American Reform and the Religious Imagination*. New York: Oxford University Press, 1994.

Aptheker, Herbert. *American Negro Revolts*. New York: International Publishers, 1974.

Barnes, Gilbert H. *The Antislavery Impulse, 1830–1844*. Gloucester, MA: Peter Smith, 1973.

Dillon, Merton. *The Abolitionists: The Growth of a Dissenting Minority*. New York: Norton, 1974.

Egerton, Douglas R. *Gabriel's Rebellion: The Virginia Slave Conspiracies of 1800 and 1802*. Chapel Hill, NC: University of North Carolina Press, 1993.

Harding, Vincent. *There is a River: The Black Struggle for Freedom in America*. New York: Harcourt Brace Jovanovich, 1981.

Hunt, Alfred N. *Haiti's Influence on Antebellum America: Slumbering Volcano in the Caribbean*. Baton Rouge: Louisiana University Press, 1988.

Lofton, John. *Denmark Vesey's Revolt: The Slave Plot that Lit a Fuse to Fort Sumter*. Kent, OH: Kent State University Press, 1983.

Oates, Stephen B. *The Fires of the Jubilee: Nat Turner's Fierce Rebellion*. New York: Harper and Row, 1975.

Stuckey, Sterling. *Slave Culture: Nationalist Theory and the Foundations of Black America*. New York: Oxford University Press, 1987.

Winch, Julie. *Philadelphia's Black Elite: Activism, Accommodation, and Struggle for Autonomy, 1787–1840*. Philadelphia: Temple University Press, 1988.

Chapter Time Markers

1851	Frances Ellen Watkins Harper vows to fight slavery
1862	Robert Smalls, 23 years old, captures a Confederate ship and sails it to the Union side
1863	Massachusetts 54th board ships in Boston to sail to war in South Carolina
1866	Charlotte Forten teaches recently freed Africans at the Port Royal School in the Sea Islands
1897	Richard T. Greener successfully completes the raising of funds to build a monument in honor of Ulysses Grant

The Great Freedom War 5

Important Terms and Names

Frederick Douglass

Frances Harper

Richard T. Greener

The Columbian Orator

Robert Smalls

Freedmen's Bureau

Thomas Mundy Peterson

Enter Frederick Douglass

When the Civil War broke out, Frederick Douglass was the most formidable black leader in the United States.[1] Douglass was born on the Eastern Shore of Maryland near the town of Easton. He was raised by his grandparents, having been separated from his natural mother when he was only weeks old. Douglass's grandmother kept him until he was six years old. His slave-master sent him to live as a houseboy with Hugh and Sophia Auld when he was eight years old. Douglass was taught the alphabet by the compassionate wife of the slaveholder until he forbade her from instructing the young African since it was illegal to teach enslaved Africans how to read. However, Douglass had learned enough to teach himself. He bargained with young white boys, giving them food in exchange for lessons in reading and writing. When he was thirteen he came into the possession of *The Columbian Orator*, a schoolbook that was famous at the time, and it helped him gain an appreciation for words, language, and oratory.

When Douglass was fifteen years old he was sent back to the Eastern Shore and became a field slave, where he experienced first-hand the most horrible abuses of the system of slavery. It was during this time that he encountered the slave-breaker Edward Covey, who would become a catalyst for Douglass's love for freedom and hatred for slavery. Covey tried to whip Douglass, but the young Douglass fought the slave-breaker. Douglass took the resulting draw as a victory and planned his escape. He was caught and brought back to the slave plantation. However, he was later returned to Baltimore to the Auld family and in early

1838 he escaped at the age of twenty by disguising himself as a sailor. Douglass went north to New Bedford, Massachusetts, and married Anna Murray. By 1841 he was a frequent participant in abolitionist meetings and was soon asked to become a lecturer for the Massachusetts Anti-Slavery Society. The already famous William Lloyd Garrison was pleased to call him a colleague.

Douglass was an inspiring orator and intelligent editor, and one of the first public men to support women's rights. His newspaper, the *North Star*, became a powerful abolitionist instrument. He wrote three autobiographies and was thrust into the leadership of the black community in the United States by his constant protest against slavery in America and in Europe.

From the very beginning of the American nation in the eighteenth century the thinking among white Americans had been corrupted by the overbearing presence of the enslavement of Africans. It entered every door where serious discourse was present and it warped the thinking of the most intelligent of white politicians and often left them bereft of rationality. Most of the signers of the Constitution were slaveholders and some, like Thomas Jefferson, although quite clear on many issues, were bogged down when it came to race. Neither Jefferson nor Washington abandoned slavery during their lifetimes.

Perhaps no president seemed to wrestle more with the question of race than Abraham Lincoln, and in the end Lincoln also arrived at the conclusion that the two races were fundamentally different and unequal. Yet the same Abraham Lincoln consulted Douglass on occasion and appointed him to several posts. Douglass was United States Marshal for the District of Columbia, the Recorder of Deeds for Washington, DC, and Minister-General from the United States to the Republic of Haiti. Nothing was as monumental, however, in Douglass's career as his call of black men to arms. He believed that it was essential that black men fight for their freedom. In one of the most moving calls to arms, Douglass produced a statement that caused many of the 186,000 blacks that fought in the Civil War to risk, and in some cases lose, their lives. This is Douglass's brilliant call:

Men of Color, To Arms!

When first the rebel cannon shattered the walls of Sumter and drove away its starving garrison, I predicted that the war then and there inaugurated would not be fought out entirely by white men. Every month's experience during these dreary years has confirmed that opinion. A war undertaken and brazenly carried on for the perpetual enslavement of colored men, calls logically and loudly for colored men to help suppress it. Only a moderate share of sagacity was needed to see that the arm of the slave was the best defense against the arm of the slaveholder. Hence with every reverse to the national arms, with every exulting shout of victory raised by the slaveholding rebels, I have implored the imperiled nation to unchain against her foes, her powerful black hand. Slowly and reluctantly that appeal is beginning to be heeded. Stop not now to complain that it was not heeded sooner. It may or it may not have been best that it should not. This is not the time to discuss that question. Leave it to the future. When the war is over, the country is saved, peace is established, and the black man's rights are secured, as they will be, history with an impartial hand will dispose of that and sundry other questions. Action! Action! not criticism, is the plain duty of this hour. Words are now useful only as they stimulate to blows. The office of speech now is only to point out when, where, and how to strike to the best advantage. There is no time to delay. The tide is at its flood that leads on to fortune. From East to West, from North to South, the sky is written all over, "Now or never." Liberty won by white men would lose half its luster. "Who would be free themselves must strike the blow." "Better even die free, than to live slaves." This is the sentiment of every brave colored man amongst us. There are weak and cowardly men in all nations. We have them amongst us. They tell you this is the "white man's war"; and you will be "no better off after than before the war"; that the getting of you into the army is to "sacrifice you on the first opportunity." Believe them not; cowards themselves, they do not wish to have their cowardice shamed by your brave example. Leave them to their timidity, or to whatever motive may hold them back. I have not thought lightly of the words I am now addressing you. The counsel I give comes of close observation of the great struggle now in progress, and of the deep conviction that this is your hour and mine. In good earnest then, and after the best deliberation, I now for the first time during this war feel at liberty to call and counsel you to arms. By every consideration which binds you to your enslaved fellow-countrymen, and the peace and welfare of your country; by every aspiration which you cherish for the freedom and equality of yourselves and your children; by all the ties of blood and identity which make us one with the brave black men now fighting our battles in Louisiana and in South Caroline, I urge you to fly to arms, and smite with death the power that would bury the government and your liberty in the same hopeless grave. I wish I could tell you that the State of New York calls you to this high honor. For the moment her constituted authorities are silent on the subject. They will speak by and by, and doubtless on the right side; but we are not compelled to wait for her. We can get at the throat of treason and slavery through the State of Massachusetts. She was the first in the War of Independence; first to break the chains of her slaves; first to make the black man equal before the law; first to admit colored children to her common schools, and she was first to answer with her blood the alarm cry of the nation, when its capital was menaced by rebels. You know her patriotic governor, and you know Charles Sumner. I need not add more.

Massachusetts now welcomes you to arms as soldiers. She has but a small colored population from which to recruit. She has full leave of the general government to send one regiment to the war, and she has undertaken to do it. Go quickly and help fill up the first colored regiment from the North. I am authorized to assure you that you will receive the same wages, the same rations, and the same equipments, the same protection, the same treatment, and the same bounty, secured to the white soldiers. You will be led by able and skillful officers, men who will take especial pride in your efficiency and success. They will be quick to accord to you all the honor you shall merit by your valor, and see that your rights and feelings are respected by other soldiers. I have assured myself on these points, and can speak with authority. More than twenty years of unswerving devotion to our common cause may give me some humble claim to be trusted at this momentous crisis. I will not argue. To do so implies hesitation and doubt, and you do not hesitate. You do not doubt. The day dawns; the morning star is bright upon the horizon! The iron gate of our prison stands half open. One gallant rush from the North will fling it wide open, while four millions of our brothers and sisters shall march out into liberty. The chance is now given you to end in a day the bondage of centuries, and to rise in one bound from social degradation to the place of common equality with all other varieties of men. Remember Denmark Vesey of Charleston; remember Nathaniel Turner of Southampton; remember Shields Green and Copeland, who followed noble John Brown, and fell as glorious martyrs for the cause of the slave. Remember that in a contest with oppression, the Almighty has no attribute which can take sides with oppressors. The case is before you. This is our golden opportunity. Let us accept it, and forever wipe out the dark reproaches unsparingly hurled against us by our enemies. Let us win for ourselves the gratitude of our country, and the best blessings of our posterity through all time. The nucleus of this first regiment is now in camp at Readville, a short distance from Boston. I will undertake to forward to Boston all persons adjudged fit to be mustered into the regiment, who shall apply to me at any time within the next two weeks.[2]

Frances Ellen Watkins Harper

Participation in the movement to end slavery was not simply a male affair. Women were actively engaged in the struggle for freedom and no woman, with perhaps the exception of Harriet Tubman, stood so tall as Frances Ellen Watkins Harper.[3] She was born a free woman in Baltimore, Maryland, on September 24, 1825. It is believed that her father was a white man and her mother an African woman who went by the last name of Watkins. Harper was formally educated by her uncle, William Watkins, who taught at a local Baltimore school for free African children. By the age of fourteen Frances Harper was employed as a servant to the Armstrong family of Baltimore. She was allowed to use their small library and bookstore to further her interest in literature. This inspired a love for fiction and poetry. Harper began writing poetry and prose and published her first book of poetry, entitled *Forest Leaves*, by 1846.

Frances Harper took a job as the first female faculty member at Union Seminary in Columbus, Ohio. It was during this time that her interest in the anti-slavery movement intensified and finally consumed her public and private life until her death. According to a letter written by Harper in 1851, "Upon the grave, I pledged myself to the anti-slavery cause."[4] In 1854 she went to live in Philadelphia and work for the Underground Railroad station. While in Philadelphia she produced her second book of poetry, *Poems of Miscellaneous Subjects*. Harper was often sent to Maine between 1854 to 1864, to speak against slavery.[5] Harper was married to Fenton Harper for a few years before he died. They had one daughter, Mary, and Frances Harper was forced by circumstances into a brief retirement in Columbus, Ohio. However, in 1864 Harper returned to Philadelphia with Mary. Phebe Hanaford wrote in the book *Daughters of America* that Frances Harper was one of the most eloquent lecturers in the country. Furthermore, she said that Frances Harper was "one of the colored women of whom white women may be proud, and to whom the abolitionists can point and declare that a race which could show such women never ought to have been held in bondage."[6] In 1896 Frances Harper participated in the First Congress of Colored Women in the United States. When she died, in 1911, her life had spanned the time of slavery, anti-slavery protest, the Civil War, and Reconstruction, but it was as an impassioned promoter of Union causes that she was known as the radically eloquent orator of reason. In fact, some have gone so

Figure 5.1
Frances Ellen
Watkins
Harper, poet,
abolitionist,
and writer.
Image courtesy
of Charles L.
Blockson Afro-
American
Collection,
Temple
University
Libraries.

far as to say that her radical political involvement and ideological maturity were the foundations for the modern concept of women's rights and "black power."

The Massachusetts 54th

After a long campaign to secure for Africans the privilege of fighting against the Confederacy, the Secretary of War, Edwin M. Stanton, gave the governor of Massachusetts, John A. Andrew, an abolitionist, authorization to form regiments including persons of African descent. Governor Andrew and Frederick Douglass had advocated raising troops from the free blacks of the North. It was logical, practical, and possible that Africans could participate in the war.

Andrew was given the task of choosing the white officers who would lead the black regiments since it was considered politically impossible for black officers to lead blacks against white troops. Andrew selected officers from prominent abolitionist families because

Figure 5.2 Frederick Douglass, the lion of African American affairs during the struggle to defeat the Confederacy. Image courtesy of Charles L. Blockson Afro-American Collection, Temple University Libraries.

they would most likely be supportive of paying for the outfitting of the black troops. Even whites in the North doubted the ability of blacks to be soldiers and citizens despite the history of blacks who had fought in the American Revolution. Nevertheless, the move was on to attract blacks to the war.

The 54th Massachusetts Regiment was the first black regiment. The leader of the 54th was the twenty-five-year-old son of wealthy abolitionist parents, Colonel Robert Gould Shaw. Born October 10, 1837 to Francis and Sara Shaw, Robert was raised in an environment of strong abolitionist sentiment. His father was heir to a large fortune and although he had advocated for abolition, he had also been part of the social elite of Boston progressive society. His friends included William Lloyd Garrison, Charles Sumner, Nathaniel Hawthorne, and Ralph Waldo Emerson. In 1846, Francis and Sara moved their family to Staten Island, New York. They took their son to Europe in 1851 and Robert studied abroad. Four years later the family returned to the United States and young Robert entered Harvard College, where he studied for three years before withdrawing.

Robert Gould Shaw took a position in the mercantile firm of his uncle Henry P. Sturgis. He did not like the business world and soon developed a passion for politics and the military. He supported Abraham Lincoln, and when the secession crisis occurred he hoped that the South would return to the Union. Shaw enlisted in the 7th New York State Militia in an effort to be sent to the front as soon as possible. He had responded to Lincoln's call for 75,000 volunteers to end the rebellion. His regiment was quartered in Washington and he got a chance to meet both Secretary of State William Seward and President Lincoln. He applied for a permanent position in the military and was given a commission. By the time he took over the 54th Massachusetts, Robert Gould Shaw was a dedicated warrior.[7]

The smart troops paraded on May 28, 1863 through the streets of Boston. They boarded ships for the coast of South Carolina. They fought the Confederates on July 16 and repelled an attack on James Island. Two days later a battle that would gain the 54th Regiment immortality took place when the troops were chosen to lead the charge on Battery Wagner, a Confederate fort located on Morris Island at Charleston, South Carolina. The young Colonel Shaw said to the men on the night of the battle, "I want you to prove yourselves. The eyes of thousands will look on what you do tonight." Nothing could have been truer than the words spoken by Shaw.

The 54th spearheaded the assault and lost many soldiers. Colonel Shaw fell in battle alongside twenty-nine of his troops, with twenty-four dying later of their wounds. Fifteen men were captured, fifty-two were missing in action, and 149 were wounded but recovered. The 54th was cited widely for the valor of its men; its name was enshrined in poetry by Robert Lowell, and the unit had a bronze monument dedicated to it on the Boston Commons. One of its soldiers, William Harvey Carney, was given the Medal of Honor for catching the U.S. flag as the flag-bearer fell on the field, and then carried the flag to the enemy ramparts and back, saying, "The old flag never touched the ground!"

Camp William Penn

Camp William Penn was the first and largest training camp for African troops. Located in Cheltenham, Pennsylvania, the camp held 11,000 free blacks and former slaves during its two years of operation. The camp was opened in 1863 after the United States government approved the recruitment of African troops. Although Frederick Douglass had claimed in the Call to Arms that he had been authorized to say that the black soldiers would receive the same pay as the whites, this was not to be the case. In fact, whites received thirteen dollars a month to the blacks' ten dollars a month in pay.

The recruits came from Pennsylvania, New Jersey, and Delaware, with almost 8,600 from Pennsylvania alone. They were willing volunteers, ready for war, and prepared to risk their

UNITED STATES SOLDIERS AT CAMP "WILLIAM PENN" PHILADELPHIA, PA.

Figure 5.3 Soldiers at Camp William Penn, the major Northern camp for training black soldiers for the Civil War. Image courtesy of Charles L. Blockson Afro-American Collection, Temple University Libraries.

lives to free their brothers and sisters in the Southern states. Their commander was William Wagner, a German, who had already been wounded in the war at the Battle of Chancellorsville but who volunteered to lead Camp William Penn because he wanted the men to look beyond the lack of tolerance they found in the community. The land for Camp William was leased by the government from the family of Lucretia Mott, the women's rights advocate.[8]

Frederick Douglass, a frequent visitor to the site, spoke to the troops at the camp on one occasion after seeing some unsettling actions against the troops, such as soldiers being punished for small military infractions. Douglass had worked hard to recruit black troops and believed that the many of them had the scars of slavery—a special understanding by the leadership of the camp. He told the troops, "You are a spectacle for men and angels. You are in a manner to answer the question, 'Can the black man be a soldier?' That we can now make soldiers of these men there can be no doubt."[9]

Robert Smalls and the Sailing Tradition

One of the most dazzling episodes during the Civil War was when Robert Smalls, an enslaved African, commandeered a Confederate ship, the USS *Planter*, and sailed it to freedom in

Charleston harbor. Smalls was born on April 5, 1839 and when he was twenty-three years old freed his family during a daring escape on May 13, 1862. After the war Smalls became a sea captain and a politician. In fact, he served in the South Carolina State legislature and the United States House of Representatives. Always a pioneer, Smalls authored the legislation that created the first free public and compulsory schools. He also was one of the blacks, alongside Martin Delany and Frederick Douglass, to convince President Lincoln to accept blacks into the Union army. Smalls died on February 23, 1915.

A Host of Black Fighters

Blacks had to agitate to fight in the war, but in the end Lincoln agreed. On July 17, 1862, Congress passed the Second Confiscation and Militia Act, freeing Africans whose masters were in the Confederate Army and therefore in rebellion against the United States. A couple of days later Lincoln abolished slavery in the territories of the United States, and on July 22 he was ready to present a preliminary draft of the Emancipation Proclamation to his Cabinet. When the Union Army forced back General Robert E. Lee's first invasion of the North at Antietam, Maryland, and the Emancipation Proclamation was subsequently announced, the recruitment of African soldiers took on a serious nature and thousands volunteered. Soldiers came from South Carolina, Tennessee, and Massachusetts to fill the first authorized black regiments. Two of Douglass' own sons volunteered and by May 1863 the government had to organize the Bureau of Colored Troops to manage the large numbers of recruits.

At the end of the war 186,000 black men and women had fought in the Civil War, and black troops made up nearly ten percent of the Union's Army. Nearly 40,000 black soldiers died during the war, 30,000 of them falling to infection or disease. Black soldiers served in artillery and infantry and were used to handle all non-combat jobs such as cooks, laborers, guards, carpenters, nurses, scouts, spies, steamboat operators, and chaplains. Some were even used as surgeons and many were teamsters. Eighty black commissioned officers served the black regiments. Harriet Tubman, the most famous spy, scouted for the 2nd South Carolina Volunteers.

In the combat zones African soldiers served with distinction in a number of battles such as at Milliken's Bend, Louisiana; Port Hudson, Louisiana; Petersburg, Virginia; and Nashville, Tennessee. Sixteen black soldiers were awarded the Medal of Honor for their valor.

Defeat of the Southern Confederacy and Lee's Surrender

In 1863 the 54th Regiment became the first black unit in the Union Army, as we have seen. The unit included soldiers from every state and was led by a white officer, Robert Gould Shaw. Frederick Douglass and William Wells Brown were asked to recruit soldiers and nearly 1,000 troops signed up within two months. Soon Africans were fighting on the Union's side throughout the campaign. Indeed, in the final push to defeat the Confederacy at the siege of Petersburg and the race to Appomattox, black troops were very present.

By the time Richmond, Virginia, became the capital of the Confederate States of America, Africans were thoroughly engaged in all aspects of the war. Thus, in June 1864 when the

Federal Army of the Potomac crossed over the James River on the way to Richmond, there were numerous black men and women serving as soldiers and spies for the Union forces. The Union forces had laid siege to Petersburg, the source of many supplies for the army of General Robert E. Lee. Black soldiers were involved in the cutting of General Lee's supply lines to and from Petersburg. The lines were finally severed on April 2, 1865. When the Union soldiers under Major General Philip Sheridan made a decision to assault Lee's flank at the Battle of Five Forks on April 2, 1865, they opened the way for General Ulysses Grant's army to gain a decisive victory over Confederate troops. Lee's soldiers abandoned their trenches after ten months and evacuated on April 2–3, 1865. Most of the nearly 8,000 Confederates surrendered, including nine generals. Sheridan rushed on to Appomattox Station, captured Lee's supplies, and placed defenses in his way. Lee raced to the west, seeking to supply his troops at Amelia Courthouse. He wanted to link up with Joseph E. Johnston's Army of Tennessee but when he arrived on April 4 he found no provisions for his army. He sent his soldiers around the countryside foraging for supplies. This slowed down his army for a day because he thought that by reaching the Roanoke River he could re-make his defenses. Soon he was moving farther west to Appomattox Station, where he expected a supply train. As the Confederates were retreating they were stopped by the power of Sheridan's cavalry.

When Lee left Petersburg, black soldiers as well as white chased his army. Although most of the United States Colored Troops in the Union Army were in Richmond, some did enter Petersburg when it fell, on April 3, 1865. Brig. General William Birney's second division, 25th Corps, came in from the west and was one of the first units to enter the city. The black units that were involved were the 7th U.S.C.T. regiment, recruited in Maryland, and the 8th U.S.C.T., from Philadelphia. They were on the skirmish line as early as 5 a.m. on April 3 and some of them marched into the evacuated railroad center under the leadership of Lt Colonel Oscar E. Pratt, the commander of the 7th, who wrote, "I entered the city of Petersburg at 6 a.m., amidst the joyous acclamations of its sable citizens."[10] The black inhabitants of Petersburg, some freemen but mostly enslaved Africans were overwhelmed with joy when they saw the sprightly marching black soldiers enter the city. Seven black units, about 2,000 men, or three percent of the total Union force in the region, made the march all the way to Appomattox Court House with Major General Ord's Union Army of the James. They arrived in time to be involved in the final fighting that brought Lee to the surrender table and turned the tide of the war toward total surrender of the Confederate Army.

Historians suggest that the route taken by Ord's Army of the James was through Nottoway Court, Burkeville Junction, Rice's Station, and Farmville, as well as other communities where proud black men and women could cheer the soldiers on toward victory.

General Ulysses Grant soon sent a message to General Lee saying that it was time to surrender the Army of Northern Virginia. On April 8, 1865, the Union cavalry under Brig. General George Armstrong Custer confiscated three trains waiting for General Lee at Appomattox. The end was near for Lee as the Army of the Potomac and the Army of the James converged upon the fateful station. Lee was surrounded but thought that he could make it to Lynchburg, where there were other supplies for him. His army would have to fight its way through the Union cavalry. Lee's army was being battered badly when the Confederate general finally agreed that there was nothing more for him to do than go and see General Grant.

On April 9, 1865 Grant and Lee met at Wilmer McLean's house in Appomattox station. Grant allowed Lee and his men to escape without being charged with treason. They received food, mules, and horses, but had to leave their heavy guns and artillery pieces. When Lee left the house, a defeated man, the Union troops, especially the black troops, who felt two centuries of weight lifted from their heads, began to cheer in celebration, but Grant immediately asked them to discontinue cheering. More than 500,000 people had been killed in a war that determined the fate of 4.5 million black people.

Repairing an Imperfect Document

The Thirteenth Amendment was passed by the United States Senate on April 8, 1864, exactly one year before the end of the Civil War on April 8, 1865. It was passed by the House on January 21, 1865 and adopted nearly a year later, on December 6 1865. Secretary of State William H. Seward declared it in his proclamation on December 18, 1865. The Fourteenth and Fifteenth amendments would follow as the principal Reconstructions Acts.

The U.S. Constitution

Amendment XIII

Context for the Amendment

Almost all of the action taken by the United States Congress since the establishment of the Constitution in 1789 until the outbreak of secession had protected slavery. America was a slave society. However, slave importation had basically ceased since 1808, although a few ships still made it to the Southern ports. So consequently there had never been a strong enough opposition to slavery for its cessation to be demanded in the Congress. However, as early as 1839 John Quincy Adams had made a proposal to abolish slavery in the United States House of Representatives, but it would not be taken up again until December 14, 1863. A bill was introduced to abolish slavery by Representative James Mitchell Ashley of Ohio. Representative James F. Wilson of Iowa made a similar proposal. On January 11, 1864 a joint resolution by Senator John B. Henderson of Missouri called for the abolition of slavery. Senator Lyman Trumbull of Illinois took up the issue of merging all of the proposals into one. Senator Charles Sumner of Massachusetts also sought to abolish slavery with his proposal, but he called for complete equality of the African. He was considered a radical for his position, which in hindsight appears quite rational and reasonable.

What the Amendment Says

Section 1. Neither slavery nor involuntary servitude, except as a punishment for crime whereof the party shall have been duly convicted, shall exist within the United States, or any place subject to their jurisdiction.

Section 2. Congress shall have power to enforce this article by appropriate legislation.

Amendment XIV

Context for the Amendment

The Fourteenth Amendment of the Constitution was one of the most contested pieces of legislation ever passed by the United States Congress. It represented a challenge to all of the philosophy that was responsible for the idea that Africans were not human. The amendment eventually passed both houses on June 13, 1866.

What should have been a simple idea became one of the most fractious of ideas in the legislative chambers. Africans were to be accepted as citizens inasmuch as they were born in the United States. The amendment sought to grant citizenship and protection to the Africans who had been freed from bondage. States were prohibited from denying or abridging the privileges or immunities of citizens of the United States. There had been discussion about giving Africans limited rights, certainly not the same rights as whites. The Southern whites sought every opportunity to deprive the African of all privileges of life, liberty, and property, often without due process of law. Now the law would dictate that the African had to have the same rights as anyone else within the jurisdiction of the nation.

The majority of the Southern states refused to ratify the law. It took the intervention of men such as Thaddeus Stevens, Charles Sumner, Benjamin Wade, Henry Winter Davies, and Benjamin Butler, called Radical Republicans, to force the passing of additional legislation that would impose the measures on the states in the former Confederacy. The result was the 1867 Reconstruction Acts that divided the South into five military districts controlled by martial law from Washington. Thus, universal manhood suffrage was established and the new constitutions in the old Confederacy had to honor the rights of Africans to be citizens, although most states sought in every way possible to avoid treating Africans equally.[11] There could be no reconciliation between the races, no equality that would stand the test of time, no hands reaching across the great divide because whites simply believed, even after the war and perhaps more after the war, that blacks were inferior. Such attitudes made it nearly impossible for blacks to reach back with trust despite the inclination of a few blacks to understand white anger at the loss of some privilege.

Many whites had no intention of following this law and the federal government would have to step in and protect the African's right to citizenship because whites refused to accept the law. It took a long time for the white population in the United States to come to realize that blacks had the right to equal protection under the law. In addition, every citizen had a right to due process.

Ratification of the Fourteenth Amendment was in doubt for some time. The fact that it had passed the Congress in 1866 did not stop states from delaying its ratification until July 28, 1868. Southern states were required to ratify it in order to be readmitted into the United States. However, the most ardent white supremacists tried everything they could to sap the life out of the amendment. Indeed, the Supreme Court's ruling in the 1873 Slaughterhouse cases weakened the amendment because the federal government could no longer control the police in the South. This was a victory for the states' rights doctrine and a major weakening of the equal protection under the law provision.

Even in 2010 there were Republican legislators in the United States Congress calling for the repeal of certain provisions of the Fourteenth Amendment, largely because they feared that children of undocumented aliens in the country could become terrorists or in some other way harm American society, perhaps by becoming a burden on the school and health systems of the nation. The government and progressive scholars and activists who see the attack on the Fourteenth Amendment as a racist action, fortunately, have rejected this argument.

What the Amendment Says

Section 1. All persons born or naturalized in the United States, and subject to the jurisdiction thereof, are citizens of the United States and of the state wherein they reside. No state shall make or enforce any law which shall abridge the privileges or immunities of citizens of the United States; nor shall any state deprive any person of life, liberty, or property, without due process of law; nor deny to any person within its jurisdiction the equal protection of the laws.

Section 2. Representatives shall be apportioned among the several states according to their respective numbers, counting the whole number of persons in each state, excluding Indians not taxed. But when the right to vote at any election for the choice of electors for President and Vice President of the United States, Representatives in Congress, the executive and judicial officers of a state, or the members of the legislature thereof, is denied to any of the male inhabitants of such state, *being twenty-one years of age*, and citizens of the United States, or in any way abridged, except for participation in rebellion, or other crime, the basis of representation therein shall be reduced in the proportion which the number of such male citizens shall bear to the whole number of male citizens twenty-one years of age in such state.

Section 3. No person shall be a Senator or Representative in Congress, or elector of President and Vice President, or hold any office, civil or military, under the United States, or under any state, who, having previously taken an oath, as a member of Congress, or as an officer of the United States, or as a member of any state legislature, or as an executive or judicial officer of any state, to support the Constitution of the United States, shall have engaged in insurrection or rebellion against the same, or given aid or comfort to the enemies thereof. But Congress may by a vote of two-thirds of each House, remove such disability.

Section 4. The validity of the public debt of the United States, authorized by law, including debts incurred for payment of pensions and bounties for services in suppressing insurrection or rebellion, shall not be questioned. But neither the United States nor any state shall assume or pay any debt or obligation incurred in aid of insurrection or rebellion against the United States, or any claim for the loss or emancipation of any slave; but all such debts, obligations and claims shall be held illegal and void.

Section 5. The Congress shall have power to enforce, by appropriate legislation, the provisions of this article.

Amendment XV

Context of the Amendment

Thomas Mundy Peterson was the first African American to vote after the right to vote amendment was approved. He cast his vote in a school board election in Perth Amboy, New Jersey, on March 31, 1870. It is interesting to note that more African Americans were elected to public office during the period from 1865 to 1880 than at any other time. Several states had strong African American legislative caucuses and many blacks served in the state legislatures.

What the Amendment Says

Section 1. The right of citizens of the United States to vote shall not be denied or abridged by the United States or by any state on account of race, color, or previous condition of servitude.

Section 2. The Congress shall have power to enforce this article by appropriate legislation. Passed February 26, 1869. Ratified February 2, 1870.

Acts of Reconstruction and Their Consequences

Although Congress passed the Thirteenth Amendment, abolishing slavery, prior to the end of the Civil War it took almost a full year for the amendment to be ratified by enough states to become a part of the Constitution. There were many objections and in some states the vote in favor of the amendment was quite close. Nevertheless, the Thirteenth Amendment was finally ratified. The Congress also established the Bureau of Freedmen, Abandoned Lands, and Refugees to systematically direct the progress of the freed people.

However, it would take the government two years after the close of the war to create an overall program for reconstructing the South and integrating Africans into American society. Three pieces of legislation were passed in 1867 and then one other measure was passed in 1868. Taken together, these measures were referred to as the Reconstruction Acts. They had five provisions:

1. Five military districts were to be created in the seceded states (not including Tennessee, which had already ratified the Fourteenth Amendment and had been readmitted into the Union).
2. Each district was to be headed by a military official empowered to appoint and remove state officials from office.
3. All voters had to be registered, including all freedmen as well as white men who took an extended loyalty oath to the Union.
4. All state constitutional conventions, comprising elected delegates, had to draft new governing constitutions providing for black male suffrage.
5. All former Confederate states were required to ratify the Fourteenth Amendment prior to readmission.

President Andrew Johnson vetoed these measures but Congress overrode his vetoes. This would become a familiar pattern between a strong Congress intent on repairing the damage done by slavery and the Civil War and a president with Southern sympathies.

Freedman's Bureau

On March 4, 1865, out of political turbulence and controversy the U.S. Congress eventually produced a temporary federal agency—the Bureau of Refugees, Freedmen, and Abandoned Lands, dubbed the Freedmen's Bureau—to assist 4 million freed Africans who were making the transition from slavery to freedom.[12] The bureau, although identified with reason as the Freedmen's Bureau, was really intended to serve refugees as well. Indeed, the first groups of clients were whites that had lost their livelihood because of the war. Unfortunately, few whites or blacks remembered the original name of the institution once it was operating. To a large degree, the overwhelming population to be served was the more than 4 million Africans who had been released from bondage. Once the agency was up and running it created protocols for getting food to the hungry, defending the freed Africans from spiteful white Southerners, handing out clothing and setting up shelter. The agency built hospitals for the enslaved and administered direct medical aid to more than 1 million people. The greatest successes of the Freedmen's Bureau were in the field of education. More than 4,000 schools were built and staffed with qualified instructors. Most of the major African American colleges in the United States were founded with the assistance of the bureau.

This was the first agency designed to prevent the abuse of a powerless group in society. The Freedmen's Bureau found jobs, negotiated contracts, examined the ill, sent investigators to look into cases of abuse, and became a guardian of the new reality for blacks. There were those in the bureau who had an initial sense of optimism that the government would redistribute land to the masses of blacks, making them an agricultural backbone of the country. A few Africans were settled on public lands under the Homestead Act of 1862, but extensive land redistribution never occurred. Indeed, President Andrew Johnson's plans were to restore abandoned lands to as many white Southerners as he could, so long as they applied for pardon by the government. Landless, free blacks were hardly above the slave status that they had experienced before the war, and all the arrangements of work were unequal, unfair, and unpopular with the workers.

Major General Oliver O. Howard was appointed to head the Freedmen's Bureau. Politicians, especially Southern sympathizers, found many problems with the agency. They rarely questioned Howard's personal integrity but they were severe on the actions of the agency. In some respects the critics felt that the agency acted as if it were the government in the South. They pointed to favoritism, corruption, inefficiency, and charges of misappropriation of funds. The agency also became the pawn of the corrupt Radical Republican government and was used to help maintain Republican control of the Southern states occupied by federal troops. After seven years, in 1872, Congress discontinued the Freedmen's Bureau. This untimely end to an agency that affected the lives of millions of formerly enslaved Africans created a void that would be filled by threats, displacements, abuse, lynching, and the Ku Klux Klan.

African Education in African Hands

When the Freedmen's Bureau arrived in the South, its staff soon discovered that hundreds of makeshift schools existed, created by Africans themselves. Men and women who could read and write taught others to read and write and the excitement of education was contagious, reaching to the far corners of the rural South as young people taught older people and everyone seemed to be prepared to learn "to read the Bible." Black teachers from the North and South formed the backbone of the instructional staffs at some of the more successful schools. Zion School in South Carolina is said to have had 850 students by 1866.[13] In the Sea Islands off the coasts of Georgia and South Carolina there were outstanding examples of self-sacrifice when teachers such as Charlotte L. Forten, the granddaughter of James Forten, went down to the South to teach children at the Port Royal School. She had been born in Philadelphia in 1837 to a prominent African American family, the Forten-Purvis family of strong anti-slavery sentiment. Forten attended school in Salem, Massachusetts, in 1854, where she learned critical thinking, history, cartography, and literature. As the only African student in her class she felt the necessity to achieve beyond her peers in every subject because of the pressure to demonstrate that Africans could do well in any academic subject. Thus, after attending Higginson School and Salem Normal School she was prepared to teach. In Massachusetts she met William Wells Brown, the first African to publish a novel, *Clotel,* in the United States, and the anti-slavery orators William Lloyd Garrison, Wendell Phillips, and Maria Weston Chapman.

Forten developed tuberculosis and returned to Philadelphia to recover. While at home she wrote poetry against slavery that was published in the *Liberator* and *Anglo African* magazines. Her work in South Carolina was chronicled in the essays "Life on the Sea Islands," and published in the *Atlantic Monthly* in the May and June issues of 1864. While in South Carolina she befriended Robert Gould Shaw, a Massachusetts native who was the white commander of the all-black 54th Massachusetts Regiment, famous for storming Fort Wagner on the night of July 18, 1863. The unit was repulsed in its futile attempt to take the fortress. Shaw was killed in battle and Forten volunteered to aid the wounded and to help remove the dead. At the end of the war Charlotte Forten worked for the United States Treasury Department as a teacher recruiter. She became a clerk of the Treasury in 1873. Her marriage at the age of forty-one, in 1881, to the Presbyterian minister Francis J. Grimké further established a tradition of African American scholarship and erudition. Francis J. Grimké's brother Archibald served as consul to the Dominican Republic, and Archibald's daughter Angelina Grimké lived with Francis and Charlotte while her parents were in the Dominican Republic. Angelina would later become a well-known author in her own right.

The experiences that Charlotte Forten Grimké had in South Carolina as a young woman touched her deeply and she never allowed the comforts of her life to take her far away from the conditions of her people. She organized women's groups and campaigns for the poor in the South, and wrote extensively on the subject of morality and ethics. She had witnessed the turbulence of the war years and the aftermath of the most destructive war ever fought on the North American continent, and Forten knew that the job of reconstruction would endure. One must not assume that the General Grant's receiving General Lee's surrender meant an end to all hostilities or the immediate releasing of Africans from bondage. Some did not know about the coming of freedom until June 19 although the surrender had been on

April 8, 1865. Most of the Africans who learned the news in June were in the frontier southern states such as Texas and Arkansas. Yet it is also true that in the core states of the Confederacy such as South Carolina, North Carolina, Georgia, Alabama, Mississippi, and Louisiana, blacks were still held in bondage after the signing of the surrender. In some cases, Africans did not gain freedom until Union troops occupied areas of the South and thousands of enslaved Africans ran into the Union encampments looking for refuge. The U.S. Army issued Field Order No. 15 to give temporary title of forty-acre plots of land to 40,000 Africans. All of these land grants were in Georgia and South Carolina, and most of them were along the thirty-mile inland coastal areas of these two states. White plantation owners had abandoned these lands, leaving tens of thousands of Africans to fend for themselves, which they had little trouble doing. They established community organizations, rules of behavior, functioning farms, and new schools.

The Freedmen's Bureau issued land to hundreds of thousands of Africans with the option to purchase the land. There was never enough funding for the Freedmen's Bureau to straighten out the paperwork and purchase land for Africans. Moreover, the land that was issued could be, and often was, reclaimed by the white owners with the cooperation of the whites elected to political office in the Southern states.

A severe shortage of money, the abundance of labor, and the deterioration of old farms produced a new condition for the exploitation of Africans. Convinced that the only way the South would ever rebound would be to establish an orderly system of employing the black masses, the government agreed to let whites who claimed loyalty to the Union establish a system of labor that would attract blacks back to the farms. The Union army agreed to assist the former plantation owners in getting Africans to sign annual labor contracts. If an African wanted protection from the Union Army, he had to sign a labor contract with a white farmer or a Northern investor who had purchased large tracts of land in the South. The proposition was that Africans would be paid minimal wages, have access to schools, be able to purchase foodstuffs from the plantation, and have the ability to leave the plantation with the permission of the owner. This was called compulsory free labor. One did not have to take these conditions, but then finding work on your own would be more difficult in an environment in which whites hostile to freedom would seek to harass any free black.

Soon there emerged new forms of labor arrangements. Sharecropping, where the owner of a plantation would agree to divide his land into twenty-acre plots distributed to freedmen to work so long as they agreed to give one-half or two-thirds of the harvest to the planter, became extremely popular because the owner of the land did not have to do any work in order to make money. The system was almost as good as slavery. Africans entered the system in debt because they had to purchase all goods for farming the land from the white owners. If they needed mules, wagons, hoes, shovels, or seeds, they had to purchase these on credit from the white owner, who would then make a loan at an exorbitant rate to the black farmers. Indeed, clothes and food for family members had to be purchased from the white landowner. When the harvest time came, everything owed to the white owner would be subtracted from the profit and in most cases the black farmer would be in more debt. The owners kept the loan books and could always show where the black farmer did not make enough money, regardless how large the harvest or how hard he and his family worked, to pay the debt he owed to the white owner.

Prison gang labor was hardly any different from slave labor. Blacks who were found guilty of the simplest misdemeanors could be picked up and pressed into gang labor. The white plantation owner would contract with the sheriff to have a gang of laborers plant his sugar cane, cotton, or tobacco and then contract with the sheriff to have the gang harvest it when it was ready. Sometimes these gangs were given time to fish, hunt, or grow their own food but they could not sell any of the food they grew for the white owners. The taskmasters were abusive and often punished the black workers severely for the smallest infractions. Resentment toward the white taskmasters created turbulent conditions as blacks were always disrupting the systems by complaining or protesting the harsh treatment they received at the hands of the overseers.

It was clear to most observers in the North, and to blacks in the South, that Reconstruction was never going to succeed with white attitudes as intransigent as they had ever been. When President Abraham Lincoln was assassinated and Andrew Johnson, a Southerner and former slaveholder, became president, everything changed. Johnson had appeared more liberal than he turned out to be. In fact, most politicians thought that he would follow Lincoln's plan because he said that the rebels should be punished, but by the summer of 1865 Lincoln's dreams of reconstruction were dismissed and Johnson wasted no time pardoning most of the Confederates.

President Johnson ordered that Africans return all land that they had leased, that they had been given, or that they had purchased through the Freedmen's Bureau. He objected to General Sherman setting aside lands in South Carolina, Georgia, and Florida for Africans and did not take kindly to General Oliver Howard of the Freedmen's Bureau making decisions to assist black freedmen. He would veto appropriations for the bureau in July, 1868, only to be overridden by Congress. Johnson's notorious statement on his view of the country would dog every effort at reconstruction. He said, "This is a country for white men, and by God, so long as I am President, it shall be a government for white men."[14] President Johnson was not a friend of African people and by the end of his term in office he had given 13,350 pardons to former slaveholders, including one to Jefferson Davis, the president of the Confederacy. Indeed, his last annual message to Congress, on December 25, 1868, was a blistering attack on the Reconstruction Acts. He said, "The attempt to place the white population under the domination of persons of color in the South has impaired, if not destroyed, the friendly relations that had previously existed between them."[15] In an earlier meeting between a black delegation seeking to support the right to vote and President Johnson, who opposed it, the president had lectured the delegation and prevented them from responding. Frederick Douglass, one of the delegates, wrote a powerful letter to Johnson in which he asked:

> Can it be that you recommend a policy which would arm the strong and cast down the defenseless? Can you, by any possibility of reasoning, regard this as just, fair, or wise? Experience proves that those are most abused who can be abused with the greatest impunity. Men are whipped oftenest who are whipped easiest. Peace between races is not to be secured by degrading one race and exalting another, by giving power to one race and withholding it from another, but by maintaining a state of equal justice between all classes.[16]

Time has proved Douglass, not President Johnson, to be on the right side of history.

Johnson's presidency was the turn toward the decline of optimism in the country. Southern whites formed militias to attack blacks and to intimidate Northern whites. In some

Southern states they were able to pass Black Codes to control the movement and actions of black people. They sought to regulate all social, political, and economic aspects of black life.

The Ku Klux Klan was formed in 1866. The Klan's attacks on black communities were often referred to as race riots when in fact they were deliberate plans to assault blacks. In some communities blacks fought back with limited weaponry and resources, but in mose cases homes were burned, crops destroyed, and men, women, and children lynched. The period from 1868 to 1877 was a reign of terror. The attack on the black community in Memphis in 1866 was to become a model for scores of terrorist actions. Two wagon drivers ran into each other at an intersection. One was black and the other white. When the police arrived, they arrested the black driver. Several black veterans of the Union army tried to intervene, asking for a fair hearing for the black man. A hostile white mob formed and over the next few days succeeded in killing forty-six people, burning down a Freedmen's school, black churches, and over 100 black homes.

While the Fourteenth and Fifteenth amendments created opportunities for blacks to participate in government, they also aroused envy and animosity in many southern whites. Nevertheless, in those states where blacks outnumbered whites, such as South Carolina and Mississippi, blacks were elected to high political offices. Black postmasters and school superintendents occupied positions in local communities. Two blacks were elected to the United States Senate and more than fifteen were sent to the House of Representatives. This was to be short-lived, however, as white Southerners rebounded in a terrifying current against blacks when the Union Army left the South in 1877. Yet while they were in office blacks brought about public education and public roads, helped to repeal the Black Codes, and funded new railroads.

Representative Thaddeus Stevens of Pennsylvania and Senator Charles Sumner of New York worked to get forty acres of land as a permanent part of the Reconstruction for African Americans. They were unsuccessful in convincing other white politicians to go along with the idea that blacks should have land. In fact, even though the United States Constitution made blacks citizens, many whites did not accept the idea that blacks should own land. Despite the objections and the obstacles, blacks succeeded in developing cooperatives that produced food, owned mining companies, and bought large farms. Nevertheless, by the 1870s most of the states were under the absolute control of Southern whites whose plans included ending all vestiges of Reconstruction. Black politicians were harassed, pushed out of office, and, in some cases, killed. Many African Americans saw the turn toward violence and believed that the worst was yet to come. They decided to leave the South, go to Mexico, or join the armed forces in order to have the protection of the federal government. Reconstruction ended after twelve years and the future of the country grew bleaker.

Buffalo Soldiers in Search of Survival

The end of the Civil War brought a different set of emotions than the fight for freedom itself. Black soldiers who had fought on the side of the Union as the 54th of Massachusetts or other units had grown used to their freedom of travel, new vistas, expanding possibilities for their families, and the excitement of being warriors. In 1866 a peacetime black unit, the 10th Cavalry, was established at Fort Leavenworth, Kansas. This unit was named the "Buffalo

Soldiers" as a translation of either a Cheyenne or a Comanche phrase. The issue is in dispute by writers about the origin. However, what is not in dispute is the fact that many Indians described the soldiers' dark masses of hair as looking like the hair of buffaloes and therefore nicknamed them the "Buffalo Soldiers."[17]

One year after the 10th Cavalry was founded there were four black regiments in the United States Army: the 9th and 10th Cavalry units and the 24th and 25th Infantry units. It is generally accepted that the first unit to be called the "Buffalo Soldiers" was the 10th Cavalry unit but later the name was applied to all black fighting units. When the units were sent to the American Southwest as the result of a political decision not to station black troops in the Deep South, where they could cause emotional outbreaks, they were intended to patrol the Indian lands. The soldiers were also based at Camp Wichita, later called Fort Sill, in Indian Territory. It was the forward base for fighting the Kiowa and Cheyenne nations as well as a base to prevent the white settlers called "Boomers" from entering the Indian Territory. Despite the warnings not to enter the territory, some whites at great risk to their lives tried to sneak into the territory and were forced back by the Buffalo Soldiers. Two other forts, Fort Supply and Fort Reno, were also used in missions to oppose the Boomers who were coming in through Arkansas, Missouri, and Texas. Used as guards against white settlers and fighters against Indians, the Buffalo Soldiers patrolled the area until 1885. The soldiers of the 9th Cavalry were ordered to Wyoming, becoming the presence of the American government in that part of the continent and also the origin of the Wyoming black community. The 9th was pressed into action when fighting broke out between rich ranchers and small farmers near Suggs, Wyoming. It took some time to quell the action but the 9th Cavalry, despite the regular hostility of whites at the time, succeeded in gaining control of the situation. One soldier was killed in the action but Camp Bettens became synonymous with courage and order. The 10th regiment, on the other hand, was ordered to Arizona to fight the Apache and to chase the great priest-leader Geronimo.

Congress purchased a tract of so-called unassigned land for farming from the Indian authority in an area around Oklahoma City and opened it up for settlers. On April 22, 1889 a rush of homesteaders arrived on foot, horseback, and wagons seeking to settle what was Indian Territory. The settlers pressured Congress for more power and sought to have their land recognized as separate from Indian Territory, and it was organized as the territory of Oklahoma. The white settlers were unsatisfied by the new acreage; they demanded more and the government assigned individual plots to the Indians and then took possession of all the tribal reservation lands for fifteen cents an acre, thus opening up the complete territory to white settlers. By 1907, when the land rushes ended, Oklahoma had been made the forty-sixth state of the Union. Unable to prevent the Boomers from entering Indian Territory and sent on self-deprecating missions against other discriminated-against people, the Buffalo Soldiers finally found their glory in the Spanish-American War, where they earned five medals of honor.

The Buffalo Soldiers gained respect and prestige when they fought to secure Cuba's independence from Spain. The United States sent the 9th and 10th Cavalries and the 24th and 25th Regiments to Cuba in 1898, where they fought courageously at the famed battle of San Juan Hill.

Richard Theodore Greener and the Tomb of Ulysses S. Grant

In the same year that black soldiers charged San Juan Hill in Cuba with Theodore Roosevelt, Richard T. Greener quietly entered Bombay, India, as United States consul to India. He was shortly thereafter transferred to Vladivostok, Russia, the first American to hold that post. Two years later Greener received from the Chinese the high honor of Order of the Double Dragon for his service during the Boxer War and his assistance to the poor people of Shanshi during the famine.

There are those who are outstanding in warfare, education, science, art, or religion, and then there are those who are most known for the quality of excellence in each endeavor they undertake. Richard T. Greener was clearly in the latter category during his memorable life. He demonstrated from his childhood a desire to excel in everything, letting nothing hold him back, refusing to succumb to the temptations of inferior work, laziness, or difficulty. This is the reason he was considered by his peers to be one of the greatest African Americans of his time.

Figure 5.4
Richard Theodore Greener, the first African American graduate of Harvard, dean of Howard University Law School, and inspiration for the New York monument to Ulysses S. Grant. Image courtesy of Charles L. Blockson Afro-American Collection, Temple University Libraries.

Greener was born in Philadelphia on January 30, 1844. When his father left the family to find his fortune in California during the gold rush and never returned, Greener's mother moved the family to Boston, where the young boy attended school until the age of fourteen, when he quit to help support his mother. He worked in several jobs, and one of his employers thought that he was so intelligent that college had to be in his future despite the great opposition in the country toward blacks attending college. This employer, Franklin Sanborn, a teacher and reformer, helped to secure a place for Greener at Oberlin College, the first American college to admit Africans. When he completed his work at Oberlin he entered Phillips Andover Academy to prepare for the Harvard curriculum. In 1865 he entered Harvard at the age of twenty-one, having done exceptionally well in all of his subjects at Andover Academy. He won two Bowdoin Prizes while at Harvard, one as a sophomore and another as a senior. Greener graduated from Harvard in 1870, becoming the first African person to receive a bachelor's degree from that institution.

He was offered an appointment in Philadelphia as the male principal for the famous Institute for Colored Youth, later Cheyney University. Subsequently he worked as a principal at Sumner High School in Washington, DC, and as an assistant to Frederick Douglass, who was editing the New National Era. Greener never tired of education or work, it seems, and in 1873 he was made professor of Mental and Moral Philosophy at the University of South Carolina. In 1875 he was the first African American elected to the American Philological Society because of his understanding of Greek and Latin. He took a law course at the University of South Carolina's Law School and received an LLB in 1876, with honors.

Three years later Greener took an appointment as dean of the Law Department at Howard University. He remained at Howard for nearly two years and then opened his own law practice. He was prominent in national and international meetings, conventions, and dialogues during the presidencies of William McKinley and Theodore Roosevelt. When the country wanted to create a tomb to honor the Civil War hero Ulysses Grant in New York, Richard T. Greener was chosen as the first secretary, working with former president Chester A. Arthur. Greener took on the principal burden of seeing that the money was raised for the project and succeeding in convincing many corporations, clubs, churches, and civic groups to support the Grant's Tomb idea. The New York Grant Memorial Association succeeded in completing the project by April, 1897, just a year before Greener was given the job in India. No one was more responsible for the construction of Grant's Tomb than the African American genius Richard T. Greener, whose name has often been buried under piles of more dramatic achievements by African Americans. However, Greener believed that no people should occupy the front seat of gratitude more than African Americans for the achievements of freedom that came on the points of the bayonets of men like Grant. Thus, Greener applied the same talents, savvy, and energy into raising funds for the tomb as he had shown in his ambition to assist his family, achieve academic success, and serve his nation.

Conclusion

Nearly 200,000 Africans fought in the American Civil War. During a time when 4.5 million Africans were enslaved, those not enslaved in the North volunteered at a very high rate to participate in the war against the slave states. This expression of solidarity with their fellows who were enslaved was much more the reason for black soldiers volunteering than the idea of saving the Union. In effect, the black population left the saving of the Union to the white soldiers; their aim was to save their brothers and sisters from perpetual enslavement.

This chapter also presents black activism during the Civil War with the exploits of the famous Massachusetts 54th, whose bravery became legendary when they stormed Fort Wagner. Robert Smalls sailed a Confederate ship to the Union line, becoming a young hero whose life would be celebrated by South Carolina blacks for decades. Leaders in religion and education sprang up to gather the people into meaningful communities of citizenship after the surrender of General Robert E. Lee to General Ulysses Grant. Frances Ellen Harper and a host of women rose up to educate the masses of Africans who had been freed from bondage. They knew that the Freedmen's Bureau which was established by Congress could never achieve success alone; blacks themselves had to work together in teaching one another. Schools, colleges, and institutes were created by brilliant organizers who believed that Africans could do anything anyone else could do. After the war the Thirteenth, Fourteenth and Fifteenth Amendments to the Constitution changed the status of Africans. As African Americans, hundreds of blacks gladly assumed their roles in building the nation. Buffalo Soldiers who had distinguished themselves in the Civil War went to the West to help expand the American nation. Other Africans would create churches and build community centers that would become seats of education. More than one hundred colleges were established in the black community. Some black leaders, Robert Greener for instance, would show their gratitude to the nation in civic duties. He took charge of raising funds for the erection of a statue in honor of Ulysses Grant. Greener was a harbinger of politically inclined blacks who would make their marks in diplomatic service to the nation.

Additional Reading

Bell, Howard Holman. *A Survey of the Negro Convention Movement, 1830–1861.* New York: Arno, 1969.

Childs, John Brown. *The Political Black Minister: A Study in Afro-American Politics and Religion.* Boston: Hall, 1980.

Dann, Martin E. *The Black Press, 1827–1890.* New York: Capricorn, 1971.

Harrold, Stanley. *The Abolitionists and the South, 1831–1861.* Lexington: University of Kentucky Press, 1995.

Hine, Darlene Clark, ed. *Black Women in American History: From Colonial Times through the Nineteenth Century,* 4 vols. New York: Carlson, 1990.

Horton, James Oliver and Lois E. Horton. *In Hope of Liberty: Culture, Community, and Protest among Northern Free Blacks, 1700–1860.* New York: Oxford University Press, 1997.

McFeely, William S. *Frederick Douglass.* New York: Simon and Schuster, 1991.

Painter, Nell Irvin. *Sojourner Truth: A Life, a Symbol.* New York: Norton, 1996.

Pease, Jane H. and William H. Pease. *They Who Would be Free: Blacks' Search for Freedom, 1830–1861.* New York: Athenaeum, 1974.

Schor, Joel. *Henry Highland Garnet: A Voice of Black Radicalism in the Nineteenth Century.* Westport, CT: Greenwood, 1977.

Sterling, Dorothy. *Freedom Train: The Story of Harriet Tubman.* Garden City, NY: Doubleday, 1954.

Still, William. *The Underground Railroad.* 1871. Reprint, Chicago: Johnson Publishing Company, 1970.

Ullman, Victor. *Martin R. Delany: The Beginning of Black Nationalism.* Boston: Beacon, 1971.

Chapter Time Markers

1853	The intellectual Alexander Crummell goes to Liberia
1877	Henry O. Flipper becomes the first African American to graduate from West Point Academy
1878	Benjamin Singleton leads hundreds of southern blacks to Kansas
1881	Tuskegee Institute is founded in Alabama
1895	Booker T. Washington delivers the Atlanta Exposition Speech and becomes the de facto leader of the African American community
1909	The explorer Matthew Henson plants the American flag at the North Pole
1916	Marcus Garvey arrives in New York from Jamaica
1919	Madame C. J. Walker, the first black millionaire, dies
1934	Paul Robeson sings in the Soviet Union and is pronounced one of the great voices of the century

Exploring New Routes to Equality and Justice

6

Important Terms and Names

Matthew Henson

Benjamin Singleton

Octavius Catto

Paul Robeson

Ida B. Wells

NAACP

Julian Abele

Alexander Crummell

Henry O. Flipper

Booker T. Washington

Fanny Jackson Coppin

Jack Johnson

Marcus Garvey

James Weldon Johnson

Adventure and Creativity

What could have inspired a people so recently out of bondage to explode in a hurricane of intellectual activity as if the people had been bottled up so long with ideas, thoughts, visions, and possibilities that each man and woman saw the explosive necessity of sacrificing for the uplift and mobility of the whole?[1] Such activity burst forth in a creative way with the intellectual work of numerous adventurers like the indomitable George Washington Williams, who lived a brief but powerful forty-two years from 1849 to 1891—the most exciting period of the nineteenth century. He was born in Bedford County, Pennsylvania, and joined the Union effort in the Civil War when he was fifteen years old. Subsequently he attended the Newton Theological Seminary and was ordained as a Baptist preacher. Like so many of the educated men and women of his day, Williams believed that it was his duty to create a journal or newspaper that would help the masses of blacks. He did not see himself as an island in the midst of the thousands of needy Africans in America, so he started the *Commoner*, a monthly journal based in Washington, DC. However, Williams was not content with his life as a preacher and journalist, the two areas opened to blacks who wanted to be independent, so he studied law in Cincinnati and was the first black person elected to the

Ohio state legislature. Williams wrote the first published history of blacks in the country, *The History of the Negro Race in America, 1619–1880.*

However, Williams would not be satisfied with his achievements in the writing field until he went to Congo to investigate the condition of Africans on the continent. What he discovered in Congo was enough to cause him to spend the rest of his life trying to rouse an international movement against the actions of the whites in that country. King Leopold of Belgium had hired the notorious Henry Stanley to head up his takeover of Congo. The huge country had been called the Congo Free State and what Williams discovered was that there was nothing free about it. The Africans were enslaved and beaten down so badly that many lost hands, arms, and their lives if they did not succumb to the white overseers' demand for them to tap rubber trees. This was the era of big rubber, because at the end of the age of the lavish royal carriages of Europe and the beginning of the automobile industry, rubber was in great demand. When Williams went to Congo as a journalist and reported what he had seen going on, it caused an international stir at the highest circles. He made certain that the people of Britain, France, and Belgium knew what was being carried out in the name of King Leopold. In addition, he informed the leading people of America, including Booker T. Washington and Mark Twain, and both acknowledged his work.

As Williams was demonstrating his Pan-African interests in the area of politics and journalism, other African Americans free to dream envisioned an entirely different future for African Americans than that planned by the racists in the North and the South. Men and women with hearts more expansive than the misery they saw, and with stamina equal to the destructive will of white racists, rose up sometimes one by one and then again as a collective phalanx of courage and determination to achieve the improbable.

Henry Ossian Flipper: An Officer and a Gentleman

Another African American with daring, courage, and ingenuity was the brilliant Henry Ossian Flipper. There had never been a black graduate of West Point Military Academy until the graduation of Henry O. Flipper in 1877. He had been born into enslavement around 1855 in Thomasville, Georgia, the son of Isabelle and Festus Flipper. His father was known for his ability to trim horse carriages and as a shoemaker. The Flipper family had been held by the slave dealer Edward Ponder until the end of the Civil War. Henry O. Flipper was fortunate to attend Atlanta University during the period of Reconstruction. One of the Reconstruction representatives from Georgia, James C. Freeman, appointed Flipper to West Point, where there were four other black cadets at the time. Flipper was the first of the group to graduate, becoming a second lieutenant. He was assigned to the 10th Cavalry, one of the four all-black regiments in the army.

Henry O. Flipper reported to Indian Territory (Oklahoma) and began his career as an officer, becoming the first black in charge of an army regiment. All black regiments had been led by white officers until Flipper's appointment to A Troop at Fort Concho. Prior to being given the leadership of the troop, Flipper had been asked to dig ditches, clear swamps, build roads, and construct telegraph lines. These were to be skills that would serve him well when he left the army to work in Mexico and Venezuela as an engineer. Nevertheless, as commander of the A Troop he conducted raids against the Apaches and was one of the leaders of the campaign against Victorio in 1880. Yet whatever his successes, and there were many, Flipper still had to endure the racism, wrath, and guile of some of his white colleagues. In particular, he was essentially set up by a fellow officer, William Rufus Shafter, who asked him to keep the quartermaster's safe in his room. He could not refuse a superior officer, but soon discovered that $2,000 was missing and attempted to cover it up by lying. He realized that he had been set up by Shafter, who probably had given him the safe with the $2,000 short. Other soldiers did not believe that Flipper had taken the money and within four days raised the money that was said to be missing. Nevertheless, he was court-martialed by Shafter. His fellow officers found him innocent of the main charge, but guilty of actions unbecoming an officer and gentleman. President Bill Clinton pardoned Flipper on February 19, 1999, thus clearing his record. After his honorable discharge, a bust of Flipper was unveiled at West Point Academy.

Matthew Henson and the North Pole

One of America's most courageous explorers was Matthew Henson, who was born in Baltimore in 1866, one year after the end of the Civil War. He grew up in rural Carroll County. Henson's family was harassed by the Ku Klux Klan. Matthew's mother died while he was a still a young child but his father was determined to raise him in an environment free of racial persecution, so he moved his family to Washington. While Henson's father worked, Matthew took care of his sick uncle with whom they lived. Henson's father died and the uncle turned quite mean and abusive, forcing Matthew to run away.

Henson wandered the streets of Washington like so many poor, uneducated black children of the day. He was often hungry, but he never tired of looking for work as a manual laborer. He found a job cleaning a restaurant that gave him food. The owner allowed him to sleep on the floor in the restaurant since he had no home. This experience toughened him and made him desire to succeed as a resolute young man.

He could read and write and one day he saw an advertisement for young men who wanted to go to sea, and so he applied for the job. This decision was momentous because it opened Henson to a sailing career that would put him in the history books. During the rest of his teenage years he sailed around the world learning all of the skills of the sailor. He studied geography, mathematics, navigation, cartography, the operations of a ship and how to read books and maps. By the time he was twenty-one years old, Matthew Henson was a superior sailor.

In between sailing trips he would work to earn money and in 1887 he worked in a fur and supplies shop in Washington. This was to be another historic moment in his life because while he was at the shop a man visited the store to buy some supplies. That man was Robert Peary, an engineer and explorer. He wanted to purchase supplies but he told the owner that he was looking for a servant to take with him on a trip to Nicaragua where he would explore the forest and map it for the government. Henson was immediately hired since he had already traveled around the world and he was only twenty-one years of age.

On the trip to Nicaragua he impressed Peary with his mapmaking skills and he helped Peary to chart the Nicaragua rainforest. In many ways, Henson taught Peary as much as he learned from Peary. Peary began to see him as his trusted fellow explorer. When Peary

Figure 6.1
Matthew Henson, explorer who stood on the North Pole. Image courtesy of Charles L. Blockson Afro-American Collection, Temple University Libraries.

decided to make a run for the North Pole, he asked Matthew Henson to accompany him. Henson made five trips with Peary and in the process learned additional skills for survival. The Inuit taught him how to repair sleds, build camps in the midst of a storm, drive dog teams, and make warm clothes out of animal skins. Peary felt that he could not get along in the Arctic without Henson.[2]

Peary's last trip to the North Pole was made in 1909. Henson was forty-three years old at this time and Peary was nearly ten years older. Henson and Peary took four Inuit, Ootah, Egigingwah, Seegloo, and Ooqueah, with them on their quest for the site that Peary had calculated as the North Pole. The six men rushed along toward the site with Matthew Henson in the lead, followed by the four Inuit pulling the frostbitten Peary in a sled. Henson became the first person in the team to stand on the site of the North Pole. Peary handed him the flag of the United States of America, which he proudly planted in the snow on April 7, 1909. Henson then posed with the four Inuit who had pulled Peary along to the North Pole.

It is believed that one of the reasons Peary's expedition to the North Pole was disputed by some in the scientific community was the fact that Matthew Henson, an African, was in the expedition and may have been the actual first person to step on the precise spot. However, it was proven that Frederick A. Cook, who had been a surgeon on one of Peary's earlier expeditions, had actually beaten Peary and Henson to the pole by one year. Other explorers claimed they were the first to find the North Pole, but no explorers had as detailed a narrative as that of the interracial team of Henson and Peary. Later the United States Congress would call Peary and his team "attainers" but not discoverers of the North Pole. The dispute created more controversy and basically ruined the reputation of Henson and Peary for a few years. It would not be until Henson was accepted into the Explorer's Club and the club worked to have his name and contribution restored that he would be accepted as a legitimate explorer. By 1954, a year before Henson's death, President Dwight Eisenhower was ready to present him with an award for his outstanding service to science. Henson's family donated half of his insurance money to the Explorer's Club for its efforts to help restore his name.

Matthew Henson was married twice and had no children by either of his wives, although he lived together with the second wife, Lucy Ross, for nearly fifty years in New York. They were first buried in the Bronx at New York's Woodlawn Cemetery but later reburied in Arlington National Cemetery.

However, Henson had one son by his Inuit lover, Akatingwah, in 1906. He was named Anaquak Henson. When Henson left the Arctic in 1909 he never returned to see his son, although many explorers reported news of him to Henson. Anaquak and his wife, Aviaq, had five sons, and two granddaughters, Laila Henson and Aviaq Henson. Five daughters have been named in memory of the first Aviaq Henson, wife of Anaquak, since she is revered as the first Henson female. Thus, all of Matthew Henson's descendants are Greenland Inuit. One of Anaquak's sons, Vittus Henson, moved to Denmark in 2000, but his other four brothers remained in Greenland in the area where Matthew Henson and Robert Peary first found their Inuit helpers.

Henson's life demonstrated in an unlikely area of achievement that African Americans were capable of superior accomplishments whenever the opportunity presented itself. While Henson went off to the North Pole, other African Americans had traveled and settled in Mexico, Liberia, and Kansas. Earlier an entire movement called the Black Exodusters had left the American South for Kansas.

Madame C. J. Walker: The Impossible Dream

Madame C. J. Walker became the first woman in history to become a millionaire of her own accord. She did not inherit money from either family or husband; she created products to serve what she saw as a need in the African American community. Born one year after Matthew Henson on December 23, 1867 in Delta, Louisiana, Madame Walker shared the same desire to demonstrate the ability of African people freed from the constraints and restraints of enslavement.

Her parents, Owens and Minerva Breedlove, named her Sarah Breedlove but she would later be known simply as Madame C. J. Walker. She was an entrepreneur who made her own hair products for African American women, experimenting with various oils, herbs, and

Figure 6.2 Madame C. J. Walker, first African American millionaire. Image courtesy of Charles L. Blockson Afro-American Collection, Temple University Libraries.

minerals; she discovered many formulas that seemed to work to improve the beauty and style of black women who were just emerging from decades of enslavement. Madame Walker's daughter A'Lelia became her partner in business and was one of the principal philanthropists to the arts during the Harlem Renaissance. C. J. Walker died in 1919 and the company passed to the management of A'Lelia.

The Black Exodusters

The father of the Black Exodus was the legendary Benjamin "Pap" Singleton, a man so intensely committed to a free and prosperous African American community that he actually sought to move thousands of people away from the Southern heart of the nation. The Black Exodus movement had begun in 1860 as blacks freed from slavery could now move to other parts of the country. Of course, without resources and knowledge, most remained in the places where they were born. But there were others, the visionaries who could see a more powerful society, a greater prosperity, and more racial peace, by moving out of the South.

Benjamin Singleton was the chief black exoduster.[3] Although the movement had started in the 1860s it would reach its climax in the 1880s when thousands of Africans on the move took their simple belongings and crossed the Mississippi and Ohio Rivers to resettle in Kansas, Oklahoma, Nebraska, Indiana, and other areas. It was the inspirational Benjamin Singleton, however, who led nearly 8,000 blacks to Kansas, traveling on mules, steamboats, trains, and horse-driven wagons.

Pap Singleton, as he became known, had been born in Davidson County, Tennessee, in 1809. He grew up in slavery and learned to be a cabinetmaker, a job at which he excelled. Singleton was sold "down the river" to New Orleans but escaped back to Nashville, Tennessee.[4] It is believed that Singleton became enamored of travel and adventure from the initial trip from Tennessee to Louisiana. He remembered everything about the route, memorizing the place where he saw large trees, floodplains, and small villages along the river. This would be knowledge that he would use when he returned to Tennessee. By the time he returned to Tennessee, where his family was, he could find no comfortable place to live and therefore decided to make his way farther north. He made his way to Detroit and then into Ontario in Canada.

When the Civil War started, Singleton left Detroit and returned to Nashville, which was under the protection of the Union Army. During this time he supported himself by making cabinets, tables, desks, and coffins. His living space was on the edge of a large Union camp set up for fugitive slaves along the Cumberland River bank in Edgefield, East Nashville. From this private and personal space along the riverbank Singleton would preach to depressed, downtrodden, and destitute former slaves the idea of going west to own federal homestead land. This was something that he had learned from listening to the whites talk about all the land west of the Mississippi. In September 1869 there was a massive meeting of blacks held in Nashville about migrating from the South. Among the leaders of the meeting were Randall Brown, Henry Carter, Elias Polk, Robert Knowles, and Daniel Watkins. The debate was furious, often bitter, and they argued the pros and cons of leaving the South. Some saw the condition of the freedmen as impossible. Living in squalor, sickness, and with daily threats of racial violence by whites, the proponents of migration said that they had to leave and find a space where whites could not decide their lives. They were angered that the federal troops did little to alleviate their overcrowded conditions. The white Southerners had just regained political power by defeating the Republican, pro-federal government party, and returned the city's politics to white racists.

These are the times when the visionaries step forward. The mass meeting failed to gain a majority of votes for migration and so Pap Singleton and Columbus M. Johnson, a Summer County preacher, organized a homestead association for those who wanted to migrate. Like

Singleton in Nashville, Johnson in Summer County wanted to alleviate suffering in the impoverished contraband camps of Gallatin and Hendersonville.

By 1872 the association could send a committee to investigate Kansas for settlement. Less than a year after that, Johnson and Singleton and 300 persons boarded steamboats on the Cumberland River, heading for three areas of Kansas: Cherokee County, Wyandotte, and Topeka. In the 1880s the north end of Topeka was called "Little Tennessee." Singleton found himself back and forth along the migration route. In April, 1875 Singleton, William A. Sizemore, and Benjamin Petway held a convention in the building that housed the first black bank in Tennessee, the Freedman's Savings and Trust Company, which had been built in 1872. This meeting was to discuss the migration of blacks from Tennessee to Kansas. They formed the Tennessee Emigration Society and elected delegates to send to Kansas to explore the situation. In addition, they resolved that "To the white people of Tennessee, and them alone, are due the ills borne by the colored people of this state."[5] Some whites claim that blacks wanted more pay for their labor and were discontented with the the delays in payment by white employers. There was little effort to stop the flow of blacks out of Tennessee and many looked forward to leaving the state to form new societies in Kansas.

Singleton led rallies to raise funds, charging five cents for parties and dances, and published newspapers to spread the news about migration. He criticized those who opposed migration, including Frederick Douglass, who thought that blacks should not migrate out of the South. Singleton wrote, "Such men as this should not be leaders of our race any longer."[6]

Douglass' idea was that blacks should fight racism in the South and everywhere else. Nevertheless, Singleton's campaign was relentless. He posted flyers around Nashville announcing, "Leave for Kansas on April 15, 1878." He established an African colony at Dunla, Morris County, Kansas in June 1879. Thousands of people flocked to the movement and the *Nashville Union and American* newspaper called it "a foolish project," but black exodusters were not looking to whites for suggestions. Indeed, some white employers supported a move to bring in Chinese laborers to replace blacks. By 1882 the last of the exodusters had left for Kansas and by this time the legend of Pap Singleton had reached epic proportions. He died around 1888 and was buried in an unidentified grave in Kansas.

Singleton was not alone in his singular desire and energy for raising the economic, social, and political prospects of his people. This was the age of audacity and not a few Africans stood up to be counted among the audacious. Towns and cities grew up and died in Oklahoma, with names like Marshalltown, North Fork Colored, Sanders, Wiley, Mohmer, Rentie, and Huttonville. Others survived, with names like Langston, Boley, Red Bird, Taft, Rentiesville, Tulluhassee, Vernon, and Lima. In Kansas, Nicodemus was promoted as the Promised Land, but in California the town of Allenworth, founded by Colonel Allen Allenworth, was financed, controlled, and operated by blacks until whites put arsenic in the water source and caused the people to leave the area. The state of Mississippi had one of the largest black towns, Mound Bayou, founded by Isaiah T. Montgomery and his cousin Benjamin Green. It was incorporated in 1887, as blacks sought to claim their own space away from the abuses of racism. The founders of these towns were in a class of their own—fearless, competent organizers, brilliant orators, and talented artisans who believed in the ideology of self-determination. Pap Singleton may have been the most prominent of these exodusters but there were scores of others who took it upon themselves to create "free spaces." Very little time and space would separate Singleton from such brave men and women as Octavius

Catto, Fanny Jackson Coppin, and Booker T. Washington, who would take their places alongside the town-building heroes of courage, ingenuity, and strategic action. In the 1860s Catto would not found a city, but a city would honor him as its natural hero.

Turbulence in the Political and Educational Arenas

The funeral dirges that sounded and the crowds that attended the funeral of Octavius Catto in Philadelphia in October 1871 were unlike anything seen since the funeral of President George Washington down 4th Street in Philadelphia. Catto was the the most popular figure in activist Philadelphia and the titular head of the African American Republicans, then the progressive political party.[7]

Philadelphia was the second-largest English-speaking city in the world for most of the ninteenth century. It also had the largest and most active free black population. It was in the City of Brotherly Love that Richard Allen and Absalom Jones had founded the first African American churches in 1793 and 1794, the African Methodist Episcopal Church and the African Episcopal Church of St Thomas. About the same time, a group of free blacks

Figure 6.3
Absalom Jones, co-founder with Richard Allen of the Free African Society and first black ordained Episcopal priest. Image courtesy of Charles L. Blockson Afro-American Collection, Temple University Libraries.

appealed to the Congress, meeting in Philadelphia, to abolish the Fugitive Slave Act of 1793. This issue would raise its head again in the 1850s and create an enormous reaction in the black community. Philadelphia—indeed, Pennsylvania—had outlawed slavery in its territory but even the president, George Washington, had found his way around the local laws.

When George Washington brought enslaved Africans to Philadelphia, the new capital, from New York to serve in the presidential mansion at Market and 6th, a stone's throw from the Congress, he violated the spirit of the Pennsylvania law against slavery. His argument was that he was a citizen of Virginia, although he was president, and so needed his enslaved people. He would keep the enslaved persons for the length of time it took for them to be illegal and then take them back to Virginia, where it was legal to own slaves. Once in Virginia he would have them sent back to Philadelphia for another stint of slavery. Living in the animal quarters at the back of the presidential house from 1790 to 1797, the nine Africans resented their enslavement and two of them, Oney Judge Staines and Hercules, the first master chef for the president, escaped to freedom from Washington's mansion. The seven other enslaved Africans were probably taken back to Virginia.

Nevertheless, the vitality of the black community in Philadelphia was very important to Washington's enslaved Africans' sense of the possible. They saw blacks doing things, creating havoc about racism, and petitioning the government. Before the Civil War there were numerous Africans who insisted on equality and non-discrimination, and none made this his cry more strongly than Octavius V. Catto.[8] Everywhere race was spoken about, Catto seemed to be present—speaking, debating, and creating fervent heat around the issues of human dignity. He was engaged at every level in the Republican Party and was considered one of the leaders of the Radical Republicans. By the late 1860s he emerged as the national spokesperson for civil rights for African Americans.

Octavius V. Catto was born in Charleston, South Carolina, on February 22, 1839, to William Catto and Sarah Isabella Cain. The family settled in Philadelphia by 1850 and were free blacks. In Philadelphia, Catto received the best education possible for an African, completing his work at the famous Institute for Colored Youth, which was later transformed into Cheney University. In 1858 Catto was the valedictorian of the school. He was trained in the classical languages, Greek and Latin, and also in the sciences. He was appointed assistant to the principal of the Institute for Colored Youth, Ebenezer Don Carlos Bassett, who was educated at Yale University and became ambassador to Haiti.[9]

Some have called Catto a renaissance man, with talents in many areas of knowledge, and a charismatic leader. But he was unable to break the racial barrier that held him back and also caused him deep distress. Catto organized the Banneker Literary Institute, named for the famous black scientist Benjamin Banneker, and was inducted into the famed Franklin Institute, an institute that attracted the leading scholars and scientists of the day. He became a great baseball player-coach and organized some of the earliest black baseball teams.

As committed as he was to a humanistic society, Catto met with opposition from immigrant groups when he tried to integrate the baseball clubs in 1868. The anger over Catto's strong rhetoric against racial discrimination caused the Irish immigrants to resent him for his activities on behalf of blacks. In fact, his greatest obstacle would be political as the debates moved from sports to political elections.

Catto was a great Unionist and a major supporter of the Lincoln administration, but worked for the Republican Party in support of the war and for civil rights after the war. He

Figure 6.4
Octavius V.
Catto, political
leader and
popular orator.
Image courtesy
of Charles L.
Blockson
Afro-American
Collection,
Temple
University
Libraries.

rallied the black population to fight against the Confederates in 1863 when they invaded Pennsylvania for the Battle of Gettysburg. One of the first volunteer companies of black men officered by whites, but made up of black troops, was the results of Catto's work. He supported the call by Frederick Douglass that blacks should fight in the war as a way to defeat slavery. Perhaps it was his complete belief in the Union's cause that made him such a supporter of the Republicans. He wanted them to win all the elections necessary as a way of gaining equality for blacks. He joined the Pennsylvania Equal Rights League and in 1864 he and other black leaders met at the National Convention of Colored Men in Syracuse, New York, and created the National Equal Rights League (NERL) with Frederick Douglass as president.

Catto went back to Philadelphia believing that with the passage of the Fifteenth Amendment he could convince black men to continue to support the Republicans. He worked to get Pennsylvania to ratify the Fifteenth Amendment, which was achieved in October 1870.

Whites were alarmed as it became clear that the large numbers of blacks enfranchised would give the Republicans a great election advantage. On election day, October 10, 1871, many whites threatened, abused, and killed blacks to prevent them from voting for the Republicans. Gangs of white hooligans tried to intimidate black voters, and the police in Philadelphia, many of them Irish immigrants, failed to protect black voters. Catto was violently intercepted by Frank Kelly, a Democratic Party member, as he walked out of his house. Kelly fired several shots at Catto, one hitting him in the heart. Catto died within minutes at the local police station and the public went into shock. How could a person who fought for justice and racial peace be so openly murdered on the streets of Philadelphia? A large majority turned out and voted for the Republican Party in reverence to Catto. The murderer, Frank Kelly, escaped Philadelphia and fled to Chicago, where he was found six years later. He was extradited to Philadelphia for trial. Kelly was acquitted by an all-white jury. One of Kelly's witnesses was ex-police sergeant John Duffy, who had been tried and acquitted for the murder of another black, Levi Bolden, during the election.

The black community celebrated Octavius V. Catto for generations by naming schools, lodges, and social centers after him. His intimate network of friends and acquaintances including the extraordinary Fanny Jackson Coppin, a mother of African American education, spurred the popularity of Catto.

Fanny Jackson Coppin, who was born in 1837, became one of the leading educators of her day. Her aunt purchased her freedom when she was twelve years old. After completing Oberlin College, the first school to admit both blacks and females, she became a teacher. However, she stepped onto the stage of effective African American education in the Philadelphia black community with a missionary's zeal, becoming the first black woman to head a major educational institution. She was the director of the Institute for Colored Youth, which became Cheyney University. Coppin died in 1913 after an illustrious career.

By the time of her death, African Americans had created nearly 100 institutions of higher learning and over 500 private and religious schools. Such an outburst of intellectual and social activity by one ethnic group had rarely been recorded in history. Tuskegee, of course, became the standard, and its leader, Booker T. Washington, who died two years after Fanny Jackson Coppin in 1915, achieved superstar status.

Booker T. Washington's philosophical and practical base would be Tuskegee Institute.[10] The school helped catapult Washington into the top ranks of African American leaders. Tuskegee's founding date is July 4, 1881. Fourteen years later, when Washington gave the Atlanta Exposition Speech, famous for the "cast down your buckets where you are" and "as one as the hand and as separate as the fingers" statements, he had risen to the top of the heap as an African American leader. However, his Atlanta speech was the lightning rod for his controversial legacy. In fact, just a year later the United States Supreme Court announced its verdict in the *Plessy v. Ferguson* case and it seemed they were reading from Washington's text as they reinforced the idea of "separate but equal" in all social matters.

Homer Plessy was a thirty-year-old shoemaker who sought to challenge the separate but equal provisions of Louisiana state law. A number of Southern states had rushed in the 1890s to institute such laws to prohibit the intermixing of blacks and whites. Louisiana's law meant that blacks riding on the local trains had to sit in the colored section, which was inferior to the white section of the train. Plessy was arrested when he sat in a car for whites only. He refused to move to the colored coach. Although he was seven-eighths white and only one-eighth black he was thrown into jail for violating the race regulations. Louisiana had decreed that if you had black ancestors then you were black. Plessy took this to court and argued that the Thirteenth and Fourteenth amendments to the Constitution had been violated. The judge, John Howard Ferguson, had recently ruled that it was unconstitutional to discriminate on trains that traveled through many states, but that in this case Plessy was guilty of violation

Figure 6.5 Fanny Jackson Coppin, missionary and educator. Image courtesy of Charles L. Blockson Afro-American Collection, Temple University Libraries.

Figure 6.6 Booker T. Washington, major African American leader of the turn of the twentieth century and founder of the Tuskegee Institute. Image courtesy of Charles L. Blockson Afro-American Collection, Temple University Libraries.

of the law because the train ran in only one state, and the state had a right to make its own laws. When the *Plessy v. Ferguson* case was brought to the United States Supreme Court, Ferguson was upheld and it would take until 1954 for the *Brown v. Topeka Board of Education* case to eliminate the separate but equal doctrine.

Washington did not make this context, but he was integrally involved in operationalizing it or, as some would insist, maneuvering through it. Thus, when he had arrived in Alabama and met his students in a one-room wooden, unpainted shack, he knew well the lingering effects of losing the Civil War on the ego of the white Southerner and tried to give his students a vision larger than the shack and broader than anything they could imagine. It was then that he began to develop his passionate philosophy that the students had to achieve something for themselves. If they wanted school buildings, they would learn how to build them, and they would build them themselves.

It is important, however, to understand that in 1881 Washington walked into a social environment that had been prepared for him by the local African people. Lewis Adams' name is rarely heard but it was Adams' dream to have a school in rural Alabama for children of formerly enslaved Africans. By all accounts Adams, who had never had a day of formal education, was an intelligent man. He could read and write. He had several skills, being a tinsmith, a shoemaker, and harness-maker.

W. F. Foster, a white politician, was a candidate for re-election to the Alabama senate when he approached Lewis Adams and asked for his support in the election. Foster wanted Adams to encourage blacks in Macon County to vote for him. He asked Adams what he would want in exchange for his political support. To his eternal glory Lewis Adams did not ask for money, prestige, or position, but told W. F. Foster that he wanted to see an educational institution for his people. Foster was elected to the Alabama Senate and, with the support of Arthur L. Brooks, to the Alabama House of Representatives. Legislation was passed to establish a "Negro Normal School in Tuskegee." It included $2,000 for teachers' salaries. Lewis Adams, Thomas Dryer, and M. B. Swanson comprised the board of commissioners delegated to organize the school. They were given this charge without students, buildings, or teachers; only the authorization. George W. Campbell soon replaced Dryer as a commissioner and it was Campbell's nephew who sent word to Hampton Institute in Virginia that the board was looking for a teacher. Booker T. Washington was selected, and when he arrived in Alabama he was offered space in the Butler Chapel AME Zion Church. It did not take him long to find a hundred-acre abandoned plantation, which became, with its one building, the new site for Tuskegee. Washington also worked to have the legislature grant Tuskegee the right to act independently of the state of Alabama. In 1892 the school became independent and Washington went into action as its most important fundraiser. Booker T. Washington was succeeded by several important leaders, including Robert Moton, who created the Tuskegee Veterans' Administration Hospital, and Frederick D. Patterson, who created the school of veterinary medicine and the United Negro College Fund, and brought the Tuskegee airmen program to the Institute. Luther Foster, the president of Tuskegee during the Civil Rights Movement, made the university a focal point of voting registration activities. He insured that Tuskegee would remain in the forefront of advancing African American interests.

The Emergence of Tuskegee

Tuskegee's impact was seen in the great number of imitators. Scores of communities organized to create schools, colleges, and institutes on the Tuskegee model. The founders of the schools were mainly preachers because these were the most independent skilled members of the African American community. Their salaries were paid not by whites but by blacks, and they had access to the black community on a regular basis, making them the opinion leaders in their cities.

The appearance of Tuskegee was electric for the nation, not so much because of its presence, since Cheyney, Lincoln, and Hampton had already been established, but because of the dynamism of its leadership. In 1890 A. K. Smiley had called the First Mohonk Conference on the Negro Question at his home on Lake Mohonk, New York. He was a genuine Christian liberal committed to doing something about the "Indian Question" and the "Negro Question." Smiley had called seven Indian conferences before he called the First Mohonk Conference on the Negro Question and asked ex-president Rutherford B. Hayes to chair the conference, which met on June 4–6, 1890. By this time Tuskegee was eight years into its training program and the idea of education was at the center of the discourse on the future of Africans in the United States.

In his introduction A. K. Smiley laid out the task in these words:

> I trust that every one who is here agrees with me that it is exceedingly important for the Negroes to be elevated in every direction, that it is necessary that they should be practically educated, that they shall learn to be thrifty and taught industries, that they shall do away with all drinking habits, shall save money, accumulate property, be law-abiding citizens: that the family relations shall be well observed, and thus be a credit to our country. I believe, if they are not so educated, that they will become a dangerous element to the community, liable to be thrown at any moment into the hands of demagogues who may use them for bad purposes. I believe that our only safety is to give the Negro a Christian education.[11]

However, it was the former president, Hayes, who had gotten to the crux of the matter. In his opening remarks he made it quite clear what the issues were with the Negro. Hayes said that although half of the Africans could read and write, illiteracy remained the chief problem with the Negro. Despite the fact that in 1865 at the end of the enslavement only five percent of the black population was literate, in 1890 it was estimated that there was about fifty percent literacy. This was the fastest leap from illiteracy to literacy the world had ever seen, but nevertheless the former president, descendant of those who had conspired to keep blacks ignorant, went on to say that

> Iliteracy in their case, we are told, means far more than ignorance of letters. It means a condition . . . compounded of ignorance, superstition, shiftlessness, vulgarity, and vice. There may be gross exaggerations in the tales we hear of the Voodoo paganism which, under the name of religion, lurks, if it does not prevail, in the cotton and cane growing districts of the South known as the *black belt*. There is, however, enough of truth in these statements to call for investigation and action.[12]

There is no condemnation of the whites for perpetrating the crime of enslavement and the inflicting of ignorance upon Africans. Nevertheless, Hayes made it clear that the problem had to be attacked at the level of education and religion. It was his belief and that of other authorities that Voodoo might *prevail* among African people in 1890.

No wonder Washington was such a magnetic presence in 1895 when he gave his Atlanta Exposition Speech—he touched upon all the issues that had been raised at First Mohonk Conference in 1890 as well as the subsequent conference in 1891, where attendees adopted a platform that included support for industrial education for black people. The path for Washington's brand of African self-help had been cleared of the boulders of politics and discussions of equality—now religion and industrial education or, perhaps, Christian education as a combination would rule the upward spiral to American citizenship.

In the early twentieth century in Nashville, Tennessee, the outstanding preachers G. P. Bowser and Marshall Keeble started the Nashville Christian Institute, a school following the model of Tuskegee Institute. Others started independent colleges in the basements of their churches, where they taught literacy, history, literature, science, and practical professions in the Tuskegee mode.

One of the most successful schools began soon after Tuskegee, not in the South but in the North. This was the Bordentown School, founded in 1888 by the Reverend Walter Rice, seven years after Tuskegee. This popular minister of the African Methodist Episcopal Church had been enslaved in Laurens, South Carolina. He was born in 1845 and fought as a volunteer with the Union Army during the Civil War. When the war was over, Rice made his way northward to New Jersey, where he sought his own education.

The school that the Reverend Rice founded was initially called the Ironsides Normal School. Like Tuskegee, the INS was to concentrate on industries that would enable students to become self-supporting. Rice was a popular African Methodist Episcopal Church preacher who saw the school as an answer to the problem of unemployment, ignorance, and indiscipline in many young people. Rice was convinced that he could create a school equal to any among the whites in discipline, scholarship, skills, and sports. His religious denomination, the African Methodist Episcopal Church, founded in 1793 by Richard Allen, would dominate the leadership of the black community during the second half of the nineteenth century. The school's success was immediate and authentic. Students did extremely well in scholarship, agriculture, and athletics. As Washington had done in Alabama to make Tuskegee independent, so Rice did in New Jersey to make his school a state project. Rice appealed to New Jersey to legislate state control of the school, just the opposite of what Washington had asked Alabama to do. New Jersey accommodated Rice and made the school New Jersey's vocational institution. Its motto was that "knowledge without goodness is dangerous." As a boarding school, Bordentown Manual and Industrial School, as it was called, was able to provide sound educational and moral supervision to its 400–500 selected students on a year-round basis.

James Gregory, a colleague and disciple of W. E. B. Du Bois, was the next leader of the school. However, as a graduate of Howard University and a believer in equal political rights for African Americans, Gregory brought some intense anti-discrimination rhetoric to his speeches. Booker T. Washington was invited to Bordentown School by the New Jersey state legislature in 1913. Soon thereafter the board of the school chose a disciple of Washington's, William Valentine, who had taught at Tuskegee, to lead the school. Bordentown was paid visits by Paul Robeson and Albert Einstein, and many other famous people visited and lectured at the school. One of the legendary leaders of Black Studies, Barbara Wheeler, who taught at City University, the University of South Florida, and Kean University, was a student in the school in 1948. The staff were expected to keep the school impeccably clean, and the students were required to hold up the school's reputation for orderliness. When it declined during the period of integration and finally closed its doors in 1955, many African Americans considered it a loss to the development of black leadership in New Jersey. All across the United

States there were schools such as Bordentown, Piney Woods, and the Nashville Christian Institute started by dedicated men and women who made personal sacrifices of time, money, and emotion to insure the success of their community members who had been enslaved, segregated, and discriminated against. These men and women were heroes of the Golden Order, a name I have given to those who without national fame or prestige put their own lives at risk in order to save others, often in large numbers.

Alexander Crummell and the Negro Academy

To the degree that Walter Rice was an institution builder committed to discipline and excellence, Alexander Crummell, the epitome of ethics and philosophy, was destined to become the late nineteenth century's African intellectual par excellence. Older than Walter Rice, Booker T. Washington, or W. E. B. Du Bois, Crummell was the embodiment of their examples of educational refinement and cultural complexity.[13] Crummell was a per-aa of knowledge, wisdom, experience, and majesty that made him the epitome of erudition and good manners. Indeed, when he died in 1898 in Red Bank, New Jersey, three years after Washington's fateful speech at the Atlanta Exposition, his life had been a glittering example of humanity's best attempt at perfection. This is not to say that Crummell did not have his critics or did not possess a stubbornness that often led to mistakes, but rather to say that few persons of his day—or any day—ever lived so fully for the intellect as Crummell.

Alexander Crummell was born to a free woman, Charity Hicks, and an enslaved African, Boston Crummell. His parents taught him very early that he was the equal to any human ever born. He did not grow up with feelings of inferiority or self-hatred. He thought of himself as a pure African and believed that his contributions in scholarship, ethics, or philosophy should be put to the use of raising the level of consciousness of the African world. Abolitionism was the earliest political doctrine taught in his home and it was the wisdom, politics, arguments, and values he learned at an early age that set his direction for life. In fact, Samuel Cornish and John Russwurm, the founders of the first black newspaper in America, *Freedom's Journal*, were no strangers to the Crummell family and the paper was often published within Crummell's home.

It is easy to imagine the conversation between the Crummells and their editor friends about the state of the African people. At an early age Alexander heard stories about Africans who achieved extraordinary feats, who escaped their captors to fly to freedom, or who fought against their enslavers to gain victory. Toussaint L'Ouverture, Dessalines, and Christophe were as eagerly discussed as the insurrections of Nat Turner, Denmark Vesey, and Gabriel Prosser. Few young blacks had ever had such intense training in race pride and race knowledge, that is, the history of the African people, as did Crummell. He was fitted out with a Pan-African spirit, a self-determining attitude, and a strict discipline even before he left home to begin his work with the American Anti-Slavery Society in New York City.

Alexander Crummell's father, Boston, shaped him as one would shape an athlete for a contest or a warrior for battle. Apart from his parents and their abolitionist comrades, Crummell's education was in the African Free School No. 2 and the Canal Street High School in New York. When Crummell finished Canal High School he attended the Noyes Academy in New Hampshire at the same time as his friend Henry Highland Garnett, who would distinguish himself as an orator and anti-slavery fighter. Northern whites who disliked the education of blacks, especially in integrated schools, burned the Noyes Academy to the ground, Crummell and Garnett barely escaping with their lives. Soon afterwards Crummell was enrolled in the Oneida Institute in New York State. Perhaps he reasoned, while a student at Oneida, that becoming a minister might help him teach the values that would allow whites to see that blacks were just as deserving of the respect that whites wished for themselves. He wanted to pursue the Episcopalian faith because of its relatively liberal position within the Protestant Movement. One more racist reaction to his ambition, however, caused him to re-examine his path. The General Theological Seminary refused to admit him, solely because he was African. Nevertheless, he would not be deterred and with the assistance of several Episcopalian clergymen who tutored him and gave him instructions he was able to gain an ordination in 1842.

Crummell found that many whites would not come to listen to him preach. With low attendance and some outright hostility among Episcopalians, Crummell made his way to Philadelphia, where he met with one of the leading bishops in the church, Bishop Onderdonk, to ask for a larger audience for his message. Onderdonk replied to this request with this stipulation: "I will receive you into this diocese on one condition: No Negro priest can sit in my church convention and no Negro church must ask for representation there."[14] Crummell, seeing this as the marginalization of himself and the black race, said, "I will never enter your diocese on such terms." Angered by the stance of the American Episcopalians, Crummell took his campaign for support to the very doors of the Church of England, from which the Episcopalian Church in the United States gained its authority. In 1847 he was given an audience at the Church of the Messiah and was able to raise £2,000 to support his congregation. He inquired into study at Oxford or Cambridge and when Benjamin Brodie, Wilberforce, Stanley Froude, and Macaulay sponsored him to Queens' College, Cambridge, he took the opportunity and completed the program, although he had to take the finals twice to obtain his degree. Because he was such a compelling speaker, traveling a tried-and-true route among English liberals that had seen the likes of Charles Remond, Frederick Douglass, and a host of other Africans from the United States, Alexander Crummell became an expert on all issues related to blacks in the United States. He answered numerous questions, gave speeches on the future of the race, and discussed the opposition to freedom among Southern whites.

However, British liberalism could not cure Crummell of the belief that whites, even in England, felt that blacks were inferior. They would never concede to the idea of racial equality despite the fact that whites in Britain as well as in America had contributed to the dangerous doctrine of white racial supremacy by promoting the enslavement of Africans. White liberals seemed to be at odds with the promotion of African freedom, liberation, and equality. Their objectives appeared more paternalistic to Crummell, who began to formulate his own ideas of Pan-Africanism.

Alexander Crummell, like Martin R. Delany, was a prototypical Pan-Africanist. Crummell's belief was that in order to achieve racial advancement in the arts, sciences, culture, or religion, blacks had to form a worldwide union because the condition of blacks in Great Britain, the Caribbean, Africa, and South America was the same as the situation in North America. This realization was monumental and would become one of the leading edges of a new African way of thinking about racial advancement. With such a fierce determination to forge racial solidarity there was but one action to take: he had to relocate to Liberia.

Alexander Crummell arrived in Liberia in 1853. Already the colony of Americo-Liberians had been established for a few years. But Crummell felt that it was better late than never for him to join the great movement for racial advancement. He would be a missionary for the Episcopal Church of the United States to work among the non-Christian populations. Influenced by some of the early teachings in his home, especially the idea that colonization was a ruse to send troublesome Africans to Africa while holding a servile population in slavery in perpetuity, Crummell had been against the colonization scheme. Now he was convinced that it had benefits worthy of his time and talents. Crummell has been criticized for seeking to Christianize, enlighten, and civilize Africans. He believed that he had a duty, along with other Africans who had learned the information that the West had to teach, to return to Africa to spread the knowledge of civilization. He neither understood nor appreciated the majesty and complexity of African civilization and made no attempt apparently to master the intricacies of local ethnic histories and identities of Africans. This would be a mistake that would return to haunt the Liberian colony on numerous occasions.

After twenty years of serving as a successful pastor and professor in Liberia, Crummell returned to the United States in 1873, having missed the turbulence of the Civil War and much of the Reconstruction. Liberia proved not to be the Promised Land, although he still had his doubts about the possibilities for Africans in the United States. When he returned to America, Crummell ran St Mary's Episcopal Mission until he took over as rector of St Luke's Episcopal Church in Washington, DC, from 1875 to 1894, making it one of the most influential churches in the city. He was able to meet the leading African Americans of his day while serving at St Luke's and he never stopped talking about racial solidarity as a way to advance the entire African population. He had seen many disappointments and experienced the frustrations of trying to bring consciousness to an entire black nation, yet he never tired of the dream of a disciplined, proud, audacious people who would work for black nationalism, self-determination, and economic uplift. One last effort at solidarity near the end of his life would inspire him and rally black intellectuals to his call like nothing else had done, and that was the creation of the American Negro Academy in 1897. Crummell gave the ANA its mission and objectives and within a year, exhausted, he passed away, in Red Bank, New Jersey.

By the time of his death he had revolutionized the thinking of leading Africans and influenced thousands, including Du Bois, James Weldon Johnson, Marcus Garvey, Paul Laurence Dunbar, and others. Du Bois wrote of him in his brilliant essay "Of Alexander Crummell" in the twelfth chapter of *The Souls of Black Folk*, as follows:

> Out of the tempation of Hate, and burned by the fire of Despair, triumphant over Doubt, and steeled by Sacrifice against Humiliation, he turned at last home across the waters, humble and strong, gentle and determined. He bent to all the gibes and prejudices, to all hatred and discrimination, with that rare courtesy which is the armor of pure souls. He fought among his own, the low, the grasping, and the wicked, with that unbending righteousness which is the sword of the just. He never faltered, he seldom complained; he simply worked, inspiring the young, rebuking the old, helping the weak, guiding the strong. So he grew, and brought within his wide influence all that was best of those who walk within the Veil.[15]

The Episcopal Church honors Crummell with a feast day on its liturgical calendar on September 10.

Du Bois was twenty-nine years old when Crummell died, and the death of the great man deeply impacted him. Five years later he would publish *The Souls of Black Folk*, with his assessment of Crummell. Born in Great Barrington, Massachusetts, in 1868, educated at Fisk, Harvard, and Berlin, Du Bois claimed the mantle of intellectual leadership by both the force of his personality and his prolific pen. Inspired by the same desire to excel, and to demonstrate in excellence the potential of the African person, Du Bois championed all causes, took on every debate, and scored success after success with his argumentative skill. Perhaps as Du Bois himself would see it, one could say that from the depths of his emotional feeling, agitated by the system that would deny him and others justice because of color or creed, angered by the incompetence and insolence of racism, and stung by the spirit of eternal optimism, he focused his exceptionally powerful intellect on recovery and revision of the African historical text. He refused all attempts to put him in his place and with a unique and unyielding character he ascended over all those who would drag his feet in the mud of ignorance, and showered those who knew him, who read him, and who spoke to him, with his own generosity and unfaltering sense of righteousness and truth.

The Baton is Passed to a New Class of Geniuses

As destiny would have it, a year after Crummell's death Percy Lavon Julian was born on April 11, 1899 and would become one of the greatest African American scientists, ushering in a new era in chemical synthesis of medicinal drugs from plants. Julian was the fulfillment, in many ways, of Crummell's man of science and knowledge, because he applied himself to his studies diligently and demonstrated by his work on human hormones, steroids, progesterone, and testosterone that plants could reveal their secrets for science and health. It was his discovery of cortisone, which laid the basis for birth control pills, that made him the dean of African American chemists. He received more than 130 patents for his chemical work and was the first African American to receive a doctorate in chemistry. Julian was the first African American chemist inducted into the National Academy of Sciences.

This was an era of grand men and women who had high purposes. One sees this in the work of James Weldon Johnson and Julian Abele among others. They took their race consciousness seriously because they knew how much the white community despised African Americans. Johnson, for example, was a genius whose expertise as an author, critic, politician, diplomat, journalist, poet, anthologist, educator, lawyer, songwriter, and activist was unassailable. Johnson demonstrated his versatility in literature and music very early in his career and was among the first black professors at New York University.

Johnson was born to Helen Louise Dillet and James Johnson in Jacksonville, Florida, on June 17, 1871. In 1887 Johnson enrolled at Atlanta University. His experience teaching children in rural Georgia inspired him to do as much as he could to raise the level of his people. He was self-confident and smart, and pursued a professional career with the idea of being the best example of his race he could.

In 1897 he was the first black to be admitted to the Florida Bar Exam since Reconstruction. Johnson was given a two-hour examination before three white attorneys and a judge.

In the year 1901, Johnson moved to New York City, along with his brother, J. Rosamond Johnson, who wrote music. They produced popular theater pieces such as "Tell Me, Dusky Maiden" and "Nobody's Looking but the Owl and the Moon." He also wrote the lyrics "Lift Ev'ry Voice and Sing," which was later adopted by the National Association for the Advancement of Colored People, called the Negro National Anthem, and soon became, after "Happy Birthday," the most popular song among African Americans.

The U.S. government sent James Weldon Johnson to Puerto Cabello, Venezuela, as the U.S. consul in 1906. He was later transferred to Nicaragua after serving for three years in Venezuela. While in Latin America he published the successful *Autobiography of an Ex-Colored Man* in 1912.

In 1916 Johnson was commissioned as the national organizer for the National Association for the Advancement of Colored People (NAACP) and was later promoted to executive secretary. As soon as he took over as national organizer, he changed the agenda by involving people in parades, and brought about more legal involvement. He brought 10,000 African Americans to 5th Avenue on July 28, 1917.

Johnson was sent to Haiti by the U.S. government in 1920 to investigate the conditions since the U.S. Marines had occupied the country from 1915. At this time he published a series of articles in *The Nation*, where he wrote about reformation of the economic life of Haiti. He criticized the brutality he had seen against the Haitians by Americans. A year later he agitated for the Dyer Anti-Lynching Bill of 1921.

In the 1920s his works as a poet, editor, and critic made him one of the most influential leaders in the Harlem Renaissance. In 1930 Johnson resigned from the NAACP to accept the Spence Chair of Creative Literature at Fisk University. In the university he lectured on literature and also on a wide range of issues related to the life and civil rights of black Americans. He held the chair until 1938.

James Weldon Johnson was killed on June 26, 1938 when his car was struck by a train near his summer home in Wiscasset, Maine. Thousands attended his funeral in Harlem, where he was eulogized as one of America's top intellectuals.

One of Johnson's contemporaries was Julian Abele (1881–1950), who emerged as a leading architect after graduating from the Pennsylvania School of Fine Arts. Abele was the first black to be admitted to the architecture school and he demonstrated extraordinary brilliance from the beginning of his academic career. After graduating, he joined an architectural firm that gave him control over many of its projects, including designing many buildings on the campus of Duke University. Abele helped design the Philadelphia Museum of Art and the Free Library of Philadelphia, and would become one of the inspirations for outstanding African American architects and artists.

Philip Freelon, also born in Philadelphia, who is well known as the founder and designer of the Freelon Group of award-winning architects, along with Max Bond and David Adjaye, of the Smithsonian National Museum of African American History, created an international stir in museum designs with the creation of the Reginald F. Lewis Museum of African American History and Culture of Baltimore. However, although Phil Freelon received some of his inspiration for excellence from Julian Abele, it was clearly a part of his family tradition to see all art forms as expressions of dignity and spirit. Freelon married the six-time Grammy nominee Nnenna Freelon, and each of their three children shows artistic strength in either art, music, or communication. Indeed, Freelon's daughter, Maya, traveled to Madagascar in 2010 to become one of the first African Americans to open an exhibit of art in that country. Notwithstanding the more contemporary examples of this African American family, it was

Philip Freelon's grandfather, the impressionist Allan Randall Freelon Sr, who established the family's artistic tradition.

While Julian Abele was mastering architecture at the Pennsylvania School of Fine Arts, another artistic talent, Allan Randall Freelon (1895–1960) was becoming a master impressionist artist. Although his name may not be as famous as that of Horace Pippin (1888–1946) or Henry Ossawa Tanner (1859–1937), Freelon was another highly gifted black artist who made his way in the art world of America against all the odds. He had been inspired as others had been by the genius of Tanner and Pippin, two early black masters. In fact, Henry Ossawa Tanner had been, like Freelon, raised in an affluent home among highly educated people and was dedicated to the making of pictures. In 1879 Tanner enrolled at the Pennsylvania Academy of Fine Arts and once he graduated moved to Atlanta, in 1889, to find his place in the world among middle-class blacks. He was disappointed by the lack of interest the people had in art; he himself saw it as one of the great instruments of knowledge and refinement. Tanner was not the first and would not be the last artist to leave the United States and move to Paris. He left for the City of Light in 1891. Two years later he was back in the United States due to illness.

In 1893 most American artists painted African Americans negatively but Henry Ossawa Tanner wanted to represent black subjects with dignity, writing, "Many of the artists who have represented Negro life have seen only the comic, the ludicrous side of it, and have lacked sympathy with and appreciation for the warm big heart that dwells within such a rough exterior." The banjo had become a stereotypical symbol of imbecility and childlikeness, so Tanner took the symbol and created *The Banjo Lesson*, which showed the dignity of a man teaching his young son in a loving way.

Figure 6.7 Albert Barnes and Horace Pippin, benefactor and artist. Image courtesy of Charles L. Blockson Afro-American Collection, Temple University Libraries.

In much the same way, Allan Freelon, the impressionist, went in the opposite direction from most of the artists of the Harlem Renaissance. His idea was to faithfully capture the impression of an object, a scene, a person. When Horace Pippin, who was born in 1888, came into human consciousness as a self-taught black artist, he painted "Domino Players" and "John Brown Going to His Hanging." Pippin fought with the famous 369th Infantry regiment in World War I and was awarded the Croix de Guerre after being shot in the arm a month before the ending of the war. He died in 1946.

By 1940 Freelon was operating in the highest elite circles of the African American community. He knew that his art was different from what was expected of the black artists of the day, yet he felt free enough to produce a work condemning racial oppression for the NAACP-sponsored exhibit called "Barbecue—American Style" on the injustice of lynching. While Freelon may have disagreed with certain aspects of Alain Locke's renaissance, he found himself in his own historical experiences and activities.

Lois Maillou Jones and Elizabeth Catlett, one as a painter and the other principally as a sculptor, carved their own pathways through the abundance of art forms and expressions during and after the Harlem Renaissance. They internationalized their art by evoking themes from Haiti, Jamaica, Brazil, and Mexico. During the 1950s and into the 1960s these innovative artists revolutionized the thinking of the African American community. Jones lived in Haiti, painted there, and returned to the States to live in Washington, DC, where she continued her dramatic Haitian-influenced and -inspired work. Catlett married a Mexican and moved to Cuernavaca, Mexico. One could never record the work and names of the thousands of other artists who contributed to the grand flow of African American history in the latter half of the twentieth century, but these two giants stand out as the precursors and inspirations to Faith Ringgold, Varnette Honeywood, Pheoris West, Richard Wyatt, Maya Freelon Asante, Bing Davis, Charles Searles, and Jeff Donaldson.

History is never made in a vacuum. What the Harlem Renaissance and earlier artists and writers recognized was that all achievements of Africans were interconnected in the minds of the black community. If enslavement did anything concretely for representatives from more than one hundred African ethnic groups, it made common achievements of individual successes. In the artistic field this was quite true. One could not look at Abele, Freelon, Pippin, and Tanner as being detached from those who were artists before them.

Thomas Day was the first recorded African American artist. Day was a free man who moved to North Carolina from the North in the 1820s. He had been educated in Boston and Washington, DC. By 1823, when he moved to North Carolina and opened his own studio to make furniture, he had already acquired a reputation. Day's artistic designs, reflecting entrenched African ideas, almost as if he was intent on repeating from memory the designs and concepts that had been passed to him from his African forebears, made him a unique furniture- and cabinetmaker.

Of course, it is not a long stretch of the imagination to realize that there were other artists, many of whose names are lost in eternal anonymity, and others whose reputations survived them but whose real essence was distorted by the slave experience. One early African American artist, for example, is David the Potter, who may have been the first to mark the ceramic tradition among Africans in America.

However, by the middle of the nineteenth century the talent of Africans was being displayed in many circles outside of the plantation. Robert Duncanson painted romantic landscapes in the style of the Hudson River school. For example, by 1851 he had painted "Blue Hole Flood Waters, Little Miami River," which showed a wilderness scene quite familiar to many Africans who had escaped from bondage. Edward Bannister and Edmonia Lewis were dominant at the 1876 U.S. Centennial Exposition, held in Philadelphia. Edmonia Lewis exhibited her powerful sculpture "The Death of Cleopatra," which made a historically accurate but controversial point about the African queen's race. According to the black press, Lewis' sculpture, the only one by a black person of nearly seven hundred on display, received the greatest attention and generated the most discussion during the Centennial. However, the excitement of her work did not bring her financial stability and she moved to Italy to continue her work. William Wetmore Story, a Bostonian, had created a sculpture of Cleopatra nearly twenty years earlier, expressing in his portrayal the African-ness of the queen, but he never received the criticism that Lewis provoked. Instead, Story's 1858 work was called one of archaeological exactitude.

Paul Robeson and the Continuing Fight for Dignity

If there had been no blacks to fight for justice then the system of oppression that existed in America from the seventeenth to the twentieth centuries would have been perfected and a race of humans of servile in nature and forever enslaved would have become common. But this was not to be, because too many Africans with the love of self, and what little culture remained after the enslavement, stood up against all forms of oppression ready to fight for human rights. African Americans did everything conceivable to demonstrate prowess and intelligence in any walk of life. Indeed, Elizabeth "Bessie" Coleman, born on January 26, 1892, literally flew into history by becoming the first female pilot of African descent, and the first person of African descent to gain an international pilot license. After taking French lessons and flight lessons in Paris, Bessie Coleman returned to the United States and entered the business of barnstorming flights. She died on April 30, 1926 in a barnstorming plane crash at the age of thirty-four. Her courage and adventurous nature defied the stereotypes of her birth, race, and class, and she added to the incredible record of African American liberation. So many African American men and women challenged the restrictions of race that the sieve of freedom ran openly toward the eventual end of oppression. Of course there were those who felt that it had to be helped on its way, and no one was a more focused champion of freedom than Paul Leroy Robeson, six years junior to Bessie Coleman.

Paul Robeson was born in Princeton, New Jersey, on April 9, 1898, the last of five children. His birth in New Jersey, coming in the year of the death of Alexander Crummell, was like the passing of a baton from one giant heroic figure to another. Robeson's father, William Drew Robeson, had escaped slavery from Matins County, North Carolina, as a teenager, joined the Union Army, and worked his way through Lincoln College in Pennsylvania. He received his divinity degree in 1873. He was a man of powerful ambitions and an intellect to accompany his work. He preached for the Princeton Presbyterian Church and later for the African Methodist Episcopal Zion Churches in Somerville and Westfield, New Jersey. Robeson's mother, Maria Bustill, a Philadelphia schoolteacher, was from a noted free black family that included a grandfather who is reputed to have baked bread for George Washington's troops during the Revolutionary War. Unfortunately for Robeson, his mother died from burns received in a household fire when he was only six years old. His father became his model for manhood, dignity, erudition, and outspokenness. Learning the lessons of discipline and hard work early in life from his father and his older siblings prepared Paul Robeson for a productive life.[16]

Writing in his revealing autobiography *Here I Stand*, Robeson said, "The glory of my boyhood years was my father. I loved him like no one in all the world . . . How proudly, as a boy, I walked at his side, my hand in his, as he moved among the people."[17]

Yet Robeson's life was like that of many other black youths in New Jersey and other Northern states. At the turn of the twentieth century he attended New Jersey public schools and was one of only two African Americans in high school, but always felt the pressure to succeed in a positive way to demonstrate the dignity and intelligence that he saw in his father. He was a star athlete in four sports: football, basketball, track, and baseball. In addition to these achievements he was also one of the top students in the school. He won a a four-year state scholarship to attend Rutgers despite the attempt of his bigoted high school principal to prevent him from taking the qualifying examination. Robeson believed that this experience convinced him that even if he was denied equality he was not inferior. This recognition of personal worth despite bigotry has steeled numerous blacks against personal bias on the parts of those in authority. It is a realization that bigots have no other way to feel powerful except to deny opportunity to those who should have received it. Nevertheless, the principal's reaction should have prepared Robeson for the more intense racism he would face at Rutgers. There had been no question of his entering Princeton College in his own hometown, whose racist policies persisted well into the twentieth century, but at the small Rutgers in New Brunswick Robeson was still shocked by the hostility. He could not live in the dormitory because the white students objected, so he found a black family in the city who rented a room to him during the entire four years of his college experience. There were only two blacks on campus during his entire college time. Nevertheless, he was prepared to demonstrate his ability in sports and in the classroom. However, during the tryout for the football team he was targeted by the other players for especially rough play and sustained injuries that required hospitalization. Robeson said his brother, Benjamin, urged him not to quit the team because it was a matter of race pride and he had to show that he was not a quitter.

When he returned to the team one player purposely stomped on his hand between plays. When the bigot tried it again, Robeson in one motion picked him up over his head and was about to slam him to the ground when the coach, fearing for the man's life, yelled, "Robeson, you are on the team."[18]

Robeson became the team's star, but his locker always stood separate from the white boys', and when they traveled he had to room with one of the assistant coaches. Some called Robeson a superman because of his speed and strength, and he also had the quality of determination that had been encouraged by his father. In college he earned fourteen varsity letters in football, baseball, basketball, discus, shot put, and the javelin.

Racism conspires to distort reality and to cripple rationality everywhere, and it did so in Robeson's college life. He was a leading singer in the Glee Club and one of Rutgers' best debaters, but he did not forget his commitment to his family and to the African American community to excel in everything he did. He was elected to the highest academic honor society, the Phi Beta Kappa, during his junior year, and in his senior year was the class valedictorian. So impressive was Robeson and so much more dignified and advanced than his peers that the class prophecy was that he would be governor of New Jersey by 1940 and a significant leader of the African Americans. He became neither the governor nor the leader of any movement but he was clearly one of the most outstanding artists and opinion-leaders of his century.

Robeson started Columbia Law School in 1920 and managed to support himself financially by working at the post office, acting, coaching basketball teams, and playing professional football. Of all of his extramural activities it seemed that Robeson preferred acting—or perhaps it was just the easiest way to financially support his educational objectives. Whatever the case, he secured a role in the play *Voodoo* in New York and then went with the company to London to act in the play there with a new name, *Taboo*. He was a successful actor—not since Ira Aldridge, the African American actor who had played in Shakespeare dramas long before, had England been so taken by the charisma of an African actor. It was during this journey that Robeson's long-time musical associate and accompanist Lawrence Brown became his friend and leading musician for thirty years. Robeson married Eslanda Cardozo Goode, a vivacious and dynamic woman, in August 1921. She graduated from Columbia University in the same year with a degree in chemistry, and worked at Presbyterian Hospital as the first black analytical chemist in pathology. She had planned to attend medical school but decided that working alongside her husband was the best possible world for the two of them. She became Robeson's agent and manager. Robeson received his law degree in 1923 and was immediately hired by a white law firm that confined him to researching briefs. Whites considered it unwise to have a black lawyer represent a client in court. When a white secretary refused to take dictation from him, he simply put on his hat and walked out of the door, ending his legal career.

If Robeson had not left the job as an attorney, the world would not have known the magnificence of his ethos. Harlem was the center of the intellectual and artistic African world at this time and Robeson needed it as much as it needed him. His marriage to Eslanda was fortuitous because she was a graceful and dynamic personality in her own right who enjoyed managing her husband's affairs and setting the social agenda. They knew numerous leading figures in the Harlem Renaissance and, of course, those people knew them. Among the names mentioned in Eslanda's diaries are black and white personalities of the time such as Langston Hughes, Countee Cullen, Theodore Dreiser, James Weldon Johson, Eugene O'Neill, Carl Van Vechten, George Gershwin, Walter White, and many others. The force of Paul Robeson's vast charisma was enough to indicate to all those he met that his intentions were to become a successful leader in the African community. His confidence, quiet internal strength, eagerness to succeed, and vitality of spirit constituted inner knowledge of his own destiny.

Robeson opened in two of Eugene O'Neill's plays in 1924—*The Emperor Jones* and *All God's Chillun Got Wings*. The plays evoked powerful emotions in the American nation, with the second play and its interracial marriage causing some whites to issue death threats to Eugene O'Neill's son for his father having written the play! Yet the audiences loved the work of Robeson. His colleagues would bring him out to the applause of people who shouted thanks for his having given them a chance to see a master perform. His intense emotional control and powerful delivery were evidence of his mastery of the stage. However, this was only a prologue to the majesty of Robeson's art because the next year, on April 19, 1925, he sang a repertoire of African American Spirituals that established him as one of the premier concert soloists in the country.

Figure 6.8 Walter White, fearless leader of the NAACP during its toughest period of fights against racism. Image courtesy of Charles L. Blockson Afro-American Collection, Temple University Libraries.

Already an international presence, at least in London with his stage acting, Robeson went on a national tour in 1926–1927 to sing before sold-out American audiences and then decided to move to London after landing the leading role in *Show Boat*'s spectacular opening at Drury Lane Theatre in April 1928. It was here that he first sang the song "Ole Man River," written especially for him. In London, Robeson was lionized by the public. His son, Paul Jr, was born in London and his mother-in-law traveled there to assist with the child. Robeson performed all over Western and Central Europe, with audiences standing at the end of his performances, demanding more from one of the major superstars of the era. Some audiences said that he had surpassed the great Russian singer Feodor Chaliapin in his range and depth, but Robeson simply sought to define the African culture through his personality and his music. The roots of his culture were long and deep and his soul was equal to those roots.

The political sentiments expressed by the poor, the downtrodden, and the social outcasts touched him emotionally and he felt, as a black American, that he could not escape the shared suffering of the world; Robeson threw himself into the issues that confronted the poor and working-class people of Europe. This was when his social feelings began to express themselves in an intellectual way. George Bernard Shaw and other socialists had an immediate impact on his political spirit.

For more than ten years Robeson was based in London, touring both the United States and Europe. He opened in *Othello* on May 19, 1930 at London's Savoy Theatre, becoming, after Ira Aldridge, one of the key black interpreters of the role. There were twenty curtain calls on the opening night, indicating that the performance had struck a chord with the audience.

Robeson also made nine feature films in the United States and London. In his films he tried to personify the dignity that he believed was essential for humanity. He saw his role expand to support the Irish people, the Welsh people, and the Russian poor. As his social consciousness grew, so did his repertoire. He put the African American Spirituals and the songs of Mozart, Beethoven, and Mussorgsky on the same level as folksongs of the Welsh and Russian masses, showing always the universality of emotion. He took courses in African and world cultures at the School of Oriental Studies at the University of London. He studied more than twenty languages, including Arabic, Japanese, Chinese, Czech, Danish, Efik, Finnish, French, German, Greek, Hebrew, Hindustani, Hungarian, Italian, Japanese, Kiswahili, Norwegian, Polish, Russian, Spanish, and Yiddish.

In Berlin in 1934 on his way to Moscow, Robeson felt the racism of fascist Germany, yet he was overwhelmed by the Russians' warmth and their respect for him.

There was something profoundly human in the way Robeson saw the world. He was affected by the injustice in the political, social, and economic realms. When he appeared at the 1937 rally at London's Albert Hall in support of the Spanish Civil War, Robeson made a signature statement that was to become his standard. He said, "The artist must take sides. He must elect to fight for freedom or slavery. I have made my choice, I had no alternative." The audience erupted in thunderous applause and when he went to the front lines in Spain and sang his freedom songs it is reported that the guns fell silent as the soldiers listened.

At the end of the war the great Robeson returned to New York and lived there from 1940 to 1947. He believed that the United States had to defeat fascism and he wanted to encourage the fight against Nazi Germany. Both black and white Americans saw Paul Robeson as a hero who had taken up the broad fight against discrimination, slavery, and fascism both at home and abroad. In the spirit of President Franklin Delano Roosevelt's New Deal policies, Robeson delved into the political fray, speaking about progressive social and economic rights. He sang to armed forces at overseas bases and participated in war bond rallies to fire up the nation against the Nazis. He received commendations from outstanding politicians and public figures, including First Lady Eleanor Roosevelt. Immensely popular, Robeson was certain, however, given his outspokenness, to run afoul of the conservative sentiments in his own country, although he was still the highest-paid concert performer in 1941. On his forty-sixth birthday tribute at New York City armory, 12,000 people showed up, including Joe Louis, Duke Ellington, Lillian Hellman, and Mary McLeod Bethune, who said of Robeson that he was "the tallest tree in our forest."

In the midst of the war efforts there were attempts to advance racial progress in the United States. A. Philip Randolph and the Brotherhood of Sleeping Car Porters as well as the National Association for the Advancement of Colored People were making noises about the discrimination against black soldiers who were fighting to liberate other people.

In October 1943, Paul Robeson opened in the Theater Guild's production of *Othello* to ten curtain calls and nearly thirty minutes of applause. The production broke the record for the longest-running Shakespearean play ever on Broadway. It was accepted that Robeson was the greatest actor on the American stage, and Margaret Webster said that at "the moment he stepped on that stage, he was not only a black man, but a great black man, a man of stature." A critic writing in *Variety* magazine is quoted as saying that "Robeson's performance is of such a stature that no white man should ever presume to play it again."

Robeson's script for life would ultimately become the script for the most authentic African American heroes. He was a courageous person with an enormous capacity to sense the emotional reactions of his people, and yet balance his art and his politics in the most productive manner. This would become in thirty years or so the predominant pattern of Muhammad Ali, speaking from a pinnacle of greatness about the distress of his people. Like Ali later, Robeson would have to fend off his enemies. He was a leader of the Council of African Affairs, a progressive and liberal group of intellectuals and artists devoted to advancing African and African American liberation from colonialism and segregation. The NAACP named him the winner of the Spingarn Medal in 1946 for his concern about "the common man of every race, color, religion, and nationality."

During the same year Paul Robeson, Albert Einstein and W. E. B. Du Bois led an integrated delegation to President Harry Truman's office to petition him to support anti-lynching legislation. Truman's response was that this was not the appropriate time for legislation. His reaction angered the delegation and Robeson's response was that if the government did not protect blacks then they would have to resort to armed defense of themselves. President Truman ended the meeting abruptly.

This might have been the point at which Robeson's popularity and influence threatened the established order, and he was hounded by reporters asking him if he were a Communist. He was subpoenaed by the California legislature to answer questions, ostensibly about the Ku Klux Klan, that turned out to be about his own activities, which some had labeled "un-American" because of his attacks on racism. Thus, in 1947 he announced at a concert in Salt Lake City that he would suspend his performing career in order to fight against racism.

When he sought to return to his concert schedule he found that all of his engagements had been cancelled. The Federal Bureau of Investigation is believed to have been responsible for censoring Robeson. If a concert promoter attempted to rent an auditorium to host Robeson the FBI would visit the promoter and the offer would be withdrawn. In 1949 he attended the World Peace Congress in Paris and told the audience that "It is unthinkable that American Negroes could go to war on behalf of those who have oppressed us for generations against the Soviet Union which in one generation has raised our people to full human dignity." He was immediately labeled a traitor to his country and denounced by some of the leading African American organizations. Robeson's income dropped from $150,000 to $6,000 by 1952 and he had lost a lot of his friends. The FBI documents found through the Freedom of Information Act show that in 1943 FBI Director J. Edgar Hoover placed him on the custodial detention list as a threat to national security. The American surveillance agencies considered him to be brilliant but naïve, and hateful of America because of its racism. His passport was canceled in 1950 because United States officials thought that it was not in the best interest of the nation to have him travel abroad where he had been for years extremely active politically in behalf of the independence of the colonial peoples of Africa. Then began a period of intense persecution of Robeson as the United States authorities sought to isolate and destitute him. He was prevented from traveling and pursuing his performance career, so he organized the Othello Recording Corporation to produce his own albums. The House Committee on Un-American Activities in 1956 questioned Robeson and then accused him of being a Communist. He invoked the Fifth Amendment and argued for his right to express his opinions. Always a student of history and a scholar of culture, Robeson pursued every conceivable relationship between folk and classical music, studied the five-tone pentatonic scale, examined aspects of African folk culture, wrote on the origin and power of jazz, and prepared himself for an eventual return to the stage.

Progressive elements around the world protested the taking of the Robesons' passports. In 1958 they were finally able to travel again and they went to Europe, where Paul was greeted by admiring audiences throughout England, France, and the Soviet Union. He spoke and sang of freedom to massive audiences, some who had only heard of him by reputation. The extent of his power as an artist and as a human being of dignity has yet to be revealed in the literature. Europe loved him probably because he was to the Europeans what they had hoped the American vision would be of the world. He was the new, the innovative, the possible, and the future of the world. Britain equaled the Soviet Union in respect for Robeson and he took tea at the House of Lords, read scripture from the pulpit of St Paul's Cathedral, and sang on national television. Most of all, for his stature and his economic situation, he accepted to star in *Othello* at the Shakespeare Memorial Theatre at Stratford-upon-Avon. The performance and the play were both successful and he played for seven months in England. At the end of the run Robeson and Eslanda traveled to Australia and New Zealand, where, as he usually did, he commented on the local situation of discrimination against the Aborigines and the Maoris.

The relentless pursuit of Robeson by the Central Intelligence Agency is attested to by the data. He wanted to return to the States after a world tour that was to include African countries, Cuba, and the Soviet Union. However, in the Soviet Union he had an emotional breakdown. Based on Freedom of Information Act documents, some believe that the incident may have been created by the CIA's "MKULTRA" project with the administering of a hallucinatory drug, LSD. Robeson recovered in Moscow but then went to London, where he had a relapse in a British hospital and was given fifty-four electroshock treatments. As he convalesced in East Berlin the doctors were amazed that he had survived the excessive shock therapy. In fact, a brain scan revealed that the treatment had damaged a significant area of his brain. Obviously—droopy, with permanent drowsiness—the great Robeson was

Figure 6.9 Charles Blockson, legendary African bibliophile. Image courtesy of Charles L. Blockson Afro-American Collection, Temple University Libraries.

nothing but a shell of his former self. Nevertheless, in 1962, under the heading of "Internal Security," the FBI noted, "We will continue to follow Robeson's activities closely." When Robeson returned to the United States in 1963, the year of the march on Washington and the year of the death of Du Bois, he was still a giant symbol of determination and nobility. As the genealogist and historian Charles Blockson has said, "Never have we seen such magnificence in one human being."[19]

The periodical *Freedomways* saluted him in 1965 for his sixty-seventh birthday and Robeson traveled to New York to speak in honor of those who came to remember him as well as the freedom fighters for African liberation. His wife, Eslanda, died in 1965 and he moved to Philadelphia to live with his sister, Marian. An elegant celebration of Paul Robeson was organized at the Carnegie Hall as a seventy-fifth birthday recognition. Produced by Harry Belafonte in collaboration with Paul Robeson Jr, the people who attended or sent greetings included the stellar figures of the African culture and art community, including Coretta Scott King, Sidney Poitier, and James Earl Jones. Paul Robeson died on January 23, 1976 at the age of seventy-seven, but clearly, *Ol' Man River, he just keeps rolling along!*

Figure 6.10 Coretta Scott King (center), civil rights leader, with two Philadelphia admirers. Image courtesy of Charles L. Blockson Afro-American Collection, Temple University Libraries.

Ida B. Wells Countering the Klan and Lynching

Ida B. Wells was born July 16, 1862 in Holly Springs, Mississippi. Her enslaved parents, James and Elizabeth Wells, were in no position to tell that the fate of all the enslaved would be decided by a war that was in its second year. This child, Ida, would become the firebrand for black men and women throughout the nation with her unswerving dedication to freedom. Her parents are said to have taught her to see herself as the equal of any other person, to respect those who respected her, and to fight evil until the end. Her life became a symbol of this determination to smash injustice and to promote good.[20]

James Wells followed politics closely and just as soon as the war was over he joined the loyal league, a black political group, and learned how to give political speeches and support candidates. His intense participation—going to meetings, having discussion groups in his house, and talking about the future of the race—all had a potent impact on Ida B. Wells. Her mother, Elizabeth Wells, was a firm Christian, believing so abundantly in the Holy Scriptures that she would often say that "The good Lord does not like ugly behavior which means he does not like the way whites are treating black people down here on this earth."[21] Her discipline, strict work ethic, and love of education became important aspects of Ida B. Wells' inheritance.

Wells came of age during a period of enormous illiteracy among the black population. After 246 years of enslavement the African population was freed, with nearly a ninety-five percent illiteracy rate, and although freedom allowed the creation of black schools and colleges, the task was overwhelming. Deliberately kept uneducated and illiterate in the South, the African population knew neither its rights nor its potential. Occasionally, strong and naturally gifted men and women would come along and point the masses in a direction of freedom. Those who would stand for truth, steel the backs of the weak, and condemn segregation and brutality made a nobility among a downtrodden people. Ida B. Wells was an icon of such nobility. She attended Shaw University, which had been set up in Holly Springs, Mississippi, in 1866 to provide education for the rural black community. Wells, her sibling, and her mother all attended Shaw University. In her autobiography Ida B. Wells wrote that "our job was to go to school and learn all we could." She developed a love for words, essays, articles, books, and it is said that she read every book in the school library from the novels of Charles Dickens to books for young boys and girls. When she studied at Shaw she discovered that few books discussed Africa or Africans and there was nothing on African civilization or contributions to world history. A blank page existed in her training and she was committed to filling it with study. Wells complained that she had read the Bible and Shakespeare but had never read a book by an African or one about Africans.

When a yellow fever epidemic struck in 1878 and killed her parents and a younger sibling, Ida Wells was visiting her grandmother's farm. She was urged to remain with the grandmother until the epidemic was over. However, the devotion to her family caused her to throw caution to the wind and return home to be with the other children, despite the doctors' warnings. She writes in her autobiography that "the conviction grew within me that I ought to be with them . . . I am going home. I am the oldest of seven living children. There's nobody but me to look after them now." She did not want her family split up and refused all suggestions that she should allow other people to raise her siblings. Thus, at sixteen years of age, without a job or any prospects of support, Ida B. Wells was thrust into leadership of a family. The local black Masonic lodge where her father was a member encouraged her to seek a job as a teacher in the country since she was so well-read. She was given a job teaching at a school six miles away from her home. During the week friends and relatives stayed with her brothers and sisters and she worked all week, returning home on Friday. She writes in her autobiography that "I came home every Friday afternoon, riding the six miles on the back of a big mule. I spent Saturday and Sunday washing and ironing and cooking for the children and went back to my country school on Sunday afternoon."[22] In 1883 Ida Wells was encouraged by her Aunt Fannie to move to Memphis because she would find better opportunities. The aunt offered to care for the two younger girls while Ida worked. She started teaching at a school in Woodstock, Tennessee, ten miles away from Memphis. This job allowed her to expand her horizons, take classes at Fisk University and Lemoyne Institute in the summers, and qualify to teach in the city schools. In 1884 she qualified to teach first grade in Memphis schools.

Ida B. Wells by all accounts was an excellent teacher, but an incident on May 4, 1884 changed her forever. While riding a train from Memphis to Woodstock, she was asked by a conductor to move from her seat in the ladies' car to the smoking car in the front of the train. She refused. The conductor tried to physically remove her but she fought him. Finally, he asked assistance from two other men and when they removed her from the seat, instead of going to the smoking car she got off the train at the next stop.

Once she had returned to Memphis she immediately hired an attorney and brought charges against the Chesapeake and Ohio Railroad Company. The court returned a verdict in favor of Wells and awarded her £500 for damages. The judge said that the company had violated the separate but equal clause by forcing blacks to ride in smoking cars that were separate but not first class, and Wells had paid for a first-class ticket. However, the railroad company appealed the verdict and in 1887 the Tennessee Supreme Court reversed the decision and ordered Wells to pay court costs. The case created lots of interest and made Ida B. Wells a household name in the black community. She wrote an article for *The Living Way Magazine*, a black weekly, and the editor asked her to continue working for them, writing an article a week. She called her column "Iola" and tried to write for the people who had little or no schooling. She wanted to write something that the people would understand and see as simple and helpful. The column was written in simple, plain sentences, and it had a powerful effect in the black community. Soon her articles were appearing in Chicago, Philadelphia, Pittsburgh, Atlanta, and other places where there were black newspapers. Wells attacked racism, poverty, segregation, and all forms of inequality. In 1889 she was offered the editorship of the *Memphis Free Speech and Headlight*, becoming a part-owner of the paper soon thereafter. Because of her fiery editorials against racial oppression, Wells was fired within two years from her teaching position in the Memphis schools, once again proving the axiom that reactionary whites do not appreciate blacks who speak against their racism. Indeed, racist whites have historically done everything in their power to unseat blacks that fought for and demonstrated their equality.

An era of unrelenting violence spiraled out of control in the American South as the awakened white supremacist ideology, defeated in the war, found new energy in the secret society called the Ku Klux Klan. This organization, based loosely on the Greek term for circle, *kuklos*, was responsible for numerous acts of violence against blacks who had begun to exercise the rights that had been guaranteed in principle by the amendments to the

Constitution. A reign of terror or a regime of brutality, one could say, took over all legitimate forms of law. Once again, Ida B. Wells, the champion of champions, faced tragedy with steadfastness and earnestness in what became known as the "Lynching at the Curve." In March 1892 Thomas Moss, Calvin McDowell, and Henry Stewart, three friends of Wells, opened the People's Grocery Store, located directly across from a white grocery store that was selling items at an exorbitant price to black people. In the spirit of capitalism and competition the three black men believed that they could supply their community with cheaper and better food. The whites were angered by this act of black self-determination in an area that was predominantly black and therefore organized a mob to frighten the black grocers. Having been informed by local blacks who overheard whites talking about running the grocers out of town with guns, the black community also armed itself and prepared for the mob. In the ensuing confrontation three white men invaded the store and the black men, standing their ground on their own property, shot and injured the invaders. When the chaos was over three blacks had been taken to jail. White newspapers sensationally claimed that "Negro desperadoes" had shot white men, without mentioning the mean-spirited and racist intentions of the invading white mob. When the newspapers hit the stands they caused even more white anger and gave rise to the formation of another white mob, this time outside the jail where the three blacks were being held and resulting in their murder.[23]

The lioness of Memphis struck once again with a power and bravery that became another mark on her dagger for dignity. Wells wrote a vicious attack on the authorities, the press, and the attitude of whites in the area. In *Free Speech* she urged blacks to leave Memphis, stating, "There is therefore only one thing left to do; save our money and leave a town which will neither protect our lives and property, nor give us a fair trial in the courts, but takes us out and murders us in cold blood when accused by white persons." Whites couldn't care less about Wells' plea to the black population to out-migrate; they were convinced that in order to keep exploiting black people they had to maintain control over the economic situation and they did not want any competition. It was vile and vicious, and the assaults on black people who spoke up and defended their rights were atrocious. Two months after Ida B. Wells wrote her editorial, 6,000 blacks left Memphis for Oklahoma Territory. With roots planted firmly in Tennessee, Wells remained in Memphis and helped organize boycotts of racist, white-owned businesses in response to the lynching of the black grocers. This incident marked the beginning of Wells' national campaign against lynching of blacks.[24]

Nothing a lone writer today can say captures the immense sound of Ida B. Wells speaking and writing about the evil of lynching. Her aim was to mobilize the nation against the practice and have Congress abolish it by law. Later, in 1892, a black women's group collected £500 and gave it to Wells to investigate the causes of lynching. This was one of the first times that blacks had donated money to an independent researcher to examine an issue that impacted on the black community. They asked her to publish her findings, which she did in a pamphlet entitled *Southern Horrors: Lynch Law in All Its Phases*, and they were highly influential. Wells discovered that most lynchings had nothing to do with sex or sexual assaults, but rather were rooted in economics and white emotions. Blacks were lynched for competing with whites, for opening businesses or farms near whites, for not paying a debt, for stealing animals for food, for testifying in courts against whites, for disrespecting whites, and for being drunk in public.

She found that one-third of all the charges against black men were for raping white women. White mobs believed that they were defending "white womanhood" by lynching blacks who had been accused of rape. In many of these cases, however, Wells discovered that there was evidence of a consensual sexual relationship between black men and white women. The black man was often caught in an impossible drama of passion, belief, and incredulity. White men did not want to think that white women could want black men; it was always that the black man wanted the white woman. Sometimes the woman, believing that she might be caught or might have a black child, told the whites that a black man had raped her. One can imagine what a white Southern community would think of Wells' study. A mob attacked her newspaper building, threatened to kill her, and put out a reward for her death. She had been speaking to a black group in Philadelphia when her paper was attacked. She did not return to Memphis but settled in Chicago and kept moving with her anti-lynching campaign. She found a sympathetic ear in the North, and the *New York Age* printed her articles after the demise of *Free Speech*. In addition to acquiring the column at the *New York Age*, Wells began her speaking career in the Northeast. She was a stunning lecturer, perhaps having only Anna Julia Cooper or Maria Stewart, the first black female political writer, as equals on the platform.[25] A woman of unusual natural beauty, grace, and charm, Wells appealed to the mind and spirit with her encyclopedic facts about lynching and her stirring personal accounts of involvement with white supremacy in Memphis. Her speeches and writings harked back sixty years to the work of anti-slavery activists who had challenged the American nation to discover its better self before the Civil War. Wells would enlist Booker T. Washington in the drive against lynching and would urge Congress to pass a law outlawing the practice, something it did not do during her lifetime.

The Complex Character of Booker T. Washington

Booker T. Washington was one of the more complex leaders of the late nineteenth and twentieth centuries.[26] Fame had been thrust upon him by the white power brokers who saw in his philosophy a method to maintain white economic and political control while opening space for blacks to be self-determining within their own communities. Washington had been born in slavery but would demonstrate that the place of one's birth has little to do with where one lands in life.

He had come of age at a time when the white South was still bitter over the loss of privilege and enslaved domestic and farm help. He soon mastered the psychology of the white supremacist and used his knowledge to advance his own institutional interest at Tuskegee. If whites believed that blacks were inferior then Washington's strategy was to feed them this inferiority and ask them to support his college. If whites wanted to insure that blacks would not integrate socially with whites, then Washington could assure them that he supported their ideology and would steer Tuskegee students away from any social integration. If whites thought that all political power should rest with whites and that blacks could be servants, waiters, cooks, farmhands, but not judges, lawyers, or politicians, then Washington assured them that this was exactly what he wanted. In operating in this fashion he became the darling of the white establishment in the North and South. Nevertheless, Washington was not unaware of the problems of racism in the American society. In one poignant expression he compared the situation in France with that in the United States, writing that "Here in France no one judges a man by his color. The color of the face neither helps nor hinders."[27]

Washington's focus on service rather than politics and scholarship, on manual labor rather than political leadership, on owning property rather than civil rights, meant that as he was capturing the imagination of the white establishment he was angering and isolating the black establishment, especially in the Northern states. His running battle with W. E. B. Du Bois was ultimately over the direction of black progress in the nation. Although at times the two protagonists, Washington and Du Bois, collaborated, as in the book they wrote together, *The Negro in America*, for most of his life Washington was opposed to the objectives of the Niagara Movement and Du Bois' drive for black political and civil rights and responsibilities.

The strident rhetoric and dirty tactics used in the battle over the future of the black community often spilled over into local communities. Surrogates and associates of both men sought to soften the ideological split that existed in the black leadership. Yet Washington, as the most visible, to whites, leader among blacks, was also the wealthiest, the most capable of supporting his people and institutions, and perhaps the most willing to attack the Du Boisian school of thought.

The Clash of Philosophies and Personalities

Who was the legitimate leader of African Americans? Which force would conquer the other to establish a solid direction for the future? No more tragic engagement between the sides occurred than when Washington clashed swords of words and actions with his detractors over just such questions. In a series of events the trouble multiplied and caused unusual bitterness. William Monroe Trotter, editor of the Boston newspaper *The Guardian*, emerged at the beginning of the twentieth century as Washington's most persistent attacker. According to Washington, most of the black newspapers supported his position and understood that he did not support Jim Crow cars or unjust election law in the South.[28] In what was probably an exaggeration, Washington claimed that nearly 200 black newspapers agreed with his position and only three—those in Chicago, Washington, and Boston—disagreed with his policies. In fact, Boston was at the epicenter of distaste for Washington's ideas, and the grand wizard of the activities was Trotter. He had graduated from Harvard and founded *The Guardian* in 1901 to defend black civil and political rights. *The Guardian* was without fear of attacking presidents, politicians, or peons who did not stand for full black equality. In fact, Trotter had severely criticized Theodore Roosevelt, William Taft, and Woodrow Wilson in turn and therefore he would not spare Washington.

What bothered Trotter was Washington's subservience to whites, his acceptance of violations of black rights, and his advocacy of second-class citizenship for African Americans. One of Trotter's colleagues, George Forbes, was accused of saying that it would be a blessing if Tuskegee should burn down. Nevertheless, Washington persevered, seeking to control as much of public opinion as he could by setting up meetings in different sections of the country to expound his views.

The unrelenting attacks by Trotter so disturbed the Washington brain trust that Robert W. Taylor, a Tuskegee supporter, recruiter, and fundraiser, proposed bringing a libel suit against *The Guardian*. However, Roscoe Conkling Bruce, whose father had been a Reconstruction Era United States senator from Mississippi and whose mother was the dean of women at Tuskegee, had another plan. The young Bruce was a student at Harvard and felt that Trotter was a fanatic and unrestrained in his attacks, but that George Forbes was more tolerant and less vitriolic than Trotter. Bruce went to the librarian, James Whitney, of the West End Branch of the Public Library, for whom Forbes was an assistant and told him of Booker T. Washington's appreciation for his work. This was intended to put pressure on Forbes to rein in his criticism of Booker T. Washington. Boston seethed with black venom against black venom, and in the process networks of opposition appeared on both sides.

Trotter sent William H. Ferris, a Yale graduate, around to speak out against the Tuskegee model. He gave speeches in the Trotterite vein, mocking Washington personally and attacking the Tuskegee experiment. A major debate took place a few weeks later at the Bethel Literary and Historical Association. Invective flew like poisoned arrows in the meeting and when it was over, both sides, those defending Washington and those against Washington, claimed victory.

The Afro-American Council was established to support all political positions in the black community. Since 1899 it had been under the control of Washington, who had funded many of its projects, devoted money to individuals who believed in the Washington scheme for black economic development, and elected Washington's friends to office. In 1902 an effort was made to take control away from Washington and his followers at the St Paul, Minnesota, meeting of the council. Ida B. Wells-Barnett, the militant anti-discrimination and anti-lynching campaigner, and the president of the council, Bishop Walters, were both replaced by Washington supporters. A series of meetings occurred in following years in which Washington's Tuskegee machine overwhelmed its opposition. The 1903 meeting in Louisville, Kentucky, of the Afro-American Council was typical. Washington was able to pay the transport of several indigent supporters who vowed their commitment to him. At the meeting a paper on literature that praised Washington's writings drew the ire of William Ferris, who disagreed with the premise and the conclusion of the paper. In addition, a large portrait of Booker T. Washington sat on the stage, which drew the attention and anger of William Monroe Trotter and George Forbes. They attacked the organizers for showing Washington's picture without also depicting alongside Washington a black person who represented intellectual development. They created a ruckus that was not resolved until a proposal was made and accepted that the portrait of the late Joseph C. Price be placed on the stage as well.

When the Louisville meeting ended, with Washington's cadre in complete control, Trotter and his supporters decided that they should call a meeting in Boston, the heart of the educated black intelligentsia and the home base of *The Guardian*. Although Washington was opposed to the idea it went ahead and he tried to pack the meeting with his supporters. Trotter wanted to bring a halt to what he called the black monarchy of Washington. When the National Negro Business League, a group formed with the support and patronage of Washington, invited him to Boston to speak at the Columbus Avenue AME Zion Church, on July 30, 1903, Trotter planned to pursue Washington with nine pointed questions. T. Thomas Fortune set the tone for a turbulent meeting by praising Washington as a great leader.[29] Along with the hisses from the audience came outpourings of love for Washington, and a man stepped forward to challenge Fortune. At that moment policemen came in and removed Granville Martin, a Trotterite, and an outburst of sneezing and coughing occurred on the stage, with Fortune being rendered unable to continue to speak. It was later reported that someone had put cayenne pepper in the water on the platform. Trotterites disrupted the introduction of Booker T. Washington, shouting "We do not want to hear you, Booker T!" Nevertheless, Washington got up to speak and all hell broke loose in the church once again—Trotter leaped on a pew and shouted out his nine questions, and Bernard Charles, of the protesters, was cut with a knife and then arrested by the police. Soon Trotter's sister Maude was taken by the police, on the charge of stabbing a policeman with her hat pin, causing more confusion in the church. Washington's people told the police to arrest Trotter: "He's the ringleader. Throw him out of the window!" The police accommodated them and led Trotter, his sister Maude, Granville Martin, and Bernard Charles to the police station. More than any other incident this put Booker T. Washington on a course of conflict with the black educated elite.

Washington was accused of running a political dictatorship supported by the paternalistic white establishment to control the black community. Newspapers attacked the spectacle, laying as much blame on Trotter as on Washington. Whites were appalled that there were blacks who disagreed with Washington, whom they thought of as being very appropriate and a man of decent understanding and good character.

A cadre of men including George Forbes, an associate editor of *The Guardian,* William Ferris, Archibald H. Grimké, Clement G. Morgan, and W. A. Shaw would continue to promote the higher intellectual, political, and legal pursuits of equality and justice. Trotter's bitterness grew the more he thought of the fact that Washington had occupied the central role in the creation of a black agenda. Washington's retaliation toward Trotter showed that he could dish it out as well as receive it. He had a white spy agency follow Trotter's wife to see whom she worked for, how much she was paid, and what her role was. Of course, it was discovered that she worked for her husband at *The Guardian* and there were no white employers that could fire her or cause Trotter any trouble.[30]

Du Bois was not in Boston when the riot broke out—he had been teaching at the Tuskegee Summer School. He had once praised Washington for his compromise speech, but seven years later, in 1903, Du Bois had no part in Washington's doctrine. In fact, he had turned down an appointment at Tuskegee as a full-time faculty member and had become a critic of Washington's, saying in 1902 that he deplored the emphasis on materialism in Washington's autobiography *Up from Slavery* when he reviewed it.[31] The pattern was set. Du Bois would not be a friend to Washington when it came to the ideas of political and civil rights. They would be on opposite sides. In one sense, Washington had leanings that would appeal to Marcus Garvey and set the stage for a later argument between Du Bois and Garvey. However, at the turn of the century it was Du Bois' turn to support the Trotter initiative in attacking Washington. In fact, there is evidence that Washington believed Du Bois to be behind the conspiracy to destroy Washington's legitimacy, and it was Du Bois that was to receive lots of attention from the Tuskegee machine. Harlan reports that although Du Bois was not in Boston when the riots occurred, he stayed at the home of the Trotters for the entire summer. In the final analysis both traditions—the strong, separatist tradition and the integrationist tradition—would survive and continue to inform the struggle for equality and justice.

The persistent struggle to determine the best method of confronting a racist society involved the activities of a multitude of Africans. Not least to exhibit their own individual and collective will to equality by their superior work were the artists of the early twentieth century. One such artist was Meta Warrick Fuller, who was born in Philadelphia in 1877. By the time of her death in 1968 she had established an international reputation as one of the greatest sculptors of her generation. Following the master, Henry O. Tanner, of equal fame, she studied in Philadelphia and went to France to study with the French giant Auguste Rodin and mastered the "Beaux Arts" style of sculpture. Perhaps she was convinced by Tanner's admission that he had been on his way to Rome to study when he landed in France and found the country much freer in its attitude toward blacks. In fact, Tanner recalled, "Strange that after having been in Paris a week, I should find conditions so to my liking that I completely forgot when I left New York I had made my plans to study in Rome and was really on my way there when I arrived in Paris."[32] Following in Tanner's footsteps, Fuller made her way to Paris and became the first African American woman to receive a United States government art commission in 1907.

The Arrival and Meaning of Jack Johnson

In sports, especially in boxing—the game of physical domination of the other with gloved hands—the appearance of John Arthur "Jack" Johnson in the ring during the early part of the twentieth century announced a masculine challenge to the doctrine of white supremacy. Johnson was born March 31, 1878 in the small fishing town of Galveston, Texas. In the same year the three queens, Queen Mary, Queen Agnes, and Queen Bottom Belly, with machetes, kerosene, and matches crossed the island of St Croix destroying enough sugar cane farms that the Danish authorities had to immediately stop the practice of slavery which they had re-instituted on the island thirty years after the emancipation. The birth of Jack Johnson at the end of the American Reconstruction period would mean he would live through turbulent times, the parallel of which was in the glory of the queens of the Virgin Islands, whose campaign against an invidious system signaled the end to white domination in the islands.

Whether Johnson's parents knew of the struggles of other blacks in the Caribbean or elsewhere, they certainly knew of the conditions in Texas. Their son, Jack Johnson, would become the strong, tough, invincible icon of the black people of his day. As the first black world heavyweight champion of the world, Johnson held his title from 1908 to 1915. He had won fifty fights against white and black opponents by 1902 and beat Denver Ed Martin on February 3, 1903 in a twenty-round fight to win his first title, "World Colored Heavyweight Champion." Because of racism and perhaps fear, the "World Heavyweight Champion," James J. Jeffries, refused to fight Johnson. Although the system allowed black and white boxers to meet in some matches, the heavyweight championship was off-limits to blacks. What would it have meant for a black man to beat a white man in the boxing ring at the start of the twentieth century?

Undeterred in his quest to be the world champion, Jack Johnson fought anyone who wanted to get in the ring with him, including the former white world champion Bob Fitzsimmons in July 1907, knocking him out in two rounds.

Thus, when the Canadian Tommy Burns became world heavyweight champion, James Jeffries retiring, he tried to avoid a contest but eventually knew that he could not dodge Jack

Johnson. To be the world champion he believed that he had to defeat the Galveston Storm, who had followed him around the world, taunting his claim to be world champion. The match was held in Sydney, Australia, on December 26, 1908 and went for fourteen rounds. Twenty thousand spectators came to see the "fight of the ages." The police intervened and stopped the fight after Burns had been so badly beaten by Johnson that he could hardly stand. The title was awarded to Johnson on a referee's decision as a technical knock-out (TKO), but it was a massive defeat for Burns and white racial thinking.

Nevertheless, it caused an enormous outpouring of white racial animosity against blacks. One famous writer, Jack London, called for a "great white hope," but while there would be white champions the century would belong to a parade of black heavyweights who would dominate the sport, with names like Joe Walcott, Joe Louis, Ezzard Charles, Sonny Liston, Floyd Patterson, Muhammad Ali, Larry Holmes, George Foreman, and Joe Frazier.

The boxing promoters threw truckloads of "great white hopes" at Jack Johnson, seeking to take the title away from him. In 1909, just a year after the won the title, he fought four white boxers, Frank Moran, Tony Ross, Al Kaufman, and the middleweight champion Stanley Ketchel. One of his most daring competitors, however, was the Philadelphian Jack O'Brien, who gave away forty pounds to Johnson, weighing 160 lb to Johnson's 205 lb, yet managed to stay on his feet in the battle with Johnson. The fight was declared a draw. With

Figure 6.11 Joe Louis, one of the most celebrated heavyweight champions in history. Image courtesy of Charles L. Blockson Afro-American Collection, Temple University Libraries.

no white boxers seemingly capable of defeating the Galveston Storm, the former champion, James J. Jeffries, who had avoided fighting Johnson when he was world champion, felt obligated to the sporting public to fight him once more. Jeffries is reported to have said that he wanted to "reclaim the heavyweight championship for the white race." His goal was to demonstrate that "the white man is king of them all."[33] Thus, after six years in retirement the previous lion of the heavyweight division decided that it was time to show the black man who was king. The fight was widely promoted and it took place on July 4, 1910 in front of 20,000 people, almost all of them whites. The ring was especially built for the fight in downtown Reno, Nevada. The aging Jeffries was no match for the strong, nimble, and skillful fighter from the Texas coast. Jack Johnson knocked James Jeffries down twice in the fifteenth round, the first time Jeffries had hit the floor in his career. After he went to the floor the second time, Jeffries' managers threw in the towel to signal defeat. The former champion had been devastated by the power of Jack Johnson, who was then in everyone's mind the king of the heavyweight division. Johnson earned $65,000 for his victory and silenced the critics who had argued that Jeffries was the real champion and that Tommy Burns was a false champion. Of course, there was an element in the country that could not stand the fact that Johnson had vanquished "the champion," and riots broke out all across the United States. Some whites felt humiliated by Johnson's victory, and to the degree that they were depressed the black community rejoiced, for it proved a victory for racial progress. To the black communities across America it was as if the collective voice was saying, "There is no race any better than any other, and no race that is king forever; we are all equal." They probably waved their hands in the air and declared a great big "Hallelujah!" William Waring Cuney's poem "My Lord, What a Morning" was written to celebrate the day after the victory. Riots occurred in twenty-five states and fifty cities, and twenty-three blacks died while only two whites were killed. Many more blacks were injured during the white riots.

The Brownville Raid and American Episodic Violence

White racial hatred ran high in 1910 and Jack Johnson's defeat of James Jeffries did not help matters, not even in Johnson's native Texas. White public officials accelerated the segregation of all public facilities and the state legislature in 1910 and 1911 also legislated that railroad stations must have separate water fountains, waiting rooms, and restrooms. Texas declared that no blacks could stay at major hotels or eat in restaurants that served whites, and that blacks had to attend cultural events in inferior conditions to those of whites. The idea was to insure that whites knew they were superior and that blacks knew they were inferior.

Texas, although not considered one of the Deep South states (Louisiana, Mississippi, Alabama, Georgia, and South Carolina), was ranked number three in the lynching of blacks between 1900 and 1910. White mobs killed over one hundred blacks between those years. This was not simply random violence; it was an attack on every symbol of black pride and service in the interest of the country. Black troops were especially sought out for abuse.

The famous 25th Infantry, an all-black unit, had been stationed at Fort Brown in Texas in 1906 when white Brownville citizens claimed that the troops had raided the city in protest at discriminatory practices. Although the charges were later considered exaggerated, President Theodore Roosevelt dishonorably discharged 160 of the black troops. Anger over this unfairness persisted for years and in 1917 flamed into clashes between black soldiers and white citizens in Houston, Texas. By this time the NAACP had become involved in fighting for the rights of African Americans in the state, and the Houston chapter, founded in 1912, became one of the principal opponents of racism in the state.

Marcus Garvey and the UNIAACL Herald a New Day

On March 23, 1916 Marcus Garvey of Jamaica came to the United States, six years after Jack Johnson defeated James Jeffries and one year after the death of Booker T. Washington. Garvey stepped into the cauldron already brewing with venomous odors of segregation, white supremacy, and lynching to announce that the black man and woman only wanted "Africa for the Africans, at home and abroad!"[34] His message was simple and clear: "if white America does not want black people, then support the Back to Africa Movement."[35] A year after arriving in the United States he established a chapter of Universal Negro Improvement Association and African Communities League and opened it for business in Harlem. An intelligent man with a broad understanding of world history and the transformation of societies, Garvey was pro-African, committed to the salvation of a race that had been downtrodden everywhere in the Americas. He was concerned about blacks not simply in the United States and Jamaica, but in Colombia, Belize, Costa Rica, and Panama as well. Wherever blacks and whites existed side by side in the Americas the military and political dominance of whites led to economic subjugation and physical abuse of blacks. He could not discover one exception to his rule.

Born on August 17, 1887, in St Ann's Bay, Jamaica, he attended school for seven years and then worked as a printer and became active in trade unionism as a way to fight against the racism of the British colonial masters in Jamaica. In 1907 he was elected vice president of the compositors' branch of the printer's union and participated in a strike, but the union collapsed. Garvey, always a student, learned a lot about organization from the mistakes that were made in the union. In 1911 he traveled to England and studied at Birkbeck College, which had a major impact on him because he met Africans who had experience in trying to fight the colonial power of Britain in their own African homelands. This is what inspired him to organize the Universal Negro Improvement Association and African Communities League (UNIA-ACL). He wanted to follow the ideas of Booker T. Washington and demonstrate what blacks could do for themselves without any assistance from whites.

Garvey found it necessary to have his own journal and so he published the *Negro World* to promote African nationalist thinking. By 1919 the UNIA, as it had become known, could boast thirty branches and over 2 million members. Garvey fought vigorously against all forms of discrimination and argued that lynching and Jim Crow laws were nothing more than indications that whites and blacks could not live together in peace. He preached separation from whites and wrote in the *Negro World* that "Europe is for the Europeans, Asia for the Asians, and Africa for the Africans." Recruits to his cause came from all corners of the black world as his message rang true for millions. He formed an army to liberate Africa, gave his followers weapons and uniforms, created a Black Cross organization to care for black people, started an African Orthodox Church, and asked Africans, at the end of the First International European War (World War I), to stand for themselves as they had stood for America by joining his organization. In 1919 he succeeded in creating the Black Star Lines and with $10 million invested by his supporters he purchased two ships, *Shadyside* and *Kanawha*, for commerce and to take Africans to Africa.

Garvey had formidable enemies in the United States. The white establishment was obviously anxious to entrap him and to keep him from developing his organization, and some elite black people, such as W. E. B. Du Bois, believed that Garvey had the wrong idea and did everything they could to slow his movement. In fact, in 1925 the United States indicted and tried him for fraud. Garvey defended himself, was found guilty of mail fraud, and was sentenced to five years in prison. He served half the term; President Calvin Coolidge commuted the rest of his prison term and deported him to Jamaica.

During the year that Garvey was released from prison, Hubert Harrison, a Virgin Islander who had been one of Harlem's most passionate socialists and, at times, defender of Garvey, died, on December 27, 1927. While Garvey had been released from prison and living his new life outside the United States, the young Harrison, at the age of forty-four, passed away at the end of a turbulent socialist history. He had written for most of the black newspapers, debated with most contemporary speakers, argued for solidarity with the masses of all races, and projected, alongside Garvey, the ultimate rise of the African people.

Out of jail and out of America, Garvey went on a lecture tour of Britain, France, Belgium, Switzerland, and Canada in 1928, staying just outside the reach of the American government in an effort to continue to build his organization. He created the paper *The Black Man* when he returned to Jamaica. In 1932 he organized another paper that he called *The New Jamaican*. In March 1935 he moved to England. He died on June 10, 1940 in England, soon after publishing *The Tragedy of White Injustice*.

The work of Garvey, Washington before him, and scores of other black leaders was rooted in their belief in the ultimate reign of justice. It was the same case with David Hamilton Jackson of the Virgin Islands. Enslavement, racism, segregation, and brutality went hand in hand in all societies where there was unequal access to justice by whites and blacks. Jackson had been born in St Croix when it was a Danish-owned and -controlled territory. He fought to reverse the prohibition against blacks owning newspapers and succeeded by going to the Danish king and pleading his cause personally. Once the king of Denmark had removed the onerous law, Jackson started his own newspaper, *The Herald*. In the Virgin Islands the celebration of Liberty Day is a commemoration of the deed done by David Hamilton Jackson. He remains one of the Virgin Islands' greatest heroes. Jackson supported Queen Coziah and the women who rallied against the low wages being paid to coal workers. Most of the coal workers in 1892 were women, and when they gathered at Market Square with sticks and other weapons to make their point about wages, it was the foundation that had been laid down by Jackson that made militancy seem quite reasonable to the authorities. Soon the Danish government sold the Virgin Islands to the United States and it was Jackson again who worked to get citizenship for the residents of the new territory. When David Hamilton Jackson died, in 1946, six years after the death of Garvey, he was not as famous as Marcus Garvey had been, but within his community he had led a stellar life as an editor, labor leader, lawyer, judge, and legislator. Jackson would be the pioneer for people such as editor and journalist Daisy Lafond, a Virgin Islander who argued for the promotion of an Afrocentric culture during the 1990s. Other important Virgin Islanders would see the need for Africans to achieve self-determination, agency, and centeredness and run away from marginalization in European culture. Some would criticize them, but the classic book by Carter G. Woodson *The Mis-education of the Negro* would become the key to understanding contemporary history and politics throughout the African world.

Conclusion

The strong racial consciousness that emerged after the end of the winter of resurgent racism during the last quarter of the nineteenth century and the first part of the twentieth century would propel African Americans to new heights in resistance and self-determination. Already having to confront the KKK and other white supremacist organizations, African Americans were busy creating their own institutions to uplift the people. In some areas of the South the economic system that replaced slavery was little more than enslavement by another name as sharecropping became the normal pattern of agricultural farming. Blacks essentially did all of the work on the farms and white farmers reaped all of the benefits. African Americans were indebted to the white farmers for food, lodging, and clothing. The condition of the African American in the South during the early part of the twentieth century was nearly identical, in some places, to that during slavery. Nevertheless, the strong men and women kept coming along. The assault on the system of enslavement had begun with black resistance to bondage; the attack on the system of segregation and white supremacy would begin with education. The idea would be to teach African Americans about their own history and culture before the enslavement and to prepare them to use their skills to advance themselves economically and socially.

Booker T. Washington brought education to the forefront of the struggle when he established the Tuskegee Institute in Alabama. He listened to the sounds of his century and created a philosophy he thought would allow blacks to develop their own communities. Much maligned by some Northern blacks, Washington was embraced by blacks and whites in the South. The whites liked the idea of "separate as the fingers" in social situations, a doctrine espoused by Washington at the Atlanta Exposition of 1895. He believed that blacks and whites could be as "one as the hand" in other matters but socially, and even politically, he saw distinctions between white society and black society.

In this chapter we have seen how Marcus Garvey, a Jamaican, came to Harlem a year after the death of Washington to carry on the great work of organizing the black population. Garvey made Harlem his headquarters and from this pinnacle of the black world at the time he created companies, newspapers, and a shipping line to spread the word of the rise of the African people. No African American leader had the kind of charisma that Garvey brought to the discourse on African consciousness. Meanwhile, many blacks had gone over to the ideas of Marx and some, like Hubert Harrison, thought that class consciousness was the answer to the problems of the African American community. For Garvey, it was not class consciousness but race first. Finally, this chapter concludes with information about the dissemination of the most salient ideas of African self-determination to other parts of the Black World.

Additional Reading

Berlin, Ira and Leslie Rowland, eds. *Families and Freedom: A Documentary History of African American Kinship in the Civil War Era*. New York: Cambridge University Press, 1997.

Du Bois, W. E. B. *Black Reconstruction in America: An Essay toward a History of the Part which Black Folk Played in the Attempt to Reconstruct Democracy in America, 1860–1880*. New York: Russell and Russell, 1935.

Foner, Eric. *Reconstruction: America's Unfinished Revolution, 1863–1877*. New York: Harper and Row, 1988.

Gutman, Herbert. *The Black Family in Slavery and Freedom, 1750–1925*. New York: Oxford University Press, 1976.

Hunter, Tera W. *To Joy My Freedom: Southern Black Women's Lives and Labors after the Civil War*. Cambridge, MA: Harvard University Press, 1997.

Litwack, Leon F. *Been in the Storm Too Long: The Aftermath of Slavery*. New York: Knopf, 1979.

Chapter Time Markers

1904	Real estate and insurance mogul Philip Payton becomes a major promoter of Harlem
1912	Claude McKay moves to the United States from Jamaica and becomes a leading writer of the Harlem Renaissance
1915	Billie Holiday is born as Eleanora Fagan
1932	Howard Thurman is appointed dean of the Rankin Chapel at Howard University
1960	Samuel Proctor becomes the president of North Carolina A and T University
1967	The nation mourns the death of the poet Langston Hughes

From Harlem We Charge Up the Racial Mountain

7

Important Terms and Names

Harlem Renaissance
Claude McKay
Langston Hughes
Alain Locke

Countee Cullen
Philip A. Payton
Howard Thurman
W. E. B. Du Bois

The Harlem Renaissance

It is easy to speak of the Harlem Renaissance as taking place in a location, Harlem, as if that was its only location. From the very moment in 1904 when the Afro-American Realty Company, led by Philip A. Payton, bought apartments at 13 West 131st Street, Harlem was destined to become identified with upward mobility because it was uptown from lower New York where the black community had been concentrated since colonial times—many successful blacks preferred to move to the larger, more spacious apartments of uptown. Harlem would also become the first cosmopolitan African gathering place in the Americas and its energy was fueled by the combination of the exposure of the World War I veterans to cultures outside the United States, the movement of Africans from Lower Manhattan to better housing conditions in Harlem, and the rise of New York City as a commercial capital of the world.[1] Such dynamics produced a draw that was irresistible to any black person who had the ability "to get up and leave" Georgia or Kansas and make it to the most liberal, progressive, creative, artistic, and success-oriented African community in the world. Harlem attracted not just artists and poets, but preachers and gangsters, soldiers and farmers, and blacks from every part of the globe, many coming as sailors on ships that docked in New York harbor. So colorful was the city in the late 1920s and early 1930s that African Americans from other cities, particularly the East Coast cities of Boston, Philadelphia, and Baltimore, found their way to the beautiful, stately streets of Harlem.

Alain Locke from Philadelphia, editor of *The New Negro*, found his passage to the broad avenues of New York. Langston Hughes of Missouri would eventually find his own way to the "Black Mecca" of America. Harry Herbert Pace was born in Georgia in 1884 and he would become an educator, a promoter, a businessman, a publisher, and lawyer. In 1912 Pace would travel to New York and create one of the first publishing companies, an insurance company, printing companies, and magazines for the new blacks congregating in New York. He collaborated with W. E. B. Du Bois in creating the *Moon Illustrated* magazine, and with W. C. Handy in the Pace and Handy Music Company and with Elizabeth Taylor Greenfield, who was called the Black Swan, in establishing the Black Swan Record Company. It recorded and produced many African American musicians and was eventually sold to Paramount Records in 1924.

Harlem was the center of the world. The Apollo Theater would later become the center for black performing culture. All roads led to excitement brought by a powerful mélange of skills, colors, and talents. Nowhere else could one see the dance, hear the music, or feel the throbbing heartbeats of optimism that came across in the nightclubs and churches of Harlem. Here was a kingdom ruled by mythical figures of African American history such as Adam Clayton Powell Sr, and later his famous son, Adam Clayton Powell Jr, guarded by the fiercely independent Abyssinian Baptist Church that they both pastored, and the Apollo Theater open for the business of making new stars. Musical giants strode the stage at the Cotton Club and all clubs that sought to become like it. White fans and fanatics went uptown to be entertained, cajoled, and comforted, both before and after the Great Depression.

However, there were long lines of extraordinarily talented men and women who ruled their own fiefdoms, made their own ways, and created the life that was to be known as the Harlem Life. In reality, the Harlem Renaissance was about an idea that had captured the minds of African Americans throughout the county and had become so intense that other Africans in Jamaica, Trinidad, Barbados, Haiti, Brazil, Colombia, Panama, Costa Rica, and Cuba caught wind of the same social and cultural breeze and found their way to *quilombismo*, *indiginistes*, *Negritude*, and other national expressions. Parades of thinkers, activists, cult leaders, and would-be messiahs came to Harlem along with the masses of Southern seekers in search of something more than misery, poverty of spirit, and despair. Hubert Henry Harrison, the fiery socialist, joined one movement and then another in the early part of the twentieth century, and finally broke with Marcus Garvey. Two extremely charismatic speakers with internationalist elements in their nationalism championed the rights of a black population that had not yet reaped the benefits of America's industrial growth. Like Garvey, Hubert Harrison was from the Caribbean. He was born on April 27, 1883 in St Croix, Virgin Islands. By the time he was seventeen years old this charming, brilliant, explosive orator was one of the best platform speakers the socialist movement had in Harlem. Once called by Asa Philip Randolph "the father of Harlem radicalism," he was later referred to as "the foremost intellect among Afro-Americans" by Joel Augustus Rogers. John Jackson, the author of *Introduction to African Civilization*, saw him as one of the best debaters in Harlem. When he was thirty-four years old he created the Liberty League organization and the *The Voice* newspaper as the first instruments of class consciousness among Africans. Ten years later, at the age of forty-four, Harrison was dead.

Harrison would lead a short activist career that would create a model for Arthur Schomburg, John Jackson, John Henrik Clarke, J. A. Rogers, and Yosef ben-Jochannan. They

Figure 7.1 Adam Clayton Powell Jr, the Harlem legislator who became the first "national" black congressman. Image courtesy of Charles L. Blockson Afro-American Collection, Temple University Libraries.

would be master lay teachers of urban black America throughout the twentieth century and their influence would rival and often excel that of the most successful academics.

Poets have been as numerous as musicians among African Americans and the two have often merged into one. Paul Laurence Dunbar, Phillis Wheatley before him, and scores of others had taught the world that poetry was at the core of the African's soul. But it would not be until the presence of the persistent poet, the authorial voice of a nation of people,

Figure 7.2
Paul Lawrence
Dunbar, one of the
most gifted poets
of his century.
Image courtesy of
Charles L. Blockson
Afro-American
Collection, Temple
University Libraries.

and the always "right on" tone of Langston Hughes that America would have a black national poet.[2] He came to Harlem to sing a new song in a cultural note so clear and authentic that he would become the voice of millions. Rarely had an American poet captured the hearts of masses of people as electrically as Langston Hughes. Just as Paul Laurence Dunbar was the folk voice and James Weldon Johnson the classical voice, Langston Hughes was the elegant voice of black people. He wrote his lyrics so sincerely that everyone believed he or she could have written the same.[3]

Langston Hughes would burst onto the poetry scene not through some promotional activities of the white world but by writing for black journals, newspapers, and magazines. He would capture the verse, the voice, and vibrations of a generation and turn them into the classical words of an entire people.

Langston Hughes was born in Joplin, Missouri, in 1902 to a family with a long history of fighting against slavery.[4] His grandfather was Charles Henry Langston, the brother of John Mercer Langston of Ohio, who in 1855 became the first African American elected to public office. After high school, Hughes went on to Columbia University to study engineering, but soon dropped out to pursue his first love: poetry. Infected with the sweet sting of Harlem

Figure 7.3 Langston Hughes, the most powerful poet of the Harlem Renaissance and the titular head of African American writers of the twentieth century. Image courtesy of Charles L. Blockson Afro-American Collection, Temple University Libraries.

and its exciting streets, Langston Hughes also looked back on his Missouri and Kansas past as roots for ideas and values, but found in the lives of the black people just up from Georgia, North Carolina, or Virginia enough power to weave golden stanzas of truth good enough to remember. Acknowledging the influence of the blues, jazz, and other rhythmic forms from the Southern African experiences made Hughes the most remarkable talent among an entire regiment of poets with names like Countee Cullen, Claude McKay, and Arna Bontemps.

What made Hughes so important over five decades, the 1920s to the 1960s, is that he had inherited a mantle that he enlarged, embellished, and sold to the world as the literature of

Figure 7.4
Countee Cullen, major Harlem Renaissance poet. Image courtesy of Charles L. Blockson Afro-American Collection, Temple University Libraries.

the African American people. As early as 1926, while still a young man, Hughes had written in *The Nation*, "We younger Negro artists now intend to express our individual dark-skinned selves without fear or shame. If white people are pleased, we are glad. If they aren't, it doesn't matter."[5] This is the gauntlet that must be thrown down by the oppressed, and when it is, the oppressed are pleased, but so often the oppressors even more so. In the case of Langston Hughes there was acceptance in the wild and swinging 1920s of the fact that blacks just might want to do their own writing and speaking for themselves. As a consequence, Hughes wrote proposals that were accepted by the Guggenheim and Rosenwald foundations. Soon he had the title the "Poet Laureate of Harlem," when in actuality black people throughout the United States moved to his rhythms.

As a teenager in 1920 Hughes had traveled by train to Mexico to visit his father. Looking out of the window at the Mississippi River as the train made its way across the bridge at St Louis he could see the vastness of the water and thought about the great expanse of African history, the depth of Africans' emotions, the longevity of the river, the ultimate blues victory of a people reverberating with the beat of soul, and penned the famous words to the poem "The Negro Speaks of Rivers," which begins:

I've known rivers, ancient, dusky rivers and my soul has grown deep like the rivers.[6]

Few seventeen-year-olds, or indeed writers of any age, have ever written a poem so inclusive and comprehensive of a people's journey through the world. He captured on paper what he had felt in his heart and what he knew to be the sentiment, historically and metaphorically, of the African American community. Hughes was a mesmerizing poet and a master of wit who must be considered among the greatest American writers. When Hughes died in 1967 he had personally written more books than any African American writer of his generation. Hughes' life was intertwined with that of other active Harlemites such as Countee Cullen and Zora Neale Hurston. They debated, competed, and supported each other and in the end helped to create elegant African American culture.

Countee Cullen's precise date and place of birth are unknown, although there has been considerable speculation due to the numerous accounts, some given by Cullen in his adult life, about his origins. Some sources say that he was born in Baltimore, Maryland, and still others say that he was born in Louisville, Kentucky. What seems to be agreed upon is that when he was nine years old a woman, Mrs Porter, who may have been his paternal grandmother, brought him to Harlem. Neither his mother nor his father seemed to play an important role in his development. However, Mrs. Porter raised him as her own son until she died in 1918. At that time, the Reverend F. A. Cullen, the minister of Salem African Methodist Episcopal Church in Harlem, officially adopted the fifteen-year-old Countee and gave him his surname.[7]

Cullen succeeded in school, winning poetry contests throughout the city. He went to De Witt Clinton High School and then entered New York University. His poetry created a sensation in the university. His first collection of poetry, *Color*, was published in 1925 as he graduated from NYU. Among the poems were historical favorites "Incident," "Heritage," and "Yet Do I Marvel."

Although Jean Toomer of Pennsylvania had published the influential *Cane* in 1923, the year 1925 was extremely important for the Harlem Renaissance Movement. Some writers

Figure 7.5 Zora Neale Hurston, novelist, folklorist, and philosopher. Image courtesy of Charles L. Blockson Afro-American Collection, Temple University Libraries.

like to start the Renaissance with *Cane* but others saw the coalescing of the movement in another event. With the publication of Cullen's *Color* and the Philadelphian Alain Locke's *New Negro* in 1925 the race to reach the top of the racial mountain was clearly on and the rules of the game were solidly set. Thus, when Claude McKay, Langston Hughes, Wallace Thurman, Arna Bontemps, Zora Neale Hurston, and James Weldon Johnson seemed to come with one major work after another in rapid succession, the Harlem Renaissance was in full swing and Countee Cullen was the leading light.

In many ways, Cullen, a Phi Beta Kappa student, helped other writers to find access to the publishing world in New York. After graduating from New York University he attended Harvard, where he earned a Master's degree in 1926. Finding work difficult in the field of literature, he succeeded in working for *Opportunity* magazine, published by the Urban League, as an assistant editor. Cullen wrote a column called "The Dark Tower" which contrasted with the Ivory Tower of the Ivy League education he had received, but showed his brilliance and breadth of knowledge of the world of culture. A year on the job and a year after leaving Harvard he published *The Ballad of the Brown Girl* and *Copper Sun*, two strong collections of poetry. White critics did not like these poems, but blacks appreciated them and considered Cullen one of the most innovative writers in Harlem. Notwithstanding, the Guggenheim gave him a fellowship that he used to travel and study in France.

Countee Cullen married Nina Yolande Du Bois, daughter of W. E. B. Du Bois, after winning her from a popular bandleader. Between 1928 and 1934 he made several trips to France. By 1929 he had published the book *The Black Christ and Other Poems*, whose title poem compared the lynching of black men to the crucifixion of Jesus Christ. His marriage did not succeed and he divorced in 1930 at the height of the Great Depression. Ten years later he married Ida Mae Robertson.

Cullen was a promoter of African American artists and writers and although he only wrote one novel, *One Way to Heaven*, he was pushing novelists to sell their works to publishers. He taught English and French at Frederick Douglass Junior High School from 1934 until his death. He never gave up writing and wrote more poems and a couple of children's books during his life. Perhaps his major collaboration was with Arnaud Bontemps when they adapted Bontemps' novel *God Sends Sunday* for the stage. The adaptation was called *St Louis Woman*. Both Cullen and Bontemps were roundly criticized by other black intellectuals for writing a play situated in the poor neighborhood of St Louis. Why would they show the poorest elements of the society and not the best? This play was embarrassing to a class of African Americans who believed that it was necessary to always show blacks at their best. Bontemps never recovered emotionally or psychologically from this attack and years later I met him at Fisk, where he was the librarian, and he seemed quite fearful of black critics. His friend Cullen continued to write, even translating the Greek dramatist Euripides' tragedy *Medea* as *The Medea and Some Poems*. In the end, Arna Bontemps would collaborate with Langston Hughes as a way to overcome his experience with Cullen, but Cullen would become more famous than Bontemps. The poem that thrust him permanently into African American history was "Yet Do I Marvel."

It is believed that Zora Neale Hurston was born on January 7, 1891. Older than Countee Cullen, she would prove to be one of the savviest of the Harlem writers. Her early life did not indicate her future success. Her father was a Baptist preacher and the family moved to Eatonville, Florida, the first incorporated black town in the United States, when she was three years old. She spent her school days reading and daydreaming and it would not be until she was already a woman that Hurston's talent would bloom. She attended Morgan College in Baltimore in 1918, and at various times Howard University, but eventually won her BA in anthropology from Barnard College, Columbia University, in 1928. She became one the first blacks to delve deep into the meaning of African cultural retentions in the United States. She refused to imitate white writers; she sought to explore her own cultural experiences. Being a Southerner, Zora Neale Hurston was a teller of stories, fantastic tales, imaginative dramas, and spiritual mysteries. During the Harlem Renaissance she was the spokesperson for the agrarian, rural, small-town Africans who lived on by the authority of their experiences. In her writings we see the merger of anthropology, literature, and drama.[8] Her short stories "John Redding Goes to Sea" and "Spunk" were two of her earliest. They attracted attention, and once she had gained anthropological knowledge, she applied for grants and fellowships to further her study into black culture. She published *Jonah's Gourd Vine* in 1934 and wrote a critical assessment of voodoo, *Mules and Men*, in 1935. After these works Hurston was an established writer with strong credentials. Nevertheless, it was not until she published *Their Eyes were Watching God*, in 1937, that she gained the recognition that would make her one of the greatest writers of her era. A year later she wrote *Tell my Horse*, a travelogue and analysis of Caribbean voodoo. In 1939 she wrote and published *Moses, Man of the Mountain*, a novel that got mixed reviews. *Dust Tracks on a Road*, her autobiography, was published in 1942. In 1948 she wrote *Seraph on the Suwannee*, a novel, which was considered a failure from a critical and commercial perspective. Hurston left the stage and resorted to living in the South, mainly in Florida.

Hurston's political beliefs were considered conservative because she never dealt with racism, especially the way whites treated blacks. Her solution appeared to be utopian in the sense that she conceived of a world where blacks would live among themselves, as her family had done in Eatonville. Her influence waned during the years after World War II and into the civil rights era. There had been rumors of her reactionary stands in the debates she had with Langston Hughes in the 1930s, but in the 1950s Hurston attacked the Civil Rights Movement and its leaders and came out in support of ultraconservative white politicians in what were considered bizarre actions by her fellow authors. These actions created animosities, bitterness, and black nationalists' anger against Hurston. Her waning influence was nearly gone before she died penniless and in obscurity. It is believed that Alice Walker and Robert Hemenway are responsible for the revival of Hurston's star in the 1970s. Alice Walker published an essay, "In Search of Zora Neale Hurston," in *Ms. Magazine* in 1975 that stirred a new interest in the author. Robert Hemenway's *The Harlem Renaissance Remembered* positioned Hurston as the keeper of the African traditions during the renaissance.[9]

The international aspect of the Harlem Renaissance was accentuated by a number of writers, including preeminently by Claude McKay.[10] He was born in Jamaica on September 15, 1890 and given the name Festus Claudius McKay. He was the youngest of the eleven children of Thomas McKay and Hannah Ann Elizabeth Edwards. His older brother was a schoolteacher and his parents sent him to stay with his brother so that he could receive a good education. By the time he was ten years old he was writing poetry, and his love of words was an early indication that he would someday be an excellent poet, novelist, or journalist. However, the prospects of a young Jamaican making a living as a writer did not seem promising and when he could not enter a boarding school because an earthquake destroyed it, he found himself apprenticed to a carriage and cabinetmaker. When he was seventeen years old he was encouraged by an Englishman to write not in English, but in the language of the ordinary Jamaican. Some of these poems were put to music and found audiences in Jamaica.

In 1912, at twenty-two years of age, Claude McKay finally moved to the United States. By this time he had already published two volumes of poetry in Jamaica, *Songs of Jamaica* (1912) and *Constab Ballads* (1912). Although McKay never lost touch with his writing, he was drawn to Tuskegee Institute, a school that had a wide reputation throughout the African world. Booker T. Washington and his followers had popularized the name of the school and its successes in Jamaica. Therefore, a brilliant young student such as McKay felt that entering Tuskegee, the epitome of black education, was the proper action. He sought to major in agronomy. He did not remain in Alabama long, however, due to the prejudices he found among the white teachers and in the Alabama community. He left Tuskegee after a year and entered Kansas State College in Manhattan, Kansas. A financial gift from the Englishman who had encouraged him to write in Jamaican language helped him move from Kansas to New York City. He married Eulalie Imelda Lewars, his childhood girlfriend, and invested in a small restaurant. Neither the marriage nor the restaurant venture lasted very long. Lewars returned to Jamaica to give birth to their daughter and McKay took jobs as janitor, dishwasher, and street sweeper. He published two poems, "The Harlem Dancer" and "Invocation," under a pseudonym in 1917 and this gave him exposure as a writer in the Harlem community. Frank Harris, the editor of *Pearson's Magazine*, and Max Eastman, the editor of the socialist *Liberator*, pushed him to write more. Soon McKay began to express himself as a socialist, so strongly had the Russian Revolution of 1917 impressed itself on his thinking. He was asked to serve as an editor of the *Liberator*, which he did, and began to write for left-wing publications.

However, the situation in the United States seemed to be deteriorating just as the masses of Russian people were creating their soviets. The Red Summer of 1919 was one of the worst periods in African American history as racial violence, with abnormal venom, poured forth from all corners of the white community in America. It was at this time that Claude McKay wrote his most memorable poem, "If We Must Die." It would reverberate throughout the world, and during the darkest days of World War II in England the eloquent prime minister Winston Churchill would resort to quoting the words ("If we must die") of this African American poet. This poem was an anthem of genuine resistance, written to capture the feeling of the African American people who found themselves battling in their own country as they had fought in Europe trying to make the world "safe for democracy" (in Woodrow Wilson's terms) but were unfree, discriminated against, and killed in their own nation. McKay's conclusion was that black people had to fight back even unto death.

McKay would also be recognized for the poems "Baptism," "The Lynching," and "The White House." By the time Harlem was brimming with the highest concentration of poets anywhere in the black world, Countee Cullen and Langston Hughes had found McKay one of their leading voices, although his poetry, mainly sonnets and not modern verse, harked back to an older school of literature. Yet even so, critics saw his contribution as a direct, frontal assault on racism and an appeal to the ordinary African person to stand his ground against all forms of degradation. He was the best protest poet of his generation.

McKay, like many African American writers of the segregation era, believed that they would find appreciation for their talents in Europe more quickly than they would among white Americans, so he left for England, where he remained from 1919 to 1921. However, while working with socialist journals in England he wrote poetry for both the British and American publics. By the time he arrived in the United States he had completed *Spring in New Hampshire* and had begun *Harlem Shadows*, his best collection of poetry.

Now wanderlust, as he said himself—a troubadour wanderer, with a pocket full of literary achievements, Claude McKay began a twelve-year sojourn across Europe and Africa. He went first to Hamburg, where he met several African and African American communists and spoke at their 1922 meeting along with his friend Otto Huiswood of Surinam. He then traveled to the Soviet Union to experience the revolution first-hand. It is possible that McKay, a former student at Tuskegee, mentioned to Lenin the possibility of asking George Washington Carver to come to the Soviet Union as the minister of agriculture. It is reported that Carver, the indomitable agricultural scientific inventor, decided to remain at Tuskegee. Nonetheless, McKay was infatuated with the Soviet Union, but found himself often ill and penniless. Looking to make money the only way he could, McKay compiled a set of essays, *The Negroes in America*, that were published in the Soviet Union, and finally published in the United States in 1979. In 1928, the year before the Great Depression, McKay's first novel, *Home to Harlem*, was published. It brought him some money and some success as a novelist but he was attacked for his severe critique of the underworld life of Harlem. As it turns out, his next novel, *Banjo: A Story without a Plot*, which follows an African American through the French city of Marseilles, one of McKay's favorite cities, ultimately had more impact on the black world. The French-speaking African intelligentsia such as Léopold Sédar Senghor, Alioune Diop, and Aimé Césaire were moved by McKay's portrayal of the black experience. They would become the leaders of the *Negritude* movement and McKay, along with Hughes, would become two of the best-known African American writers among these French-speaking Africans.

In 1930 Claude McKay moved to Morocco and wrote several other books, including the short stories collection *Gingertown* in 1932, and *Banana Bottom*, a novel, in 1933. However, by 1934 he had to return to the United States to seek employment; he was broke. Fortunately, after two years he gained a grant from the Federal Writers Project in 1936 that allowed him to complete his autobiography, *A Long Way from Home*, in 1937. By now his travels throughout Europe and Africa and his intense journeys in the Soviet Union had convinced him that he could not be a communist, although he was sympathetic to socialism. He began to write for *The Nation*, *The New Leader*, and *The New York Amsterdam News*. His work *Harlem: Negro Metropolis* (1940) remains one of his most important contributions to the history of Harlem.

McKay's absence from Harlem denied him the stature he had achieved during the 1920s. He was never able to regain the spark of his earlier years and found himself chronically short of cash. He blamed his condition on racism and his lack of academic credentials, notwithstanding his financial situation during his life; however, his fame has continued to grow among African American literary critics. He never returned to the Jamaica he had left in 1912—becoming an American citizen in 1940, he abandoned his lifelong agnosticism and became a Catholic. Then, almost desperately, as a surprise to his friends, he moved to Chicago in 1944 to work for the Catholic Youth Organization. He died on May 22, 1948. His second autobiography, *My Green Hills of Jamaica*, was published in 1979.

While Claude McKay was living his own personal blues, the Empress of the Blues, Bessie Smith, born on April 15, 1894, was becoming the most popular female singer of the 1920s

Figure 7.6 Bessie Smith, blues legend called the Empress of the Blues. Image courtesy of Diane D. Turner.

and 1930s.[11] This was the era of the blues since the Great Depression sent the vast majority of people into a tailspin economically and African Americans were already uncontrollably, it seems, in a downturn long before most others. Bessie Smith was the iconic voice of pain and suffering. Of course she was unique, but in the peculiarity of her style she influenced many other artists in jazz and blues.

Bessie Smith was born in Chattanooga, Tennessee. She lost her mother and father before she had any good memory of them and was raised by her older sister, Viola. In 1903 Bessie Smith and her brother Andrew danced and sang on the streets of Chattanooga as a duo to earn funds for the family. Andrew was an excellent guitar player and Bessie would sing and dance right in front of the White Elephant Saloon in the African American community. Her oldest brother, Clarence, ran away from home in 1904 to join a traveling troupe of singers. It was reported that Clarence ran away covertly because he did not want his sister following him, which everyone knew she would. However, in 1912 Clarence returned to Chattanooga with the Moses Stokes troop and arranged for the managers to allow Bessie to audition. She was hired as a dancer, not as a singer, because the legendary Ma Rainey was the lead female singer for the group.

Nevertheless, Bessie Smith made her own way to Broadway, singing in the musical *How Come?* starring Sidney Bechet. She lived in Atlanta and played clubs up and down the East Coast while still performing in *How Come?* until she had a financial dispute with show's producer, left *How Come?* and moved to Philadelphia. Alberta Hunter, another noted singer, replaced her on Broadway.

In 1923 Columbia Records released Bessie Smith's first recordings. Soon she was the biggest black star on the stage and the highest-paid performer of her day. When Bessie Smith

Figure 7.7 Billie Holiday, famed as "Lady Day" Holiday, captured the jazz singing world with her elegant style. Image courtesy of Charles L. Blockson Afro-American Collection, Temple University Libraries.

died, on September 26, 1937, she had already influenced a generation of singers, and none so much as Lady Day, Billie Holiday.

The twenty-one-year-old Eleanora Fagan, whose name was changed to Billie Holiday, had been born April 7, 1915.[12] She followed Ma Rainey and Bessie Smith to the top of the blues and jazz ladder by pioneering her own style of phrasing, inspired by the trumpet, saxophone, and piano. Her singing was intimate, sensual, soulful, and personal in a way that brought her audiences into her emotions. Soon everyone knew her songs "God Bless the Child," "Don't Explain," "Lady Sings the Blues," "Fine and Mellow," "Easy Living," and "Strange Fruit."

Billie Holiday's career reached from the Harlem Renaissance to the Civil Rights Era and although she lived a short life, dying in 1959, it was outstanding in its underscoring of the dynamism of African American culture.

Art and Politics in Abundance

Each age, regardless of humble location and ordinary people, can organize itself into the most extraordinary assemblage of personalities. Harlem was a formidable cradle for culture and politics, and where African Americans gathered, neither culture nor politics was far behind. The cultural soldiers who assaulted the racial mountain were too numerous to count. Consider Langston Hughes, Claude McKay, Bessie Smith, W. E. B. Du Bois, James Weldon Johnson, Zora Neale Hurston, Arna Bontemps, Billie Holiday, and then Duke Ellington, Louis Armstrong, and Cab Calloway at the same dinner table and you have just a sampling of the soldiers who attacked the racial mountain, some, of course, in their own unique way.

Louis Armstrong often claimed that he was born on July 4, 1900 but baptismal records indicate that he was born on August 4, 1901. By the time he died, on July 6, 1971, Armstrong had revolutionized the jazz trumpet.[13] He was born in New Orleans and is responsible for making the city one of the greatest jazz destinations of all. Satchmo, as he was called, was a trumpeter and a cornet player of the most creative and inventive quality. His influence is still felt in the music today because although he never left the improvisational nature of jazz, he shifted its focus to the individual performer. He stood out himself as an artist, a trumpeter, and he mastered improvisation from a solo performer's stance. Often adding "scats," vocalization of syllables, to his songs, he bent the tones and twisted the lyrics in such a way that the audience felt it was in the presence of the greatest ever musical dexterity. One never knew precisely what Armstrong would do next since his charisma on stage as a communicator was equal to his playing as a musician.

The challenges confronted by Louis Armstrong were enormous. He was the grandson of enslaved Africans; his father, William, left his mother, Maryann Albert, when he was an infant; his mother left him with his grandmother, Josephine Albert. He moved back with his mother when he was five years old and saw his father only during the carnival parades. In order to assist the family he became a paperboy and a scrounger for discarded food that he could sell to restaurants. Armstrong was introduced to all kinds of licentious dancing in the clubs and dance halls as a child, but he also heard the great Joe "King" Oliver perform in Storyville, the red-light district.

Figure 7.8 Louis Armstrong, king of the New Orleans trumpet sound. Image courtesy of Diane D. Turner.

Louis Armstrong dropped out of school at eleven years of age and joined a group of young singers and dancers busking in the streets of New Orleans. He was taught to play music by ear by Bunk Johnson and King Oliver. However, Armstrong was unable to sustain himself economically until he started to work for the Karnofsky junk hauling business. With odd jobs from the Karnofskys he was soon able to make ends meet, but he saw how other whites treated these Lithuanian Jews. He was only a child but reports that he understood that other whites considered the Jews inferior. He wore a Star of David the rest of his life out of respect for the Karnofskys.

Criticized by other musicians for playing in front of segregated audiences and not being actively involved in civil rights, Armstrong was often considered an Uncle Tom.[14] Yet during the 1950s, Louis Armstrong sent donations to Martin Luther King Jr in support of the movement, preferring to work quietly and not mixing his art with politics. He did, on one occasion, call President Dwight Eisenhower "two-faced" and "gutless" because he did not speak out against the racism over school integration in Little Rock, Arkansas, in 1957.[15] He also cancelled a Department of State-sponsored trip to the Soviet Union, saying, "The way they're treating my people in the South, the government can go to hell."[16] He did not believe he could represent the United States abroad when he felt that the government was not doing enough to support black people. Raised a Baptist, wearing a Star of David, and being a friend to the Pope made Armstrong one of the most complicated entertainers of his day, yet his international reputation as a showman surpassed that of any other jazz musician. The most dominant names in the field of jazz and blues paid respect to Louis Armstrong even though they may have disagreed with his politics.

However, Edward Kennedy "Duke" Ellington, born on April 29, 1899, who was possibly one year older than Satchmo, matched him in elegance and audience appeal. Ellington, of course, was not born in poverty. He came from a rather middle-class background in

Figure 7.9 Duke Ellington, one of the most prolific composers in history. Image courtesy of Diane D. Turner.

Figure 7.10 Cootie Williams, jazz and blues trumpeter. Image courtesy of Diane D. Turner.

Washington, DC. Nevertheless, he came to music early, much like Armstrong, and remained all of his life the most prominent figure in the history of jazz, which he called American music. He was a prolific composer, perhaps America's most productive composer, with more than 3,000 songs to his credit. He covered all musical genres in his creativity from gospel to film scores, popular to classical, blues to jazz.[17]

Duke Ellington's career was extraordinarily meritorious. In fifty years he composed his inexhaustible songbook, scored music for movies, and led his big band. Ellington was called Duke because of his elegance, eloquence, charisma, and dynamic persona. He pioneered so many different uses of the band, creating the Ellingtonian type of orchestral music. No other jazz leader elevated the music to the international stage like Ellington. He was so special in his contribution to American culture that the Pulitzer Prize board felt the need to bestow upon him a posthumous honor in 1999. The musicians who played with him were some of the greatest musicans in their own right, yet they stuck with him for many years. He was beyond categorizing, but his music's acceptance had a lot to do with the fact that his musicians were superstars as well. Ellington knew the skills and talents of his musicians so well that he would often compose something just for a particular musician. Famous among the special compositions were "Concerto for Cootie," for Cootie Williams, "Jeep's Blues," for Johnny Hodges, and "The Mooche," for Tricky Sam Nanton and Bubber Miley. Yet it was his work with Billy Strayhorn, himself a genius, which made Duke and Strayhorn two of the most productive composers in jazz history. Not until Kenneth Gamble and Leon Huff of the Philadelphia Sound would there be a duo of writers so gifted and productive. Gamble and Huff are said to have created more than 2,500 songs. When Ellington died, on May 24, 1974, he left behind an immense collection of creative artifacts and a massive record of his creative gifts.

Although Cabell "Cab" Calloway III was eight years younger than Duke Ellington, and maybe nine years younger than Armstrong, few critics considered him anything but a peer. Nevertheless, Calloway often deferred to his older colleagues for what they taught him. It was Louis Armstrong, for example, who taught him how to scat. Therefore, when he became a jazz singer and bandleader he elevated scat singing to such a degree that it became essential for other musicians to introduce scat into their sessions.

Cab Calloway was born on December 25, 1907 in Rochester, New York, and raised in Baltimore, Maryland. He lived until November 18, 1994. His father was a lawyer and his mother was a church organist and public school teacher. Thus, much like the older Ellington, Calloway was of middle-class origin.[18] His love of music came from watching and listening to his mother play in church. His parents gave him music lessons and put him in voice classes. Although they disproved of jazz music, their son gravitated easily toward performing in jazz clubs. Drummer Chick Webb and pianist Johnny Jones mentored him in performance and entertaining.

Calloway attended Lincoln University but left in 1930 before graduating from college. His sister, Blanche, was already in show business and she inspired him to follow her lead.

Figure 7.11 Cab Calloway, a powerful big band leader. Image courtesy of Diane D. Turner.

Calloway's parents refused to give up on his becoming a lawyer like his father so they pressured him to enter Crane College in Chicago. He would find himself at the Dreamland Ballroom, the Club Berlin, or the Sunset Café performing as a singer, drummer, or emcee. It was in these clubs that he met Armstrong and learned how to scat. The next move for him was to organize his own band.

His band included some of the greatest musicians ever organized in America. The band members often saw themselves in competition with Duke Ellington's band. Calloway had his own style and personality and was a showman with infinite graces. His band featured giants such as Adolphus "Doc" Cheatham and the incredible Dizzy Gillespie, two phenomenal trumpeters. Milt Hinton, bass, and Danny Barker, guitar, were also feature artists with the Cab Calloway Band.

Figure 7.12 Dizzy Gillespie, developer of bebop and modern jazz. Image courtesy of Charles L. Blockson Afro-American Collection, Temple University Libraries.

Just as Calloway, or "His High-de-Highness of Ho-de-Ho," as he was sometimes called, was impacted by Louis Armstrong, he was also influenced by Duke Ellington. In the 1930s the Cotton Club was the place to play and Duke Ellington had it nearly locked down. However, Calloway had taken over a faltering band company called the Missourians in 1930 and transformed it into his own band. While Ellington's band was traveling, the Cotton Club hired Calloway's band. He became so popular that the bands became "co-house" bands. Calloway played at the Cotton Club while Duke Ellington was traveling and vice versa. The two bandleaders broke the broadcast network color barrier on NBC radio with live music twice a week. The two bands appeared on Walter Winchell's radio program and with Bing Crosby, but their home audiences were the scores of black nightclubs that gave them their soul.

Calloway's genius emerged in 1931 in his "Minnie the Moocher," "St James Infirmary Blues," and "The Old Man of the Mountain," songs which were all performed with animated shows. In many ways, when Calloway died, at 86, an era had passed, but no narrative of African American history is complete without an appreciation of the complex situations in which Armstrong, Ellington, and Calloway found themselves and how they each, out of the peculiar conditions of their times, responded to their challenges and demonstrated, through personal diligence, discipline, and grace, the charisma that is at the core of artistic success.

In their own ways the artists, especially the musicians, too many to name—from John Coltrane to Nat King Cole, from Ma Rainey to Ethel Waters, from Ella Fitzgerald to Dinah Washington—all have to be claimed for their deliberate and consistent production of African culture. They were not alone in their challenges or in their successes; they were but one chord being played as the entire orchestra of a people participated from whatever venue they occupied. So the philosophers came with their gifts just as the plaster artists, painters, and sculptors, Augusta Savage, Meta Warrick Fuller, Jacob Lawrence, Edmonia Lewis, Allan Freelon, Charles White, John Biggers, Elizabeth Catlett, Aaron Douglas, Romare Bearden, and others, had placed their spears in the ground to stake out the territory of their genius.[19] The future would belong to Harry Belafonte, Ruby Dee, Ossie Davis, Sammy Davis Jr, Max Roach, Otis Redding, Sam Cooke, Sidney Poitier, and scores of other artists and actors who would sing, act, and dance their way across the stage of African American history. Audiences would be chilled by the awesome artistic talents of Art Tatum, and say, "God has entered the building," and call Riley B. King, stage name B. B. King, "the king of the blues." Deities, gods and angels, monarchs, kings, queens, and princesses would multiply and people the performing spaces of America with talent so genuine that it would have to be called soulful. Their legacy would reach back to the beginning of the twentieth century and reach forward to the end of that victorious age. Thus, anchored firmly to the past, new artists would be able to make something out of the rich materials they had inherited.

No wonder the generation of the first half of the twentieth century can be called the "Children of Miracles," because they were the children of those who would not allow them to die. Their parents had seen the best and the worst of the African American sojourn in the United States. They had often witnessed the beginning and the end of Reconstruction.

Howard Thurman was born on 1899 in Daytona Beach, Florida, and nothing in his family's life or in his circumstance of being born in a segregated and ignorant South could foretell his greatness. Thurman's birth in the small town of Daytona Beach did not prevent him from being the valedictorian at Morehouse College in 1923. A couple of years later, after completing

Figure 7.13 Nat King Cole, entertainer. Image courtesy of Charles L. Blockson Afro-American Collection, Temple University Libraries.

Figure 7.14 Ethel Waters, the master of gospel, blues, and jazz. Waters merged the vocal elements of the African American in her style. Image courtesy of Charles L. Blockson Afro-American Collection, Temple University Libraries.

his study at Colgate Rochester Theological Seminary, he was ordained as a Baptist preacher. An avid reader and a pursuer of knowledge, especially philosophical history, he entered Haverford College in Pennsylvania as a special student of the famous Quaker mystic philosopher Rufus Jones. He completed his work and earned a doctorate at Haverford College.

Howard Thurman became dean of Rankin Chapel at Howard University in 1932 and served for twelve years. During his time at Rankin Chapel, Thurman began to win followers for his deeply moving ethical insights into religion. He traveled to Europe and Asia, holding conversations with Mahatma Gandhi on the nature of the human condition and non-violence. When Thurman left Howard University he took up a post at the Fellowship of Reconciliation and established the Church for the Fellowship of All Peoples in San Francisco. Some have claimed that this church, founded in 1944, was the first fully integrated church in the United States. Thurman's co-pastor was the white preacher Alfred Fisk.

In 1953 Thurman was invited to Boston University to become the dean of Marsh Chapel. He served in that post for twelve years, becoming the first black person to be named a tenured dean at a majority-white university. When he left Boston in 1965 he returned to San Francisco as the chairman of the board and director of the Howard Thurman Educational Trust until his death in 1981. A prolific author, Howard Thurman wrote twenty books on ethics and philosophy, the most famous being *Jesus and the Disinherited,* which was read by Martin Luther King Jr and influenced many of the leaders of the Civil Rights Movement. Indeed, well-known preachers and ethicists such as Dr Henry Mitchell, Dr Catherine Iles Godboldte, Dr Gardner Taylor, Dr Jeremiah Wright, and Dr Cornel West count Howard Thurman as one of their influences.[20]

African American history is abundant with men and women who have been noted as sages or activists or both. Many African Americans knew Adam Clayton Powell Jr as "the black congressman" for so long that some of them did not know his identity as a pastor of Harlem's largest church, a role he inherited from his father, Adam Clayton Powell Sr. Born on November 29, 1908, Powell represented Harlem from 1945 to 1971 with a fierce independence, deep dedication to fighting against racism, and with a personality that irritated the white establishment. When he died, on April 4, 1972, he had experienced the roller-coaster ride that had become the standard for black public figures that challenged racism and prejudice.[21]

Powell was the first African American elected to the House of Representatives from New York City. In Congress, Powell was assertive, strong, and firm; he refused to take any subservient roles to white Congressmen and this created friction with some of them, who felt that he was uppity, that is, arrogant. When he became chairman of the Education and Labor Committee in 1961 he was able to pass several important pieces of social legislation. Chuck Stone, Powell's chief of staff, and an important person in the history of African American journalism, left politics and entered the academy as a professor at the University of North Carolina at Chapel Hill. He often complained that Powell's contributions had been underestimated and not truly appreciated, but Powell, who had graduated from Colgate, was a preacher who mastered audience analysis and generated strong attachments with black communities throughout the nation. His marriage to Hazel Scott, a jazz singer, placed him directly in the limelight of the entertaining world.

As intriguing as Powell's life was between Harlem and Washington, his Abyssinian Baptist Church flock felt the dynamism of his preaching, with its curious turns on the scriptures and his use of contemporary political events to elucidate his messages. In a similar fashion

Gardner Calvin Taylor, often called the greatest African American preacher—even more so than the legendary John Jasper, whose sermon "And the Sun Stood Still" was a nineteenth-century phenomenon—was creating an aura of philosophical and practical ethics at Concord Baptist Church in the Brooklyn section of New York.

Taylor was born June 18, 1918 in Baton Rouge, Louisiana, the son of a famous preacher, Washington Taylor.[22] Gardner Taylor's father died when Taylor was thirteen, and his mother, Selina Taylor, raised him to love books and knowledge. He went to Leland College, where he earned a BA degree, and then enrolled at Oberlin Graduate School of Theology. Preaching at Concord during the time that Powell was at Abyssinian meant that Taylor had to become as active in the Civil Rights Movement as any other preacher. He was a leader, giving the first anniversary address, for the Montgomery Bus Boycott. He involved himself in every issue related to human rights in the city of New York, including supporting Latinos and African Americans who experienced housing discrimination. Only a conservative group of black Baptist preachers kept Gardner Taylor from being elected as head of the National Baptist Convention on a platform that would have merged the efforts of the Civil Rights Movement with the ethical purpose of the Convention. They did not see a political and racial agenda as a part of the religious mission. Nevertheless, Taylor became a per-aa of the pulpit, a remarkable leader with a golden tongue and a gift for poetry. He was an academic, an activist, a poet, a dramatist, and the best model of the radical progressive African American philosopher of religion.

While Adam Clayton Powell had been born in the North and Gardner Taylor in the South, both had attended school at Northern colleges, Colgate and Oberlin respectively. C. Eric Lincoln, one of the most popular religious authors, was born on June 23, 1924 in Athens, Alabama, and went first to two African American colleges, LeMoyne and Fisk. However, in elementary school he had attended a missionary school in Alabama founded by the New England Congregational Church. Although he was abandoned by his parents and left to his grandparents to raise, C. Eric Lincoln never gave up on himself or knowledge. He became the valedictorian of his school and worked as a milk bottle washer and a cotton picker to help his grandparents survive the hardships of poverty. Eventually Lincoln would attend the University of Chicago and Boston University, where he would receive his doctorate. Once he had completed his education, Lincoln became a professor at several colleges: Boston, Portland State, Union Theological Seminary, Fisk, and Duke. Among his books were *The Black Muslims in America*, *My Face is Black*, *Martin Luther King Jr.: A Profile*, *This Road since Freedom: Collected Poems*, and *Coming Through the Fire: Surviving Race and Place in America*. He wrote or edited more than twenty books, including a novel for which he won the Lillian Smith Book Award. A prodigious thinker and writer, C. Eric Lincoln befriended many younger scholars and theologians as well as supporting the work of friends such as Alex Haley, Malcolm X, Martin Luther King Jr, and others. Often considered alongside James Weldon Johnson, Howard Thurman, John Hope Franklin, Yosef ben-Jochannan, John Jackson, Chancellor Williams, and John Henrik Clarke, C. Eric Lincoln was one of the first African American thinkers to be read by ordinary people. Lauded as a poet, hymnist, novelist, horticulturist, gourmet cook, and lover of architecture, Lincoln was the complete philosopher of the African American experience.[23]

In 1996 Samuel DeWitt Proctor and Gardner Taylor, two of the towering intellectual leaders of the African American church, wrote a book, *We Have This Ministry*, in which they

Figure 7.15 Dr Martin Luther King Jr, civil rights leader and martyr for justice. Image courtesy of Charles L. Blockson Afro-American Collection, Temple University Libraries.

discussed the abiding legacy of C. Eric Lincoln. Woven together as if of one fabric, Taylor, Lincoln, and Samuel DeWitt Proctor represent the finest tradition of the black church, an institution that despite its woefully inadequate foundation continued to produce committed religious thinkers deep into the twentieth century. Separately and together these three theologians are responsible for more theological development among African American preachers than any other three scholars. Proctor was born in Norfolk, Virginia, on July 13, 1921. Both of his parents were college educated and his grandparents, maternal and paternal, had university educations. Proctor's father, Hughes, worked at the Norfolk Naval Shipyard and he grew up in the church that had been founded by his great-grandfather, Zachariah Hughes.[24]

Proctor attended Virginia State College on a music scholarship and played with Billy Taylor in a jazz band. In 1939, after two years, he left the college to try his hand at shipfitting, but after a year he was back at college at Virginia Union University, where he became a devout Christian. He married Bessie Tate and after graduating from Virginia Union he entered the University of Pennsylvania and then moved to Crozer Theological Seminary in Upland, Pennsylvania, to pursue a degree in religion. When he completed Crozer in 1945 he had been influenced by the higher criticism, the questioning of the literal truth of the Bible. He left to take a pastor position in Providence, Rhode Island, and also to study ethics at Yale University. Instead of completing his work at Yale, he moved to Boston and received his PhD in 1950 from Boston University School of Theology.

It was when he was invited to his alma mater to give a lecture that he met Martin Luther King Jr, who was a student at Crozer Theological Seminary. Proctor introduced King to the works of Reinhold Niebuhr and Harry Emerson Fosdick. In 1955 at the age of thirty-three, Samuel Proctor was appointed the president of Virginia Union University. King invited Proctor to Montgomery to speak at the Spring Lecture Series during the bus boycott.

In the heated environment of civil rights during the 1950s President Eisenhower asked several leaders, including Proctor, to come to the White House for a meeting in which the president urged them to ease up on their pressure for civil rights. The black leaders refused the president's request and Proctor, while president at Virginia Union, traveled to the Soviet Union, Poland, and Germany, and attended conferences in Africa and Asia.

Proctor became president of North Carolina A&T University in 1960. Jesse Jackson was the president of the student body at the time as well as the quarterback for the football team. Proctor took a leave from the presidency to serve as associate director of the Peace Corps during the Kennedy administration. The March on Washington for Jobs and Freedom had a significant conscious-raising effect on Proctor. He decided to move his family to Nigeria for a year, and upon his return went back to his presidency at North Carolina A&T. However, after a year back on the job he became head of the National Council of Churches.

In 1969 Proctor gave a lecture at Rutgers on the one-year anniversary of the death of Martin Luther King Jr, and the administrators asked him to serve as the first Martin Luther King Distinguished Professor of Education. Proctor accepted their offer and held this position until his retirement in 1984. Upon the death of the famed Adam Clayton Powell Jr, the Abyssinian Baptist Church called him to its pulpit, where he served until 1989, when he resigned and was replaced by Calvin O. Butts. Proctor died in 1997 while lecturing at Cornell University.

History is never written in a straight line. There are many complexities to the global narrative of African Americans, and this is as true in the history of religious thinkers as it is in the history of political activists. If one considers the fact that Albert Cleage, later named Jaramogi Abebe Agyeman, was a revolutionary thinker and activist whose experiences with formal education were far less stilted and disciplined than that of Proctor, Lincoln, or Powell, then it is possible to see how he was able to advance a nationalist religious ideology created out of the realities of ordinary people.[25] Cleage was born in 1911 in Detroit and grew up in a middle-class home, his father being a physician.

Cleage became a black nationalist in the 1970s and rejected the basic principles of integration because he saw it as a way to make blacks think and act like whites, in effect losing their own identities and culture. He is responsible for preaching a Christian doctrine where the Savior is black, the Madonna is black, and the basic virtues, values, and principles of the religion are taken from African culture. He founded the Shrine of the Black Madonna, which was later renamed the Pan African Orthodox Christian Church, in Detroit. He founded two additional shrines, one in Houston and another in Atlanta. He believed that it was essential that Africans return to a more aware position about circumstances and conditions of their oppression. This emphasis on self-determination and self-definition would become a central part of the ideology of younger, more educated theologians who followed closely the developments in Agyeman's circle.

204 From Harlem We Charge Up the Racial Mountain

It is possible to see Agyeman's book *The Black Messiah* (Sheed and Ward, 1968) as the work that separated him from more traditional black theologians. Nevertheless, there were some theologians such as Archbishop George Augustus Stallings of the independent African American Catholic congregation (Imani Temple, 1989) and James Cone, a professor at Union Theological Seminary who attempted to refine Cleage's thinking and create their own avenues to self-definition.

Cone is seen as a major thinker in the tradition of black liberation theology. He was born on August 5, 1938. His book *Black Theology and Black Power* came out a year after Cleage's *The Black Messiah*. In some ways it might be said that Cone's work was more important among professional theologians while Cleage's work appealed to the masses. There was a utility to Cleage's ideas that was different from the intellectual influence of Cone's work. As the Charles Augustus Briggs Distinguished Professor of Systematic Theology at Union Theological Seminary, James Cone has been a key player in the orchestration of black religious ideas.[26]

Cone was born in Fordyce, Arkansas, and raised in Bearden, Arkansas, where he attended the African Methodist Episcopal Church. Thus, before he attended Philander Smith College, Garrett-Evangelical Theological Seminary, or Northwestern University, he had been introduced to a church with a self-defining history. The AME was not a branch of a white denomination, but an independent black church. Cone used his academic appointments at Philander Smith, Adrian College in Michigan, and Union Theological Seminary to advance his philosophy that Christianity, to be meaningful for Africans, had to address the injustices and inequalities confronted by blacks; it had to be liberating.

Therefore, it was not a mystery when Jeremiah Alvesta Wright Jr began his own interpretations of sacred texts in a similar fashion and often quoted James Hal Cone. Wright, an eloquent speaker with a charismatic style, became one of the most influential pastors and theologians in the African American community during the 1980s and 1990s while preaching for the powerful Trinity United Church of Christ of Chicago. Wright's expression of black liberation theology was the most practical and visible manifestation of what Cone's theories would look like in reality. The power of the idea in the hands of Wright was spectacular. The fact that Barack Obama sat at the feet of Jeremiah Wright is often mentioned, but what is not mentioned is that most of the leading theologians and activist philosophers spoke at the church and many of the leading citizens of the nation were pleased to be in the presence of Dr Wright.

Wright's understanding of the religious tradition that most blacks accepted in the United States was critical to his construction of a new approach. He did not want an oppressive religion, one where blacks accepted a God that was against black people or a God that despised the language of black people, or one resigned to black subservience. He wanted to see an activist God who believed in the ultimate victory of truth over falsehood, of justice over injustice, and good over evil. Wright's theology was formed in the crucible of the experiences of the people who came to him for advice and counseling and in the veritable strength of his own mother and father, who instilled in him the values of self-determination.

Jeremiah Wright left college in 1961 to serve in the United States Marine Corps. After two years of service he joined the United States Navy and trained as a cardiopulmonary technician, assisting on the team that cared for President Lyndon Baines Johnson after his 1966 surgery. Ironically, those who resented his prophetic call for America to live up to its founding documents would question Wright's patriotism.

Once Wright had left military service he entered Howard University and earned a Bachelor's degree and a Master's degree in English. He also graduated with a Master's degree from the University of Chicago's Divinity School. He later won his doctorate from United Theological Seminary studying under the famous Samuel DeWitt Proctor, already mentioned, who had mentored Martin Luther King Jr.

The title of President Barack Obama's book *Audacity of Hope* is thought to be taken from a sermon that was delivered by Jeremiah Wright on the audacity to hope, based on a lecture by Frederick G. Sampson on the G. F. Watts painting "Hope." The painting shows a woman "with her clothes in rags, her body scarred and bruised and bleeding, her harp all but destroyed and with only one string left, she had the audacity to make music and praise God. To take the one string you have left and to have the audacity to hope . . . that's the real word God will have us hear from this passage and from Watts' painting."[27]

It is often said that the world is small but it can truly be said that the world of black theologians and philosophers of ethics is a small world. Calvin O. Butts III, who was born in New York in 1949 of parents with roots in rural Georgia, has a connection to most of the major thinkers of his generation. As pastor of Abyssinian Baptist Church, heir to the pulpit of Adam Clayton Powell and Samuel D. Proctor, Butts was thrust into the leadership cadre of the black intelligentsia. He serves as president of the State University of New York at Old Westbury as well as pastor of the famed church.[28]

Butts grew up in Queens and attended Flushing High School. He earned his Bachelor's in philosophy from Morehouse College. Afterwards, he received a Master's in Divinity from Union Theological Seminary and a doctorate in ministry and public policy from Drew University. He founded the Abyssinian Development Corporation (ADC) in 1989, a unit of the church that has contributed to community development of schools, businesses, and housing developments. Serving in numerous capacities as a religious leader and a political opinion-maker and educator has made Butts one of the central figures in the redevelopment of Harlem. But with the pressures of society, the demands of communities, and the contradictions of politics, how does one really balance all the acts and become a moral agent? It is precisely this question that Katie Cannon has answered in her own life as an intellectual.

Katie Cannon was born on January 3, 1950, in Kannapolis, North Carolina. She would turn her love of inquiry into a thirst for higher education, going first to Barber-Scotia College, where she obtained a Bachelor's in 1971, then to the Johnson C. Smith Seminary of Interdenominational Theological Center for her MDiv in 1974, and finally to the Union Theological Seminary for her MPhil and PhD in 1983. Her role in Christian ethics has been fundamental.[29] She took the position of being a theological ethicist as well as a pastor and has merged the two roles in a powerful presentation of the reformation of the church.

Katie Cannon has taught at the New York Theological Seminary, Yale Divinity School, Harvard Divinity School, Wellesley College, Episcopal Divinity School, Temple University, and other colleges. Cannon was the first black woman to be ordained a Presbyterian minister. What was magnificent in the manner that Cannon approached her position was her attention to meditation and reflection on the nature of progressive spirituality. She had always been open to various perspectives on the meaning of life and human destiny; it was the influence of radical thinkers, some feminists and others—Afrocentrists—who provided her the plinth from which to launch her own explorations into the mysteries of human nature. Overcoming both race and gender discrimination is a tradition with Cannon, who has been an inspiration for hundreds of female theologians of all races and classes.

Perhaps because Cannon was the first female ordained in the Presbyterian Church, she felt the necessity for intellectual and historical success. She was, however, the first black female to get a doctorate in the Old Testament and she has used her vanguard position since to challenge the discrimination against females in churches and society, becoming a standard-bearer for various issues of inequality.

Among the awards that have been given to Katie Cannon are the Isaac R. Clark Preaching Award, Young Scholar Award, Fellow, the Rockefeller Protestant Fellow Fund for Theological Education, Ford Foundation Fellow National Fellowships Fund, and the Radcliffe College Bunting Institute Award. On the path to receive even more awards, Katie Cannon has become an internationally recognized phenomenon in religion.

What rendezvous or combination of circumstances in one's life will lead to the creation of an institution? Who can say why the same set of meetings and circumstances may lead one person to succeed and another person to allow the moment to pass? The life of John Harold Johnson, in many ways, parallels the lives of African Americans who fled the poor and segregated South for the more liberal North during the lowest period of the Great Depression and yet through sheer determination to achieve accomplished the most unexpected victories.

John H. Johnson was born in Arkansas City, Arkansas, on January 19, 1918. His father was killed in a sawmill accident when Johnson was six years old and his mother and stepfather raised him. Johnson was an excellent student and when he had completed the eighth grade, the highest grade at his school, he continued in the eighth grade another year just so he could continue his education.

Several events occurred that changed the direction of Johnson's life. First, when he was a teenager his mother took him to Chicago to visit the World's Fair. The Fair opened both his mother's and his mind to the possibilities of living in the North. It seemed that the North would afford Johnson a better opportunity for education and his parents greater access to jobs. So in 1933 he enrolled at DuSable High School, named for the African founder of Chicago, Jean du Sable, although at the time Johnson did not know this.[30]

The family found jobs hard to come by. His stepfather and mother went out every day looking for work but every day came back empty-handed. The family was forced to accept welfare for two years when they could not find even domestic work, normally available at all times. Then both Johnson's stepfather and mother found jobs with the government program the Works Progress Administration and the young Johnson found work with the National Youth Administration. Nevertheless, Johnson felt the sting of being a recent immigrant to Chicago as the students at DuSable teased him and he found it difficult to cope with the taunts he received for his ragged clothes. He was the classmate of Nat King Cole and Redd Foxx; both would become outstanding entertainers. Johnson's will to succeed appeared to grow the more he saw the quality of his classmates. He was eventually elected the student council president, the editor of the school newspaper, and the editor of the yearbook. He was offered a tuition scholarship to attend the University of Chicago but he did not have the funds to pay for the rest of the fees or for housing, so he declined his admission.

However, the second event that impacted his life occurred about this time, when he was invited to give a speech at the annual Urban League dinner. When Harry Pace, the legendary founder of the Supreme Life Insurance Company, heard Johnson speak, he immediately hired him to work for his company so that he could pay for his college education. Working for a black-owned business fueled his own desire to be an entrepreneur.

Johnson started the newspaper *Negro Digest* in 1942 when his mother allowed him to use her furniture as collateral for a $500 loan. He was met by the perennial publisher's problem—poor distribution. He asked a magazine distributor named Joseph Levy to assist him in getting his *Negro Digest* to urban markets. This was extremely valuable as Levy took a personal interest in the product himself and within six months the *Negro Digest* had reached 50,000 copies. It covered history, drama, novels, essays, and politics. The name was later changed to *Black World*. While the *Negro Digest* had a circulation of over 100,000, it never did reach the popularity of Johnson's later publication, *Ebony Magazine*. Johnson would go on to launch *Tan Magazine*, *Jet Magazine*, *African American Stars*, and *Ebony Jr.*

If there had not been a Johnson Publishing Company the need would have been so compelling that someone would have had to create one. Johnson used his publications to create a tapestry of African American life that was positive, inspiring, and factually accurate. His magazines and journals avoided the fantastic and the bizarre, but gave a view of African achievements, sometimes those of Africans from other nations, that challenged the stereotypes preferred by racists. He hired good editors and writers—some of them, such as Lerone Bennett and Hoyt Fuller, most famous editor of *Negro Digest* and *Black World*, achieved superstar status among the black intelligentsia. Bennett, a fellow Southerner to Johnson, is most known for being the executive editor of *Ebony*. He was born on October 17, 1928 in Clarksdale, Mississippi, and always kept his deep Mississippi Delta roots close to his writing style. He was a graduate of Morehouse College. Johnson promoted him to the executive editor position in 1958 and he essentially stamped *Ebony*'s imprint on every issue. Using his position much like W. E. B. Du Bois had done as editor of *Crisis*, Bennett became the most popularly known African American historian of his time. He wrote regularly on major subjects in African American culture. His books *Before the Mayflower: A History of Black America, 1619–1962* and *Forced into Glory: Abraham Lincoln's White Dream* are his most important works.[31] Both Bennett and Fuller were talented, brilliant even, in their portrayals of art, culture, and literature, always showing by example the possibilities of economic and cultural success, but they were not the only writers Johnson employed. The company hired more than 2,600 people, many of them writers, essayists, and editors, but all of them dedicated to the common mission to make the Johnson publications appeal to the black masses.

While it is true that Johnson's company was sometimes criticized for concentrating too much on the material possessions of athletes and entertainers and not enough on intellectuals and more philosophical or ethical accomplishment, his publications touched nerves in the African American experience that made people respond, especially to *Ebony*. Sadly, for many scholars and artists, neither the *Negro Digest* nor its successor, *Black World*, was able to survive economically.

By the time of his death, on August 8, 2005, Johnson had done more than any other publisher to attack what Langston Hughes had once called the "racial mountain." He had challenged it, conquered its sharpest peaks, and fought off all the unsuspected dangers connected with a bold black man developing and sustaining a business in the United States. Individually, he had amassed numerous awards, including in 1972 Publisher of the Year by the leading publishers in the United States, the NAACP's Spingarn Medal, and the

Figure 7.16
Alain Locke, one of the
intellectual leaders of
the Harlem Renaissance.
Image courtesy of
Charles L. Blockson
Afro-American
Collection, Temple
University Libraries.

Presidential Medal of Honor, bestowed by President William Clinton in 1997. He wrote in his 1989 autobiography, "If it could happen to a black boy from Arkansas it could happen to anyone."[32] Of course, as we have seen, it was his ability to take advantage of the challenges placed in front of him and to make the best of them that distinguished his commercial and social journey to overcome the economic deprivations of his youth.

Conclusion

This chapter has revealed a parade of champions under the panoply of difficulties brought about by the vagaries of an unjust system. Yet in no uncertain terms these champions marched toward the prize of genuine American citizenship, undaunted by the obstacles that were placed in front of them. They were first in art and culture, with the express train of productivity having been unleashed by the writings of Alain Locke and W. E. B. Du Bois on culture. They would climb the mountain as Langston Hughes wanted them to do and they would work tirelessly to overcome all of the handicaps of segregation. The fight was on and there was never a time when the right person did not step into the arena to continue until the bell sounded. Each man or woman in turn preached, wrote, sang, built, danced, or spoke themselves into the history of struggle.

Everything in this chapter teaches us that discipline, willpower, intellect, and a masterful commitment to justice can overcome numerous barriers. These champions shared one common trait—they were unafraid to venture their own ideas and opinions and to stand for the collective rise of African people, whether they were in athletics, theology, arts, or business. Their objective was to convey a redemptive message of possibilities—unlimited possibilities—for the black population if racism did not exist.

John Johnson became one of the greatest purveyors of African American contributions to American life with the establishment of the Johnson Publishing Company. In Johnson's company were some of the best writers in the nation, led by Lerone Bennett and Hoyt Fuller. The historian Bennett and later the literary person Fuller dominated the making of opinions and ideas in the African American community, although they were often challenged for this leadership by other voices and institutions. The dominant position of the Johnson Publishing Company as a maker or breaker of black fame and celebrity would last until the emergence of new information technology and the rise of the Internet.

Additional Reading

Anderson, James D. and V. P. Franklin, eds. *New Perspectives on Black Education*. Boston: G. K. Hall, 1978.

Chalk, Ocania. *Black College Sport*. New York: Dodd, Mead, and Co. 1976.

Jaynes, Gerald D. *Branches without Roots: Genesis of the Black Working Class in the American South, 1862–1882*. New York: Oxford University Press, 1986.

Lomax, Alan. *Mr. Jelly Roll: The Fortunes of Jelly Roll Morton, New Orleans Creole and "Inventor of Jazz."* New York: Grove Press, 1950.

Mays, Benjamin E. *Born to Rebel*. New York: Scribner, 1971.

Weaver, John. *The Brownsville Raid*. New York: Norton, 1971.

Chapter Time Markers

1937	Joe Louis becomes the heavyweight champion of the world
1938	Marian Anderson sings at Carnegie Hall
1941	Dorie Miller shoots down Japanese planes attacking Pearl Harbor
1944	Richard Wright breaks with the Communist Party
1947	Jackie Robinson becomes the first black player in modern major league baseball

Trouble in Paradise 8

Important Terms and Names

Hubert Harrison
Universal Negro Improvement Association
Great Depression
Scottsboro Case
Joe Louis
Marian Anderson
Mary McLeod Bethune
Eartha Kitt
Alcan Highway

Charles Drew
Jackie Robinson
99th Pursuit Squadron
Ralph Ellison
Lena Horne
Oscar Micheaux
Dorie Miller
Richard Wright

The Inevitable Confrontations

Racism was no respecter of centuries, and so at the start of the twentieth century Eugene Bullard, the Columbus-born military pilot, was denied opportunity to serve in the United States forces. He had been born on October 9, 1884 and when he was in his teen years he stowed away aboard a ship that took him to Scotland. Later he made a trip to Paris, where he joined the French air force and flew as a member of the Lafayette Flying Club. He married in France and had two daughters whom he raised alone. When the Germans invaded Paris in 1940 Bullard took his daughters to the south of France. Bullard died in New York in 1961. By the time Bullard died, Harlem had already gone through the height of its own glory. Trouble in paradise was right around every corner in the most socially liberal city in the country. However, in the decade prior to Bullard's death New York blacks had asserted their strength in demonstrations and organizations. A. Philip Randolph's plan for a March on Washington had established a major tactic that could be used to draw attention to the issues that affect African Americans. It would reappear in 1963 when Martin Luther King would join A. Philip Randolph and other civil rights leaders to plan a march on Washington. Harlem

Figure 8.1
A. Philip Randolph, founder of the Brotherhood of Sleeping Car Porters. Image courtesy of Charles L. Blockson Afro-American Collection, Temple University Libraries.

was the nerve center for many African American ideas, and this had been so for a considerable time.

Harlem in the decades 1920–1940 may have had a life filled with work and fun, poetry and business, politics and dance, but the fact is that most of the African American population still suffered at the bite of the arrows of racism that pierced the soul. Harlem boiled over with the rhetoric of Hubert Harrison, Marcus Garvey, James Weldon Johnson, and W. E. B. Du Bois as blacks in the *ile ife*, place of heaven, explored socialism, communism, nationalism, and integrationism as avenues for liberation. Nothing was untouched and no river raged so fiercely that it could not be crossed. The inspiration fueled by the achievements of blacks in New York and Chicago and other large cities could not eliminate the problems of racism. Almost every day somewhere in the United States during the first half of the twentieth century there were incidents of harassment, murder, conspiracy, and abuse of black people. There were no islands of solitude for black Americans. There were no courts of appeal, especially in the South, that would listen to reason when it came to a black and a white person arguing over a case. Whites controlled all of the instruments of power and privilege and they maintained those instruments close to their own chests. No wonder African Americans started seeing other nations as being more liberal and progressive in race relations. The venerable James Weldon Johnson, Executive Secretary of the NAACP, wrote in his autobiography, *Along this Way*:

> From the day I set foot in France, I became aware of the workings of a miracle within me . . . I recaptured for the first time since childhood the sense of being just a human being. I need not try to analyze this change for my colored readers; they will under-stand in a flash what took place . . . I was suddenly free; free from conflict within the Man–Negro dualism and the innumerable maneuvers in thought and behavior that it compels; from the problem of the many obvious or subtle adjustments to a multitude of bans and taboos; free from special scorn, special tolerance, in thought special condescension, special commiseration; free to be merely a man.[1]

If a white person were a racist with a strong belief in the inferiority of black people, there would be few actions that the African American could take to dispel that feeling. No achieve-ment would amount to anything, whether in the arts, sciences, sports, music, education, or politics. All could be dismissed or argued against in the most sincere fashion. Approaching the ignorance of white racism meant that the collective energy, not merely the individual energy of one person or the strivings of one personality, but the group's energy and responsibility, had to be turned toward all fronts. It was inescapable that blacks would have to excel at any station, whether in war or peace, in sports or science, in order to redeem the race, and even then redemption might be postponed. The dilemma was real, however, because whites would hardly accept any proof that blacks were equal to whites, and yet blacks felt the need to continue to excel in a sort of "in your face" manner. *Not* showing whites that blacks could achieve as much as, or more than, they could was not an option, but showing them did not mean that blacks would be accepted by whites. Therefore, the task became black acceptance of blacks' achievements; this was a victory in itself because it meant that blacks were finally overcoming the prejudice that had also been grafted into social development and maturity.

Dangers lurked in the economic crisis of Great Depression and its aftermath as whites, feeling less powerful economically, lashed out at blacks within their midst. When Africans pressed for the same menial jobs as the poor whites the friction was palpable. There were no escape routes for individuals seeking to feed their family but through the valley of racial despair.

Consequently, blacks, and particularly young African American males seeking work, were at risk all the time in the society and there was no way to escape the inevitable confrontations so long as you lived in the South. When several young African Americans decided to go to look for work in another city, they ran headlong into the white supremacists' machine. History refers to one of the worst events in this era as the *Scottsboro Boys Case* but the hysteria surrounding the situation reverberated across the nation.[2]

The Scottsboro Case

No trial had ever created as much fury, frenzy, or fanciful notions about sex and race as the case of the Scottsboro Boys, as they were called. When it was all said and over, there were numerous trials, reversals, retrials, convictions, and exonerations. The case started when two white girls alleged that nine black teenagers on a Southern Railroad freight train had raped them on March 25, 1931. The case lasted for twenty years in a search for justice for the nine young African Americans, who had been, as it turned out, falsely accused.

The lives of many people were destroyed in the course of the two decades it took to finally conclude all the deliberations in the case. Some people became immediate celebrities, others found themselves chastised for their opinions and their decisions, and through it all the Scottsboro Boys themselves suffered the most and felt the animosity, hatred, and mean-spiritedness of the white Southern population as racial strife, and indeed, sectional and regional strife, as few persons had ever suffered.

The nine boys were hoboes, that is, they had hitched a ride on a freight train in the middle of the Great Depression. With some vague idea of going somewhere, anywhere, to make their lives better, the young men had hopped aboard the Chattanooga to Memphis train. Nearly two dozen young men, white and black, were riding the train. Four of the blacks were from Chattanooga and the other five were from various places in Georgia. They were heading to Memphis to investigate the story of government jobs hauling logs on the Mississippi. Four young whites, two males and two females, dressed in overalls, also rode the train. They were returning home to Alabama after an unsuccessful search for cotton mill jobs in Chattanooga. When the train got to Alabama a white youth walking across a tank car stepped on the hand of a black youth hanging onto the side of the train. A stone-throwing fight erupted between the youths. At some point in the struggle the blacks forced all of the whites but one off the train. The white youths forced off the train went and reported it to the stationmaster in Stevenson, Alabama. They said a gang of black boys had assaulted them for no reason. The stationmaster wired ahead and had the train stopped by a white posse at Paint Rock, Alabama. Scores of armed whites rushed the train and made it stop. The whites then rounded up all of the young black men they could capture. They were tied together with a rope and put on a flat-back truck and driven to a prison in Scottsboro. Two female mill workers from Huntsville, Victoria Price and Ruby Bates, greeted the posse and, in response to a question or on their own initiative, told the whites that they had been raped by a gang of about twelve blacks with pistols and knives. Taken to the prison, Price pointed out six of the nine boys and said they were the ones who had raped her. Then the guard replied, "Well, it stands to reason that the other had Miss Bates." When Clarence Norris, one of the accused, called the girls liars, a white guard pricked him with a bayonet.[3]

Crowds gathered at the jail hoping for a lynching. However, the governor foiled the plans to lynch the young men when he asked the National Guard to go to the town and protect the jail. Twelve days after their arrest the nine were on trial. The conclusion that the young men were guilty had already been made by white public opinion. A local newspaper, the *Jackson County Sentinel*, had a headline which read: "ALL NEGROES POSITIVELY IDENTIFIED BY GIRLS AND ONE WHITE BOY WHO WAS HELD PRISONER WITH PISTOL AND KNIVES WHILE NINE BLACK FIENDS COMMITTED REVOLTING

CRIME."[4] The lawyers representing the nine were incompetent. Stephen Roddy and Milo Moody had an impossible task. Roddy was neither paid nor ready for the trial—he was a real estate attorney who appeared visibly drunk on the first day of the trial. The second attorney, Milo Moody, was seventy years old and had not tried a case in several decades.

The defense lawyers were willing to try all nine together, despite the fact that the youngest of these defendants was only twelve years old. They decided to try the case in groups of three. The white accuser, Victoria Price, was on the stand no more than ten minutes. Neither Price nor Bates was asked about contradictions in their stories. Crowds roared with approval as the young men were found guilty. When the trials concluded, eight of the Scottsboro Boys had been convicted and sentenced to death. Twelve-year-old Roy Wright had eleven jurors seeking to give him the death penalty even as the prosecutor pled with them to give him a life sentence instead of death.

The Communist Party moved aggressively to support the young boys. While the NAACP was interested in the case and followed it, the Communists made it their own cause. In some circles it is thought that the NAACP did not want to enter a rape case because they could have been damaged in other areas of their fight for justice if it turned out that some of the boys were guilty. This case became one of the instruments for recruiting Southern blacks and Northern liberals to the side of the Communist Party.

Using their legal section, the International Labor Defense (ILD), the Communist Party worked strenuously to be named the lawyers for the young men. Once the NAACP made further assessment of the case it came to the conclusion that it should secure the famous lawyer Clarence Darrow to handle the case. The Communists had already been selected as lawyers for the boys and in January 1932, after arguments, the Alabama Supreme Court affirmed all but one of the eight death sentence convictions. It ruled that Eugene Williams, age thirteen, should not have been tried as an adult.

The United States Supreme Court overturned the convictions in the landmark *Powell v. Alabama* decision. The Court ruled 7–2 that the defendants had the right to have competent attorneys and should not have been convicted in the first place.

Samuel Leibowitz, an extraordinary lawyer, served as the lead defense attorney. He had amassed an enviable record of seventy-seven acquittals and one hung jury out of seventy-eight murder trials. Joseph Brodsky, the ILD's chief attorney, was to assist Leibowitz. The Scottsboro Boys had spent two years between their first and second trials. The trial started in 1933 in Decatur, Alabama.

There would be at least five trials and reversals. Ultimately the Scottsboro Boys would be released, escape, be shot, or be mentally damaged, and their story is one of shame for a nation of laws. Trials run by judges whose intent was to punish young African American men regardless to the testimony were nothing more than sham dramas.

One cannot write about the injustice of this case without thinking that white jurors were unable to accord a black man charged with raping a white woman any presumption of innocence. If anything, they assumed the black man was guilty. Evil is the face of ordinary frightened human beings, and the case of the Scottsboro Boys reminds us that the face was shown to the nine teenagers in its most monstrous form. Haywood Patterson, the most tried of the Scottsboro Boys, escaped from prison in 1948 and went to live in Michigan. The governor of that state refused to grant Alabama's request to extradite him. Patterson wrote a book in 1950 called *Scottsboro Boy*.[5]

Joe Louis and the Strong Keeps Coming Along

Joseph Louis Barrow was born on May 13, 1914. He would become the longest-reigning heavyweight boxing champion in history, from 1937 to 1949, during one of the most racist decades in American history. His reign would cover some of the most tumultuous times in the nation and he would join his place alongside 1936 Olympic champion Jesse Owens, singer Paul Robeson, poet Langston Hughes, actor Lena Horne, and scholar W. E. B. Du Bois as standards of excellence to whom African Americans could point to indicate equality. In the field of athletics, Joe Louis would add verve to the tradition that had been reinvigorated by Jesse Owens' victory in the face of Hitler at the Olympics. Nothing could endanger Owens' place in the hall of victors but Louis would certainly rival him, and perhaps equal him, in the hearts of the people. From humble beginnings in Alabama, Louis grew up in Detroit, Michigan, and earned the nickname "The Brown Bomber."[6] Louis's journey from Alabama to Michigan, from the South to the North, at a time that saw a massive migration of African Americans from the agrarian life of the South to the urban life of the North, was the signature of the era. Mobility, migration, and the use of the railroad as the single biggest mover of Africans since the slave ships were the calling cards of a time of complex struggle against racism on all fronts. Louis would take on the physical world, continuing where Jack Johnson had left off, demonstrating that whites could not always be stronger than blacks, that boxers of skill came in all colors, and that no master race existed.

Early in the 1930s Louis signed a contract with the black bookmaker John Roxborough for his fights when Roxborough convinced him that most white promoters would have no interest in seeing Louis work his way toward the title fight. Roxborough joined with Chicago promoter Julian Black, who had already signed a group of fighters with whom Louis could be paired. Joe Louis's first fight in 1934 was against Jack Kracken, whom he knocked out in the first round. In that year he won all twelve of his professional bouts and by September 1934 was ready to fight the Canadian Alex Borchuk. The Michigan State Boxing Commission tried to force Roxborough to have Louis sign with a white management team while promoting the fight. This was an attempt to have whites control the financial end of the transactions but Roxborough refused and scheduled bouts with Art Sykes and Stanley Poreda. Thus, even in the North, while the racism was different and the venues more varied, racist actions against blacks were frequently attempted.

Soon Louis would become the dominant boxer of his time and be called the greatest heavyweight champion of all time by the International Boxing Research Organization. He was champion for 140 consecutive months, participated in twenty-seven championships, which included twenty-five successful defenses of his title. *The Ring* magazine list of one hundred greatest punchers ranked Joe Louis number one on the list. While his boxing skills were indisputable and his winning ways made him famous and rich at a time when African Americans were struggling for basic rights, Louis' value to the black community and ultimately to the nation went far beyond his titles and his prowess in the ring.

He embodied the popular values of the hard-working American. He was devoted to his family, devoted to his country, willing to serve in the war effort, and God-fearing. Those who knew him attested to his honesty, although those who were often around him may have been less than honest. Indeed, Joe Louis achieved not just African American hero status but also American hero status. Among his social achievements were integration of the game of golf and breaking the color bar in sports by appearing under a sponsor's exemption in a Professional Golf Association event in 1952.

Joe Louis stepped into the boxing game with superior skills at a time that white America was wary about the rise of another Jack Johnson. Indeed, Johnson's turbulent reign had shattered the image of the invincible white and had breached the racial divide between black men and white women causing deep resentment in the white community. Thus, Joe Louis' prowess as a boxer was always shadowed by the strong image of Jack Johnson. To protect him from what they saw as the failures of Jack Johnson, his black advisors, Roxborough and Black, developed Seven Commandments for Louis when he turned twenty-one years of age. Among the commandments were that he should "never have his picture taken with a white woman," "never gloat over a fallen opponent," "never engage in fixed fights," "live and fight clean."

There were several fights that made him a household name before he won the championship. He fought Primo Carnera and beat him in six rounds; Carnera had been the former heavyweight champion and was 269 pounds and 6'6". The black community saw the defeat of the Italian Carnera as an instance where African Americans could show solidarity with the Ethiopian community that had been invaded by Mussolini, the Italian dictator. The fact that Louis was now being called the "Mahogany Mauler" or the "Chocolate Chopper" indicated growing affection by the press. In some ways, it was the naïveté of Louis that the press seemed to prefer. He was strong, powerful, but gentle and unassuming, not a threat to white manhood, except in the ring, and certainly no threat to white womanhood.

Not since the retirement of Jack Dempsey in 1929 had there been any cheer in the boxing ranks. There was no heroic figure and even if Louis were black, the white American boxing public was looking for someone to demonstrate American virility. The argument was that boxing had become a cesspool of gamblers and fixers and needed someone to rescue the game from organized crime. That the rescuer would be black had not been anticipated, yet the strength and clean-cut quality of Louis made him the champion to rescue the sport.

Joe Louis fought Max Schmeling, the former world champion from Germany, in June 1936. This proved to be a challenge, although prior to the fight some people said that this was just a tune-up for Louis and not a threat. Louis had a record of 27–0 and no one thought of Schmeling, already thirty years old, as a major threat. Schmeling prepared and Louis played golf, not taking the fight too seriously. On June 19, 1936, Louis was knocked out in the twelfth round by Max Schmeling. This brought everything back into focus and Louis had to recast his training style and concentrate on overcoming his mistakes. Nevertheless, he went on to fight Braddock for the championship and on June 22, 1937 he knocked out Braddock in the eighth round. He was now heavyweight champion of the world, just a year after Jesse Owens' conquering running and jumping in Berlin. Celebrations took place all over America as black people ran through the streets shouting, "I told you so, I told you so!" to anyone who would listen. Louis was now at the pinnacle of the heavyweight division and his journey was complete. Langston Hughes, the black poet laureate, said that thousands of blacks lived each day because of the victories of Joe Louis. Out of the depths of economic depression they could see one black man's triumph and feel good about themselves. The effect that Joe Louis had on the emotions of African Americans was unbelievable. In small towns in the South, enterprising business people started companies that sold "Joe Louis Cookies" to capitalize on the "greatest" black man of his time. His victory inspired Africans on the continent of Africa as well, and colonized Africans in Nigeria, South Africa, and East Africa gloried in the ascent of a black man to the top of the heavyweight division in boxing.[7]

Louis knew, however, that there would always be those who would say that he had been beaten by Max Schmeling. Louis wanted to beat Schmeling to solidify in his mind and that of the public that he was the legitimate champion. Schmeling could not reach terms with Louis on the money. Instead, Schmeling maneuvered to fight the British Empire champion, Tommy Farr, but when Louis' people offered Farr a guaranteed $60,000 he chose to fight Louis instead. On August 30, 1937 more than 32,000 people went to Yankee Stadium to see Louis fight one of the toughest opponents he had ever faced. The battle went the entire fifteen rounds. Louis had not knocked Farr down and the referee was apparently congratulating Farr after the bout only to hear a controversial decision announced that gave Louis the win. The enormous crowd booed the decision; they had expected Louis to at least knock Farr down.

Even with the controversial win over Farr, Louis was not satisfied with himself. He believed that he had to fight Schmeling once again, a match which would be considered one of the most famous battles of all time. It is a signature event in sports for the twentieth century for several reasons. In the first instance, it took place during the rise of the doctrine of Aryan superiority when *der Führer* of Germany, Adolf Hitler, preached the dominance and superiority of the pure white man. Secondly, most black Americans felt that they were the equal to any whites and believed that the "deliverer" had come to prove this fact. As far as the white Americans were concerned, the threat of a Nazi Germany with the audacity to enslave "whites" as they and other Europeans had enslaved Africans and Asians was too much to accept. Nazism had to be defeated and if it took an African to do it in the boxing ring, they would accept the arrows of their dismay and support Joe Louis.

The fight was set for 1938 and Joe Louis set about training with a renewed purpose. President Franklin D. Roosevelt told him, "Joe, we need muscles like yours to beat Germany." Louis knew that the nation was depending upon him to teach the German Nazi a lesson. Two years earlier Jesse Owens, the fastest human alive, had smashed the Aryan dream four times at the Summer Olympics in Berlin when in August 1936 he won four gold medals in the 100 meters, 200 meters, long jump, and as a part of the 4×100 meter relay team. Now the pressure was on another black man to demonstrate that there was nothing to the spurious allegations of racial supremacy and racial superiority of whites.[8]

The Germans came to New York with a publicist who immediately announced that a black man could never defeat Schmeling and that when Schmeling won, his money would be used to build war tanks. This caused many Americans, whites and blacks, to protest the presence of the Nazi ideology in New York.

On June 22, 1938 Joe Louis met Max Schmeling for the second time at Yankee Stadium before a sell-out crowd of 70,043 people. Millions of people heard the broadcast in numerous languages around the globe. The world was on edge. Here was the contest of the age between good and evil, between racial animus and racial harmony, between threats, bombast, and taunts and calm, resolve, and dignity. A black man, Joe Louis, an American national, the most dominant fighter of the era, was in the ring with a white man, a German national, Max Schmeling, who was the only man to have defeated Louis.

The fight started and ended in two minutes and four seconds. Louis brutalized Schmeling with a series of thunderous poundings that forced him against the rope, where he received paralyzing blows to the mid-section. In two minutes and four seconds, Schmeling was knocked to the canvas three times, only managing to throw two punches during the entire boxing match. The fight was stopped when Schmeling's trainer threw in the towel, announcing that Schmeling's resistance was over.

Joe Louis would fight many outstanding boxers such as Billy Conn and a lot of "bums of the month" types but his most challenging battle would always be against racism and discrimination. While Louis was shielded from the most serious aspects of racism most of his life as a heavyweight, his last years were spent living off the largesse of sponsors who sympathized with his situation. Indeed, here was an authentic, genuine American national hero who experienced the angst and conflict of living in a racially divided society while at the same time seeking to promote the good. On one occasion Joe Louis had to argue with two MPs who sought to move him and Sugar Ray Robinson to the back of an Alabama military bus. He was successful in doing so on that occasion, though on another occasion he had to resort to bribery to persuade an officer to drop charges against Jackie Robinson for punching a racist captain for calling him a "nigger." Louis fought in ninety-six boxing exhibitions with friends like Sugar Ray Robinson, called "pound for pound the greatest fighter in the world," before 2 million soldiers. By the end of the war Louis had fought in many charity events raising money for various causes and had championed the war effort,

Figure 8.2
Jackie Robinson and Mary McLeod Bethune, two of the most iconic African personalities. Image courtesy of Charles L. Blockson Afro-American Collection, Temple University Libraries.

but the Internal Revenue Service credited all of the money raised by the charity events as taxable income. The government pursued him relentlessly for tax evasion during the 1950s.

Defeats by Ezzard Charles and Rocky Marciano sealed the boxing career of Joe Louis. He had sought to fight to earn money to pay a $500,000 tax liability to the IRS, which later grew to over $1,000,000 by the late 1950s. He was nothing of his old self when he stepped into the ring for the last time in the United States against Marciano, who beat him badly, closing both eyes, and then weeping with him about the loss. Marciano had knocked Louis out of the ring in the eighth round. He would fight again in Taipei, Taiwan, in December 1951 against Corporal Buford DeCordova, but for all real purposes the career of Joe Louis as a boxer was over.

It is believed that he made nearly $5,000,000 in purses but only received $800,000. Investing in a restaurant, an insurance company, a softball team, a milk company, a punch drink company, a horse farm, a public relations firm, Louis sought ways to preserve the money he did receive from his purses, only to see the businesses fail because of poor management and corruption on the part of employees. He also repaid the city of Detroit the welfare money it had paid his family when he was a child.

Nevertheless, Louis seldom received grace or mercy from the IRS. It was through his army friend Ash Resnick that he eventually got a job as an official greeter to the Caesar's Palace in Las Vegas. He had to resort to wrestling in the 1950s and 1960s, and again in 1972, to make ends meet. Even Max Schmeling, the former Nazi and the first man to beat Louis, provided financial assistance during Louis' retirement. In the 1960s an agreement with the IRS, negotiated by his friends, helped Joe Louis live out his life quite comfortably until his death of a heart attack in Desert Springs, California, on April 12, 1981. President Ronald Reagan waived the eligibility rules to allow Louis to be buried in the Arlington National Cemetery with full military honors. Trapped as he was, an African American in a predominantly white nation with powerful anti-black sentiments, Louis was destined, even with all of his grandeur as a person and athlete, to be relegated to the margins of American life. There would be some belated attempts to accord him his rightful place, but had he been a white boxer with such records there would have been hundreds of films, study guides, and workshops about style, determination, and skill, based on his life. Yet Louis lived a life of few regrets and by the time of his death he was a respected figure throughout the African world. Younger boxers, like Nelson Mandela, grew up on the lore of Joe Louis. His inspiring story, despite some attempts to minimize his achievements, would help break the barriers of race and racism long after he had left the public stage.

Marian Anderson Confronts Racism in the Arts—and Wins

At the time Joe Louis was rising in the ranks of great boxers, the great mezzo-soprano Marian Anderson, born in Philadelphia on February 27, 1897, would be rising to become one of most impressive singers of any generation. It would be said that a voice like hers would not be heard in another one hundred years. In September 1930 she and Paul Robeson were both performing in London, Robeson in the production of *Othello* at the Savoy and Anderson at London's Wigmore Hall. Two African Americans on stage in the most cosmopolitan city of the Western world represented an expression of the indomitable will of African people to

Figure 8.3
Marian Anderson, contralto with the "voice of a thousand birds." Image courtesy of Charles L. Blockson Afro-American Collection, Temple University Libraries.

express themselves in the arts. Rarely had the stage of London seen such masterful performances by a man and a woman acclaimed as the greatest artists in their fields.[9]

Anderson had received a scholarship from the National Association of Negro Musicians to study in Great Britain. She, like other artists before her, would return to Europe again and again, feeling often that there was more acceptance of blacks in Europe than in America. Marian Anderson studied on a Julius Rosenwald Fund grant while she was perfecting her language skills in Italian and German. Because most operas were written in these languages she felt that it was essential to master them. Of course, it did not hurt her to also learn the art of lieder singing—from England she traveled to Germany and began a Scandinavian tour from Berlin.

Marian Anderson was the oldest daughter of John and Anna Anderson. Her father, John, worked at the large Reading Terminal Market in Philadelphia as a laborer, loading and unloading fruits and vegetables, while her mother, Anna, who had been a schoolteacher, found work as a domestic, as did a majority of black women in Philadelphia during that time.

Her father died when she was fifteen years old and she sought to prepare herself for the labor market to assist her mother with the younger children until she discovered that her music was her first love. When she applied for admission to music school she was rejected because she was black, thus setting up the epic battle of another African American making the long journey of liberation. She decided that her dreams would not be shattered by racism and took the path of thousands of other talented blacks—to master her skills by any means necessary. It was important that she had the backing of her family. If they knew anything, they knew she could sing.

Marian Anderson had achieved high recognition as a young singer at her church and in school assemblies prior to her father's death, and used the piano that he bought for her from his brother to teach herself how to play. She excelled as a young singer and finally, at the age of twenty-two, she sang at the National Baptist Convention. She soon began to tour black colleges, singing, among other songs, "Deep River," which often brought audiences to tears. At $100 dollars a concert she was on her way to becoming a significant professional when on April 23, 1924 she held a concert in New York at the Town Hall. This concert nearly caused her to end her career because the audience was lacking and so was her voice, according to critics. But undeterred, Marian entered the Philadelphia Philharmonic Society contest in 1925, winning first place among 300 competitors. She then sang in New York with the Philharmonic Orchestra accompanying her.

By 1926 Anderson was touring the eastern and southern United States as a major musical discovery. Her appearance on December 30, 1928 at Carnegie Hall was hailed for its power, range, and delicacy. Thus, her performance in London in 1930 was a remarkable demonstration of an artist's stride toward success. She performed 142 concerts in Scandinavia and sang before King Gustav in Sweden and King Christian in Denmark. By 1935 Arturo Toscanini, the Italian conductor, could exclaim, "Yours is a voice such as one hears once in a hundred years."

Marian Anderson was an international star when she returned to New York's Town Hall on December 20, 1935 and sang with tremendous applause to an appreciative audience. Nevertheless, four years later she would experience the reality of being black in America when Sol Hurok tried to rent Constitutional Hall for an Anderson concert. But the hall's policy was that it should not be rented to blacks. The fact that the Constitutional Hall refused to allow Marian Anderson to book the stage caused First Lady Eleanor Roosevelt to resign from the Daughters of the American Revolution, who controlled the hall. Mrs Roosevelt, Sol Hurok, and Walter White, the Executive Director of the NAACP, arranged with Secretary of the Interior Harold Ickes to open the steps of the Lincoln Memorial for a free concert on Easter Sunday. Marian Anderson sang before a live audience of 75,000 people with millions more listening by radio.

Four years later, in 1943, Marian Anderson performed at Constitutional Hall at a benefit for a Chinese relief effort. Later Anderson was appointed to the United Nations Human Rights Committee by President Dwight Eisenhower and sang at the inauguration of John F. Kennedy in 1961. Marian Anderson was considered a national treasure and received the Spingarn Medal, the Bok Award, the American Medal for Freedom, a gold medal from Congress on her seventy-fifth birthday, and the National Medal of Arts. Disinclined to be combative, Marian Anderson was often criticized for not speaking out more vigorously against racism. She would take her meals in her rooms instead of fighting to eat in the restaurants at hotels. She tried to avoid situations that proved uncomfortable or stressful from a racial perspective. Although Marian Anderson insisted on vertical seating where blacks would be allotted seats in all parts of the auditorium, she nevertheless tried to avoid difficult situations until 1950, when she made it clear that she would not sing to segregated audiences. Anderson died of heart failure in Portland, Oregon, on April 8, 1993.

Lena Horne and Eartha Kitt: Princesses of the Performing Stage

Two important performers, Lena Horne and Eartha Kitt, defined and reoriented the concept of style for the stage during their careers. Lena Horne, more than any other woman, was the pin-up queen for African American servicemen during World War II. Key to her acceptance by black servicemen was her commitment to African American culture. She refused to perform for audiences of soldiers where black troops were barred, thus underscoring her intent not to be used against her people. Horne was deeply involved in the creation of early black films, becoming one of the best-known early stars. She performed with many black male stars on the stage as an actor as well as a singer. Lena Horne was a friend of Paul Robeson's during the worst period of his isolation and marginalization after he was accused

Figure 8.4
Lena Horne, actress and singer. Image courtesy of Charles L. Blockson Afro-American Collection, Temple University Libraries.

of being a communist. As a member of the NAACP she was urged by the organization to allow it to use her talents to break the color bar in the film industry. Prior to Lena Horne most jobs for blacks in the movies had been menial. She refused these roles and demanded to be treated with dignity and respect. There would not have been a Dorothy Dandridge had Lena Horne not plowed the fields for new seeds to be sown in the industry, As early as 1938 she appeared in the musical *The Duke is Tops* as the Bronze Venus. Thus, when the first significant roles written for blacks appeared in the big studios, *Cabin in the Sky* and *Stormy Weather*, for example, Lena Horne appeared with Eddie "Rochester" Anderson, Ethel Waters, Duke Ellington, and Louis Armstrong. Because of her strength she was able to let the frequent abuse and negative comments roll off her like water from a duck's back, unfazed by the ignorance of many whites. When Lena Horne died in 2010 at the age of ninety-two she left behind one of the most varied and impressive résumés of any African American performer.

Her contemporary, to some extent, was Eartha Kitt. While Horne was active all of her life in the African American struggle, even receiving a compliment for her style and beauty in an early book by W. E. B. Du Bois, Eartha Kitt, who was tremendously successful, has been interpreted as a much less activist talent.

Eartha Kitt was born in South Carolina after the white man who owned the farm where they worked raped her mother. She was raised in New York City and as a teenager joined the Katherine Dunham Dance troupe until 1948. Subsequently she performed in France and

Figure 8.5
Eartha Kitt, actress, singer, and cabaret star. Image courtesy of Charles L. Blockson Afro-American Collection, Temple University Libraries.

throughout Europe as a singer and dancer with a distinctive style. In 1950 she was given a role as Helen of Troy in the staging of *Dr Faustus*, which initiated a long career on stage and in films. Her candor about the Vietnam War is reported to have brought tears to the eyes of Lady Bird Johnson, the president's wife, when she complained in 1968 that America sent off its best young people to be maimed and killed in a war. Her comments caused many companies to withdraw from supporting her performances but she continued, always with the capacity to perform in nightclubs throughout the world. After a triumphant and enthusiastic reception in Moscow she returned to New York and was offered numerous parts in plays and films, once again proving that maintaining a sense of purpose and principles was necessary for personal success. By the time Eartha Kitt died in 2008 she had received hundreds of honors, awards, and prizes.

Exploring the Celluloid Media

Like Lena Horne and Eartha Kitt, Oscar Micheaux, a few years before them, sought ways to express the durable qualities of the black soul in an artistic manner. Often criticized for some of his images and characters, Oscar Micheaux nevertheless emerged as the major producer of African American films during the twentieth century. Although it is conceded by scholars that William D. Foster started creating films about a decade earlier than Micheaux, no one doubts the prolific work of this early black filmmaker. After forming his own company in 1910, the Foster Photoplay Company, in Chicago, the sports writer for the newspaper *Chicago Defender* became the first independent black filmmaker in history. He produced the film *The Railroad Porter* in 1912. When D. W. Griffith produced the racist fantasy *The Birth of a Nation* in 1915 he inspired blacks to make their own films. The negative stereotypes in that film are as much a part of the racist imagination of white Americans as any book written by the most vile and obscene of authors. Every negative image of blacks appeared in Griffith's film. Celebrated by whites as one of the greatest films made, *The Birth of a Nation* motivated two brothers, George Perry Johnson and Noble Johnson, to create the Lincoln Motion Picture Company in 1916. They produced films like *The Realization of a Negro's Ambition* in 1916, *Trooper of Troop K* in 1917, and *The Birth of a Race* in 1918. A year later Oscar Micheaux produced the film *The Homesteader* and began his career as the most prolific black filmmaker. He made more than forty films and cast Paul Robeson in the film *Body and Soul*, which was produced in 1925.

The legacy of black filmmakers acting in their own interest and within a framework of liberation visions may be traced from the beginning of the twentieth century to the creation of a Los Angeles School of African American filmmakers that gave us Pamela Jones, Jamaa Fanaka, Billy Woodberry, A. Sharon Larkin, Larry Clark, Charles Burnett, and the incredibly focused work of Haile Gerima and Julie Dash. To be sure, there are hundreds of filmmakers who do independent work or who work admirably for large studios, but the ability to connect historical, cultural, and social values to the ultimate advancement of the African American community is a special characteristic of the best filmmakers. Increasingly, filmmakers are discovering the historical narratives that have remained untold in the media of film, for example the obstacles that confronted Harriet Tubman in her underground railroad journeys, the religious imagination of Nat Turner, the dramatic confrontations between

Figure 8.6 Paul Robeson and Marian Anderson, two giants of the singing world, both with voices that were considered rare in musical history. Image courtesy of Charles L. Blockson Afro-American Collection, Temple University Libraries.

civil rights leaders over tactics, the real secrets of the plantations' social life where one person could own another, and so forth. What we cannot doubt, however, is the value of examining the lives of heroes, and no people has ever had any more heroes who exhibit courage and bravery under stress than the African American people. Doris"Dorie" Miller is one such hero.

Doris "Dorie" Miller and the Narrative of Courage

War tends to produce opportunities for humans to carry out extraordinary tasks. During World War II the second great international war, Doris Miller, often called "Dorie" Miller, emerged as the great black hero of the era. While Dorie Miller was a long way from being the only African American hero of the war, nor was he the first to gain recognition, he was truly the person who captured the imagination of the black community. An individual with limited—almost deliberately limited—knowledge of warfare, but with enormous courage and powerful natural instincts, he shot down Japanese planes at Pearl Harbor. It was a remarkable narrative of nobility and majesty.

Miller was not the only hero of World War II. There were others, many other blacks, who distinguished themselves in their bravery and valor. Indeed, in 1997 President Clinton recognized seven additional heroes in one of the most sobering occasions in the nation's military history. These were men who, because of their race, did not receive recognition for their courage. They were denied the Medal of Honor until 1997, when only one of the men, Vernon Baker, was still living. Near Viareggio, Italy, Baker had distinguished himself by taking out two German machine gun nests and had drawn enemy fire to himself to permit others to evacuate. Captain David Williams, the white commander of A Company, 761st Tank Battalion, said of his black soldiers, "I had the best tank company in the whole 3rd Army."[10] He recommended Ruben Rivers, who always wanted to point the attack, in the fight with the Germans. He was killed in fierce action on November 19, 1944. President Clinton said these men "are among the bravest of the brave."[11] Although Clinton pointed out that President Truman had given out twenty-eight Medals of Honor after the war but no black was in the group, it was time to rectify that historical situation. The president said, "Today, we fill the gap in that picture."[12] There were numerous rumors of heroes and reports of exceptional exploits circulating in the African American community about the war. Nothing captured the population more than the story of Dorie Miller, probably because of the Pearl Harbor catastrophe and its significance to the national narrative. It was whispered that a black man, a cook, had shot down Japanese planes and had saved his captain's life.

Doris "Dorie" Miller was born in Waco, Texas, on October 12, 1919, to Henrietta and Conery Miller. He had three brothers, one who also served in the army during World War II. A natural athlete with strong competitive interests, Miller achieved a reputation in Moore High School as a fullback on the football team. His father was a farmer and Dorie spent most of his youth working on the farm until he enlisted into the U.S. Navy as a Mess Attendant, Third Class. He thought that by joining the navy he would be able to travel the world, earn a living, and make his family proud. He joined the navy in September, 1939, Second Class and First Class, and subsequently was promoted to Cook, Third Class. Miller took training at the Naval Training Station, Norfolk, Virginia, and was then assigned to the ammunition ship USS *Pyro* (AE-1), where he served as a Mess Attendant, and on January 2, 1940 he was transferred to USS *West Virginia* (BB-48) as Mess Attendant, but while on board the USS *West Virginia* he soon became the ship's heavyweight boxing champion. Joe Louis had defeated Max Schmeling in 1938 and many black men had decided to go into the boxing ring. Miller, strong and sturdy, took up the sport and developed a fairly good reputation as a pugilist.

Miller was sent to temporary duty aboard USS *Nevada* (BB-36) at Secondary Battery Gunnery School in July 1940. He returned to the *West Virginia* on August 3 and was serving on that battleship when the Japanese attacked Pearl Harbor on December 7, 1941.

The story of Miller's heroics began when he awoke at 6 A.M. and while collecting his laundry heard the alarm for general quarters. He headed for his battle station, which was the anti-aircraft battery nearest him. When he arrived he noticed that a torpedo had wrecked it, so he went up on deck and began to carry wounded sailors to safety. He was ordered to the deck to retrieve the mortally wounded captain of the battleship. After moving the captain's body, Miller rushed to man a fifty-caliber Browning anti-aircraft machine gun that had not been damaged. He fired until he ran out of ammunition and the call came to abandon the ship. Miller had never been trained on the machine gun but he said that it was not difficult since he had watched others fire the guns. Miller claims to have shot down one plane, but by the time the story reached the African American community the hero had shot down five Japanese attack planes. The battleship was severely damaged and flooded below deck, and when Miller and others finally got off, it settled slowly to the bottom of the harbor. The West Virginia carried 1,541 men and in the attack 130 were killed and fifty-two were wounded.[13]

The Secretary of the Navy, Frank Knox, commended Dorie Miller, and he also received the Navy Cross, personally presented by Fleet Admiral Chester W. Nimitz, the Commander-in-Chief, Pacific Fleet. Nimitz said, "This marks the first time in this conflict that such high tribute has been made in the Pacific Fleet to a member of his race and I'm sure that the future will see others similarly honored for brave acts."[14]

Miller subsequently perished aboard the *Liscome Bay*, to which he had been assigned in the spring of 1943. A single Japanese torpedo destroyed the ship on November 24, 1943 while it was cruising near Butaritari Island. In 1973 the United States Navy commissioned a ship, the USS *Miller* (FF-1091), a Knox-class frigate, in honor of Doris "Dorie" Miller.

No Lesser Distinction in Valor

Every time the nation called, and everywhere the battle was, the black soldier was there. Black women served in the Women's Army Auxiliary Corps (WAACs) from its inception in 1942 during World War II. Later, in 1943, when the Women's Army Corps (WACs) was approved and the bill signed into law, black women again signed up and remained in the service at a higher rate than white women. They operated in the theaters of war with bravery and valor equal to that of any man. Forty African American women had entered the WAAC officer candidate class 1942 and had been segregated from whites into a separate platoon. These women were allowed to attend classes and share the dining facilities with white officer candidates but were segregated from the service clubs, cosmetic shops, and movie theaters. Black women served in the Navy's Women Accepted for Volunteer Emergency Service (WAVES) as well as the Coast Guard.

The African American women who served in World War II were the forerunners for those who would be fully committed in the succeeding wars. Since the Revolutionary War, when black women served beside men, according to Lucy Terry's account, dressing themselves like males, and the Civil War, where the service of Harriet Tubman and other women as spies and sabotage experts helped the Union troops to win the war, the black woman as soldier has distinguished herself.[15] In fact, during the 1990s African American women served with remarkable talent during Operation Desert Storm. They were officers, noncommissioned officers, and enlisted soldiers, who fought in the battles just as the men fought. It is reported that of the 35,000 females who were sent to Desert Storm, an estimated forty percent of them were African American women. They were soldiers who went through the same privations as the men, with little electricity, blistering desert heat, no running water, and elementary toilet facilities. One woman, Lieutenant Phoebe Jeter, headed an all-male platoon, and ordered thirteen Patriots launched (anti-missile missiles), destroying at least two Scuds (Iraqi surface-to-surface missiles). During Desert Storm another African American woman, Captain Cynthia Mosely, commanded Alpha Company, 24th Support Battalion Forward, 24th Infantry Division (Mechanized), a hundred-person unit that brought fuel, water, food, and ammunition to the front lines. On foreign battlefields African Americans have shown their willingness to sacrifice to protect the country of their birth but also to fight for the economic, cultural, and mental liberation of African people inside the nation. These

Figure 8.7
Harriet Tubman, called by some the greatest African American because of her feat of traveling to the South and rescuing more than 300 enslaved Africans. Image courtesy of Charles L. Blockson Afro-American Collection, Temple University Libraries.

women did not serve their nation unaware of the indignities suffered at home by their families; they served because they believed that in their service and in their commitment to fight for freedom for others they would insure their will to resist discrimination and make an America that lived up to its founding documents. They were patriots, clear and simple.

Overcoming the Odds

History never takes a straight line and the experiences of African Americans have rarely followed any predictable course except that of African agency. Black women and men have stepped up whenever they felt that their service or action would insure a better life for their posterity. In 1942 the American government, fearing the invasion of Alaska by the Japanese, decided to complete the much-discussed highway linking Alaska to the forty-eight states. When 10,000 soldiers were ordered to the North to build the Alcan Highway, often called one of the ten most significant construction projects in the twentieth century, more than 3,900 of the troops were black.[16] In fact, so many African Americans worked on that 1,600-mile highway that some people believed only blacks worked on it. Of course that was not true, yet nearly a half of the troops of the engineering corps, the 93rd, 95th, and 97th regiments, were African Americans. Congress approved a law that allowed African Americans to work alongside white soldiers for the first time, and the achievements of black soldiers in taking a leading role in building the highway across the cold terrain of the North in eight months, crossing over 200 raging rivers, and often having only dog sleds to supply them with food, music, and news of home, made such an impression on the American nation that by 1947 the United States integrated the armed forces. Barriers based on race fell daily in the midst of a national emergency.

When some whites argued that African Americans could not fly airplanes, Tuskegee set up a flying school and trained hundreds of African Americans to be flyers and took the First Lady, Eleanor Roosevelt, for a flyover. The Tuskegee flyers distinguished themselves during World War II.[17]

The men came from every section of the nation to train as pilots, navigators and bombardiers. They put themselves through the most rigorous training, believing that black soldiers or airmen had to be twice as good as the whites to succeed in a racist society. They were academically well prepared for their tests and endurance. They studied engine mechanics, radio communications, control tower operations, and expert flying.

Those who became flyers were trained at the Tuskegee Army Air Field in Alabama. The aviation cadets started in 1941 and the program lasted for nine months. Thirteen started the first class and five completed the training. Soon thereafter the program began to receive many new recruits, and eventually 996 pilots got their licenses from the TAAF program. Black pilots, navigators, and bombardiers were necessary in the minds of the black

Figure 8.8 Eleanor Roosevelt and Marian Anderson. Marian Anderson was a magnificent contralto. Image courtesy of Charles L. Blockson Afro-American Collection, Temple University Libraries.

community. Over half of the pilots served overseas, most notably in Europe. They were in the 99th Pursuit Squadron or the 332nd Fighter Group, trained and led by the brilliant Benjamin O. Davis Jr. The 99th, later called Fighter Squadron, trained in P-40 Warhawk aircraft and flew in North Africa, Italy, and Sicily. They often had to suppress their rage but they showed great signs of skill and ingenuity as pilots.

Scientists Multiply to Defeat Racism

The history of the African American scientist has not been fully written and cannot be completed here, but it is essential to understand that blacks were not simply isolating themselves in a few sectors of the society. Men and women were asserting intelligence and drive in all avenues of American society. One such individual was Ernest Just, who was born on August 14, 1883 in Charleston, South Carolina.[18] Growing up in a segregated and racist society did not prevent Just from seeking to achieve at the highest levels. His gift for academic research and intellectual inquiry led him ultimately to Dartmouth College. In 1907 he graduated from that Ivy League college as the only student to be accorded the title *magna cum laude* with a degree in Zoology. He had taken honors in botany, sociology, and history as well. Just went on to teach at Howard University and to becoming the first African American to write books on cell theory. In fact, he was one of the first Americans of any race to achieve original research in cell theory. As head of the Department of Physiology at Howard University until his death, Dr Just, as he was known, was considered one of the first pure scientists produced in the country. He won the first Spingarn Medal by given the NAACP in 1915 for his accomplishments. In 1916, Just demonstrated his genius once again, graduating *magna cum laude* from University of Chicago with his doctorate in experimental embryology. At the Marine Biological Laboratory (MBL) in Woods Hole, Massachusetts, Just carried out hundreds of experiments studying the fertilization of the marine mammal cell. Based upon his research conducted at Wood's Hole, Just published his first book, entitled *Basic Methods for Experiments on Eggs of Marine Mammals*. As brilliant as he was, Just experienced the ignorance of racial prejudice in the United States and in 1930 decided to study in Europe, mainly France, and published his second book, *The Biology of the Cell Surface*. In 1938 he went to France with the idea of continuing his research in that country. Although he published a number of papers and lectured on the topic of cell cytoplasm, he was eventually driven out of the country and back to America. Just died October 27, 1941 in Washington, DC, two months before the bombing of Pearl Harbor.

Charles Drew and Blood Plasma

As in previous wars, African Americans kept distinguishing themselves during the World War II years. While Ernest Just had died broken-hearted because his achievements were not truly recognized by the American population as they had been by the French, other scientists kept expressing their genius in no uncertain terms. No one added more to the discourse over race and blood than Charles Drew. Like Ernest Just, he was to become a hero of science and medicine to the African American community.

Drew was born on June 3, 1904 in Washington, DC, twenty-one years the junior of Ernest Just. Like Just, Charles Drew excell academically and eventually went to Amherst College in Massachusetts, where he was an honors student. Finding it difficult to attend medical school in the United States, he entered McGill University Medical School in Montreal, majoring in physiological anatomy.[19]

Charles Drew left medical school and researched blood plasma and transfusions in the United States. While working at Columbia University he made discoveries relating to the preservation of blood. Separating the liquid red blood cells from the near-solid plasma and freezing the two separately, he discovered that blood could be preserved and reconstituted for later use.

His work with the storage of blood led to the blood plasma preservation process, later called the blood bank system. With this discovery Charles Drew revolutionized medical treatment and made it possible during World War II for soldiers to be helped on the battlefield. Dr Drew also founded the American Red Cross blood bank, becoming the first director, and he organized the world's first blood bank drive, "blood for Britain."

The American Red Cross established blood donor stations to collect plasma for the U.S. armed forces. After the war, Charles Drew became head of Surgery at Howard University. Like Ernest Just before him, he received the Spingarn Medal for his contributions to medical science in 1944. Charles Drew died at the early age of forty-six from injuries suffered in a car accident near Burlington, North Carolina. He had been driving with three other black doctors to a meeting in Tuskegee, Alabama, when the car skidded and flipped over, pinning Drew under the steering wheel. He had severe injuries but his companions escaped with minor physical injuries. Drew was rushed to the hospital but died thirty minutes after receiving treatment. Over the years, disputes have raged as to whether or not a white hospital refused to see him for treatment and to give him a blood transfusion. According to one account by Scot Morris, the author of *Omni Games*, Charles Drew was not denied treatment by the white hospital. In fact, Morris claims that one of the doctors traveling with Drew was Dr John Ford. He is reported to have told Scot Morris that

> We all received the very best of care. The doctors started treating us immediately. He had a superior vena caval syndrome—blood was blocked getting back to his heart from his brain and upper extremities, and to give him a transfusion would have killed him sooner. Even the most heroic efforts couldn't have saved him. I can truthfully say that no efforts were spared in the treatment of Dr Drew, and, contrary to popular myth, the fact that he was a Negro did not in any way limit the care that was given to him.[20]

This account by the science fiction pundit Scot Morris is now given as the evidence that the legendary account of the white hospital refusing to treat Charles Drew in 1950 is apocryphal. The issue is not closed as some writers have rushed to conclusions based on the reported interview with Dr John Ford. There are several reasons that some African Americans question the authenticity of this conclusion that there was no racism involved in the treatment. In the first place, if Scot Morris interviewed Dr John Ford just prior to the publication of his book in 1983, Dr Ford would have probably been an octogenarian. While this does not necessarily mean that he could not remember all the details of the accident, it does raise the issue of Scot Morris not providing any collaborative proof on this issue. I am inclined to believe that there was more than a kernel of truth in the reports of African Americans in North Carolina during that time. Segregation was the law of the South. Blacks could not be treated in white hospitals and vice versa unless the circumstances were highly unusual. Four black doctors traveling to Tuskegee with Washington, DC, license plates would have been quite suspicious to whites in the South. Given the ignorance that accompanies racism, the whites probably had no idea about the significance of Charles Drew's discovery of blood plasma preservation techniques. It is more likely that they considered him just another black man in a car accident. Morris claims that Dr Ford said that a blood transfusion would not have saved Drew, but the African American mythmakers see the irony in the fact that a black man who created methods to save people dying from the loss of blood could not have those methods used in his case, probably because of the deep racist reaction to blacks in the South in 1950. Whatever the truth of this story, the irony will never disappear from the imagination of those who study discrimination and prejudice.

Mary McLeod Bethune

Like Charles Drew, Mary McLeod Bethune was a believer in education and the virtue of hard work and discipline, and became one of the iconic figures of her time. Often mentioned in the same category as Charles Drew, Booker T. Washington, and W. E. B. Du Bois, Bethune was the queen mother of African American education and politics for more than a half a century.[21] The fact of the matter is that there have always been black men and women of superior energy, intelligence, and expertise despite the intense racist propaganda to the contrary. In the United States it took a long time for the general white population to appreciate the fact that the enslaved Africans and their descendants were no less human and no less capable than whites. Given the hand that had been dealt to some African Americans, it was almost miraculous what they did with their circumstances.

For example, Mary McLeod Bethune, who was born on July 10, 1875, one of seventeen children to Samuel and Patsy McLeod, in Mayesville, South Carolina, would become one of the most important persons in the pantheon of great African Americans.[22] After receiving an education in religious schools Bethune began teaching and eventually founded her own college called Daytona Normal and Industrial Institute for Negro Girls (now Bethune-Cookman) in 1904. Bethune was president of the school from 1904 to 1942 and then again from 1946 to 1947. She became a leader of the black women's club movement and served as president of the National Association of Colored Women. President Franklin Roosevelt made her the Director of Negro Affairs in the National Youth Administration from 1936 to 1944. In this position Bethune was able to influence the hiring of blacks in many federal capacities, including being the consultant for the first female officer candidates. She founded the National Council of Negro Women and became a vice president of the NAACP. Her work resonated throughout the black world; the Haitian government gave her the Haitian Medal of Honor and Merit and the country of Liberia made her Commander of the Order of the Star of Africa. Her travels took her to Switzerland, Canada, and any place where people were interested in hearing the narrative of the rise of African people. She died on May 18, 1955. A few months before her death she had *Ebony* magazine publish her Last Will and Testament in which she outlined the nine principles that she left her people:

I leave you love.

I leave you hope.

I leave you the challenge of developing confidence in one another.

I leave you a thirst for education.

I leave you respect for the uses of power.

I leave you faith.

I leave you racial dignity.

I leave you a desire to live harmoniously with your fellow men.

I leave you finally a responsibility to our young people.[23]

Few women or men of any culture ever felt the suffering and the pain of her people as deeply as Mary McLeod Bethune and she exclaimed often, in the words of Margaret Walker, the author of *Jubilee*, that "the black man and woman will rise with education and dedication to purpose."[24] Neither Bethune nor Walker or any of the giants who stroked our sense of wonderment with their achievements ever felt that blacks could or should not play, have fun, or participate in sports. They believed that the African person was capable of mastering any sport, any science, and any art; everywhere they looked they could see solid athletic prowess equal to the intellectual accomplishments of the race.

Baseball: The African Americans are Coming

Since its inception baseball has been called the American pastime. The implications of this designation had as much to do with whiteness as with the sport itself. There were black baseball clubs and black players long before there was a black player in the major leagues of baseball, so the issue of America's pastime had more to do with symbolism than with substance. Whites had established in their minds certain barriers that could not be broken if they were to maintain social control. Black men could never have sex with white women (although white men could and did have sex with black women from the earliest periods of enslavement), blacks could never be quarterbacks on football teams, black soldiers could never command white soldiers, blacks could never be allowed to eat in restaurants with whites, and blacks could never play major league baseball.[25] Of course, as various barriers are broken then others are created; for example, blacks can never be pitchers on baseball teams or coaches of white players, and so forth. Nothing could have been a greater signature in the sports world for racism than the idea that baseball, that is, "real" baseball, was a white man's sport.

Yet it was clear that even prior to 1890 there were blacks who played baseball with whites despite the popular illusion. Although one could not say there was integrated baseball during this period, there were blacks that eventually played alongside white athletes in the minors. For example, while the National Association of Base Ball Players had been formed in 1867, it still banned black athletes.[26] However, a few years later in 1870 a few blacks appear on the roster of minor league teams. Racism was horrible, and most quit rather than take the abuse. Among these early players was John W. "Bud" Fowler, a second baseman who played in 1884 for the Stillwater, Minnesota, club. Moses "Fleetwood" Walker played with Toledo and was called one of the best catchers in the Northwestern League. In the late 1880s a number of African Americans played alongside whites, including Fowler and Walker, and George Stovey and Frank Grant. Some played for barnstorming outlaw minor clubs that would roll into a town, set up a game with the locals, and then leave. But in 1890 the white clubs of the International League, the most famous of the minor leagues, established a rule that barred black players from any white teams for fifty-five years. It was a gentlemen's agreement that forced clubs to dismiss the black players that they already had on their rosters.

Most black players did not pursue the white clubs since there were more than 200 all-black independent teams in the country, many organized in direct competition to the ban. Some of the early teams were the popular Cuban Giants, Cuban X Giants, Harrisburg Giants, Kansas City Monarchs, Chicago Giants, Indianapolis ABCs, Lincoln Giants, Brooklyn Royal Giants, Cuban Stars, St Louis Giants, and Homestead (Pennsylvania) Grays. There were other teams such as the Nashville Standard Giants and Birmingham Black Barons, and Andrew Foster's Chicago American Giants.

Foster was the motivator and organizer of the Negro National League in 1920. The League was born in Kansas City with eight teams: Chicago American Giants, Chicago Giants, Cuban Stars, Dayton Marcos, Detroit Stars, Indianapolis ABCs, Kansas City Monarchs, and St. Louis Giants. Additional entrepreneurs followed with other leagues. For example, the Nashville Elite Giants became the centerpiece for the Negro Southern League, with teams in Nashville, Atlanta, Birmingham, Memphis, Montgomery, and New Orleans. The Eastern Colored League was formed in 1923, featuring the Hilldale Club, Cuban Stars (East), Brooklyn Royal Giants, Bacharach Giants, Lincoln Giants, and Baltimore Black Sox.

The Negro National League lasted from 1920 until the economic pressures of the Great Depression exhausted it, in 1931. Two years later the Second Negro National League was established by Gus Greenlee, who became the dominant personality in black baseball from 1933 to 1949. Other leagues appeared, such as the Negro American League in 1937 and the Negro Southern League. Among the Hall of Famers were players such as Satchel Paige, the legendary pitcher Josh Gibson, called the greatest baseball player ever, Cool Papa Bell, Judy Johnson, Buck Leonard, and Oscar Charleston.

Jackie Robinson—The Barrier Falls

On April 15, 1947 Jackie Robinson became the first black person to play major league baseball in the twentieth century. As a member of the famed Brooklyn Dodgers team, Robinson, after being hired by Branch Rickey, took his place against the Boston Braves at Ebbets.[27] Robinson's appearance had shown the world that having a black player on the field would not cause the earth to come to a halt. Blacks marveled at the fact that whites had made such a big fuss about a black baseball player being able to participate in the major leagues. Indeed, most black communities knew players who were equal or superior to the white players who were making big salaries in the majors. Furthermore, there were some in the black community who believed that although Robinson was an excellent player he was not the very best that the black community had to offer. Yet Robinson had attended college at UCLA and had the look, the manner, and the proper temperament for the times to be the first black major leaguer. Pride ran down the smiling faces of black America when Robinson showed that he was not intimidated by the circumstances. Of course, the white players and white crowds did not make it easy for the twenty-eight-year-old Robinson when he stepped onto the field. He was taunted, booed, and called nasty names during his first few games.

Nevertheless, he proved to be a stunning base runner, a first-rate line-drive hitter, and a man of dignity who had to withstand criticism and ostracism from even his own teammates. Robinson's victory was the achievement of an entire black nation waiting to hear each day about the success or failure of a lone warrior in the camp of the enemy. How could he sustain his mental focus? What were his deepest thoughts on the field when he saw the snarling faces of those who wished that he would fail? Rarely in African American history has a burden weighed so heavy upon one man—with perhaps the exceptions of the black defenders of the heavyweight boxing division, Jack Johnson and Joe Louis, or the first African American president, Barack H. Obama—as upon Jackie Robinson.

Robinson played second base and often teamed with Pee Wee Reese to make an outstanding double play combination. The Brooklyn team was successful and won six pennants and a World Series during his early years. Robinson became the National League's most valuable player in 1949, when he batted a league-leading .342. Robinson left baseball in the 1956 season and joined the work for civil rights. He was a regular speaker against racism and discrimination and supported Martin Luther King Jr, and Roy Wilkins and other leaders in sounding the call for strong economic development in the black community.[28] Robinson was a cofounder of the Freedom National Bank in Harlem. As a writer for the *New York Post* and *Amsterdam News* he could be counted on to write about housing, education, and economic development. He was inducted into the Baseball Hall of Fame and died in Stamford, Connecticut, in October 1972 at the age of 53. Robinson's legacy was so well ingrained in the psyches of African Americans that most people could not think of baseball without thinking of Jackie Robinson. He was before Babe Ruth, Mickey Mantle, or any of the great white players that became household names in America. In a powerfully lyrically manner he became the metaphor for superior achievement and the substance of new magical, even mystical, narratives. Sixty years after Robinson became the first black player in the major leagues, his third child by Rachel, David Robinson, a coffee farmer in Tanzania, returned to the United States to attend a game between the Houston Astros and the Philadelphia Phillies. On April 23, 2007 the Phillies were honoring Robinson, four living members of the Negro League Philadelphia Stars, Tuskegee airmen who fought in World War II, and Jim Ellis, who created a black swim team that became the inspiration for the movie *Pride*. David Robinson, who threw out the ceremonial first ball, said at the Philadelphia ballpark that Jackie Robinson Day was not enough to honor the man who was a social changer. Instead he asked the professional baseball teams to contribute to the Jackie Robinson Fund, founded by his mother, Rachel, to provide education for African American, Latino, Native American, and other children who were financially strapped. David Robinson said he wanted the foundation to become a living legacy for his father.[29]

By the time Hank "Hammerin" Aaron had broken Babe Ruth's homerun record in 1973, major league baseball had come a long way since the first years of Jackie Robinson. Aaron, the gentle champion, would be the first player to hit thirty or more homeruns in fifteen seasons of play, making him the most dominant homerun hitter of his time. Other players would see Hank Aaron as the target to make, as Aaron had seen Babe Ruth or others had seen Jackie Robinson. Barry Bonds would eventually surpass the sheer number of homeruns hit by Aaron but controversy would cloud the achievement. In many respects, especially in terms of historical action, memory, and superstition, the world of baseball as reflected in the life of Jackie Robinson and Hank Aaron was singular in the way it merged with the world of other athletes, the Tuskegee flyers, and eventually the genius of writers such as Richard Wright, Ralph Ellison, John O. Killens, and Ralph Waldo Ellison.

Richard Wright Finding a Home Away from Mississippi

One of America's most poignant writers, Richard Wright, was also among the first African American writers to achieve international literary fame and fortune, but his reputation has less to do with his blackness than with the substantive imagination and strong literary quality of his work. He spent the first years of his life on a plantation in Mississippi. The state of his birth played a massive role in inspiring the imagination of Richard Wright, as seen in his two most important and famous works: *Native Son*, a novel, and his autobiography, *Black Boy*. These works established him as one of the most compelling novelists in America.[30]

Wright was a Southerner in his sentiments, sensibilities, and resonances about race and racism. He was born on a plantation near Natchez, Mississippi, on September 4, 1908 to Nathaniel and Ella Wilson. His father was bright but illiterate and his mother was a well-educated schoolteacher. When Richard Wright was six years old the family moved from Mississippi to Memphis, considered by many Mississippi blacks at the turn of the century the haven of all things good. Ida B. Wells had journeyed to Memphis from Mississippi years earlier and thousands of other blacks had made their way to the American Mennefer (*Memphis* is the Greek rendering of the ancient African city of *Mennefer*, meaning "Beautiful Wall"). Whether it was the bright lights or more likely the good times of Memphis streets, Wright's father left the family for another woman and his mother took a job as a cook to support the family. Wright was placed in an orphanage for a short period until his mother could organize her work schedule. Soon, however, it became impossible for Wright's mother to maintain the two of them in Memphis and she returned to Mississippi, this time to Jackson, to live with her mother. It was in this rich, spiritual, and deeply imaginative cauldron of worry and want that Richard Wright began to write. His first story was published in 1924 in the *Southern Register*, a local black newspaper. It was called "The Voodoo of Hell's Half Acre." As he got older he moved between Jackson and Memphis, working in the cotton fields and doing other menial work while all the time reading H. L. Mencken, Sinclair Lewis, and Theodore Dreiser. These writers would have a powerful effect on him and his thinking about writing with purpose and impact.

Perhaps the crucial decision for Richard Wright was his 1927 move to Chicago, because he made a break with the physical state of the South while carrying around in his head all of the accumulated wisdom, information, and ideas that he had received as a child. He took a job at the post office in Chicago and soon the Great Depression took its toll on everyone. He was forced to take extra jobs to survive economically. Out of the turmoil of the Depression he was drawn to the Communist Party, which welcomed him because he was bright, conversant with literature and ideas, and eager to write. He wrote articles and stories for the *Daily Worker* and the *New Masses*. His first major story, "Superstition," was published in the *Abbot's Monthly* in April 1931.

After living in Chicago for ten years Richad Wright moved to New York and became the Harlem editor for the *Daily Worker*. He also edited a short-lived literary magazine called *New Challenge*. He published *Uncle Tom's Children* in 1938 and this enabled him to secure a Guggenheim Fellowship on which he completed his novel *Native Son*.

Wright ended his ties with the Communist Party in 1944 and moved to Paris in 1946, where he met Albert Camus and Jean-Paul Sartre, the two French existentialist writers who were commanding lots of attention in war-torn France. His novel *The Outsiders*, published in 1953, is an icon of his existentialist phase. Wright, like other African Americans during this period, found freedom in Paris, or at least felt free to work and to think in Paris without the added burden of racism. Indeed, Wright wrote, "Every Negro in American carries all through his life the burden of race consciousness like a corpse on his back. I shed that corpse when I stepped off the train in Paris. Half a lifetime is long enough to carry it. I don't intend to pick it up again."[31] Six years earlier he had become a French citizen and traveled from Paris throughout the world to see the condition of poor and African people. Wright wrote several nonfiction books but he was plagued with financial problems during the last years of his life because none of the books brought much financial gain. He wrote nearly 4,000 haiku poems, several major novels, many nonfiction books, and short stories. His novel *The Long Dream* was published in 1958 and a book of short stories came out after his death, which happened on November 28, 1960. By the time Wright passed away, a new African American writer had assumed center stage in the literary pantheon; his name was Ralph Waldo Ellison.

Ralph Waldo Ellison and Invisibility

Ralph Waldo Ellison was born on March 1, 1914 in Oklahoma City, Oklahoma, seven years after Oklahoma became the forty-sixth state. His father named him for the writer Ralph Waldo Emerson, whom he admired. The Ellisons would bring their children, Ralph and Herbert, second-hand toy sets, books, and old typewriters to provide them with as much orientation to success as they could. Ellison was quite studious and wanted to be what he called a "Renaissance man." He studied cultures, values, and behaviors of the three groups of people he knew in Oklahoma: the Native Americans, the African Americans, and the white Americans.[32]

As a student at Douglass High School in Oklahoma City, Ellison thought that he would be a musician, music being one of his many inclinations and a great love of his life. However, when he went to Tuskegee Institute on a scholarship with the idea of writing a great symphony, he ran into problems immediately because the school seemed to have confused the terms of the scholarship. Instead of returning to Oklahoma City, Ellison chose to go to New York City. He found the city to be a great challenge. He could not find work as a musician and ended up doing many menial jobs in Harlem in order to live. He was a file clerk at the Harlem YMCA psychiatrist's office.

As fortune would have it, however, he met Richard Wright in New York and it was Wright who influenced him to become a writer rather than a musician. The two writers would become the major influences on black literature for a generation until the appearance of James Baldwin and Toni Morrison. Ellison's literary reputation rests largely upon his great novel *Invisible Man*, which was published in 1952. The truth is that Ellison decried literature for the sake of social transformation and participated in it purely, it seems, for the sake of literature. This was counter to the way Richard Wright saw literature and different even from the work of James Baldwin and Amiri Baraka, for example. One could say, almost as an understanding of Ellison, that when he left Oklahoma to arrive at New York he left his social and racial feelings either in the tragic ditches of a Tuskegee scholarship misunderstanding or in some other strange and isolated place. Whatever that place was that Ellison left, he never regained an African sensibility, it seems, in the way that African Americans had experienced Wright to have or were to experience Toni Morrison to have. Nothing in his college teaching experience seemed to point to clarity on the identity issue, although he taught at Rutgers, Bard, and New York University at various times during his career. Ellison, uniquely gifted as a writer, left a mixed legacy as an intellectual when he passed away, on April 16, 1994. One is left with the fact that this grand genius never truly managed to conquer the monster of identity in his writings or within himself. His confrontation with racism had made him, it seemed, a casualty of the race wars and he had slipped by the ultimate civil rights struggle of his time, invisible to his own people.

History has always taken care of its own narrative, filling in the gaps, the lapses, and the non-sequiturs with substance, and so it was with the literary history of African Americans. If those who had fostered the notion of African invisibility by awarding Ellison with prizes and placing his image, however powerful, at the center of black literary tradition had thought they had succeeded in moving Africans from a sense of agency, they would be disappointed by the appearance of the Macon, Georgia, born John O. Killens. He moved to New York in 1948 and soon established the Harlem Writers Guild. Two of his novels received nominations for Pulitzers: *And Then We Heard the Thunder* and *The Cotillion or One Good Bull is Half the Herd*. While neither received the prize, Killens was seen as a folk hero in the African American community, commanding crowds of people whenever he spoke and wherever he appeared, so definite was his word in support of the agency of African people. Always concerned about the entire literary scene in the African American community, Killens sought to open doors to other artists, planting seeds of self-determination in schools, community groups, and churches.

And so as it had been before the giants came and blasted racism, so it was when they departed for those who came after them. The battle was not won, although segregation in its most blatant form was surely mortally wounded and would not appear frontally except in some isolated clubhouses or secret societies run by ardent white racists. For the most part, a society freed of overt racist behavior has existed since the 1980s. However, the uglier elements have not completely disappeared, as in the suspected Mississippi lynching of a twenty-six-year-old black man, Frederick James Carter, on December 3, 2010. Consequently, the worst elements occasionally appear, but in the twenty-first century African Americans primarily confront process racism, where administratively those who are racist can effect their wills by denying promotions, acceptance of applications, salary raises, or other benefits. Young black men can still be treated unequally in the prison system, receiving harsher sentencing from racist judges than those same judges would give to white males.

Conclusion

African American entertainers became the world's first international celebrities. Lena Horne, Eartha Kitt, John O. Killens, Paul Robeson, and Jackie Robinson were the names of a new people. Their art and culture, their athletics and recreation, were combined with the rigor of training and exercise for the purpose of demonstrating that they were no less capable than the next person. In accomplishing their goals they were carrying on their shoulders the weight of their much-maligned people. Nothing was so difficult that they would run away from confronting it and nothing more rewarding than jobs well done and positions filled with excellence.

Chapter Time Markers

We Will be Free

9

The African Resistance

Important Terms and Names

Congress of Racial Equality
Southern Christian Leadership Conference
Black Panthers
Nation of Islam
Franklin Florence
Fannie Lou Hamer

Malcolm X
Martin Luther King Jr
Asa Philip Randolph
Charles Houston
Urban League
Thurgood Marshall

In Defense of Human Dignity

Oppression breeds subservience, and the habit of servility invites more brutal oppression. Breaking this cycle in the history of African Americans did not come easily since it had been institutionally established for several centuries. From the first capture in a physical sense and the mental imprisonment by demanding that Africans accept the names given to them by the white enslavers, the cycle had been set in place, as in stone, by the perpetuation of African enslavement. Of course, the African was not only separated from his or her own land but also separated from his or her sense of identity. It was as if one's name was no longer Mandela but Madison, no longer Baraka but Barber, no longer Adusei Peasa but Arthur Price, and so forth. Africans had lost not just physical place but mental place, a loss that meant the people could no longer see themselves as assertive. Therefore, the process of enslaving Africans was as much a psychological one as it was a physical one.

To break the habits that had been instilled in Africans to make slaves had to be a collective response on the part of the African population. One could not do it individually because all were victims of the same oppressive situation. It was this groupness, this collective suffering, that gave birth to the African American identity. The abiding problem was that the masses did not see often enough the possibility of such a rise, could not imagine what it would look like, and had seen every attempt to change the psychological condition challenged by the overwhelming power of the white established order. Various cadres of white racists often physically and economically decimated blacks that stood up to assert dignity. The crimes against blacks were numerous and were the common knowledge of the masses from their own local examples of the many lynchings of blacks who had spoken up against abuse, against wage cheating, against white children swearing at old women and men, against indignities meted out to black women, and against assaults on black males for appearing to be uppity. They knew the realities of living in the United States under the regime of white supremacy and they did not forget these lessons.

Blues singers like B. B. King, Leadbelly, Etta James, and Lightnin' Hopkins would remix personal and public pain in serious interpretations of the black condition during the twentieth century. In many respects their art would anticipate a new, awakened, and virile African American committed to speaking up and speaking out against all forms of racism, personal, and public. What had been spoken indirectly or in riddle or jest would soon be spoken directly, boldly, and thereby create what has been called the Malcolmian Moment.

When Malcolm X in the early 1960s began *to speak the soul* of African Americans, to be the voice that had been silenced for too long, to state clearly and forcefully the deepest emotions of the black community, to demand an end to indignity and white racism, and to say that blacks would be free by any means necessary, he had announced a new dispensation.[1] This was the break with the past. He was an example of a black man talking like a black man who had experienced the worst of segregation and discrimination and not wrestling with either his identity or his ethics. Malcolm X was simply tied of bending over for beatings that he did not deserve, and in speaking this way he was the mouthpiece of a generation of frustration. Eventually the outburst of talented, willful, and determined black men and women would engulf an entire nation and help to radicalize blacks living in the most isolated parts of the American South. Television, itself maturing along with the movement, would send the images of blacks demanding justice and equality to a wider world, and the *New Negro* of Alain Locke would become the *New Black Person*. No one seemed to capture the spirit of the era any better than Muhammad Ali, who had followed Malcolm into the Nation of Islam, started by the Honorable Elijah Muhammad.

Muhammad Ali and the Dream of Freedom

As muscular as the writers have been in the African American experience, their prowess has often been captured in the victories of athletes more than any other class. Boxing at the top weights has proven the purview of the greatest athletes and the most important of these in the second half of the twentieth century was Muhammad Ali. He had no peer in talent or drama and exercised the "pulpit" of the greatest boxer better than any other heavyweight had ever done.[2] Indeed, Ali established the model that has to be overcome in order for a fighter to declare his individuality in the sport.

Rising to the top of his career just as Malcolm X was becoming the most electric intellectual activist in the Civil Rights Movement made Muhammad Ali ultimately the inheritor of the tradition of *Shine*, the smart black but also the proud and defiant black. This was the Malcolmian Moment that we saw also in the politics of parades, marches, and street protests.

Figure 9.1 Muhammad Ali, hugely colorful and effective heavyweight champion. Image courtesy of Charles L. Blockson Afro-American Collection, Temple University Libraries.

Now was the time for true, authentic human beings willing to lay their lives down for what was just and fair; Ali did not shirk from this duty.

Muhammad Ali was born in Louisville, Kentucky, on January 17, 1942 and named Cassius Marcellus Clay. He would start boxing when he was in junior high school and won the Amateur Athletic Union light heavyweight and Golden Gloves heavyweight championships in 1960. He would go on to vanquish all his opponents at the Rome Olympics and win the gold medal.

Ali, still called by his "slave" name, turned professional after the Olympics and defeated his first opponents but it was not until his fight with Sonny Liston on February 25, 1964 that he attracted serious attention. A young Ali showed his cockiness, poetic proclivities, and boxing skill in knocking Liston out in the seventh round. It had been thought that Sonny Liston was unbeatable. Once Ali defeated Liston he defended the title nine times as heavyweight champion from 1965 to 1967, becoming the most active heavyweight champion since Joe Louis. He united the heavyweight division by beating Ernie Terrell, the World Boxing Association champion, in fifteen rounds on February 6, 1967. With Ali's victories came a new assertiveness of African Americans, who felt that he had demonstrated for the world the ability of blacks to defend themselves because he had done it for himself. At one time it was as if the entire globe knew the name of Muhammad Ali, champion of the world. So famous had he become that the original Muhammad Ali, an Albanian pasha of modern Egypt, paled in comparison to the African American Muhammad Ali's luster.

After becoming sole champion, Ali received the affection of millions of fans around the world for his charm, charisma, and boxing ability. The African American people embraced him as the representative athlete of the people. Even when he changed his name from Clay to Muhammad Ali and joined the Nation of Islam, the black community saw him as following in the legacy of the great resisters to racism and discrimination.

The Vietnam War was raging and the television reports every evening on the number of killed and injured pasted the pictures and words in the minds of the nation. The war greatly divided the United States, pitting various political groups against each other and creating splits in families and communities. There was a belief, borne out in the deaths of soldiers, that African Americans were bearing the brunt of the attacks at the front lines.[3] The Vietnam War effort saw blacks make up nearly twenty-seven percent of the soldiers in combat, twelve percent of the fatalities, about the same as the percentage of blacks in the nation's population.[4] Added to the general controversy in the society about the war was the belief by many African Americans that it was an unfair war against a colored people.

Thus, in 1967, when Muhammad Ali was inducted into the army, he refused to go, saying that the Vietnamese had never used a derogatory term against him. This action brought strong animosities as some declared that he was unpatriotic. Others acclaimed his decision as one of the most progressive actions ever taken by an African American. He was praised for risking his championship for his beliefs. Ali was prepared mentally for the challenges of the government. He was charged with violating the Selective Service Act; his titles were taken from him and he was not allowed to fight. The case went to court and after several months he was convicted of draft evasion and given five years in prison plus a $10,000 fine. Ali never went to prison but could not box during the legal actions. A judge ruled in 1970 that Ali could box professionally in Georgia because it had no state commission of boxing, and his managers quickly arranged a match in Atlanta against Jerry Quarry, whom Ali knocked out in three rounds. Soon afterwards Ali's managers set up a bout for March 8, 1971 between Ali and Joe Frazier. It was called the "The Fight of the Century." The boxers seemed evenly matched and Frazier proved himself an outstanding puncher, knocking Ali down in the fifteenth round. Ali bounced back up but in the end the judges gave Frazier the win.

Finally, after appeal, the United States Supreme Court agreed that he was not guilty of draft evasion and should not have been drafted at all. Ali felt that a large part of his career in the ring had been damaged and so he fought as many opponents as would put themselves forward. He fought Jerry Quarry, Floyd Patterson, Joe Bugner, and Ken Norton. Only Norton defeated him. He fought Frazier in 1974 but then, when Frazier lost the heavyweight champion to George Foreman, Ali decided to go after Foreman.

Billed as "The Rumble in the Jungle," the Don King-promoted fight attracted 60,000 fans to the Kinshasa stadium on October 30, 1974. Millions more watched the fight on television. The experts favored George Foreman, who was seven years younger and seen as stronger. On the other hand, Ali had the African people behind him, the children in the streets of Kinshasa, and the millions of African Americans who wanted to see justice done by Ali regaining his championship. Ali fought one of the most brilliant battles ever performed in the ring. He allowed the less experienced Foreman to throw heavy blows to his body until Foreman was exhausted. Then Ali went to work on Foreman, "floating like a butterfly and stinging like a bee," as he would say, until he knocked Foreman out in the eighth round.

Ali had several additional fights, another one with Frazier, and then he lost to Leon Spinks on February 15, 1978 in a split decision. In 1979, after having lost three bouts, Ali announced that he was finished. Unfortunately, he returned to fight Larry Holmes in 1980 and Trevor Berbick of Canada in 1981, losing both fights. He retired permanently after those fights. Soon he was stricken with Parkinson's disease, an illness of the nervous system, for which he was under doctor's care. His mind, ever quick with the iconic Ali wit, remained sharp. During the Atlanta Olympics of 1996, Muhammad Ali, the beloved warrior who threw only punches in a legal ring, received the honor of lighting the Olympic torch. At the moment Ali appeared, the world seemed to break into a broad grin as the champion, his gait now slower but his will as determined as ever, drove on toward the lighting of the flame. All that Ali had fought for in his life could be summed up as a chapter in the epic of the African American in quest for justice. The struggle was more legal, political, and activist than boxing, but what Ali did was to use his heavyweight pulpit to preach the gospel of equality; others would take the battle to more traditional venues.

Although to Muhammad Ali's generation he seemed to have taken on the establishment alone, even he knew that the struggle for equality and justice had gone on for decades. Indeed, the roots of the civil rights battles and the legal opposition to discrimination were in the bold organizations created to challenge the traditional patterns of segregation and prejudice.

Civil Rights and Labor Unions: Joining the Struggle for Justice

The NAACP

Widely regarded as the premier civil rights organization in America's history, the National Association for the Advancement of Colored People started improbably on February 12, 1909, making it the oldest continuous rights group in the United States.[5] The NAACP was founded by an integrated cadre of progressives who believed that the time had come for a final push against the last vestiges of racial prejudice. They had hoped to attack discrimination at the social, legal, and educational levels, knowing full well that racism was entrenched in the psyche and practice of many Americans. They would seek all the rights of citizenship, conduct voter mobilization, and monitor discriminatory practices in the society. The legal arm of the organization would grow and gain independent status over the years while the main body, rarely over 600,000 members, would hold steady to attacking racism and discrimination anywhere.

The NAACP was formed as a response to lynching, other forms of brutality, and rampant voter fraud. Ida B. Wells had brought the issue of lynching to the forefront, and the creation of the NAACP, partly in response to her campaign and the violent and horrific acts of cruelty seen in the American nation, was a rational act. There had to be a response to the forces of violence. Blatant disregard for the rights of blacks had to stop. If the clarion voice of Ida B. Wells could not be heard then progressives and liberals heard the cries of black people during the 1908 race riot in Springfield, Illinois, the resting place of President Abraham Lincoln's body. Terrified at what the nation was becoming and shocked at the violence committed against defenseless black people, a handful of whites, including Mary White Ovington, Oswald Garrison Villard, descendants of radical abolitionists, and William English Walling, and Henry Moscowitz, called a group of sixty people to discuss the future of civil rights in the nation. When the group finally met, it included only seven African Americans, including the already well-known Ida B. Wells-Barnett, W. E. B. Du Bois, and Mary Church Terrell. The last-named of these was a formidable lecturer and leader who traveled to Europe several times. Indeed, Terrell once wrote after traveling to France:

> What joy, what rapture to return to my old French camping grounds after an absence of fifteen years! How I love France and the French people! . . . The country I was born and reared and have lived is my fatherland, of course, and I love it genuinely, but my motherland is dear, broadminded France in which people with dark complexions are not discriminated against on account of their color.[6]

Terrell was not an exception, because the vast majority of the sixty people were public intellectuals and dedicated justice seekers. Notable among the early members of this group of civil rights advocates were Mary McLeod Bethune, Charles Darrow, Lillian Wald, George Henry White, Sophonisba Breckenridge, John Haynes Holmes, John Dewey, Lincoln Steffens, Ray Stannard Baker, Josephine Ruffin, Mary Talbert, Inez Milholland, Florence Kelley, William Dean Howells, Fanny Garrison Villard, Charles Edward Russell, and Jane Addams. No greater group of human rights advocates with personal stock in the future of race relations had ever existed in the nation.

The idea behind what was called the Niagara Movement, because the first meeting took place across the Niagara River from Buffalo, New York, in Fort Erie, Ontario, in 1905, was the protection of the rights guaranteed by the Thirteenth, Fourteenth, and Fifteenth Amendments. Since its inception the NAACP has remained focused on ending racial discrimination in all of its guises. When the organization established its national office in New York in 1910 it also named a board of directors and Moorfield Storey, a white lawyer and former head of the American Bar Association, as its first president.

The paternalistic nature of the organization showed itself early in the fact that the only black person among the executives was the young William Edward B. Du Bois, who was made the director of publications and research. W. E. B. Du Bois used his office to dominate the ideological direction of the organization, to advance African American history, to inspire literary and social criticism, and to promote resistance to discrimination and racial prejudice. He founded *The Crisis*, the official journal of the NAACP, almost as soon as he took over publications in 1910. Through *The Crisis* DuBois fought every battle worth fighting for black rights, defended the dignity of Africa, and championed the Harlem Renaissance by publishing works by the greatest writers of the era.

A series of outstanding executive secretaries of the NAACP would push the organization into battle against all forms of racial oppression. Legendary black leaders like Walter White and James Weldon Johnson would prepare the way for masterful practitioners of civil rights advocacy such as Roy Wilkins, who would lead the civil rights group during the critical period of the Civil Rights Movement in the 1950s and 1960s.

Figure 9.2
W. E. B. Dubois, perhaps the most prolific writer of his age. Image courtesy of Charles L. Blockson Afro-American Collection, Temple University Libraries.

The National Urban League

Another organization that found its origins in fighting against racism and social deprivation in the early twentieth century was the Urban League. Its history was somewhat different from that of the NAACP, but it was just as committed to struggle. The Urban League was founded in New York City on September 29, 1910 by Ruth Standish Brown and Dr George Edmund Haynes.[7] The Urban League merged with two older groups, the Committee for the Improvement of Industrial Conditions among Negroes in New York, which had been founded in 1906, and the National League for the Protection of Colored Women that had been organized in 1905. Thus, its focus was more social, economic, and industrial than that of the NAACP. Furthermore, it had more blacks in positions of influence and power in its structure than the NAACP. The organization never had the same kind of cachet among African Americans as the NAACP, however, because its mission was less public, more subtle, and mainly economic and social, rather than political and legal as seen in the NAACP.

When Eugene K. Jones took over the leadership of the group in 1918 he expanded its operations and vision. The Urban League sought to eradicate discrimination in employment and housing and to provide assistance to the needy during the trying times of the Depression. Two years after Jones assumed the leadership, the organization changed its name to the National Urban League, suggesting that its scope was larger than its New York City base and indeed more expansive than urban areas in the northeast. The NUL sought to enable African Americans to achieve power, parity, and civil rights. To this end, by 1941, when Lester Granger, one of the organization's most outspoken leaders, assumed leadership, he joined with Asa Philip Randolph's plan to march on Washington.[8] Bayard Rustin and A. J. Muste developed a strategy based on Randolph's idea and in the process got the full support of Lester Granger to fight for self-determination and against racial discrimination in the Armed Forces. Granger, although outspoken, often spoke for conciliation and persuasion rather than confrontation. The National Urban League would not be projected as one of the leading civil rights organizations until 1961, when Whitney Young became the executive director. The NUL had to change, given the rhetoric of revolution and the eloquence of the aggrieved against the established order. Young was an expansive leader. He brought in more people to the ranks of the National Urban League and made the organization a much more nimble and flexible instrument of social transformation. He hosted the planning meetings of the 1963 March on Washington that was proposed by Asa Philip Randolph, Martin Luther King Jr, and John Lewis, leader of the Student Nonviolent Coordinating Committee.

The NUL started "street academies" and "new thrusts" to galvanize the African American masses from the urban neighborhoods. It sought to open alternative education to thousands of young people, teaching them values and skills. In addition, the NUL prepared as many school dropouts for college as it could and opened the door to economic advancement by those who wanted to improve their lot.

The Urban League and other civil rights groups defined an aggressive mission for equality and justice during the 1950s, 1960s, and the 1970s by insisting on economic, social, and political fairness. Already on the cultural side, for some time artists like Sammy Davis Jr, James Brown, Ray Charles, Mahalia Jackson, Nina Simone, Duke Ellington, Cab Calloway, Dizzy Gillespie, John Coltrane, Dinah Washington, and Ella Fitzgerald had had national and international appeal. The political and economic opportunities were rushing to catch up

Figure 9.3 Ella Fitzgerald, one of the great jazz vocalists of all time, with a reputation in Europe as well as the Americas. Image courtesy of Charles L. Blockson Afro-American Collection, Temple University Libraries.

with the cultural and, indeed, athletic advances. This would mean new methods of struggle, new avenues of protest, and the flexing of different muscles.

Prelude to Action

The twentieth century opened with white privilege intact in the North and in the South notwithstanding the Civil War, the Reconstruction, and the Amendments to the United States Constitution that would grant citizenship and voting rights to blacks. Whites never willingly rejected their privilege; for the most part, many whites accepted it as a fact that they should be first, they should be served, and they should see blacks only as servants and assistants. But the black community never lacked individuals of unusual courage and mastery of the United States Constitution. Nothing prevented blacks in the North and some in the South from fulfilling dreams of education and knowledge and joining the fight against the last vestiges of white privilege.

During the second half of the nineteenth century and early part of the twentieth century, Mary Eliza Church Terrell, who had been one of the founders of the NAACP, was one such outsize individual who spoke up for equality and justice. She had been born in 1863 and grew up during the most difficult period of African American advancement, the Reconstruction

Era. She was a young girl, only fourteen years old, when the Union Army was removed from the occupation of the South. She heard the most awful stories of persecution, beatings, and death in the South. What ungodly and frightening men and women these must be who drape themselves in white sheets and tear into the night with loud noises and burning crosses! Erudite beyond any of her peers, Mary Eliza Church Terrell began writing in the interest of equality and justice as a young woman and did not end her quest for true liberation until she expired, in 1954. Others would come, almost as if called into action by the awful conditions of their lives, to rescue the black masses from whatever station they could muster their forces.

Asa Philip Randolph and the Brotherhood of Sleeping Car Porters

It was into this type of world that Asa Philip Randolph had been born, on April 15, 1889 in Crescent City, Florida. His father, James William Randolph, was a preacher for the African Methodist Episcopal Church and his mother, Elizabeth Robinson, a highly skilled seamstress. Randolph's family moved to Jacksonville, Florida, a relatively prosperous black community, two years after his birth. He learned lessons from his father and mother that were to stay with him through all of his struggles. His father told him that character and conduct were the two most important qualities that a young African American could have and his mother taught him that he must get an education and be prepared to defend himself from those who would seek to do him or his family harm.[9]

One of his most compelling accounts is about the time his mother sat in the front room of their house with a shotgun while his father with a pistol in his coat pocket walked to the local jail to prevent a mob from lynching a black man. This incident had a profound character-building impact on Randolph and he vowed to do his best as a student. He exceled in public speech, drama, and literature in high school at the Cookman Institute. An impressive athlete, singer, and scholar, Randolph was a standout on the baseball team and a soloist in the school's choir. He was valedictorian of the 1907 graduating class of his school.

Reading Du Bois' *The Souls of Black Folk* changed Randolph's life. He was convinced after reading the book that he wanted to do something important in the fight for equality, but believed that he had to travel to the North because blacks in the North seemed to have more freedom to advance the race. He moved to New York in 1911 to become an actor. His parents frowned upon his career choice and he decided to spend time working for socialist politics. He married Lucille E. Green in 1914. She was a Howard University graduate and an entrepreneur who made enough money to support the family while the baritone-voiced Southerner made his way on stage. Randolph played Hamlet, Othello, and Romeo in several Shakespeare plays in Harlem. He was not satisfied just acting so he joined a political movement. In 1912, as a young member of the Socialist Party led by Eugene V. Debs, Randolph pushed the change agenda through trade unionism and organization, believing that the more moderate form of change sought by Du Bois and others would never bring reform and racial integration. With his strong beliefs he went to the Socialist Party and it assisted him in founding *The Messenger*. This was a monthly magazine that espoused socialist solutions to social issues. Once he had established name recognition Randolph ran for New York State Comptroller in 1920 and two years later for the position of Secretary of State for New York.

Clearly, Randolph did not come to organizing without experience. He is best known for organizing the Brotherhood of Sleeping Car Porters (BSCP) in 1925. He had organized a union of elevator operators in 1917 and was elected president of the BSCP. Organizing the Pullman Company employees would become one of the most progressive actions to be taken by African Americans. Presidency of the group made A. Philip Randolph a national leader in the black community. He was an elected leader of a union that had good wages and good benefits and relative freedom of expression. The union supported the newspaper *The Messenger* until 1928.

Success did not come easily for the Brotherhood of Sleeping Car Porters since the Pullman Company fought the unionization long and hard. However, the amendments to the Railway Labor Act of 1934 caused the membership in the union to increase to 7,000 members. Randolph called a march on Washington in the 1940s that was only cancelled because President Franklin Roosevelt issued Executive Order 8802, the Fair Employment Act, to stop discrimination against blacks in war industries. By the time of the merger with the American Federation of Labor, Randolph and the BSCP were solidly on the side of progressive politics. A. Philip Randolph had emerged as the leading anti-segregationist voice of his time. He was resolute and firm, giving in to no one on the question of equality, and with money and people behind him he remained above intimidation. While no one would consider Randolph a black nationalist, he was nevertheless one of the quickest minds among the black leadership and championed the best values of a self-determining people. In some regards, Randolph, booming his indignation about segregation and discrimination, was the connective tissue between the nationalist sentiment of the believers in self-defining and self-determining and the purely integrationist sentiments. His BSCP organization represented black assertiveness in the interest of black workers along lines that brought nationalist and socialist sentiments quite close to each other.

A New Black Nationalism

If ever there was a set of circumstances orchestrated to create a revolutionary approach to repression, segregation, and discrimination, it was the array of racial situations in Georgia when Elijah Poole was born in Sandersville on October 7, 1897. He lived a life of farming and self-study until he moved to Detroit in 1923 and joined an organization started by Walid or Wallace Fard. In fact, Fard had found a following among many disaffected blacks who had moved to Detroit for industrial jobs. When Poole joined the group he soon became one of the best students of Fard, preaching that African Americans had to learn discipline in order to separate from whites. As Fard's assistant, Poole took the name Elijah Muhammad and became a leading member of the Nation of Islam. When Fard disappeared mysteriously, Muhammad took leadership of the organization and enlarged its membership, purchased property, and created an ideology around the life and teachings of Wallace Fard. In fact, Muhammad claimed that Fard was God and that Fard as God had selected Muhammad as his messenger.[10] Indeed, he would name one of his sons Wallace, thus keeping alive the name of the mystery man, who had probably come from North Africa.

The Nation of Islam appealed to thousands of blacks who believed that racism was a permanent aspect of American life because of the inherent evil of whites, who would never see blacks as equal. Many African Americans sought to join a group that would create a moral high place for blacks. In fact, the group found a self-defense organization, abstained from drugs, and taught respect for women. In addition, the Nation of Islam taught that blacks should not fight in any of America's wars because those wars did not advance black rights. In fact, Elijah Muhammad was charged with violating the Selective Service Act and put in prison between 1942 and 1946. War spirit was high and the United States government did not want any challenges to its ability to draft young men into the military service. As far as Muhammad was concerned, the United States had not treated blacks as citizens, indeed had oppressed blacks, and should not be expected to have the patriotism of intelligent blacks. He described African Americans as the chosen people who should have their own nation.

The conversion of Malcolm X to the Nation of Islam was one of the organization's most important moments. Malcolm's charisma elevated the Nation of Islam to a higher level of visibility and gave it respectability among international figures in the African world that it did not have prior to Malcolm. By 1958 Malcolm X was second only to Elijah Muhammad in the hierarchy of the Nation. He became the greatest recruiter of Muslims, the most ardent developer of the ideology, and the founder of many new mosques. He took over the important New York City mosque and from that powerful pulpit commanded national and international attention, bringing high-visibility blacks in entertainment and athletics into his circle. In fact, the writers Muriel Feeling and Tom Feeling, the historian John Henrik Clarke, the educator Brother James Smalls, the professor Leonard Jeffries, the attorney Percy Sutton, and the dancer Pearl Reynolds were all friends of Malcolm X. He attracted the political and national stars of black intellectual progress because he spoke without hesitation against injustice and vowed to fight it to the end.[11] With his magnetism Malcolm X preached a promising Islam with an emphasis on the words of Elijah Muhammad.

Malcolm X had been born Malcolm Little on May 25, 1925 in Omaha, Nebraska, where his father, Earl Little, had tried to make a living as a spiritual leader in the tradition of Marcus Garvey. He was a militant Baptist preacher, meaning he spoke up for the rights of black citizens. Malcolm's mother, Louise Norton Little, was a homemaker with seven other children.

Racism was not unknown to Malcolm's family in a personal way and his father moved the family twice before Malcolm was four years old. In 1929 the family home in Lansing, Michigan, was burned to the ground. Earl Little felt the pressures of his outspokenness but always wanted to be independent of white economic control and kept speaking up for the rights of blacks. In 1931 Earl Little's mutilated body was found lying across the Lansing trolley tracks. Although the white police force called the death an accident the family members believed that it was the results of Earl's militant voice. This entire episode would affect the family and have a particularly strong impact on the way Malcolm saw himself and his life. A further blow would occur, however, a few years later when Louise would have to be committed to a mental institution after a psychological breakdown. The Little children were sent to orphanages, other family members, and foster care.

Malcolm X was intelligent and graduated at the top of his junior high class. Yet he was not considered bright enough for college and his white teacher told him that his dream of being a lawyer was "not realistic for a nigger."[12] Perhaps because of this experience Malcolm left school and went to live with his older sister in Boston but soon found himself on the wrong side of the law, involved in petty crimes in Boston and later in New York. He was charged and convicted of burglary in 1946 and received a seven-year sentence. His brother

Reginald visited him in prison and told him about the Nation of Islam. It was the first time that Malcolm had heard a coherent theory of white racism and black oppression. He found the doctrine of Elijah Muhammad to be consistent with his experiences and took on the ideology with eagerness.

When Malcolm came out of prison in 1952 he had changed his name to Malcolm X to indicate that no blacks in America knew their real names and he did not know his but he would no longer bear the name of his enslaver. Few people could compete with him as a debater and orator of wit, ingenuity, and knowledge. Malcolm X became a minister of the Nation of Islam and caused the movement to grow from 500 members in 1952 to over 30,000 by 1963. Elevated to a position of honor and leadership by the masses of blacks who were not even members of the Nation of Islam, Malcolm X began to develop an iconic personality long before his death in 1965. His vivid personality was combined with a strict adherence to the teachings of Elijah Muhammad. But when Malcolm discovered that his teacher was having sexual relations with as many as six women it shattered his faith in the Nation's leader. Agents of the Federal Bureau of Investigation sought to exploit the differences and divisions and soon there was a major split in the organization.

Malcolm X married Betty Shabazz in 1958 and they had four daughters. In 1992 the acclaimed director Spike Lee directed a movie, *Malcolm X*, starring the indefatigable Denzel Washington. The brilliant actor received an Oscar nomination as Best Actor for his role but it is widely believed that the industry felt it could not reward a film that highlighted the militancy and brilliance of Malcolm X. Washington would later receive an Oscar for a film with lesser social impact. At the funeral of Malcolm X, Ossie Davis, the great actor, called him "our shining black prince."[13] Manning Marable's *Malcolm X: A Life of Reinvention* sought to do his own reinvention of Malcolm's persona by demonstrating that Malcolm was simply as full of faults as the people he criticized. Marable's work has been heavily questioned by some of the top black intellectuals such as Amiri Baraka, Herb Boyd, and Maulana Karenga.[14] Some have claimed that Manning Marable's *Malcolm*, published immediately upon Marable's death in April 2011, was an unfortunate deconstructive biography of one of the major figures of the twentieth century. Malcolm was buried at Ferncliff Cemetery in Hartsdale, New York.

After the deaths of Malcolm X in 1965 and Elijah Muhammad in 1975, the Nation of Islam suffered setbacks in its agenda and doctrinal purity. It was an organization essentially up for grabs. However, Wallace D. Muhammad, a son of the founder, took over the reins of one group, renounced the Nation of Islam doctrine of his father, and renamed himself Warith Deen Mohammed, and Louis Farrakhan took over the remnants of the Nation of Islam.[15] When Warith died in 2008 he had completed his rejection of his father's ideology and the mainstream Nation of Islam fell to Louis Farrakhan.

Farrakhan had been born Louis Eugene Walcott on May 11, 1933 in the Bronx, New York, and raised in Boston by parents from St Kitts.[16] He became a member of the Nation of Islam in 1955. He was known as a calypso singer, dancer, and violinist in Boston but was told by Elijah Muhammad that he could not both be in the entertainment field and be a member of the Nation. He turned down offers to perform and became a devout follower of the Nation of Islam.

Farrakhan struck two new chords in the Nation of Islam's doctrine. First, he would engage the entire black community as a political leader, not merely as the leader of the Nation of Islam. Secondly, he would propose bold new adventures that would capture the imagination of the masses in a way that would attract attention. From these two bases he would carve out an international ethos that would allow him to deal with Muslim leaders in Africa.

He founded the newspaper *The Final Call* in 1979. It was modeled after *Muhammad Speaks*. In 1988 a resurgent and revitalized Nation of Islam repurchased its Chicago Temple and moved to introduce the concept of re-training and re-educating the black world. By 1995 Farrakhan was ready to introduce the Million Man March.[17] He was the inspiration for the meeting of more than a million black men who came to Washington to voice their concern over the negative portrayals of blacks in U.S. society. The philosopher Maulana Karenga would be asked to write the mission statement for this movement. With his long history of ethical struggle and commitment to African people, Karenga emerged as the best person to capture the rationale for the march.[18]

The Gathering of Warriors

It goes largely without saying that any people confronted with as many enemies, personal and national, as African Americans have faced over the years in America would have had to create institutions, organizations, and societies devoted to resistance and liberation. The battlefield was on many fronts. There were no isolated patches of American society where the Africans were not attacked and provoked because of color and race. On the other hand, there were few, if any, Pulwes (a city in Guadeloupe where all of the streets are named after African revolutionaries), even where the cities were all-black, that allowed for the free expression of the deepest patriotic and ancestral emotions of Africans. Yet in the midst of political anomie, social chaos, and economic exploitation, African Americans continued to devise instruments for freeing themselves from the clutches of white racial domination. Among these institutions to infuse the Civil Rights Movement with moral and spiritual energies were the Congress of Racial Equality and Southern Christian Leadership Conference. They took strong views, often opposite each other, yet with vigor that spoke of determination and faith.

The Congress of Racial Equality

The Congress of Racial Equality (CORE) was founded in Chicago in 1942 by four social activists, namely, James L. Farmer Jr, George Houser, James R. Robinson, and Bernice Fisher. They remain the guiding lights of the organization and James Farmer, of course, the central figure in the organization's history. They were pacifist and their ideology was meant to influence the right behavior of the nation toward blacks and other oppressed groups. It is believed that the idealism of this quartet of leaders led to the organization's difficulties during the height of the Black Power Revolution when masses of blacks were calling for a more militant stance toward the government and society.[19]

CORE's intellectual energy and philosophical inspiration derived from Krishnalal Shridharani's *War without Violence*, a 1939 essay that relied upon the ideas of Gandhi. Indeed, many African Americans, unaware of Gandhi's own prejudice against Africans during his South African days, believed that Gandhi was the model of the successful moralist against racist violence. Shridharani's work suggested that there could be a direct procedural advance toward justice based on the philosophy of Gandhi.

Probably because the name of Gandhi was in the news during the years of CORE's formation, he was considered quite relevant. Yet as Gerald Horne understands, Gandhi was problematic when it came to his positions on the equality of the races. In fact, in *The End of Empires: African Americans and India*, Horne claims with good evidence that the histories of African Americans and Indians intertwine at certain points during the fight for human equality; this is true despite the fact that Gandhi, for example, had advanced only the rights of Indians, and not Africans, in South Africa.[20]

One could have thought, for example, of Asa Philip Randolph, of the Brotherhood of Sleeping Car Porters, as an example just as important as others. He was brilliant as an organizer, a radical free thinker not tied up in knots by the Christian, Muslim, or Jewish faith, and a philosopher of social and racial peace. Perhaps seeking to avoid any taint of social activism tied to the socialist or communist ideal, the founders of CORE found inspiration in Gandhi's ideology, one that might be seen as serving the specific needs of the Indian people.

CORE, however, must not be thought of as being anti-activist; it was pro-activist but believed that civil disobedience was the best way to oppose racial doctrines. The organization had to be organized in a manner that was consistent with the objectives of social trans-formation. Therefore, chapters taught lessons of nonviolence and were required to meet monthly like a trade union organization. The officials were elected and unpaid and the group's agenda was run by volunteers committed to the philosophy. CORE opposed racial segregation and paid particular attention to housing and job discrimination.

CORE's philosophy often caused friction with other black groups. For example, when the Deacons of Defense in the South wanted to protect CORE's people who were registering voters, the leaders of CORE rejected protection because they wanted to demonstrate the power of pacifism. Younger members of CORE were affected by the teachings of Malcolm X, Huey Newton, Bobby Seale, and Maulana Karenga, who believed that it was essential for African Americans to defend themselves against all forms of violence—social, racial, psychological, physical, or cultural. Indeed, when the venerable James Farmer could no longer hold his membership to the pacifist course, he resigned the leadership in 1966, the height of the Black Power era, and was replaced by Floyd McKissick.[21]

It was under the tutelage of McKissick that CORE seemed to have lost its way. It was no longer what it set out to be in the 1940s and it expressed no clear ideological position that gave it a limited following among the emerging conscious class of African Americans. McKissick was involved in several large and important building projects supported by Republican politicians. His "Soul City" development, in some senses, usurped his strategic position in the movement for civil rights. By the time Roy Innis took charge of CORE in 1968 the organization had lost all legitimacy with the masses of black people. It had become reactionary and conservative and advanced nothing positive or progressive on the American social, legal, or civil agenda.

The Southern Christian Leadership Conference

The SCLC was formed out of another organization that was a direct result of action during the Montgomery Bus Boycott in 1955. On December 5, 1955 the black population in

Montgomery, Alabama, instituted a boycott of public transportation that would last for 381 days, ending on December 21, 1956. It would serve as a wake-up call for segregationists around the nation because the economic boycott of an economic sector by a sizable number of African Americans could close vulnerable businesses.

When Rosa Parks was arrested for refusing to give up her seat for a white man on a bus in Montgomery she was carrying out the strategy of the Montgomery Improvement Association (MIA). It had two main principals, Martin Luther King Jr, its president, and Ralph David Abernathy, the program director. Their collective decision to state a boycott was one of history's most dramatic actions against an entrenched racist system. Without resorting to weapons that were unavailable to blacks in large supply, and without venom that would cause the objective to be lost, the MIA controlled a series of protests that stunned the nation.[22]

Out of this movement came the modern civil rights movement. It was an important struggle and a necessary stage in the confrontation with white racism in the South. More boycotts spread across the nation as black people felt their economic power. In nonviolent action after action, the civil rights movement marched to a new, more authoritative chant for civil rights: "If you do not give us our rights, we will not buy from you. We will close you down."

On January 10–11, 1957 the Montgomery Improvement Association met with other protest groups in Atlanta to coordinate their activities. Sixty people from ten different states came to the meeting in Atlanta under the threat of the bombing of Ralph Abernathy's home. When the meeting was over, the group had formed the Southern Leadership Conference on Transportation and Nonviolent Integration. They declared that civil rights were essential for democracy, that segregation had to end, and that all blacks should reject all forms of segregation absolutely and with nonviolence. A month later, in New Orleans on February 14, 1957, the organizers shortened the name to Southern Leadership Conference and voted for Martin Luther King Jr to be president, Ralph David Abernathy to be Financial Secretary-Treasurer, C. K. Steele to be vice president, T. J. Jemison to be Secretary, and I. M. Augustine to be the general counsel.

In August 1957 the group met in Montgomery and renamed the organization the Southern Christian Leadership Conference (SCLC). They sought to enshrine their doctrine in the chartering documents of the organization. King had been a young graduate of the Morehouse College of Benjamin Mays and a graduate student at large of the philosophy of nonviolence. One cannot ignore the impact of his theological training at Crozer Theological Seminary, where he was awarded the degree of a Bachelor of Divinity and his study for the doctorate in Systematic Theology at Boston University, where he was awarded a degree on June 5, 1955 after completing the dissertation "A Comparison of God in the Thinking of Paul Tillich and Henry Wieman." However, it is generally agreed that it was the Mayes–Gandhi influence that permeated the movement led by King.[23] Among the organization's tenets were nonviolent mass action as the cornerstone of strategy, which seemed like a nod to the old pacifist idea of the Congress of Racial Equality, but was dusted off under the new rhetoric of nonviolence coming from the philosophy of Martin Luther King, the attachment of all protests to local community groups, and a determination to make the organization open to all races, religion, and background, even with the "Christian" in the name. The organization has had a series of well-known leaders such as:

- Rev. Dr Martin Luther King Jr: 1957 to 1968
- Rev. Ralph D. Abernathy: 1968 to 1977
- Rev. Joseph E. Lowery: 1977 to 1997
- Mr Martin L. King III: 1997 to 2004
- Rev. Fred Shuttlesworth: February 2004 to November 2004
- Mr Charles Steele Jr: November 2004 to 2008
- Dr Byron C. Clay: January 2009 to January 2010

Charles Hamilton Houston, Thurgood Marshall, and New Law

Very few individuals are able to have such a profound impact on the character of their societies as Charles Hamilton Houston.[24] Probably not since the legislative era after the Civil War, or even since the creation of the Constitution, had an individual affected the legal direction of the nation by his actions in the way that Houston managed to do without being eiher a judge or a legislator. He merely found new avenues to justice in the Constitution of the United States and thus changed forever his society.

The fact that few people know his name or have his name and résumé at the top of their lists attests to the strength and popularity of his ideas rather than to anything else. He is so well known in our law that it is like breathing air without knowing all of its chemical parts. In fact, on the occasion of Amherst College's celebration of Houston, Thurgood Marshall would say, "You have a large number of people who never heard of Charles Houston. But you're going to hear about him, because he left us such important items."[25] He could continue his praise of Houston by saying that of the two dozen lawyers representing the side of Brown in *Brown v. Topeka Board of Education*, perhaps only two had not come under the influence of Charles Hamilton Houston.[26] Justice William O. Douglas said that Charles Houston was one of the ten top advocates ever to appear before the Supreme Court.[27] Indeed, the historian Genna Rae McNeil says, "Charles Hamilton Houston cut through the bitterness that racism and the absence of authentic freedom in the United States might have made a permanent malady for African Americans and affirmed his own values. The price exacted by American society was great. Relentless struggle brought him to this death at the age of fifty-four."[28] What Houston achieved with a cohort of young lawyers he taught and mentored was the breakdown of legal segregation that had stood since the *Plessy v. Ferguson* decision. By exploring in his classes and his legal offices various methods of attacking the heart of legal segregation, Hamilton constructed strategies and tactics that live in the arguments of all those fighting for social, cultural, gender, or racial justice.

Charles Hamilton Houston was born in Washington, DC, on September 3, 1895 to a lawyer, William Lepre Houston, and a hairdresser, Mary Ethel Hamilton Houston. A brilliant student from his earliest years at the M Street High School, where he graduated at the top of his class, he also completed his Bachelor's as *magna cum laude* from Amherst College at the age of nineteen, and was one of six valedictorians.

When he finished Amherst he went to teach at Howard University but after two years enlisted in a segregated officers' training school for World War I and became a second lieutenant in a U.S. Army field artillery unit. Houston left the army to attend law school at Harvard, where he became the first black editor of the *Harvard Law Review*. Supreme Court

Figure 9.4
Thurgood Marshall, indomitable lawyer, effective Solicitor General, and first African American Supreme Court justice. Image courtesy of Charles L. Blockson Afro-American Collection, Temple University Libraries.

Justice Felix Frankfurter had taught Houston at Harvard, where he considered Houston to be one of the most brilliant students he ever taught.

Houston returned to Washington to practice law with his father and to teach at Howard University. He also was dean of Howard Law School from 1929 until 1935. Houston was responsible for leading the case for Howard Law School's accreditation by the Association of American Law Schools and the American Bar Association. Some of the most distinguished

Figure 9.5
William Hastie, legal mind and judge. Image courtesy of Charles L. Blockson Afro-American Collection, Temple University Libraries.

and influential civil rights lawyers in the nation studied at Howard during Houston's tenure as vice-dean. They included *Brown v. Topeka Board of Education* lawyer Thurgood Marshall, who later became a Supreme Court Justice. James Nabrit, William Hastie, Spottswood Robinson, A. Leon Higginbotham and Robert Carter, all superior lawyers and judges, also studied at Howard under Houston's mentorship during the time civil rights law was being invented.

At the time of Houston's death on April 22, 1950 it was as if the heavens had called home the brightest star in the civil rights firmament because the loss of Houston dimmed the gaze upon the law for all other lawyers. Four years later his protégé Thurgood Marshall would win the case *Brown v. Topeka Board of Education* and finally write into law a new chapter based on Houston's strategies. Five United States Supreme Court justices attended Houston's funeral, the most ever at the time to attend the funeral of a black law professor. The NAACP posthumously gave him its highest award, the Spingarn Medal.

Figure 9.6 Leon Higginbotham and Georgie Woods, famous legal scholar and outstanding impresario. Image courtesy of Charles L. Blockson Afro-American Collection, Temple University Libraries.

Houston's student and intellectual heir Thurgood Marshall was the grandson of enslaved Africans. Marshall was born on July 2, 1908 in Baltimore, Maryland. He attended Lincoln University in Pennsylvania, where his classmates included Langston Hughes, Kwame Nkrumah, and Cab Calloway, all of whom would make their marks on society. On completion of Lincoln, Marshall applied to enter law school at the University of Maryland, but this event more than anything else convinced him that he would work to destroy racism. In fact, the university's denial of admission because of his race was considered truly unacceptable. Marshall would never forget the racial discrimination shown by the University of Maryland. Instead he entered Howard University's Law School. To his delight he was accepted and immediately came under the influence of the most powerful legal mind in the African American community.[29]

Houston's challenge to his students was for them to apply the tenets of the Constitution to everyone alike. He believed, and taught Marshall and other students, that the doctrine

Figure 9.7 Kwame Nkrumah (center) and Horace Mann Bond (far left) at Lincoln University. Nkrumah became the leading Pan-Africanist of his time as well as the president of Ghana; Bond was head of Lincoln University, where Nkrumah received one of his degrees. Image courtesy of Charles L. Blockson Afro-American Collection, Temple University Libraries.

called "separate but equal" had to be attacked at its core and it and all other attachments would come falling down. Thus, Thurgood Marshall in 1933 successfully sued the state of Maryland to admit a student, Donald Gaines Murray. H. L. Mencken wrote in the Maryland Law School's journal that the segregation was "brutal and absurd." He said that the state of Maryland should not object to a self-respecting black student who graduated from Amherst.

When Charles Hamilton Houston was called to become the Chief Counsel for the NAACP he took Thurgood Marshall with him. Marshall was asked by the United Nations to help draft the Constitutions of Ghana and Tanzania. Marshall and Houston continued to amass great records as lawyers. Marshall had an enviable record as a civil rights lawyer, winning twenty-nine of thirty-two cases that he argued before the Supreme Court. In 1965 President Lyndon Johnson appointed Marshall to the office of U.S. Solicitor General, where he argued and won fourteen of the nineteen cases before the Supreme Court on behalf of the government. Marshall received the nomination to the United States Supreme Court in 1967, the year John Coltrane made his transition, and it was a sign that one spirit was leaving and another was ascending because after the death of Coltrane, Marshall, who was a lover of African American jazz and blues, expressed his sense of loss. Indeed, Thurgood Marshall represented and won more cases before the United States Supreme Court than any other American lawyer. Marshall died on January 24, 1993 after having retired from the court and insuring his legacy with wit, charm, and intellect.[30]

There was a Voice Crying in the Wilderness

Mississippi, the poorest of the Deep South states, and the least educated, was also the most entrenched in the doctrine of white racial supremacy during the twentieth century. Members of the Ku Klux Klan paraded the streets of small towns to demonstrate their intentions to maintain the racial structure that had been in place since the collapse of the Reconstruction at the turn of the century. Nonetheless, blacks in Mississippi, as in other states, resisted every attempt to reverse the tide of progress. Elements in the white community who had inherited the power given to them by their parents and grandparents felt that it was their duty to "keep blacks in their place," and that place was one of subservience and ignorance. On the other hand, African Americans in the state that had seen two blacks go to the United States Senate during the Reconstruction were just as adamant that they would fight with all their ingenuity to overcome the stranglehold the whites had on their consciousness, political rights, education, and economic liberation.

A series of draconian laws had been passed in the Mississippi legislature that had made it almost impossible for blacks to exercise their constitutional rights, especially the Fifteenth Amendment. Black voting rights had been reduced to almost nothing. It could be said that a dog had more privilege in being able to go to the voting polls than blacks because even a dog could go with its owner and lie around on the ground as the whites voted. Blacks were shut out, with one regulation after another, from the right to vote, and the fierce determination of some blacks to overcome these prescriptions meant death. They were sacrificial lambs on the altar of American justice, their lives given up for the privilege of casting a vote for one candidate or another, sometimes both equally racist. Yet for the mere casting of such a vote the African American was often beaten, harassed, or killed.

There is no wonder that Fannie Lou Hamer, famous for her statement that she was "sick and tired of being sick and tired," was a necessary intervention into the life of the American nation. She had been born many times before in the courage and determination of her mothers and fathers and yet in the personal manifestation of the woman born on October 6, 1917 in rural Montgomery County, Mississippi, the spirit of indignation came into full bloom. She was the granddaughter of enslaved Africans and her family was captured by the sharecropping system of Mississippi, not much above enslavement, where blacks worked on large farms for whites with the expectation that they would be able to plant and harvest a small plot of land for their personal and family needs while getting all of their supplies and food from the white man's store. The ultimate objective of this situation was the total control of the black family. Every sharecropping family owed the white planters more than they could pay and therefore were tied to the land like landless serfs. No European serf during the darkest days of medieval serfdom experienced as much social and economic hell as Africans in American under the sharecropping system. The system was simply created to reintroduce permanent slavery.

A corollary system was the political control of blacks equal to the economic and social control. In Mississippi, as in most of the Southern states, a person could not vote unless they satisfied several conditions: (1) the voter had to be literate; (2) if the voter were literate he would have to know the Constitution; (3) if the voter could quote the Constitution he would have to be able to interpret the Constitution, any article or clause; (4) if the voter could interpret the Constitution, then the voter would have to show the receipt from the previous election to demonstrate that he had paid his poll tax the previous year; and (5) if the voter had managed to keep his receipt from the last poll tax, he would have to prove that his grandfather voted in the elections in that district (the grandfather clause). Of course, few blacks were able to meet all of these qualifications, which whites did not have to prove, and therefore few blacks were ever granted the absolute right to vote in elections during the early part of the twentieth century. This is why the Civil Rights Movement concentrated on voting rights so heavily during the 1960s. The struggle remained one for human dignity.

Fannie Lou Hamer

Fannie Lou Hamer had nineteen brothers and sisters who lived through the most horrendous parts of segregation. And most of her life, Hamer had sacrificed in the same way to the same oppressive system until 1962. She came from the cotton fields of Mississippi with freedom on her mind and she would not let anything or anybody turn her around once she became conscious of her rights and privileges as a citizen. Hamer became the custodian of dignity and in her royal way she elevated what some called the pedestrian tasks of farm life and made them the platform for her eloquence.[31]

Young students from the Student Nonviolent Coordinating Committee came to her town to register voters. Fannie Lou Hamer was forty-four years old when she learned that African Americans had a constitutional right to vote. She had been held back so long and her family kept ignorant so long that she expressed surprise that blacks could actually be defended by the Constitution. When the SNCC workers asked for volunteers to go to the courthouse to register voters, Hamer was the first one to step forward. The decision was risky for her family and herself but at the time she did what she had to do. Later she reflected, "The only thing they could do to me was to kill me, and it seemed like they'd been trying to do that a little bit at a time ever since I could remember."[32]

The white authorities met the blacks at the courthouse with billy clubs and guns, and, after beating them simply for trying to register people to vote, placed them in jail. Immediately Hamer's plantation owner threw her family out of its shack and left her homeless and without work even as a sharecropper. They had worked on the same farm for thirty years. They moved in with friends until sixteen shots were fired into the friends' house. Fannie Lou Hamer then went to a nearby town where she found shelter and a job with the voter registration campaign run by SNCC. She taught other African Americans how to read and vote.

This was to be a lesson to any other black person who tried to register or encourage others to vote. Threats against her were numerous as whites wanted to make an example out of her. She was arrested and beaten almost to death in front of black male prisoners to show what could happen to any black who tried to get out of his or her place.

A few months later she and Annelle Ponder were arrested and badly beaten for trying to use a "whites only" restroom in Winona, Mississippi. Hamer's kidneys were permanently damaged and she lost the sight of one eye.

An assassin on June 12, 1963 gunned down the charismatic and confident Medgar Evers.[33] He had served in Normandy defending the rights of Europeans during World War II. When he came home he attended Alcorn College and started to establish local chapters of the

NAACP because he saw that the conditions he left in Mississippi had not changed much, and although he had risked his life for whites it was about time he risked his life for himself. In 1954 he applied for and was denied admission to the University of Mississippi Law School. The NAACP made him its first Mississippi field representative. His boycotts and school integration battles, based on the law, made him the most hated black man in Mississippi. It would take thirty-one years before his murderer, Byron De La Beckwith, would be brought to trial and convicted. He is buried in Arlington National Cemetery. It is in this context that Fannie Lou Hamer found her strength and her voice. If fear existed in her, it no longer ruled her. If she could vote, she would; if others could risk their lives and die for the just cause, then she would be willing to do the same.

But, above all, she would not be intimidated and said that with all that her grandparents and parents had given to Mississippi, she was not going to move out of the state. "The white man is the scariest person on earth. Out in the daylight he don't do nothing. But at night he'll toss a bomb or pay someone to kill. The white man's afraid he'll be treated like he's been treating Negroes, but I couldn't carry that much hate," Hamer said.[34]

Such was the courage of this indomitable woman that she was not frightened even of death, and became a Field Secretary for the SNCC effort to register voters. After working with the SNCC for a few months she became one of the most important voices of the Civil Rights Movement.[35] She was an electrifying speaker, quick of wit, intelligent in her profound African American sensibility, and sharp in repartee.

Hamer co-founded the Mississippi Freedom Democratic Party (MFDP), which was to make history itself when in 1964 the Party challenged the all-white Mississippi delegation to the Democratic National Convention. Hamer spoke in front of the Credentials Committee in televised proceedings that reached millions of viewers and made her an instant hero in the African American community. In fact, she became a star for the progressive wing of the Democratic Party. She told the committee how African Americans in many states across the country were prevented from voting through illegal tests, poll taxes, and physical intimidation. As a result of her speech, two delegates of the MFDP were given speaking rights at the convention and the other members were seated as honorable guests. Like the martyred Medgar Evers of the Mississippi NAACP, Fannie Lou Hamer is among the most revered figures in civil rights. She died on March 14, 1977 at the age of fifty-nine, and a committee led by scholar and author Patricia Reid-Merritt and Patricia Thompson organized a committee to erect a statue of Hamer in the town of Ruleville, Mississippi.

Word Warriors Emerge with the Pen

One could write an entire twenty-volume history of African American writers and not complete a comprehensive treatment of the literary compendium of the people. So richly textured is the literature and *orature* of African Americans that one cannot think of American culture devoid of African contributions. From the use of the West African words "OK," "go-go," "goober," and other creative words from Ebonics, the African presence has made American language ripe and expressive. In nearly the same way the myths, speculations, imaginations, and experiences of African Americans have also contributed to American society. However, it is in the expansion of human consciousness, the advancement of freedom, and the expression of humanity's desire for fulfillment that African Americans have made their greatest contribution. During the 1960s the cultural and political consciousness of African Americans was cultivated and expressed by some of the most important writers since the Harlem Renaissance.[36] Indeed, the abundance of skills and talents was unequalled even by the Harlem Renaissance. James Baldwin was the best example of this spirit but he was certainly not alone.

James Baldwin Emerges as a Spokesman

James Baldwin, the brilliant essayist, published his book *The Fire Next Time* in 1964, and immediately became the new voice crying in the wilderness. Almost prophetically he anticipated the fury that was raging in the black community. When a white policeman killed a fifteen-year-old student in Harlem in July, 1964, the anger had reached boiling point and an uprising occurred that would be repeated in Rochester, New York, Philadelphia, Brooklyn, Newark, and Camden. Cities burned and local leaders like Franklin Florence in Rochester, New York, and Cecil B. Moore in Philadelphia tried to articulate the sentiments of the masses to the white establishment. Florence created an organization called FIGHT in Rochester and forced Kodak and other companies to get involved in the economic empowerment of the African American community. Cecil B. Moore led demonstrations against segregated private schools and a public school system that were unresponsive to the African American community's interests. This was occurring throughout the nation as numerous local men and women took to the streets to rally the masses against prejudice, discrimination, and the more odious forms of racial segregation.

Periodically in African American history some person or persons hear the call of the times and step forward, from some improbable nexus of circumstances, and present a persona that defies place of origin, station in life, and expectation. James Arthur Baldwin was such an individual. Baldwin, who was born in Harlem, New York, on August 2, 1924 and died on November 30, 1987, was an emergent voice with a sharp literary style that was both combative and vibrant at the critical moment when individual and collective freedom collided. It was as if his style had been created especially for the political foliage that had to be cleared away during the Civil Rights Era. Growing up in an intensely religious home where he was the eldest of nine children, Baldwin was destined to become a Pentecostal preacher at the age of fourteen. The religious cadences found in his literary style lend credence to the idea that he had imbibed the best periods of the preaching sermon and the King James Bible to become a writer who could bridge gaps between the Northern and Southern blacks as well as reach whites in regions of their moral consciousness that they might have forgotten. *Go Tell It on the Mountain* (1953), his first novel, is considered autobiographical and his first real play, *The Amen Corner* (1954), had autobiographical elements. Baldwin's essay collections *Notes of a Native Son* (1955), *Nobody Knows My Name* (1961), and *The Fire Next Time* (1963) were thought of as his intellectual appeal, from deep within the African American soul and aesthetic, to reasonable whites.[37]

Baldwin heard the call of France when he was twenty-four years old. This is the same voice that Richard Wright had heard two years earlier in 1946 at the age of thirty-eight. Like so many African Americans, particularly writers, they felt that the French were different from other whites, more congenial, more socially accepting of blacks, and more capable of laying aside racial notions to allow others to succeed. Whether they were right or wrong in this estimation, they had the examples of Josephine Baker and Félix Éboué, two blacks, one from the United States and the other from South America (French Guiana) who had risen to achieve national recognition by the French. Indeed, a year after Baldwin arrived in France, the multifaceted French African Félix Éboué was buried in the Pantheon, France's national cemetery for its greatest heroes. Baldwin made his home mainly in the south of France, often returning to teach and lecture in the United States. Although he loved France, he spent time in Turkey and Switzerland, where he found a different environment but still an atmosphere that was freer, in his mind, than that of his own country. In 1957 he made a decision to spend half a year in New York and half a year outside of the United States. His novels include *Giovanni's Room* (1956), about a white American expatriate who deals with his homosexuality, and *Another Country* (1962), about the conflicts between race and homosexuality among New York intellectuals. Baldwin's homosexual writings stirred lots of discussion, some of it negative, in the African American community, but he maintained his place as the leading essayist on race during the 1960s. While Eldridge Cleaver, at the time Minister of Information for the Black Panthers and chairman of the Black House Council, said that Baldwin's writing displayed an "agonizing, total hatred of the blacks," others believed that he had demonstrated enormous courage in laying bare issues often concealed in society.[38] Baldwin's plays *Blues for Mister Charlie*, produced in 1964, *Going to Meet the Man* (1965), and *Tell Me How Long the Train's Been Gone* (1968) showed him to be an extremely powerful dramatist.

Figure 9.8 Josephine Baker, the legendary singer and dancer who stole the heart of the French, at the Pyramid Club. Image courtesy of Charles L. Blockson Afro-American Collection, Temple University Libraries.

Conclusion

The three-quarters of the twentieth century covered by this chapter was filled with action against racism. One might say that this was the period when African Americans took the heart out of the system of segregation and discrimination by refusing to accept being treated as second-class citizens. It was impossible for the system to maintain itself after it had been assaulted by so many thousands of blacks attacking every vestige of inequality in transportation, lodging, education, and other sectors of society. Quite literally every day in the nation thousands of individuals resisted the attempt to inferiorize them. The future became brighter although there were setbacks, revolts, riots, and lynchings deep into the century. During this period of intense agitation for equality and justice, the African American population also played roles in the expansion of democracy, the building of highways, the participation in the international wars, and the struggle against fascism in Europe and colonization in Africa. Indeed, Brenda Gayle Plummer's *Rising Wind* is a remarkable testimony to the various ways in which African Americans made their mark on the major issues of the day. A people asserting its agency in the most vigorous manner defined the spirit of this period.

Additional Reading

Bond, Horace M. *The Education of the Negro in the American Social Order*. New York: Octagon Books, 1966.

Conyers, James E. *Malcolm X: An Historical Reader*. Durham, NC: Carolina Academic Press, 2008.

Harris, William H. *The Harder We Run: Black Workers since the Civil War*. New York: Oxford University Press, 1982.

Goings, Kenneth W. *"The NAACP Comes of Age": The Defeat of Judge John J. Parker*. Bloomington: Indiana University Press, 1990.

Kellogg, Charles F. *NAACP: A History of the National Association for the Advancement of Colored People*. Baltimore: Johns Hopkins University Press, 1967.

McNeil, Genna Rae. *Groundwork: Charles Hamilton Houston and the Struggle for Civil Rights*. Philadelphia: University of Pennsylvania Press, 1983.

Painter, Nell Irvin. *The Narrative of Hosea Hudson: His Life as a Negro Communist in the South*. Cambridge, MA: Harvard University Press, 1979.

Pfeffer, Paula F. *A. Philip Randolph, Pioneer of the Civil Rights Movement*. Baton Rouge: Louisiana State University, 1990.

Tillotson, Michael. *Invisible Jim Crow: Contemporary Ideological Threats to the Internal Security of African Americans*. Trenton: Africa World Press, 2011.

Wilkins, Roy with Tom Mathews. *Standing Fast: The Autobiography of Roy Wilkins*. New York: Da Capo Press, 1994.

Chapter Time Markers

1955	Emmett Till murdered in Mississippi
1963	March on Washington
	Martin Luther King Jr gives "I have a Dream" speech
1964	Council of Federated Organizations (COFO) leads voter registration in the South
1965	Voting rights law passed
	Malcolm X assassinated in New York
1966	Maulana Karenga creates Kwanzaa
1968	Martin Luther King Jr assassinated in Memphis

Social and Moral Challenges are Everywhere

10

Important Terms and Names

Oliver Ollie Harrington

Josephine Baker

Freedom Summer

Rosa Parks

Emmett Till

Fred Hampton

Maulana Karenga

Muhammad Ali

Us Organization

Kwame Nkrumah

Ella Jo Baker

Student Nonviolent Coordinating Committee

James Brown

Black Panthers

March on Washington

Montgomery Bus Boycott

Selma March

Irene Morgan

Challenging Racism

Racial segregation produced its own internal laws. One of the most predictable was that people who felt betrayed by the national creeds on civil and social rights would eventually, sooner rather than later, explode into resistance. In 1944 Irene Morgan, a twenty-seven-year-old Baltimorean, was arrested and jailed in the state of Virginia for refusing to give up her seat to a white person on the interstate Greyhound bus. The white driver stopped the bus and summoned the sheriff, who tried to arrest her. Morgan tore up the arrest warrant, kicked the sheriff in the groin, and fought the deputy who dragged her off the bus. The case went to court. Two years later the U.S. Supreme Court ruled 7–1 that Virginia's law enforcing segregation was illegal on interstate buses. Irene Morgan was born in 1917 and died in 2007.

On March 2, 1955 Claudette Colvin, a fifteen-year-old student, was physically removed from a bus in Montgomery, Alabama. Eight months later eighteen-year-old Mary Louise Smith was ejected from another Montgomery bus. Both had been sitting in the "whites only" section of the bus.

Rosa Parks Frustrates White Privilege

By December 1955 the Montgomery black community was ready to mount a sustained boycott against the Montgomery Bus Company, and Rosa Parks, a college-educated secretary, rode into history and began a season of discontent that would lead to a new dispensation in the South.

Often called the "Mother of Freedom" and recognized by the U.S. Congress as "the First Lady of Civil Rights," Parks' bravery became iconic for the Civil Rights Movement largely because it was also backed by the Montgomery Bus Boycott.[1] It was the insistence of the movement that projected her case into the national limelight. Her attorney, the brilliant Fred Gray, who had quickly become a student of the new Houstonian uses of the Constitution to fight segregation, pursued the last vestiges of transport discrimination. Defiance of the racist policies of all Southern-state bus and transport systems became a part of the framework of breaking apart the superstructure of racism in the United States.

Rosa Parks was also the secretary of the Montgomery chapter of the NAACP and had attended a session at the famed progressive Highlander Folk School, which had gained a reputation for working for equality. Parks lost her job as a seamstress at a department store because of her activism against segregation. She soon moved to Detroit, where she found work and became an important part of the Detroit political community. She served as the receptionist and secretary to U.S. Representative John Conyers from 1965 to 1988. She lived her final years as a private citizen and received hundreds of awards and honors, including the Spingarn Medal and the Congressional Gold Medal, and a statue was placed in the National Statuary Hall after her death in 2005.

Two years before Rosa Parks' historic ride into history, Sarah Keys, who was a private in the Women's Army Corps (WAC), filed a segregation complaint against the Carolina Coach Company in 1953. Using the non-discrimination language of the Interstate Commerce Act, Keys' attorneys argued that segregation of black passengers was banned. Washington lawyer Julius Winfield Robertson and his partner, Dovey Johnson Roundtree, a former WAC, who had taken on the case with personal zeal because she had been discriminated against when she served in the WAC, won their legal case in 1955, just six days before Rosa Parks' refusal to give up her seat to a white man in Montgomery. The intent of the civil rights lawyers was to use the U.S. Supreme Court's logic in the *Brown v. Topeka Board of Education* case to close the loop used by private bus companies to discriminate in interstate travel. Ultimately, all of these segregation cases must be viewed as collectively contributing to the rise of a national consciousness against racial discrimination.

The Lynching of Emmett Till

The scholar Clenora Hudson-Weems insists in *Emmett Till: The Sacrificial Lamb of the Civil Rights Movement* that the murder of Emmett Till in August 1955 should rightly be called the beginning of the end of segregation in the South.[2] Hudson-Weems' argument rests on the irrational behaviors of the bigoted Southerners who killed Till and the subsequent rush of condemnation from around the world at the savage beating of the young boy. Emmett Louis "Bobo" Till was lynched at the age of fourteen in Money, Mississippi, for speaking to a white woman in a grocery store.

Emmett Till, who lived in Chicago, went to Mississippi in the summer of 1955 to visit his cousins. When the fourteen-year-old went into a store owned by Roy Bryant to buy candy, he is alleged to have said to Carolyn Bryant, the wife of Roy, "Bye bye, baby." Coming from the North, Till had no real understanding of how violent would be the whites' reaction to this perceived violation of their white supremacy doctrine. A black male could never speak or whisper to a white woman in a social manner. A few days later, while Till slept in the bedroom at his relatives' house, he was awakened in the middle of the night when two white men, Roy Bryant and John William Milam, armed with guns broke into the house and kidnapped him. They killed Till and then tied his body to a seventy-pound cotton gin fan with barbed wire around his neck and dumped him into the Tallahatchie River. However, two boys discovered the mangled body three days later while fishing in the river.

The corpse showed evidence of a brutal beating and torture. The body was badly mutilated, with one eye beaten or shot out, a bullet lodged in his brain, and signs of vicious torture on his upper and lower body. Although the killing of Till occurred after the murders of many other African Americans, it was the brutality of the hatred as exemplified by the badly abused and mutilated body of Emmett Till that struck the world with the barbarity of the hatred whites in the South held against blacks. Roy Bryant and John Milam were arrested and put on trial.

A courageous and straightforward Mose Wright, Till's uncle, testified that he had seen Roy Bryant and John Milam take his nephew from the house at gunpoint, but the all-white jury acquitted the two men, who would later confess to *Look Magazine* in 1956 that they killed Emmett Till. The fact that they could boast of their actions and their ability to outwit justice showed the state of the American nation in 1956.

The funeral was held in Chicago, his hometown, and Till's mother, Mamie Bradley, demanded that the body be funeralized in Chicago with an open casket because she wanted the whole world to see how the murderers mangled the body of her son. The photographs appeared in newspapers around the world and black parents held their young children closer and told them that they loved them. There was a spirit of resolve in the many thousands who viewed the body of Emmett Till in the casket in Chicago. Nothing could erase the image of the badly beaten, shamelessly tortured body of the young man from the brains of those who saw the image. Bradley's wish that the world would see came true, and even today the name of Emmett Till stirs the emotions and causes contemporaries to contemplate the cruelty of human beings toward each other. Memorials to Emmett Till exist throughout the nation in statues, streets, and schools. Till's death had made him, in the words of the scholar Clenora Hudson-Weems, "the sacrificial lamb of the Civil Rights Movement."

The March on Washington

The background to the August 28, 1963 March on Washington was filled with activism, sit-ins, marches, protests, petitions, and freedom rides. We had not come to Washington for a social party; we had come to Washington to present the people's case to the national leaders.

In 1958 nine black students had demonstrated incredible courage by walking through a canyon of angry whites to enroll at Central High School in Little Rock, Arkansas. Daisy Bates, the leader of the NAACP, took up the students' case and led the NAACP in a heroic assault against segregated schools.[3] The students showed poise and discipline under threats and shouts of intimidation hurled at them by white parents who threatened defiance of the federal government. They strategized in a states' right defense, meaning essentially that the state had power to determine what went on in its jurisdiction, harking back to the secessionists who precipitated the Civil War. However, Governor Faubus had to retreat from his challenge to the federal government and the "Little Rock Nine" became enshrined in the history of the march to liberty.

Then, on February 1, 1960, four students of the North Carolina Agricultural and Technical College in Greensboro decided to challenge public segregation of eating facilities by employing the technique of the sit-in, that is, remain seated until they were served or arrested. This protest action created a whole new wave of mass action against segregated establishments and brought out the full anger of whites who wanted to retain segregation. Thousands of black and white students joined the protest trail against segregated eating facilities. They were often beaten and taken to jail singing "freedom songs" and showing a willingness to stand up for what they believed to be right. As Forman and Younge would record, black students were threatened and beaten; indeed, many suffered head and brain injuries and other students died.[4]

King Enters Birmingham

A few months later, in early 1963, the Reverend Fred Shuttlesworth invited Martin Luther King to Birmingham. Shuttlesworth's church had been bombed and he had been arrested for assisting student freedom riders. On April 3, 1963, King came to Birmingham with his top lieutenants to begin preparations for a nonviolent campaign. During the next few weeks Shuttlesworth and King prepared their nonviolent troops for a full-scale assault on the bastions of segregation. They identified the top players in the segregation structure, tallied the numbers they could depend upon for marches, organized transportation, and discussed the primary objectives for the demonstrations. They recognized that the leading face of segregation in Birmingham had become Bull Connor, a pugnacious and radical racist whose intent was to prevent integration by all means.

Bull Connor, the Birmingham sheriff, had committed himself to upholding segregation. He outfitted his men with K-9 dogs, fire hoses, tear gas, and electric prods that could send a person into shock, and sent them to patrol the demonstrators. Neither King nor Shuttlesworth was scared of Bull Connor or the segregationists; they had seen many battles and had won most of them. King told reporters that he planned to be in Birmingham until "Pharaoh lets God's people go."[5]

The Letter from a Birmingham Jail

Finally, on April 12, 1963, King began the demonstrations in Birmingham. Bull Connor's forces were out in full regalia, loading down with whips, electric prods, and tear gas. King was arrested and thrown into jail. Many of the demonstrators were arrested and some were injured. The Birmingham white ministers denounced the marchers and asked King why he had come to Birmingham. Dr King was moved while in prison to write a "Letter from a Birmingham Jail" to the white ministers in which he defended the right of oppressed people to protest their condition.[6]

He began his letter on April 16, 1963:

> My Dear Fellow Clergymen: While confined here in the Birmingham city jail, I came across your recent statement calling my present activities "unwise and untimely." Seldom do I pause to answer criticism of my work and ideas. If I sought to answer all the criticisms that cross my desk, my secretaries would have little time for anything other than such correspondence in the course of the day, and I would have no time for constructive work. But since I feel that you are men of genuine good will and that your criticisms are sincerely set forth, I want to try to answer your statement in what I hope will be patient and reasonable terms.

King wrote to the preachers in a language that they could understand:

> I am in Birmingham because injustice is here. Just as the prophets of the eighth century BCE left their villages and carried their "thus saith the Lord" far beyond the boundaries of their home towns, and just as the Apostle Paul left his village of Tarsus and carried the gospel of Jesus Christ to the far corners of the Greco-Roman world, so am I compelled to carry the gospel of freedom beyond my own home town. Like Paul, I must constantly respond to the Macedonian call for aid.

King's forces made a direct challenge to Bull Connor's bigotry and were effective in casting the city of Birmingham as the laughing stock of the South. It was a bigoted, racist city that would even command dogs to attack schoolchildren. The shocking images shaped the national and international perception of the struggle for freedom and helped to accelerate the passage of the 1964 Civil Rights Act.

By May, 1963 more than 3,000 people had been arrested in Birmingham. The town had acquired the nickname "Bombingham" because there had been so many unsolved shootings and bombings. Theophilus "Bull" Connor, the public safety commissioner, and Governor George Wallace conspired to put an end to the civil rights protest. The governor sent state patrolmen to reinforce Bull Connor's prohibition of the marches. The semi-literate Connor, who had had limited schooling, believed that his white constituents would support him in keeping the black population in a subservient position. He ordered his men to do everything to insure that the marches would be unsuccessful. Water hoses and attack dogs were turned on the marchers and among those arrested was a fourteen-year-old girl. The attacks on the demonstrators in Birmingham sparked activists across the nation and more than 930 public protests were held in more than one hundred cities. Birmingham was a symbol of defiance to racism. Finally, the white leaders in Birmingham made concessions and the demonstrations ended.

King and his civil rights lieutenants knew that things would be difficult in the South. As they were preparing for the March on Washington, in August 1963, they heard the sad news that Medgar Evers, the field secretary for the NAACP, had been assassinated, yet they were determined that they had come this far and they had to go farther, and indeed Evers would have insisted that they go farther. From Alabama, Georgia, and Mississippi, Jesse Jackson,

Andrew Young, James Bevel, Ralph Abernathy, and Wyatt T. Walker, and other lieutenants of Dr King, fanned out to other cities and other battles. Soon the March on Washington would be a reality and the "justice troopers" of the movement would present their case to the nation at the memorial honoring Abraham Lincoln.

August 28, 1963: An Event for History

On August 28, 1963, exactly seven years after the funeral of Emmett Till, blacks and whites, men and women, Christians and Jews, workers and executives, who believed that the time was ripe for the final push to justice and equality combined forces for the March on Washington. Bayard Rustin and A. Philip Randolph, veteran organizers, were enthusiastic when they looked at the thousands of citizens who had come to the Lincoln Memorial to demand jobs and freedom. Between them they had been the main planners and organizers, pulling together union and religious leaders as well as civil rights and political leaders in a dramatic demonstration of racial unity.

The "Big Five" civil rights leaders were Whitney Young of the Urban League, John Lewis of SNCC, Roy Wilkins of the NAACP, Floyd McKissick, representing James Farmer of CORE, and Martin Luther King Jr of the SCLC. Farmer had been arrested and had sent McKissick to read his speech.

The most memorable event of the 1963 March on Washington was Martin Luther King Jr's "I have a Dream" speech. To have heard it, as I heard it on that summer day as a college student, was to have been in the presence of the most memorable oratorical performance of the century. Only Marcus Garvey, Frederick Douglass, or Booker T. Washington could have rivaled King's cadence, his measured eloquence, and his passionate commitment to his ideas. But they spoke before the days of television, and their gifts of speech could only be reported. King's speech was instantaneously a national event.

A quarter of a million demonstrators listening to Martin Luther King's every word, agreeing with his sentiments, and feeling a sense of euphoria meant that the march had brought many blacks and whites together on a historical occasion. There would be only one other march, the Selma March, two years later, where this degree of racial unity would be demonstrated in the Civil Rights Movement. Beyond the sense of unity was the definite feeling that something had been concretely accomplished. It would not be long before the national leaders were pressured to introduce the most comprehensive Civil Rights Bill in history.

The coalition of the black and white civil rights workers that produced the March on Washington was shattered in the months after the demonstration. Racism did not abate, but neither did the demands of the African Americans for freedom. The rhetoric of anger coming from young blacks, heavily influenced by the sharp arguments of Malcolm X, and the resistance of the white establishment to granting more opportunities forced the civil rights leaders to reassess their strategies.

President John Kennedy was thought by many black leaders to be a friend to the African American community, yet this new sense of urgency on the part of the civil rights leaders puzzled him. Dr King warned the president, "If something isn't done to give the Negro a new sense of hope and a sense of protection there is a danger we will face the worst race riot we have ever seen in this country."[7]

Kennedy asked King and the other leaders to try to forestall any violence while he attempted to get the civil rights legislation passed: "Tell the Negro communities that this is a very hard price which they have to pay to get this job done." Kennedy could not foretell how hard and how difficult it would be for African Americans to wait for justice. The Birmingham bombers kept up their assaults on the innocent.

Author's Reflection

On August 28, 1963 I stood with 250,000 other people at the Lincoln Memorial in Washington, DC, having answered the call for a March on Washington. I had persuaded my Chinese college roommate, John Lye of Singapore, to make the trip with me and we had driven my 1957 Chevrolet to Washington for the historic event. Through the crush of people we had found positions near the stage. As a young college student I felt a moral obligation to travel to the capital city to register my voice against racism. John was enthusiastic about the occasion. We were close enough to see John Lewis, Roy Wilkins, Whitney Young, and Martin Luther King Jr as they spoke from the platform. It was a glorious day but it had come as a conclusion to a summer of discontent, which unfortunately was just a prelude to an autumn of more unrest.

On September 15, 1963 four young girls gathered for Sunday School at the 16th Street Baptist Church in Birmingham were killed in a bomb attack on the church.

Two months later, on November 22, 1963, President Kennedy was assassinated in Dallas, Texas. The United States was undergoing a change in its political culture. Since the society had not responded aggressively against social violence aimed at African Americans it had allowed a violent atmosphere to flourish.

In some circles, however, violence would be met with violence and the rhetoric in the African American community matched that in the white communities. Black people did not intend to roll over and be killed or maimed; the age of nonviolence appeared to be fast disappearing. Groups of interracial citizens sought to place brakes on the rapidly deteriorating conditions in the country but soon the African American struggle was internationalized and became for many people the *cause célèbre* of the age. Black Americans, with dignity and nonviolence, had begun the struggle for civil rights, and now the aim was to hold back all forms of prejudice while advancing human rights. All hands would be needed on the wheel of progress. So infectious was the drama of the movement that Africans in Europe and Asia responded with positive energy to request to hold candlelight sympathy protests for various events. Kennedy's death had struck deep into the heart of America's destiny; it had galvanized the left wing and created the possibility that those who had been nonaligned to the progressive movement would now get involved. Less than a year after the assassination of the president, racists struck in Mississippi against three civil rights workers. On June 21, 1964 white supremacists murdered James Chaney, a twenty-one-year-old African American from Meridian, Mississippi; Andrew Goodman, a twenty-year-old Jewish student from New York; and Michael Schwerner, a twenty-four-year-old Jewish organizer for the Congress of Racial Equality, also from New York. The lynching of the three young men occurred as they were investigating the burning of a church involved in the civil rights movement. They knew they would be followed because the infamous White Citizens' Council and Ku Klux Klan had been given their license number, so they told colleagues who worked for the Council of Confederated Organizations where they were going. Nevertheless, their courage, which was sterling, and their intense faith in the rightness of their actions to support voter registration, carried them to Neshoba County, where the deputy sheriff, Cecil Price, a member of the White Knights of the Ku Klux Klan, stopped their car. He arrested Chaney for driving above the speed limit and then held Goodman and Schwerner for further investigation.[8]

None of the prisoners was allowed to make telephone calls. However, their colleagues from COFO made attempts to inquire about them when they did not return. The jail secretary lied about their presence in the jail. During the time they were being held, the white supremacist organizations gathered to discuss how to kill them. An ambush was planned for them on the road back to Meridian.

They were released with a twenty-dollar fine for speeding, but when they drove away, the deputy sheriff who pulled them over again followed them. He kept them waiting until Klan members arrived and then the three were taken to an isolated area where Chaney was beaten and all three of them shot to death. The car they were driving was set on fire and driven into Bogue Chitto swamp. The bodies were buried in a shallow grave. Chaney had a left arm broken in one place and a right arm broken in two places, a broken jaw, a marked disruption to the left elbow joint, a crushed right shoulder, and trauma to the groin area. This information was not released until 2000, nearly thirty-three years after the trial.

Ultimately the U.S. Justice Department charged eighteen individuals with conspiring to deprive the three of their civil rights. Those found guilty on October 20, 1967 were Cecil Price, Klan Imperial Wizard Samuel Bowers, Wayne Roberts, Jimmy Snowden, Billy Wayne Posey, Horace Barnett, and Jimmy Arledge. They were sentenced to three to ten years, but no one served more than six for the murders. Considered an outrage by millions of people around the world, the lynching of the three civil rights activists united African Americans and progressive whites in a determined challenge to all forms of racism. In the process of investigating the case the Federal Bureau of Investigation had uncovered seven other bodies from the swamps and waterways of Mississippi, showing that there was a pattern of murdering of blacks who threatened the system of white supremacy. Activists regained their footing and added new recruits to the civil rights organizations, African Americans who lived overseas, like James Baldwin and Josephine Baker, reiterated their commitment to the struggle, although they made their financial and moral contributions from abroad.

Josephine Baker and the International Call to Participate

The rampant racial attacks against blacks in the United States upset even those African Americans who had chosen to make Europe or Africa their homes. They were just as eager to see an end to racial injustice in their native land as others. One of these was the performer Josephine Baker.[9] She was born Freda Josephine McDonald in June 3, 1906 in St Louis, Missouri, the daughter of Carrie McDonald and Eddie Carson, and grew to become of the world's most powerful entertainers. When Baker died, on April 12, 1975, she had spent most of her life in France, her adopted country. She started her career as a vaudeville star in a Harlem club. She was an extraordinary dancer and entertainer who captivated the audiences of the twentieth century. When Baker first went to France she was only nineteen years old and her performance in Paris in *La Revue Nègre* tantalized the French audiences, who considered her beautifully exotic. The French had rarely seen black performers and they had not seen one so attractive and skilled in her dance routine. She became the idol of the young French intellectuals and artists. Josephine Baker's dance performance was different from the classical French ballet. She was a dancer but was always in motion, something that was different from the movement and pose style of most ballet dancers. Soon the French called her the "Bronze Venus," the "Black Pearl," and the "Creole Goddess." She remained, however, in her own mind a humanitarian committed to justice who used her art to win friends for her various causes. By 1937 Baker had become a French citizen. She became Europe's highest-paid entertainer, the first African American female to star in a major film, and the first African American female to integrate a concert hall in the United States. When World War II broke out in Europe, Baker assumed the mantle of a dedicated French citizen, serving as a spy for the French Resistance and sheltering French Jews at her Château des Milandes.

When the war ended, Baker, a French hero, used her popularity to advance her humanitarian interest in adopting poor children. Her own life had been filled with abuse, hard work, and poverty. When she was eight years old the white woman whom she worked for burned her hands because she used too much soap while washing the laundry. Furthermore, after she dropped out of school at the age of twelve she had become homeless, living in cardboard shelters and searching for food in trash heaps. However, her brilliant street corner dancing attracted recruiters, who took her to New York to perform *Shuffle Along* (1921) and *The Chocolate Dandies* (1924) at the Plantation Club.

On October 2, 1925 Josephine Baker opened her dance performance in Paris at the Théâtre des Champs-Élysées. After her immediate success she was asked to tour Europe with her act. The call of France was too strong for her to complete her tour of Europe and when she returned to Paris she starred at the Folies Bergère, creating the role that would make her famous. The costume she wore in the performances was made out of a string of artificial bananas. Because her performance success coincided with the Exposition Internationale des Arts Décoratifs or "Art Deco" as well as European artistic interest in African art, Baker was enthroned as the queen of entertainment.

Because she was famous in Europe, Baker's fame spread in the United States, the country of her origin, as American writers and artists visiting Paris saw her perform. The famous author Ernest Hemingway is reported to have said that she was the most sensational woman he ever saw on stage. Baker was an extraordinary figure. In 1931 "J'ai deux amours" became her most financially successful song. Among her friends in Paris, including Ernest Hemingway, were Langston Hughes, F. Scott Fitzgerald, Pablo Picasso, and Christian Dior.

Baker's stage performance went through various transformations and in most cases she stretched the limits of popular performance. She also went through several managers but in 1934 she hired Giuseppe Pepito Abatino, a Sicilian stonemason, to be her manager and she immediately began to find new roles. She was given the lead in a revival of a musical by Jacques Offenbach called *La Créole*. It was an 1875 opera which had premiered at the Champs-Élysées and was seeing a revival in 1934 with the most visible Paris performer taking the lead. She would emerge from this experience as a magnificent diva and not simply a "petite danseuse sauvage," as she had been previously called. Those who witnessed the performance of Baker thought that they had seen the greatest, most spectacular singer and performer of all time. She was immediately pressed into service by the French government. It is reported that the Germans who occupied France during World War II steered clear of her because of her popularity with the people. However, Baker became a loyal member of the French Underground working to defeat the Nazis. Cleverly sending coded messages to the Underground resistance in Portugal in her sheet music, Baker became a legend in the Underground. The grateful French leader, General Charles de Gaulle, made her a Chevalier of the Légion d'honneur and she also received the Croix de Guerre and the Rosette de la Résistance.

Although widely popular in France, Josephine Baker never achieved the same power or prestige in the United States. In fact, in 1936 she performed in a version of *Ziegfeld Follies* that failed at the box office and the famous American Gypsy Rose Lee replaced her. Of course, Baker always believed that American society was less open, less progressive, and less liberal than French society and felt that the racism and discrimination in the United States had something to do with the failure of the show.

Fidel Castro, the leader of the Cuban Revolution, invited Baker to perform at the Teatro Musical de La Habana in April 1966 and her tremendously successful show broke all records in attendance. She would return to the United States in 1973 and open at Carnegie Hall to a standing ovation in a certain measure of redemption for the American audience.

Baker's distaste for racism was at the heart of her protest against discrimination. During the 1950s, while the demonstrators against segregation were shaking the American nation, Baker began to adopt twelve multi-racial orphans as a show of her humanity. Her rainbow group included Janot (Korean son), Akio (Japanese son), Luis (Colombian son), Jari (Finnish son), Jean-Claude (Canadian son), Moïse (French Jewish son), Brahim (Algerian son), Marianne (French daughter), Koffi (Ivorian son), Mara (Venezuelan son), Noël (French son), and Stellina (Moroccan daughter). Her only natural child had been stillborn in 1941, yet she had wanted to have a family that symbolized her belief in a common humanity. Thus, long before entertainers such as Angelina Jolie, Mia Farrow, and Madonna started adopting children from different nations, Josephine Baker had raised each of her children to speak his or her own language and to practice his or her own religion. However, Château des Milandes, the French estate the entertainer owned from 1947 to 1968, was to slip through her hands more quickly than her fame slipped from the mind of the French. La Baker, as the French called the star, could not afford the estate when her finances deteriorated.

While living in Château de Milandes, in Dordogne, with her children, Baker refused to play before segregated audiences in the United States. She demanded that all of her performances be integrated, and this insistence helped to integrate the shows in Las Vegas. Nevertheless, in 1951 she charged Sherman Billingsley's Stork Club in New York with racism for refusing to serve her. Grace Kelly, who happened to be in the club, walked out of the club with her entire entourage because of the incident. The two women became close friends thereafter.

Josephine Baker always kept the Civil Rights Movement on her agenda, enlisting to work against racism whenever her schedule permitted. In fact, she was asked to speak at the famous 1963 March on Washington, the only one on the program. Baker chose to speak dressed in her Free French uniform that was emblazoned with the Légion d'honneur. Baker's influence was international but no one ever denied her impact on the country of her birth. She influenced the styles of Whitney Houston and Diana Ross. In addition, other American dancers and performers used techniques that had been pioneered by Baker in her European performances.

The honors dedicated to Baker are numerous. Memorialized in the Montparnasse Quarter of Paris with her own "Place Josephine Baker," she also appears on the St Louis (Missouri) Walk of Fame. Josephine Baker died at Pitié-Salpêtrière Hospital in Paris at age sixty-eight on April 12, 1975. Services for the first American woman to receive full French military honors were held at L'Église de la Madeleine and she was buried in Monte Carlo at the Cimetière de Monaco.

Racism ain't Funny: Oliver Ollie Harrington and the East Berlin Exile

Numerous other famous African Americans looked askance at the situation in the United States. Chester Himes and John A. Williams had also absconded to Europe. But Oliver Harrington, who was born in Valhalla, New York, on February 14, 1912, was there before them. He was educated at the Yale School of Fine Arts and the Natonal Academy of Design. When he was in school, Harrington had started to draw cartoons of one of his teachers whom he considered a racist. The arrogance and ignorance of the teacher fired his imagination and he vowed to attack racism indirectly through his art. Soon thereafter he began to submit cartoons to newspapers in Harlem. They were accepted and considered brilliant. In 1935 Harrington joined the *Amsterdam News* and created the character called Bootsie, a sturdy, bald man from Harlem. This was the first black comic to receive national attention and Harrington was considered an excellent talent. He took the most unbelievable situations and came up with characters to fit the situations. His work soon appeared in the *Chicago Defender*, the *Pittsburgh Courier*, and the *People's Voice* newspapers. He worked with the NAACP as a cartoonist against racism. Harrington's anxiety about racism was so strong that he began to think about leaving the United States. His opinions brought him to the attention of J. Edgar Hoover and the FBI, which seemed in the late 1940s and early 1950s to be interested in following the activities of all leading African Americans. Harrington went to live in Paris, finally convinced that the American government was seeking to entrap him. Harrington was friends with other expatriates in Paris such as Chester Himes, Richard Wright, and Langston Hughes, who would occasionally visit. As his politics grew more socialist and his attacks on the West more virulent, Harrington later moved to East Berlin but continued to write cartoons for United States newspapers. Always attacking established systems of oppression, self-serving politicians, racists, imperialists, and capitalists, Harrington's work took on a sharpness that was often bitter. He published hundreds of cartoons and some of these were published in books, including *Dark Laughter*, the collection of his best cartoons. He died in East Berlin on November 2, 1995 at the age of eighty-four.

Freedom Summer

In 1964 the Council of Federated Organizations (COFO), under the leadership of Robert Moses, began a campaign to empower the grassroots, the impoverished black Southern farm families. The Mississippi Summer Project attracted students from across the nation to volunteer to investigate the status of civil rights and to register voters. In June, three volunteers, James Chaney, Michael Schwerner, and Andrew Goodman, were slain and their bodies buried in a shallow grave. Their bodies were recovered in August after a massive search. The killers were arrested but never tried on state murder charges. Twenty men were convicted on federal charges of interfering with the victims' civil rights.

The Civil Rights Act of 1964

President Lyndon Johnson, a Texan, not known for a strong stand on civil rights, became an advocate for the strong civil rights legislation initiated under President Kennedy. Johnson knew that blacks were fed up with segregated and inferior facilities in public places. He mounted a strong campaign to see the legislation pass. The Civil Rights Act of 1964 was the most comprehensive civil rights legislation since the end of slavery. It immediately ended "whites only" signs in public places. Furthermore, it became the Twenty-Fourth Amendment to the Constitution. This is what the Act did:

- strengthened previous civil rights acts;
- outlawed devices such as the poll tax and literacy tests which were designed to keep African Americans from voting;
- barred discrimination in public places such as restaurants, hotels, and theatres;
- banned segregation in parks, stadiums, and swimming pools;
- gave financial assistance to all schools in the process of desegregation;
- withheld funds from schools and programs that discriminated;
- prohibited discrimination by employers and unions;
- extended the life of the Civil Rights Commission for four more years;
- prevented a federal court from sending a civil rights case back to state or local courts;
- established the Community Relations Service to arbitrate local race problems;
- provided the right of a jury trial for any case brought under the protection of the Civil Rights Act of 1964.

Malcolm X and the Ballot or the Bullet

One could say that progress was being made but it was being made slowly, almost reluctantly, and would never have happened without a push. Malcolm X saw that whites in the Congress were moving slowly about the Voting Rights bill and so he raised the level of his rhetoric and imposed a threat on the society. "It will be the ballot or it will be the bullet," said Malcolm X, calmly, as he gave a lecture to a Detroit audience. "We have not seen an American Dream, we have only known the American nightmare," he stated.[10]

The year 1965 was an intense one. Malcolm X was at the height of his power. By now he had broken with Elijah Muhammad, the leader of the Nation of Islam, and had begun to expand his audience. A gifted orator, Malcolm X was the epitome of the modern African American: proud, noble of carriage and countenance, and capable of defending himself against all enemies. His voice was like a staccato machine as he laid arguments upon arguments for a revolution in American society.

On a cool February 21, 1965 Malcolm X spoke to an audience of about 400 faithful followers at the Audubon Ballroom in Harlem, New York. His wife, Betty Shabazz, was sitting near the front in the center of the room. Several gunmen suddenly stood up and began to fire toward Malcolm X. He was hit several times and died, at the age of thirty-nine, in a hail of bullets.

Selma and the Confrontation at the Pettus Bridge

There was urgency about the events of 1965 that made it seem like everything was coming to a head. A volcano was beginning its angry bellow. Either the society would accept peaceful change or there would be violent change, but there could be no going back to a time when African Americans did not speak up and out. Time was out for second-class citizenship.

After the death of Malcolm X, the Student Nonviolent Coordinating Committee decided to take its campaign into the heart of Alabama. The Southern Christian Leadership Conference also planned a voter registration drive in Selma. A combination of forces from the SNCC and SCLC planned a march from Selma to the state capital at Montgomery.

On Sunday, March 7, 1965 the marchers, without Dr King, who had a previous engagement, were met at Pettus Bridge on the outskirts of Selma with whips, tear gas, clubs, and guns at the ready. The police attacked the marchers when they did not turn back toward town. John Lewis, the leader of the SNCC, was beaten and suffered a fractured skull. He later said, "I don't see how President Johnson can send troops to Vietnam . . . and can't send troops to Selma, Alabama." After "Bloody Sunday" the activists were more inclined than ever to march to Montgomery. Another march was planned for March 10. King was asked to defy the police and march along with the young activists. He informed them that the main objective now was to gain a voting rights bill and he did not want to do anything that would lessen the public support for the legislation. Nevertheless, the marchers went ahead with the demonstration and once again were met by the police at Pettus Bridge and turned back. That night a white mob killed the Reverend James Reeb, a white civil rights worker. The murder, unlike the killing of Jimmy Lee Jackson a few weeks earlier, brought a national outcry against the segregationists. Five days later, President Lyndon Johnson went on national television to announce why he supported the voting rights bill. Finally, court permission was granted for the march from Selma to Montgomery. And on March 25 more than 25,000 marchers crossed Pettus Bridge and later entered Montgomery with Ralph Bunche, the venerable diplomat, and Martin Luther King Jr, the two African American Nobel Peace Prize winners at the head of the march. No more powerful point could have been made for justice and peace. Bunche, the older of the two, had won his award for negotiating peace between Israel and her neighbors, and leaned toward King's domestic politics, underscoring the younger man's nonviolent approach to racism.[11]

King's speech at Montgomery was awesome: encouraging, proud, and philosophical. He said, "Our aim must never be to defeat or humiliate the white man but to win his friendship and understanding . . . We must come to see that the end we seek is a society at peace with itself, a society that can live with its conscience."[12]

The national leadership was ready to accede to the justice of a voting rights act. King's words regarding the struggles were prophetic: "however difficult the moment, however frustrating the hour, it will not be long, because truth pressed to earth will rise again."[13] Soon thereafter the Voting Rights Act of 1965 was passed.

The Voting Rights Act of 1965

In 1965 there were hundreds of thousands of African Americans in the South who had never voted. In fact, they believed, like Fannie Lou Hamer, that it was impossible for blacks to vote without being killed. Whites had effectively closed off all avenues for the African Americans to have a say in politics by insisting that there were no reasons for blacks to vote or want to vote. Paternalism was the order of the day and was nothing short of slavery in another style.

The 1965 Voting Rights Act provided for direct federal examination of voter registration and voting procedures. This was necessary because Southern whites had often rigged the voting registration procedure so that it would be almost impossible for an African American to qualify to vote. Among the ways that white Southerners kept African Americans from voting were (1) the grandfather clause, (2) the poll tax, and (3) the literacy test.

If blacks still wanted to register and vote, they would be threatened with the loss of their job or their life. However, the Voting Rights Act made it possible for the federal government to intervene directly if a problem of discrimination existed.

Fighting Racism

Victories were being won in the South at a steady pace. However, all was not well in the nation and the condition of African Americans in the urban North was becoming increasingly difficult economically and socially. Police brutality appeared to be on the increase and black men complained bitterly about harassment they received from local officers. Suggestions were made that the KKK had become the police force in the South. Segregated police forces often felt the greatest pressure from the black community for being racist in their application of the laws.

Less than a week after the Voting Rights Act of 1965 was passed into law, all hell broke out in Watts, a densely populated section of South Central Los Angeles in California.

Marquette Frye, a young, virile African American, had been pulled over by the Los Angeles police in the early evening of August 11, 1965 because of suspicion of driving while intoxicated (DUI). Police surrounded his car and crowds surrounded the police. Tempers and charges flew. By late evening thousands of angry African Americans had assembled in the streets.

The African American community was incensed. Stores and other businesses in South Central Los Angeles were burned to the ground. A local disk jockey had popularized the slogan "Learn, baby, learn." It had now become "Burn, baby, burn" in the language of the streets. At least thirty people were killed over the six days of rebellion. Nearly $50 million of property was burned, ransacked, or looted. The Watts Rebellion, as it was called, came to be seen as a preview of other outbreaks of social and civil violence because for the next four years each summer brought waves of unrest in the urban areas.

Black Power and Black is Beautiful

Willie Mukasa Ricks, also known simply as Muksasa, one of the leaders of the SNCC, had conceived the idea that the term "Black Power," which had been used by Harlem, New York, Congressman Adam Clayton Powell at the Howard University commencement in 1966 would be electrifying on the tongue of the national leader, Stokely Carmichael (Kwame Ture). Ricks tried the term out on groups of people in Mississippi. "What do we want?" he shouted. The people responded as prompted, "Black Power!" It worked.[14]

Powell was the most outspoken black Congressmen since the Reconstruction Era and he had become an icon in the black community for his role in peppering the racists in Congress with his quick wit and sharp repartee. Hounded by his enemies, he was eventually forced to relinquish his powerful committee assignment and to leave Congress.[15]

At a reception for Stokely Carmichael in Washington, DC, in 1998, Willie Ricks indicated that the shooting of James Meredith had sparked anger and outrage among young African Americans and there had to be some way to vent this penned-up anger that would be productive in the long run. Black Power was what was needed and demanded.

On June 5, 1966 James Meredith, the courageous student who had integrated the law school at the University of Mississippi, planned to walk 220 miles from Memphis, Tennessee, to Jackson, Mississippi. Two days into his March Against Fear, gunshots rang out and Meredith was hit with birdshot from a sixteen-gauge shotgun. Those who saw him lying on the ground in a pool of blood vowed that the march would continue. Blacks were no longer afraid to stand up and march for their rights. They felt that the shooting of weaponless marchers was an indication of weakness. They would not be intimidated.

The organizers of the "Finish the Meredith March" found the march to Jackson to be just the thing they needed to demonstrate to black people in the South that they should not fear white people. Martin Luther King Jr, Floyd McKissick of CORE, and Stokely Carmichael decided that the march should commence on June 7.

The occasion of the march was to be a classic changing of the rhetoric. Martin Luther King Jr, spoke of "Freedom Now!", the slogan that brought black and white people together in the previous marches. But Stokely Carmichael, armed with Willie Ricks' research and term, announced that "What we're gonna start saying now is Black Power!" The new term electrified the crowds. Willie Ricks took up the chant, "What do you want?" Without pausing, the people responded, "Black Power!"

Many of the leaders of the Civil Rights Movement were disappointed with Carmichael's use of the term. They were at pains to explain it to reporters and white sympathizers. But Carmichael would not give up the use of the term. He said that African Americans were defined by "their blackness and their powerlessness." He understood it to mean a call to black people "to define their own goals, lead their own organizations, and to support these organizations."

Stokely Carmichael had tapped into the same cultural pool that had given Malcolm X his position as a leading spokesperson for black pride. Malcolm X had argued that African Americans had to accept their color and heritage as Africans. "Black is Beautiful" took hold in the society and became the slogan of a new generation of pride. Along with the pride came a renewed commitment to struggle for total liberation from racism and discrimination. This would involve Malcolm X's call for blacks to defend themselves against racist attacks.

As never before, the giant of black consciousness was awakened and popular culture, religion, music, art, and athletics dressed themselves in the new symbols of awareness. African American athletes John Carlos and Tommy Smith, at the Mexico City Olympics in 1968, stood on the winners' stand and gave the Black Power salute. They drank from the same well of knowledge and emotion that fed a revolution in attitude throughout the United States.[16] The year of 1968 was important because it was critical to the direction of the human rights movement. It was the year that the largest number of major universities started Black Studies programs and it was the year that blacks throughout the world announced their separation from all forms of subservience; indeed, they created Black Power organizations and self-expression venues in a more energetic fashion than ever before.

Pushed by the assassination of Martin Luther King Jr in April 1968 and the Orangeburg Massacre of the South Carolina State University students in February 1968, Shakur Afrikanus, an African American born in South Carolina, went to live in London right after the Tet Offensive in Vietnam in August 1968. Afrikanus felt that racism was a permanent factor in American life and that the only way to conquer it was through a determined attempt to transform the society. He wanted to know as much as he could about other systems of government, believing that there must be something better than the racist system in place throughout many parts of the United States. Having served in the American armed forces, in the Air Force, Afrikanus was sure that the future of African Americans was in a return to culture and African history. He believed that the most authentic representation of African culture in the United States was James Brown. He was struck by Brown's mastery of the ordinary emotions of Africans, at home and abroad, when he came to play at the Royal Albert Hall in London. At this time Brown's song, "Say It Loud, I am Black and I am Proud," was the popular uniting anthem of the blacks living in London. It represented blacks taking agency. It was a predictor of an Afrocentric revolution. He would take his records of James Brown to parties that featured Africans, and the response to African American music emboldened him because he saw it as a contribution to the global revolution in African thought.

In many respects, Afrikanus is typical of the ordinary African American immigrant to Europe or Africa. Shakur Afrikanus was born in Gaffney, South Carolina, on August 5, 1947. He discovered his political energy from attending sessions at the Africa House and also attending the Speaker's Corner lectures by people like the Guyanese activist Roy Sawyer.

Studying and learning about political organizations, Afrikanus found his compatriots at the Q Club in London. When Muhammad Ali and other African Americans traveled to London they felt the need to visit the Q Club on their way to Africa and other parts of Europe. Continental Africans such as Chenhamo Chimutengwende established an African information desk that allowed Africans from various countries to communicate with each other. Afrikanus spent four years in London before returning to the United States. Nkrumah's little *Black Book: Axioms of Kwame Nkrumah*, full of quotations from Nkrumah, became a part of his theoretical practice alongside knowledge of the socialist tradition. Thus, uniting his socially conscious work in the South as a part of the Civil Rights Movement with his study of world systems and his concentration on African culture, Afrikanus was able to achieve a higher consciousness of transformation and power among the poor.

In the progressive circles of London, Afrikanus met numerous Africans who helped to educate him about the continent itself. He connected with Africans who were from

Barbados, Jamaica, Guyana, Nigeria, Ghana, Zimbabwe, and South Africa. Once back in the United States he became a Woodsonian Afrocentric lay scholar.

A Nation Remembers Martin Luther King Jr

After a tumultuous debate the nation passed a law to celebrate the birthday of Martin Luther King Jr as a federal national holiday to be observed on the third Monday of each January. A coalition of progressive organizations pushed for the King Holiday. Two African Americans, Congressman John Conyers, Democrat of Michigan, and Senator Edward Brooke, Democrat of Massachusetts, sponsored the bill to make King's birthday a national holiday. This bill did not pass when it was first introduced in 1979, failing by five votes.

Subsequently, The King Center of Atlanta joined with civil rights organizations and labor groups to pressure Congress to support the holiday. The great singer Stevie Wonder wrote the song "Happy Birthday" to further advance the campaign for the holiday. In fact, 6 million signatures were collected for the holiday, making it one of the largest petitions in favor of an issue in the United States. Although the campaign for Martin Luther King Jr's Day generated lots of political heat, ultimately the law was passed and signed by President Ronald Reagan in 1983. It was first celebrated in 1986. Representative Katie Hall, Democrat of Indiana, had sponsored the bill that was signed into law by President Reagan. Some states refused to celebrate the holiday and Arizona especially became the bedrock of opposition; only in 2000 did all fifty American states celebrate the holiday.

The Evolution of the Student Nonviolent Coordinating Committee (SNCC)

Perhaps the most distinctive change in the history of black liberation in the United States occurred in the 1960s with the establishment of the Student Nonviolent Coordinating Committee. With so many students involving themselves in the movement, the older organizations such as CORE, NAACP, and SCLC attempted to provide guidance to this new, dynamic part of the movement. The students honored and respected the older leaders but wanted to remain independent of any one of the established groups.

James Lawson, who had been dismissed from Vanderbilt Divinity School because of his activism, wrote the statement of purpose for a new organization to be called the Student Nonviolent Coordinating Committee. He said in part, "Nonviolence as it grows from Judaic-Christian traditions seeks a social order of justice permeated by love."[17] Not all of the students agreed with all of the principles in Lawson's statement of purpose. It would be debated on several occasions. He had been trained in India and had declared nonviolence to be his life's mission, but the majority of the students were simply concerned with over-throwing the racist regime of segregation. Fortunately, some elders came to the aid of the students as they were organizing. Chief among these elders was Ella Jo Baker.

Ella Baker had been a long-time activist with a career in the NAACP and was the office manager for the Southern Christian Leadership Conference's Atlanta headquarters. She knew all the players in the Civil Rights Movement, understood the intricacies of the political situation, and had some idea of what the students would confront as they traveled around the South. As a woman in the male-dominated arena of the movement, Ella Baker demonstrated more than once her ability to handle any situation as well as the leaders. Baker invited the leading student activists to a meeting at Shaw University, her alma mater, on Easter weekend in 1960. At this meeting she encouraged them to form their own organization and to practice a group-centered leadership. She did not want any one person to feel left out of the leadership and although personal issues would emerge between different groups of students they could be settled by consensus. Ella Jo Baker was trying to institute a traditional African leadership style in the organization. She said what the organization needed were "people who were not so interested in being leaders as developing leaders among other people."[18]

Finally, the SNCC emerged from a series of student rallies, seminars, and organizational meetings led by Ella Baker at Shaw University in Raleigh, North Carolina. For the first time, black students would be thrust out front in the attempt to change the segregation policies of the United States. No longer would students be protected from the sharpest elements of racism by their parents and other adults who had taken the brunt of the attacks by racists as a way to protect their children. Fathers had often kept their humiliations to themselves, not venturing to tell either their wives or their children, and mothers who had been abused as domestic workers by white males frequently held their tongues. But now, a new ethic and dispensation had appeared, and young people were ready to take on the burdens of transformation.

Ella Baker was born on December 13, 1903 in Norfolk, Virginia, and died on December 13, 1986 in New York. Between those dates she was a whirlwind of activism, being influenced by Martin Luther King, A. Philip Randolph, W. E. B. Du Bois, and influencing Diane Nash, Bob Moses, Marion Barry, H. Rap Brown, Kwame Ture (Stokely Carmichael), and Marimba Ani. Her role as an activist rose from the soil of North Carolina, where she attended college, and her most important achievement was the founding of the Student Nonviolent Coordinating Committee at Shaw University in Raleigh, North Carolina, her alma mater. Convincing the Southern Christian Leadership Conference to call a meeting of young activists from college campuses in 1960, Ella Baker became the catalyst for the creation of a new form of participatory democracy. In fact, she would be so identified with this doctrine that when the Students for Democratic Action organization was formed, it had to give credit to the vision of Ella Baker. Baker's role in SNCC is inescapable and its history cannot be written without attention to the "godmother of the movement," who devoted hours to historical training, organizational education, and matters of etiquette of confrontation to the students over the long days of the organization of SNCC.

The SNCC was led by a series of charismatic and dynamic leaders such as Marion Barry, its first chairperson, and other chairpersons such as John Lewis, who became a distinguished U.S. Congressman, Stokely Carmichael (Kwame Ture), founder of the All African Peoples Revolutionary Party, H. Rap Brown (Jamil Abdullah al-Amin), Julian Bond, the SNCC first communication director; and James Forman, first executive secretary.

In 1969 the organization changed its name to the Student National Coordinating Committee to reflect the challenges from the Black Panthers and the Us Organization (pp. 289–290), groups that had outflanked SNCC on the left with a move toward thrusting the student movement into the international liberation arena. In many ways, the SNCC's response may have sealed the fate of the organization as members who were committed to the idea of nonviolence, as had been preached by Martin Luther King Jr, and members of the pacifist CORE, dropped away and other organizations picked up the SNCC's fiery militants. In fact, the SNCC sought to merge with the Black Panthers but in the end the organization lost its focus and its political will.

Without any question the student movement, building upon the dynamic postures and courageous actions of young people, had injected energy into the movement for justice that was contagious. Diane Nash, a Fisk University student who had led demonstrations in Nashville, had organized a group of students to continue the CORE freedom ride into Jackson, Mississippi, after the original interracial CORE group had to cancel their ride because of white mobs. Immediately after they were arrested, Diane Nash became a symbol of the new black woman in America. She was proud of her blackness and committed to liberating all the people from segregation. Of course, not all student activists were members of SNCC and some created different organizations.

The young people of the movement exhibited unusual courage in the face of mob violence. None showed more tenacity than James Meredith. He had tried to integrate the University of Mississippi in 1962 when 3,000 white people rioted in protest. President John Kennedy had to order federal troops to the campus in Oxford, Mississippi. It took more than 23,000 federal troops to bring peace to the town. By October 1962 James Meredith had to be escorted to class by federal marshals.

The Black Panthers Emerge

By October 1966, two Merritt College students in Oakland, California, Huey Newton and Bobby Seale, had created an organization called the Black Panthers which demanded that the black community take control of its own destiny. The Black Panthers captured the imagination of many young people, who flocked to an organization that promised that black men would defend black women and that if the police brutalized black people they would have to suffer the consequences.

The philosophy of the Black Panthers was contained in their 1966 platform and stated the following demands:

- We want freedom. We want power to determine the destiny of our black community.
- We want full employment for our people.
- We want an end to the robbery by the white man of our black community.
- We want decent housing, fit for shelter of human beings.
- We want education for our people that exposes the true nature of decadent American society.
- We want all black men to be exempt from military service.
- We want an immediate end to police brutality and murder of black people.
- We want freedom for all black men held in federal, state, county and city jails and prisons.
- We want all black people, when brought to trial, to be tried by a jury of their peer group.
- We want land, bread, housing, education, clothing, justice, and peace.

This platform was considered radical by most of the civil rights leadership. However, there was nothing in the Black Panther Party's platform that had not been discussed in other venues in the black community. Huey Newton, Bobby Seale, David Hilliard, and Erica Huggins were soon joined by a host of intelligent and creative colleagues who flocked to the organization from all across the nation. Some would become scholars, such as Regina Jennings, FeFe Dunham, Kathleen Cleaver, and Maat Ka Re Monges; others would become judges, like Judge Joe Brown; and yet others would become politicians.

The shooting death of Lil' Bobby Hutton on April 6, 1968 was a major turning point for the Black Panthers. Many members of the party believed that the police were out to assassinate as many of the party's leaders as possible. The Black Panther Party believed that black people had to carry guns in order to defend themselves. They argued that until the laws in America were changed then it was legal for blacks to own and carry guns so long as they were not concealed. However, Hutton, aged seventeen years, was not carrying a gun when the police killed him.

The *Black Panther* newspaper told the story like this:

> The circumstances surrounding the death, the murder, the crucifixion, have often been told. How the pigs [police] in an effort to destroy the leadership of the Black Panther Party, ambushed Eldridge Cleaver and a group of Panthers including Lil' Bobby. How the pigs fired hundreds of rounds of ammunition into the house where Lil' Bobby and Eldridge had sought shelter. How Lil' Bobby and Eldridge emerged from the house and were beaten brutally by the pigs: Lil' Bobby was murdered by a fusillade of fire from the pigs. How Lil' Bobby had his hands in the air and was obeying the pigs' orders when they fired on him. This is all history, not to be forgotten, but to inflame and inspire.[19]

Repeatedly the Black Panther Party would come into conflict with the police because the Panthers believed that the police needed policing. In Chicago, Los Angeles, Philadelphia, and other cities, the police attacked the Panthers. Mark Clark and Fred Hampton, two of the most talented of the Panthers, were killed in Chicago on December 4, 1968. Just two months earlier I had hosted Fred Hampton at the West Lafayette campus of Purdue University. As always, he was talking about the need for black students to understand the nature of American society and to give back to the community. The Breakfast program through which his chapter fed hundreds of poor black children was his pride. His death was another blow to civility as the police surrounded the headquarters of the Black Panther Party in Chicago and fired hundreds of rounds of ammunition. In Philadelphia the police chief, Frank Rizzo, had his police raid the Panthers headquarters and order the members to strip naked. In subsequent months many Panthers were injured, killed, or jailed. This intensi-fication of the assaults on the Panthers only served to make them more attractive to the black community. Financial support to the Panthers for their Breakfast program for black children was forthcoming from many sources.

An FBI program initiated in the late 1960s called COINTELPRO (covert intelligence program) was designed to pit one black group against another. This strategy was introduced to undercut the two most powerful movements among black youth, the Black Panthers and the Us Organization. The suspicions and tensions generated by the FBI lingered into the twenty-first century long after the death of J. Edgar Hoover and the other initiators of the covert program.

Conflict between the Panthers and the Us Organization remained as the FBI COINTELPRO attempted to infiltrate black groups. Shootings between the two organizations were responsible for a period of disunity. However, the proper analysis of the UCLA shooting that left two members of the Black Panthers dead did not take place till years later, when it was discovered that the FBI had provoked confrontations between black groups. On January 17, 1969 the head of the Los Angeles chapter of the Black Panthers, the popular Bunchy Carter, and Deputy Minister John Huggins were killed in a gun battle in Campbell Hall at UCLA during a meeting to discuss the control of the UCLA Center for African American Studies. The alleged shooters were members of the Us Organization. There was another shoot-out between the two groups on March 17 that led to more injuries. The FBI had sent a provocative letter to the Us Organization to create chaos and antagonism between it and the Black Panthers. A similar strategy had seen the FBI telling the Black Panthers that they would be under attack by the Us Organization. Thus, stuck in the rut of FBI intrigue the black organizations looked at each other with suspicion and the ultimate objective was to prevent the unity of the most powerful wings of the African American student revolution.

Maulana Karenga and the Kawaida Movement

The Us Organization, founded by Maulana Karenga in 1965, reflected the growing feeling that culture was essential to the re-education of the black community. Thus, it was from a reflection on culture that Karenga advanced the Kawaida idea. After the Watts Rebellion, Karenga analyzed the situation and determined that many African Americans had been killed because they were not operating with cultural guidelines. They reacted but they did not reflect on the deeper meanings of actions by the police or by the society. What Karenga taught the members of his organization was that it was essential to know the enemy. He was determined to help create a conscious and aware community.

Maulana Karenga had been a doctoral student at the University of California, Los Angeles, majoring in political science, when he dropped out of UCLA to form a community-based organization dedicated to the transformation of the African American population. The philosophy of Kawaida, customs and traditions, would be the centerpiece for the Us Organization. In Karenga's words, "We can only depend upon us." His discourse was bent toward a self-determining and self-defining philosophy. He would say consistently, "If you do not know who you are, you may think your friend is your enemy."[20]

Young students and older activists joined the Us Organization and made it the cornerstone group for building cultural competence. The group did not concentrate on legal issues; this was left to the NAACP. The Us Organization did not concentrate on voting rights; this was left to the SNCC. It did not concentrate on social welfare; this was done by CORE and Urban League. The Black Panthers sought to pose a physical threat to the police by defending the community if necessary but also feeding hungry children breakfast. What the Us Organization sought to do was to establish a solid base for all political actions through the proper training and educating of a cadre of knowledgeable militants. No African American group in history had covered this aspect of the struggle for liberation, although such a

Figure 10.1 Carter G. Woodson, Father of Black History. Image courtesy of Charles L. Blockson Afro-American Collection, Temple University Libraries.

movement had been anticipated in Carter G. Woodson's *Miseducation of the Negro* and in Malcolm X's speeches.

In 1966 Karenga established Kwanzaa, a national holiday, celebrated December 26– January 1, to commemorate the activities and achievements of African people. The seven principles of Kwanzaa included *umoja*, unity; *kujichagulia*, self-determination; *ujima*, collective work and responsibility; *ujamaa*, cooperative economics; *nia*, purpose; *kuumba*, creativity; and *imani*, faith.

Several chapters of the Us Organization were set up across the nation. In addition to the Los Angeles chapter the most important were the San Diego, Buffalo, Brooklyn, and Newark groups. Maulana Karenga and Leroi Jones, who later took on the Kawaida name Amiri Baraka, were the two leading figures in the late 1960s and early 1970s. While Karenga was imprisoned for three years because of a trumped-up charge of brutality and torture, Baraka, the well-known poet and playwright, was the chief spokesperson for the organization. Baraka would later abandon the movement for more Marxist orientations. Karenga had maintained his innocence and as soon as he came out of prison he resumed leadership of the organization with the support of Amen Ra, Segun Shabaka, John Tambuzi, Tiamoyo Karenga, Tulivu Tjadi, and Chimbuko and Limbiko Tembo.

The Vietnam War

Very few African Americans felt good about the war in Vietnam. The casualties for black soldiers were out of all proportion to the numbers of blacks in the American population. The French had lost a guerrilla war to the Vietnamese several years before the Americans had entered the fray. Vietnam had been a colony of France's until a massive grassroots war led to France's defeat at Dien Bien Phu in 1954. When the French were gone a civil war broke out, pitting the North of the country against the South of the country. Both sections served as surrogates or stand-ins for major powers. The North was aligned with the Chinese and Russians and the South was aligned with the French and Americans.

In August, 1964, ten years after the defeat of the French at Dien Bien Phu, the North Vietnamese were alleged to have attacked an American destroyer in the Gulf of Tonkin. This allegation, later proved to be false, gave President Lyndon Johnson the leeway to declare war on North Vietnam. Suddenly America was at war with Vietnam in a massive way. Black soldiers were among the first to volunteer for the war. African Americans did not complain much about discrimination in the United States Armed Forces, as had been the case in previous wars. This was due in part to the fact that there was almost no obvious racism. Nevertheless, blacks still constituted less than five percent of the more than 11,000 officers serving by 1967.

What concerned the African American leaders was the high rate of casualties among black troops. There was an indication that the 50,000 African Americans who served in that war were being treated unfairly on the fighting lines. Although blacks made up a percentage of the fighting forces close to the national level in the population, more than twenty-two percent of those killed in combat were African Americans. Another issue that concerned some African Americans was the fact that sixty-four percent of all African Americans found acceptable for the army were drafted while only thirty-one percent of the acceptable whites were drafted. Some black leaders charged that African Americans were used for the most dangerous missions, such as serving as point on search and destroy missions.

Nevertheless, African American soldiers displayed valor and courage in the face of a persistent enemy. In 1968 *Time Magazine* wrote that re-enlistment rates of blacks were three times those of whites.[21]

Some African Americans took their lead from Muhammad Ali and refused to fight the Vietnamese because of the racism they found in the United States. For his refusal, Ali was stripped of his heavyweight championship in April 1967 by the World Boxing Association and many African Americans were put in jail for refusing to serve. A year earlier, Julian Bond had been denied his seat as Georgia state representative because of comments he made against the war in Vietnam.

The Vietnam War took its toll on the political climate in the country. African Americans felt that President Lyndon Johnson's domestic programs had been weakened by the war because the nation no longer focused on the civil rights issue. Martin Luther King Jr had grown increasingly critical of the war, claiming that the war drained money from the War on Poverty. The president then announced, on March 31, 1968, to a stunned nation, that he would not seek re-election.

The Death of King

On April 3, 1968, Martin Luther King Jr told a mass meeting in Memphis, Tennessee, where he had gone to support the sanitation workers, that "We've got some difficult days ahead, but it really doesn't matter with me now because I've been to the mountaintop." He indicated to his audience that he might not get to the Promised Land with them, but they would get there. Whether King was conscious of his impending death or not, no one can say for certain.

However, the very next day an assassin, James Earl Ray, shot King as he stood on the balcony of the Lorraine Hotel in Memphis. Members of the King family, some claiming that James Earl Ray may not have been the killer, have debated the facts of this case. Nevertheless, as Kennedy's death had earlier shocked the nation, so now did the death of King. African Americans registered the depth of their hurt by burning down stores and refusing to go to work in hundreds of cities. Nothing could have been so devastating to the black community at that time in history as the death of King. Malcolm X had been assassinated in 1965 and now King was gone too. Two giants, bending toward each other at the end, one remaining upright longer than the other, but both enshrined in the hearts of a proud people, had left the earth during the same decade. Once again the urban areas took the heaviest toll of burned-out stores and gutted dwellings as a nation severely injured by prejudice and inequality limped painfully toward resolution of its most persistent crimes against its black citizens.

Conclusion

Notable individuals and organizations came forward during the period covered in this chapter to assert that nothing would stop the campaign for freedom. Black men and women pushed the suffocating blanket of racism back in every field. Len Miller and his son, Len Jr, showed the world that blacks could race automobiles and then created a company to sponsor their own racers. The smell of segregation and discrimination was still alive when Josephine Baker went to France, where she would remain and become a citizen. Oliver Ollie Harrington would find his place in Berlin, Germany. These expatriates would be joined by thousands of others who would seek to improve their lives in Ghana, Tanzania, Nigeria, Britain, France, the Soviet Union, Turkey, and other countries. However, those who did not and could not flee the country of their birth dug in and created civil rights organizations that spoke to the conditions, injustices, and situation faced by African Americans. They voted, demonstrated, petitioned, and maintained a group discipline that allowed group remedies around racism.

Soon the student groups would be transformed into full-fledged civil rights groups. Activists such as Kwame Ture, Maulana Karenga, and Bobby Seale, who often stood in for the imprisoned Huey Newton on the platform, led these groups. Who could have thought that the legacy of the Freedom Summer when young black and white students risked their lives in the South to gain the right to vote for Southern blacks would lead to a genuine transformation of the South? Nothing could slow down the march for justice as Ella Jo Baker in political organization helped to establish the Student Nonviolent Coordinating Committee and James Brown, the King of Soul, joined the chorus with "I'm black and I'm proud!"

Additional Reading

Asante, M. K. Jr *Bigger than Hip Hop*. New York: St Martin's Press, 2008.

Barlow, William. *Looking Up at Dawn: The Emergence of Blues Culture*. Philadelphia: Temple University, 1989.

Egerton, John F. *Speak Now against the Day: The Generation before the Civil Rights Movement in the South*. New York: Knopf, 1994.

Jones, James H. *Bad Blood: The Tuskegee Syphilis Experiment*. New York: Free Press, 1981.

Kelley, Robin D. G. *Hammer and Hoe: Alabama Communsts during the Depression*. Chapel Hill: University of North Carolina Press, 1990.

O'Reilly, Robert G. *Lady Day: The Many Faces of Billie Holiday*. New York: Arcade Publishers, 1991.

Sammons, Jeffrey T. *Beyond the Ring: The Role of Boxing in American Society*. Urbana: University of Illinois Press, 1988.

Walker, Margaret. *Richard Wright, Daemonic Genius: A Portrait of the Man, a Critical Look at His Work*. Philadelphia: Temple University Press, 1988.

Chapter Time Markers

1967	Nathan Hare becomes the head of the Black Studies program at San Francisco State University
1978	Award-winning playwright August Wilson moves from Pittsburgh to St Paul, Minnesota
1989	David Dinkins becomes the first black mayor of New York City
1993	Novelist Toni Morrison receives the Nobel Prize for Literature
1995	Million Man March in Washington, DC
2008	Oprah Winfrey's DNA test reveals her Kpelle (Liberian) roots
2011	Afrocentricity International is founded on April 9 in Philadelphia

The Rise of Social Consciousness

11

Important Terms and Names

Black Studies Movement
Bill Sutherland
St. Clair Drake
Nathan Hare
Introduction to Black Studies
Afrocentricity International

Kwanzaa
Cornel West
Journal of Black Studies
Black Scholar
Charles Fuller
August Wilson

African American Public Intellectuals

During the 1960s it was often said that African Americans had one civil rights leader, Martin Luther King, one political leader, Adam Clayton Powell, and one public intellectual, James Baldwin. However, by the 1990s there were scores of African Americans seeking to become public intellectuals, many of them quick with words and eloquent in speech but with no practical activist traditions. A few of them became quite popular on the public platform with commentaries, public announcements, and debates. Darlene Hines, bell hooks, Nell Irvin Painter, Frances Cress Welsing, Ama Mazama, Joyce King, Marimba Ani, and Patricia Hill-Collins were the leading women speakers. James Turner, James Stewart, Leonard Jeffries, Jacob Carruthers, Asa Hilliard, Cornel West, Ismael Reed, Stanley Crouch, Michael Eric Dyson, Charles Johnson, John Edgar Wideman, Manning Marable, Henry Louis Gates Jr, Maulana Karenga, Na'im Akbar, and Wade Nobles represented a host of male lecturers named as public intellectuals. However, almost all of them were associated with universities. Perhaps the people poet Gil Scott-Heron, who died on May 27, 2011, may have escaped the branding as a school intellectual, finding his public statements in the dire historical realities of African people and speaking his words as poetry with music.

In America it seems the media has depicted two groups of public intellectuals: those who speak to mostly white audiences and those who speak to mostly African American audiences.

It would not be surprising that African Americans are more familiar with Maulana Karenga, for example, than Cornel West, because of the nature of word-of-mouth dissemination of ideas. Na'im Akbar speaks to hundreds of African American audiences but is not known as extensively among whites. The opposite is true with public figures such as Henry Louis Gates and Shelby Steele.

Maulana Karenga, the most influential contemporary African American philosopher of culture, and founder of Kwanzaa in 1966, puts it this way: "The African American suffers from a cultural crisis. If we cannot solve the cultural crisis, we cannot hope to solve any other."[1] Karenga's influence on education, cultural practice, language, and drama is overwhelming, dominating all language of African American cultural reconstruction. By the end of the 1990s he had already assumed the dominant position in the contest for cultural and political influence on the masses of African Americans. Today he stands as a link to the best traditions of past African scholarship and activism as well as a link to the technological and ethical future of a people fighting for true mental and cultural liberation. As one among many public intellectuals, Karenga continued to write scholarly books and articles refining the meaning of race, identity, culture, and ethics.

To an extent that is not normally recognized, musicians took their places as spokespersons for change during the same period as we saw the public intellectual rise to the forefront of the rhetorical tradition. Who is to say that Curtis Mayfield, Oscar Brown Jr, Pharaoh Sanders, Isaac Hayes, Odetta, and Miriam Makeba did not challenge African Americans to reach new levels of consciousness?

The Black Studies Movement

"We want courses that are relevant to our lives, taught from a black perspective, and anti-racist," a black student demonstrator at UCLA said in 1967.[2]

She was expressing a desire for something that she could identify with as deriving from her own cultural experience. This was not cultural chauvinism, which is the belief that one's culture is better than anyone else's. Rather, it was what many African American writers call *cultural nationalism*, which is the acceptance of one's historical experiences as valid and beneficial for inspiration, motivation, and a healthy self-concept.

The Black Studies Movement was just one example of cultural nationalism. Other examples were demonstrated by Pan-African activists such as Bill Sutherland, who had moved in the 1950s to Ghana to assist in the setting up of a new government. A friend to Kwame Nkrumah, Sutherland married Efua Theodora, a Ghanaian playwright, and made a commitment to the revolutionary liberation of the African continent. Just as the Civil Rights Movement was in full swing in the United States, Sutherland gave up the idea that America would ever change, made his peace with Ghana, and decided to move to Tanzania in 1963. He became the unofficial ambassador for African Americans for more than fifty years. His history in Dar es Salaam, Tanzania, where he fled to find his liberation from the prejudice and discrimination of America, was rich with the details of politics, intrigue, and rendezvous. He had been born in New Jersey, imprisoned at Lewisburg Federal Correctional Facility in the 1940s, where he met Bayard Rustin, Dave Dellinger, and other pacifists who protested the Second International European War (World War II), and radicalized by the nuclear bomb experiments of the United States and Soviet Union. His answer was to find a peaceful, creative, enlightened society. While it escaped him most of his life, he never tired of dancing to the music of genuine peace.

I remember his meeting me at the airport late one night in 1972 when I flew in from Nairobi. I did not know who this tall, slim gentleman was who had offered to drive me to my hotel, but I soon discovered that he had been in the country for ten years and had started a chicken farm. Sutherland was not a simple farmer, he was a civil servant and supporter for numerous independent organizations and governments in exile. He befriended all of the liberators from Mozambique, Zimbabwe, Angola, and South Africa, and his name reverberated around the tables of the expatriates, exiles, and nationalists with enthusiasm. Julius Nyerere of Tanzania considered Sutherland a friend and Kenneth Kaunda of Zambia helped him to form the Pan-African Freedom Movement of East and Central Africa (PAFMECA). Sutherland was made the hospitality officer for the Sixth Pan African Congress held in Dar es Salaam in 1974. He worked with C. L. R. James, the Trinidadian Marxist who resided in Britain, to connect continental Africans with diasporan Africans. Few expatriate Africans have ever had as much influence on their adopted nations as Bill Sutherland did in Tanzania. When Malcolm X visited Tanzania he was hosted by Sutherland, and when Stokely Carmichael (Kwame Ture) visited the country he would find the home of Bill Sutherland. Never a person to forget where he came from, Bill Sutherland spread the love of jazz music, his classical African American music, to every African who visited him. When he died at the age of ninety-one on January 2, 2010, Sutherland had rewritten the legacy of African Americans in East Africa. Indeed, Bill Sutherland was the living example of a conscious, activist African who believed in Black Studies and kept the university students in Dar es Salaam focused on their own involvement in the general rise of the African people.

Of course, in the United States the Black Studies movement on campuses around the nation sent shockwaves though the academic community.[3] Challenging colleges to be more pro-active toward introducing courses that dealt with the black experience, Black Studies activists pushed the civil rights agenda into the corridors of the best universities. Black Studies is the name given to the movement in schools and colleges to teach African and African American experiences as subjects in their own right and not simply as a minor branch of white American culture and history. Among the names of departments and programs are Black Studies, African American Studies, Africana Studies, and Africology.[4] They all refer to the teaching of courses that relate to African Americans and Africans from an Afrocentric standpoint. Maulana Karenga published the most comprehensive textbook in Black Studies and created a discourse around the substance of the field.[5] Afrocentric means viewing Africans as subjects of history rather than objects of history. This implies that Africans have acted and done things, not just had things done to them.

Nathan Hare at San Francisco State University

Nathan Hare, a sociologist and professor, was the leading voice in the Black Studies movement in 1967. Hare had been a student of the famous sociologist E. Franklin Frazier at Howard University and had written a book, *The Black Anglo-Saxons*.[6] As a result of the student protest, Hare was hired by San Francisco State College to help ease the tension between the

African American students and the administrators. Hare was the most prominent faculty voice in support of the Black Studies curriculum. His advocacy and the students' persistence led to the opening of the first "autonomous" department of Black Studies in the nation in 1968. Nathan Hare became the voice of the new movement to transform American education. Soon after the San Francisco State victory, departments and programs were set up at University of California campuses at Los Angeles (UCLA) and Berkeley, Cornell University, Northwestern, Ohio State, and the University of Wisconsin.

The First Generation of Leaders

The first generation of leaders of the Black Studies field included many scholar-activists, students who had been active in the Civil Rights Movement but were now college professors. Some of these early leaders had organized student protests on the very campuses where the demonstrations for Black Studies were occurring. Outstanding figures in this first generation included Leonard Jeffries, who began his career at San Jose State; Robert Singleton of UCLA; Sonja Stone of the University of North Carolina; Edward Crosby of Kent State University; James Turner of Cornell University; Talmadge Anderson of Washington State University; William Nelson of Ohio State University; and Ewart Guinier of Harvard University.

Among the scholars who wrote for the new and exciting field were Maulana Karenga, Harriette McAdoo, Robert Harris, Robert Staples, Charles White, Gerald A. McWorter, Winston Van Horne, and Linda James Myers. Karenga's book *Introduction to Black Studies* soon became a classic text for majors. It explained the need for the study of African Americans and placed the entire movement in the general framework of culture and activism. McWorter, writing as Abdul Alkalimat, published *Introduction to Afro-American Studies: A Peoples College Primer* in 1986.

The UCLA Case

A university can organize the teaching of a subject in two important ways administratively. It can create a department or it can create a program. Most professors believe that the creation of a department is more permanent and permits more control over curriculum and faculty than a program.

UCLA's struggle to develop a Black Studies program was typical of many other campuses. Students had debated the issue with numerous administrators. In 1968 the University relented and set up an Afro-American Studies Center under the general umbrella of an Institute of American Cultures. It was a research center with some funds for grants and awards but no faculty and no right to control curriculum. It was therefore without the traditional elements of power in a university.

Nevertheless, Robert Singleton, a doctoral student in economics, was asked to be the interim director of the Center. He was quite persuasive and managed to get the Center space in Campbell Hall. In addition, the *Journal of Black Studies* was created when Singleton as chairman of the board and Molefi Kete Asante, then called Arthur L. Smith, as editor was able to convince Sara Miller McCune at Sage Publications to publish the journal. Later, when a search was completed in 1969, the same year the journal was found, Asante was made the first permanent director of the Center for Afro-American Studies at UCLA, instituting a Master's degree program and establishing a library. However, Asante would eventually realize that a program, such as the UCLA center, would never compete with a department for focus, courses, and faculty because it did not control faculty, degrees, or course offerings.

Across the nation new programs or departments were being created at Northwestern, Cornell, Albany, Yale, Temple, Harvard, Massachusetts, Ohio State, and numerous other colleges. Soon there would be over 200 programs and more than forty departments. Like most centers and departments, the UCLA center celebrated African American life and culture and challenged the reigning ideologies of racism by producing scholarly essays and monographs to refute them. The center also promoted the integration of African culture on overwhelmingly white campuses by providing African art, dance, and cultural programming as well as political and social seminars.

Never had major universities, almost all of them in the North or West, entertained so many significant scholars of African descent. Regularly St. Clair Drake, Langston Hughes, Arna Bontemps, Harold Cruse, Yosef ben-Jochannan, John Henrik Clarke, John Hope Franklin, and Benjamin Quarles lectured on college campuses. Clarke, who had been born in Alabama in 1915, became an outspoken advocate of African American Studies once he moved to Harlem as a young man in the 1930s. Clarke wrote short stories and had been an associate editor with the progressive arm of *Freedomways*. But his first love was African and African American history and the article by Arturo Schomburg entitled "The Negro Digs Up His Past" so captivated him that he began a journey to recover as much of that history as he could.[7] Clarke had been inspired to devote his life to the creation of African American Studies programs when a white man in Georgia had told him that "black people have no history." Clarke later taught at Hunter College in New York.

Colleges like UCLA, Berkeley, and Stanford in the West and Temple, SUNY-Albany, Yale, Harvard, and Cornell in the East became the leaders in African American Studies. In the North, Wisconsin, Kent State, Indiana, and Ohio State created departments. The Southern institutions such as Emory, Duke, Georgia, Vanderbilt, Rice, and Baylor made no early commitment to African American Studies.

Pan-African Connections

It was only logical that there would be an outreach to the African world. African American students not only learned more about the United States in African American Studies programs, they learned about Africa and became involved in the struggles of Africa. Already Ghana had gained its independence in 1957, Nigeria in 1960, but there were other issues that had to be dealt with on the continent. The racist system of apartheid was still in full swing in South Africa, Portugal remained in control of Mozambique and Angola, and the Rhodesians were fighting to hold onto their minority regime in Zimbabwe.

African Americans were among the most passionate defenders of the rights of Africans to be free in their own lands. Support groups were established in almost all major cities and on many college campuses to fight against apartheid. Students worked with African

American politicians and activists as well as white activists to force schools, colleges, corporations, and cities to divest and deprive South Africa of its dollars. In the end South Africa was free and Nelson Mandela walked out of prison with the well-wishes of millions of African Americans.

Winnie Mandela, Nelson's first wife, was the spirit behind the international campaign to free him. She was a welcomed guest in the homes of the leading African American activists and a regular lecturer on the college circuit. She kept Nelson's memory alive for twenty-seven years.

Once elected to the presidency of South Africa, Nelson Mandela never forgot those who supported him and his people during the lowest ebb of their social and political lives. He made many visits to the United States, speaking at churches, community meetings, and in conferences. When some Cuban politicians in Miami demonstrated against his visit to Miami because of his friendship with Fidel Castro, there was a serious rift between the African American and Cuban communities. Mandela argued that when his people were fighting against the racist South African regime, Castro supported the African masses and he would not turn his back on a friend. Of course, the Cuban Americans have numerous complaints against the Cuban government and vice versa. Fortunately, Miami is a city of great diversity and people are learning to live together and respect each other in ways that might be instructive for other communities.

In 2011 Afrocentricity International, a worldwide Pan-African organization founded in Philadelphia, announced a ten-point program between the United States and Africa with the following points:

- Cancel all African debt to American financial institutions.
- Support African peacekeeping by terminating all military aid programs.
- Support free and open elections in African and Caribbean nations.
- Support aggressive steps to wipe out AIDS.
- Support all reparations for hundreds of years of African underdevelopment.
- End slavery by boycotting countries such as Sudan and Mauritania.
- Remove all sanctions from nations that have defended their liberty against racism, e.g., Zimbabwe.
- Create an "Africa Plan" for transportation, education, communication, and end inequality by gender, region, race, and class.
- Work with African governments to insure fair trade in farming and mineral products.
- Create an African advisory commission that would inform American policy toward Africa in a unified manner.

African Americans have become increasingly interested in African matters. In fact, cases like the Amadou Diallo case energize segments of the African American population that have rarely been concerned with international issues. Earl G. Graves of *Black Enterprise* said of the acquittal of the four police officers that killed the Guinean:

> Today is another sad day in the history of America. It's obvious that the scales of justice are not balanced nor are they blind. How we as a nation can allow the senseless murder of an innocent human being is fathomless to those capable of logical thinking. At the

onset of this tragedy, I, along with many others, took a visible and vocal stand on police brutality and the use of excessive force. No matter the level of our success in this country the only thing that matters—is race.[8]

This was the assessment of a reflective African American entrepreneur who has made it to the economic top of the nation. His solidarity with a West African immigrant was based on the fact that Amadou Diallo was killed because he was a black man in a predominantly black neighborhood. Few African American people believed an Albanian or Yugoslavian or Irish person would have been gunned down in the same manner in a white neighborhood.

Using Culture as a Tool for Empowerment

During the period in the late 1960s and early 1970s that saw the renaissance of American education brought about by the entry of thousands of black students into predominantly white colleges after the assassination of Martin Luther King Jr in 1968, academic departments produced conferences and seminars demonstrating that they were capable of engaging debate and discourse on the leading topics of the day. Many students came to departments and programs with interest in their own cultural backgrounds. The first black female astronaut, Mae Jemison, majored in Black Studies and chemical engineering at Stanford University, and First Lady Michelle Obama also took classes in Black Studies at Princeton. Whites too took the courses in Black Studies to learn about a part of the American experience that had been denied them.

A cultural revolution was born as books and articles about Africa and African Americans began to pour forth like a mighty rush of water. The foundations had been set in the works of W. E. B. Du Bois, Carter G. Woodson, Anna Julia Cooper, J. A. Rogers, Edward Wilmot Blyden, Martin Delany, Arturo Schomburg, and Yosef ben-Jochannan. Everywhere, it seemed, people were reading, interpreting, and discussing the meaning of the African cultural and social influences in the United States and the Caribbean. The *Journal of Black Studies*, the *Western Journal of Black Studies*, and *Black Scholar* dedicated their pages to the social, cultural, and behavioral research in the field. A powerful and new perspective emerged in literature, art, science, and history. This was the beginning of "a black perspective," later identified as the Afrocentric idea, that is, the acceptance of African agency. Agency means that African people are studied as subjects rather than as objects, as actors rather than people who are acted upon. This perspective on history is an exercise in Afrocentricity because it is written from the standpoint of African Americans as doers, builders, and achievers. One must never underestimate the resilience of people who are centered, located in the middle of their own historical experiences. To be heroic is to be able to teach and to write from the standpoint of humans as agents, not as victims or objects, but genuine subjects who have done and will do important and significant works.

Black Studies created, *inter alia*, institutions and programs that enshrined a new historiography in the annals of disciplines. The National Council of Black Studies, a professional organization, was formed in 1974 as the professional organization of faculty committed to advancing the field. Fourteen years later, in 1988, Molefi Kete Asante created at Temple University's Department of African American Studies the first doctorate program in African American Studies. By 2000 there were three other programs offering the doctorate: the University of Massachusetts at Amherst; the University of California at Berkeley; and Harvard University. By 2010 there were ten PhD programs, the additions being Michigan State, Northwestern, Yale, Indiana, Wisconsin at Milwaukee, and the University of Pennsylvania.

The Black Arts Movement

Several African American playwrights, poets, and artists opened the doors to a new world of African American writing in the late 1960s and early 1970s. They formed what was called the Black Arts Movement. One of the most inspiring organizers of this movement was Hoyt W. Fuller. He was a poet, educator, critic, and author who brought his editorial talents to the promotion of outstanding black writers. In fact, Fuller provided a platform for poets such as Haki Madhubuti and Nikki Giovanni by setting up the Organization of Black American Culture. Born in 1923, Fuller edited the *Negro Digest*, published by Johnson Publishing Company, and when the *Negro Digest* ended because of lack of financial support from the company, he published his own journal called *First World*. He taught literature, criticism, and fiction writing at Columbia College in Chicago, Northwestern, and Cornell. Erudite, serious, and committed to the promotion of African culture from a Pan-African perspective, Hoyt Fuller exercised unusual influence in the field of poetry, publishing the best and brightest of a generation of writers. At the height of his work he was impacted by the dynamic rhetoric and action of the Nation of Islam's most articulate speaker, Malcolm X, and like many intellectuals of his period, Fuller used the times wisely to advance black literary artists.

No single period in the history of American letters was as defining as the years from the death of Malcolm X to the late 1970s. This period is usually referred to as the Black Arts Movement but might be better seen as an arm of the Black Liberation Movement because it was the artistic wing of the movement to bring about social, cultural, economic, and artistic justice. At its core was the redefining of the idea of the "Negro" in American society. Thus, its militant thrust was not an unexpected part of the movement, nor yet was it something that could be avoided. The reality was that black people in every sector of the society, including economics, religion, education, and art, were tired of serving as the doormats for white people. They insisted on carrying out Langston Hughes' earlier sense of agency. Among the voices that called for a new aesthetic were those of Larry Neal, Amiri Baraka, Ed Bullins, Mari Evans, Charles Fuller, and Sonia Sanchez. One of the most outspoken leaders of the Black Arts Movement was Amiri Baraka. He had been one of the young poets of the 1950s and 1960s to define a cultural renaissance. He is a poet, writer, political activist, teacher, and one of the nation's most influential and prolific artists. He founded his own press, *Totem*, in 1958. Baraka, who had been born Everett LeRoi Jones on October 7, 1934, assumed the leadership of the Black Arts Movement through sheer will to rescue black culture from the doldrums. Larry Neal is usually associated with him during the movement's early years because of the 1969 co-edited volume *Black Fire: An Anthology of Afro-American Writing*. However, it was Baraka, the author of more than forty different works, who became the most prominent writer of the period, dominating drama and poetry and assuming a leading role as an essayist. In fact, Baraka is credited with founding several organizations, including the Black Arts Repertory Theatre/School of Harlem (BARTS), where he produced plays and taught the principles of cultural development. Influenced by Askia Toure and Maulana Karenga, Amiri Baraka made major achievements in cultural nationalist art. His idea was to advance art in order that it might arm the people against racism. Among the writers and artists who are also called Black Arts Movement artists are Ismael Reed, Haki Madhubuti, Sonia Sanchez, Ed Bullins, Charles Fuller, and August Wilson. Both Fuller and Wilson saw drama in another key and raised it to a profound level of feeling and emotion at one with the intellect and vision, the most intense vision, Africa had to offer to the world.

Sonia Sanchez, a poet, is one of the early members of the Black Arts Movement. She is the author of thirteen books including *Homecoming, I've Been a Woman: New and Selected Poems* and *Under a Soprano Sky*. She brought a literary laser beam to gender and women's issues to the Black Arts Movement that had not surfaced as powerfully before her writings. In some ways, Toni Cade Bambara and Toni Morrison might be seen as useful contrasts to the more people-oriented style of Sanchez, who has been known for her readings as much as her writings.

The Black Arts Movement had many elements. It showed itself in the African cultural styles that people used in dress, such as the wearing of *kente* cloth and African outfits, as well as in how they wore their hair, or purchased products. Wearing the natural "Afro" style was thought to be the most radical thing that an African American woman could do personally to express self-love. Popularized by people like Angela Davis and the poets Gwendolyn Brooks and Maya Angelou, the natural style became widely acceptable. Davis, a Marxist professor, and a revolutionary who was a friend of George Jackson, widely believed to have been a political prisoner, wore the iconic Afro hairstyle and mesmerized thousands of black youth.[9] In many ways the Black Arts Movement was aligned with the "Black is Beautiful" and "Black Power" movements under the umbrella of African Consciousness. African Americans felt an increasing need to accept culture as one way to keep the traditions. Gwendolyn Brooks won the Pulitzer Prize for poetry in 1950, becoming the first African American to win the award, but she refused to allow the accolades of society to change her strong attachment to African American culture. Leading and influencing younger writers like Amiri Baraka and Haki Madhubuti, Brooks charted new imagery and metaphors for cultural audacity. This movement, however, would include ultimately people in the plastic arts, dance, and film, although it started with literature. For example, Jeff Donaldson would lead a community of plastic artists in demonstrating the power of the conscious canvas from his base at Howard University's Department of Art. John Biggers would do the same from Texas Southern University's art department, and throughout the nation African Americans leaped to the challenge of producing socially and culturally relevant art.

Ed Bullins, another pioneer of the Black Arts Movement of the late 1960s and 1970s, made drama of the ordinary lives of African people. Few writers had so much influence on a generation of playwrights as Bullins. He has continued to be a prolific playwright, scholar, and black activist. Plays like *The Taking of Miss Janie, In New England Winter*, and *The Gentleman Caller* served to usher in a new era for African American plays.

Charles Fuller also emerged as a major playwright during this period.[10] He had been a close friend of Larry Neal's in Philadelphia when much of the philosophy of the movement was being created. Charles Fuller was born in Philadelphia in 1939. He was only the second African American playwright to receive a Pulitzer Prize for Drama (Charles Gordone had received it for *No Place to be Somebody* in 1970) when he won the award in 1980 for *A Soldier's Play*. Fuller began to attract critical notice in 1969 with *The Perfect Party*. Along with Larry Neal he participated in the direction of the Afro-American Arts Theatre in Philadelphia, 1967–1971. Suzan Lori Parks, the first black female to receive the Pulitzer for Drama, is a protégée of Fuller's richly textured, highly informative, instructive style of dramatic writing. You will never leave a play by Parks or Fuller without learning something. Charles Fuller was one of two playwrights who dominated the stage in the 1980s and 1990s. He was born in Philadelphia, Pennsylvania, on March 5, 1939 to Charles H. Fuller Sr and Lillian Anderson. The second dominant playwright was August Wilson, who was born in Pittsburgh to Frederick Kittel and Daisy Wilson on April 27, 1945. Both Pennsylvanians went on to become winners of the Pulitzer Prize for drama and Wilson won the award twice—in 1987 for *Fences* and 1990 for *The Piano Lesson*, which also won Best Play awards.

Fuller won the Pulitzer Award in 1982 for his play *A Soldier's Story*. He was educated at Roman Catholic High School in Philadelphia and Villanova University. In 1959 he joined the United States Army and served in Japan and Korea. When he completed his service in the army he went to LaSalle University in 1965–1967, where he received a DFA. During 1967 he co-founded the Afro-American Arts Theatre in Philadelphia. In the late 1960s he teamed with Larry Neal as Philadelphia's dynamic duo in the arts.

Fuller knew from his early childhood that he was interested in how people formed their opinions and ideas, and carried out their actions. He knew this from watching the drama of ordinary lives and from listening to the provocative conversations that took place in his house when he was still a young man. Fuller sought to create an art form that would allow African Americans to respond to every challenge as ordinary human beings who achieve extraordinary levels of understanding, empathy, and power, noting always that African Americans had to confront the existential problems of being black humans. He often used his military experience to probe the mind of African Americans in the army. *The Brownsville Affair*, an 1975 play, dealt with the struggle between black and white civilians in 1906. When the dust had settled on the Brownsville Raid an entire black regiment had been discharged dishonorably from the United States Army.

Charles Fuller would become the most important playwright associated with the venerable Negro Ensemble Company (NEC). It had been founded by Douglas Turner Ward, Robert Hooks, and Gerald Krone in the late 1960s, and had produced memorable plays such as Lorraine Hansberry's *A Raisin' in the Sun*, Lonnie Elders' *Ceremonies in Dark Old Men*, and Joe Walker's *The River Niger*. Associating with the NEC and writing for it were conscious decisions by Fuller to insure the continuation of black theatre. He would accumulate accolades for the realistic style of his writing and the remarkable depth of his dramatic work. In 1980 he won the Obie Award for *Zooman and the Sign*, a spectacular examination of how easily humans can resort to violence and how willing humans are to demand justice if they have been wronged. In *Zooman*, which was produced by the NEC, a Philadelphia teenager kills a young girl outside of her house. The neighbors are baffled and afraid at first but soon are provoked to collective anger when the girl's father places a sign outside the house. Although Fuller does an exceptional job showing how *Zooman* is a product of society, he also strongly suggests that society has the capacity to produce justice. The play has a currency that has made it a standard of the college theatre circuit. It is also popular with community theatres.

The election of Barack Obama may have finally made the last line in the play, "You'll have to get used to Black people being in charge," acceptable, or at least tolerable, to many people. It is this line that was most criticized by some who feared black assertiveness. What was Fuller predicting about the future of the United States? The fear of blacks being in charge not only is irrational but has been demonstrated to be overblown in the imagination of racists because where African Americans have been in charge they have rarely expressed the same hatred toward whites that was historically aimed at blacks. In a very meaningful way, Charles Fuller is the ultimate American playwright because he understood the psychological make-up of humans.

Fuller wrote the screen adaptation for the movie *A Soldier's Story* in 1984. For his work he was nominated for an Academy Award, a Golden Globe Award, and a Writers Guild of America Award, and his screenplay won the Edgar Award. A world traveler and an avid reader, Fuller is one of the most erudite authors of his generation. He is a philosopher with a tremendous grasp of history, which is the best art to assist in understanding the complexities of life.

Charles Fuller is one of the most philosophical writers of his generation. He is attuned to the profound emotions of ordinary people and he brings the widest possible brush and the most authentic personal engagement with words to his writing. In effect, he is the intellectual's artist, committed to getting right the most powerful attitudes and thinking in the community as a barometer of humanity. While he may have been brought to drama by seeing a Yiddish play, it was directing at the Afro-American Arts Theatre in Philadelphia and writing and directing *Black Experience* for WIP radio that endeared him to his audiences.

Probably since Fuller's Pulitzer Prize in 1982, he has been known simply as a master playwright, but he is in fact a comprehensive and multi-talented genius. His early writings included poetry, essays, and short stories. An acute ability to hear dialogue and to sense conflict propelled him into drama. He created skits, sometimes from his short stories, and one-act plays and then full-length dramas. In 2010 he published the novel *Snatch* for young people. It is a powerful and suspense-filled narrative created around two brothers in colonial New York. Here perhaps is Fuller's keenest demonstration of his gift for character, plot, action, suspense, and metaphor within a historical context.

Charles Fuller demonstrates the multidimensional literary personality of the greatest writers in the African American tradition. He challenges the anticipated outcomes in the lives of everyday African Americans and thereby projects in his brilliant writing the most human example of our lives. As the second African American playwright to receive the Pulitzer Prize for Drama, Charles Fuller solidified his place in the literary pantheon in which he continues to shine so brightly.

August Wilson, six years younger than Fuller, was a prolific playwright who left an immense body of work when he died in 2005. Influenced by the poetry of Amiri Baraka and the conversations of elderly black men in restaurants, August Wilson began in the late 1960s to jot poetic and dramatic notes on paper. However, it was the cultural nationalism of Malcolm X that gave him an intellectual direction. Although he was not formally educated, Wilson studied enough of Langston Hughes, Ralph Ellison, Richard Wright, James Baldwin, John Berryman, Chris Brown, Malcolm X, Baraka, and Dylan Thomas to become an expert on the nature of writing and racism in contemporary society. His intense hatred of racism, stemming from incidents with his schoolteachers, one of whom thought that a paper he had done was too good not to have been plagiarized, soured him on school. With Rob Penny, one of the great drama teachers and playwrights of Pittsburgh, Wilson founded the Black Horizons on the Hill theatre and company, which allowed him to produce some of his works on the stage. He always believed that he could become a writer if he were willing to put the time in his craft that it demanded.

Moving to St Paul, Minnesota, in 1978, Wilson would write every day, for ten days, in a fish and chip restaurant from noon till evening and then type his manuscripts until 4 A.M. until he had completed a draft of the play *Jitney*. When *Jitney* was accepted by the Minneapolis Playwright Center and brought him a $200-a-month fellowship, he knew that he could write. Wilson began an intense period of research and writing that ultimately saw him become one of the most important writers ever to live in the United States of America. Often compared with the most important dramatists of the nation, August Wilson produced a series of ten plays, each for a decade in African American life, often referred to as "The Pittsburgh Cycle." The plays, according to decades, are: 1900s: *Gem of the Ocean* (2003); 1910s: *Joe Turner's Come and Gone* (1988); 1920s: *Ma Rainey's Black Bottom* (1984); 1930s: *The Piano Lesson* (1990, Pulitzer winner); 1940s: *Seven Guitars* (1995); 1950s: *Fences* (1987, Pulitzer winner); 1960s: *Two Trains Running* (1991); 1970s: *Jitney* (1982); 1980s: *King Hedley II* (1999); and 1990s: *Radio Golf* (2005).

Oprah Winfrey and the Creation of Style

"Can any good come out of Mississippi?" This was a question that many African Americans asked about the state of Mississippi in the 1950s. The answer was always "yes." Despite the oppressive conditions in Mississippi, the state produced numerous outstanding African Americans. Oprah Winfrey was born in the small community of Kosciusko, Mississippi, on January 24, 1954. Her mother was Vernita Lee and her father Vernon Winfrey. Her maternal grandmother, Hattie Mae, and her father, Vernon, raised her. According to a DNA test in 2008, Winfrey's African ancestry includes the Kpelle, Bamileke, and Nkoye peoples.

Oprah Winfrey's life changed dramatically when she entered Tennessee State University. Her experiences at the university prepared her to overcome the disadvantages of a poor African American woman. She won many contests in college, was a reasonably good student, and participated in the social and cultural life of the campus. All of these activities prepared her to assume the role that would be hers a few years after college: the richest black woman in the United States of America.

Nothing was offered to Oprah Winfrey on a golden plate; she had to work hard for what she earned. When she was thirty years old she became the hostess for a Chicago morning talk show called *A. M. Chicago*. Within months she had outstripped her competition, *The Phil Donahue Show*, in the number of viewers. Her show was increased from thirty minutes to one hour and renamed *The Oprah Winfrey Show*. Soon the program was syndicated nationally and was a big hit.

Winfrey has become one of the biggest people in the entertainment industry. In 1985 she acted in *The Color Purple*, a movie adapted from Alice Walker's book by the same name, and was nominated for Best Supporting Actress for her role as Sofia in the movie. The next year she formed a production company called HARPO (Oprah spelled backward). Three years later, in 1989, she acquired a television and movie production studio to go along with her production company. By the end of 2010 she had accumulated numerous Emmy Awards, the Emmy Lifetime Achievement Award, and recognition by the NAACP and other organizations as one of the most influential women of the century.

Attracting a broad audience of women of all colors, Oprah Winfrey has demonstrated that concentration on the lives of women, especially the overcoming of pain, suffering, destitution, and psychological abuse, is something that people want to hear. Winfrey established herself in a short time, eighteen years, as the most dominant African American woman and one of the most prominent people in America.

The Million Man March

My thirteen-year-old son, M. K., and I took a 6 A.M. Amtrak train from Philadelphia to Washington on October 16, 1995 to be a part of the largest gathering of black men in history. We were not surprised that the train was full of African American men, some coming from as far away as Boston, on the way to Washington. We all wanted to be there early in order to get a good spot from which to see the stage and hear the speakers. When we got off the train at the beautiful Washington train terminal, we walked the distance to the Capitol area, where we saw hundreds of thousands of men who had beaten us to the right spots. We worked our way through the crowd, sometimes being helped up and over by groups of men, all singing, praying, or simply reflecting on the meaning of a million black men in front of the Capitol.

The leader of the Nation of Islam, a religious group that believes in Islamic values, Louis Farrakhan, called for a monumental statement of atonement, making amends, by African American men.

A national council of more than seventy leaders accepted the challenge to bring a million black men to Washington for this massive demonstration. Around the nation, churches organized to send delegations of their members, adults and children, to the march. Radio stations and newspapers reported frequently on the plans for the march. Money was taken up within the community and donated to the March organization. African American corporations and individuals gave large amounts of cash to underwrite the activities of the march. Most people donated their time and energy to planning for a successful demonstration.

Perhaps the most stirring speech was made by a twelve-year-old named Ayinde Shomari Jean-Baptiste from Chicago. He approached the podium with confidence and courage. Looking out over the 1 million men before him, he spoke with a strong and moving voice: "My fathers, you must shape the vision of tomorrow." This was enough for Allen Johnson, a postman from a rural town in Georgia, who turned to us and others with tears in his eyes, singing, "I will begin to shape the vision."

When all the speeches were over and as the debate raged about whether there were 1 million, half a million, or 2 million men present at the march, I read the official mission statement written by the philosopher Maulana Karenga, which said in part:

> This Mission Statement is on one hand the product of the ongoing concern and conversation in the African American community about who we are as a people, where

we stand and what we are compelled to do in view of our self-under-standing and the condition confronting us.

Clearly, Karenga wanted to challenge the million men to be conscious of the challenges which history posed for African Americans and to be committed to working for a better world. In a ten-page, carefully worded document, "The Million Man March/Day of Absence Misson Statement," he emphasized all the themes that had been roundly debated a year earlier as preparation for the March was under way.[11]

The Executive Council for the Million Man March included Minister Louis Farrakhan, Maulana Karenga, Benjamin Chavis, Ron Daniels, Ms Mawina Kouyate, Bob Law, Haki Madhubuti, Leonard Muhammad, Imari Obadele, Frank Reid, Willie Wilson, and Conrad Worrill.

The Million Woman March

Just two years later, on October 25, 1997, Phile Chionesu pulled off the Million Woman March along the magnificent Benjamin Franklin Parkway in Philadelphia. Chionesu had always tried to be a role model for young black women and, as a business owner in Philadelphia, sought to do something for history's sake. Using all of her personal resources as well as the contributions of time and money of her friends and colleagues, Chionesu was able to raise most of the money to support the event. Her reputation as an organizer and leader grew daily as she dealt with internal problems of organization and external criticism from more well-known women that they did not have anything to do with the march. Keeping her eye on the goal and her focus clear, Chionesu had formed a small cadre of sisters who supported the purpose of the march.

On the day of the march it rained a little, but the sunshine was in the hearts of the demonstrators. Many people were surprised that Chionesu could have brought about such an event, but those who knew her said that she should never be underestimated. Congresswoman Maxine Waters of California agreed early to be the keynote speaker. Other powerful figures from various organizations of African American women, and others, joined the movement to produce the largest gathering of women in the history of the nation. Personal narratives were as compelling as those from the Million Man March. For example, a group of five women from Oklahoma City drove to Philadelphia to the march. They told their friends that they came with a cavalier, casual attitude but they left with the feeling that "black women can make things happen."[12]

The Cultural Diversity of the African American Community

In 2001 I was invited to speak at District 17 of the New York Public Schools. Although I knew that New York, particularly the Brooklyn area, was a diverse community, I did not know so many different groups of people had now come to comprise the African American community. There were Jamaicans, Haitians, Dominicans, Puerto Ricans, Barbadians, Trinidadians, Guyanese, Costa Ricans, Panamanians, Nigerians, Senegalese, Ghanaians,

Kenyans, South Africans, Ethiopians, and Brazilians, all participating in the life of the African American community.

What this meant to New York and the nation was that there was a richer, denser African culture evolving in terms of music, art, and cuisine. The languages of Senegal and Ghana are as present on the streets of urban America as Ebonics or Spanish. In a city such as Brooklyn the voices and music of Haiti and Jamaica on Fulton Street are as real and authentic as any that you will hear in Port-au-Prince or Kingston. But this is not merely true in the north-east urban areas; one finds similar evolutions in Atlanta, Los Angeles, Chicago, Detroit, and Houston, although with different populations. Houston, for instance, has been dubbed "Little Lagos" because there are so many successful Nigerians there. Wherever you are in the United States or the world you will see how beautifully the African American community is evolving. I have seen this evolution in Miami, Tampa, San Francisco, Washington, Fort Lauderdale, West Palm Beach, and the crosscurrents are reverberating in Accra, Jo'burg, Dakar, Cape Town, and Abuja.

One must not assume that this is merely recent history. While the pace of the evolution has quickened in the twenty-first century, it is in reality a twentieth-century initiative. When Marcus Garvey arrived from Jamaica in 1916, he was at the vanguard of a new African American community from the Caribbean where people like Gil Nobles, Patrick Bellegarde Smith, Stokely Carmichael, Colin Powell, Ama Mazama, Shirley Chisholm, Garvey Lundy, would be joined by athletes and entertainers from all over the African world.

Shirley Chisholm: Gender and Politics

The little girl looked up at the tall black woman and said, "I have never seen a black Congresswoman before." Shirley Chisholm looked down at the nine- or ten-year-old child and said, "Well, dear, you are looking at one now." The little girl beamed.[13]

One wonders if the child realized the history she was seeing. Shirley Chisholm had represented her home district in Brooklyn in the New York State Assembly and now, in 1968, she was the first African American female elected to Congress. She was one of nine African Americans elected to the House of Representatives in 1968. Eight years later she would be joined by three additional black female legislators, including Yvonne Braithwaite of California, Barbara Jordan of Texas, and Cardiss Collins of Illinois. In 1976 the "unbought and unbossed" Shirley Chisholm ran for the presidency. However, despite her outspoken manner and determined attitude, she did not get the support from blacks and women she expected.[14]

By 1971 there was enough common sentiment among the African American legislators in the nation's capital that they formed the Congressional Black Caucus. It became a major instrument for expressing the sentiment and opinions of the African American community. In many ways, the Congressional Black Caucus replaced the old-line civil rights leaders as the voice of the black community, and among the new leaders were women such as Shirley Chisholm.

Shirley St. Hill Chisholm was born on November 30, 1924 in Brooklyn, New York, to Charles and Ruby St. Hill. Her father was from British Guiana (Guyana) and her mother was from Barbados. Her parents sent her to Barbados in 1927 to live with her maternal grandmother. She received a sound grounding in the British system of education and when she returned to New York was quite accomplished as a student. She attended Girls High School in 1934 and graduated in 1942.

Chisholm matriculated in Brooklyn College after graduation and met numerous students and colleagues who would become lifelong friends. At Brooklyn, for example, she met Adelaide Sanford, who would later become one of the longest-serving members of the New York State Board of Regents.[15] Neither Chisholm nor Sanford liked racism and they fought against it at Brooklyn College. Blacks were denied entrance into social clubs and so Shirley Chisholm organized an alternative club for black students. Although she graduated with honors in 1946 it was hard for her to find a job equal to her training. After being rejected by numerous companies she finally landed a position with Mt Calvary Childcare Center in Harlem. Soon Chisholm believed that she could do more for her community if she became a politician. She ran for the General Assembly of the state and won the election, serving from 1964 to 1968. After serving in the state legislature she decided to run for the Twelfth Congressional District with the slogan "Fighting Shirley Chisholm—Unbought and Unbossed." Of course, she won the election and immediately hired an all-female staff. Her philosophy was progressive and her agenda items included withdrawing troops from Vietnam, women's rights, and civil rights. She was a co-founder of the National Organization for Women. She announced her candidacy for president on January 25, 1972. She declared:

> I stand before you today as a candidate for the Democratic nomination for the Presidency of the United States. I am not the candidate of black America, although I am black and proud. I am not the candidate of the women's movement of this country, although I am a woman, and I am equally proud of that. I am not the candidate of any political bosses or special interests. I am the candidate of the people.[16]

The 1972 Democratic National Convention in Miami was the first major political convention in which any female was considered for the presidential nomination. Chisholm won 151 of the delegates' votes. She continued to serve in the House of Representatives until 1982. Shirley Chisholm passed away on January 1, 2005.

Jesse Jackson, one of the heirs of Martin Luther King Jr, and Al Sharpton, a powerful orator and activist, would both run for political office. Jackson would run for the nomination to be the presidential candidate for the Democrats in both 1984 and 1988. Ronald Walters, one of the outstanding African political scientists, would bolster his chances for sound international understanding of the African world as his advisor. Sharpton would run for the New York senatorial seat in 1992 and 1994. However, Jackson would not win his bids for the presidency and Sharpton would not win his bid to be senator for the State of New York, but both would continue to be vibrant voices against police violence, discrimination in jobs, housing discrimination, and economic exploitation. It might well be said that if they did not exist they would have had to be created to stand up in every sector of the society to fight for African rights.

Jesse Jackson would eventually see the mainstream Democrats choose Ron Brown, a politically connected Washington, DC, attorney to be the chairperson of the Democratic National Committee in 1989. Brown would be killed in an airplane crash on the way to Bosnia in 1995 while serving in the administration of President William Clinton. Ron Brown, as Secretary for the Department of Commerce, had emerged to become a power broker nationally and internationally, and his success as a political leader would help to establish the format for the rise of black leadership of the Republican National Committee. Michael Steele had a tempestuous tenure at the helm of the Republican organization from January 2009 until January 2011, when he stepped aside after four rounds of voting for a new head of the RNC.

TransAfrica and Political Activism

Randall Robinson, Hershelle Challenor, and Willard Johnson created the design for a global African American organization that would promote justice throughout the African world. When TransAfrica was incorporated in 1977, a year after the three principals had met at the Black Leadership Conference convened by the Congressional Black Caucus in 1976, it was a powerful symbol that blacks would be involved in international discussions about the affairs in the African world. As an advocacy organization headed by Randall Robinson, TransAfrica would make its voice heard loudest in the battle to defeat apartheid in South Africa. Robinson as executive director was relentless in fighting in the American Congress for the rights of Africans in South Africa. In an effort to expose the secret agreements and meetings between President Reagan's administration and the white minority regime's representatives, TransAfrica increased its media attack on all support for the minority regime. Demonstrations were held almost daily by TransAfrica and soon the organization had the reputation of being the most adamant defender of majority rights in South Africa. Among the leaders of TransAfrica have been Danny Glover, Harry Belafonte, Chuck D, Johnetta B. Cole, Walter Mosley, Manthia Diawara, and Nicole Lee. They have inherited an organization that has established its place in the ranks of strong African American organs for justice and fairness.

The Hip Hop Nation Arises

Hip hop is the name given to a genre of music and its accompanying culture. It is defined by five key elements: djing, mcing, breaking, graffiti, and knowledge. Other concepts that are often tied to hip hop are turntablism and beatboxing. Most experts agree that the movement began in South Bronx in New York City in the 1970s when young African Americans and Latinos began to express themselves in the African rap style. The writer M. K. Asante Jr explains in his seminal book *It's Bigger than Hip Hop* that the word "hip" comes from the Senegalese Wolof verb "hipi," that is, to open one's eyes. He explains that with "hop-hop," coming from the Old English word "hoppian," meaning to spring forward into action, the result is enlightened action. Furthermore, Asante Jr writes, "the force that created Malcolm was the same force that created hip hop."[17] The combination of action and enlightenment constitutes the core of hip hop. Asante Jr. says that when KRS-ONE raps "I Am Hip-Hop" he's also saying "I Am an enlightened actor."[18]

Common, Omar Tyree, and Rah Digga were being interviewed at the Philadelphia Community College back in 2000 and the young crowd was just as excited to see the artists of their generation as their older siblings had been to hear Chuck D of Public Enemy, KRS-One, and Run DMC. By late 2010 Common and Rah Digga had to move over for newer artists. Some artists such as Kanye West, Lil Wayne, and Jay-Z searched for ways to remain relevant to the ever-changing artistic environment. New artists like Jay Electronica, J Cole, and Lupe Fiasco were laying the foundations for an entirely new generation of artists, younger, and happy to push the art to new levels based on the revolutionary cultural mix happening in the African American community. International and diasporan rappers—Senegalese like Akon, Duggy Tee, Didier Awadi; Ghanaians like Obrafour, Samini, Sarkodie, Okyeame Kwame; South Africans like Pro, Abdus Jr, Jabba, Sixfo, and Teargas; and Nigerians like Ubani, Mister, Modenine, Ruggedman, the brilliant Afrocentric Nigerian female rapper Word MC—are topping charts all over the world and daring to invent the future. The hip hop world is a fluid one where those who are here today are gone tomorrow, but the search for a positive soulful music never ends as moguls such as Russell Simmons, Sean Coombs, and Jay-Z keep discovering new talents.

When the Sugar Hill Gang came out with *Rapper's Delight* in 1979 it was the beginning of the hip hop revolution where a whole nation of youths would arise and call themselves hip hoppers. The term *hip hop* was in the air and the rhythmic poetry of the young poets was called rap. The rappers articulated the concerns of the youth community in terms of their social and cultural concerns. They spoke about the drugs and violence in the urban community and the racism and prejudice in the larger society. The most authentic voices of the early rappers were those like Gary Byrd (Imhotep, he later called himself), Grandmaster Flash, and the Furious Five. But the field soon grew to include various styles of rap. But the one common denominator was the use of the technique of scratching, moving a record back and forth under a needle to create a staccato, metallic sound that reproduced the urban sounds of subways, trains, and community activity. Sometimes they connected two turntables to the same set of speakers and would switch from one to the other to create a new composition. Flash is given credit for this innovation. Many other disc jockeys experimented with rap styles.

Ten years after *Rapper's Delight*, gangsta rap came about with N.W.A., a Los Angeles-based group that produced *Straight Outta Compton*. Struggles between the so-called East and West ends of the music caused rifts between some of the entertainers, and Tupac Shakur and Notorious B.I.G. were killed in a feud. Rap continued to influence the dress styles and language of young African Americans. Films such as *Boyz N the Hood*, *He Got Game*, *Menace II Society*, *Soul Food*, *New Jack City*, and *Romeo Must Die* used much of the language and style of the contemporary African American rap rhythms. However, by 2011 the field had matured so that the various styles of rap could coexist with rhythms from Senegal, Nigeria, Cuba, Haiti, Mexico, Puerto Rico, as well as the urban African American community.

The Afrocentric Future

Counting the battles won and lost, the African American community record book is weighed on the side of victory. All of the strife, tension, pain, suffering, and ill will can never be fully explained, but one thing is certain: African Americans are respected throughout the world for consistent and persistent struggle against all forms of racial prejudices and discrimination.

Phases taken from the language of the African American Civil Rights Movement—"We Shall Overcome," "Justice Now," and "Nobody Can Turn Us Around"—have become resilient expressions in activist struggles for respect and humanity in settler South Africa and Rhodesia, in turbulent Palestine, in France, especially in Martinique and Guadeloupe, among the indigenous communities of East Timor, in Australia among the Aborigines, and in Ecuador and Bolivia by the native people. Unquestionably, people in other nations use the themes and the songs of the African Americans' freedom movement as their own. The Chinese students who protested against the communist regime in Beijing's Tiananmen Square in 1990 sang "We Shall Overcome," the classic African American freedom song. Undoubtedly African Americans have come a long way when the world now sings the songs their ancestors sang in their struggle for equality and justice.

African Americans represent nearly twelve percent of the U.S. population but the cultural, intellectual, and artistic impact has been far greater than the numbers. The diversity of the African American population reflects the energy and dynamism of today's society. There are African people from the Caribbean, Africa, Central and South America, the Middle East, Alaska, Europe, and Asia. One of the leading African American cinematographers is Haile Gerima, who was born in Ethiopia. Shirley Chisholm, first black congresswoman and the first female to run for president, was from Barbados. Colin Powell, former chairman of the Joint Chiefs of Staff for the U.S. military, and Secretary of State, was born in the United States of Jamaican parents. Carlos Moore, a leading African American intellectual, is Cuban. Ama Mazama, the distinguished linguist, is from Guadaloupe. Mustafa Hefny, the African educator who fought to have his racial classification changed from white to African, was born in Egypt. Marta Vega, the founder of the Caribbean Cultural Center of New York, is Puerto Rican. Yet all of these individuals participate in the traditional African American community.

Today, African Americans stand firmly on the foundations of struggle laid by a diverse group of committed individuals who were driven by the demands of their community.

But full equality has not been achieved. We have a long way to go. African Americans and whites still come up with different answers to national questions such as "Does discrimination still exist?" "Are whites given greater opportunities than African Americans?" Whites and African Americans hold different political views on many issues. This is seen quite often in politics, where opinion polls show that whites and African Americans have opposite views on individual freedom and fair play.

African Americans are concerned about police brutality, the United States' unequal treatment of Haitian refugees, economic support for Africa, and racial profiling, the practice of stopping African American or Latino drivers because they fit a certain profile established by the police. African Americans are also continuing the struggle against economic discrimination. There are a large number of African Americans who remain outside the economic avenue of power. Sometimes, entire families have been so victimized or abused by the legacies of enslavement that they cannot see themselves ever rising beyond their current circumstances.

History has shown that without government support, equal opportunity for African Americans stuck at the bottom of the economic ladder will be difficult. In fact, banks still discriminate in loaning money to African Americans. On home mortgages, for example, many large banks deny mortgages more frequently to African Americans than whites. When mortgage loans are approved, African Americans are charged a higher rate of interest than whites. The Center for Responsible Lending found that black people were 34 percent more likely to receive higher-rate subprime loans.[19] African American anger, given the incredible sacrifices generations of Africans have made to the United States, has certainly been normal and justified. If African Americans did not express any signs of anger, perhaps they would need to have their sanity questioned.

Civil rights legislation created opportunities and made it illegal for whites to discriminate against African Americans. But the law has its limits. Discrimination exists when individuals use every means at their disposal to get around the law. Many people have found new ways to obstruct the law and frustrate justice. This kind of discrimination is so subtle that it is very difficult to prove. For example, if the law says that African Americans must be admitted into public hotels, an owner can choose to turn the hotel into a private club with restrictions that are guaranteed to keep African Americans out. If the law says that it is illegal to deny African Americans access to employment, a company can create artificial requirements such as a recommendation from someone who has worked in the position being filled or some other requirement that has little to do with the candidate's ability to perform that job. Failure to meet these and other obscure requirements allows the discriminating company to argue that African Americans do not meet company standards. This kind of reasoning is no different from the logic that nineteenth-century whites used when they created the Grandfather Clause that allowed an African American to vote only if his grandfather had voted before 1876. Yet while civil rights legislation did not change people's prejudices, it did restrict their ability to discriminate openly against African Americans as they had done in the past.

Supreme Court Justice Clarence Thomas, the Gerrymander Law, and the Danger of Race

Soon afterwards the nation entered a new, more conservative era, in which presidents Reagan and the first Bush appeared to hold back on the forward progress that was made by the previous administration of Jimmy Carter. President George H. W. Bush's appointment of Clarence Thomas as an associate justice of the Supreme Court solidified in the minds of African Americans the disdain that the Republican president held for the black community and for the fabled seat of the beloved Thurgood Marshall. Clarence Thomas did not overcome the initial apprehensions concerning his appointment among blacks, who predicted he would become a right-wing judge.

Thomas' confirmation hearing in 1991 before the Senate was embarrassingly dramatic as Anita Hill gave damaging testimony about Thomas' moral behavior. Hill had been an attorney who worked with Clarence Thomas at the United States Department of Education and at the Equal Employment Opportunity Commission. Hill testified that Thomas had made sexually explicit statements and sexual overtures, and had sexually harassed her when she worked for him. Thomas was born in Georgia and educated at Holy Cross and Yale Law School. He became an assistant attorney general for the state of Missouri in 1974 and in 1979 was a legislative assistant to Missouri's senator John Danforth. In 1981 he was made Assistant Secretary for Civil Rights at the U.S. Department of Education and a year later President Ronald Reagan made him chairman of the Equal Employment Opportunity Commission. In 1990, President George H. Bush nominated him for a seat on the Supreme Court.

During the 1990s the Congressional Black Caucus would have to confront new forms of racism and new challenges to the position of African Americans in the legislatures of the nation. One of the first cases that Thomas had to hear as an associate of the Supreme Court was about political districts. Gerrymandering, dividing a political district to benefit one party, became an issue when whites claimed that the Democratic majorities in some states had redrawn districts to benefit African Americans.

Two cases, *Bush v. Vera* and *Shaw v. Hunt*, became the defining cases. The Supreme Court ruled against the plans by North Carolina and Texas to strengthen the likelihood of African American participation in the political process. Among the justices in the 5–4 decision voting with the majority was Justice Clarence Thomas, who argued that the "the law cannot make us equal." Of course, most African Americans believed that the case was decided wrongly because for many years whites had gerrymandered blacks out of political power. They saw no reason why African Americans could not be considered voting majorities in some districts. After a succession of Thomas' votes on the side of the Court's right wing, the term *clarencization* became a slang expression to describe a black person who had lost their mind.

Clarence Thomas was neither distinguished among American jurists nor significant in African American history during his first twenty years on the Supreme Court. He was consistently among the most conservative of judges, creating a well of negative opinion within the African American community because of his lack of social and historical consciousness. In effect, Clarence Thomas' race made no difference on the Court and he became precisely what the whites who championed him expected him to become, a person devoid of psychological consciousness about his own history. On the other hand, Leon Higginbotham, who many thought should have been appointed to the bench, remained even in death the most heralded black legal mind during the first part of Thomas' tenure on the bench. Higginbotham had been appointed to the federal bench when he was thirty-five, one of the youngest federal judges in history, and published more than one hundred articles and books on various legal and historical subjects. Clearly, Thomas did not fall in the same category as Higginbotham, and had neither the charisma, intellect, nor sense of social purpose of Higginbotham.[20]

The Anita Hill/Clarence Thomas Affair

African Americans, like other Americans, were glued to the television set during one of the most dramatic moments of American television, the Anita Hill/Clarence Thomas affair being discussed and debated on national television in 1991. It occurred during the hearing on Thomas' nomination by President George H. W. Bush to serve on the Supreme Court.

The drama had been set up by the resignation from the Supreme Court of the venerable jurist Thurgood Marshall. His reputation as a fighter for civil rights and as an advocate of human dignity was unquestioned. To replace him, Bush had nominated Clarence Thomas, who many saw as intellectually weak, morally suspect, and uncommitted to the historic African American objective of making society better for those worst off. In fact, some people thought that there could be no greater anti-Thurgood Marshall than Clarence Thomas.

However, Anita Hill, a law professor at the University of Oklahoma, who had worked with Clarence Thomas, and indeed had completed Yale Law School, as had Thomas, created the most difficult challenge for Thomas' confirmation. Hill took a polygraph test and passed it; Thomas refused to take a polygraph. Thomas argued that he was a victim of "a high-tech lynching," meaning that the media had created a stir where there was none. He felt that he was being mistreated by the television and newspaper industry as a black man. Some prominent blacks such as Maya Angelou, the writer, and Niara Sudarkasa, president of Lincoln University, supported Thomas, believing that no black who sat on the Supreme Court could be unconscious of the history of the appointment and ignorant of the legacy of Thurgood Marshall. Most African Americans did not support him, believing that Thomas had a history of conservative policies. Indeed, the progressives within the African American community believed Anita Hill's story and saw Thomas' later confirmation by the all-white Senate Committee and then by the Senate as an indication that the Republicans wanted a black person they could trust to carry out their agenda.

A large host of African American leaders voiced their objection to appointing Thomas to the Supreme Court. The objection was based on the belief that Thomas would advance the Republican political agenda and turn a blind eye toward the African American community. This indeed proved to be the case. Other leaders in the black community chose at this time to concentrate on the economic development of the black community since the political sector was often too full of politics. Kenneth Gamble, who along with Leon Huff had created the Philadelphia Sound, started a revolution in the housing industry in South Philadelphia by purchasing old housing stock and refurbishing it to improve the living standards of the community and to beautify the living spaces of the people. Gamble recovered more than 400 houses during the 1990s and 2000s.

The Election of African American Mayors

The black political candidate often received unexpected results, sometimes beneficial and at other times not so good. When Carl Stokes was elected to the mayoralty of Cleveland in 1967 he was the first African American to be elected mayor of a major city. Richard Hatcher of the small industrial city of Gary, Indiana, had been elected at the same time and both took their offices in January 1968. Stokes' election was made possible because he received a good percentage of white votes. This would be a pattern that would hold when blacks became mayors of other large cities. By 2000, African Americans had been elected mayors in Los Angeles, New York, Chicago, Philadelphia, Detroit, Washington, Baltimore, San Francisco, Denver, and Atlanta. Richard Hatcher used his political base to advance the cause of African American social and economic gains.

Detroit, the Motor City, was thrust into the forefront of the news when Coleman A. Young was elected the first black mayor of a world-class American city in 1974. Young was born in Tuscaloosa, Alabama, in 1918. Young was elected to the mayoralty in 1974 and served until 1993. Already known for its music industry led by the Motown Corporation, Detroit was now embarking upon a new course in governance. White flight to the suburbs had taken place rapidly and would increase when blacks took over the city government. Young was determined to make the city responsive to the needs of its citizens and his leadership allowed African Americans to participate in the economic life of the city. This would be a pattern repeated by Mayor Harold Washington of Chicago and Mayor Goode of Philadelphia. Mayor

Thomas Bradley, who won office with a larger white vote than Young, Washington, or Goode, would have less success in securing economic opportunities for black citizens.

By 1989, when David N. Dinkins was elected as the head of the nation's largest city, there were more than 300 African American mayors of towns and cities in the United States, including Philadelphia. Since that time, black mayors and governors have been elected in many cities and several states.

The Governor's Seat

In the 1970s, running for governor of a state was another matter. In 1971 Charles Evers, the brother of the slain civil rights leader Medgar Evers, and mayor of Fayette, Mississippi, ran a losing effort for the governorship of Mississippi. Kenneth Gibson, mayor of Newark, ran for and lost the governorship of New Jersey in 1981, after serving for three terms as mayor. Thomas Bradley lost by a close vote in the 1982 election for the governorship of California.

It would not be until the election of Lawrence Douglas Wilder of Virginia as lieutenant governor in 1985 and then as governor in 1990 that an African American would capture a governor's seat as an elected official. Wilder was born on January 17, 1931, and became the first African American to be elected governor of a United States state, and the second to serve as governor. P. B. S. Pinchback was govenor of Louisiana for thirty-five days, December 9, 1872 to January 13, 1873, during the Reconstruction. Wilder's election demonstrated that it was possible for blacks to win statewide elections because he won in a state that was eighty-one percent white.

Two additional governors of African American descent have held their state's highest office. Deval Laurdine Patrick, who was born in Chicago on July 31, 1956, was elected governor of Massachusetts in 2006. Patrick had served in Clinton's administration as a United States assistant attorney general. He became the first African American to hold the office of Massachusetts' governor. However, Massachusetts elected an African American U.S. Senator, Edward Brooke, in 1966, making him the the first black to sit in the Senate in the twentieth century.

Another black governor, David Alexander Patterson of New York, took over the reins of the most populous northern state when he was sworn in on March 17, 2008 after Eliot Spitzer stepped down from the governorship due to a sex scandal. Patterson was the first black governor and only the second legally blind person to hold a governorship.

Jesse Jackson and the Rainbow Coalition

The popularity of Jesse Jackson, who had been at King's side when he was slain, remained consistent during the 1980s and 1990s. Jackson became adept at finding ways to expand the interests of the black community, even making forays into the economic arena and international policy.

Jackson used the Rainbow Coalition, his political organization, as his launching platform for political operations. He had been born in 1941 in Greenville, South Carolina, and had attended school at North Carolina Agricultural and Technical University. Later he completed a course of study at the Chicago Theological Seminary. In 1960 he became one of the closest aides to Dr Martin Luther King Jr, and a prominent member of the Southern Christian Leadership Conference. Jackson, always articulate and ready with a speech, modeled his early speeches after those of Dr King. He loved the technique of the figure of speech, used so eloquently by King. Jackson could say, "We go from the doghouse to the White House," or "we leave street language in the street" and be understood clearly by the African American audience. In an expansive way, he would say, "Our flag is red, white, and blue, but our nation is a rainbow—red, yellow, brown, black, and white." With this type of national rhetoric, Jesse Jackson decided to become a traditional politician, shedding his civil rights image. In 1984 he entered the Democratic National Convention with 300 delegates and was defeated on the floor. In many ways, Jackson followed the same path as Shirley Chisholm, but he would have another chance. In 1988 he enlarged his electoral base by demonstrating that he could attract a broader segment of the population. Thus, by keeping his core African American base and expanding it with voter registration campaigns, he was able to win 1,200 delegates in thirteen state primaries for the nomination to be the Democratic nominee, though still not enough to win. However, he had established himself as a legitimate power-broker, someone who could help make other candidates winners. Individuals who managed the Jackson campaign became bona fide, genuine, leaders in the Democratic Party. Chief among these was Ronald Brown, who would go on to become the first black person to hold the title of chairperson of a national political party when he was elected the head of the Democratic National Committee in 1989.

When Jesse Jackson Jr became a United States representative from Illinois in 1996 he reflected his father's determination and passion. Thirty-eight other African Americans entered Congress at the time of Jesse Jackson Jr. Thirteen of the African American legislators were women and one of them, Carol Moseley-Braun, Democrat of Illinois, was the first African American elected to the Senate.

Congresswoman Maxine Waters rose to prominence in the House of Representatives after many years as an elected official. She had been elected to the California State Assembly in 1976, re-elected every year until she joined the 102nd Congress in 1990. In 1997 she became leader of the Congressional Black Caucus. As a leader of the CBC she was an outspoken opponent of the forces that sought to impeach President Clinton. Her husband, Sidney Williams, a wealthy businessman, was United States ambassador to the Commonwealth of the Bahamas in the 1990s.

The Death of Affirmative Action

Slavery set back the African American community by more than 250 years. Deprivation, discrimination, segregation, and racism combined to disadvantage African Americans in industry, education, science, and technology. One of the ways that the government in the 1970s and 1980s tried to deal with the discrimination against African Americans was to create opportunities for the public agencies, organizations, corporations, and educational institutions to respond to the lack of African Americans in various sectors of the society. This program was called *Affirmative Action* because it meant that an organization would agree to affirmatively act in the interest of allowing those who had been discriminated against to enter the organization.

Affirmative action expanded to include women, other minority groups, and the handi-capped. Soon white males, believing that the beneficiaries of affirmative action were taking over society, reacted to the idea of assisting these groups to become integrated into American society. Public policy changed and the pressure for affirmative action was removed. A black man, Ward Connerly, led a campaign in California to eliminate affirmative action. He was successful in getting the state of California to abandon its commitment to affirmative action at the University of California. By 2000 the number of African Americans admitted to the University of California, Los Angeles, and the University of California, Berkeley, had dropped to less than 300 each. The blow was devastating to the African American and Hispanic communities.

The elimination of affirmative action has generated a louder call for *reparations*, the paying of descendants of enslaved Africans for the work that was done by their ancestors. The proponents argue that the government of the United States at one time sanctioned slavery and now it should try to remedy the effects of the enslavement by paying the descendants of the enslaved people for the unpaid labor of their ancestors. It is a moral argument that has gained momentum since the faltering of affirmative action.

The Conservative Challenge

The defeat of Jimmy Carter by Ronald Reagan in the 1980 presidential election signaled a sharp right turn in American politics. Black conservatives were quite prominent in the Reagan administration as leaders of a few agencies as well as academic supporters of the conservative position of the government under Reagan. Conservatives were generally opposed to abortion rights, affirmative action for African Americans and other discriminated-against persons, and equal rights for women. The African American conservatives believed that the philosophy of individualism was superior to what they called group rights. In other words, many conservatives believed that the fact that African Americans were descendants of people who were enslaved had nothing to do with the present state of black people in America. The conservative view was not popular among African Americans. However, Ronald Reagan played on the new sentiment among a small cadre of black conservatives by appointing some of them to high posts. For example, Eleanor Holmes Norton was replaced as chair of the Equal Employment Opportunity Commission (EEOC) with William Bell, an African American conservative. When he was challenged because of his limited quali-fications, Reagan appointed Clarence Thomas, who was later nominated to be a Supreme Court justice.

Thomas Sowell, Ann Wortham, Shelby Steele, Glenn Loury, Armstrong Williams, and Walter Williams were the most prominent names among the African American conservatives during both the Ronald Reagan and the George Bush administrations. They were rarely powerful within the political ranks of the Republican Party and had little influence on policy, but they became useful instruments in carrying the Republican message to the public. They were ineffective with the masses of African Americans, who remained firmly entrenched within the liberal camp of American politics.

African Americans and President William Clinton

Ronald Brown was the chairperson for the Democratic National Committee and the engineer behind Bill Clinton's capture of the White House in 1992. African Americans voted for Clinton in record numbers in 1992. Four years later, when he was elected for the second time, the African American community again demonstrated its support of the Democratic candidate to a degree higher than any other segment of the voting population.

President Clinton responded to this outpouring of support in several symbolic and concrete ways. He asked Maya Angelou (b. 1928), the writer who became famous after writing *I Know Why the Caged Bird Sings*, to write his inaugural poem. She was the first African American and the first woman to receive such a presidential honor. She wrote the poem "On the Pulse of the Morning" and recited it at Clinton's 1993 inauguration. Once he was inaugurated, President Clinton named more African Americans to high-level appointments than any president. The cabinet-level positions given to African Americans included:

- Ronald Brown, Secretary of Commerce
- Rodney Slater, Secretary of Transportation
- Jesse Brown, Secretary of Veterans Affairs
- Hazel O'Leary, Secretary of Energy
- Mike Espy, Secretary of Agriculture
- Alexis Herman, Secretary of Labor
- Jocelyn Elders, David Satcher, Surgeon General.

Clinton named fellow Arkansan Jocelyn Elders to the post of Surgeon General. She resigned under fire from critics because she was considered "too forthright" on health issues. She "told it like it was" regarding the nation's health. Most people give her high marks for straight talk and good science. Another African American, David Satcher, an eminent scientist who had led the Center for Disease Control and Prevention in Atlanta, was named to the post.

From the time Lyndon Baines Johnson named Robert Weaver to the post of Secretary of Housing and Urban Development in 1966, each president has had African Americans in cabinet-level or sub-cabinet-level positions. President Ronald Reagan's administration was considered by most blacks to be the nadir, lowest point, for African American appointees in government since 1966.

President Ronald Reagan's most significant African American appointment was that of General Colin Powell to be President of National Security Affairs in 1987. Never before had an African American risen so high in the American military establishment. However, in 1988 President George Bush appointed Powell to the position of chairman of the Joint Chiefs of Staff, the highest military advisory group. The chairman is the chief military advisor to the president. General Powell played a leading role in planning the invasion of Panama in 1989 and was the chief strategist of Operation Desert Storm during the Persian Gulf War. There were 132,300 African Americans who served in the Persian Gulf conflict, constituting a quarter of all the military personnel who served. They were extremely proud of the way General Powell conducted himself in the course of the war, although about fifty percent of the African Americans at home opposed the war. Nevertheless, Powell went on to distinguish himself in winning the war. In 1991 he won the Spingarn Medal from the NAACP and retired from the military in September, 1993.

President George W. Bush would have two star African American figures. Colin Powell would serve the president as Secretary of State until he resigned after his fervent speech at the United Nations claiming that Iraq had weapons of mass destruction. That speech, Powell's most widely watched and heard, led him to his political nadir. He later resigned and Condoleazza Rice replaced him, making it the first time in history that one African American secretary in the cabinet had replaced another.

Maya Angelou and the Poetry of Life

Maya Angelou (Marguerite Annie Johnson) was born in St Louis, Missouri, and grew up in Stamps, Arkansas, where she felt the sting of racial discrimination at an early age. Living with her grandmother, she was indoctrinated in the tradition of southern African American culture. Her mother's boyfriend sexually assaulted her when she was seven and visiting her mother in Chicago. She confided in her brother and later on discovered that her uncle had killed the attacker. She attended school in San Francisco when she rejoined her mother, who now lived on the West Coast. Dropping out of school, Maya became the first African American cable car conductor. She had a son when she was sixteen and then took on the life of a single mother. When she met a Greek sailor, Anastasios Angelopolos, she married him and then began her career as Maya Angelou. She studied dance with Martha Graham and Alvin Ailey, seeking to develop her skills. Discovering that the stage was where her talents were, Maya started to write and perform.

She was attracted to Vusumzi Make, a South African, who brought her into the circle of South African civil rights. They moved in 1960 to Cairo, Egypt. After living in Cairo for a while, Angelou moved with her son Guy to Ghana and got involved in the political transition taking place in that independent African nation. She was an assistant administrator at the University of Ghana's School of Music and Drama.

Maya Angelou enlarged her art and her mind, and read voraciously. She could read two or three newspapers a day. She studied Arabic, French, Spanish, Italian, and Fante. Returning to the United States in 1964, Maya wanted to assist Malcolm X in building the Organization of African American Unity. She worked with artists, and the writer James Baldwin in her writing projects. *I Know Why the Caged Bird Sings* is her autobiographical novel.

Angelou is an exceptional artist, writer, personality, and icon of culture. She has an enormous international audience as a result of her writings and her performances. In 1972 she wrote a screenplay, *Georgia, Georgia*, and it was nominated for a Pulitzer Prize. She wrote poetry, films, short stories, and essays. Some of her books include *I Wouldn't Take Nothing for My Journey Now* (1993), *Even the Stars Look Lonesome* (1997), *Most Gather Together in My Name* (1974), *Singin' and Swingin' and Getting' Merry Like Christmas* (1976), *The Heart of a Woman* (1981), *All God's Children Need Traveling Shoes* (1987), and *A Song Flung Up to Heaven* (2002).

Angelou was appointed to various committees by successive American presidents. She has worked for President Gerald Ford, President Jimmy Carter, and President William Clinton. Her poem "On the Pulse of the Morning" brought her an instant world audience and fame. In 2009 Angelou narrated M. K. Asante Jr's award-winning documentary film *The Black Candle*. She was appointed to the distinguished title of Reynolds Professor at Wake Forest University in Winston-Salem, North Carolina. Angelou's legacy is not just as a poet, but as a philosopher who has walked in the path of Zora Neale Hurston as the interpreter of the most intricate aspects of African American culture.

Toni Morrison and the African American Imagination

Much like Maya Angelou, Toni Morrison, the first black woman to receive the Nobel Prize for Literature, is a phenomenal person with numerous artistic gifts as a writer. She was born Chloe Anthony Wofford on February 18, 1931 in Lorain, Ohio. Morrison was the second of four children of George Wofford, a shipyard welder, and Ramah Willis Wofford. At home, Chloe heard many songs and tales of Southern black folklore because the Woffords were proud of their African heritage and frequently used stories to stress cultural values of discipline, trust, and character.

In her first grade, Morrison was the only black student in her class and the only one who could read. She was friends with many of her white schoolmates and did not encounter discrimination until she started dating. Morrison's favorite writers were the Russian writers Tolstoy and Dostoyevsky, French author Gustave Flaubert, and English novelist Jane Austen. Morrison attended Howard University and majored in English with a minor in classics. Toni Wofford graduated from Howard University in 1953 with a BA in English. She then attended Cornell University in Ithaca, New York, and received a Master's degree in 1955.

After graduating, Morrison was offered a job at Texas Southern University in Houston, where she taught introductory English. In 1957 she returned to Howard University as a member of faculty. This was the time of the Civil Rights Movement and she met several people who were later active in the struggle. She met the poet Amiri Baraka (at that time called LeRoi Jones) and Andrew Young (who later worked with Dr Martin Luther King, and later still became a mayor of Atlanta, Georgia). Two of her students, taught at Howard also by Nathan Hare, became quite famous; Stokely Carmichael, who became a leader of the Student Nonviolent Coordinating Committee (SNCC), and Claude Brown, author of *Manchild in the Promised Land*, published in 1965.

In the fall of 1964 Morrison went to work for Random House in Syracuse, New York, as an associate editor. In 1967 she was transferred to New York and became a senior editor at Random House. Her first book, *The Bluest Eye*, was published in 1970. Morrison taught at State University of New York at Purchase for a year in 1971–1972. Her second book was *Sula*, published in 1973. *Song of Solomon* was published in 1977. In 1981 she published her fourth novel, *Tar Baby*, where for the first time she wrote of interracial relations. In 1984 Morrison was named the Albert Schweitzer Professor of the Humanities at the State University of New York in Albany. She wrote her first play, *Dreaming Emmett*, which premiered on January 4, 1986 at the Marketplace Theater in Albany. Morrison's next novel, *Beloved*, was influenced by a published story about a slave, Margaret Garner, who in 1851 escaped from slavery in Kentucky with her children to Ohio. In 1988 *Beloved* won the Pulitzer Prize for fiction.

In 1987 Toni Morrison was named the Robert F. Goheen Professor in the Council of Humanities at Princeton University. She became the first black woman writer to hold a named chair at an Ivy League University. She published *Jazz* in 1992. In 1993 Toni Morrison received the Nobel Prize for Literature.

A Nation of Classical Artists

A great host of African American artists, choreographers, and musicians spread African American culture worldwide. Katherine Dunham, often called the Queen Mother of African American Dance, stormed into the world of theatre and dance in the 1940s as a choreographer, dancer, and author. She maintained her prominence during a life that spanned almost a century, from her birth on June 22, 1909 to her death on May 21, 2006. Dunham's fame was widespread in Europe, Latin America, and the United States. She was, in the words of one writer, "Dance's Katherine the Great." Dunham set the model for choreography, creating more than ninety dances. It would be years before her record would be exceeded. One of Dunham's younger contemporaries was Pearl Primus. In the powerful biography of Pearl

Figure 11.1
Katherine Dunham, considered the most important choreographer of African American dance. Image courtesy of Charles L. Blockson Afro-American Collection, Temple University Libraries.

Primus, *The Dance Claimed Me*, written by Peggy and Murray Schwartz, one discovers that Primus, one the best dancers in African American history, was born in New York of Trinidadian parents in 1919 but found her true mission as a dancer when she visited Liberia in 1948–1949. After a phenomenal career as a dancer and anthropologists, Primus died in 1994, but her legacy from the 1940s and 1950s moved swiftly to other choreographers and dancers. Clyde Morgan, one of the most electric dancers and choreographers, moved to Brazil and maintained residences on two continents and two cities for thirty years. As the "mayor" of Salvador, Brazil, Clyde Morgan has presided over scores of festivals, international meetings, and dances. His wife, Lais, and their children are the unofficial ambassadors of culture between the United States and Brazil.

By the 1980s a host of African Americans would move to Africa to find their places in the societies. For example, the choreographer Kariamu Welsh would travel to Zimbabwe and be asked by Prime Minister Robert Mugabe to create the National Dance Company of Zimbabwe in 1981. She would later head the Department of Dance at Temple University and create more than 140 dances. A large number of African Americans abandoned the comforts and discomforts of American life to discover the limits and possibilities opened to them in other nations. Chester Higgins Jr, an eminent photographer for the *New York Times*, would travel and live in Europe and Africa and take some of the most memorable photographs of African people. Ife Nii Owoo, the artist and illustrator, moved to Ghana in the 1974 after studying in Philadelphia and London and married Ghanaian filmmaker Nii Kwate Owoo. While studying African Visual Arts at the Institute of African Studies, University of Ghana, Legon, she developed a love and passion for the Adinkra symbols and wrote and illustrated an acclaimed book for children called *A is for Africa*. African American jazz musicians made Paris their second home, and from that city they traveled throughout Europe disseminating African American classical music. Furthermore, contemporary jazz artists like Wynton Marsalis and Chinyere Nnenna Pierce Freelon have traveled throughout the world, in Europe, Africa, Asia, and South America, following in the well-worn paths of Duke Ellington, Nina Simone, Billy Eckstine, and Thelonious Monk.

One cannot fully understand the charisma, art, and dynamism of Michael Jackson without having some appreciation for the foundation from which he built his career. The Motown machine, as it might be called, that was founded by Berry Gordy and produced so many famous artists was itself in the vein of many independent-minded black entrepreneurs. Kenneth Gamble and Leon Huff of the Philadelphia Sound, for instance, would make their name and history on the basis of their productive writings of songs for outstanding artists. Thus, James Brown, the King of Soul, and Chuck Berry, the authentic King of Rock, were the forerunners of Michael Jackson, the King of Pop, and the performance, theatrics, dramatics, and range of voice of Michael Jackson had been anticipated in the dance moves, sexuality, and rhythms of Chuck Berry and James Brown.

The death of Michael Jackson on June 25, 2009 after he suffered a cardiac arrest shocked his fans and led to an intensive investigation into his personal physician, Conrad Murray. Murray had claimed that he found Jackson in his bedroom, not breathing but with a faint pulse. Murray said he administered CPR to no avail. Paramedics came to the home and administered CPR but Jackson was pronounced dead at the Ronald Reagan UCLA Medical Center. Reports claimed that Jackson probably died from an overdose of the anesthetic propofol (Diprivan).

Jackson, born in 1958, had been a superstar all of his adult life and most of his youth. He was in a class by himself as an entertainer. In 2009 he was preparing for a comeback concert tour that was to reintroduce him to a new audience and new fans. Hounded by charges of child molestation, which were never proven, and money problems, which disappeared after his death, Jackson was a man in search of himself and any island of stability. In the end, although he had a great host of family, friends, producers, and followers, from the record producer Berry Gordy to his three children, Michael Jackson, the greatest performer of the twentieth century, died alone.

African American in Afrocolombia

Msomi Mauer, a scholar and writer, lived in Colombia in South America from 2004 to 2007. While studying at the University of the West Indies Mauer discovered Colombia, neighboring Ecuador, and Venezuela and decided to go to the La Universidad del Pacífico, located in Colombia's principal port and majority in the Afrocolombian city of Buenaventura. This university was one of the first devoted to the African community; it is considered an ethnic institution of higher learning that wholeheartedly embraces the formation of an Afrocentric curriculum. Mauer also discovered that there was another college with strong African emphasis, La Universidad Tecnológica del Chocó–Diego Luis Córdoba, named after the Afrocolombian responsible for the creation of the Department of the Chocó.

What Mauer learned was that from the sixteenth century onward Africans from the Senegambia, Sierra Leone and the Rice Coast, Lower Guinea, and the Congo–Angola regions of Africa were being shipped to Cartagena—which was for a time the largest slaving entrepôt in the hemisphere (only Veracruz, Mexico, imported more Africans until the 1580s and 90s). Afrocolombians are still referred to as *Negros*, which was the shortened form used to refer to them on the slaving ships—*bozales negros*—or savages the color of death. Colombia's African population is nearly thirty percent of the total population, yet the role of blacks in the country is quite limited because of prejudice and discrimination.

In 2008 the African Colombian politicians formed a Black Caucus comprising four male legislators and one female senator—the world-renowned Piedad Córdoba, who made it her mission to resurrect the consciousness and the self-determination of the African people. Senator Córdoba has been actively involved in the construction of community educational programs and youth consciousness-raising sessions to bring the young people face to face with their history as African people.

Launching Afrocentricity International in Paris

On July 9, 2010 Basil Davidson, the British historian of Africa, died in England and a group of African activists and intellectuals, from the continent, the Caribbean, and the Americas, met at La Maison des Mines in Paris. They represented the United States, Guadeloupe, Cameroons, and Mali. The meeting was held to initiate the organization Afrocentricity International. Molefi Kete Asante and Ama Mazama, two of the leading members of the Philadelphia Afrocentric Circle, called the meeting with G. S. Modeste, Saloman Mezepo,

Kalala Omotunde, and Demba Coulibaly, stalwarts of the AfricaMaat group in France, in an effort at international solidarity for a central idea. After the presentations by Asante and Mazama the floor was opened for discussion of a mass movement organization as a historic step beyond the nationality boundaries that had plagued our institutions in the past.

Jean-Philippe Omotunde spoke in support of the idea for a mass organization. Demba Coulibaly was eager to create a data list based on what he knew about the movement's Pan-African philosophy. G. S. Modeste spoke with caution about the organization, seeking to insure that the group did not make the mistakes that had been made in previous attempts at international African organization. Saloman Mezepo spoke with quietness and spirit. He told of the creation of AfricaMaat because of the Cheikh Anta Diop conference held by African Americans in Philadelphia. The seventh of his Menaibuc Africa Maat conferences in Paris was an extension of the Diop idea from Philadelphia. Once again this idea of a global reach for African American networks and intersections with other Africans appears to be one of the driving forces of African American history. While the Pan-African movement at the international level has increased enormously over the past twenty years, the struggle at home, and especially since the election of Obama, has confounded many African Americans. One sees it in the extraordinary number of threats made to the life of the president. Is it because he is black? Many blacks complained that during the Obama years racist incidents increased.

Police Brutality

Police brutality and false imprisonment remain among the lingering complaints in the black community. Indeed, the case of Mumia Abu Jamal is considered one of the most celebrated instances of false imprisonment in America's history. Mumia was a well-known journalist in Philadelphia when he was arrested and put in prison for allegedly shooting police officer Daniel Faulkner in December, 1981. Because many people believed that Mumia had been unjustly convicted he became an international *cause célèbre*. As president of the Association of Black Journalists and a founding member of the Philadelphia Chapter of the Black Panthers, Mumia was already visible to the police before his trial. He was the news director for WHAT radio station in the city and a commentator on National Public Radio.

Mumia worked as a taxi driver to supplement his income. On December 9 he was driving his cab through downtown Philadelphia around 4 A.M. when he let off a fare and parked his car near 13th and Locust Streets. He heard gunshots and turned to see his brother staggering in the street. He left the taxi, ran toward his brother, was shot by a uniformed police officer, and fell down unconscious. Within minutes police arrived and found both Faulkner and Mumia shot. Faulkner later died. Mumia was arrested, brutally beaten, and driven to a hospital. According to testimony, although the hospital was only a few blocks away, it took the police thirty minutes to make the journey. Mumia survived and was charged with murder. The trial began in 1982. The judge had sent more blacks to death row than any other judge. Mumia wanted to represent himself but the court revoked his rights and appointed a lawyer for him.

The prosecution claimed that the bullet that killed Faulkner came from Mumia's gun. However, Mumia's gun, legally registered, was a .38-caliber weapon when the medical examiner said the bullet removed from Faulkner's body was a .44-caliber. This fact was kept from the jury. The police at the scene did not test Mumia's gun to see if it had been recently fired. The prosecution claimed that Mumia had confessed at the hospital but this was not reported until two months after the December 9 incident, when Mumia filed a brutality suit against the police. Gary Wakshul claimed to have heard the confession but on the day of the shooting wrote in his police report that "the Negro male made no comments." The attending physician, Dr Coletta, said that he never heard Mumia say a word. There were many other contradictions in this case and once the word was spread about it, there was a growing and continuing mass of supporters for freedom for Mumia, who in 2010 had been on death row since 1983.

In many respects the police have appeared to be the continuation of the padder-rollers of the slave system. Many believe they have been entrusted to use any method necessary to keep blacks in line. Sometimes the actions are dramatic and tragic, as in the case of Oscar Grant, killed by an Oakland, California, policeman. Maulana Karenga commented prior to the verdict on Johannes Mehserle's killing of Oscar Grant:

> Moreover, in a context of racialized and criminalizing interpretations of Black behavior, the tendency is to accept the police accounts of their conduct and their claims to be simply protecting themselves and society against constant threats from the Outer Limits. And when their acts seems too savage, even to supporters, the police need only transform themselves into untrained members of F-Troop, making unintended tragic mistakes or into sympathetic wimps, whining about perceived and contrived threats.[21]

The jury in Los Angeles produced a verdict of guilty of manslaughter, not murder, and the community of Oakland, 300 miles away, erupted in an outpouring of destructive anger. The fact that the United States Department of Justice quickly indicated that it would investigate the case may have prevented more widespread riots in the black community. Nearly one hundred people were arrested in Oakland when the state court returned a guilty verdict of involuntary manslaughter rather than murder, the nation having seen on video how the policeman pulled the trigger on the twenty-two-year-old unarmed Oscar Grant. Police are often the most visible arm of the racist engine that fires the hatred in the urban communities.

Beatings, murders, and widespread arrests of black people for questioning police actions constitute reason for continuing concern. In Detroit the police shot and killed a seven-year-old girl, Aiyana Stanley Jones, during an early morning raid on a home on the city's east side on May 16, 2010. The child was struck in the head and neck area while sleeping on a couch at the home. Assistant Police Chief Ralph Godbee said police were executing a "no-knock" search warrant for a homicide suspect in the two-apartment home. He said the police—members of the heavily armed Special Response Team—threw a flash grenade through an unopened window around 12:45 A.M. before charging in with guns drawn.[22] On the morning of July 22, 2010, a fifteen-year-old youth, James Rivera, was shot dead in Stockton, California, when police surrounded a car he was driving. Apparently the police had cornered the van Rivera was driving because they thought it had been used in a carjacking hours previously. Rivera's parents said that the police visited their home around 1 A.M. and told them that they were looking for their son and that they were going to kill him.[23] After spotting him, the police stopped Rivera and then released him. As he drove away they chased him and rammed his van until he lost control. They asked him to come out of the van. However, as he was getting out, and within seconds of their command, the officers shot thirty rounds with 7mm handguns and automatic M-16 rifles. It is reported that fifteen bullets tore into the body of Rivera. A crowd of people assembled and began to chant out of their rage, "No justice, no peace!"

Achieving Anyway: The Competitive Spirit

Civil rights legislation helped create more African American millionaires, more middle-class professionals, and more avenues for social and economic advancement for those with ambition and education. Over the last two decades, some African Americans have had exceptional personal achievements. For example, Oprah Winfrey, Michael Jackson, and Bill Cosby are among the most successful entertainers in history. They have achieved international fame because of their exceptional talent, intelligence, and ability to communicate with millions of viewers. Some have argued that this is not necessarily the goal for which African Americans have struggled and yet one cannot deny that wealthy African Americans have added to the possibilities for fulfillment and enlarged the boundaries of workable freedom within the American nation.

Willis Gary, for example, was one of eleven children born to a farm family in Eastman, Georgia, in 1947. He worked in sugar cane fields as a young man, but he always wanted to have enough money to help the poor people he saw around him. He attended Shaw University and then got his Juris Doctorate from North Carolina Central University and became a lawyer. In 1995 he won a $500 million judgment for a Mississippi firm that had been the victim of unscrupulous, that is, unfair, business practices. The case was settled for $175 million. Gary has become one of the most generous African American philanthropists, giving $10 million to his alma mater, Shaw University.

Johnnie Cochran, another lawyer, was born in Shreveport, Louisiana. He graduated from UCLA in 1959 and then entered Loyola Law School. He was appointed to the American College of Trial Lawyers, an honor reserved for about 1 percent of American lawyers. Cochran's list of clients, people he defended, included some well-known individuals like Todd Bridges, Jim Brown, Latrelle Sprewell, Michael Jackson, and O. J. Simpson. It was the O. J. Simpson case, where Simpson was accused of murdering his wife and another person, that made Cochran internationally famous. Cochran demonstrated his legal knowledge, organization, strategy, and eloquence in defending his client. O. J. Simpson was found not guilty of the murders. Cochran subsequently wrote a book, *Journey to Justice*.

Reginald Lewis was born in 1942 and died in 1993. By the time of his death he had become one of the richest African Americans, worth more than $400 million. At his funeral, Bill Cosby said, "Reggie Lewis played the hell out of the hand he was dealt." Lewis, it was said, did not want to have the largest black business; he wanted the largest business. This was the spirit of competition that drove him to success in the business world. He acquired Beatrice Foods, a Fortune 100 company, for $985 million. The Harvard University International School of Law is named in his honor. The city of Baltimore has a museum designed by the award-winning Freelon Group named after him.

Robert Johnson was born in Hickory, Mississippi, one of nine children. He was educated at Illinois and Princeton. He always wanted his own cable company and in 1980 he organized

Black Entertainment Television (BET). The company employs 600 people and publishes three magazines, *EMERGE, BET Weekend,* and *Heart and Soul.*

Berry Gordy was born in Detroit, one of eight children. He began writing music and working on the Ford Motor Company assembly line. When he met Jackie Wilson in 1957, he liked the way Wilson sang the songs he had written. He produced four songs and they were well received. He also met Smokey Robinson in 1957 and asked him to join with him in producing songs.

On January 12, 1959, Gordy formed Motown Records with $800 he had borrowed from family. Motown produced the Supremes, who had been called the Primettes. He molded the Temptations from the Distants, and signed Gladys Knight and the Pips, Martha and the Vandellas, the Four Tops, Marvin Gaye, and Stevie Wonder. He had captured the best talents in the country.

Earl G. Graves is a remarkable entrepreneur. He attended Morgan State University. In 1970 he formed the *Black Enterprise* magazine, which has grown into the major African American business magazine in the country. Since that time he has been involved in numerous business ventures including the purchasing of the Pepsi-Cola franchise for Washington, DC, in conjunction with his partner, Earvin "Magic" Johnson. The list of African American corporate executives who have led companies like Honeywell, American Express, Fedex, Xerox, Time-Warner, and numerous other big-board entities is long and growing. In effect, a strong managerial class has entered the structure of the African American middle class and changed the dynamics for the American nation.

Other African Americans are recognized for their intellectual, scientific, and artistic, gifts demonstrating that the achievements of African Americans are much broader and deeper than some would have us believe. Mae Jemison, Cornel West, Maulana Karenga, Asa Hilliard, Ben Carson, Iyanla Vanzant, Henry Louis Gates Jr, Wynton Marsalis, Lewis Gordon, Manning Marable, as well as Common, Khnum and Dead Prez, NAS, Tupac, Public Enemy, Mos Def, among hundreds of others are now household names. The hip hoppers have taken the music to a new level and their scene is now merging one form with another form. The poets of the contemporary period are the rappers. They are the singers, the ones who "tell us what time it really is," according to Big D. Artists with names like Tupac, 50 Cent, Lil' Wayne, and Notorious B.I.G. created emotional sensations that captivated masses of young people and created an entire community of hip hoppers devoted to the latest in the culture. M. K. Asante Jr writes in his book *It's Bigger than Hip Hop* that "Hip hop like the Black musical oxygen that preceded it—blues, gospel, jazz, soul—cannot be looked at in a vacuum because the artists owe their lives to the context of their births."[24] What Asante Jr recognizes is the fact that contemporary hip hop artists are indebted to Muddy Waters, Aretha Franklin, Billie Holiday, Ray Charles, James Brown, Ethel Waters, Stevie Wonder, and John Coltrane among others. No art is without antecedent in the African American community. So the accomplishments of African American people are lined up like lights on a dark street where aura succeeds shadow, one after the other.

One can say that the achievements in the arts are not without their counterparts in the sciences. This is especially true in astronautic sciences. There are now more than twenty African American astronauts. Following Dr Bernard Harris' historic walk in space on February 10, 1995, Winston Scott and Robert Curbeam and others have made multiple walks in space. African Americans are visible in every aspect of space exploration, information technology, and nanotechnology. Dedicated and skilled scientists are found in every American sector. Charles Drew, Percy Julian, and Meredith Gourdine have inspired organizers of large laboratories in chemistry and biology. Gourdine's work in electro-gas dynamics, Julian's in the discovery of cortisone, and Charles Drew in blood plasma and blood transfusion methodologies are not only historic but phenomenal, given the racial ignorance with which they had to deal. Ernest Just, the first truly important American cell biologist, was not only an African American but an African American who had to overcome the barriers of race and the burdens of white animosity and ignorance. Just succeeded despite the spikes placed in his path to science, and his success inspired numerous other African scientists from the surgeon Ben Carson to the biologist Fatimah Jackson.

In athletics, perhaps more than any other field, the African American has excelled since the breakdown of Jim Crow sports. African American athletes are found in nearly all world-class athletic competitions. The list of world-class athletes and their sports is too long to

Figure 11.2
Sugar Ray Robinson, pound-for-pound called the greatest boxer who ever lived. Image courtesy of Charles L. Blockson Afro-American Collection, Temple University Libraries.

discuss in a history book. However, consider Sammy Sosa, Ken Griffey Jr, Venus Williams, Serena Williams, Jacqueline Joyner-Kersee, Eldrick "Tiger" Woods, Althea Gibson, Arthur Ashe, Michael Jordan, Kobe Bryant, Bill Russell, Bernard Hopkins, Sugar Ray Robinson, Sugar Ray Leonard, Joe Louis, Lebron James, Allen Iverson, and Shaquille O'Neal as a few symbols of excellence.

At the beginning of the twenty-first century Muhammad Ali's daughter, Khalilah Ali, became one of the first women boxers to popularize boxing among women. In politics, numerous elected officials attest to the power of the vote and the eagerness with which African Americans have entered the arena of civic responsibility. By 2010, African Americans held more than 12,100 elective offices in the United States, including the presidency of the United States. While this number reflects a growing willingness by African Americans to be involved in the political process, it is still only about 1 percent of all elected officials. African Americans constitute nearly thirteen percent of the American population. In science, there are hundreds of active practitioners in every branch of human sciences. In law, African Americans have made steady progress in the legal field. In art and literature, works of painters, sculptors, writers and filmmakers excel in almost all genres or categories. Toni Morrison, Alice Walker, Charles Fuller, and August Wilson are among the most powerful writers in contemporary literature. Wilson established himself as one of the greatest dramatists of his era with a startlingly successful series of ten plays about African American life. He won two Pulitzer Prizes for drama to his credit.

Wesley Snipes' *A Great and Mighty Walk*, documenting the life of John Henrik Clarke, is a monument to the late historian. Other filmmakers such as Spike Lee, John Singleton, and Gordon Parks have made contributions to the flow of African American history.

Hollywood remains a bastion of whiteness but it is slowly opening up to African American artists. Spike Lee and John Singleton remain prominent names among directors, but it is in the arena of acting that blacks continue to distinguish themselves. Carl Franklin, Charles Burnett, Tyler Perry, Halle Berry, and Eddie Murphy have made successful feature movies much like Singleton and Lee have done during the past twenty years as directors. There are some actors who are regularly cast in movies, not all of them made by African Americans. Will Smith and Denzel Washington are two of the most prominent actors but Morgan Freeman, Whitney Houston, Whoopi Goldberg, Wesley Snipes, Ruby Dee, and the late Ossie Davis remain among the leaders in successful Hollywood performances. One abiding difficulty is that Hollywood has very few roles for African American females apart from stereotypical parts. There are a few major talents who do succeed in getting work. Perhaps Halle Berry or Beyoncé, of the contemporary beauties, rival the attractiveness of Lena Horne, Dorothy Dandridge, and Cicely Tyson of earlier generations, but the skill, talent, style, and presence of the older actors have endured as classic for many years.

Not since the early days of Sidney Poitier has an African America male actor commanded as much attention as Denzel Washington. He has chosen excellent characters to demonstrate the breadth of his showmanship as an actor. From playing Malcolm X to Hurrricane Carter, from commanding submarines to directing wars against evil, Washington has been all over the movie screen. Yet he has remained one of the most enigmatic actors of all time, protecting his own privacy and that of his family from the spotlight of Hollywood. Admired as an actor and a person, Denzel Washington has become one of the most durable of black stars.

Figure 11.3 Sidney Poitier, phenomenal actor. Image courtesy of Charles L. Blockson Afro-American Collection, Temple University Libraries.

Conclusion

The preceding chapter has shown the extremely complex and dynamic universe of African American activities from the 1960s to the early part of the twenty-first century. It is a large swath of the rich history of African Americans but one could hardly write a history of this period without examining the role of Black Studies in the nation's educational system. Without Black Studies agitation, the nation would be different. In fact, when Nathan Hare ran the Black Studies department at San Francisco State University he became the first modern public intellectual among African American academics, defining and agitating, explaining and creating a strong academic base for studying phenomena from the standpoint of Africans. But while Black Studies appears to have dominated this era, this was not the case because the artists, in every genre, were making their marks as well.

Playwrights such as August Wilson, Ed Bullins, Charles Fuller, and scores of others stormed the stage with new insights into the intricacies of African American life. The chapter shows that as David Dinkins was governing New York City as its first black mayor, Toni Morrison was on an award-winning path as one of America's best novelists, winning the Nobel Laureate for fiction, and black men were stirred to action by the call for a Million Man March on Washington. Rarely had African Americans descended upon the capital city with such enthusiasm. There had been the 1963 March on Washington, which is said to have attracted 250,000, but the Million Man March brought more than one million men. From 1989 to 2008, African Americans were in an intense state of searching for linkages inside and outside of the United States. Oprah Winfrey discovered that her DNA took her to the Kpelle people of Liberia, and others, lesser known, paid thousands of dollars to discover their likely places of origin. Moreover, this period of great international activity and saw the emergence of Afrocentricity International as the most ambitious unity project since the Honorable Marcus Garvey attempted it.

Additional Reading

Bogle, Donald. *Brown Sugar: Eighty Years of America's Black Female Superstars*. New York: Crown Publishers, 1980.

Drake, St. Clair and Horace R. Cayton. *Black Metropolis: A Study of Negro Life in a Northern City*. New York: Harper and Row, 1962.

Karenga, Maulana. *Introduction to Black Studies*. Los Angeles: University of Sankore Press, 1993.

Levine, Lawrence. *Black Culture and Black Consciousness: Afro-American Folk Thought from Slavery to Freedom*. New York: Oxford University Press, 1977.

Lott, Tommie L. *The Invention of Race: Black Culture and the Politices of Representation*. Malden, MA: Blackwell, 1999.

Patton, Sharon F. *African American Art*. New York: Oxford University Press, 1998.

Schwartz, Peggy and Murray Schwartz. *The Dance Claimed Me: A Biography of Pearl Primus*. New Haven, CT: Yale University Press, 2011.

Chapter Time Markers

An Unfinished Agenda 12

Important Terms and Names

Shirley Sherrod

Barack Obama

Mumia Abu Jamal

Dante Carver

Aaron Vessup

Kenneth Gamble

Charles Fuller

Walter P. Lomax

An Array of Challenges

The robust African American narrative has taken many routes to the present, but the journey is not over. Take the example from a Chattanooga, Tennessee, courtroom. In February 2000 a judge overturned the rape conviction of Ed Johnson, ninety-four years after Johnson was lynched by an angry white mob as police stood silently by. Johnson had been convicted of raping a white woman in 1906. He had won a stay of execution from the U.S. Supreme Court on the grounds that he had not received a fair trial from the all-white jury. The following night he was dragged from his cell by a mob of white men who demanded that he confess to the rape. Johnson told them, "God bless you all, I am innocent." During the twentieth century scores of black men were lynched for crimes that they did not commit.[1]

Geronimo Ja Jiga Pratt, a former Black Panther leader from Los Angeles, died at his farm in Tanzania in May 2011 at the age of sixty-two. Pratt was arrested and falsely convicted of murder in 1971 because of lies told against him by an undercover agent during the trial. He was held in prison until 1997, when he was released. Pratt had maintained his innocence for twenty-seven years, claiming that he was nearly 400 miles away when the murders happened. He was awarded $4.2 million for false arrest, and while declaring that he held no animosity, immediately made preparations to live in East Africa. Pratt and many other blacks who struggled to expand democracy and increase freedom were often taken for common criminals because they argued against the marginalization of African Americans.

Yet the steadfastness of the warriors for freedom brought some victories in places like Mississippi; the *New York Times* on February 27, 2000 published "Student Body at Ole Miss Elects First Black Leader" about the election of the first black student body president. Although events such as this election were commonplace throughout the United States during this era, the fact that Ole Miss elected a black student body president challenged the reigning notions of black inferiority in a state that had one of the most severe histories of racial domination. Of course, Mississippi is not alone in its history of race oppression and even into the twenty-first century there are cases where negative racial sentiments are still expressed at the national level.

Consider the 2010 Shirley Sherrod incident, where a conservative blogger sent Fox News a modified video clip of Shirley Sherrod, a low-level United States agricultural officer, speaking about racism to an NAACP conference. Sherrod was heard saying in the speech, which had been given twenty years earlier, that she had some emotions over a white man asking her help when she knew that black people had been treated so badly by whites. This clip was disseminated with the implication that she was racist against whites.

The outpouring of vitriol against Sherrod forced the head of the Department of Agriculture, Tom Vilsack, to ask for her immediate resignation. The NAACP reacted quickly, saying that Sherrod should lose her job. Other progressives joined with conservatives in attacking Shirley Sherrod. However, when the full forty-minute speech was viewed it was clear that she was not a racist but had begun her speech explaining how she felt as a young officer, then explaining how she arrived at the position of believing that racism was wrong, and that everyone should be treated the same. When this was explained and the video viewed, many people and organizations, including the government, had to apologize to Sherrod. Indeed, she was offered another job at the Department of Agriculture and President Barack Obama called her personally and apologized. What these incidents show is that there are still contradictory actions in the country even while the course of African American history is on the upward swing.

Even so, the nagging issues of economic justice and police brutality still haunt the African American community. African Americans still earn far less than whites and the net worth of the average African American family is far below that of the white family. Between 1992 and 2000 the United States experienced the longest period of prosperity without a recession and yet the unemployment of the African American community remained around 10 percent. It is no wonder that President Clinton was moved to call for a racial initiative at the 1997 NAACP convention. He wanted to promote "racial healing" in order to bring African Americans and white Americans closer to a true national dialogue. The eminent African American historian John Hope Franklin was asked by President Clinton in 1997 to head "One America: The President's Initiative on Race." This great scholar had been named in 1978 by *Who's Who in America* as one of eight Americans who had made a particularly significant contribution to society. His credentials were impeccable, yet even Professor Franklin's commission could not deliver the transforming bullet that would reshape society. Racism had to be rooted out at the grassroots, at the elementary schools, in the religious institutions, and in the homes.

However, President Obama on July 30, 2010 told the Urban League meeting in Washington, DC, that the discourse on race should not be directed by the President's Office but should be held over the kitchen table and at the barbershops and in the basements of meeting places by the ordinary people. This question of race and racism is not simply a presidential matter; it is profoundly a matter for the entire nation. To the degree that such a conversation can be generated, it will introduce a more serious discourse among the ordinary people, many of whom harbor racial animosities and do not know how they have acquired them or from whence they have come. Tim Wise, Erika Vora, Sidney Wilhelm, and Joe Feagin are some of the white scholars and authors who have tried to rid the country of racism by raising the hard questions that often lurked in the most inaccessible places in the minds of the common people. While some of the more liberal professors have been seen as encouraging intercultural and interracial communication, African Americans have seen the police as an institution as a protector of racist beliefs.

Confrontations between the police, often seen as occupying forces by the African American community, and black males have long been at crisis levels. Hatreds built up over the years because fear, guilt, and mistrust often boil over in society. The televised beating of Rodney King in 1991 by the Los Angeles police brought calls for punishment of the police. The exoneration of the officers brought about one of the most intense uprisings in an urban community in twenty years. African Americans could not believe their eyes. They had seen Rodney King beaten with batons by several officers while he lay on the ground. How could they get off? Many African Americans believed that justice for the black man was not to be found in America. However, in 1994 a jury did award Rodney King $3.4 million for the beating he suffered. Of course, freedom is better than money.

The case of Wesley Cook, who goes by the name of Mumia Abu Jamal, in Philadelphia became an international *cause célèbre*. Mumia was a well-respected journalist, a father, a husband, and a former member of the Black Panther Party. As was discussed in the previous chapter, he was accused of shooting to death a policeman, Daniel Faulkner, on a corner in downtown Philadelphia on the night of December 8, 1981. Mumia had maintained his innocence from the day he was arrested. He was convicted in 1982 and sentenced to death. A hearing was held in which lawyers for Mumia indicated that they had evidence of false testimony in the previous trial. The judge, Albert Sabo, who had a reputation for sending more people to the death sentence than any judge at the time, ruled against the appeal. The Pennsylvania state court denied an appeal in 1999.

The Burning of Black Churches

Writing for the *New World Outlook* for September–October, 1999, Sandra Peters said, "Hate, violence, racism, religious intolerance, prejudice, and bigotry—these words have been used to characterize the burnings and desecrations of churches or other houses of worship during the 1990s and earlier decades. However, our understanding of the depth of violation caused by these attacks broadens considerably if we use an expanding lens—a lens that amplifies civil rights and views hate as a violation of human rights."[2]

An outbreak of church burnings during the 1990s caused consternation and considerable anger in the African American community. Who would stoop so low as to desecrate a church, some would ask. But in a society where synagogues and churches reflect an emphasis on morality and a common humanity, those who oppose those values seek to destroy churches and synagogues.

Many programs were instituted to rebuild churches in the late 1990s. Some of these programs have been remarkable because of the human relations that have gone into the process of rebuilding. For example, a project attracting volunteers rebuilt the Apostle Faith Church of Jesus, an African American church in Indiantown, Florida, in an area that was considered an economic backwater region of the state. Some churches received grants from charitable organizations to rebuild their sanctuaries. African Americans led the way in rebuilding over one hundred churches that had been bombed or burned to the ground in the 1990s. There is still a long way to go before we African Americans achieve the kind of freedom and liberation hoped for by generations of our enslaved ancestors. Nevertheless, Benjamin Quarles said it best: "it is the centrality of the Afro-American experience that makes its past so significant, a past that has sobering but redemptive quality for our nation."[3]

Nevertheless, the centrality of the African American experience is one that must be asserted each day because America is not a static idea but a dynamic project, and each day there are individuals, domestic or foreign, who live in this society without any rational understanding of African American history. In New York, a city that still remains at the heart of African American protest against injustices, the names of Charles Barron, James McIntosh, Leonard Jeffries, James Smalls, Solomon Goodrich, Julius Garvey, Viola Plummer, Shakur Afrikanus, Camille Yarbrough, Betty Dopson, Donald Smith, Herb Boyd, James Turner, Omowale Clay, Adelaide Sanford, and Alton Maddox have become international symbols of righteous anger against all forms of racial and social injustice. Some, like Alton H. Maddox Jr, who defended Tawana Brawley, a young African American woman who accused police of sexually abusing her, paid an extraordinary price for aggressively going after the law enforcement officers. Maddox, who was born in Newnan, Georgia, in 1945, and educated at Howard University and Boston College Law School, began practicing law in 1976 and immediately assumed the role of defender of the disdained. The New York State Supreme Court suspended his legal license in 1990 because he failed to appear before a disciplinary board to answer charges of unprofessional conduct. Maddox's circumstance caused an enormous outpouring of African American support for him and he soon became the inspiration and hero of the United African Movement. Few attorneys have ever taken on the burden to defend clients more directly and personally than Alton Maddox. The New York City Council supported his reinstatement in 2006.

Activists of the new century do not come only from the legal ranks; they have also been physicians, educators, bus drivers, authors, nurses, construction workers, and priests, but they have all been active in support of human dignity. Who are the real heroes of a nation? Those ardent defenders of individual and collective freedom who are willing to risk their careers and lives to make justice substantive and to instill equality with content are the true heroes of a nation whose laws insist on liberty. What is the meaning of America as seen through the eyes of African people? Who constitutes the matter of a rational political text written in the lives of active votarists?

Local leaders emerge from the cauldrons of regional economic and political pressures but often assume national dimensions. Such is the case with Walter P. Lomax in Philadelphia, one-time physician to Martin Luther King Jr. There are hundreds of cases in other cities that might be cited for this national trend, but the Lomax example is particularly important for its historic dimensions. Walter P. Lomax was born in 1933 in South Philadelphia. He became a medical doctor working for three decades in the community where he was born. His practice grew to more than twenty doctors when he established Lomax Health Systems, concentrating on health care and recruiting physicians to supplement the staff in the city prison system. By 1994 he was able to purchase the plantation where his great-grandmother was enslaved, in King William County, Virginia. It is a property with grave sites dating to 1732, just a little over one hundred years after Africans landed in Jamestown. What singles Walter Lomax out for merit as a historical figure, however, is the fact that he excelled at his practice, leaped at the chance to revise the historical text of African people by purchasing the plantation where his ancestors served, and returned numerous resources to his community through communication stations, family businesses, and venture capital for promising and talented African American enterprises. This method of protest and construction is the principal mode of change in the economic condition of the black community. When the economic action is joined with political activism it creates multiple avenues for social and cultural advancement because in the final analysis it is the control of resources, as in the securing and direction of resources, that allows the development and advancement of communities.

Toward a Global Presence

In addition to the increasingly flexible expressions of African American culture in domestic economic development, the last twenty-five years have seen many African Americans seeking their fortunes and objectives in international areas. For example, Aaron Vessup, a retired professor from Elgin Community College, took his teaching and writing skills to China, where he immediately became an honored teacher of English in Changsha University in Hunan, and then at Jilin University in Changchun. He has taught in China since 2005 and has been the recipient of several awards for his work. Vessup is also a distinguished author of five books, including *Beyond Cultural Anxieties*, and a professional photographer. There is also Dante Carver, a native of New York, who decided to emigrate to Japan to follow his dreams. By 2010 Dante Carver had become the number one TV commercial actor in Japan, breaking through the racial barriers that have prevented many non-Japanese from ascending the ladder of success in the country. Carver's experience demonstrates that the African American is willing to travel to other lands to discover success. In 2008 Douglas Ashby taught in Bangkok, Thailand, working for corporations such as Sony Vector, Toyota, and Hewlett-Packard. Like many African American educators in Asia, Douglas Ashby taught the English language. The African American presence in Asia comes much later than that presence in Europe.

Most African Americans went to England, France, Russia, and Sweden, although there is evidence of Africans in other Western European countries. Sweden's most famous African person, Adolf Badin, originally came from the Danish colony of St Croix, in what is now the United States Virgin Islands, during the period of enslavement. He was taken to Sweden in 1747, educated in the royal court, made an emissary of Queen Lovisa Ulrika, and was the protector of King Gustav III, with whom he was raised in the palace. However, the great bulk of African Americans who entered Sweden did so as artists and musicians during the 1950s and 1960s. Later there would be a sizable population of blacks arriving in Sweden during the Black Power Era. More than one hundred African American and African Caribbean artists, singers, dancers, actors, and filmmakers lived in Sweden during the 1970s. Among the most famous were Jack Jordan, who produced "Georgia-Georgia," in 1972, and anti-war journalist and activist Sherman Adams, but Huey Newton, Bobby Seale, and Stokely Carmichael all had limited stints in Sweden. Two deserters from the Vietnam War, Ray Jones and Terry Whitmore, were some of the first blacks to enter Sweden in protest at the war. Jack Jordan, the filmmaker, spent $200,000 to open a restaurant, "The Best of Harlem," in Stockholm. It failed after three months because of a disagreement with the Swedish chef. Thus, African Americans in Sweden, as in other European nations, did not necessarily find total acceptance.

France has been the magnet for African American visitors for two centuries. In fact, nearly 50,000 Africans left Louisiana for France in the two decades after Napoleon sold the territory to the United States. Since slavery did not end in the United States until 1865, blacks who traveled to France in the early nineteenth century went in search for freedom. Nevertheless, the pull of the French Revolution was so strong that after World War I many blacks remained in the country and became citizens. Jazz entered Paris in the 1920s, with traveling musicians coming to play to the increasingly large communities of Africans. Famous African Americans, in addition to Josephine Baker, who found their lives enriched and who enriched life in France were jazzman Sidney Bechet, guitarist Mickey Baker, writers James Baldwin and Richard Wright, painter Henry Ossawa Tanner, author Barbara Chase-Riboud, and the world's first black military pilot, Eugene Bullard. Thousands of African Americans have lived or live in Paris, making it the first city of African American art in Europe. While Britain has attracted African Americans as well, the city of London, home to many African Americans, has never possessed the draw of Paris for black Americans.

The Soviet Union also had an impact on the movement of African Americans. Some African Americans found in the promise of the Russian Revolution of 1917 the possibility of a society without racism. Others went to the Soviet Union to escape the deep poverty of the Great Depression that had destroyed the market economy. Among this number of African Americans who migrated to the Soviet Union in the quest for a better economic life was a young actor. Lloyd Patterson, a twenty-two-year-old African American, who married the theatre artist Vera Ippolitovna Aralova soon after he arrived in Moscow, believed that the Soviet Union offered him a chance to advance in his art without facing racism. Patterson and Aralova had three children; the oldest, born in Moscow on July 17, 1933, was named James Lloydovich Patterson. As a baby, James Lloydovich appeared in the popular Soviet film *Circus* in 1936, the first child of African descent to appear in a Soviet movie. He was cast as a biracial child of an interracial couple being raised in the egalitarian manner of the new Soviet society.

Vera evacuated her children, James Lloydovich and his siblings, to the eastern part of the country once the Germans invaded the Soviet Union. Lloyd Patterson, who had a position as an English radio reporter with Soviet radio, remained in Moscow and died during the German bombardment of the city in 1942. However, Lloyd's son, James Lloydovich, became a member of the Komsomol and graduated from Riga Nakhimov Naval School, a military academy for high school boys, in 1951. Patterson became an excellent cadet and later trained in St Petersburg (then Leningrad) as a submariner. He was commissioned as an officer of the Soviet Navy and given command with the Black Sea Fleet in 1955. By 1961 he had begun to write poetry and published a book of poems called *Russia*. When he left the navy in 1963 he published a collection called *Africa*. After graduating from the Maxim Gorky Literature Institute in 1964 Patterson wrote on racism in the United States, the space age, civil rights demonstrations, and other subjects. In addition to *Russia* and *Africa*, Patterson became well known for *Chronicles of the Left Hand*, *The Red Lily*, *Birth of the Rain*, *Interaction*, and *Winter Swallows*. In 1987 Patterson had written enough poetry and other works to be granted entry into the Union of Writers of the USSR. During the tremendous changes occurring in his own country in the 1990s, James Lloydovich and his mother immigrated to his father's homeland, the United States.

It should be obvious that the presence of African Americans in different parts of the world means that the influence of African Americans eventually shades the discourse on culture and identity in the adopted nations. In Africa, for example, the large colonies of African Americans in Ghana, Senegal, Nigeria, Zimbabwe, Tanzania, and South Africa are involved in music, business, art, filmmaking, painting, dancing, and research. There is no wonder that this very global community has engaged in disseminating African and African American culture in a dynamic manner. With the election of President Barack Obama, the worldwide African American community joined in pride with the domestic black community to share a political achievement that raises the bar for everyone. From Adolf Badin to Barack Obama may be more than two centuries, but whether in Europe, Asia, Africa, South America, or Australia, wherever African Americans live, the history of the people is still being written in their incredible contributions to their societies.

President Barack Hussein Obama

The campaign for the presidency in 2008 was extraordinarily exciting for millions of Americans and people around the world. In fact, no political candidacy had ever attracted as many African Americans as Obama's campaign. When it was finally announced that Barack Obama, Democratic senator from Illinois, had defeated the chameleonic Arizona Republican senator John McCain to become the forty-fifth president of the United States, many people felt that the journey of liberation had ended. Celebrations took place not only in the United States, but also throughout the world, especially in Africa, as a son of Africa was elected to the highest office in the United States of America.

Barack Obama's stride to the White House had been quick and certain, with the candidate not missing a step toward his goal. He had won the hearts of the Democratic Party with an electrifying speech at the 2004 convention. His eloquence and charisma had established him as a major force in the political pantheon of the Democratic Party. It would take him only four years to consolidate his base and launch his thrust for the White House. Obama, with a black father, Barack Hussein Obama, and a white mother, Ann Dunham Stanley, one from the Luo ethnic community of Kenya and the other from Kansas, had defied the irrationality of racism in the United States to become the first black president of the strongest nation on the earth. The narrative of the new president's origin was repeated in the media as a unique American story. President Obama was born on August 8, 1961 in Honolulu, Hawaii.

While progressives applauded the election of Barack Obama to the presidency, some citizens went so far to suggest that the election would lead to a post-racial America, by which they meant that race would no longer have any value in the American nation. This thesis was tested several times during the first 200 days of Obama's presidency as some protesters against his health bill initiative succumbed to the temptation to introduce negative racial tones in their demonstrations. By the time the bill was passed into law, Obama had spent a great deal of political capital; nevertheless, he had managed against his enemies and all odds to achieve something that had proved elusive in the past. Those who had wishful thinking about America overcoming racism would prove to be wrong, but what was right was the fact that race was beginning to have a decreasing influence on the fundamental political issues of the national life of the United States. To others, the election of Barack Obama was the epitome of racial progress. They would have a point, but the election would neither bring about a post-racial society nor would it mean that hatred and bitterness about race had disappeared. On the other hand, no cynic could doubt the importance of an election where many young whites, African Americans, Mexican Americans, Asian Americans, and women would combine to create an energetic political coalition to elect the first black president.

Establishing a Tradition of Electoral Politics

Since 1970 thousands of African Americans have been elected to various posts in legislative, judicial, and executive offices throughout the nation. In fact, there were 1,469 black elected officials in 1970. By 2001 the number of black elected officials had reached 9,101.[4] By 2008 the number of black elected officials had passed 15,000. This rapid progress toward participation laid the basis for campaigns for the presidency. There were several black candidates for president or vice president before Barack Obama, including Angela Davis, Shirley Chisholm, Lenora Fulani, Jesse Jackson, Carol Mosely-Braun, J. C. Watt, and Al Sharpton. Most of these individuals entered either the Democratic or Republican primaries, but some were candidates of third parties. The vast majority of African Americans are registered Democrats and most of the candidates have been Democrats. However, each of these candidates had a defined agenda, mainly social, that spoke to the issues of race and discrimination in American society or, as in the case of Watt, Davis, and Fulani, articulated strong partisan issues of party politics outside of the usual race and cultural discourse.

The first serious black candidate for the presidency was a woman, Shirley Chisholm, who was also the first African American congresswoman, and a powerful representative for New York. Those who followed her believed that a person should be able to run for the presidency regardless of race or gender. They also accepted the fact that there were so many whites who believed in the inferiority of blacks that it would be hard for a black person to be elected to the presidency. This coin of campaign logic, nevertheless, was not enough to prevent very qualified candidates from running in the primaries or general elections. Their running, in some respects, broke down the barriers about black capabilities and opened the doors for wider ambitions and participation. Whites saw, some for the first time, blacks on the political platforms with whites in debate and discussion. None of the black candidates that ran for president was incompetent; each had the intellectual ability to be president, although their policies were often very different. They cleared the path for Barack Obama's candidacy in ways that had not happened before. They also opened the country up to the possibility of innovations in the discourse around the presidency.

With Shirley Chisholm, Jesse Jackson, Angela Davis, Lenora Fulani, Ron Daniels, and other blacks assuming that the post was within their capability if not their grasp, it was just a matter of time before an African American candidate would appear who would take on the conventional wisdom and beliefs of a nation and shatter them with his powerful rhetoric and brilliant intellect. It was said that Barack Obama may have been among the sharpest and most intelligent presidential candidates to have run for the office; whether or not that was true, what *was* true was that phenomenal challenges stared him in the face once he was elected.

When Barack Obama became president he faced several major problems simultaneously: (1) a budget that was out of control and a growing national deficit; (2) a military that could not support the political and military commitments made by the government; (3) a broken immigration policy; (4) an increasingly criminalized society with prisons being built at an accelerated rate; (5) failing education standards; (6) an excessively close relationship between the military and huge corporations; (7) the health care and housing needs of millions of citizens; (8) a loss of American moral leadership in the world because of deception, lies, and corruption in the national administration around the Iraq invasion; and (9) the persistence of income and wealth differentials between whites and African Americans.

On the wintry January day in 2009 when Barack Obama took the oath of office he may not have had, probably could not have had, a full appreciation of the severity of the budget and financial crisis facing the nation, the impending financial collapse, and the runaway speculation produced by the deregulation of the market. He was a rapid learner, however, and that allowed him to move toward a clearer picture of reality as president. He managed to place before Congress and the nation the most sweeping progressive reform agenda since the presidency of Franklin Delano Roosevelt. He would insist that there be a national health plan, although he was unable to get the votes to have the one for which the Democrats had campaigned. He would insist on creating a financial reform that would be transparent and clear to the consumers. In addition, he saved the economy from hemorrhaging with bankruptcies and closures when he took office by intervening in the financial process and introducing tighter rules and regulations. Obama's "Race to the Top" plan for schools sought to take the education department in a new direction. While it was criticized as not having enough money to pay for the programs, it did constitute a positive change in the system of rewards. Nevertheless, presidential administrations are often evaluated on forces that appear capricious, unexpected, and unanticipated. Just as President George W. Bush did not expect the September 11, 2001 attack on the World Trade Center and the Pentagon or the aftermath of the Katrina Hurricane in New Orleans, President Obama did not anticipate the flow of hundreds of thousands of barrels of oil into the Gulf of Mexico because of the British Petroleum well disaster. The best advice given to the administration was to avoid the mistake of President Bush during the Katrina crisis; the president had to gain control of the situation immediately. However, in the case of an oil leakage deep in the ocean floor it was not so easy to determine what action to take. There were no emergency plans for this disaster and each day the oil spilled into the Gulf meant that the president, although not directly responsible, was seen as attached to this tragedy. With the November 2010 mid-term elections looming, the Obama administration did everything it could to prevent the disaster from being charged to his office. Yet in reality voters have proven to be fickle and the fact that the leakage occurred on Obama's watch is an associative factor in the analysis of his presidency. One expects, however, that there will always be intervening factors, and sometimes the factors are extraordinarily useful to the administration.

Turbulence and Continuity

The year 2010 began with a tragedy of major proportions. The Haitian earthquake of January 12 changed African Americans perception of the interconnection of African populations in ways that had begun with the Katrina Hurricane. When thousands of people were buried in their homes, killed by falling buildings, and made homeless by the earthquake, African Americans felt a kinship with Haitians that was reminiscent of the spirit that connected people during the aftermath of Hurricane Katrina. Haiti is a special place for African Americans and has a unique position in the history of the world. As the second republic in the Americas, having gained its independence from France in 1804, Haiti has always been a lodestone for African people. The fact that it was isolated by European nations and forced to pay the French nation for the loss of their plantations and enslaved Africans robbed Haiti of the necessary resources to build its economy. The nation has suffered many crises during its history but none equaled the impact of the 2010 earthquake. The African American community was joined by the rest of the world in an outpouring of generosity that has rarely been exceeded. People in Haiti called for the return of their last democratically elected president, Jean-Bertrand Aristide, a man of profound courage and deep intellect. In the time of distress and at the moment of their gravest crises, the people yearned for the leader who had brought the nation together and who had twice been ousted from power by *coup d'état*. In exile in South Africa, the president of Haiti grieved with his suffering nation but there was no invitation, either from any world body or from the Haitian government, for him to return. African Americans such as Congresswoman Maxine Waters, Harry Belafonte, Danny Glover, Bill Fletcher, and Randall Robinson all supported the return of Aristide. The international spirit and commitment to assist Haiti relit the fire of Pan-African solidarity in the Americas. Jamaicans, Costa Ricans, Colombians, Cubans, and Dominicans came to the rescue of Haitians.

But the year saw the black unemployment rate leap through the window as more than fourteen percent of the black population was unemployed. President Obama succeeded, in the waning days of the summer of 2010, getting the Congress to support an extension of unemployment insurance, thereby saving millions of Americans from sinking under the burden of a lack of funds. In addition, Obama was able to secure the passage of several key bills during the lame duck session of Congress late in 2010.

Potentially one of the most far-reaching actions of 2010 was the census because it could determine the rate of increase in the population of blacks, the comparative level of population increase or decrease among various segments of the society, and the amount of resources the nation would have to spend in given regions. Which cities now have the largest concentrations of African Americans? Which states have the greatest percentage of middle-class blacks? These and a myriad of other questions are raised by the census. Yet the census, as always, had its political and symbolic dimension.

Because 56,000 blacks self-identified in 2000 as *Negroes*, the United States Census Bureau decided to use *Negro* as a designation in 2010. Of course, the politically conscious African Americans used the term *African*, which will probably mean, if the Census Bureau uses the same logic a decade later, that the term *African* will be the term of choice. Considered archaic, even anachronistic, the term *Negro* generated enormous resentment against the government, many blacks insisting that they would write in *African*. The census was expected to reveal that the African American population had reached 40 million.

The African population in the United States is only surpassed in Africa by Nigeria, Ethiopia, Sudan, Democratic Republic of the Congo, Kenya, and South Africa. All other African nations have fewer people of African descent. In the Americas, only the country of Brazil has a larger black population than the United States. The African American people, as a nation, would be more populous than the European nations of Poland, Canada, Australia, Greece, Hungary, or Portugal, among others. Yet as this narrative history of the global reach of the African American people has shown, the story is not merely about numbers but about a collective sense of responsibility and nobility born of the rugged journey framed at the hearth of difficult and demanding times. Thus, a vision of the possible, despite the crippling effects of the cataracts of racism, is tightly focused among some of the keepers of the dream whose journey, while not yet completed, will continue to inspire those who are the children of a hard-won freedom.

Conclusion

The globalization of American culture meant that African American experiences were also made available to a massive world audience. One of the attributes of the American culture is its ability to disseminate its ideas widely. African Americans had always been a people of several continents, whether Africa, Europe and America, or North America and South America, or Africa and Asia. This chapter shows the reader how the lives of Mumia Abu Jamal, Shirley Sherrod, Aaron Vessup, Walter Lomax, Charles Fuller, Lloyd Patterson, and others have been internationalized. Mumia Abu Jamal became a *cause célèbre* throughout the world because many people, especially in France and the United Kingdom, became convinced that he was not given a fair trial.

On the other hand, Aaron Vessup in China, Kevin Caudle in Germany, and Dante Carver in Japan are just a few examples of a new movement among younger African Americans to discover their careers, vocations, and futures on other continents. As in the case of these three individuals, the choice was private and personal. They were able to maneuver the rules and protocols of their host cultures to carve out a space for themselves. This means that they had to learn the language, master the etiquettes of the society, and establish good relationships with local people. Sizable populations of African Americans are now appearing in newer expatriate sites such as Salvador, Brazil; Guangzhou, China; Madrid, Spain; and Johannesburg, South Africa. In fact, the older sites of Paris, France; Accra, Ghana; Stockholm, Sweden; Dar es Salaam, Tanzania; and London, England have more established enclaves of African Americans but the newer sites appear to provide better opportunities for persons with information technology skills. African Americans can be found who speak French, Spanish, Russian, Twi, Kiswahili, Mandarin Chinese, Japanese, and Portuguese in almost every major American city. These linguistic skills provide new expatriates with useful tools for integrating into the host societies. Of course, everywhere African Americans reside in the world, they carry with them the memories of Harriet Tubman, Nat Turner, Frederick Douglass, Booker T. Washington, W. E. B. Du Bois, Sojourner Truth, Martin Luther King Jr, Marcus Garvey, Malcolm X, and now President Barack Obama, the most global of American presidents.

Additional Reading

Asante, Molefi Kete. *Maulana Karenga: An Intellectual Portrait*. Cambridge: Polity Press, 2010.

Asante, Molefi Kete and Ama Mazama, eds. *Encyclopedia of Black Studies*. Thousand Oaks, CA: Sage Publications, 2004.

Asante, Molefi Kete and Ama Mazama, eds. *Encyclopedia of African Religion*. Thousand Oaks, CA: Sage Publications, 2009.

Baldwin, James. *Notes of a Native Son*. New York: Dial, 1955.

Baldwin, James. *The Fire Next Time*. New York: Dial, 1963.

Baraka, Amiri. *The Autobiography of LeRoi Jones*. New York: Freundlich Books, 1984.

Foner, Philip. *The Black Panthers Speak*. Philadelphia: Lippincott, 1970.

Hay, Samuel A. *African American Theatre: A Historical and Critical Analysis*. Cambridge: Cambridge University Press, 1994.

Jones, LeRoi. *Home: Social Essays*. New York: William Morrow, 1966.

Muhammad, Khalil Gibran. *The Condemnation of Race*. Cambridge, MA: Harvard University Press, 2011.

Neal, Larry. *Visions of a Liberated Future: Black Arts Movement Writings*. New York: Thunder's Mouth Press, 1989.

Karenga, Maulana. *Introduction to Black Studies*. Los Angeles: University of Sankore Press, 2010.

Seale, Bobby. *Seize the Time*. New York: Random House, 1970.

Weiss, Nancy. *Whitney M. Young Jr and the Struggle for Civil Rights*. Princeton, NJ: Princeton University Press, 1989.

West, Cornel. *Race Matters*. Boston: Beacon, 1993.

Appendix I

A Chronology of African American History

1444	The Portuguese succeed in capturing unprotected Africans in Senegal
1482	Nana Kwame Ansah meet the Portuguese at Elmina
1488	Africans meet Columbus at Elmina
1570	20,000 Africans are already in Mexico
1594	Ahmed Baba, vice chancellor of the university at Sankore, is arrested by Arabs
1619	Twenty Africans arrive in Jamestown, Virginia
1641	Massachusetts becomes the first state to legalize perpetual enslavement
1663	Africans revolt against enslavement in Gloucester, Virginia
1664	All English colonies legalize African enslavement
1670	The French legalize slavery in all colonies
1676	Africans take a leading role in Bacon's Rebellion in Virginia
1680	One million Africans are in Spanish-held territories
1687	Africans run away to Florida from English colonies
1688	Africans and Quakers make first formal protest against slavery
1712	Africans in New York revolt against slavery, killing nine whites
1739	Violent African revolt in Stono, South Carolina, kills thirty white overseers
1741	Several Africans are executed for general insurrection against slavery
1760	Jupiter Hammons, of New York, publishes first writings by an African in North America
1775	Crispus Attucks is killed by the British at the start of the American Revolution
1777	Vermont is first state to abolish enslavement of Africans
1783	Massachusetts abolishes enslavement of Africans
1787	Richard Allen and Absalom Jones organize Free African Society in Philadelphia
1793	Richard Allen founds the African Methodist Episcopal Church
1800	Gabriel Prosser organizes a slave revolt in Richmond, Virginia
1804	Dessalines declares Haiti a Free Republic, first successful slave revolution in history
1808	Importation of Africans for enslavement is prohibited by law
1812	Twenty percent of the U.S. Navy is made up of Africans
1816	Andrew Jackson destroys Fort Apalachicola, occupied by Africans and Native Americans

1817   John Russwurm and Samuel Cornish organize against American Colonization Society

1821   Thomas Jennings is the first African to receive a patent for an invention, a dry cleaning machine

1822   Denmark Vesey organizes a revolt in Charleston, South Carolina

1827   John Russwurm and Samuel Cornish publish *Freedom's Journal*, first black newspaper

1829   David Walker writes a militant appeal to the colored citizens of the world

1831   Nat Turner leads the most successful revolt against slavery in Virginia

1839   Sengbe leads a revolt aboard the ship *Amistad*

1842   Henry Highland Garnett calls for Africans to revolt

1843   Sojourner Truth starts her journeys to tell the truth

1848   Harriet Tubman escapes from slavery in Maryland

1852   Institute for Colored Youth is founded in Philadelphia, forerunner of Cheyney University

1853   William Wells Brown publishes the novel *Clotel*, the first by an African in North America

1857   Supreme Court decides against rights for Africans in the Dred Scott decision

1859   John Brown leads raid on Harpers Ferry. Five blacks and twelve whites join him

1860   South Carolina secedes from the Union

1863   President Lincoln signs the Emancipation Proclamation

1865   John S. Rock, Boston attorney, admitted to practice at the Supreme Court

1865   General Grant accepts General Lee's surrender of the Confederacy, April 8, 1865

1867   Congress divides the Confederacy into military districts

1870   Richard Greener of Philadelphia becomes the first black graduate of Harvard

1871   Fisk Jubilee Singers begin national tour

1872   Charlotte Ray becomes first African American lawyer, graduating from Howard University

1876   Henry Flipper graduates from West Point

1878   Lewis Latimer works with Max Hiram to invent the incandescent lamp

1879   Pap Singleton leads Africans from Tennessee to Kansas

1880   Burrett Lewis becomes the first black jockey to win the Kentucky Derby

1881   Booker T. Washington opens Tuskegee

1893   Daniel Hale Williams performs first open-heart surgery

1895   W. E. B. Du Bois becomes the first African to receive a doctorate from Harvard

1905   Niagara Movement organized as forerunner to NAACP

1909   Du Bois and others found the National Association for the Advancement of Colored People

1909   Matthew Henson becomes the first human to reach the North Pole

1910   Jack Johnson becomes the heavyweight champion of the world

1915   Carter G. Woodson organizes the Association for the Study of Negro Life

1919   Eighty-three African Americans are lynched in the "Red Summer of Hate"

1920   Marcus Garvey convenes the international meeting of the UNIA in Harlem

1923   George Washington Carver receives the Spingarn Medal from NAACP

1923   Garrett Morgan invents the traffic light

1924   Asa Philip Randolph organizes the Brotherhood of Sleeping Car Porters

1931   Elijah Muhammad founds the Nation of Islam

1935	Mary McLeod Bethune founds the National Council of Negro Women
1936	Jesse Owens captures four Olympic medals
1937	Joe Louis wins the heavyweight title
1941	Charles Drew organizes the blood bank after developing technique to separate and preserve blood
1947	Jackie Robinson joins the Brooklyn Dodgers
1949	Wesley Brown is first African American to graduate from Annapolis Naval Academy
1950	Ralph Bunche wins Nobel Prize for Peace for mediating in Palestine
1954	U.S. Supreme Court decides in *Brown v. Topeka Board of Education* that separate but equal is invalid
1955	Emmett Till is kidnapped and murdered in Mississippi
1960	North Carolina A and T students stage first sit-ins in segregated stores
1962	James Meredith enters the University of Mississippi with federal troop protection
1963	250,000 people attend the March on Washington and hear King's "I have a Dream"
1964	Martin Luther King Jr receives Nobel Prize for Peace
1965	Malcolm X is assassinated
1966	Bobby Seale and Huey Newton start Black Panthers
1966	Maulana Karenga founds the Us Organization and Kawaida Movement
1966	Robert Weaver is first African American in the presidential cabinet as Secretary of Housing
1967	Thurgood Marshall is appointed to the Supreme Court
1968	Shirley Chisholm is first African American woman in House of Representatives
1969	Molefi Kete Asante becomes the editor of the *Journal of Black Studies*
1970	James Williams receives a doctorate in engineering from Cambridge University
1973	Coleman Young is elected mayor of Detroit
1974	Henry Aaron hits 715 homeruns to become the all-time leader
1978	Muhammad Ali becomes the first person to win heavyweight title three times
1979	Franklin Thomas is named head of Ford Foundation
1979	Arthur Lewis is named Nobel awardees for Economics
1982	Charles Fuller wins Pulitzer Prize for Drama for *A Soldier's Story*
1983	Guion Bluford becomes first African American in space
1984	Jesse Jackson, head of Operation Push, runs for Democratic nomination for presidency
1987	Mae Jemison becomes first African American woman in space
1988	Toni Morrison wins Pulitzer Prize for the novel *Beloved*
1988	Temple University receives first PhD class for African American program
1989	David Dinkins elected first African American mayor of New York
1989	Douglas Wilder elected first African American governor of Virginia
1993	Toni Morrison wins Nobel Prize for Literature
1995	More than a million black men meet in Washington
1997	One million black women meet in Philadelphia
1997	Tiger Woods wins the Masters golf tournament
2004	Molefi Kete Asante and Ama Mazama publish *Encyclopedia of Black Studies*
2008	Barack Obama becomes first African American elected to the presidency
2010	Charles Fuller publishes the novel *Snatch*, to rave reviews

Appendix II

Some Notable African Americans in Space

Arnaldo Tamayo Mendez
b. January 29, 1942
Soyuz 38
(September 18, 1980)
Cuban cosmonaut, first person of African
descent in space

Guion Bluford
b. November 22, 1942
STS-8 (August 30, 1983)
STS-61-A (October 30, 1985)
STS-39 (April 28, 1991)
STS-53 (December 2, 1992)
First African American in space

Ronald McNair
b. October 21, 1950
STS-41-B (February 3, 1984)
STS-51-L
(January 28, 1986)
Died on *Challenger*

Frederick D. Gregory
b. January 7, 1941
STS-51-B
(April 29, 1985)
STS-33
(November 22, 1989)
STS-44 (November 24, 1991)
Acting NASA Administrator from 2005

Charles F. Bolden
b. August 19, 1946
STS-61-C
(January 12, 1986)
STS-31 (April 24, 1990)
STS-45 (March 24, 1992)
STS-60 (February 3, 1994)
NASA Administrator from 2009

Mae Jemison
b. October 17, 1956
STS-47 (September 12, 1992)
First African American woman in space

Bernard A. Harris Jr
b. July 18, 1953
STS-55 (April 26, 1993)
STS-63 (February 3, 1995)
First African American to walk in space

Winston E. Scott
b. August 6, 1950
STS-72 (January 11, 1996)
STS-87 (November 19, 1997)
Three space walks

Robert Curbeam
b. March 5, 1962
STS-85 (August 7, 1997)
STS-98 (February 7, 2001)

STS-116 (December 9, 2006)
Seven walks in space

Michael Phillip Anderson
b. December 25, 1959
STS-89 (January 22, 1998)
STS-107 (January 16, 2003)
Died on *Columbia*

Joan Higginbotham
b. August 3, 1964
STS-116 (December 9, 2006)

Alvin Drew
b. November 5, 1962
STS-118 (August 8, 2007)

Stephanie Williams
b. September 27, 1966
STS-121 (July 4, 2006)
STS-120 (October 23, 2007)

Appendix III

African American Inventors and Technologists

- James S. Adams—airplane propeller
- George E. Alcorn—semiconductors
- Virgie M. Ammons—fireplace damper tool
- Charles S. Bankhead—composition printing
- Benjamin Banneker—America's first clock
- James A. Bauer—coin changer
- Charles R. Beckley—folding chair
- Alfred Benjamin—scouring pads
- Miriam E. Benjamin—signal chair
- J. W. Benton—oil derrick
- Henry Blair—corn and cotton planters
- Sarah Boone—folding ironing board
- Otis Boykin—artificial heart stimulator
- Henrietta Bradbury—torpedo discharger
- Phil Brooks—disposable syringe
- Marie Van Brittan Brown—home security system
- Robert F. Bundy—signal generator
- J. A. Burr—lawn mower
- W. Montague Cobb—color chart of the human heart
- Cap B. Collins—portable electric light
- David N. Crosthwait—vacuum heating system
- Charles Richard Drew—blood bank
- Albert Y. Garner—flame retardant
- Sarah E. Goode—folding bed
- Meredith C. Gourdine—smoke control, electradyne paint spray gun
- Solomon Harper—thermostatic hair curlers
- Lincoln Hawkins—coatings for communication cable
- Edward Hawthorne—heart monitor, blood pressure control
- Dorothy E. Hoover—aeronautical research

- Harry C. Hopkins—hearing aid
- Thomas L. Jennings—dry-cleaning process
- Frederick M. Jones—truck refrigeration, starter generator, portable X-ray machine
- Percy Lavon Julian—glaucoma treatment, synthetic cortisone
- Ernest Everett Just—studies of cell division
- Samuel L. Kountz—improved kidney transplants
- Robert Benjamin Lewis—oakum picker
- J. L. Love—pencil sharpener
- Elijah J. McCoy—automatic locomotive lubricator
- James Winfield Mitchell—method of purifying chemicals
- Garret Augustus Morgan—gas mask, four-way traffic signal
- Benjamin T. Montgomery—boat propellor
- George Olden—postage stamp
- W. B. Purvis—fountain pen, machine to make paper bags
- J. W. Reed—dough roller and kneader
- Norbert Rillieux—sugar refiner
- G. T. Sampson—folding clothes dryer
- Dewey S. C. Sanderson—urinalysis meter
- C. B. Scott—street sweeper
- J. H. Smith—lawn sprinkler
- P. D. Smith—mechanical potato digger
- Richard Spikes—automatic carwash, car directional signals, automatic transmission, beer keg
- J. A. Sweeting—cigarette roller
- Stewart and Johnson—metal bending machine
- Lewis Temple—improved whaling harpoon
- Anthony Weston—improved threshing machine
- Daniel Hale Williams—first emergency open-heart surgery
- Ozzie S. Williams—radar search beacon
- J. R. Winter—fire escape ladder
- Granville T. Woods—railroad telegraph
- Louis Tompkins Wright—treatment for head and neck injuries

Appendix IV

African American Firsts

- **Local elected official:** John Mercer Langston, 1855, town clerk of Brownhelm Township, Ohio.
- **State elected official:** Alexander Lucius Twilight, 1836, the Vermont legislature.
- **Mayor of major city:** Carl Stokes, Cleveland, Ohio, 1967–1971. The first black woman to serve as a mayor of a major U.S. city was Sharon Pratt Dixon Kelly, Washington, DC, 1991–1995.
- **Governor (appointed):** P. B. S. Pinchback, served as governor of Louisiana from Dec. 9, 1872 to Jan. 13, 1873, during impeachment proceedings against the elected governor.
- **Governor (elected)** L. Douglas Wilder, Virginia, 1990–1994. The only other elected black governor has been Deval Patrick, Massachusetts, 2007–
- **U.S. Representative:** Joseph Rainey, became a congressman from South Carolina in 1870 and was re-elected four more times. The first black female U.S. representative was Shirley Chisholm, congresswoman, New York, 1969–1983.
- **U.S. Senator:** Hiram Revels, became senator from Mississippi from Feb. 25, 1870, to March 4, 1871, during Reconstruction; Edward Brooke became the first African American senator since Reconstruction, 1966–1979. Carol Moseley Braun became the first black woman senator, serving from 1992 to 1998 for the state of Illinois. (There have only been a total of five black senators in U.S. history: the remaining two are Blanche K. Bruce [1875–1881] and Barack Obama [2005–2008]).
- **U.S. cabinet member:** Robert C. Weaver, 1966–1968, Secretary of the Department of Housing and Urban Development under Lyndon Johnson; the first black female cabinet minister was Patricia Harris, 1977, Secretary of the Department of Housing and Urban Development under Jimmy Carter.
- **U.S. Secretary of State:** General Colin Powell, 2001–2004. The first black female Secretary of State was Condoleezza Rice, 2005–2009.
- **Major Party Nominee for President:** Senator Barack Obama, 2008. The Democratic Party selected him as its presidential nominee.
- **U.S. President:** Senator Barack Obama. Obama defeated Sen. John McCain in the

general election on November 4, 2008, and was inaugurated as the 44th president of the United States on January 20, 2009.

- **Editor, Harvard Law Review:** Charles Hamilton Houston, 1919. Barack Obama became the first president of the *Harvard Law Review.*
- **Federal Judge:** William Henry Hastie, 1946; Constance Baker Motley became the first black woman federal judge, 1966.
- **U.S. Supreme Court Justice:** Thurgood Marshall, 1967–1991. Clarence Thomas became the second African American to serve on the Court in 1991.
- **U.S. diplomat:** Ebenezer D. Bassett, 1869, became minister-resident to Haiti; Patricia Harris became the first black female ambassador (1965; Luxembourg).
- **U.S. Representative to the UN:** Andrew Young (1977–1979).
- **Nobel Peace Prize winner:** Ralph J. Bunche received the prize in 1950 for mediating the Arab–Israeli truce. Martin Luther King Jr became the second African American Peace Prize winner in 1964.
- **Combat pilot:** Georgia-born Eugene Jacques Bullard, 1917, denied entry into the U.S. Army Air Corps because of his race, served throughout World War I in the French armed forces. He received the Legion of Honor, France's highest honor, among many other decorations.
- **First Congressional Medal of Honor winner:** Sergeant William H. Carney for bravery during the Civil War. He received a Congressional Medal of Honor in l900.
- **General: Benjamin O. Davis Sr:** 1940–1948.
- **Chairman of the Joint Chiefs of Staff:** Colin Powell, 1989–1993.
- **First patent holder: Thomas L. Jennings:** 1821, for a dry-cleaning process. Sarah E. Goode, 1885, became the first African-American woman to receive a patent, for a bed that folded up into a cabinet.
- **MD degree:** James McCune Smith, 1837, University of Glasgow; Rebecca Lee Crumpler became the first black woman to receive an MD degree. She graduated from the New England Female Medical College in 1864.
- **Inventor of the blood bank:** Dr Charles Drew, 1940.
- **Heart surgery pioneer:** Daniel Hale Williams, 1893.
- **First astronaut:** Robert H. Lawrence Jr, 1967, was the first black astronaut, but he died in a plane crash during a training flight and never made it into space. Guion Bluford, 1983, became the first black astronaut to travel in space; Mae Jemison, 1992, became the first black female astronaut. Frederick D. Gregory, 1998, was the first African American shuttle commander.
- **College graduate (BA):** Alexander Lucius Twilight, 1823, Middlebury College; first black woman to receive a BA degree: Mary Jane Patterson, 1862, Oberlin College.
- **PhD:** Edward A. Bouchet, 1876, received a PhD from Yale University. In 1921, three individuals became the first U.S. black women to earn PhDs: Georgiana Simpson, University of Chicago; Sadie Tanner Mossell Alexander, University of Pennsylvania; and Eva Beatrice Dykes, Radcliffe College.
- **Rhodes Scholar:** Alain L. Locke, 1907.
- **First PhD created in African American Studies:** Dr Molefi Kete Asante, 1987, at Temple University
- **College president:** Daniel A. Payne, 1856, Wilberforce University, Ohio.

- **Ivy League president:** Ruth Simmons, 2001, Brown University.
- **Novelist:** Harriet Wilson, *Our Nig*, 1859
- **Poet:** Lucy Terry, 1746, "Bar's Fight." Her only surviving poem.
- **Poet (published):** Phillis Wheatley published *Poems on Various Subjects, Religious and Moral* in 1773.
- **Pulitzer Prize winner:** Gwendolyn Brooks, 1950, won the Pulitzer Prize in poetry.
- **Pulitzer Prize winner in Drama:** Charles Gordone, 1970, for his play *No Place to be Somebody*.
- **Nobel Prize for Literature winner:** Toni Morrison, 1993.
- **Poet Laureate:** Robert Hayden, 1976–1978; first black woman Poet Laureate: Rita Dove, 1993–1995.
- **Member of the New York City Opera:** Todd Duncan, l945.
- **Member of the Metropolitan Opera Company:** Marian Anderson, 1955.
- **Male Grammy Award winner:** Count Basie, 1958.
- **Female Grammy Award winner:** Ella Fitzgerald, 1958.
- **Principal dancer in a major dance company:** Arthur Mitchell, 1959, New York City Ballet.
- **First Oscar:** Hattie McDaniel, 1940, supporting actress, *Gone with the Wind*.
- **Oscar, Best Actor/Actress:** Sidney Poitier, 1963, *Lilies of the Field*; Halle Berry, 2001, *Monster's Ball*.
- **Oscar, Best Actress Nominee:** Dorothy Dandridge, 1954, *Carmen Jones*.
- **Film director:** Oscar Micheaux, 1919, wrote, directed, and produced *The Homesteader*, a feature film.
- **Hollywood director:** Gordon Parks directed and wrote *The Learning Tree* for Warner Brothers in 1969.
- **Network television show host:** Nat King Cole, 1956, "The Nat King Cole Show"; Oprah Winfrey became the first black woman television host in 1986, "The Oprah Winfrey Show."
- **Star of a network television show:** Bill Cosby, 1965, "I Spy."
- **Major league baseball player:** Jackie Robinson, 1947, Brooklyn Dodgers.
- **Elected to the Baseball Hall of Fame:** Jackie Robinson, 1962.
- **NFL quarterback:** Willie Thrower, 1953.
- **NFL football coach:** Fritz Pollard, 1922–1937.
- **Golf champion:** Tiger Woods, 1997, won the Masters golf tournament.
- **NHL hockey player:** Willie O'Ree, 1958, Boston Bruins.
- **World cycling champion:** Marshall W. "Major" Taylor, in 1899.
- **Wimbledon and the United States national tennis championships:** Althea Gibson. She won both tournaments twice, in 1957 and 1958. In all, Gibson won fifty-six tournaments, including five Grand Slam singles events. The first black male champion was Arthur Ashe, who won the 1968 U.S. Open, the 1970 Australian Open, and the 1975 Wimbledon championship.
- **Heavyweight boxing champion:** Jack Johnson, 1908.
- **Olympic gold medalist (Summer games; individual):** DeHart Hubbard, 1924, for the long jump; the first woman was Alice Coachman, winner of the high jump in 1948.

- **Olympic medalist (Winter games):** Debi Thomas, 1988, won the bronze in figure skating.
- **Olympic gold medalist (Winter games):** Vonetta Flowers, 2002, bobsled.
- **Olympic gold medalist (Winter games; individual):** Shani Davis, 2006, 1,000 m speedskating, and 2010.
- **Licensed Pilot:** Bessie Coleman, 1921.
- **Millionaire**: Madame C. J. Walker.
- **Billionaire:** Robert Johnson, 2001, owner of Black Entertainment Television; Oprah Winfrey, 2003.
- **Portrayal on a postage stamp:** Booker T. Washington, 1940 and 1956.
- **Explorer, North Pole:** Matthew A. Henson, 1909, accompanied Robert E. Peary on the first successful U.S. expedition to the North Pole.
- **Explorer, South Pole:** George Gibbs, 1939–1941 accompanied Richard Byrd.
- **Flight around the world:** Barrington Irving, 2007, from Miami Gardens, Florida, flew a Columbia 400 plane named *Inspiration* around the world in 96 days, 150 hours (March 23–June 27).

Notes

1 Time before the Time

1 Vincent Macaulay et al., Letters, *Science*, vol. 309, September 23, 2005, speak directly to this issue.

2 Ayele Bekerie, *Ethiopic, an African Writing System: Its Principles and History*. Trenton, NJ: Africa World Press, 1997.

3 Christy G. Turner II, "A dental anthropological hypothesis relating to the ethnogenesis, origin, and antiquity of the Afro-Asiatic language family: Peopling of the Eurafrican–South Asian Triangle IV," in John D. Bengston, ed., *In Hot Pursuit of Language in Prehistory: Essays in the Four Fields of Anthropology in Honor of Harold Crane Fleming*. Amsterdam: John Benjamins, 2008, pp. 17–23

4 Shomarka Keita, "Geography, selected Afro-Asiatic families, and Y chromosome lineage variation: An exploration in linguistics and phylogeography," in John D. Bengston, ed., *In Hot Pursuit of Language in Prehistory: Essays in the Four Fields of Anthropology in Honor of Harold Crane Fleming*. Amsterdam: John Benjamins, 2008, pp. 3–16

5 Miriam Maat Ka Re Monges, *Kush: The Jewel of Nubia*. Trenton, NJ: Africa World Press, 1997.

6 Monges, *Kush: The Jewel of Nubia*, pp. 56–61.

7 Robert Draper, "The black pharaohs," *National Geographic Magazine*, February, 2008. The assumption behind Draper's article is that most of the kings of Egypt were not black; this is a false assumption. In fact, all of the kings of Egypt were African, black by America's standards, with the few exceptions of the invaders into Africa. The Nubians were merely leaders of one African nation conquering another, just as the Germans might conquer the French and we would see it as one white nation overcoming another. The Egyptians and Nubians were of the same race, continental gene pool: African people.

8 Bruce Williams, "The lost pharaohs of Nubia," in Van Sertima, Ivan, ed., *Egypt Revisited*. New Brunswick, NJ: Transaction Publishers, 1991. Williams began studying hundreds of fragments of pottery, jewelry, stone vessels, and ceremonial objects such as incense burners, that had been recovered from the Qustul cemetery by Keith C. Seele, a professor at the University of Chicago, when the Aswan High Dam was being built. The cemetery dug up by Seele contained thirty-three tombs that were heavily plundered in ancient times. Williams interpreted the incense burner as manifesting the first elements of a monarchy with its palace façade.

9 James Henry Breasted, *Ancient Records of Egypt Part I*.

10 Herodotus, *Histories*, Book II.

11 Molefi Kete Asante, *Classical Africa*. Saddle Creek, NJ: PPG, 1993, p. 28.

12 Asante, *Classical Africa*, p. 34.

13 Asante, *Classical Africa*, p. 45.

14 Asante, *Classical Africa*, p. 57.

15 Pekka Masonen, "Trans-Saharan trade and the West African discovery of the Mediterranean world," in M'hammad Sabour and Knut Vikør, eds, *Ethnic Encounter and Culture Change*. Bergen/London: Nordic Society for Middle Eastern Studies, 1997, pp. 116–42.

16 Pekka Masonen, "Trans-Saharan trade."

17 Djibril T. Niane, *Sundiata: An Epic of Old Mali*. London: Longman, 1965.

18 Al-Omari, *Masalik el absār fi mamālik el-amsār*, translated and annotated by M. Gaudefroy-Demombynes. Paris: Paul Guethner, 1927.

19 Al-Omari, *Masalik el absār fi mamālik el-amsār*.

2 The Broken Links

1 Basil Davidson, *The Lost Cities of Africa*. Boston: Back Bay, 1959; Paul Bohanon, *Africa and Africans*. Prospect Heights, IL: Waveland Press, 1995; Molefi Kete Asante, *The History of Africa*. London: Routledge, 2007.

2 The Greeks called the clan groups *nomes* but the ancient Africans referred to them as *sepats*.

3 Molefi Kete Asante and Ama Mazama, eds, *Encyclopedia of African Religion*, 2 volumes. Thousand Oaks, CA: Sage Publications, 2009.

4 See Maulana Karenga, *Maat: The Moral Ideal in Ancient Egypt*. Los Angeles: University of Sankore Press, 2006.

5 Karenga, *Maat*, p. 10.

6 Cheikh Anta Diop, *Cultural Unity of Black Africa*. Chicago: Third World Press, 1969.

7 Maulana Karenga, "Odu Ifa," in Asante and Mazama, eds, *Encyclopedia of African Religion*.

8 Maulana Karenga, *Odu Ifa: The Ethical Teachings*. Los Angeles: Kawaida Publishers, 1999, 31:3.

9 Karenga, *Odu Ifa*, 70:1.

10 Pekka Masonen, "Trans-Saharan trade and the West African discovery of the Mediterranean world," in M'hammed Sabour and Knut S. Vikør, eds, *Ethnic Encounter and Culture Change*. Bergen/London: Nordic Society for Middle Eastern Studies, 1997, pp. 116–142.

11 Masonen, "Trans-Saharan trade," p. 126.

12 Aboubacry Moussa Lam, *De l'origine égyptienne des peuls*. Dakar: Éditions Présence Africaine, 1993.

13 See Herodotus, *Histories*, Book II.

14 Masonen, "Trans-Saharan trade," p. 132.

15 Richard Hakluyt, *The Principal Navigations Voyages Traffiques & Discoveries of the English Nation*, etc. (Hakluyt Society; Extra Ser., nos. 1–12). Glasgow: James MacLehose & Sons for the Hakluyt Society. 12 vols. 1903–1905. X, 15.

16 Hayluyt, *The Principal Navigations*, VI, 270.

17 Oscar Handlin and Mary Handlin, "Origin of the Southern labor system," *William and Mary Quarterly*, vol. 7, 1950, pp. 199–222.

18 Eugene Genovese, *Roll, Jordan, Roll: The World the Slaves Made*. New York: Vintage, 1974. Although Genovese later turned in temperament and politics to the right, the data he provided in this earlier work, for which he won the Bancroft Prize, are usually accepted as solid.

19 Phillis Wheatley, *Memoir and Poems of Phillis Wheatley, a Native African and Slave*. Boston: G. W. Light, 1834.

20 In a letter to Baron Constant de Rebecq, Voltaire opined that Fontenelle should never have said that there would never be black poets since "il y a actuellement une Négresse qui fait de très bon vers anglais." This is reported by Edward D. Seeber in his book on the French anti-slavery movement. See Edward Derbyshire Seeber, *Anti-Slavery Opinions in France during the Second Half of the Eighteenth Century*. New York: Burt Franklin Publishers, 1971. Seeber takes a cautious view of Voltaire's statement because of the low estimation Voltaire had of Africans, saying that Voltaire considered them as different from whites in intelligence as they were in physical appearance.

21 Thomas Hutchinson, "Strictures upon the Declaration of the Congress at Philadelphia," London, 1776, in Hans L. Eicholz, *Harmonizing Sentiments: The Declaration of Independence and the Jeffersonian Idea of Self-Government.* New York: Peter Lang, 2001, appendix, pp. 177–199. See also Jeremy Bentham's attack on the Declaration in Robert Ginsberg, ed., *A Casebook on the Declaration of Independence.* New York: Thomas Y. Crowell Company, 1967, pp. 9–17.

22 John Blackman, *A Memoir of the Life and Writings of Thomas Day.* London: John Bedford Leno, 1862; also Peter Rowland, *The Life and Times of Thomas Day, 1748–1789: English Philanthropist and Author, Virtue Almost Personified.* Lewiston, NY: E. Mellen Press, 1996.

3 Africans Confront the American Situation

1 George Quintal believes that there were at least 103 black patriots at the Battle of Bunker Hill. Given the fact that 3,000 Americans are said to have participated in the battle, nearly five percent were Africans. Later, at the Battle of Monmouth, New Jersey, 800 Africans participated, about seven percent of the 12,000 soldiers. See George Quintal, *Patriots of Color: A Peculiar Beauty and Merit, African Americans and Native Americans at Battle Road and Bunker Hill.* Washington, DC: United States Department of the Interior, 2005. See also Benjamin Quarles, *The Negro in the American Revolution.* Chapel Hill: University of North Carolina Press, 1961, pp. 4–45.

2 Emma Nogrady Kaplan and Sidney Kaplan, *The Black Presence in the Era of the American Revolution.* Amherst: University of Massachusetts Press, 1989.

3 Kaplan and Kaplan, *The Black Presence*, pp. 23–45.

4 Lord Dunmore, Proclamation of John Murray, Fourth Earl of Dunmore, November 7, 1775, Archives of the University of Virginia, Charlottesville, Virginia. This was the first mass emancipation of Africans in North America. The response of the Virginia Assembly was to denounce the declaration as an attack on the foundation of Virginia's society.

5 Kwando Mbiassi Kinshasa, *African American Chronology.* Westport, CT: Greenwood Press, 2006.

6 Meriwether Lewis and William Clark, *The Journals of Lewis and Clark* (Lewis & Clark Expedition), ed. Bernard DeVoto. Boston: Mariner Books, 1997. See also http://lewisandclarkjournals.unl.edu/namesindex/index.php?name=Y.

7 Lewis and Clark, *Journals* 1997.

8 Lewis and Clark, *Journals* 1997.

9 Lewis and Clark, *Journals* 1997.

10 Lewis and Clark, *Journals* 1997.

11 Lewis and Clark, *Journals* 1997.

12 Lewis and Clark, *Journals* 1997.

13 Lewis and Clark, *Journals* 1997.

14 Henry Adams, *The War of 1812.* New York: Cooper Square Press, 1999, pp. 12–34.

15 Thomas H. Huxley, *Lay Sermons, Addresses and Reviews.* New York: Appleton, 1871.

16 Georg Hegel, *The Philosophy of History.* New York: IAP, 2009.

17 Hegel, *The Philosophy of History*, p. 154.

18 Hegel, *The Philosophy of History*, p. 156.

19 Hegel, *The Philosophy of History*, p. 167.

20 Cheikh Anta Diop, *The African Origin of Civilization: Myth or Reality.* New York: Lawrence Hill, 1989; see also Cheikh Anta Diop, *Civilization or Barbarism.* New York: Lawrence Hill, 1991.

21 Marcus Junianus Justinus, *Epitome of the Philippic History of Pompeius Trogus,* translated, with notes, by the Rev. John Selby Watson. London: Henry G. Bohn, 1853, 18:4–6.

22 George G. M. James, *Stolen Legacy: Greek Philosophy is Stolen Egyptian Philosophy.* Trenton, NJ: Africa World Press, 1993. Much maligned, James' book, however, is one of the first to question the dominant paradigm of a miraculous Greek philosophical tradition. Whatever else one can say of *Stolen Legacy*, one must accept the fact that James takes on an entire school tradition of Greek

exceptionalism and succeeds in raising enough questions that scholars after him had to return to the original texts rather than merely accept the received interpretations.

23 John Jackson, Chancellor Williams, and Yosef ben-Jochannan, alongside John Henrik Clarke, would be called by Jacob Carruthers and Martin Bernal, "the Old Scrappers." They popularized the cutting-edge research on Africa during their age as well as providing new interpretations that challenged the received versions of African history. They were champions of the masses, committed to educating the millions of Africans who had been left out of the discourse about their own history. Although seldom schooled in the same sense as the later African American historians, they were more original, less hampered by traditional European explanations. See John Jackson, *Introduction to African Civilization*. New York: Citadel, 2001; Chancellor Williams, *The Destruction of Black Civilization: Great Issues of a Race*. Chicago: Third World Press, 1987; and Martin Bernal, *Black Athena*. New Brunswick, NJ: Rutgers University Press, 1984.

24 Eric Williams, *Capitalism and Slavery*. Chapel Hill: University of North Carolina Press, 1994.

25 Matt Wrack, "Slavery and the rise of capitalism," a review of *The Making of New World Slavery: from the Baroque to the Modern, 1492–1800*. By Robin Blackburn, Verso, 1997. *Socialism Today*. Issue 33, November, 1998.

26 Angelo Costanzo, *Surprising Narrative: Olaudah Equiano and the Beginnings of Black Autobiography*. Westport, CT: Greenwood Press, 1987.

27 David Walker, *An Appeal to the Coloured Citizens of the World*, 1829.

28 Williams, *Capitalism and Slavery*, pp. 45–67.

29 Williams, *Capitalism and Slavery*, p, 74.

30 James M. Blaut, *The Colonizer's Model of the World: Geographical Diffusionism and Eurocentric History*. New York: The Guilford Press, 1993.

31 Angel Rosenblat, *La población indígena y el mestizaje en América*. vol. 1, Buenos Aires, 1954.

32 Blaut, *The Colonizer's Model of the World*, p. 170. See also R. C. Smedley, *History of the Underground Railroad in Chester and the Neighboring Counties of Pennsylvania*. New York: Beaufort Books, 1982, p. 104.

33 Smedley, *History of the Underground Railroad in Chester*.

34 Smedley, *History of the Underground Railroad in Chester*, p. 104.

35 William Waller Hening, *The Statutes at Large, being a Collection of All the Laws of Virginia from the First Session of the Legislature in the Year 1619*, 13 volumes. Richmond: W. Gray Printers, 1819. 3:252.

36 Hening, *The Statutes at Large*, 3:255.

37 The Negro Act of 1740 in South Carolina.

38 *Slave Code of Barbados, 1661*. This code was adopted by South Carolina in 1696. It permitted slave-owners to mutilate, brutalize, and burn Africans alive without fear of reprisal.

39 Grant Gilmore and Charles L. Black, *The Law of Admiralty*, 2nd edition. St. Paul, MN: West Publishing Company, 1975.

40 Gilmore and Black, *The Law of Admiralty*, pp. 12–34.

41 Audrey Smedley, *Race in North America: Origin and Evolution of a Worldview*, 3rd edition. Boulder, CO: Westview Press, 2007; see Theodore W. Allen, *The Invention of the White Race*. London: Verso, 1994; also Noel Ignatiev, *How the Irish Became White*. London: Routledge, 1995; also Karen Brodkin, *How Jews Became White Folks: And What That Says about Race in America*. New Brunswick, NJ: Rutgers University Press, 1998.

42 Joseph Feagin, *Racist America: Roots, Current Realities and Future Reparations*. 2nd edition. London: Routledge, 2010, pp. 56–89.

43 James Weldon Johnson, *Lift Every Voice and Sing: Quartet for Mixed Voices*. New York: Edward B. Marks Music Company, 1928.

44 David Walker's *Appeal, in Four Articles; Together with a Preamble, to the Coloured Citizens of the World, but in Particular, and Very Expressly, to Those of the United States of America*, revised edition with an Introduction by Sean Wilentz. New York: Hill and Wang, 1995, pp. 4–5.

45 David Walker's *Appeal*, 1995, pp. 7–8.

46 Lamont D. Thomas, *Rise to be a People: A Biography of Paul Cuffee*. Urbana: University of Illinois Press, 1986, pp. 3–14.

4 Freedom and Revolution without End

1 John K. Thornton, "The African roots of the Stono Rebellion," in Darlene Clark Hine and Earnestine Jenkins, eds, *A Question of Manhood*. Bloomington: Indiana University Press, 1999, pp. 116–123.

2 Peter Charles Hoffer, *Cry Liberty: The Great Stono River Slave Rebellion of 1739*. Oxford: Oxford University Press, 2010.

3 Silvio A. Bedini, *The Life of Benjamin Banneker, the First African American Man of Science,* 2nd edition. Baltimore: Maryland Historical Society, 1999.

4 Bedini, *The Life of Benjamin Banneker*, pp. 7–12.

5 Herbert Marshall, *Ira Aldridge: Negro Tragedian*. Washington, DC: Howard University Press, 1993.

6 Douglas R. Egerton, *Gabriel's Rebellion: The Virginia Slave Conspiracies of 1800 and 1802*. Chapel Hill: University of North Carolina Press, 1993.

7 Arna Bontemps, *Black Thunder: Gabriel's Revolt, Virginia, 1800*. Boston: Beacon, 1992

8 James Sidbury, *Ploughshares into Swords: Race, Rebellion, and Identity in Gabriel's Virginia, 1730–1810*. Cambridge: Cambridge University Press, 1997.

9 Sidbury, *Ploughshares into Swords*, pp. 13–23.

10 Egerton, *Gabriel's Rebellion*, pp. 101–142.

11 See Herbert Aptheker, *American Negro Slave Revolts*. New York: International Publishers, 1974, pp. 219-226. In fact, Aptheker also says, "James Monroe wrote to Thomas Jefferson asking his advice about the execution of the Negro leaders. Mr. Jefferson replied: "The other states & the world at large will forever condemn us if we indulge a principle of revenge, or go one step beyond absolute necessity. They cannot lose sight of the rights of the two parties, & the object of the unsuccessful one." Aptheker, pp. 223–224. So massive was the conspiracy that accurate figures have been difficult to come by since reports range from two thousand Africans to fifty thousand being involved in some way or another with the plot.

12 Aptheker, *American Negro Slave Revolts*, p. 220.

13 Aptheker, *American Negro Slave Revolts*, pp. 220–226.

14 David M. Robertson, *Denmark Vesey: The Buried History of America's Largest Slave Rebellion and the Man Who Led It*. New York: Knopf, 1999, pp. 126-145.

15 Junius P. Rodriguez, "Rebellion on the River Road: The ideology and influence of Louisiana's German Coast slave insurrection of 1811," in John R. McKivigan and Stanley Harrold, *Antislavery Violence: Sectional, Racial, and Cultural Conflict in Antebellum America*. Knoxville: University of Tennessee Press, 1999. See also Thomas Marshall Thompson. "National Newspaper and Legislative Reactions to Louisiana's Deslonde Slave Revolt of 1811," *Louisiana History*, vol.33, Winter 1992, pp. 5–29.

16 There is no way to know for certain and it could easily have been more than 500 people involved, given the extent of the reaction and retaliation.

17 Eric Foner, *Nat Turner*. Englewood Cliffs, NJ: Prentice-Hall, 1971.

18 Aptheker, *American Negro Slave Revolts*.

19 Helen Kromer, *The Amistad Revolt 1839: The Slave Uprising aboard the Spanish Schooner*. New York: Franklin Watts, 1973. Reprinted Pilgrim Press, 1997, as *Amistad: The Slave Uprising aboard the Spanish Schooner*. See also Donald Dale Jackson. "Mutiny on the Amistad," *Smithsonian*, December, 1997, pp. 114–124; Howard Jones, "All We Want is to Make Us Free," *American History*. January–February 1998, pp. 22–28, 71.

20 Erlene Stetson and Linda David, *Glorying in Tribulations: The Lifework of Sojourner Truth*. East Lansing: Michigan State University Press, 1994. See also Nell Irvin Painter, *Sojourner Truth: A Life, a Symbol*. New York: Norton, 1997.

21 Henry Box Brown, *Narrative of Henry Box Brown: A Memoir*. New York: Oxford University Press, 2002. Originally published in 1851.

22 Eric Foner, *Free Soil, Free Labor, Free Men: The Ideology of the Republican Party before the Civil War*. New York: Oxford University Press, 1995. Also Stanley Campbell, *The Slave Catchers: Enforcement of the Fugitive Slave Law, 1850–1860*. Chapel Hill: University of North Carolina Press, 1970.

23 Charles Fuller, *Snatch*. Philadelphia: David and Me, Publishers, 2010.

24 Chris Dixon, *African Americans and Haiti: Emigration and Black Nationalism in the Nineteenth Century*. Westport, CT: Greenwood Press, 2000, pp. 75–106.

25 Victor Ullman, *Martin R. Delany: The Beginnings of Black Nationalism*. Boston: Beacon Press, 1971, p. 112.

26 *News and Courier*, Oct. 18, 24, 1876.

27 *News and Courier*, Oct. 18, 24, 1876.

28 *News and Courier*, Oct. 18, 24, 1876.

29 Ullman, *Martin R. Delany*, p. 419.

30 Benjamin A. Quarles, *Allies for Freedom & Blacks on John Brown*. New York: De Capo, 2001.

31 Edwin S. Redkey, *Black Exodus: Black Nationalist and Back to Africa Movements*. New Haven, CT: Yale University Press, 1969.

32 Stephen Ward Angell, *Bishop Henry McNeal Turner and African American Religion in the South*. Knoxville: University of Tennessee Press, 2001.

33 Dorothy Sterling, *Freedom Train: The Story of Harriet Tubman*. New York: Scholastics, 1987; see also Sarah Bradford, *Harriet, the Moses of Her People*. New York: Lockwood and Sons, 1886.

34 Josiah Henson, *Uncle Tom's Story of His Life: An Autobiography of Rev. Josiah Henson*. London: Christian Age Office, 1877.

35 George Fredrickson, *White Supremacy: A Comparative Study in American and South African History*. Oxford: Oxford University Press, 1981.

36 *Dred Scott v. Sanford*, United States Supreme Court, 1857.

37 *Dred Scott v. Sanford*, United States Supreme Court, 1857.

38 *Dred Scott v. Sanford*, United States Supreme Court, 1857.

39 Frederick Douglass, *Life and Times of Frederick Douglass: His Early Life as a Slave, His Escape from Bondage, and His Complete History to the Present Time*. Hartford, CT: Park Publishing Co., 1881, p. 23.

40 Quarles, *Allies for Freedom*, pp. 59–87.

41 David S. Reynolds, *John Brown, Abolitionist: The Man Who Killed Slavery, Sparked the Civil War, and Seeded Civil Rights*. New York: Vintage, 2006.

5 The Great Freedom War

1 Douglass had succeeded the brilliant Charles Lenox Remond on the antislavery stage as the leading African speaker years earlier. Even on the eve of the Civil War, Douglass had his challengers for the leadership of the African community but he had outflanked and out performed most of them by the time the war began.

2 http://www.historynet.com/camp-william-penn-training-ground-for-freedom.htm

3 Frances Smith Foster, *A Brighter Coming Day: A Frances Ellen Watkins Harper Reader*. New York: Feminist Press, 1990.

4 William Still, *The Underground Rail Road*. Philadelphia: Porter and Coates, 1872, p. 786.

5 Maryemma Graham. *The Complete Poems of Frances E. W. Harper*. New York: Oxford University Press, 1988.

6 Phebe A. Hanaford, *Daughters of America*. Augusta, ME: True and Company, 1882.

7 Peter Burchard, *One Gallant Rush: Robert Gould Shaw and His Brave Black Regiment*. New York: St Martin's Press, 1990; see also Russell Duncan, *Where Death and Glory Meet: Colonel Robert Gould Shaw and the 54th Massachusetts Infantry*. Athens: University of Georgia Press, 1999.

8 The nearly all-black town of La Mott, Pennsylvania, took its name from the Mott family.

9 John Blassingame et al., eds, *The Frederick Douglass Papers: Series One—Speeches, Debates, and Interviews*. New Haven, CT: Yale University Press, 1979. vol. I, p. 407.

10 http://www.nps.gov/archive/apco/blacks.htm (accessed December 11, 2010).

11 Eric Foner, *Reconstruction: America's Unfinished Revolution, 1863–1877*. New York: New American Nation Series, Harper and Row, 1988.

12 Lieberman, Robert C., "The Freedmen's Bureau and the politics of institutional structure," *Social Science History,* vol. 18, no. 3, 1994, pp. 405–437. See also Richard Lowe, "The Freedmen's Bureau and Local Black Leadership," *Journal of American History,* vol. 80, no. 3, 1993, pp. 989–998; also J. Thomas May, "Continuity and Change in the Labor Program of the Union Army and the Freedmen's Bureau," *Civil War History,* vol. 17, September 1971, pp. 245–254.

13 Martin Abbott, *The Freedmen's Bureau in South Carolina, 1865–1872.* Chapel Hill: University of North Carolina Press, 1967, esp. pp. 37–48.

14 Eric Foner, *A Short History of Reconstruction, 1863–1877.* New York: Harper and Row, 1990.

15 Foner, *A Short History of Reconstruction,* pp. 45–48.

16 Frederick Douglass, *Life and Times of Frederick Douglass: His Early Life as a Slave, His Escape from Bondage, and His Complete History to the Present Time.* Hartford, CT: Park Publishing, 1881.

17 William Loren Katz, *Black Indians: A Hidden Heritage.* New York: Atheneum, 1997.

6 Exploring New Routes to Equality and Justice

1 Frantz Fanon, *The Wretched of the Earth.* New York: Grove, 1963; London: Penguin, 1983.

2 Matthew A. Henson, "The Negro at the North Pole: The story of the last dash, told by Commander Peary's only American companion at the top of the Earth," *The World's Work: A History of Our Time,* vol. 19, April 1910, pp. 12825–12837.

3 Robert G. Athearn, *In Search of Canaan: Black Migration to Kansas, 1879–80.* Lawrence: The Regents Press of Kansas, 1978.

4 Gary R. Entz, "Benjamin 'Pap' Singleton: father of the Kansas exodus," in Nina Mjagkij, ed., *Portraits of African American Life since 1865.* Wilmington, DE: Scholarly Resources, 2003.

5 http://www.robinsonlibrary.com/america/unitedstates/afroamericans/singleton.htm

6 Entz, "Benjamin 'Pap' Singleton," p. 56.

7 R. Lane, *William Dorsey's Philadelphia and Ours: On the Past and Future of the Black City in America.* New York: Oxford University Press, 1991.

8 Daniel Biddle and Murray Dubin, *Tasting Freedom: Octavius Catto and the Battle for Equality in Civil War America.* Philadelphia: Temple University Press, 2010.

9 Biddle and Dubin, *Tasting Freedom,* pp. 32–67.

10 Booker T. Washington, *An Autobiography: The Story of My Life and Work.* Toronto: J. L. Nichols and Company, c. 1901. See also Louis Harlan, *Booker T. Washington: The Wizard of Tuskegee, 1901–1915.* New York: Oxford University Press, 1983.

11 Isabel C. Barrow, *First Mohonk Conference on the Negro Question.* Boston: George Ellis, 1890, p. 3.

12 Barrow, *First Mohonk Conference,* p. 10.

13 Alfred Moss, "Alexander Crummell: Black Nationalist and Apostle of Western Civilization," in August Meier and Leon Litwack, eds, *Black Leaders of the Nineteenth Century.* Champaign: University of Illinois, 1991.

14 http://www.bartleby.com/114/12.html

15 W. E. B. Du Bois, *The Souls of Black Folk.* New York: Fawcett, 1903, pp. 18–20. Also New York: New American Library, 1969.

16 Paul Robeson, *Here I Stand.* Boston: Beacon Press, 1970; Philip Foner, *Paul Robeson Speaks.* New York: Citadel Press, 1978.

17 Robeson, *Here I Stand,* 1970, p. 23.

18 Robeson, *Here I Stand,* p. 45.

19 Charles Blockson, "Robeson: The grand example," a lecture at Temple University, September 27, 1996.

20 James West Davidson, *"They Say": Ida B. Wells and the Reconstruction of Race.* New York: Oxford University Press, 2009.

21 P. J. Giddings, *Ida: A Sword among Lions.* New York: HarperCollins, 2008.

22 Giddings, *Ida,* 2008. See also Davidson, *"They Say."*

23 Robert L. Zangrando, *The NAACP Crusade against Lynching, 1909–1950*. Philadelphia: Temple University Press, 1980.

24 Zangrando, *The NAACP Crusade*.

25 Maria W. Stewart, *America's First Black Woman Political Writer: Essays and Speeches*. Edited by Marilyn Richardson. Bloomington: Indiana University Press, 1987.

26 Harlan, *Booker T. Washington*, p. 36.

27 *The Booker T. Washington Papers*, volume 5, 142.

28 Harlan, *Booker T. Washington*, p. 36.

29 Emma Lou Thornbrough, *T. Thomas Fortune, Militant Journalist*. Chicago: University of Chicago Press, 1972.

30 Harlan, *Booker T. Washington*, pp. 50–123.

31 Book review by Du Bois of Washington's *Up from Slavery*, *Dial*, July 16, 1901. Reprinted In Herbert Aptheker, ed., *Book Reviews by W. E. B. Du Bois*. Millwood, NY: Kraus-Thomson, 1977, pp. 1–3.

32 Marcia Mathews, *Henry Ossawa Tanner, American Artist*. Chicago: University of Chicago Press, 1995.

33 Tim Joyce, "Jack Johnson deserves a Pardon," *Real Clear Sports*, February 22, 2011; see also: http://www.realclearsports.com/articles/2011/02/22/its_time_to_pardon_jack_johnson_97228.html

34 Tony Martin, *Marcus Garvey, Hero: A First Biography*. Dover, MA: Majority Press, 1983.

35 Amy Jacques-Garvey, *The Philosophy and Opinions of Marcus Garvey*. New York: Atheneum, 1969.

7 From Harlem We Charge Up the Racial Mountain

1 Walter Dean Myers and Christopher Myers, *Harlem*. New York: Scholastic, 1997.

2 Arnold Rampersad, *The Life of Langston Hughes*. New York: Oxford University Press, 2002.

3 Arnold Rampersad, *The Poems of Langston Hughes*. Columbia: University of Missouri Press, 2007.

4 Langston Hughes, *The Big Sea: An Autobiography*. New York: Alfred A. Knopf, 1940; New York: Thunder's Mouth Press, 1986. See also *I Wonder as I Wander: An Autobiographical Journey*. New York: Rinehart, 1956; New York: Hill and Wang, 1964; New York: Thunder's Mouth Press, dist. by Persea Books, 1986.

5 Langston Hughes, "The Negro Artist and the Racial Mountain," *Nation*, June 23, 1926.

6 Langston Hughes, "The Negro Speaks of Rivers," *The Crisis*, June, 1921.

7 See Shirley Washington, *Countee Cullen's Secret Revealed by Miracle Book: A Biography of His Childhood in New Orleans*. New York: AuthorHouse, 2008. Washington claims that Cullen was born in 1906 and that she is his niece, the daughter of one of Cullen's sisters. Most writers put his birth date in 1903. There is no way to confirm either of these claims.

8 See Alice Walker, "In Search of Zora Neale Hurston," *Ms. Magazine*, March, 1975, pp. 74–n79, 84–89; also Robert E. Hemenway, "Zora Neale Hurston." In Paul Lauter and Richard Yarborough, eds, *The Heath Anthology of American Literature*, 5th edition, vol. D. New York: Houghton Mifflin Co., 2006, pp. 1577–1578. The best biography is probably Valerie Boyd's *Wrapped in Rainbows: The Life of Zora Neale Hurston*. New York: Scribner's, 2004.

9 Walker, "In Search of Zora Neale Hurston"; also Hemenway "Zora Neale Hurston," pp. 1577–1578.

10 Among the best sources for information on McKay are these: Wayne F. Cooper, *Claude McKay: Rebel Sojourner in the Harlem Renaissance, a Biography*. Baton Rouge: Louisiana State University Press, 1987; Tyrone Tillary, *Claude McKay: A Black Poet's Struggle for Identity*. Amherst: University of Massachusetts Press, 1992; and James R. Giles, *Claude McKay*. Boston: G. K. Hall, 1976; Stephen H. Bronz, *Roots of Negro Racial Consciousness: The 1920s, Three Harlem Renaissance Authors*. San Diego, CA: Libra Publishers, 1964; Addison Gayle, *Claude McKay: The Black Poet at War*. Detroit: Broadside Press, 1972; and Wayne F. Cooper, ed., *The Passion of Claude McKay*. New York: Schocken Books, 1973, provide bibliographic resources. McKay's obituary appears in the *New York Times*, May 24, 1948.

11 Jackie Kay, *Bessie Smith*. New York: Absolute Press, 1997. Also, Chris Albertson, Bessie (Revised and Expanded Edition). New Haven, CT: Yale University Press, 2003. See also Paul Oliver, "Bessie Smith," in Barry Kernfeld, ed., *The New Grove Dictionary of Jazz*, 2nd edition, vol. 3. London: Macmillan, 2002. p. 604.

12 Robert O'Meally, *Lady Day: The Many Faces of Billie Holiday*. New York: Da Capo, 2000. See also Donald Clarke, *Billie Holiday: Wishing on the Moon*. New York: Da Capo, 2002.

13 Gary Giddens, *Satchmo: The Genius of Louis Armstrong*. New York: Da Capo, 2001. See Laurence Bergreen's *Louis Armstrong: An Extravagant Life*. New York: Broadway Books, 1998, for a detailed discussion of Armstrong's background.

14 See Alfred Apfel Jr, "Louis Armstrong, Race and the Power of Song," *The New Republic*, 31 August 1995, pp. 31–38. No one ever accused Louis Armstrong of being a militant race man although he had often been a victim of racism. His song "What Did I do to be So Black and Blue?," has to be seen as an indication of the effect of negative self-concepts on his own thinking. Why would any black person see blackness as something which he or she as human would have to decry?

15 "Louis Armstrong, Barring Soviet Tour, Denounces Eisenhower and Gov. Faubus," *New York Times*, September 19, 1957. In Grand Forks, North Dakota, Armstrong talked extensively about race and racism, saying that "It's getting almost so bad a colored man hasn't got any country." This was a rare expression of his anger at the treatment that blacks received at the hands of the state and federal government.

16 *New York Times*, September 19, 1957.

17 Ken Rattenbury, *Duke Ellington: Jazz Composer*. New Haven, CT: Yale University Press, 1990; also Stanley Dance, *The World of Duke Ellington*. New York: Da Capo, 2000. See also G. E. Lambert, *Duke Ellington*. London: Cassell, 1959. I would also advise readers to consult Peter Gammond, ed., *Duke Ellington: His Life and Music*. New York: Roy, 1958, reprint Da Capo, 1977. For a juvenile introduction to the composer, please see Andrea Pinkney and Brian Pinkney, *Duke Ellington: The Piano Prince and His Orchestra*. New York: Hyperion, 2006.

18 See Alyn Shipton, *Hi-De-Ho: The Life of Cab Calloway*. New York: Oxford University Press, 2010. Also, Ismael Reed, *Cab Calloway Stands In for the Moon*. New York: Bamberger, 1988.

19 *Beyond the Blues*. New Orleans: Amistad Research Center and the New Orleans Museum of Art, 2010. See also David Driskell, *Narratives of African American Art and Identity*. Petaluma, CA: Pomegranate Communications, 1998.

20 Thurman's list of religio-philosophical books has almost no peer among the works of his contemporaries. His great books had names like *The Inward Journey, The Creative Encounter, The Mood of Christmas, The Search for Common Ground, Meditations of the Heart,* and *Jesus and the Disinherited*. There is hardly a modern African American preacher who has not been impacted by the works of Thurman.

21 Charles V. Hamilton, *Adam Clayton Powell, Jr.: The Political Biography of an American Dilemma*. New York: Cooper Square Press, 2002. Perhaps it is Powell's autobiography that best traces his ambitions in support of his community. It is here that we see the author's own explanations for his behaviors and activities. The book *Adam by Adam: An Autobiography of Adam Clayton Powell, Jr.* was published in New York by Kensington Books, and reissued in 2002.

22 W. Virgie, "Dean of Black Preachers," *Los Angeles Sentinel*, July 28, 2005; Ronnetta Slaughter, "Dr. Gardner Taylor inspires fellow ministers: Pastors attend 'Preaching with Passion and Purpose' conference," *Indianapolis Recorder*, October 5, 2001; and Kim Lawton, "A preacher for the ages; Gardner Taylor raised the art of the sermon," *Washington Post*, September 9, 2006.

23 See these books by C. Eric Lincoln for a more profound insight into his philosophy of knowledge and consciousness: C. Eric Lincoln, *Black Muslims in America*. Grand Rapids, MI: Eerdsman Publishing, 1994; *The Black Church in the African American Experience*. Raleigh, NC: Duke University Press, 1990; and *Coming Through the Fire: Surviving Race and Place in America*. Raleigh, NC: Duke University Press, 1996.

24 See Samuel DeWitt Proctor, *The Substance of Things Hoped For: A Memoir of African American Faith*. New York: Putnam, 1996.

25 Albert G. Cleage, *The Black Messiah*. Trenton, NJ: Africa World Press, 1989. Agyeman, the name taken by Cleage, was a powerfully eloquent voice against the idea of a white Jesus until his death at the age of eighty-eight in 2000. Agyeman claimed that the worldwide existence of the Black Madonna image demonstrated the ubiquity of the Black Messiah long before the creation of the

American nation. Strong communities in Detroit, Atlanta, and Houston still teach his doctrines and practice an African version of Christianity.

26 Cone is perhaps the single most important African American theologian of his generation because of his influence on what is called progressive theology or the theology of liberation. The reader will find Cone's books quite helpful in understanding the nexus between his form of black liberation theology and Agyeman's notion of a Black Messiah. See for example, Cone's *A Black Theology of Liberation*, 40th anniversary edition. Maryknoll, NY: Orbis, 2010; *God of the Oppressed*. Maryknoll, NY: Orbis, 1997; *Martin and Malcolm and America*. Maryknoll, NY: Orbis, 1992; and *My Soul Looks Back*. Maryknoll, NY: Orbis, 1985.

27 Retrieved on December 17, 2010 from http://sweetness-light.com/archive/wrights-sermon-the-audacity-to-hope

28 Calvin O. Butts redefined the role of the Abyssinian Baptist pastor. While his predecessors could be counted on to be radically democratic and progress, Butts introduced a cautious pragmatism into the political equation in New York. Ken Schacter, writing in the *Long Island Magazine*, entitled his article "The many faces of Reverend Calvin O. Butts, III," April, 2006. In many respects Butts has been seen as the Henry Gates Jr of the ministry, that is, a personality who easily bridges the worlds of blacks and whites, mostly leaning toward white privilege and power, to the dismay of politically progressive African Americans.

29 Sara Lawrence-Lightfoot, *I've Known Rivers: Lives of Loss and Liberation*, Reading, MA: Addison-Wesley, 1994.

30 Douglas Martin, "John Johnson, 87, founder of *Ebony*, dies," *New York Times*, August 9, 2005.

31 Lerone Bennett was for more than fifty years the most widely read popular historian in the African American community. With a platform provided by John H. Johnson, Bennett was able to produce articles and books and get them distributed at will by the formidable circulation machine of the Johnson Publishing Company. His position as the house historian at Johnson provided Bennett with an unusual independence and guarantee of wide readership that could not be claimed by any comparable author.

32 John H. Johnson, and Lerone Bennett Jr, *Succeeding against the Odds: The Inspiring Autobiography of One of America's Wealthiest Entrepreneurs*, New York: Warner Books, 1989.

8 Trouble in Paradise

1 James Weldon Johnson, *Along This Way*, New York: Da Capo, 2000, p. 209.

2 Dan T. Carter, *Scottsboro: A Tragedy of the American South*. Baton Rouge: Louisiana State University Press, 2007. Carter's scholarly treatment of the case is remarkable for its detail.

3 See Carter, *Scottsboro: A Tragedy of the American South*, p. 233.

4 Lita Sorensen, *The Scottsboro Boys Trial*. New York: Rosen, 2004, p. 16.

5 Haywood Patterson, *Scottsboro Boy*. Washington, DC: American Council of Learned Societies Humanities, 2008.

6 Gerald Astor, *"And a Credit to His Race": The Hard Life and Times of Joseph Louis Barrow , a.k.a. Joe Louis*. New York: Saturday Review Press, 1974.

7 African leaders such as Nelson Mandela, Robert Mugabe, Kwame Nkrumah, and Julius Nyerere would credit Joe Louis with making Africans throughout the world proud and confident.

8 Jesse Owens and Paul Neimark, *The Jesse Owens Story*. New York: Putnam's 1970.

9 Pam Muñoz Ryan, *When Marian Sang*. New York: Scholastic, 2002; and Russell Friedman, *The Voice that Challenged a Nation: Marian Anderson and the Struggle for Equal Rights*. New York: Sandpiper, 2011.

10 Retrieved on December 19, 2010 from http://www.defense.gov/news/newsarticle.aspx?id=43307

11 American Forces Press Service. Washington, January 16, 1997

12 Rudi Williams, "Seven black heroes of World War II receive medals," American Forces Press Service. Washington, DC, January 16, 1997.

13 Retrieved on December 21, 2010 from http://www.history.navy.mil/faqs/faq57-4.htm. The government was quick to use the achievements of this Cook Third Class sailor as an example of patriotism. A 1942 United States War propaganda poster "Above and Beyond the Call of Duty" featured Dorie Miller. In addition, a ship commissioned on June 30, 1973, USS *Miller* (FF-1091), a Knox-class frigate, was named in honor of Doris Dorie Miller. Then, on October 11, 1991, the Alpha Kappa Alpha Sorority dedicated a bronze commemorative plaque of Miller at the Miller Family Park located on the U.S. Naval Base, Pearl Harbor.

14 See http://www.history.navy.mil/faqs/faq57-4.htm

15 J. Bellafaire (n.d.) *Volunteering for Risk: Black Military Women Overseas during the Wars in Korea and Viet Nam*. Retrieved on December 21, 2010 from http://www.womensmemorial.org/Education/BWOHistory.html. Randolph, L. B. "The untold story of black women in the Gulf War." *Ebony* magazine, September, 1991. Retrieved on December 21, 2010 from http://findarticles.com/p/articpes/mi_m1077/is_n11_v46?ai_11256190/ See also P. T. Tucker *Cathy Williams: From Slave to Female Buffalo Soldier*. Mechanicsburg, PA: Stackpole Books, 2002. For a good general history of women in the military see S. A. Sheafer, *Women in America's Wars*. Springfield, NJ: Enslow Publishers, 1996.

16 E. Valerie Smith, "The black Corps of Engineers and the construction of the Alaska (ALCAN) Highway," *Negro History Bulletin*, vol. 51, December 1993. The Alaska portion of the road, which also went through British Columbia and the Yukon, the most dangerous, rugged, and hazardous section, was built by the all-black 93rd, 97th and 95th Army Engineer General Service Regiments of the Corps of Engineers over the objections of the United States Army commander for Alaska, General Simon Buckner, Jr.

17 Chuck Roberts, "Tuskegee airmen," *Air Force News Agency*, September, 2004. Also read Lynn Homan and Thomas Reilly, *Black Knights: The Story of the Tuskegee Airmen*. New York: Pelican, 2001. See also J. Alfred Phelps, *Chappie: America's First Black Four-Star General, the Life and Times of Daniel James, Jr*. Novato, CA: Presidio Press, 1992.

18 Kenneth R. Manning, *The Black Apollo of Science: The Life of Ernest Everett Just*. New York: Oxford University Press, 1985. See also Robert C. Hayden, *Seven Black American Scientists*. Reading, MA: Addison-Wesley, 1970. See also W. Montague Cobb, "Ernest Everett Just 1883–1941," *NMA Journal*, National Medical Association. Vol. 49, September, 1957, pp. 349–351.

19 Spencie Love, *One Blood: The Death and Resurrection of Charles R. Drew*. Chapel Hill: University of North Carolina Press, 1997. See also Linda Trice, *Charles Drew: Pioneer of Blood Plasma*. New York: McGraw-Hill, 2000.

20 Scot Morris, *Omni Games: The Best Brainteasers from* Omni *Magazine*. New York: Holt, Rinehart, and Company, 1983.

21 John H. Bracey Jr and August Meier, gen. eds, *Mary McLeod Bethune Papers: The Bethune Foundation Collection*. Bethesda, MD: University Publications of America, 1997. This is the finest collection of Bethune's papers. One can see the full extent of her activities in the interest of the African American community.

22 Rackham Holt, *Mary McLeod Bethune: A Biography*. Garden City, NY: Doubleday, 1964.

23 Mary McLeod Bethune, "My Last Will and Testament," *Ebony*, August, 1955.

24 Soon after I created the Ph.D. program in African American Studies at Temple University in 1988 I invited Margaret Walker Alexander to speak to our students and her words at that time were the same as she had always given, "Our rise will come when we have educated several generations."

25 Lillian Smith, *Killers of the Dream*. New York: Norton, 1994; Jo Ann Robinson, "Lillian Smith: Reflections of race and sex," *Southern Exposure* vol. 4, 1997, pp. 43–48. See also Tim Wise's writings on white privilege, especially *White like Me: Reflections on Race from a Privileged Son*. New York: Soft Skull Press, 2007.

26 Among the best books on this history are the following: Marshall D. Wright, *The National Association of Base Ball Players, 1857–1870*. New York: McFarland and Company, 2000; Warren Goldstein, *Playing for Keeps: A History of Early Baseball*. Ithaca, NY: Cornell University Press, 1991; Harold Seymour, *Baseball: The Early Years*. New York: Oxford University Press, 1960; David Block, *Baseball Before We Knew It: A Search for the Roots of the Game*. Lincoln: University of Nebraska Press, 2005.

27 Harvey Frommer, *Rickey and Robinson*. New York: Macmillan, 1982.

28 Arnold Rampersad, *Jackie Robinson: A Biography*. New York: Ballantine, 1998.
29 Associated Press, April 23, 2007.
30 See the Richard Wright Papers at the Beinecke Rare Book and Manuscript Library, Yale University Library; also see Sarah Relyea, *Outsider Citizens*. New York: Routledge, 2006, for a discussion on Richard Wright.
31 *Ebony*, July 1953, p. 32
32 Mark Busby, *Ralph Ellison*. Boston: Twayne, 1991.

9 We Will be Free

1 George Breitman, ed., *Malcolm X Speaks*. New York: Grove, 1994.
2 Thomas Hauser, *Muhammad Ali: His Life and Times*. New York: Simon and Schuster, 1992.
3 Robert W. Mullen, *Blacks and Vietnam*. Alexandria, VA.: University Press of America, 1981.
4 Charles C. Moskos and John Sibley Butler, *All that We Can Be: Black Leadership and Racial Integration the Army Way*. New York: Basic Books, 1997.
5 Gilbert Jonas, *Freedom's Sword: The NAACP and the Struggle against Racism in America, 1909–1969*. New York: Routledge, 2005.
6 Mary Church Terrell, *A Colored Woman in a White World*. Amherst, NY: Humanity Books, 2005, p.209.
7 *National Urban League 40th Anniversary Yearbook*. New York: National Urban League, 1950.
8 Bayard Rustin, *Down the Line: Collected Writings*. New York: Quadrangle, 1971.
9 Paula F. Pfeffer. *A. Philip Randolph: Pioneer of the Civil Rights Movement*. Baton Rouge: Lousiana State University, 1996.
10 E. U. Essien-Udom, *Black Nationalism: The Search for an Identity*. Chicago: University of Chicago Press, 1995; see also C. Eric Lincoln, *Black Muslims in America*. Grand Rapids, MI: Eerdmans Publishing, 1994.
11 Malcolm's presence and charisma spoke to the millions of black youth who were disaffected with the scenes of blacks being beaten, water-hosed, and bitten by dogs. The Northern black population was seething with anger that the nonviolent movement had allowed black men and women to be humiliated. Malcolm was the voice of action and resolve.
12 Malcolm X, *The Autobiography of Malcolm X: As Told to Alex Haley*. New York: Ballantine, 1997.
13 Richard Severo and Douglas Martin, "Ossie Davis, actor, writer, and eloquent champion of justice, dies at 87," *New York Times*, February 5, 2005.
14 Manning Marable, *Malcolm X: A Life of Reinvention*. New York: Viking, 2011.
15 George Breitman, Herman Porter, and Baxter Smith, *The Assassination of Malcolm X*. New York: Pathfinder Press, 1991; first published in 1976.
16 See Manning Marable, *Speaking Truth to Power: Essays on Race, Resistance, and Radicalism*. Boulder, CO: Westview Press, 1996.
17 Marable, *Speaking Truth to Power*, especially chapter 13.
18 Molefi Kete Asante, *Maulana Karenga: An Intellectual Portrait*. Cambridge: Polity Press, 2009.
19 Charles V. Hamilton and Stokely Carmichael, *Black Power: The Politics of Liberation in America*. New York: Random House, 1988; first published in 1966.
20 Gerald Horne, *The End of Empires: African Americans and India*. Philadelphia: Temple University, 2009.
21 Perhaps the most useful research information about Floyd B. McKissick can be found in his papers housed at the University of North Carolina, Chapel Hill, as *Floyd B. McKissick Papers, 1940s–1980s*, Collection Number: 04930. McKissick's change of direction for CORE was in line with his more Republican leanings as well as a more conservative politics. Roy Innis would later articulate what he called a "pragmatic nationalism" that kept CORE activist but still tainted with its McKissick years.
22 Ralph Abernathy, *And the Walls Came Tumbling Down: An Autobiography*. New York: HarperCollins, 1990; see also James A. Colaiaco, *Martin Luther King, Jr.: Apostle of Nonviolence*. New York: Grolier, 1988.

23 Benjamin E. Mays, *Born to Rebel: An Autobiography*. New York: Scribner, 1971; reprint, with a revised foreword by Orville Vernon Burton, Athens: University of Georgia Press, 2003.

24 Genna Rae McNeil, *Groundwork: Charles Hamilton Houston and the Struggle for Civil Rights*. Philadelphia: University of Pennsylvania Press, 1984. There is no more passionate and powerful treatment of Charles Hamilton Houston than this penetrating study by an impressive author.

25 Thurgood Marshall, "College honors Charles Houston, '15,'" *Amherst Magazine*, Spring 1978, p. 12.

26 Marshall, "College honors Charles Houston," p. 12.

27 Justice William O. Douglas to J. Clay Smith, 19 April 1974, as reported by Genna Rae McNeil in *Groundwork*, p. 3.

28 McNeil, *Groundwork*, p. 224.

29 Rawn James, Jr, *Root and Branch: Charles Hamilton Houston, Thurgood Marshall, and the Struggle to End Segregation*. London: Bloomsbury Press, 2010. See also Barbara Ransby, *Ella Baker and the Black Freedom Movement: A Radical Democratic Vision*. Chapel Hill: University of North Carolina Press, 2005.

30 Mark V. Tushner, *Making Civil Rights Law: Thurgood Marshall and the Supreme Court, 1936–1961*. Oxford: Oxford University Press, 1994.

31 Chana Kai Lee, *For Freedom's Sake: The Life of Fannie Lou Hamer*. Urbana: University of Illinois Press, 2000. See also Maegan Parker Brooks and Davis W. Houck, eds, *The Speeches of Fannie Lou Hamer: To Tell It Like It Is*. Oxford, MS: University Press of America, 2010.

32 Brooks and Houck, *The Speeches of Fannie Lou Hamer*, p. 123.

33 Myrlie Evers-Williams and Manning Marable, eds, *The Autobiography of Medgar Evers: A Hero's Life and Legacy Revealed through His Writings, Letters, and Speeches*. New York: Basic Civitas Books, 2005.

34 Brooks and Houck, *The Speeches of Fannie Lou Hamer*, p. 128.

35 Clay Carson, *In Struggle: SNCC and the Black Awakening of the 1960s*. Cambridge, MA: Harvard University Press, 1981.

36 Chief among these were Charles Fuller, Mari Evans, Alice Childress, Nikki Giovanni, Larry Neal, Amiri Baraka, Haki Madhubuti, and Sonia Sanchez. In many instances the earlier work of Lorraine Hansberry, especially "A Raisin' in the Sun," predicted or anticipated a more militant art and literary form, which emerged in the Black Arts Movement of the late 1960s and early 1970s.

37 David Leeming. *James Baldwin: A Biography*. New York: Henry Holt, 1994. For a perspective on Baldwin's time in Turkey, see Magdalena Zaborowska, *James Baldwin's Turkish Decade: Erotics of Exile*. Durham, NC: Duke University Press, 2008. Baldwin's own account of identity, especially what it means to be an American, can be seen in James Baldwin, "The Discovery of What It Means to be an American," in *The Price of the Ticket: Collected Nonfiction, 1948–1985*. New York: St Martin's/Marek, 1985.

38 Eldridge Cleaver, *Soul on Ice*. New York: Laurel, 1970. One could contrast Baldwin's *The Fire Next Time* with Cleaver's *Soul on Ice* to ascertain two very different views to the issue of race and identity in America. Baldwin's work is personal, provocative in an individualistic sense with importance collectively, while Cleaver's vision is clouded by sex in a way that Baldwin's is not, and yet Cleaver's passions are enormously personal and private and he shares them with us without our asking. We are captive to his own prejudices and vices and see his powerful, lyrical voice fade into irrationality. On the other hand, Baldwin's anger, while personal, boils to the point that if the society does not correct racism, then there will be fire the next time from the black masses.

10 Social and Moral Challenges are Everywhere

1 Rosa Parks with Jim Haskins, *Rosa Parks: My Story*. New York: Puffin, 1999.

2 Clenora Hudson-Weems, *Emmett Till: The Sacrificial Lamb of the Civil Rights Movement*. Bloomington, IN: AuthorHouse, 2006.

3 Daisy Bates, *The Long Shadow of Little Rock: A Memoir*. Fayetteville: University of Arkansas Press, 1987.

4 Bruce Dierenfield, *The Civil Rights Movement*. Harlow, UK: Longmans, 2008. Also see John Lewis with Michael D'Orso, *Walking with the Wind: A Memoir of the Movement*. New York: Simon and Schuster, 1998.

5 Editors, "Martin Luther King, Jr., Person of the Year, 1963," *Time* magazine, January 1, 1964.

6 Martin Luther King Jr, "Letter from a Birmingham Jail," April, 1963.

7 David J. Garrow, *Bearing the Cross: Martin Luther King, Jr., and the Southern Christian Leadership Conference*. New York: Harper Perennial, 1999.

8 Ben Chaney, *Schwerner, Chaney, and Goodman: The Struggle for Justice*. American Bar Association, Fall, 2009.

9 Ean Wood, *The Josephine Baker Story*. New York: Sanctuary Publishing, 2002.

10 George Breitman, ed., *Malcolm X Speaks*. New York: Grove, 1994.

11 Benjamin Rivlin, ed., *Ralph Bunche, the Man and His Times*. Foreword by Donald McHenry. New York: Holmes and Meier, 1990.

12 Martin Luther King, *Stride toward Freedom: the Montgomery Story*. New York: Harper, 1958.

13 King, *Stride toward Freedom*, pp. 78–80

14 Clayborne Carson, *In Struggle: SNCC and the Black Awakening of the 1960s*. Cambridge, MA: Harvard University Press, 1981. See also Vincent Harding, *There is a River*. New York: Harcourt, Brace, 1981; John Lewis with Michael D'Orso, *Walking with the Wind*; and see Vanessa Murphree, *The Selling of Civil Rights: The Student Nonviolent Coordinating Committee and the Use of Public Relations*. New York: Routledge, 2006. Also of interest is the site: http://panafrican news.blogspot.com/2007/11/mukasa-dada-aka-willie-ricks-originator.html

15 Adam Clayton Powell. *Adam by Adam: the Autobiography of Adam Clayton Powell, Jr.* New York: Dial Press, 1971.

16 Harry Edwards, *The Revolt of the Black Athlete*. Foreword by Samuel J. Skinner Jr. New York: The Free Press, 1969; see also Harry Edwards, *The Struggle that Must Be: An Autobiography*. New York: Macmillan, 1980.

17 Manning Marable and Leith Mullings, eds, *Let Nobody Turn Us Around: Voices of Resistance, Reform, and Renewal*. Alexandria, VA: Rowman and Littlefield, 1999.

18 Carson, *In Struggle*, pp. 201–202.

19 *The Black Panther Newspaper*, April, 1968.

20 Molefi Kete Asante, *Maulana Karenga: An Intellectual Portrait*. Cambridge, UK: Polity Press, 2009.

21 *Time* magazine, March 24, 1968; see also "Why Blacks Reenlist?" *Ebony Magazine*, Volume 23, Number 10, August 1968.

11 The Rise of Social Consciousness

1 See Molefi Kete Asante, *Maulana Karenga: An Intellectual Portrait*. Cambridge, UK: Polity Press, 2009.

2 If the reader will permit a personal reference: During the late 1960s I was a student at UCLA and the president of the Student Nonviolent Coordinating Committee for a couple of years. Our emphasis as students was to secure a curriculum at UCLA that would be relevant to our lives both in the present and in the future. Resistance at UCLA to this idea was like it was at hundreds of other universities and colleges: rather pedestrian and without sensitivity to the thousands of African students who had entered the universities.

3 Maulana Karenga, *Introduction to Black Studies*. Los Angeles: University of Sankore Press, 2002.

4 Ama Mazama, "Naming and Defining: A Critical Link," *Western Journal of Black Studies*, Volume 34, Number 2, Summer 2010.

5 See Karenga, *Introduction to Black Studies*; also Asante, *Maulana Karenga*.

6 Nathan Hare was born in 1933. He became, by virtue of his age, inclination, scholarship, and activism, the "father of Black Studies," while working at San Francisco State University in 1968, where he organized the first Black Studies program. He is credited with first using the term "Ethnic

Studies," in reaction to "Minority Studies," a term that was being used by white professors. Hare had established a strong record of teaching at Howard University prior to his appointment to San Francisco State. Among his students at Howard had been Claude Brown, who wrote *Manchild in the Promised Land*, and Stokely Carmichael, who became one of the greatest leaders of the Student Nonviolent Coordinating Committee. A critical sociologist with a Ph.D. from the University of Chicago, Nathan Hare was already popular in the black community with his book *Black Anglo-Saxons*, prior to his ascendancy at the top of Black Studies.

7 Elinor Dee Verney Sinnette, *Arthur Alfonso Schomburg, Black Bibliophile & Collector: A Biography*. New York: New York Public Library, 1989.
 8 Earl Graves, "Amadou Diallo," *Black Enterprise*, May, 1999. See also "Thousands Protest Acquittal of Police Officers who Killed Amadou Diallo," *Democracy Now*, February 28, 2000.
 9 Angela Davis, *Angela Davis: An Autobiography*. New York: International Publishers, 1989. An earlier work by Davis, *If They Come in the Morning*. New York: J. Opaku, 1991, first published in 1971, remains one of the most authentic pieces on the sixties revolution because of the original voices of the writers.
10 Wanda Macon, "Charles Fuller," in Linda Metzger et al., *Contemporary Authors New Revision Series*. Detroit: Gale, 1990, pp. 206–208.
11 Maulana Karenga, "The Million Man March / Day of Absence Mission Statement," in Haki R. Madhubuti and Maulana Karenga, eds, *Million Man March / Day of Absence: A Commemorative Anthology; Speeches, Commentary, Photography, Poetry, Illustrations, Documents*. Chicago: Third World Press, 1996, p. 147.
12 These women were my friends and they spent time with my family in Philadelphia. Hotel space was limited but the energy of the women who had come to the march was electrifying.
13 Shirley Chisholm, *Unbought and Unbossed*. Boston: Houghton Mifflin, 1970.
14 Chisholm, *Unbought and Unbossed*.
15 Born in Brooklyn, November 27, 1925, Adelaide Sanford became an effective vice chancellor of the New York State Board of Regents, assuming leadership of the Regents' Committee for Low Performing Schools. She essentially reshaped the education for students in New York State. Often referred to by African Americans as the "Queen Mother" for her active support of self-determination, dignity, nobility, and excellence as the keys to success, Adelaide L. Sanford came out of the same activist tradition as Shirley Chisholm. She received the Congressional Black Caucus Humanitarian Award, and outstanding alumna awards from Wellesley and Brooklyn College, among numerous others. Sanford was interviewed by *The HistoryMakers* on September 19, 2003.
16 Chisholm, *Unbought and Unbossed*.
17 M. K. Asante Jr, *It's Bigger than Hip Hop*. New York: St Martin's Press, 2008, p. 10.
18 Asante, *It's Bigger than Hip Hop*, p. 10.
19 Carey Alexander, "HSBC, Wells Fargo Accused of Racism in Mortgages," *The Consumerist*, March 15, 2009.
20 See Leon Higginbotham, *Shades of Freedom: Racial Politics and Presumptions of the American Legal Process: Race and the American Legal Process 2*. New York: Oxford University Press, 1998; also Leon Higginbotham, *In the Matter of Color: Race and the American Legal Process 1: The Colonial Period*. New York: Oxford University Press, 1980.
21 Maulana Karenga, "Oscar Smith Case," *Los Angeles Sentinel*, June 8, 2010.
22 *Uhuru News*, May 17, 2010
23 *Uhuru News*, July 27, 2010.
24 Asante, *It's Bigger than Hip Hop*, p. 4.

12 An Unfinished Agenda

1 Anne P. Rice, *Witnessing Lynching: American Writers Respond*. New Brunswick, NJ: Rutgers University Press, 2003.

2 Sandra Peters, *New World Outlook*, September–October, 1999.
3 Benjamin Quarles. *Black Mosaic: Essays in Afro-American History and Historiography.* Introduction by August Meier. Amherst: University of Massachusetts Press, 1988.
4 Joint Center for Political and Economic Studies, Washington, DC, 2001, www.jointcenter.org

Bibliography

Abbott, Martin. *The Freedmen's Bureau in South Carolina, 1865–1872*. Chapel Hill: University of North Carolina Press, 1967.

Abernathy, Ralph. *And the Walls Came Tumbling Down: An Autobiography*. New York: HarperCollins, 1990.

Adams, Henry. *The War of 1812*. New York: Cooper Square Press, 1999.

Albertson, Chris. *Bessie*, revised and expanded edition. New Haven, CT: Yale University Press, 2003.

Allen, Theodore W. *The Invention of the White Race*. London: Verso: 1994.

Anderson, Marian. *My Lord, What a Morning: An Autobiography*. New York: Viking Press, 1956.

Angell, Stephen Ward. *Bishop Henry McNeal Turner and African American Religion in the South*. Knoxville: University of Tennessee Press, 2001.

Aptheker, Herbert, ed. *A Documentary History of the Negro People in the United States*. New York: Citadel Press, 1951.

Aptheker, Herbert. *American Negro Slave Revolts*. New York: International Publishers, 1974.

Aptheker, Herbert, ed. *Book Reviews by W. E. B. Du Bois*. Millwood, NY: Kraus-Thomson, 1977.

Asante, Molefi Kete. *Classical Africa*. Saddle Creek, NJ: PPG, 1993.

Asante, Molefi Kete. *African American History: A Journey of Liberation*. Saddle Creek, NJ: PPG, 2001.

Asante, Molefi Kete. *Cheikh Anta Diop: An Intellectual Portrait*. Los Angeles: University of Sankore Press, 2006.

Asante, Molefi Kete. *The History of Africa*. New York: Routledge, 2007.

Asante, Molefi Kete. *The Afrocentric Manifesto: Toward an African Renaissance*. Cambridge: Polity Press, 2008.

Asante, Molefi Kete. *Maulana Karenga: An Intellectual Portrait*. Cambridge: Polity Press, 2009.

Asante, Molefi Kete. *As I Run toward Africa*. Boulder, CO: Paradigm, 2011.

Asante, Molefi Kete and Mark Mattson. *African American Atlas*. New York: Simon and Schuster, 1999.

Asante, Molefi Kete and Ama Mazama, eds. *Encyclopedia of African Religion*. Thousand Oaks, CA: Sage Publications, 2009. 2 Volumes.

Asante, Molefi Kete and Emeka Nwadiora. *Spear Masters: Introduction to African Religion*. Lanham, MD: Rowman and Littlefield, 2007.

Asante, Molefi Kete and Maulana Karenga, eds. *Handbook of Black Studies*. Thousand Oaks, CA: Sage Publications, 2005.

Asante, Molefi Kete and Ama Mazama, eds. *Encyclopedia of Black Studies*. Thousand Oaks, CA: Sage Publications, 2005.

Asante, M. K. Jr. *It's Bigger than Hip Hop*. New York: St Martin's Press, 2008.

Astor, Gerald. *"And a Credit to His Race": The Hard Life and Times of Joseph Louis Barrow, a.k.a. Joe Louis*. New York: Saturday Review Press, 1974.

Athearn, Robert G. *In Search of Canaan: Black Migration to Kansas, 1879–80*. Lawrence: The Regents Press of Kansas, 1978.

Baldwin, James. *Notes of a Native Son*. Boston: Beacon Press, 1955.

Baldwin, James. *Nobody Knows My Name: More Notes of a Native Son*. New York: Dial Press, 1963.

Baldwin, James. *The Price of the Ticket: Collected Nonfiction, 1948–1985*. New York: St Martin's/Marek, 1985.

Barrow, Isabel C. *First Mohonk Conference on the Negro Question*. Boston: George Ellis, 1890.

Bates, Daisy. *The Long Shadow of Little Rock: A Memoir*. Fayetteville: University of Arkansas Press, 1987.

Batuta, Ibn. *Travels in Asia and Africa, 1325–54*, trans. H. A. R. Gibb, New York: Routledge, 1957.

Bauval, Robert and Thomas Brophy. *Black Genesis: The Prehistoric Origins of Ancient Egypt*. Rochester, VT: Bear and Company, 2011.

Bedini, Silvio A. *The Life of Benjamin Banneker, the First African American Man of Science*, 2nd edition. Baltimore: Maryland Historical Society, 1999.

Bekerie, Ayele. *Ethiopic, an African Writing System: Its History and Principles*. Lawrenceville, NJ: The Red Sea Press, 1997.

Bengston, John D., ed. *In Hot Pursuit of Language in Prehistory: Essays in the Four Fields of Anthropology in Honor of Harold Crane Fleming*. Amsterdam: John Benjamins, 2008.

Bennett, Lerone Jr. *Before the Mayflower: A History of Black America*. Chicago: Johnson, 1982.

Bergman, Peter. *The Chronological History of the Negro in America*. New York: Mentor Books, 1969.

Bergreen, Laurence. *Louis Armstrong: An Extravagant Life*. New York: Broadway Books, 1998.

Berlin, Ira and Ronald Hoffman, eds. *Slavery and Freedom in the Age of the American Revolution*. Charlottesville: Published for the United States Capitol Historical Society by the University Press of Virginia, 1983.

Bernal, Martin. *Black Athena*. New Brunswick, NJ: Rutgers University Press, 1987.

Biddle, Daniel and Murray Dubin. *Tasting Freedom: Octavius Catto and the Battle for Equality in Civil War America*. Philadelphia: Temple University Press, 2010.

Blackman, John. *A Memoir of the Life and Writings of Thomas Day*. London: John Bedford Leno, 1862.

Blassingame, John et al., eds. *The Frederick Douglass Papers*. Series One, 5 vols, 1979–1992; Series Two, 2 vols, 1999–2003.

Blauner, Bob. *Black Lives, White Lives: Three Decades of Race Relations in America*. Berkeley: University of California Press, 1989.

Blaut, James M. *The Colonizer's Model of the World: Geographical Diffusionism and Eurocentric History*. New York: The Guilford Press, 1986.

Blight, David W. *Frederick Douglass' Civil War: Keeping Faith in Jubilee*. Baton Rouge: Louisiana State University Press, 1989.

Block, David. *Baseball Before We Knew It: A Search for the Roots of the Game*. Lincoln: University of Nebraska Press, 2005.

Blyden, E. W. *Christianity, Islam and the Negro Race*. Edinburgh: Edinburgh University Press, 1967.

Bohanan, P. *Africa and Africans*. London: Routledge, 2007.

Bond, Julian. *A Time to Speak, a Time to Act: The Movement in Politics*. New York: Simon and Schuster, 1972.

Bontemps, Arna. *Black Thunder: Gabriel's Revolt, Virginia, 1800*. Boston: Beacon, 1992.

Boyd, Valerie. *Wrapped in Rainbows: The Life of Zora Neale Thurston*. New York: Scribner's, 2004.

Bracey, John H. Jr and August Meier, gen. eds. *Mary McLeod Bethune Papers: The Bethune Foundation Collection*. Bethesda, MD: University Publications of America, 1997.

Bradford, Sarah. *Harriet, the Moses of Her People*. New York: Lockwood and Sons, 1886.

Bradley, Michael. *Dawn Voyage: The Black African Discovery of America*. New York: A and B Distributors, 1992.

Breitman, George, ed. *Malcolm X Speaks*. New York: Grove, 1994.

Breitman, George, Herman Porter, and Baxter Smith. *The Assassination of Malcolm X*. New York: Pathfinder Press, 1991. First published in 1976.

Brodkin, Karen. *How Jews Became White Folks: And What That Says about Race in America*. New Brunswick, NJ: Rutgers University Press, 1998.

Bronz, Stephen H. *Roots of Negro Racial Consciousness: The 1920s, Three Harlem Renaissance Authors*. San Diego, CA: Libra Publishers, 1964.

Brooks, Maegan Parker and Davis W. Houck, eds. *The Speeches of Fannie Lou Hamer: To Tell It Like It Is*. Oxford, MS: University Press of America, 2010.

Brown, Henry Box. *Narrative of Henry Box Brown: A Memoir*. New York: Oxford University Press, 2002. Originally published in 1851.

Burchard, Peter. *One Gallant Rush: Robert Gould Shaw and His Brave Black Regiment*. New York: St Martin's Press, 1990.

Busby, Mark. *Ralph Ellison*. Boston: Twayne, 1991.

Butzer, K. W. *Early Hydraulic Civilization in Egypt*. Chicago: University of Chicago Press, 1976.

Campbell, Stanley. *The Slave Catchers: Enforcement of the Fugitive Slave Law, 1850–1860*. Chapel Hill: University of North Carolina Press.

Carson, Clay. *In Struggle: SNCC and the Black Awakening of the 1960s*. Cambridge, MA: Harvard University Press, 1981.

Carter, Dan T. *Scottsboro: A Tragedy of the American South*. Baton Rouge: Louisiana State University Press, 2007.

Carter, Hodding. *The Angry Scar: The Story of Reconstruction*. Garden City, NY: Doubleday, 1974.

Cary, Lorene. *Black Ice*. New York: Knopf, 1991.

Casely Hayford, J. E. *Gold Coast Native Institutions*. London: Frank Cass, 1970.

Cavalli-Sforza, L. L. "Genes, peoples and languages," *Scientific American*, 265, 5 (November 1991).

Chaney, Ben. *Schwerner, Chaney, and Goodman: The Struggle for Justice*. American Bar Association, Fall, 2009.

Chinweizu, I. *The West and the Rest of Us*. New York: Vintage, 1975.

Chisholm, Shirley. *Unbought and Unbossed*. Boston: Houghton Mifflin, 1970.

Clarke, Donald. *Billie Holiday: Wishing on the Moon*. New York: Da Capo, 2002.

Clarke, John Henrik. *African World Revolution*. Trenton, NJ: Africa World Press, 1992.

Cleage, Albert G. *The Black Messiah*. Trenton, NJ: Africa World Press, 1989.

Cleaver, Eldridge. *Soul on Ice*. New York: McGraw-Hill, 1967.

Colaiaco, James A. *Martin Luther King, Jr.: Apostle of Nonviolence*. New York: Grolier, 1988.

Cone, James H. *My Soul Looks Back*. Maryknoll, NY: Orbis, 1985.

Cone, James H. *Martin and Malcolm and America*. Maryknoll, NY: Orbis, 1992.

Cone, James H. *God of the Oppressed*. Maryknoll, NY: Orbis, 1997.

Cone, James H. *A Black Theology of Liberation*, 40th anniversary edition. Maryknoll, NY: Orbis, 2010.

Cooper, Wayne F., ed. *The Passion of Claude McKay*. New York: Schocken Books, 1973.

Cooper, Wayne F. *Claude McKay: Rebel Sojourner in the Harlem Renaissance, a Biography*. Baton Rouge: Louisiana State University Press, 1987.

Costanzo, Angelo. *Surprising Narrative: Olaudah Equiano and the Beginnings of Black Autobiography*. Contributions in Afro-American and African Studies, vol. 1. New York: Greenwood Press, 1987.

Cottrell, John. *Muhammad Ali, Who Once was Cassius Clay*. New York: Funk & Wagnalls, 1968.

Davidson, Basil. *The Lost Cities of Africa*. Boston: Back Bay, 1959.

Davidson, Basil. *The African Past*. New York: Penguin, 1966.

Davidson, Basil. *Black Mother*. London: Longman, 1970.

Davidson, Basil. *Old Africa Rediscovered*. London: Longman, 1971.

Davidson, Basil. *Africa in History*. London: Paladin, 1975.

Davidson, Basil. *The History of Africa, 1000–1800*. London: Longman, 1977.

Davidson, Basil. *The Growth of African Civilization: East and Central Africa to the Nineteenth Century*. London: Longman, 1977.

Davidson, James West. *"They Say": Ida B. Wells and the Reconstruction of Race*. New York: Oxford University Press.

Davis, Angela. *If They Come in the Morning*. New York: J. Opaku, 1991; first published 1971.

Davis, Angela. *Angela Davis: An Autobiography*. New York: Random House, 1974.

Davis, Arthur P., J. Saunders Redding, and Joyce Ann Joyce, eds. *The New Cavalcade: African American Writing from 1760 to the Present*. Washington, DC: Howard University Press, 1991.

Dei, George Sefa. *Rethinking Schooling and Education in African Contexts*. Trenton, NJ: Africa World Press, 2001.

Dierenfield, Bruce. *The Civil Rights Movement*. Harlow, UK: Longmans.

Diop, Cheikh Anta. *Cultural Unity of Black Africa*. Chicago: Third World Press, 1969.

Diop, Cheikh Anta. *Civilization or Barbarism: An Authentic Anthropology*. New York: Lawrence Hill, 1991.

Diop, Cheikh Anta. *The African Origin of Civilization: Myth or Reality*. New York: Lawrence Hill, 1989, originally published in 1974.

Dixon, Chris. *African Americans and Haiti: Emigration and Black Nationalism in the Nineteenth Century*. Westport, CT: Greenwood Press, 2000.

Douglass, Frederick. *Life and Times of Frederick Douglass: His Early Life as a Slave, His Escape from Bondage, and His Complete History to the Present Time, Including His Connection with the Anti-Slavery Movement*. Hartford, CT: Park Publishing Co., 1881.

Dove, Nah. *Afrikan Mothers: Bearers of Culture, Makers of Social Change*. Albany: SUNY Press, 1998.

Driskell, David. *Narratives of African American Art and Identity*. Petaluma, CA: Pomegranate Communications, 1998.

Duberman, Martin B. *Paul Robeson*. New York: Knopf, 1988.

Du Bois, W. E. B. *The Souls of Black Folk*. New York: New American Library, 1969.

Duncan, Russell. *Where Death and Glory Meet: Colonel Robert Gould Shaw and the 54th Massachusetts Infantry*. Athens: University of Georgia Press, 1999.

Dunn, Ross. *The Adventures of Ibn Battuta: A Muslim Traveler of the 14th Century*. Berkeley: University of California Press, 2005.

Edwards, Harry. *The Revolt of the Black Athlete*. New York: The Free Press, 1969.

Edwards, Harry. *The Struggle that Must Be: An Autobiography*. New York: Macmillan, 1980.

Egerton, Douglas R. *Gabriel's Rebellion: The Virginia Slave Conspiracies of 1800 and 1802*. Chapel Hill: University of North Carolina Press, 1993.

Ehret, Christopher. *The Civilizations of Africa: A History to 1800*. Charlottesville: University Press of Virginia, 2002.

Ehret, Christopher and Mary Posnansky, eds. *The Archaeological and Linguistic Reconstruction of African History*. Los Angeles and Berkeley: University of California Press, 1982.

Eicholz, Hans L. *Harmonizing Sentiments: The Declaration of Independence and the Jeffersonian Idea of Self-Government*. New York: Peter Lang, 2001.

Essien-Udom, E. U. *Black Nationalism: The Search for an Identity*. Chicago: University of Chicago Press, 1995.

Evers, Mrs Medgar. *For Us, the Living*. Garden City, NY: Doubleday, 1967.

Evers-Williams, Myrlie and Manning Marable, eds. *The Autobiography of Medgar Evers: A Hero's Life and Legacy Revealed through His Writings, Letters, and Speeches*. New York: Basic Civitas Books, 2005.

Fairclough, Adam. *To Redeem the Soul of America: The Southern Christian Leadership Conference and Martin Luther King, Jr.* Athens: University of Georgia Press, 1987.

Falola, Toyin. *Nationalism and African Intellectuals*. Rochester, NY: University of Rochester Press, 2001.

Falola, Toyin, ed. *Tradition and Change in Africa: The Essays of J. F. Ade Ajayi*. Trenton, NJ: Africa World Press, 2000.

Fanon, Frantz. *The Wretched of the Earth*. London: Penguin, 1983.

Feagin, Joseph. *Racist America*. London: Routledge, 2010.

Finch, Charles. *Echoes of the Old Dark Land*. Atlanta, GA: Khenti Inc., 1991.

Foner, Eric. *Reconstruction: America's Unfinished Revolution, 1863–1877*. NY: Harper and Row, 1988.

Foner, Eric. *A Short History of Reconstruction, 1863–1877*. New York: Harper and Row, 1990.

Foner, Eric. *Free Soil, Free Labor, Free Men: The Ideology of the Republican Party before the Civil War*. New York: Oxford University Press, 1995.

Foner, Philip. *Paul Robeson Speaks*. New York: Citadel Press, 1978.

Foster, Frances Smith. *A Brighter Coming Day: A Frances Ellen Watkins Harper Reader*. New York: Feminist Press, 1990.

Franklin, John Hope. *Reconstruction: After the Civil War*. Chicago: University of Chicago Press, 1961.

Franklin, John Hope. *The Emancipation Proclamation*. Garden City, NY: Doubleday & Company, 1963.

Franklin, John Hope. *George Washington Williams: A Biography*. Chicago: University of Chicago Press, 1985.

Franklin, John Hope. *From Slavery to Freedom: A History of Negro Americans*. New York: Alfred A. Knopf, 1988.

Frazier, E. Franklin. *The Negro in the United States*. New York: Macmillian, 1957.

Frazier, E. Franklin. *Black Bourgeoisie*. New York: Collier Books, 1962.

Frederickson, George. *White Supremacy: A Comparative Study in American and South African History*. Oxford: Oxford University Press, 1981.

Friedman, Russell. *The Voice that Challenged a Nation: Marian Anderson and the Struggle for Equal Rights*. New York: Sandpiper, 2011.

Frommer, Harvey. *Rickey and Robinson: The Men Who Broke Baseball's Color Barrier*. New York: Macmillan, 1982.

Fuller, Charles. *Snatch*. Philadelphia: David and Me, Publishers, 2010.

Gammond, Peter, ed. *Duke Ellington: His Life and Music*. New York: Roy, 1958; reprint, Da Capo, 1977.

Garrow, David J. *Protest at Selma: Martin Luther King, Jr. and the Voting Rights Act of 1965*. New Haven, CT: Yale University Press, 1978.

Garrow, David. *Bearing the Cross: Martin Luther King, Jr. and the Southern Christian Leadership Conference*. New York: Morrow, 1986.

Gayle, Addison. *Claude McKay: The Black Poet at War*. Detroit: Broadside Press, 1972.

Genovese, Eugene. *Roll, Jordan, Roll: The World the Slaves Made*. New York: Vintage, 1974.

Gentile, Thomas. *March on Washington, August 29, 1963*. Washington, DC: New Day Publications, 1983.

Giddens, Gary. *Satchmo: The Genius of Louis Armstrong*. New York: Da Capo, 2001.

Giddings, P. J. *Ida: A Sword among Lions*. New York: HarperCollins, 2008.

Giles, James R. *Claude McKay*. Boston: G. K. Hall, 1976.

Gilmore, Grant and Charles L. Black. *The Law of Admiralty*. 2nd edition. St Paul, MN: West Publishing Company, 1975.

Goldstein, Warren. *Playing for Keeps: A History of Early Baseball*. Ithaca, NY: Cornell University Press, 1991.

Graham, Maryemma. *The Complete Poems of Frances E. W. Harper*. New York: Oxford University Press, 1988.

Gutman, Herbert George. *The Black Family in Slavery and Freedom, 1750–1825*. New York: Pantheon Books, 1976.

Hakluyt, Richard. *The Principal Navigations Voyages Traffiques & Discoveries of the English Nation*, etc. 12 vols. Glasgow: James MacLehose & Sons for the Hakluyt Society, 1903–1905.

Hamilton, Charles V. *Adam Clayton Powell, Jr.: The Political Biography of an American Dilemma*. New York: Cooper Square Press, 2002.

Hamilton, Charles V. and Stokely Carmichael. *Black Power: The Politics of Liberation in America*. New York: Random House, 1988; first published in 1966.

Hanaford, Phebe A. *Daughters of America*. Augusta, ME: True and Company, 1882.

Harding, Vincent. *There is a River*. New York: Harcourt, Brace, 1981.

Harlan, Louis R. *Booker T. Washington: The Wizard of Tuskegee, 1901–1915*. New York: Oxford University Press, 1983.

Hauser, Thomas. *Muhammad Ali: His Life and Times*. New York: Simon and Schuster, 1992.

Hayden, Robert C. *Seven Black American Scientists*. Reading, MA: Addison-Wesley, 1985.

Hening, William Waller. *The Statutes at Large, being a Collection of All the Laws of Virginia from the First Session of the Legislature in the Year 1619*. 13 vols. Richmond: W. Gray Printers, 1819.

Henson, J. *Uncle Tom's Story of His Life: An Autobiography of Rev. Josiah Henson*. London: Christian Age Office, 1877.

Higginbotham, A. Leon Jr. *In the Matter of Color: Race and the American Legal Process 1: The Colonial Period*. New York: Oxford University Press, 1980.

Higginbotham, A. Leon Jr. *Shades of Freedom: Racial Politics and Presumptions of the American Legal Process: Race and the American Legal Process 2*. New York: Oxford University Press, 1998.

Hine, Darlene Clark, ed. *The State of Afro-American History: Past, Present, and Future*. Baton Rouge: Louisiana State University Press, 1986.

Hine, Darlene. *Black Women in United States History*. Brooklyn, NY: Carlson, 1990.

Hine, Darlene Clark and Earnestine Jenkins, eds. *A Question of Manhood: A Reader in U.S. Black Men's History and Masculinity*. Bloomington: Indiana University Press, 1999.

Hochschild, Adam. *King Leopold's Ghost*. New York: Houghton Mifflin, 1998.

Hoffer, Peter Charles. *Cry Liberty: The Great Stono River Slave Rebellion of 1739*. Oxford: Oxford University Press, 2010.

Holt, Rackham. *Mary McLeod Bethune: A Biography*. Garden City, NY: Doubleday, 1964.

Homan, Lynn and Thomas Reilly. *Black Knights: The Story of the Tuskegee Airmen*. New York: Pelican, 2001.

Horne, Gerald. *Black and Red: W.E.B. Du Bois and the Afro-American Response to the Cold War, 1944–1963*. SUNY Series in Afro-American Society. Albany: State University of New York Press, 1985.

Horne, Gerald. *The End of Empires: African Americans and India*. Philadelphia: Temple University, 2009.

Hudson-Weems, Clenora. *Emmett Till: The Sacrificial Lamb of the Civil Rights Movement*. Bloomington, IN: AuthorHouse, 2006.

Hughes, Langston. *The Big Sea: An Autobiography*. New York: A. A. Knopf, 1940.

Hughes, Langston. *I Wonder as I Wander: An Autobiographical Journey*. New York: Hill and Wang, 1956.

Hughes, Langston and Milton Meltzer. *A Pictorial History of the Negro in America*. New York: Crown, 1963.

Huxley, Thomas Henry. *Lay Sermons, Addresses and Reviews*. New York: Appleton, 1871.

Ignatiev, Noel. *How the Irish Became White*. London: Routledge, 1995.

Irwin, Graham W. *Africans Abroad: a Documentary History of the Black Diaspora in Asia, Latin America, and the Caribbean during the Age of Slavery*. New York: Columbia University Press, 1977.

Jackson, Blyden. *A History of Afro-American Literature*. Baton Rouge: Louisiana State University Press, 1989.

Jackson, John. *Introduction to African Civilizations*. New York: Citadel Press, 2001.

Jacques-Garvey, Amy. *The Philosophy and Opinions of Marcus Garvey*. New York: Atheneum, 1969.

James, George M. *Stolen Legacy: Greek Philosophy is Stolen Egyptian Philosophy*. Trenton, NJ: Africa World Press, 1993.

James, Rawn Jr. *Root and Branch: Charles Hamilton Houston, Thurgood Marshall, and the Struggle to End Segregation*. London: Bloomsbury Press, 2010.

Johnson, James Weldon. *Lift Every Voice and Sing: Quartet for Mixed Voices*. New York: Edward B. Marks Music Company, 1928.

Johnson, James Weldon. *Along This Way*. New York: Da Capo, 2000.

Johnson, John H. and Lerone Bennett Jr. *Succeeding against the Odds: The Inspiring Autobiography of One of America's Wealthiest Entrepreneurs*. New York: Warner Books, 1989.

Jonas, Gilbert. *Freedom's Sword: The NAACP and the Struggle against Racism in America, 1909–1969*. New York: Routledge, 2005.

Justinus, Marcus Junianus. *Epitome of the Philippic History of Pompeius Trogus*, trans. John Selby Watson. London: Henry G. Bohn, 1853.

Kaplan, Sidney. *The Black Presence in the Era of the American Revolution*. Amherst: University of Massachusetts Press, 1989.

Karade, Baba Ifa. *Imoye: A Definition of the Ifa Tradition*. Brooklyn: Athelia Henrietta Press, 1999.

Karenga, Maulana. *Maat: The Moral Ideal in Ancient Egypt*. Los Angeles: University of Sonkore Press, 2006.

Karenga, Maulana. *Odu Ifa: The Ethical Teachings*. Los Angeles: Kawaida Publishers, 1999.

Karenga, Maulana. *Introduction to Black Studies*. Los Angeles: University of Sankore Press, 2002.

Katz, William Loren. *Black Indians: A Hidden Heritage*. New York: Atheneum, 1997.

Kay, Jackie. *Bessie Smith*. New York: Absolute Press, 1997.

Kenyatta, Jomo, *Facing Mt. Kenya*. New York: Vintage, 1962.

Kernfeld, Barry, ed. *The New Grove Dictionary of Jazz*. London: Macmillan, 2002.

Khaldûn, Ibn, *The Muqaddimah: An Introduction to History*, Franz Rosenthal translation, abridged and edited by N. J. Dawood, Bollingen Series, Princeton, NJ: Princeton University Press, 1967.

Kinshasa, Kwanda Mbiassi. *African American Chronology*. Westport, CT: Greenwood Press, 2006.

Ki-Zerbo, J. *Histoire de l'Afrique noire d'hier à demain*. Paris: Hatier, 1972.

Kromer, Helen. *The Amistad Revolt 1839: The Slave Uprising aboard the Spanish Schooner*. New York: Franklin Watts, 1973. Reprinted as *Amistad: The Slave Uprising aboard the Spanish Schooner*. Cleveland, OH: Pilgrim Press, 1997.

Lam, Aboubacry Moussa. *De l'origine égyptienne des peuls*. Dakar: Éditions Présence Africaine, 1993.

Lambert, G. E. *Duke Ellington*. London: Cassell, 1959.

Lane, R. *William Dorsey's Philadelphia and Ours: On the Past and Future of the Black City in America*. New York: Oxford University Press, 1991.

Lauter, Paul and Richard Yarbrough, eds. *The Heath Anthology of American Literature*, 5th edition. New York: Houghton Mifflin Co.

Lawrence-Lightfoot, Sara. *Balm in Gilead*. Reading, MA: Addison-Wesley, 1988.

Lawrence-Lightfoot, Sara. *I've Known Rivers: Lives of Loss and Liberation*. Reading, MA: Addison-Wesley, 1994.

Lee, Chana Kai. *For Freedom's Sake: The Life of Fannie Lou Hamer*. Urbana: University of Illinois Press.

Leeming, David. *James Baldwin: An Autobiography*. New York: Henry Holt, 1994.

Lewis, John with D'Orso, Michael. *Walking with the Wind: A Memoir of the Movement*. New York: Simon and Schuster, 1998.

Lewis, Meriwether and William Clark. *The Journals of Lewis and Clark*, ed. Bernard DeVoto. Boston: Mariner Books, 1997.

Lincoln, Eric C. and Lawrence H. Mamiya. *The Black Church in the African-American Experience*. Durham, NC: Duke University Press, 1990.

Lincoln, C. Eric. *The Black Church in the African American Experience*. Raleigh, NC: Duke University Press, 1990.

Lincoln, C. Eric. *Black Muslims in America*. Grand Rapids: Eerdmans Publishing, 1994.

Lincoln, C. Eric. *Coming Through the Fire: Surviving Race and Place in America*. Raleigh, NC: Duke University Press, 1996.

Litwack, Leon F. *Been in the Storm So Long: The Aftermath of Slavery*. New York: Alfred A. Knopf, 1979.

Logan, Rayford. *The Negro in American Life and Thought: The Nadir, 1877–1901*. New York: Collier Books, 1965.

Logan, Rayford W. and Michael R. Winston. *Dictionary of American Negro Biography*. New York: Norton, 1982.

Love, Spencie. *One Blood: The Death and Resurrection of Charles R. Drew*. Chapel Hill: University of North Carolina Press, 1997.

Low, W. Augustus, and Virgil A. Clift, eds. *Encyclopedia of Black America*. New York: McGraw-Hill, 1981.

Madhubuti, Haki R. and Maulana Karenga, eds. *Million Man March / Day of Absence: A Commemorative Anthology; Speeches, Commentary, Photography, Poetry, Illustrations, Documents*. Chicago: Third World Press, 1996.

Manning, Kenneth R. *The Black Apollo of Science: The Life of Ernest Everett Just*. New York: Oxford University Press, 1985.

Marable, Manning. *W. E. B. Du Bois, Black Radical Democrat*. Twayne's Twentieth-Century American Biography Series, vol. 3. Boston, Twayne, 1986.

Marable, Manning. *Speaking Truth to Power: Essays on Race, Resistance, and Radicalism*. Boulder, CO: Westview Press, 1996.

Marable, Manning. *Malcolm X: A Life of Reinvention*. New York: Viking, 2011.

Marable, Manning and Leith Mullings, eds. *Let Nobody Turn Us Around: Voices of Resistance, Reform, and Renewal*. Alexandria, VA: Rowman and Littlefield, 1999.

Marshall, Herbert. *Ira Aldridge: Negro Tragedian*. Washington, DC: Howard University Press, 1993.

Martin, Tony. *Marcus Garvey, Hero: A First Biography*. Dover, MA: Majority Press, 1983.

Martin, Waldo E. Jr. *The Mind of Frederick Douglass*. Chapel Hill: University of North Carolina Press, 1984.

Mathews, Marcia. *Henry Ossawa Tanner, American Artist*. Chicago: University of Chicago Press.

Mays, Benjamin Elijah. *Born to Rebel: An Autobiography*. New York: Charles Scribner's Sons, 1971.

Mazama, Ama, ed. *Africa in the 21st Century*. New York: Routledge, 2007.

Mazrui, Ali A., ed. *Africa since 1935. UNESCO General History of Africa VIII*. Berkeley: University of California Press, 1982.

Mbiti, John. *Introduction to African Philosophy and Religion*. London: Heinemann, 1991.

M'Bokolo, E. *Le Continent convoité: L'Afrique au Xxe siècle*. Paris and Montreal: Éditions Études Vivantes, Coll. Axes Sciences Humaines, 1980.

McKivigan, John R. and Stanley Harrold, eds. *Antislavery Violence: Sectional, Racial, and Cultural Conflict in Antebellum America*. Knoxville: University of Tennessee Press, 1999.

McNeil, Genna Rae. *Groundwork: Charles Hamilton Houston and the Struggle for Civil Rights*. Philadelphia: University of Pennsylvania Press, 1984.

McPherson, James M. *The Abolitionist Legacy: From Reconstruction to the NAACP*. Princeton, NJ: Princeton University Press, 1975.

Meier, August. *Negro Thought in America, 1880–1915*. Ann Arbor: University of Michigan Press, 1963.

Meier, August and Elliott Rudwick. *CORE: A Study in the Civil Rights Movement, 1942–1968*. New York: Oxford University Press, 1973.

Meier, August and Leon Litwack, eds. *Black Leaders of the Nineteenth Century*. Champaign: University of Illinois, 1991.

Meier, August and Elliot Rudwick. *From Plantation to Ghetto*. New York: Hill and Wang, 1976.

Miller, Kelly. *The Education of the Negro*. Washington, DC: Government Printing Office, 1902.

Miller, Kelly. *Race Adjustment: The Everlasting Stain*. New York: Arno Press and the *New York Times*, 1968.

Miller, Kelly. *Out of the House of Bondage*. New York: Schocken Books, 1971.

Mjagkij, Nina, ed. *Portraits of African Life since 1865*. Wilmington, DE: Scholarly Resources, 2003.

Monges, Miriam Maat Ka Re. *Kush, the Jewel of Nubia: Reconnecting the Root System of African Civilization*. Trenton, NJ: Africa World Press, 1997.

Morris, Scot. *Omni Games: The Best Brainteasers from* Omni *Magazine*. New York: Holt, Rinehart and Company, 1983.

Moskos, Charles C. and John Sibley Butler. *All that We Can Be: Black Leadership and Racial Integration the Army Way*. New York: Basic Books, 1997.

Mullen, Robert W. *Blacks and Vietnam*. Washington, DC. University Press of America, 1981.

Muñoz Ryan, Pam. *When Marian Sang*. New York: Scholastic, 2002.

Murphree, Vanessa. *The Selling of Civil Rights: The Student Nonviolent Coordinating Committee and the Use of Public Relations*. New York: Routledge, 2006.

Myers, Walter Dean and Christopher Myers. *Harlem*. New York: Scholastic, 1997.

Myrdal, Gunnar. *An American Dilemma: The Negro Problem and Modern Democracy*. New York: Pantheon Books, 1975.

National Urban League. *National Urban League 40th Anniversary Yearbook*. New York: National Urban League, 1950.

Niane, Djibril T., *Sundiata: An Epic of Old Mali*. London: Longman, 1965.

Niane, Djibril T., "Introduction," in J. Ki-Zerbo and D. T. Niane, *UNESCO General History of Africa IV: Africa from the Twelfth to the Sixteenth Century*. New York: James Currey; University of California Press, 1997.

Nieman, Donald G. *To Set the Law in Motion: The Freedmen's Bureau and the Legal Rights of Blacks, 1865–1868*. Millwood, NY: KTO Press, 1979.

Nkrumah, Kwame. *Africa Must Unite*. London: Panaf, 1998, new edition.

Nkrumah, Kwame. *Consciencism*. New York: Monthly Review, 1970.

Nyerere, Julius. *Ujamaa: Essays on Socialism*. London: Oxford University Press, 1977.

Obenga, Théophile. *Pour une nouvelle histoire*. Paris: Présence Africaine, 1980.

Obichere, Boniface I. *West African States and European Expansion: The Dahomey Niger Hinterland, 1898*. New Haven, CT: Yale University Press, 1971.

Ogden, Robert C., ed. *From Servitude to Service: Being the Old South Lectures on the History and Work of Southern Institutions for the Education of the Negro*. Boston: American Unitarian Association, 1905.

Al-Omari. *Masalik el absIr fi mamIlik el-ensIr*, trans. and ed. M. Gaudefroy-Demombynes. Paris: Paul Guethner, 1927.

O'Meally, Robert. *Lady Day: The Many Faces of Billie Holiday*. New York: Da Capo, 2000.

O'Reilly, Kenneth. *Racial Matters: The FBI's Secret File on Black America, 1960–1972*. New York: Free Press, 1989.

Owens, Jesse and Paul Neimark. *The Jesse Owens Story*. New York: Putnam's, 1970.

Painter, Nell Irvin. *Sojourner Truth: A Life, a Symbol*. New York: Norton, 1997.

Parish, Peter J. *Slavery: History and Historians*. New York: Harper and Row, 1989.

Parks, Rosa with Jim Haskins. *Rosa Parks: My Story*. New York: Puffin, 1999.

Patterson, Haywood. *Scottsboro Boy*. Washington, DC: American Council of Learned Societies Humanities, 2008.

Pfeffer, Paula F. *A. Philip Randolph: Pioneer of the Civil Rights Movement*. Baton Rouge: Louisiana State University, 1996.

Phelps, J. Alfred. *Chappie: America's First Black Four-Star General, the Life and Times of Daniel James, Jr.* Novato, CA: Presidio Press, 1992.

Pinkney, Andrea and Brian Pinkney. *Duke Ellington: The Piano Prince and His Orchestra*. New York: Hyperion, 2006.

Proctor, Samuel DeWitt. *The Substance of Things Hoped For: A Memoir of African American Faith*. New York: Putnam, 1996.

Poe, Daryl Zizwe. *Kwame Nkrumah's Contribution to Pan Africanism*. New York: Routledge, 2003.

Porter, Dorothy B., ed. *The Negro in the United States: A Selected Bibliography*. Washington, DC: Library of Congress, 1970.

Potts, Howard E., comp. *A Comprehensive Name Index for the American Slave*. Westport, CT: Greenwood Press, 1997.

Powell, Adam Clayton. *Adam by Adam: the Autobiography of Adam Clayton Powell, Jr*. New York: Dial Press, 1971.

Quarles, Benjamin. *The Negro in the American Revolution*. Chapel Hill: University of North Carolina Press, 1961.

Quarles, Benjamin. *Allies for Freedom & Blacks and John Brown*. New York: Oxford University Press, 1974.

Quarles, Benjamin. *The Negro in the Making of America*. New York: Collier Macmillan, 1987.

Quarles, Benjamin. *Black Mosaic: Essays in Afro-American History and Historiography*. Amherst: University of Massachusetts Press, 1988.

Quintal, George. *Patriots of Color: A Peculiar Beauty and Merit, African Americans and Native Americans at Battle Road and Bunker Hill*. Washington, DC: United States Department of the Interior, 2005.

Rabinowitz, Howard N., ed. *Southern Black Leaders of the Reconstruction Era*. Urbana: University of Illinois Press, 1982.

Rampersad, Arnold. *The Life of Langston Hughes*. 2 vols. New York: Oxford University Press, 1986.

Rampersad, Arnold. *Jackie Robinson: A Biography*. New York: Ballantine, 1998.

Rampersad, Arnold. *The Poems of Langston Hughes*. Columbia: University of Missouri Press, 2007.

Ransby, Barbara. *Ella Baker and the Black Freedom Movement: A Radical Democratic Vision*. Chapel Hill: University of North Carolina Press, 2005.

Rattenbury, Ken. *Duke Ellington: Jazz Composer*. New Haven, CT: Yale University Press, 1990.

Redkey, Edwin S. *Black Exodus: Black Nationalist and Back to Africa Movements*. New Haven, CT: Yale University Press.

Reed, Ismael. *Cab Calloway Stands In for the Moon*. New York: Bamberger, 1988.

Relyea, Sarah. *Outside Citizens*. New York: Routledge, 2006.

Reynolds, David S. *John Brown, Abolitionist: The Man Who Killed Slavery, Sparked the Civil War, and Seeded Civil Rights*. New York: Vintage, 2006.

Rivlin, Benjamin. *Ralph Bunche, the Man and His Times*. New York: Holmes and Meier, 1990.

Robertson, David M. *Denmark Vesey: The Buried History of America's Largest Slave Rebellion and the Man Who Led It*. New York: Knopf, 1999.

Robeson, Paul. *Here I Stand*. Boston: Beacon Press, 1970.

Rose, Willie Lee. *Slavery and Freedom*. New York: Oxford University Press, 1987.

Rosenblat, Angel. *La población indígena y el mestizaje en América*. Buenos Aires, 1954.

Rowland, Peter. *The Life and Times of Thomas Day, 1748–1789: English Philanthropist and Author, Virtue Almost Personified*. Lewiston, NY: E. Mellen Press, 1996.

Rustin, Bayard. *Down the Line: Collected Writings*. New York: Quadrangle, 1971.

Sabour, M'hammad and Knut Vikør, eds. *Ethnic Encounter and Culture Change*. Bergen and London: Nordic Society for Middle Eastern Studies, 1997.

Schubert, Frank N., comp. *On the Trail of the Buffalo Soldier: Biographies of African American Soldiers in the U.S. Army, 1866–1917*. Wilmington, DE: Scholarly Resources, 1995.

Seeber, Edward Derbyshire. *Anti-slavery Opinions in France during the Second Half of the Eighteenth History*. New York: Burt Franklin Publishers, 1971.

Sertima, Ivan Van. *They Came Before Columbus*. New York: Random House, 1976.

Seymour, Harold. *Baseball: The Early Years*. New York: Oxford University Press, 1960.

Sheafer, S. A. *Women in America's Wars*. Springfield, NJ: Enslow Publishers, 1996.

Shillington, Kevin. *History of Africa*. New York: St Martin's Press, 1989.

Shipton, Alyn. *Hi-De-Ho: The Life of Cab Calloway*. New York: Oxford University Press, 2010.

Sidbury, James. *Ploughshares into Swords: Race, Rebellion, and Identity in Gabriel's Virginia, 1739–1810*. Cambridge: Cambridge University Press.

Simmons, Walter J. and Henry McNeal Turner. *Men of Mark: Eminent, Progressive and Rising*. Cleveland, OH: G. M. Rewall & Co., 1887.

Sinnette, Elinor Dee Verney. *Arthur Alfonso Schomburg, Black Bibliophile & Collector: A Biography*. New York: New York Public Library, 1989.

Smedley, Audrey. *Race in North America: Origin and Evolution of a Worldview*. Boulder, CO: Westview Press, 2007.

Smedley, R. C. *History of the Underground Railroad in Chester and the Neighboring Counties of Pennsylvania*. New York: Beaufort Books, 1982.

Smith, Lillian. *Killers of the Dream*. New York: W.W. Norton, 1949.

Sorensen, Lita. *The Scottsboro Boys Trial: A Primary Source Account*. New York: Rosen, 2004.

Staples, Robert. *The Urban Plantation: Racism & Colonialism in the Post Civil Rights Era*. Oakland, CA: Black Scholar Press, 1987.

Stein, Judith. *The World of Marcus Garvey: Race and Class in Modern Society*. Baton Rouge: Louisiana University Press, 1986.

Sterling, Dorothy. *Freedom Train: The Story of Harriet Tubman*. New York: Scholastics, 1987.

Sterling, Dorothy and Benjamin Quarles. *Lift Every Voice: The Lives of Booker T. Washington, W. E. B. Du Bois, Mary Church Terrell, and James Weldon Johnson*. Garden City, NY: Doubleday, 1965.

Stetson, Erlene and Linda David. *Glorying in Tribulations: The Lifework of Sojourner Truth*. East Lansing: Michigan State University Press, 1994.

Stewart, Maria W. *America's First Black Woman Political Writer: Essays and Speeches*, ed. Marilyn Richardson. Bloomington: Indiana University Press, 1987.

Still, William. *The Underground Rail Road*. Philadelphia: Porters and Coates, 1872.

Sweeney, William Allison. *History of the American Negro in the Great World War: His Splendid Record in the Battle Zones of Europe*. New York: Johnson Reprint, 1970.

Terrell, Mary Church. *A Colored Woman in a White World*. Amherst, NY: Humanity Books, 2005.

Thomas, Lamont D. *Rise to be a People: A Biography of Paul Cuffee*. Urbana: University of Illinois Press, 1986.

Thornbrough, Emma Lou. *T. Thomas Fortune, Militant Journalist*. Chicago: University of Chicago Press, 1972.

Tillary, Tyrone. *Claude McKay: A Black Poet's Struggle for Identity*. Amherst: University of Massachusetts Press, 1992.

Trice, Linda. *Charles Drew: Pioneer of Blood Plasma*. New York: McGraw-Hill, 2000.

Tucker, P. T. *Cathy Williams: From Slave to Female Buffalo Soldier*. Mechanicsburg, PA: Stackpole Books, 2002.

Tushner, Mark V. *Making Civil Rights Law: Thurgood Marshall and the Supreme Court, 1936–1961*. Oxford: Oxford University Press, 1994.

Van Sertima, Ivan. *Egypt Revisited*. New Brunswick, NJ: Transaction Publishers, 1981.

Vansina, Jan. *Paths in the Rain Forest: Toward a History of Political Tradition in Equatorial Africa*. Madison: University of Wisconsin, 1990.

Vogel, Joseph O., ed. *Encyclopedia of Precolonial Africa: Archaeology, History, Languages, Cultures and Environments*. Walnut Creek, CA: AltaMira Press, 1999.

Walker, David. *David Walker's Appeal, in Four Articles, together with a Preamble, to the Coloured Citizens of the World, but in Particular, and Very Expressly, to Those of the United States of America*. Boston, 1829. Revised edition, New York: Hill and Wang, 1995.

Walker, E. A. *A History of Southern Africa*. London: Longman, 1957.

Washington, Booker T. *Up from Slavery: An Autobiography*. Boston: Houghton Mifflin, 1901.

Washington, Booker T. *An Autobiography: The Story of My Life and Work*. Toronto: J. L. Nichols and Company, *c.* 1901.

Washington, Shirley. *Countee Cullen's Secret Revealed by Miracle Book: A Biography of His Childhood in New Orleans*. New York: AuthorHouse, 2008.

Wheatley, Phillis. *Memoirs and Poems of Phillis Wheatley, a Native American and Slave*. Boston: G. W. Light, 1834.

White, Walter Francis. *How Far the Promised Land*. New York: Viking Press, 1955.

Wiener, Leo. *Africa and the Discovery of America*. New York: A and B Distribution, 1992.

Williams, Chancellor. *The Destruction of Black Civilization: Great Issues of a Race.* Chicago: Third World Press, 1987.

Williams, Eric. *Capitalism and Slavery.* Chapel Hill: University of North Carolina Press, 1994.

Wilson, Joseph T. *The Black Phalanx: A History of the Negro Soldiers of the United States in the War of 1775–1812, 1861–'65.* Hartford, CT: American Publishing Co., 1892.

Windley, Lathan A., comp. *Runaway Slave Advertisements: A Documentary History from the 1730s to 1790.* Westport, CT: Greenwood Press, 1983.

Wise, Tim. *White like Me: Reflections on Race from a Privileged Son.* New York: Soft Skull Press, 2007.

Wood, Ean. *The Josephine Baker Story.* New York: Sanctuary Publishing, 2002.

Woodson, Carter G. *The History of the Negro Church.* Washington, DC: Associated Publishers, 1921.

Woodson, Carter G. *The Education of the Negro prior to 1861.* New York: Arno Press, 1968.

Woodson, Carter G. *The Mind of the Negro as Reflected in Letters Written during the Crisis, 1800–1860.* New York: Russell & Russell, 1969.

Woodward, C. Vann. *The Strange Career of Jim Crow.* New York: Oxford University Press, 1974.

Wright, Bruce. *Black Robes, White Justice.* Secaucus, NJ: Lyle Stuart, 1987.

Wright, Marshall D. *The National Association of Base Ball Players, 1857–70.* New York: McFarland and Company, 2000.

Wright, Richard. *Black Boy: A Record of Childhood and Youth.* 10th ed. New York: Harper, 1945.

X, Malcolm. *Autobiography of Malcolm X.* With the assistance of Alex Haley. Introduction by M. S. Handler. Epilogue by Alex Haley. New York: Grove Press, 1965.

Zaborowska, Magdalena. *James Baldwin's Turkish Decade: Erotics of Exile.* Durham, NC: Duke University Press, 2008.

Zangrando, Robert L. *The NAACP Crusade against Lynching, 1909–1950.* Philadelphia: Temple University Press, 1980.

Index